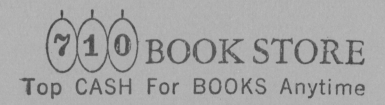

710 BOOK STORE
Top CASH For BOOKS Anytime

"YOURS — FOR LOWER COSTS
OF HIGHER EDUCATION "

MASS MEDIA RESEARCH

From the Wadsworth Series in Mass Communication

GENERAL

BROADCAST AND CABLE

JOURNALISM

MASS MEDIA RESEARCH
An Introduction
SECOND EDITION

ROGER D. WIMMER
Surrey Consulting & Research, Inc.

■

JOSEPH R. DOMINICK
University of Georgia

WADSWORTH PUBLISHING COMPANY
Belmont, California
A Division of Wadsworth, Inc.

For Chris and Joan

Senior Editor: **Rebecca Hayden**
Production Editor: **Vicki Friedberg**
Designer: **Merle Sanderson**
Print Buyer: **Karen Hunt**
Editorial Associate: **Naomi Brown**
Copy Editor: **Brenda Griffing**
Technical Illustrator: **Harry Spitzer**
Cover: **Merle Sanderson**
Signing Representatives: **Tom Orsi and Mark Francisco**
Cover photograph: **Courtesy of Apple Computer, Inc.**

Printed in the United States of America

   3 4 5 6 7 8 9 10—91 90 89 88 87

ISBN 0-534-06702-6

Library of Congress Cataloging-in-Publication Data

Wimmer, Roger D.
     Mass media research.

          Includes bibliographies and indexes.
          1. Mass media—Research.   2. Mass media—Methodology.
I. Dominick, Joseph R.   II. Title
P91.3W47   1987   001.51′072   86-4094
ISBN 0-534-06702-6

PREFACE

The media in the United States are constantly changing, and these changes have a profound effect on media researchers. For example, new FCC radio and television ownership regulations, cable television must-carry rules, buyouts of smaller media companies by larger groups, new approaches to advertising, and sophisticated public relations campaigns all change the focus and approach of research. Such changes in the media are reflected in this second edition.

One of the most dramatic changes in media research during the past 5 years is in computers, especially the introduction of microcomputers. Researchers no longer need to be tied to a mainframe computer to conduct research. The power of microcomputers and the software available for these machines have given media researchers easier access to the tools used in solving problems. In this second edition we have addressed the importance of microcomputers; however, we urge every reader to monitor a variety of computer periodicals to keep up to date with the rapidly changing hardware and software.

All the chapters in the second edition have been revised. In most cases these changes were occasioned by developments in the research field, such as microcomputers (Chapter 17) and people meters (Chapter 14); there are new chapters on longitudinal research (Chapter 9) and research in media effects (Chapter 16); and other types of qualitative research are discussed in other chapters. However, many changes were the result of readers who took the time to write and offer suggestions.

The second edition differs slightly from the first edition in organization. Part 1 contains four chapters about the fundamentals of research; Part 2, which discusses a variety of research approaches, has been expanded to include longitudinal research and other qualitative methods; Part 3 introduces basic statistics—the first edition's chapter on multivariate statistics has been shortened and placed in Appendix 2; Part 4 demonstrates research applications and includes a new chapter on mass media effects research; and Part 5 concerns the analysis and reporting of research. Each chapter has a section of problems and questions for further investigation. Appendix 1 contains tables used in statistical analysis, and Appendix 3 is a brief guide for conducting focus groups—a feature suggested by many users of the first edition. The glossary at the end of the book defines words printed in **boldface** when they are introduced in the text.

We wish to thank the following people who reviewed the manuscript and/or provided insightful comments for this second edition: John Robinson, Cox Enterprises, Inc.; Barry Sherman, University of Georgia; Alan Rubin, Kent State University; Jennings Bryant, University of Houston; and Joanne Cantor, University of Wisconsin at Madison. Also, we are grateful to the Literary Executor of the Late Sir Ronald A. Fisher, F.R.S., to Dr. Frank Yates, F.R.S., and to Longman Group Ltd, London for permission to reprint Tables 2 and 4 in Appendix 1 from their book *Statistical Tables for Biological, Agricultural, and Medical Research* (6th edition, 1974).

Our editor at Wadsworth, Becky Hayden, was the driving force behind this edition, and we owe her a debt of gratitude. We'd also like to thank Vicki Friedberg, our production editor, and Merle Sanderson, our book designer.

Finally, since this is a coauthored text, if there are any inaccuracies, omissions, or other lapses, each author will steadfastly blame the other.

Roger Wimmer
Denver, Colorado

Joseph Dominick
Athens, Georgia

CONTENTS

The Research Process

C H A P T E R 1

Science and Research

everal decades ago Richard Weaver (1953), a communications scholar, discussed the meanings of language and identified the differences between "god" and "devil" terms. A god term is positive and has connotations of strength, goodness, and significance; *democracy, innovation,* and *freedom* are god terms in the United States. A devil term, on the other hand, represents a negative image and connotes weakness, evil, or impending doom; *communist, moral decay,* and *inferior* are examples of devil terms.

One term that transcends both categories is *research.* Advertisers, for example, use research as a god term to sell products and services. Broadcast commercials and print advertisements include statements such as: "Research shows that 6 out of 10 doctors . . ." and "According to a recent survey, 80 out of 100 Cadillac owners preferred. . . ." The intention is to associate with the product a degree of importance based on the mere performance of research; research results alone are considered enough to convince consumers of the need for a product.

Research can also be a devil term, however, especially to those mass media students who consider statistics and research to be detours on the road to receiving a college degree. It is the intention of this book to help dispel the "devil" connotation of research. In communications, research need not be viewed negatively; rather it should be regarded as a tool with which to search for answers.`

Chapter 1, which introduces mass media research, includes discussions of the development of mass media research during the past 40 years, the methods used in collecting and analyzing information, and an expanded discussion of the scientific method of research. This chapter provides the foundation for topics discussed in greater detail in later chapters.

Two basic questions that the beginning researcher must learn to answer are *how* and *when* to use research methods and statistical procedures. Developing methods and procedures are valuable tasks, but the focus for the majority of research students should be on applications. This book advocates the approach of the *applied data analyst,* not the statistician.

As Figure 1.1 shows, the statistician and the data analyst belong on the same continuum, but their specialties are different. Statisticians generate statistical procedures or formulas called **algorithms**; data analysts use these algorithms to investigate research questions and hypotheses. The results of this cooperative effort are used to advance our understanding of the mass media.

Figure 1.1 Research continuum

Statistician _____ Data analyst

(Development)   (Utilization)

For example, consider the problem broadcasters once had with statistical error in audience ratings (a problem that has not been totally solved). Broadcasters and advertisers who used these ratings recognized that certain sampling procedures themselves rendered the figures they obtained highly susceptible to error. The users of ratings approached statisticians and asked them to develop a sampling error formula that would help make ratings more reliable. Several formulas were developed, and with these formulas, researchers, broadcasters, and advertisers were able to estimate the amount of error present in ratings data and help make more reliable interpretations. (In practice, however, only rarely does a broadcaster, advertiser, advertising agency buyer, or anyone else in broadcast-related industries consider sampling or statistical error when reading a radio or television ratings book. The numbers are accepted as real. One of the few times that error is considered comes when a station performs very poorly in a particular ratings book. Then the first comment from station management usually is "The numbers are wrong.")

Since the early part of the twentieth century, when it required little more than "head counts" of the audience, the mass media industry has come to rely on research results for nearly every major decision it makes. This increased demand for information has created a need for more research organizations, both public and private, as well as an increase in research specialization. There are research directors who plan and supervise studies and act as liaisons to management; methodological specialists who provide statistical support; research analysts who design and interpret studies; and computer specialists who provide hardware and software support in data analysis.

The importance of research in mass media is partly due to the realization that gut feelings or reactions are not entirely reliable as bases for decisions. Although common sense is often accurate, media decision makers need additional, more objective information to evaluate problems, especially when hundreds of thousands of dollars are at stake. Thus, the past 50 years have witnessed the slow evolution of an approach combining research and intuition to create a higher probability of success in the decision-making process.

Research is not limited to decision-making situations. It is also widely used in theoretical areas to attempt to describe the media, to analyze media effects on consumers, to understand audience behavior, and so forth. Barely a day goes by without some reference in the media to audience surveys, public opinion polls, the status or growth

Figure 1.2 Research phases in mass media

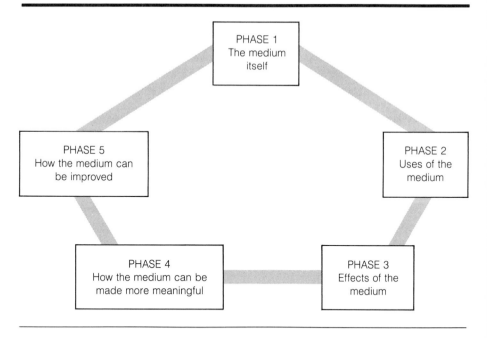

of one medium or another, or the success of advertising or public relations campaigns. Research in all areas of the media continues to expand at a phenomenal rate.

The Development of Mass Media Research

Mass media research has evolved in definable steps, and similar patterns have been followed in each medium's requirements for research (see Figure 1.2). Initially, there is an interest in the medium itself: researchers attempt to explain what the medium is, how it developed, and how it offers alternatives to the communication systems already available. This initial interest is followed by a second phase: a desire to learn more about how people use the medium for information and entertainment. A third phase involves an interest in determining what effects the medium has on people—how the medium alters or contributes to behavior patterns and attitudes.

Generally speaking, the interest in effects never subsides, but other phases quickly evolve. The broad area of policy research, for example, belongs in the phase devoted to an investigation of how to structure the medium to make it more useful or significant in the world of communication. An interest in the beneficial effects of technological developments on the medium is representative of the last phase. The importance of the fourth and fifth phase is clearly evident in studies of cable television's impact on the television industry. As Figure 1.2 indicates, mass media research is not a linear process: research emphases are continually changing. Researchers continue to apply all phases of research to a medium even decades after it has become popular.

In private sector research an additional research phase is continually present: How can the medium make money? The largest percentage of research conducted in the private sector relates in some way to finance—how to save money, make money, take money away from another source, or keep others from making money.

At least four major events or social forces have contributed to the growth of mass media research. The first was World War I, which brought about a need to further understand the nature of propaganda. Researchers working from a stimulus–response point of view attempted to uncover the effects of the media on people (Lasswell, 1927). The media at that time were thought to exert a very powerful influence over their audiences, and several assumptions were made about what the media could and could not do. One theory of mass media, known as the hypodermic needle model of communication, suggested that mass communicators need only "shoot" messages at an audience and they would receive preplanned and universal effects. The belief was that all people behave in very similar ways when they encounter media messages, though we know now that individual differences among people rule out this rather simplistic view. However, as DeFleur and Ball-Rokeach (1982) note:

> These assumptions may not have been explicitly formulated at the time, but they were drawn from fairly elaborate theories of human nature, as well as the nature of the social order. . . . It was these theories that guided the thinking of those who saw the media as powerful.

During the 1930s and 1940s, media researchers realized that early theories and assumptions about the media were limited in scope and application (see DeFleur & Ball-Rokeach, 1982). Instead of continuing to investigate other phases of the media, researchers stepped back to reexamine the media themselves—to explain the basic characteristics of the media. This was soon followed by an interest in the uses and effects of the media (Katz & Lazarsfeld, 1955; Lazarsfeld, Berelson, & Gaudet, 1948; Herzog, 1944; Klapper, 1960).

A second contributor to the development of mass media research was the realization by advertisers in the 1950s and 1960s that research data were useful in devising ways to persuade potential customers to buy products and services. Consequently, they encouraged studies of message effectiveness, audience demographics and size, placement of advertising to achieve the highest level of exposure (efficiency), frequency of advertising necessary to persuade potential customers, and selection of the medium that offered the best chance of reaching the target audience.

A third contributing social force was the increasing interest of citizens in the effects of the media on the public, especially on children. The direct result was an interest in research related to violence and sexual content in television programs and in commercials aired during children's programs. Over the past several years, some researchers have expanded their focus to include the positive (prosocial) as well as the negative (antisocial) effects of television (see Chapter 16). This phase is once again active with the heated debate over pop music lyrics and videos, which are shown on MTV and elsewhere.

Increased competition among the media for advertising dollars has been a fourth contributor to the growth of research. Media management has grown more sophisticated, utilizing long-range plans, management by objectives, and increasing dependency on data to support the decision process. Even program producers have begun to seek relevant research data, a task usually assigned to the creative side of program development. In addition, the mass media are now headed full speed into audience fragmentation; we are experiencing a "demassification" of the mass media.

The competition among the media for audiences and advertising dollars continues to reach new levels of complexity. The media "survival kit" today includes information about consumers' changing values and tastes, shifts in demographic patterns, and developing trends in lifestyles. Audience fragmentation in the media has led to an increased desire for trend studies (fads, new behavior patterns), image studies (how people perceive the media and their environment), and segmentation studies (explanations of types or groups of people). Major research organizations, consultants, and media owners and operators now conduct research that was previously considered the sole property of marketing. With the advent of increased competition and audience fragmentation, the media are more frequently using marketing strategies in an attempt to discover their position in the marketplace, and when this position is isolated or identified, the medium is packaged as an "image" rather than a product. (Similarly, the producers of consumer goods such as soap and toothpaste try to sell the "image" of these products, since the products themselves are very similar, if not the same, from company to company.) This packaging strategy involves determining what the members of the audience think, how they use language, how they occupy their spare time, and so on. Information on these ideas and behavior patterns is then woven into the merchandising effort to make the medium seem to be part of the audience. Positioning thus involves taking information from the audience, transforming it into research data, and using it to market the medium (see Ries & Trout, 1981, for more information about positioning in broadcasting and advertising).

Much of the media research up to the early 1960s originated in psychology and sociology departments at colleges and universities. Researchers with backgrounds in the media were rare because the media themselves were young. But this situation has changed. Media departments in colleges and universities grew rapidly in the 1960s, and media researchers entered the scene. Today the field is no longer dominated by researchers from allied areas. In fact, the trend is to encourage cross-disciplinary studies in which media researchers invite participation from sociologists, psychologists, and political scientists. Because of the pervasiveness of the media, researchers from all areas of science are now actively involved in attempting to answer media-related questions.

Media Research and the Scientific Method

Kerlinger (1973) defined scientific research as a systematic, controlled, empirical, and critical investigation of hypothetical propositions about the presumed relations among natural phenomena. Regardless of its origin, all research begins with a basic question or proposition about some phenomenon. For example: Why do people watch television? What section of the newspaper do people read most often? Why don't people subscribe to the most expensive cable television tier? Each of these questions could be answered to some degree with a research study.

There are several possible approaches in answering research questions. Kerlinger (1973), using definitions provided nearly a century ago by C. S. Peirce, discusses four approaches to finding answers, or "methods of knowing": tenacity, intuition, authority, and science.

The user of the **method of tenacity** follows the logic that something is true because it has always been true. An example is the store owner who says, "I don't advertise because my parents did not believe in advertising." The basic idea is that nothing changes; what was good, bad, or successful before will continue to be so in the future.

In the **method of intuition**, the a priori approach, one assumes that something is true because it is "self-evident" or "stands to reason." A claim such as "No one likes *Playboy* magazine because it contains pictures of nude women" represents the method of intuition. The speaker assumes that because he or she does not like the magazine (or television program, or newspaper editorial), everyone else holds the same belief.

The **method of authority** seeks to promote belief in something because a trusted source, such as a relative, news correspondent, or teacher, says it is true. The emphasis is on the source, not on the methods the source may have used to gain the information. The claim that "The world is going to end tomorrow because the *New York Times* editorial said so" is based on the method of authority.

The **scientific method** approaches learning as a series of small steps. That is, one study or one source provides only an *indication* of what may or may not be true; the "truth" is found only through a series of objective analyses. This means that the scientific method is self-correcting in that changes in thought or theory are appropriate when errors in previous research are uncovered. For example, scientists changed their ideas about the planet Saturn when, on the basis of information gathered by the Voyager spacecrafts, they uncovered errors in earlier observations. In communications, researchers discovered that the early perceptions of the power of the media (the "hypodermic needle" theory) were incorrect and, after numerous research studies, concluded that behavior and ideas are changed by a combination of communication sources and that people may react to the same message in different ways.

The scientific method may be inappropriate in many areas of life, such as evaluating works of art, choosing a religion, or forming friendships, but the method has been valuable in producing accurate and useful data in mass media research. The following section provides a more detailed look at this method of knowing.

Characteristics of the Scientific Method

Five basic characteristics or tenets distinguish the scientific method from other methods of knowing. A research approach that does not follow these tenets cannot be considered to be a scientific approach.

Scientific research is public. Scientific advancement depends on freely available information. A researcher (especially in the academic sector) cannot plead private knowledge, methods, or data in arguing for the accuracy of his or her findings; scientific research information must be freely communicated from one researcher to another. As Nunnally (1978, p. 8) noted:

> Science is a highly public enterprise in which efficient communication among scientists is essential. Each scientist builds on what has been learned in the past, day by day his or her findings must be compared with those of other scientists working on the same types of problems.

Researchers, therefore, must take great care in published reports to include information on their use of sampling methods, measurements, and data-gathering procedures. Such information allows other researchers to verify independently a given study and to support or refute the initial research findings. This process of **replication**, discussed in greater detail in Chapter 2, allows for correction or verification of previous research findings.

Researchers also need to save their descriptions of observations (data) and their research materials so that information not included in a formal report can be made available to other researchers on request. It is common practice to keep all raw research material for 5 years. This material is usually provided free as a courtesy to other researchers, or for a nominal fee if photocopying or additional materials are required.

Science is objective. Science tries to rule out eccentricities of judgment by researchers. When a study is undertaken, explicit rules and procedures are constructed and the researcher is bound to follow them, letting the chips fall where they may. Rules for classifying behavior are used so that two or more independent observers can classify particular patterns of behavior in the same manner. For example, if the attractiveness of a television commercial is being measured, researchers might count the number of times a viewer switches channels while the commercial is shown. This is considered to be an objective measure because a change in channel would be reported by any competent observer. Conversely, to measure attractiveness by observing how many people make "negative facial expressions" while the ad is shown would be a subjective approach, since observers may have different ideas of what constitutes a negative expression. However, an explicit definition of the term "negative facial expression" might eliminate the coding error.

Objectivity also requires that scientific research deal with facts rather than interpretations of facts. Science rejects its own authorities if their statements are in conflict with direct observation. As the noted psychologist B. F. Skinner (1953) wrote: "Research projects do not always come out as one expects, but the facts must stand and the expectations fall. The subject matter, not the scientist, knows best."

Science is empirical. Researchers are concerned with a world that is knowable and potentially measurable. ("Empiricism" is derived from the Greek word for "experience.") They must be able to perceive and classify what they study and to reject metaphysical and nonsensical explanations of events. For example, a newspaper publisher's claim that declining subscription rates are "God's will" would be rejected by scientists—such a statement cannot be perceived, classified, or measured.

This does not mean that scientists evade abstract ideas and notions—they encounter them every day. But they recognize that concepts must be strictly defined to allow for observation and measurement. Scientists must designate overt behavior patterns of certain kinds to represent abstract concepts if a link is to be provided between the metaphysical world and the physical world. Typically this linkage is accomplished by framing an **operational definition**.

Operational definitions are important in science, and a brief introduction necessitates some backtracking. There are basically two kinds of definitions. A **constitutive definition** defines a word by substituting other words or concepts for it. For example, "An artichoke is a green leafy vegetable, a tall composite herb of the *Cynara scolymus* family" is a constitutive definition of the concept "artichoke." In contrast, an operational definition specifies procedures to be followed in experiencing or measuring a concept. For example, "Go to the grocery store and find the produce aisle. Look for a sign that says 'Artichokes.' What's underneath the sign is one." Although an operational definition assures precision, it does not guarantee validity. An errant stock clerk may mistakenly stack lettuce under the artichoke sign and fool someone. This underlines the importance of considering both the constitutive and the operational definition of a concept in evaluating the trustworthiness of any measurement. A careful examination of the constitutive definition of artichoke would indicate that the operational definition might be faulty. For further discussion of operational definitions, see Chapter 3 and *Psychometric Theory* (Nunnally, 1978).

Science is systematic and cumulative. No single research study stands alone, nor does it rise or fall by itself. Astute researchers always utilize previous studies as building blocks for their own work. One of the first steps taken in conducting research is to review the available scientific literature on the topic so that the current study will draw on the heritage of past research (see Chapter 2). This review is valuable for identifying problem areas and important factors that might be relevant to the current study (see Cattell, 1966).

In addition, scientists attempt to search for order and consistency among their findings. In its ideal form, scientific research begins with a single, carefully observed event and progresses ultimately to the formulation of theories and laws. A **theory** is a set of related **propositions** that presents a systematic view of phenomena by specifying relationships among concepts. Researchers develop theories by searching for patterns of uniformity to explain the data that have been collected. When relationships among variables are invariant under given conditions (that is, when the relationship is always the same), researchers may formulate a law. Both theories and laws help researchers search for and explain consistency in behavior, situations, and phenomena.

Science is predictive. Science is concerned with relating the present to the future. In fact, scientists strive to develop theories because, for one reason, they are useful in predicting behavior. A theory's adequacy lies in its ability to predict a phenomenon or event successfully. If a theory suggests predictions that are not borne out by data analysis, that theory must be carefully reexamined and perhaps discarded. Conversely, if a theory generates predictions that are supported by the data, that theory can be used to make predictions in other situations.

Research Procedures

The use of the scientific method of research is intended to provide an objective, unbiased evaluation of data. To investigate research questions and hypotheses systematically, both academic and private sector researchers (discussed below) follow a basic eight-step developmental chain of procedures:

1. Select a problem.
2. Review existing research and theory (when relevant).
3. Develop hypotheses or research questions.
4. Determine an appropriate methodology/research design.
5. Collect relevant data.
6. Analyze and interpret the results.
7. Present the results in appropriate form.
8. Replicate the study (when necessary).

Steps 2 and 8 are optional in private sector research because in many instances research is conducted to answer a specific and unique question related to a future decision, such as whether to invest a large sum of money in a developing medium. In this type of project there generally is no previous research to consult, and there seldom is a reason to replicate (repeat) the study because a decision will be made on the basis of the first analysis. However, if the research provided inconclusive results, the study would be revised and replicated.

Each step in the eight-step research process depends on all the others to help produce a maximally efficient research study. Before a literature search is possible, a clearly stated research problem is required; to design the most efficient method of investigating a problem, the researcher needs to know what types of studies have been conducted, and so on. All the steps are interactive: the results or conclusions of any step have a bearing on other steps. For example, a literature search may refine and even alter the initial research problem; a study conducted previously by another company or business in the private sector might have similar effects.

Two Sectors of Research: Academic and Private

The practice of research is divided into two major sectors, academic and private. Both are important in mass media research, and in many cases the two work together to solve media problems.

Academic sector research is conducted by scholars from colleges and universities. It also *generally* means that the research has a *theoretical* or scholarly approach; that is, the results are intended to help explain the mass media and their effects on individuals. Some popular research topics in the theoretical area include the use of the media and various media-related items, such as video games, teletext, and multiple-channel cable systems; lifestyle analyses of consumers; media "overload" on consumers; alternatives to present media systems; and the effects of various types of programming on children.

Private sector research is conducted by nongovernmental businesses and industries or their research consultants. It is generally *applied* research; that is, the results are intended to be used in decision-making situations. Typical research topics in the private sector include analyses of media content and consumer preferences, acquisition research to determine whether to purchase additional businesses or facilities, public relations approaches to solve specific informational problems, sales forecasting, and image studies of the properties owned by the company.

There are other differences between academic and private sector research. For instance, academic research is public. Any other researcher or research organization that wishes to use the information gathered by academic researchers should be able to do so merely by asking the original researcher for the raw data. Most private sector research, on the other hand, generates **proprietary data**: the results are considered to be the sole property of the sponsoring agency and cannot generally be obtained by other researchers. Some private sector research, however, is released to the public soon after it has been conducted, such as opinion polls and projections of the future of the media; still other data are released after several years, although this practice is the exception rather than the rule.

Another difference between academic and private sector research involves the amount of time allowed to conduct the work. Academic researchers generally do not have specific deadlines for their research projects (except when research grants are received). Academicians usually conduct research at a pace that accommodates their teaching schedules. Private sector researchers, however, nearly always operate under some type of deadline. The time frame may be specified by management or by an outside agency that requires a decision from the company or business. For example, the Federal Communications Commission often indicates that a rule or regulation will be reviewed on a specific date and advises that any person, group, or entity may respond to the review. When an impending ruling may have an impact on a company's operation, the data required for the FCC hearing must be collected and analyzed in a very short time. Private sector researchers rarely have an opportunity to pursue research questions in a casual manner; a decision is generally waiting to be made on the basis of the research.

Also, academic research is generally less expensive to conduct than research in the private sector. This is not to say that academic research is "cheap"—it is not in many cases. But academicians do not need to have enormous sums of money to cover overhead costs for equipment, facilities, computer analysis, subcontractors, and personnel. Private sector research, whether it is done within a company or hired out to a research supplier, must take such expenses into account. The reduced cost is the primary reason why many of the large media companies and groups prefer to use academic researchers rather than professional research firms.

Despite these differences, it is important for beginning researchers to understand that academic research and private sector research are not completely independent of each other. The link between the two areas is important. Academicians perform many studies for the industry, and private sector groups conduct research that can be classified as theoretical (for example, the television networks have departments that conduct social research). Many college and university professors act as consultants to, and often conduct private sector research for, the media industry.

It is also important for all researchers to refrain from attaching to academic or private sector research such stereotypical labels as "unrealistic," "inappropriate," "pedantic," and "limited in scope." Research in both sectors, although differing occasionally in terms of cost and scope, uses similar methodologies and statistical analyses. In addition, both sectors have common research goals: to understand problems and to predict the future.

In conducting a study according to the scientific method, researchers need to have a clear understanding of what they are investigating, how the phenomenon can be measured or observed, and what procedures are required to test the observations or measurements. Conceptualization of the research problem in question and a logical development of procedural steps are necessary to have any hope of answering a research question or hypothesis. (See Chapter 2 for a more detailed discussion of research procedures.)

Summary

In an effort to understand any phenomenon, researchers can follow one of several methods of inquiry. Of the procedures discussed in this chapter, the scientific approach is most applicable to the mass media because it involves a systematic, objective evaluation of information. Researchers first identify a problem, then investigate it, using a prescribed set of procedures known as the scientific method of research. In addition, the scientific method is the only learning approach that allows for self-correction of research findings; one study does not stand alone but must be supported or refuted by others.

The rapid growth of mass media research is mainly attributable to the rapidly developing technology of the media industry. Because of this growth in research, both applied and theoretical approaches have taken on more significance in the decision-making process of the mass media and in our understanding of the media.

Questions and Problems for Further Investigation

1. Obtain a recent issue of *Journal of Broadcasting & Electronic Media*, *Journalism Quarterly*, or *Public Opinion Quarterly*. How many articles fit into the research phases outlined in Figure 1.2?
2. What are some potential research questions that might be of interest to both academic and private sector researchers? Do not limit the questions to the area of effects research.
3. How might the scientific research approach be abused by researchers?
4. Theories are important in developing solid bodies of information; they are used as springboards to investigation. However, there are few universally recognized theories in mass media research. Why do you think this is true?
5. During the past several years, citizens' groups have claimed that television has a significant effect on viewers, especially with regard to violence and sexual content of programs. More recently, groups are criticizing song lyrics. How might these groups have collected data to support their claims? Which method of knowing would such citizens' groups be most likely to use?

References and Suggested Readings

Brown, J. A. (1980). Selling airtime for controversy: NAB self regulation and Father Coughlin. *Journal of Broadcasting, 24*(2), 199–224.

Carroll, R. L. (1980). The 1948 Truman campaign: The threshold of the modern era. *Journal of Broadcasting, 24*(2), 173–188.

Cattell, R. B. (Ed.). (1966). *Handbook of multivariate experimental psychology.* Skokie, IL: Rand McNally.

DeFleur, M. L., & Ball-Rokeach, S. (1982). *Theories of mass communication* (2nd ed.). New York: David McKay.

Herzog, H. (1944). What do we really know about daytime serial listeners? In P. Lazarsfeld & F. Stanton (Eds.), *Radio Research 1943–44*. New York: Duell, Sloan, and Pearce.

Katz, E., & Lazarsfeld, P. F. (1955). *Personal influence.* New York: Free Press.

Kerlinger, F. N. (1973). *Foundations of behavioral research.* New York: Holt, Rinehart & Winston.

Klapper, J. (1960). *The effects of mass communication.* New York: Free Press.

Lasswell, H. D. (1927). *Propaganda technique in the World War.* New York: Knopf.

Lazarsfeld, P., Berelson, B., & Gaudet, H. (1948). *The people's choice.* New York: Columbia University Press.

Murphy, J. H., & Amundsen, M. S. (1981). The communication effectiveness of comparative advertising for a new brand on users of the dominant brand. *Journal of Advertising, 10*(1), 14–20.

Nunnally, J. C. (1978). *Psychometric theory.* New York: McGraw-Hill.

Ries, E., & Trout, J. (1981). *Positioning: The battle for your mind.* New York: McGraw-Hill.

Skinner, B. F. (1953). *Science and human behavior.* New York: Macmillan.

Sybert, P. J. (1980). MBS and the Dominican Republic. *Journal of Broadcasting, 24*(2), 189–198.

Weaver, R. M. (1953). *The ethics of rhetoric.* Chicago: Henry Regnery.

C H A P T E R 2
Research Procedures

SELECTION OF A RESEARCH TOPIC

·

DETERMINATION OF TOPIC RELEVANCE

·

REVIEW OF AVAILABLE LITERATURE

·

STATEMENT OF A HYPOTHESIS OR RESEARCH QUESTION

·

RESEARCH AND EXPERIMENTAL DESIGN

·

RESEARCH SUPPLIERS

·

DATA ANALYSIS AND INTERPRETATION

·

PRESENTATION OF RESULTS

·

REPLICATION

·

THE HAZARDS OF RESEARCH

·

SUMMARY

·

QUESTIONS AND PROBLEMS FOR FURTHER INVESTIGATION

·

REFERENCES AND SUGGESTED READINGS

The scientific evaluation of any problem must follow a sequence of steps to increase the chances of producing relevant data. Researchers who do not follow a prescribed set of steps do not subscribe to the scientific method of inquiry and simply increase the amount of error present in the study. This chapter describes the process of scientific research, from identifying and developing a topic for investigation to replication of results. The first section briefly introduces the steps in the development of a research topic.

Objective, rigorous observation and analysis are characteristic of the scientific method. To meet this goal, researchers must follow the prescribed steps shown in Figure 2.1. This research model is appropriate to all areas of scientific research.

Selection of a Research Topic

Selecting a research topic is not a concern for all researchers; in fact, only a few investigators in communications fields are fortunate enough to be able to choose and concentrate on a research area interesting to them. Many come to be identified with studies of specific types, such as focus group methodology, magazine advertising, or communications and the law. These researchers investigate small pieces of a puzzle in communications to obtain a broad picture of their research area.

In the private sector, researchers generally do not have the flexibility of selecting topics or questions to investigate. Instead, they conduct studies to answer questions raised by management. Although most private sector researchers are limited in the amount of input they can contribute to topic selection, they usually are given total control over how the question should be answered (that is, what research methodology should be used). The goal of private sector researchers is to develop a method that is fast, inexpensive, reliable, and valid. If all these criteria are met, the researcher has performed a valuable task.

However, selecting a topic is a concern for many beginning researchers, especially those writing term papers, theses, and dissertations. The problem is knowing where to start. Fortunately, there are virtually unlimited sources available in searching for a research topic; academic journals, periodicals and newsweeklies, and everyday en-

Figure 2.1 Steps in the development of a research project

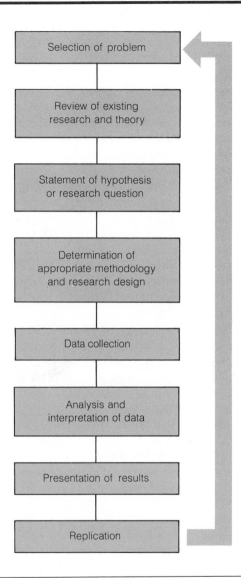

counters can provide a wealth of ideas. Some of the primary sources are highlighted in this section.

Professional Journals

Academic communication journals, such as the *Journal of Broadcasting & Electronic Media, Journalism Quarterly,* and others listed in the accompanying box are excellent sources for information. Although academic

JOURNALS SPECIALIZING IN MASS MEDIA RESEARCH

- *Critical Studies in Mass Communication*
- *Journalism Quarterly*
- *Journal of Advertising*
- *Journal of Advertising Research*
- *Journal of Broadcasting & Electronic Media*
- *Journal of Consumer Research*
- *Journal of Marketing*
- *Journal of Marketing Research*
- *Public Relations Review*

JOURNALS OCCASIONALLY PUBLISHING MASS MEDIA RESEARCH

- *American Psychologist*
- *Communication Education*
- *Communication Monographs*
- *Communication Research*
- *Feedback* (from the Broadcast Education Assocation)
- *Human Communication Research*
- *Journalism Educator*
- *Journal of Communication*
- *Multivariate Behavioral Research*
- *Politics*
- *Public Relations Quarterly*
- *Quarterly Journal of Speech*
- *Social Forces*
- *Sociology and Social Research*

---

journals tend to publish research that is 12 to 24 months old (due to review procedures and backlog of articles), the articles may provide ideas for research topics. Most authors conclude their research by discussing problems encountered during the study and suggesting topics that need further investigation. In addition, some journal editors build issues around individual research themes, which often can help in formulating research plans.

There are many high-quality journals covering various aspects of research. Some journals specialize in mass media research, and others include media research occasionally. The journals above provide a starting point in using academic journals for research ideas.

In addition to academic journals, professional trade publications offer a wealth of information relevant to mass media research. These include *Broadcasting, Advertising Age, Electronic Media, Television/ Radio Age, Media Decisions, Editor & Publisher, CableVision,* and *Media and Marketing Management.* Other excellent sources for identifying current topics in mass media are the weekly newsletters, such as *Media Industry Newsletter, Cable Digest,* and several publications from Paul Kagan and Associates.

Research abstracts, located in most college and university libraries, are also valuable sources for research topics. These volumes contain summaries of research articles published in nearly every academic journal. Of particular interest to media researchers are *Communication Abstracts, Psychological Abstracts, Sociological Abstracts,* and *Dissertation Abstracts.*

Magazines and Periodicals

Many educators feel that publications other than professional journals contain only "watered-down" articles written for the general public. To some extent this is true, but these articles tend to eliminate the tedious technical jargon and are often good sources for problems and hypotheses. In addition, more and more articles written by highly trained communications professionals are appearing in weekly and monthly publications such as *TV Guide, Time,* and *Newsweek.* These sources often provide interesting perspectives on complex problems in communication and many times raise interesting questions that media researchers can pursue.

Research Summaries

Professional research organizations irregularly publish summaries that provide a close look at the major areas of research in various fields. These summaries are often useful for obtaining information about research topics, since they survey a wide variety of studies. Good examples of summary research (also known as "metaresearch") in communication include: *Television and Human Behavior,* by George Comstock and others; *The Effects of Mass Communication on Political Behavior,* by Sydney Kraus and Dennis Davis; and *Mass Communication: A Research Bibliography,* by Donald Hansen and J. Hershel Parsons. The *Communication Yearbook,* an annual publication by the International Communication Association, has gained in popularity since its first issue in 1977 and contains a variety of media research. Another popular research source is the *Mass Communication Yearbook,* published by Sage Publications.

Everyday Situations

Each day we are all confronted with various types of communication via broadcasting and print, interpersonal communication, public relations campaigns, and so forth. These confrontations can be excellent sources of research topics for the researchers who take an active role in analyzing them. What types of messages are produced? Why are they produced in a specific way? What effects are expected from the various types of communication? These and other questions may help develop a research idea. Significant studies based on questions arising from everyday encounters with the media and other forms of mass communication have covered investigations of television violence, layout of newspaper advertisements, advisory warnings on television programs, and approaches to public relations campaigns.

Data Archives

Data archives, such as the Inter-University Consortium for Political Research (ICPR) at the University of Michigan, the Simmons Target Group Index (TGI), the Gallup and Roper organizations, and the Arbitron collection at the University of Georgia, are other valuable sources of ideas for researchers. These archives act as storage facilities where data are deposited for use by other investigators, who conduct further research or ask different questions. This process, known as **secondary analysis**, has become a major research approach because of the time and resource savings it affords.

Secondary analysis provides an opportunity for researchers to evaluate otherwise unavailable data. Becker (1981, p. 240) defines secondary analysis as:

> [the] reuse of social science data after they have been put aside by the researcher who gathered them. The reuse of the data can be by the original researcher or someone uninvolved in any way in the initial research project. The research questions examined in the secondary analysis can be related to the original research endeavor or quite distinct from it.

Advantages of secondary analysis. Ideally every researcher should conduct a research project of some magnitude, to learn about design, data collection, and analysis. Unfortunately, this ideal situation does not exist. Modern research is simply too expensive. In addition, because survey methodology has become so complex, it is rare to find one researcher, or even a small group of researchers, who are experts in all phases of large studies.

Secondary analysis is one research alternative that solves some of these problems. There is almost no expense involved in using available data. There are no questionnaires or measurement instruments to construct and validate, salaries for interviewers and other personnel are nonexistent, and there are no costs for subjects and special equipment. The only expenses entailed in secondary analysis are those for duplicating materials—some organizations provide their data free of charge—and computer time.

Secondary analysis has a bad connotation for some researchers, especially those who are unfamiliar with its potential (Becker, 1981). Although researchers can derive some benefits from developing questionnaires and conducting a research project using a small and often unrepresentative sample of subjects, this type of analysis rarely produces results that are externally valid (see p. 38). The argument here is that in lieu of conducting a small study that has limited (if any) value to other situations, researchers would benefit from using valid data that have been previously collected.

Another advantage of secondary analysis is that data allow researchers more time to further understand what has been collected (Tukey, 1969). All too often research is conducted and after a cursory analysis of the data for publication or report to management, the data are set aside, never to be touched again. It is difficult to completely analyze all data from any research study in just one or two studies, yet this procedure is followed in both the academic and private sectors.

Tukey (1969, p. 89) argues for data reanalysis especially for graduate students, but his statement applies to all researchers:

> There is merit in having a Ph.D. thesis encompass all the admitted steps of the research process. Once we recognize that research is a continuing, more or less cyclic process, however, we see that we can segment it in many places. Why should not at least a fair proportion of theses start with a reasonably careful analysis of previously collected and presumably already lightly analyzed data, a process usefully spread out over considerable time. Instant data analysis is—and will remain—an illusion.

Arguments for secondary analysis come from a variety of researchers (Glenn, 1972; Hyman, 1972; Tukey, 1969). It is clear that the research method provides excellent opportunities to produce valuable knowledge. The procedure, however, is not free from criticism.

Disadvantages of secondary analysis. Researchers who use secondary analysis are limited to the types of hypotheses or research questions that can be investigated. The data already exist, and since there is no way to go back for further information, researchers must keep their analyses within the boundaries of the type of data originally collected.

Researchers conducting secondary analysis studies also may face the problems of using data that were poorly collected, inaccurate, or flawed. Many studies do not include information about the research design, sampling procedures, weighting of subjects' responses, or other peculiarities. Perhaps it is suspected that some of the data were fabricated. Large research firms tend to explain their procedures in detail. Although individual researchers in mass media have begun to make their data more readily available (Reid, Soley, & Wimmer, 1981; Wimmer & Reid, 1982), not all follow adequate scientific procedures. This may seriously affect a secondary analysis.

Before selecting a secondary analysis approach, researchers need to consider the advantages and disadvantages. However, with the increased use of secondary analysis, some of the problems associated with research explanations and data storage are being solved. For an example of secondary analysis, see Becker, Beam, and Russial (1978).

Determination of Topic Relevance

Once a basic research idea has been chosen, the next step is to ensure that the topic has merit. This step can be accomplished by answering seven basic questions.

Question 1: Is the Topic Too Broad?

Most research studies concentrate on one small area of a field; few researchers attempt to analyze an entire field in one study. There is a tendency, however, for researchers to choose topics that, while valuable, are too broad to cover in one study—for example, "the effects of television violence on children," or "the effects of mass media information on voters in a presidential election."

To avoid this problem, the researcher should write down his or her proposed title, as a visual starting point, and attempt to dissect the topic into small questions. Figure 2.2 illustrates this dissection process with regard to the topic "Political Communication." It is an effective way to isolate a manageable topic from a broad research category.

Question 2: Can the Problem Really Be Investigated?

Aside from considerations of broadness, a topic might prove unsuitable for investigation simply because the question being asked has no answer, or at least cannot be answered with the facilities and information available. For example, a researcher who wants to know how people who have no television receiver react to everyday interpersonal communication situations must consider the problems of finding subjects without at least one television set in the home. Some may exist in re-

Figure 2.2 The development of a research topic from a broad category to a restricted analysis

Political Communication

Effects of mass media in presidential elections.

Effects of mass media in Senate elections.

Effects of mass media in local elections.

Mass media or interpersonal?

Local campaigns rely heavily on interpersonal communication in campaigns.

How effective is this interpersonal information on the outcome of the election?

What kinds of topics do the local candidates discuss during the campaign?

Where does the candidate get information on the various issues discussed in the campaign?

Conduct a survey of candidates to find out where they get information for speeches and interpersonal discussions.

Survey just one candidate about sources of information.

Conduct a field study: follow the candidate from the day he/she announces intention to run for office; analyze where he/she gets information for campaign issues.

Develop a workable hypothesis regarding how local political candidates develop information for issues.

mote parts of the country, but the question is basically unanswerable due to the current saturation of television. Thus the researcher must attempt to reanalyze the original idea in conformity with practical considerations. A. S. Tan (1977) solved this particular dilemma by choosing to investigate what people do when their television sets are turned off for a period of time. He persuaded subjects not to watch television for one week and to record their use of other media, their interactions with their family and friends, and so on.

Another point to consider is whether all terms of the proposed study are definable. Remember that all measurable variables must be operationally defined (see Chapter 3). A researcher who is interested in examining youngsters' use of the media needs to come up with a working definition of the word *youngsters* to avoid confusion. Potential problems can be eliminated if an operational definition is stated: "Youngsters are children between the ages of 3 and 7 years."

One final consideration is to review available literature to determine whether the topic has been investigated. Were there any problems in previous studies? What methods were used to answer the research questions? What conclusions were drawn?

Question 3: Are the Data Susceptible to Analysis?

A topic does not lend itself to productive research if it requires the collection of data that cannot be measured reliably and validly (see Chapter 3). In other words, the researcher who wants to measure the effects of not watching television should consider whether the information about the subjects' behavior will be adequate and reliable, whether the subjects will answer truthfully, what value the data will have once gathered, and so forth. Researchers also need to have enough data to make the study worthwhile. It would be inadequate to analyze only 10 subjects in the "television turn-off" example, since the results could not be generalized with regard to the entire population.

Another consideration is the researcher's previous experience with the statistical method selected to analyze the data. That is, does he or she really understand the proposed statistical analysis? Researchers need to know how the statistics work and how to interpret the results. All too often researchers design studies involving advanced statistical procedures that they have never used. This tactic invariably creates errors in computation and interpretation. Research methods and statistics should not be selected because they happen to be popular or because a research director suggests a given method, but rather because they are appropriate for a given study and are understood by the person conducting the analysis. A common error made by beginning researchers is to select a statistical method without understanding what the statistic actually produces. Using a statistical method without understanding what the method produces is called the *law of the instrument*. It is much wiser to do simple frequencies and percentages and understand the results than to try to use a high-level statistic and end up totally confused.

Question 4: Is the Problem Significant?

Before a study is conducted, the researcher must determine whether it has merit, that is, whether the results will have practical or theoretical value. The first question to ask is, Will the results add knowledge to the information already available in the field? The goal of all research is to help further the understanding of the problems and questions in the field of study; if a study does not do this, it has little value beyond the experience the researcher acquires from conducting it. This does not mean that all research has to be earth-shattering. Many investigators, however, waste valuable time trying to develop monumental projects when in fact the smaller problems are of more concern.

A second question is, What is the *real* purpose of the study? This is important because it helps focus ideas. Is the study intended for a class paper, a thesis, a journal article, a management summary? Each of these projects has different requirements concerning background information needed, amount of explanation required, and detail of results generated. For example, applied researchers need to determine whether any useful action based on the data will prove to be feasible, as well as whether the study will answer the question(s) posed by management.

Question 5: Can the Results of the Study Be Generalized?

For a research project to have practical value—to be significant beyond the immediate analysis—it must have **external validity**; that is, one must be able to generalize from it to other situations. For example, a study of the effects of a small-town public relations campaign might be appropriate if plans are made to analyze such effects in several small towns, or if it is a case study not intended for generalization; however, such an analysis has little external validity.

Question 6: What Costs and Time Are Involved in the Analysis?

In many cases the cost of a research study is the sole determinant of the feasibility of a project. A researcher may have an excellent idea, but if costs would be prohibitive, the project must be abandoned. A cost analysis must be completed very early on. It does not make sense to develop specific designs and the data-gathering instrument for a project that will be canceled because of lack of funds. Sophisticated research is particularly expensive: costs may easily exceed $50,000 for one project.

A carefully itemized list of all materials, equipment, and other facilities required is necessary before beginning a research project. If the costs seem prohibitive, the researcher must determine whether the same goal can be achieved if costs are shaved in some areas. Another possibility to consider is financial aid from graduate schools, funding agencies, local governments, or other groups that subsidize research projects. In general, private sector researchers are not severely constrained by expenses; however, they must adhere to budget specifications provided by management.

Time is also an important consideration in research planning. Research studies must be designed in such a way that they can be completed in the amount of time available. Many studies have failed because not enough time was allotted for each research step, and in many cases, the pressure created by deadlines creates problems in producing reliable and valid results (for example, failure to provide alternatives if the correct sample of people cannot be located).

Question 7: Is the Planned Approach Appropriate to the Project?

The most marvelous research idea may be greatly, and often needlessly, hindered by a poorly planned method of approach. For example, a researcher who wished to measure any change in attendance at movie theaters that may have accompanied the increase in television viewing in one city could mail questionnaires to a large number of people to determine how media habits have changed during the past few years. However, the costs of printing and mailing questionnaires, plus follow-up letters and possibly phone calls to increase the response rate, might prove prohibitive.

Could this study be planned differently to eliminate some of the expense? Possibly, depending on the purpose of the study and the types of question planned. The researcher could collect the data by telephone interviews to eliminate printing and postage costs. Some questions might need reworking to fit the telephone procedure, but the essential information could be collected. A close look at every study is required to plan the best approach. Every procedure in a research study should be considered from the standpoint of the **parsimony principle**, or Occam's razor: the simplest research approach is always the most efficient.

Review of Available Literature

Researchers often spend time collecting data that are already available. For example, a researcher wishing to know how much money was spent for political advertising by the presidential candidates during the 1984 election campaign might send questionnaires to all the candidates in the campaign. However, a small amount of research would reveal that this information can easily be obtained from the Federal Communications Commission. A researcher who conducts an investigation without regard to data that are already available or work that has already been done in the field is said to have fallen into the syndrome of "Ivory Tower Research." Research such as this adds nothing to our understanding of the media.

A search of the available literature saves time and money. By examining government documents, professional journals, data archives, and library sources, the researcher may find that the main portion of the data needed in a particular study has been collected. Moreover, the chosen topic may have been the subject of one or more research studies already; thus an additional investigation would be redundant.

In conducting a review of existing research, an investigator should bear in mind such questions as the following (Agostino 1980):

1. What type of research has been done in the area?
2. What has been found in previous studies?
3. What suggestions do other researchers make for further study?
4. What has not been investigated?
5. How can the proposed study add to our knowledge of the area?
6. What research methods were used in previous studies?

Answers to these questions will usually help define a specific hypothesis or research question.

Statement of a Hypothesis or Research Question

After a general research area has been identified and the existing literature reviewed, the researcher must state the problem as a workable **hypothesis** or **research question**—that is, a tentative generalization regarding the relationship between the variables that will figure in the study. A hypothesis is a testable statement, whereas a research question is a formally stated question intended to provide indications about a particular variable relationship. A research question is generally used when the researcher is unsure about the nature of the question and is merely gathering preliminary data. It is often possible to generate testable hypotheses from the data gathered during the research question phase of a study.

For example, Singer and Singer (1981) provide an excellent example of how a topic is narrowed, developed, and stated in simple terms. The authors were interested in whether television material enhances or inhibits a child's capacity for symbolic behavior. After a thorough review of available literature, Singer and Singer narrowed their study by seeking to answer three basic research questions.

1. Does television content enrich a child's imaginative capacities by offering materials and ideas for make-believe play?
2. Does television lead to distortions of reality for children?
3. Can intervention and mediation on the part of an adult while a child views a program, or immediately afterward, evoke changes in make-believe play, or stimulate make-believe play?

The information collected from this type of study could provide data to create testable hypotheses. For example, Singer and Singer might have collected enough valuable information from their preliminary study to test the hypotheses suggested below.

1. A child's capacity for make-believe play is directly related to television content.
2. A child's distortion of reality is directly related to the amount and type of television the child views.
3. Parental intervention during or after a child's exposure to television increases the child's capacity for make-believe play.

The difference between the two sets of statements is that the research questions only pose potential relationships between variables; the intention is not to support or reject the statements, but rather to gather information to enable the researchers to define testable hypotheses.

Research and Experimental Design

Given the variety of research questions in mass media, different research approaches are required. Some questions call for a survey methodology via telephone or mail; others are best answered through in-person interviews. Still other problems necessitate a controlled laboratory situation to eliminate extraneous variables. The approach selected by the researcher depends on the goals and purpose of the study and how much money is available to conduct the analysis. Even projects that sound very simple may require a highly sophisticated and complex research approach.

The process of developing or preparing a research study is referred to as "research design" or "experimental design." There is no particular agreement among researchers as to the definitions of these two terms. Although "research design" has become a generic term for any type of plan for a research study, in this book, the term refers to the plan a researcher develops for a nonlaboratory study, whereas "experimental design" designates a plan for a laboratory, or controlled, study.

The primary difference between these two types of research is that in a laboratory study, the researcher is in control of the situation. Nonlaboratory research does not generally afford the amount of control found in laboratory research.

A research or experimental design is essentially a blueprint or set of plans for collecting information. The ideal design collects a maximum amount of information with a minimal expenditure of time and resources. Depending on the circumstances, a design may be brief or very complicated; there are no specific guidelines concerning the amount of detail required for a design. However, all designs incorporate the steps in the process of collecting and analyzing the data.

Researchers must determine the methodology (the way the data will be collected and analyzed) before beginning a research project. Attempting to force a study to follow a particular approach or statistic after the data have been gathered only invites error. For example, a director of marketing for a large shopping mall was interested in finding out more about the customers who shopped at the mall (for example, where they lived and how often they shopped at the mall). With very little planning, she designed a simple questionnaire to collect the information. However, the possible answers, or response choices for respondents, to each of the questions were inadequate and the questionnaire inappropriately designed for any type of summary analysis. Thus, the director of marketing was stuck with thousands of useless questionnaires.

All research—from very simple surveys of only a few people to nationwide studies covering complex issues—requires a design of some type. All procedures, including variables, samples, and measurement instruments, must be selected or designed in light of their appropriateness to the hypotheses or research questions, and all items must be planned in advance.

There are four characteristics of research design that should be noted if a study is to produce reliable and valid results (Haskins, 1968):

1. *Naturalistic setting.* For the results of any project to have external validity, the study must be conducted under normally encountered environmental conditions. This means that subjects should be unaware of the research situation, if possible; that phenomena should not be analyzed in a single session; and that normal intervening variables, such as noise, should be included in the study. Also, long-term projects are more conducive to a naturalistic atmosphere than short-term studies.

2. *Clear cause-and-effect relationships.* The researcher must make every effort to rule out intervening or spurious independent/dependent variable relationships. The results of a study can be interpreted with confidence *if and only if* all confounding effects are identified.

3. *Unobtrusive and valid measurements.* There should be no perceptible connection between the communication presented to subjects and the measurement instruments used. Subjects tend to answer questions differently if they can identify the purpose of the study. Also, the study should be designed to assess both immediate and long-term effects on the subjects.

    To assure the validity of the measurements used, a sample should be large enough to allow detection of minor effects or changes (see Chapter 4). Additionally, the selection of dependent variables should be based on their relevance to the study and the researcher's knowledge of the area, not on convenience.

4. *Realism.* A research design must above all be realistic. This necessitates a careful consideration of the availability of time, money, personnel to conduct the study, and researchers who are competent in the proposed research methodology and statistical analysis.

Once the methodology has been properly developed, researchers must make a trial run, or **pilot study**, of the entire process. A pilot study is a small-scale version of the planned study and is designed to check for errors in the research design, measurement instrument(s), or equipment used. The mall marketing director in the previous example could have saved a great deal of time and money by running a pilot study using 10 or 20 mall shoppers. She would have quickly discovered that the questionnaire did not produce the desired results. Conducting a pilot study in research is similar to taking driver's education in high school: you are allowed to make errors without jeopardizing the final results (or the real situation).

Research Suppliers

Many researchers do not actually conduct every phase of every project they supervise. That is, although they usually design research projects, determine the samples to be studied, and prepare the measurement instruments, the researchers generally do not actually make the telephone calls or interview respondents in shopping malls. The researchers instead contract with a *research supplier* or *field service* to perform these tasks.

A research supplier is not the same as a full-service research company. A supplier merely gathers data for a client; a full-service company participates in the designing of a study, supervises data collecting, and provides an analysis of the results.

Just as there are a variety of research methodologies available for application to a given problem, there are also a variety of research suppliers to be hired for research projects. Some suppliers have only a few employees and specialize in a particular type of research, or possibly even in a specific aspect of research such as focus group recruiting (such a firm is responsible for recruiting the people for the group and providing a suitable facility for the performance of the research). Other suppliers, such as R. H. Bruskin Associates, are large companies that offer a variety of services from simple research design to the conduct of a complete study, including sample selection, questionnaire design, data collection, and preparation of a formal written analysis of the data.

Contracting with a supplier is quite simple. Most researchers know several dozen companies that provide research, but through past experience have determined which company (or companies) would be most qualified to handle a specific project. The researcher simply calls the supplier and explains the project to the appropriate person. Assuming that the supplier has the time and personnel to complete the project by the deadline, the researcher hires the company to conduct the study. This does not mean that the supplier is in complete control of the study. Quite the opposite is true. The researcher must monitor the status of the project, identify any problems with the measurement instrument, and possibly make changes in the project to solve problems that were not apparent in the original research design.

Some problems with hiring research suppliers are discussed in Chapter 7; however, two important points must be introduced here to help novice researchers when they begin to use research suppliers.

1. All research suppliers are not equal. Any person of any age, with any qualifications, can form a research supply company. There are no formal requirements, no tests to take, and no state or federal licenses to acquire. Any company can hang a "research" shingle on the door, place some advertising in research trade publications, and join one or more of the voluntary marketing research organizations (although this last step is not necessary).

Due to the lack of regulations in the research industry, it is the sole responsibility of the research user to determine which of thousands of suppliers available are capable of conducting a professional, scientifically based research project. Experienced research users develop a list of qualified companies, basically from the recommendations of other users (mass media researchers throughout the country are a very closely knit group of people who trade information almost daily).

2. The researcher must maintain close supervision over the project. This is true even with the very good companies, not because their professonalism cannot be trusted, but rather, to be sure that the project is answering the questions that were posed. Because of security considerations, a research supplier may never completely understand why a particular project is being conducted, and the researcher needs to be sure that the project will provide the exact information required.

Data Analysis and Interpretation

The time and effort required for data analysis and interpretation depend on the study's purpose and the methodology used. Analysis and interpretation may take several days to several months. In many private sector research studies involving only a single question, however, data analysis and interpretation may be completed in a few minutes. For example, a business or company may be interested in discovering the amount of interest in a new product or service. After a survey, for example, the question may be answered by summarizing only one or two items on the questionnaire that relate to demand for the product or service. In this case, interpretation is simply "go" or "no-go."

Every analysis should be carefully planned and performed according to guidelines designed for that analysis. Once the computations have been completed, the researcher must "step back" and consider what has been discovered. The results must be analyzed with reference to their external validity and the likelihood of their accuracy. Here, for example, is an excerpt from the conclusion drawn by Singer and Singer (1981).

> Television by its very nature is a medium that emphasizes those very elements that are generally found in imagination: visual fluidity, time and space flexibility and make-believe. . . . Very little effort has emerged from producers or educators to develop age-specific programming . . . it is evident that more research for the development of programming and adult mediation is urgently needed.

Researchers must determine through analysis whether their work is valid internally and externally. This chapter has touched briefly on the concept of external validity; an externally valid study is one whose results can be generalized to the population. To assess **internal validity**, on the other hand, one asks: Does the study really measure or investigate the proposed research question?

Internal Validity

Control over research conditions is necessary to enable researchers to rule out all plausible rival explanations of results. Researchers are interested in verifying that "y is a function of x," or $y = f(x)$. Control over the research conditions is necessary to eliminate the possibility of finding that $y = f(b)$, where b is an extraneous variable. Any such variable that creates a rival explanation of results is known as an **artifact**. The presence of an artifact indicates a lack of internal validity: the study has failed to investigate its hypothesis.

Suppose, for example, that researchers discover through a study that children who view television for extended lengths of time have lower grade point averages in school than children who watch only a limited amount of television. Could an artifact have created this finding? It may be that children who view fewer hours of television also receive parental help with their school work: parental help (the artifact), not hours of television viewed, may be the reason for the difference in grade point averages between the two groups.

Artifacts may arise from several sources. Ten of those most frequently encountered are described below. Researchers should be familiar with these sources to achieve internal validity in the experiments they conduct (Campbell & Stanley, 1963).

1. History. Various events occurring during a study may affect the subjects' attitudes, opinions, and behavior. For example, to analyze an oil company's public relations campaign for a new product, researchers first *pretest* subjects concerning their attitudes toward the company. The subjects are next exposed to an experimental promotional campaign (the *experimental treatment*)); then a *posttest* is administered to determine whether changes in attitude occurred as a result of the campaign. Suppose the results indicate that the public relations campaign was a complete failure—that the subjects displayed a very poor perception of the oil company in the posttest. Before the results are reported, the researchers need to determine whether an intervening variable could have caused the poor perception. An investigation discloses that during the period between tests, subjects learned from a television news story that the oil company was planning to raise gasoline prices by 20%. The news of the price increase—not the public relations campaign—may have acted as an artifact that created the poor perception. The longer the time period between a pretest and a posttest, the greater the possibility that history might confound the study.

The effects of history in a study can be devastating, as was shown during the late 1970s and early 1980s. Several broadcast companies and other private businesses perceived a need to develop Subscription Television (STV) in various markets throughout the country where cable television penetration was thought to be very low. An STV service allows a household to pick up, using a special antenna, pay television services similar to Home Box Office or Showtime. Several cities became prime targets for STV because both Arbitron and Nielsen reported very low cable penetration. Several companies conducted research in many of these cities, and results supported the Arbitron and Nielsen data. In addition, the research found that people who did not have access to cable television were very receptive to the idea of STV. However, it was discovered later that even as some of the studies were being conducted, cable companies in the target areas were expanding very rapidly and had wired many of the previously nonwired neighborhoods. What were once prime targets for STV soon became accessible to cable television. The major problem was that researchers attempting to determine the feasibility of STV failed to consider the historical changes (wiring of the cities) that could affect the results of their research. The net result was that many companies lost millions of dollars and STV soon faded from memory.

2. Maturation. Subjects' biological and psychological characteristics change during the course of a study. Growing hungry or tired or becoming older may influence the manner in which subjects respond to a research study. For example, fatigue will cause subjects who spend 3 hours analyzing television commercials to respond differently from the first commercial to the last.

3. Testing. Testing in itself may be an artifact, particularly when subjects are given similar pretests and posttests. A pretest may sensitize subjects to the material and improve their posttest scores regardless of the type of experimental treatment given to subjects. This is especially true when the same test is used for both situations. Subjects learn how to answer questions and to anticipate researchers' demands. To guard against the effects of testing, different pretests and posttests are required. Or, instead of being given a pretest, subjects can be tested for similarity (homogeneity) by means of a variable or set of variables that differs from the experimental variable. The pretest is not the only way to establish a *point of prior equivalency* (the groups were equal before the experiment) between groups—this can also be accomplished through sampling.

4. Instrumentation. Also known as **instrument decay,** this term refers to the deterioration of research instruments or methods over the course of a study. Equipment may wear out, observers may become more casual in recording their observations, and interviewers who memorize frequently asked questions may fail to present them in the proper order.

5. Statistical regression. Subjects who achieve either very high or very low scores on a test tend to regress to the sample or population mean during following testing sessions. Often *outliers* (subjects whose pretest scores are far from the mean) are selected for further testing or evaluation. Suppose, for example, that researchers develop a series of television programs designed to teach simple mathematical concepts, and they select only subjects who score very low on a mathematical aptitude pretest. An experimental treatment is designed to expose these subjects to the new television series, and a posttest is given to determine whether the programs increased the subjects' knowledge of simple math concepts. The experimental study may show that indeed, after only one or two exposures to the new programs, math scores increased. But the higher scores on the posttest may not be due to the televison programs; they may be a function of statistical regression. That is, regardless of whether the subjects viewed the programs, the scores in the sample may have increased merely because of statistical regression to the mean. The programs should be tested with a variety of subjects, not just those who score low on a pretest.

In addition, a **control group** (see Chapter 5) that receives no exposure to the program can help rule out statistical regression as the cause of higher posttest scores.

6. Experimental mortality. All research studies face the possibility that subjects will drop out for one reason or another. This is especially true in long-term studies. Subjects may become ill, move away, drop out of school, or quit work. This **mortality**, or loss of subjects, is sure to have an effect on the results of a study, since most research methods and statistical analyses make assumptions about the number of subjects used. It is always better, as mentioned in Chapter 4, to select more subjects than are actually required—within the budget limits of the study.

7. Selection. Most research designs compare two or more groups of subjects to determine whether differences exist on the dependent measurement. These groups must be randomly selected and tested for homogeneity to ensure that results are not due to the type of sample used.

8. Demand characteristics. The term **demand characteristics** is used to describe subjects' reactions to experimental conditions. Orne (1969) suggested that under some circumstances, subjects' awarenesss of the experimental purpose may be the sole determinant of how they behave; that is, subjects who recognize the purpose of a study may produce only "good" data for researchers.

For instance, research about television viewing habits often produces subjects who report high levels of public television viewing. However, when the same subjects are asked to list their favorite PBS programs, many cannot recall a single one. **Cross-validating** questions are often necessary to verify subjects' responses; by giving subjects the opportunity to answer the same question phrased in different ways, the researcher can spot discrepant, potentially error-producing responses. In addition, researchers can help control demand characteristics by disguising the real purpose of the study; however, researchers should use caution when employing this technique (see Chapter 18).

9. Experimenter bias. Rosenthal (1969) discussed a variety of ways in which a researcher may influence the results of a study. Bias can enter through mistakes made in observation, data recording, mathematical computations, and interpretation. Whether experimenter errors are intentional or unintentional, they usually support the researcher's hypothesis and are considered bias (Walizer & Wienir, 1978).

Several procedures can help to reduce experimenter bias. For example, individuals who provide instructions to subjects and make observations should not be informed of the purpose of the study; experimenters and others involved in the research should not know whether subjects belong to the experimental group or the control group (this is called a **double blind experiment**); and automated devices such as tape recorders should be used whenever possible to provide uniform instructions to subjects.

10. Evaluation apprehension. Rosenberg's (1965) concept of **evaluation apprehension** is similar to demand characteristics, but it emphasizes that subjects are essentially *afraid* of being measured or tested. They are interested in receiving only positive evaluations from the researcher and from the other subjects involved in the study. Most people are hesitant to exhibit behavior that differs from the norm and will tend to follow the group, even though they may totally disagree with the others. The researcher's task is to try to eliminate this passiveness by letting subjects know that their individual responses are important.

Artifacts are complex and may arise in all phases of research. For this reason, it is easy to see why the results from a single study cannot be used to refute or support a theory or hypothesis. As Hyman (1954) recognized:

> All scientific inquiry is subject to error, and it is far better to be aware of this, to study the sources in an attempt to reduce it, and to estimate the magnitude of such errors in our findings, than to be ignorant of the errors concealed in our data.

External Validity

External validity refers to the generalizability of the results of a study across populations, settings, and time (Cook & Campbell, 1979). The external validity of a study can be severely affected by the interaction in an analysis of variables such as subject selection, instrumentation, and experimental conditions (Campbell & Stanley, 1963).

Cook and Campbell (1979) identified three procedures that can be used to increase the external validity of a research study: (1) use random samples that are representative of the population under investigation; (2) use heterogeneous samples and replicate the study several times; and (3) select a sample that is representative of the group to which the results will be generalized. Another way to increase external validity is to conduct research over a long period of time. Mass media research is often designed as short-term projects: subjects are exposed to an experimental treatment and are immediately tested or measured. However, in many cases, the immediate effects of a treatment are negligible. In advertising, for example, research studies designed to measure brand awareness are generally based on only one exposure to a commercial or advertisement. It is well known that persuasion and attitude change rarely take place after only one exposure; they require multiple exposures over time. Logically, such measurements should be made over a period of weeks or months to take into account the sleeper effect: that attitude change may be minimal or nonexistent in the short run and still prove significant in the long run.

Presentation of Results

The format used in presenting results depends on the purpose of the study. Research intended for publication in academic journals follows a format prescribed by each journal; research conducted for management in the private sector tends to be reported in simpler terms, excluding detailed explanations of sampling, methodology, and review of literature. However, all presentations of results need to be written in a clear and concise manner appropriate to both the research question and the individuals who will read the report. A more detailed discussion of reporting is included in Chapter 18.

Replication

One important point mentioned throughout this book is that the results of any single study are, by themselves, only *indications* of what might exist. A study provides information that says, in effect, "This is what may be the case." To be relatively certain of the results of any study, the research must be replicated. Too often, researchers conduct one study and report the results as if they are providing the basis for a theory or law. The information presented in this chapter, and in other chapters that deal with internal and external validity, argues that this cannot be true.

A research question or hypothesis requires investigation from many different perspectives before any significance can be attributed to the results of any one study. Research methods and designs must be altered to eliminate **design-specific results**, that is, results that are based on, hence specific to, the design used. Similarly, subjects with a variety of characteristics should be studied from many angles to eliminate **sample-specific results**; and statistical analyses need variation to eliminate **method-specific results**. In other words, all effort must be made to ensure that the results of any single study are not created by or dependent on a methodological factor; studies must be replicated.

Researchers overwhelmingly advocate the use of replication to establish scientific fact. Lykken (1968) and Kelly, Chase, and Tucker (1979) have identified four basic types of replication that can be used to help validate a scientific test.

- **Literal replication** involves the exact duplication of a previous analysis, including the sampling procedures, experimental conditions, measuring techniques, and methods of data analysis.
- **Operational replication** attempts to duplicate only the sampling and experimental procedures of a previous analysis, to test whether the procedures will produce similar results.
- **Instrumental replication** attempts to duplicate the dependent measures used in a previous study and to vary the experimental conditions of the original study.

- **Constructive replication** tests the validity of methods used previously by deliberately avoiding the imitation of the earlier study; both the manipulations and the measures used in the first study are varied. The researcher simply begins with a statement of empirical "fact" uncovered in a previous study and attempts to find the same "fact."

Although the process of replication has not been widely used in communications research, the trend seems to indicate that more and more mass media researchers consider it an invaluable step in producing scientific data (Wimmer & Reid, 1982).

The Hazards of Research

All researchers quickly discover that research projects do not always turn out the way they were planned. It seems that Murphy's Law—Anything that can go wrong will go wrong—holds true in any type of research. It is therefore necessary to be prepared for difficulties, however minor, in conducting a research project. Planning and flexibility are essential. Presented below are what are known as the TAT (They're Always There) laws. Although these "laws" are somewhat tongue-in-cheek, they are nonetheless representative of the problems one may expect to encounter in research studies.

1. A research project always takes longer than planned.
2. No matter how many people review a research proposal and say that it's perfect before you start, people will always have suggestions to make it better after the study is completed.
3. There are always errors in data entry.
4. The data errors that take the longest to find and correct are the most obvious.
5. Regardless of the amount of money requested for a research project, the final project always costs more.
6. A computer program never runs the first time.
7. A sample is always too small.
8. Regardless of how many times a pilot study is conducted to make sure that measurement instructions are clear, there will always be at least one subject who doesn't understand the directions.
9. All electronic equipment breaks down during the most crucial part of an experiment.
10. Subjects never tell you how they really feel or what they really think or do.

Summary

This chapter has described the processes involved in identifying and developing a topic for research investigation. It was suggested that researchers consider several sources for potential ideas, including a critical analysis of everyday situations. The steps in developing a topic for investigation naturally become easier with experience; beginning researchers need to pay particular attention to material already available. They should not attempt to tackle broad research questions, but should try to isolate a smaller, more practical subtopic for study. They should develop an appropriate method of analysis and then proceed, through data analysis and interpretation, to a clear and concise presentation of results.

The chapter stresses that the results of a single survey or other research approach only provide indications of what may or may not exist. Before researchers can claim support for a research question or hypothesis, the study must be replicated a number of times to eliminate dependence on extraneous factors.

While conducting research studies, investigators must be constantly aware of potential sources of error that may create spurious results. Phenomena that affect an experiment in this way are sources of breakdowns in internal validity. If and only if differing and rival hypotheses are ruled out can researchers validly say that the treatment was influential in creating differences between the experimental and control groups. A good explanation of research results rules out intervening variables; every plausible rival explanation should be considered. However, even when this is accomplished, the results of one study can be considered only as indications of what may or may not exist. Support for a theory or hypothesis can be made only after the completion of several studies that produce similar results.

In addition, for a study to have substantive worth to the understanding of mass media, the results must be generalizable to subjects and groups other than those involved in the experiment. External validity can be best achieved through randomization of subject selection: there is no substitute for random sampling (see Chapter 4).

Questions and Problems for Further Investigation

1. The focus of this chapter is on developing a research topic by defining a major problem area and narrowing the topic to a manageable study. Follow the procedure explained in the chapter to develop two different research projects in an area of mass media research. Use either an outline or a flowchart format.

2. Replication has long been a topic of debate in scientific research, but until recently, mass media researchers have not paid it a great deal of attention. Read the articles by Reid, Soley, and Wimmer (1981) and Wimmer and Reid (1982). Explain in your own words why replication has not been a major factor in mass media research. What could be done to correct the current situation in replication?

3. In an analysis of the effects of television viewing, it was found that the fewer the hours of television students watched per week, the higher were the scores achieved in school. What alternative explanations or artifacts might explain such differences? How could these variables be controlled?

References and Suggested Readings

Agostino, D. (1980). Cable television's impact on the audience of public television. *Journal of Broadcasting, 24*(3), 347–366.

Babbie, E. R. (1986). *The practice of social research* (4th ed.). Belmont, CA: Wadsworth.

Becker, L. B. (1981). Secondary analysis. In G. H. Stempel & B. H. Westley (Eds.), *Research methods in mass communications*. Englewood Cliffs, NJ: Prentice-Hall.

Becker, L. B., Beam, R., & Russial, J. (1978). Correlates of daily newspaper performance in New England. *Journalism Quarterly, 55*, 100–108.

Campbell, D. T., & Stanley, J. C. (1963). *Experimental and quasi-experimental designs for research*. Skokie, IL: Rand McNally.

Cohen, J. (1965). Some statistical issues in psychological research. In B. B. Wolman (Ed.), *Handbook of clinical psychology*. New York: McGraw-Hill.

Comstock, G., Chaffee, S., Katzman, N., McCombs, M., & Roberts, D. (1978). *Television and human behavior*. New York: Columbia University Press.

Cook, T. D., & Campbell, D. T. (1979). *Quasi-experimentation: Designs and analysis for field studies*. Skokie, IL: Rand McNally.

Glenn, N. (1972). Archival data on political attitudes: Opportunities and pitfalls. In D. Nimmo & C. Bonjean (Eds.), *Political attitudes and public opinion*. New York: David McKay.

Haskins, J. (1968). *How to evaluate mass communication*. Chicago: Advertising Research Foundation.

Hyman, H. H. (1954). *Interviewing in social research*. Chicago: University of Chicago Press.

Hyman, H. H. (1972). *Secondary analysis of sample surveys*. New York: John Wiley.

Kelly, C. W., Chase, L. J., & Tucker, R. K. (1979). Replication in experimental communication research: An analysis. *Human Communication Research, 5*, 338–342.

Kraus, S., & Davis, D. (1967). *The effects of mass communication on political behavior*. University Park: Pennsylvania State University Press.

Lykken, D. T. (1968). Statistical significance in psychological research. *Psychological Bulletin, 21*, 151–159.

Orne, M. T. (1969). Demand characteristics and the concept of quasi-controls.

In R. Rosenthal & R. L. Rosnow (Eds.), *Artifact in behavioral research*. New York: Academic Press.

Reid, L. N., Soley, L. C., & Wimmer, R. D. (1981). Replication in advertising research: 1977, 1978, 1979. *Journal of Advertising, 10,* 3–13.

Rosenberg, M. J. (1965). When dissonance fails: On eliminating evaluation apprehension from attitude measurement. *Journal of Personality and Social Psychology, 1,* 28–42.

Rosenthal, R. (1969). *Experimenter effects in behavioral research.* New York: Appleton-Century-Crofts.

Rubin, R. B., Rubin, A. M., & Piele, L. J. (1985). *Communication research: Strategies and sources.* Belmont, CA: Wadsworth.

Singer, D. G., & Singer, J. L. (1981). Television and the developing imagination of the child. *Journal of Broadcasting, 25,* 373–387.

Tan, A. S. (1977). Why TV is missed: A functional analysis. *Journal of Broadcasting, 21,* 371–380.

Tukey, J. W. (1969). Analyzing data: Sanctification or detective work? *American Psychologist, 24,* 83–91.

Walizer, M. H., & Wienir, P. L. (1978). *Research methods and analysis: searching for relationships.* New York: Harper & Row.

Wimmer, R. D., & Reid, L. N. (1982). Willingness of communication researchers to respond to replication requests. *Journalism Quarterly, 59,* 317–319.

C H A P T E R 3

Elements of Research

CONCEPTS AND CONSTRUCTS

∎

MEASUREMENT

∎

DISCRETE AND CONTINUOUS VARIABLES

∎

SUMMARY

∎

QUESTIONS AND PROBLEMS FOR FURTHER INVESTIGATION

∎

REFERENCES AND SUGGESTED READINGS

C hapters 1 and 2 presented a brief overview of the research process. In this chapter, three basic elements of this process are defined and discussed: concepts and constructs, variables, and measurement. To conduct and understand empirical research, it is necessary to understand these elements.

Concepts and Constructs

A **concept** is a term that expresses an abstract idea formed by generalization from particulars (Kerlinger, 1973). It is formed by summarizing related observations. For example, a researcher might observe that a public speaker becomes restless, starts to perspire, and continually fidgets with a pencil just before giving an address. The researcher might summarize these observed patterns of behavior and label them *speech anxiety*. On a more concrete level, the word *table* is a concept that represents a wide variety of observable objects, ranging from a plank supported by concrete blocks to a piece of furniture typically found in dining rooms. In mass communication, terms such as *message length, media usage*, and *readability* typically are used as concepts.

Concepts are important because they facilitate communication among those who have a shared understanding of them. Researchers use concepts to organize their observations into meaningful summaries and to transmit this information to their colleagues and to the public. In addition, since concepts are abstracted from observations, they enable researchers to look for general explanations or patterns in these observations.

A **construct** is a combination of concepts created for a particular scientific purpose. Constructs are generally difficult to observe directly; their existence must be inferred from related behavior patterns. For example, in mass communication research, the term *authoritarianism* represents a construct specifically defined to describe a certain type of personality; it comprises nine different concepts, including conventionalism, submission, superstition, and cynicism. Authoritarianism itself cannot be seen; its presence must be determined by some type of questionnaire or standardized test. The results of such tests indicate what authoritarianism might be and whether it is present under given conditions, but they do not provide exact definitions for the concept.

A **variable** is a phenomenon or event that can be measured or manipulated and is used in the development of constructs. Researchers attempt to test a number of associated variables to develop an underlying meaning or relationship among them. After suitable analysis, the important variables are retained while the others are discarded. These important variables are labeled **marker variables** since they seem to define or highlight the construct under study. After further analysis, new marker variables may be added to increase understanding of the construct and to permit more reliable predictions.

Constructs and marker variables are valuable tools in theoretical research. But, as noted in Chapter 1, researchers also function at the observational or empirical level. To understand how this is done, it is necessary to examine variables and to know how they are measured.

Independent and Dependent Variables

Variables are classified in terms of their relationship with one another. It is customary to talk about **independent** and **dependent variables**: independent variables are systematically varied by the researcher, while dependent variables are observed and their values presumed to depend on the effects of the independent variables. In other words, the dependent variable is what the researcher wishes to explain. For example, assume that an investigator is interested in determining how the angle of a camera shot affects an audience's perception of the credibility of a television newscaster. Three different versions of a newscast are videotaped: one shot from a very low angle, another from a high angle, and a third from eye level. Groups of subjects are randomly assigned to view one of the three versions and to complete a questionnaire that measures credibility. In this experiment, the camera angle is the independent variable. Its values are systematically varied by the experimenter, who selects only three of the camera angles possible. The dependent variable to be measured is the perceived credibility of the newscaster. If the researcher's assumption is correct, the newscaster's credibility will vary according to the camera angle. (Note that the actual values of the dependent variable are not manipulated; they are simply observed or measured.)

Keep in mind that the distinction between types of variable depends on the purposes of the research. An independent variable in one study may be a dependent variable in another. Also, a research task may involve examining the relationship of more than one independent variable to a single dependent variable. For example, a study designed to examine the impact of type size and page layout on learning would encompass two independent variables (type size and layout) and one dependent variable (learning). Moreover, in many instances multiple dependent variables are measured in a single study. This type of study, called a *multivariate analysis*, is discussed in Appendix 2.

Other Types of Variables

In nonexperimental research, where there is no active manipulation of variables, different terms are sometimes substituted for independent and dependent variables. The variable that is used for predictions or is assumed to be causal (analogous to the independent variable) is sometimes called the **predictor** or **antecedent variable**. The variable that is predicted or assumed to be affected (analogous to the dependent variable) is sometimes called the **criterion variable**.

Researchers often wish to account for or control variables of certain types for the purpose of eliminating unwanted influences. These **control variables** are used to ensure that the results of the study are due to the independent variables, not some other source. However, a control variable need not always be used to eliminate an unwanted influence. On occasion, researchers use a control variable such as age, sex, or socioeconomic status to divide subjects into specific relevant categories. For example, in studying the relationship between newspaper readership and reading ability, it is apparent that IQ will affect the relationship and must be controlled; thus, subjects may be selected on the basis of IQ scores, or placed in groups with similar scores.

One of the most difficult aspects of any type of research is trying to identify all the variables that may create spurious (false) or misleading results. Some researchers refer to this problem as "noise." Noise can occur even in very simple research projects. For example, a researcher designs a telephone survey that asks respondents to name the local radio station listened to the most during the past week. The researcher uses an open-ended question—that is, no specific response choices are provided; thus the interviewer writes down exactly what each respondent says in answer to the question. When the completed surveys are tabulated, the researcher notices that several people mentioned radio station WAAA. But if the city has a WAAA-AM and a WAAA-FM, which station gets the credit? The researcher cannot arbitrarily assign credit to the AM or the FM station; nor can credit be split, because such a practice may distort the actual listening pattern.

The researcher could attempt call-backs of everyone who said "WAAA," but this method is not suggested for two reasons: (1) the likelihood of reaching all the people who gave that response is low; and (2) even if the first condition is met, some respondents may not recall which station they mentioned originally. The researcher, therefore, is unable to provide a reliable analysis of the data because all possible intervening variables were not considered. (The researcher should have foreseen this problem, and the interviewers should have been instructed to find out in each case whether "WAAA" meant the AM or the FM station.)

Another type of research noise is created by people who unknowingly provide false information. For example, people who keep diaries for radio and television surveys may err in recording the station or channel they tune in; that is, they may listen to or watch station KAAA but incorrectly record KBBB (this problem is partially solved by the use of people meters—see Chapter 14). In addition, people often answer a multiple-choice or yes/no research question at random because they do not wish to appear ignorant or uninformed. To minimize this problem, researchers should construct their measurement instruments with great care. Noise is always present, but a large and representative sample should decrease the effects of some research noise. (In later chapters, noise is referred to as "error.")

Many simplistic problems in research are solved with experience. In many situations, however, researchers understand that total control over all aspects of the research is impossible, and the impossibility of achieving perfect control is accounted for in the interpretation of results.

Defining Variables Operationally

In Chapter 1 it was stated that an operational definition specifies procedures to be followed in experiencing or measuring a concept. Research depends on observations, and observations cannot be made without a clear statement of what is to be observed. An operational definition is such a statement.

Operational definitions are indispensable in scientific research because they enable investigators to measure relevant variables. In any study, it is necessary to provide operational definitions for both independent and dependent variables. Table 3.1 contains examples of such definitions taken from research studies in mass communication.

Kerlinger (1973) identified two types of operational definitions, measured and experimental. A measured operational definition specifies how to measure a variable. For instance, a researcher investigating dogmatism and media use might operationally define *dogmatism* as a subject's score on the Twenty-Item Short Form Dogmatism Scale. An experimental operational definition explains how an investigator has manipulated a variable. Obviously, this type of definition is used when defining the independent variable in a laboratory setting. For example, in a study concerning the impact of television violence, the researcher might manipulate media violence by constructing two 8-minute films. The first film, labeled "the violent condition," might contain scenes from a boxing match. The second film, labeled "the nonviolent condition," could depict a swimming race. Or, to take another example, source credibility might be manipulated by alternately attributing an article on health to the *New England Journal of Medicine* and to the *National Enquirer*.

Operationally defining a variable forces the researcher to express abstract concepts in concrete terms. Occasionally, after unsuccessfully grappling with the task of making a key variable operational,

Table 3.1 Illustrations of Operational Definitions

Study	Variable	Operational definition
Atkin & Block (1983)	Celebrity status of a source endorsing an alcohol brand	Subjects saw one version of an ad featuring a famous person and a second version of the same ad with an unfamiliar person.
Burgoon & Burgoon (1980)	Time spent reading newspaper	Subjects estimated the amount of time they spent reading the paper.
Elliot & Slater (1980)	Perceived TV program realism	Subjects evaluated a program on a five-point scale ranging from "very realistic" to "very unrealistic."
Heeter et al. (1983)	Local Hispanic–American news coverage	Researchers tabulated every news mention of Hispanic surnames, Hispanic culture, Hispanic ethnicity, or Hispanic countries.
Henningham (1984)	Journalists' professional values	Subjects rated the importance of 21 job characteristics such as "opportunity to learn new skills," "opportunity for originality," and "opportunity to influence public thinking."

the investigator may conclude that the variable as originally conceived is too vague or ambiguous and that redefinition is required. Because operational definitions are expressed so concretely, they can communicate *exactly* what the terms represent. For instance, a researcher might define political knowledge as the number of correct answers on a 20-item true/false test. And while it is possible to argue over the validity of the operational definition "Women possess more political knowledge than men," there is no confusion as to what the statement means.

Finally, there is no single infallible method for operationally defining a variable. No operational definition satisfies everybody. The investigator must decide which method is best suited for the research problem at hand.

Measurement

Mass communication research, like all research, can be qualitative or quantitative. **Qualitative research** refers to several methods of data collection, which include focus groups, field observation, in-depth interviews, and case studies. Although there are substantial differences among these techniques, all involve what some writers refer to as "getting close to the data" (Chadwick, Bahr, & Albrecht, 1984).

Qualitative research has certain advantages. In most cases, it allows a researcher to view behavior in a natural setting without the artificiality that sometimes surrounds experimental or survey research. In addition, qualitative techniques can increase a researcher's depth of understanding of the phenomenon under investigation. This is especially true when the phenomenon has not been previously investigated. Finally, qualitative methods are flexible and allow the researcher to pursue new areas of interest. A questionnaire is unlikely to provide data about questions that were not asked, but a person conducting a field observation or focus group might discover facets of a subject that were not even considered before the study began.

There are, however, some disadvantages associated with qualitative methods. First of all, sample sizes are generally too small to allow the researcher to generalize the data beyond the sample selected for the particular study. For this reason, qualitative research is often used as a preliminary step to further investigation rather than the final phase of a project. The information collected from qualitative methods is often used to prepare a more elaborate quantitative analysis, although the qualitative data may in fact constitute all the information needed for a particular study.

Reliability of the data can also be a problem since single observers are describing unique events. Because a person doing qualitative research must become very closely involved with the respondents, loss of objectivity when collecting data is possible. If the researcher becomes too close to the study, the necessary professional detachment may be lost.

Finally, if qualitative research is not properly planned, the project may produce nothing of value. Qualitative research looks easy to conduct, but projects must be carefully planned to ensure that they focus on key issues.

Although this book is primarily about quantitative research methods, field observation, focus groups, and case studies are discussed in Chapter 7. For those who wish to know more about the other research techniques that make up qualitative analysis, two sources are Filstead (1970) and Schwartz and Jacobs (1979). Several examples of qualitative research are contained in the Fall 1982 issue of the *Journal of Broadcasting*.

Quantitative research requires that the variables under consideration be measured. This form of research is concerned with how often a variable is present and generally uses numbers to communicate this amount. Quantitative research has certain advantages. One is that the use of numbers allows greater precision in reporting results. For example, the Violence Index (Gerbner et al., 1980), a quantitative measuring device, makes it possible to report the exact increase or decrease in violence from one television season to another, whereas qualitative research could only describe whether violence went up or down. Another advantage is that quantitative research permits the use of powerful methods of mathematical analysis. The importance of mathematics to mass media research is difficult to overemphasize. As pointed out by measurement expert J. P. Guilford (1954):

> The progress and maturity of a science are often judged by the extent to which it has succeeded in the use of mathematics. . . . Mathematics is a universal language that any science or technology may use with great power and convenience. Its vocabulary of terms is unlimited. . . . Its rules of operation . . . are unexcelled for logical precision.

For the past several years some friction has existed in the mass communication field as well as in several other disciplines between those who have favored quantitative methods and those who preferred qualitative techniques. Recently, however, most researchers have come to realize that both qualitative and quantitative techniques are important in understanding any phenomenon. In fact, the term **triangulation**, commonly used by marine navigators, is frequently heard now in conversations about communication research. If a ship picks up signals from only one navigational aid, it is impossible to know the vessel's precise location. If, however, signals from more than one source are detected, elementary geometry can be used to pinpoint location. In the context of this book, "triangulation" refers to the use of both qualitative and quantitative methods to understand fully the nature of a research problem.

Although most of this book is concerned with skills relevant to quantitative research, it is not implied that quantitative research is in any sense "better" than qualitative research. Obviously, each technique has value, and different research questions and goals may make one or the other more appropriate in a given application. Over the past 30 years, however, quantitative research has become more and more common in mass media. Consequently, it is increasingly important for beginning researchers to familiarize themselves with common quantitative techniques.

The Nature of Measurement

The idea behind **measurement** is a simple one: a researcher assigns numerals to objects, events, or properties according to certain rules. Examples of measurement are everywhere: "She or he is a 10." "Unemployment increased by 1%." "The earthquake measured 5.5 on the Richter scale." Note that the definition contains three central concepts: numerals, assignment, and rules. A numeral is a symbol, such as V, X, C, or 5, 10, 100. A numeral has no implicit quantitative meaning. When it is given quantitative meaning, it becomes a number and can be used in mathematical and statistical computations. Assignment is the designation of numerals or numbers to certain objects or events. A simple measurement system might entail assigning the numeral "1" to the people who get most of their news from television, the numeral "2" to those who get most of their news from a newspaper, and the numeral "3" to those who get most of their news from some other source.

Rules specify the way that numerals or numbers are to be assigned. Rules are at the heart of any measurement system; if they are faulty, the system will be flawed. In some situations, the rules are obvious and straightforward. To measure reading speed, a stopwatch and a standardized message may be sufficient. In other instances, the rules are not so apparent. Measuring certain psychological traits such as "source credibility" or "attitude toward violence" calls for carefully explicated measurement techniques.

Additionally, in mass communication research and in much of social science research, investigators usually measure indicators of the properties of individuals or objects rather than the individuals or objects themselves. Concepts such as "authoritarianism" or "motivation for reading the newspaper" cannot be directly observed; they must be inferred from presumed indicators. Thus, if a person endorses statements such as "Orders from a superior should always be followed without question" and "Law and order are the most important things in society," it can be deduced that he or she is more authoritarian than someone who disagreed with the same statements.

Measurement systems strive to be isomorphic to reality. **Isomorphism** means identity or similarity of form or structure. In some research areas, such as the physical sciences, isomorphism is not a key problem, since there is usually a direct relationship between the objects being measured and the numbers assigned to them. For example, if an electrical current travels through substance A with less resistance than it does through substance B, it can be deduced that A is a better conductor than B. Testing a few more substances can lead to a ranking of conductors whereby the numbers assigned indicate the degree of conductivity. The measurement system is isomorphic to reality.

In mass media research, the correspondence is seldom that obvious. For example, imagine that a researcher is trying to develop a scale to measure the "persuasibility" of people in connection with a certain type of advertisement. She devises a test and administers it to five people. The scores are displayed in Table 3.2. Now imagine that an omniscient being is able to disclose the "true" persuasibility of the same five people. These scores are also shown in Table 3.2. For two people, the test scores correspond exactly to the "true" scores. The other three scores miss the "true" scores, but there is a correspondence between the rank orders. Also note that the "true" persuasibility scores ranged from 0 to 12, while the measurement scale ranged from 1 to 8. To summarize, there is a general correspondence between the test and reality, but the test is far from an exact measure of what actually exists.

Table 3.2 Illustration of Isomorphism

Person	Test score	"True" score
A	1	0
B	3	1
C	6	6
D	7	7
E	8	12

Unfortunately, the degree of correspondence between measurement and reality is rarely known in research. In some cases researchers are not even sure they are actually measuring what they are trying to measure. In any event, researchers must carefully consider the degree of isomorphism between measurement and reality. This topic is discussed in greater detail later in the chapter.

Levels of Measurement

Scientists have distinguished four different ways to measure things, or four different levels of measurement. The operations that can be performed with a given set of scores depend on the level of measurement achieved. The four levels of measurement are: nominal, ordinal, interval, and ratio.

The **nominal level** is the weakest form of measurement. In nominal measurement, numerals or other symbols are used to classify persons, objects, or characteristics. For example, in the physical sciences, rocks can generally be classified into three categories: igneous, sedimentary, and metamorphic. A geologist who assigns a "1" to igneous, a "2" to sedimentary, and a "3" to metamorphic has formed a nominal scale. Note that the numerals are simply labels that stand for the respective categories; they have no mathematical significance. A rock that is placed in category "3" does not have more "rockness" than those in categories "2" and "1." Other examples of nominal measurement are numbers on football jerseys and license plates, and social security numbers. An example of nominal measurement in the area of mass communications would be classifying respondents according to the medium they depend on most for news. Those depending most on TV would be in category "1," those depending most on newspapers would be in category "2," and so on.

The nominal level, like all levels, possesses certain formal properties. Its basic property is that of equivalence. If an object is placed in category "1," it is considered equal to all other objects in that category. Suppose a researcher is attempting to classify all the advertisements in a magazine according to primary appeal. If an ad has an economic appeal it is placed in category "1," if it uses an appeal to fear, it is placed in category "2," and so on. Note that all ads using "fear appeal" are considered equal even though they may differ on other dimensions, such as product type, size, or use of illustrations.

Another property of nominal measurement is that all categories are exhaustive and mutually exclusive. This means that each measure accounts for every possible option and that each measurement is appropriate to only one category. For instance, in the example of primary appeals in magazine advertisements, all possible appeals would need to be included in the analysis (exhaustive): economic, fear, morality, religion, and so on. Each advertisement would be placed in one and only one category (mutually exclusive).

Nominal measurement is frequently used in mass media research. For example, Gafke and Leuthold (1979), in their study of editorial endorsements in the 1976 presidential campaign, divided newspapers into three nominal categories: those that endorsed Ford, those that endorsed Carter, and those that made no endorsement. Wilson and Howard (1978) divided errors found in media reports of news events into two categories: factual errors and interpretative errors.

Even when it is measured at the nominal level, a variable may be used in higher order statistics by *transforming* it into another form. The results of this transformation process are known as **dummy variables**. For example, political party affiliation could be coded as follows:

Republican	1
Democrat	2
Independent	3
Other	4

However this measurement scheme can be interpreted incorrectly to imply that a person classified as "Other" is three units "better" than a person classified as a "Republican." To measure political party affiliation and use the data in higher order statistics, the variable must be transformed into a more neutral form.

One way of transforming the variable to give equivalent value to each option is to recode it as a dummy variable that creates an "either/or" situation for each option: a person is either a "Republican" or something else. For example, a binary coding scheme could be used:

Republican	001
Democrat	010
Independent	100
Other	000

This scheme treats each affiliation equivalently and allows the variable to be used in higher order statistical procedures.

Note that the final category "Other" is coded using all zeros. A complete explanation for this practice is beyond the scope of this book; basically, however, its purpose is to avoid redundancy, since the number of individuals classified as "Other" is known from the data on the first three options. If, in a sample of 100 subjects, 25 are found to belong in each of the first three options, it is obvious that there will be 25 in the "Other" option. (For more information on the topic of dummy variable coding, see Kerlinger & Pedhazur, 1973.)

Objects measured at the **ordinal level** are generally ranked along some dimension, usually in a meaningful way, from smaller to greater. For example, one might measure the variable "socioeconomic status" by categorizing families according to class: lower, lower middle, middle, upper middle, or upper. A rank of "1" is assigned to lower, "2" to lower middle, "3" to middle, and so forth. In this situation, the numbers have some mathematical meaning: families in category "3" have a higher socioeconomic status than families ranked "2." Note that nothing is specified with regard to the distance between any two rankings. Ordinal measurement has often been compared to a horse race without a stopwatch. The order in which the horses finish is relatively easy to determine, but it is difficult to calculate the difference in time between the winner and the runner-up.

An ordinal scale possesses the property of **equivalence**; thus in the previous example, all families placed in a category are treated equally, even though some might have greater incomes than others. It also possesses the property of *order* among the categories. Any given category can be defined as being higher or lower than any other category. Common examples of ordinal scales include rankings of football or basketball teams, military ranks, restaurant ratings, and beauty pageant finishing orders.

Ordinal scales are frequently used in mass communication research. Haskins and Kubas (1979) rated readers' interest in 24 comic strips to see whether readership of these comics could be predicted. Williams and Semlak (1979) ranked topics that were important to people during an election campaign to determine whether they corresponded to the relative degree of media coverage of those issues.

When a scale has all the properties of an ordinal scale and the intervals between adjacent points on the scale are of equal value, the scale is at the **interval level**. The most obvious example of an interval scale is temperature. The same amount of heat is required to warm an object from 30 to 40 degrees as to warm it from 50 to 60 degrees. Interval scales incorporate the formal property of *equal differences*; that is, numbers are assigned to the positions of objects on an interval scale in such a way that one may carry out arithmetic operations on the differences between them.

One disadvantage of an interval scale is that it lacks a true zero point, or a condition of nothingness. For example, it is difficult to conceive of a person having zero intelligence or zero personality.

The lack of a true zero point means that the researcher cannot make statements of a proportional nature: someone with an IQ of 100 is not twice as smart as someone with an IQ of 50, and a person who scores 30 on a test of aggression is not three times as aggressive as a person who scores 10.

Interval scales are frequently used in mass communication research. For example, in their study of the impact of the film *All the President's Men*, Elliott and Schenck-Hamlin (1979) constructed a scale to measure attitudes toward the press by measuring responses of "agree" or "disagree" to four separate questions. Rubin (1983) constructed a scale to measure the strength of various motivations for television viewing by presenting a list of 30 statements to respondents with five response options, ranging from "exactly" to "not at all" like their own reasons for viewing.

Scales at the **ratio level** of measurement have all the properties of interval scales plus one more: the existence of *true zero point*. With the introduction of this fixed zero point, ratio judgments can be made. For example, since time and distance are ratio measures, one can say that a car traveling at 50 miles per hour is going twice as fast as a car traveling at 25. Ratio scales are relatively rare in mass media research, although some variables, such as time spent watching television or number of words per story, are ratio measurements. For example, Gantz (1978) measured news recall ability by asking subjects to report whether they had seen or heard 10 items taken from the evening news. Scores could range from zero to 10 on this test. Giffard (1984) counted the length of wire service reports related to 101 developed or developing nations. Theoretically, scores could range from zero (no coverage) to hundreds of words.

Researchers using interval or ratio data are able to use **parametric statistics**, which are specifically designed for these data. Procedures designed for use with "lower" types of data can also be used with data at a higher level of measurement. Statistical procedures designed for higher level data, however, are generally more powerful than those designed for use with nominal or ordinal levels of measurement. Thus, if an investigator has achieved the interval level of measurement, parametric statistics should generally be employed.

Statisticians disagree about the importance of the distinction between ordinal and interval scales and about the legitimacy of using interval statistics with data that may in fact be ordinal. Without delving too deeply into these arguments, it appears that the safest procedure is to assume interval measurement unless there is clear evidence to the contrary, in which case ordinal statistics should be employed. For example, for a research task in which a group of subjects rank a set of objects, ordinal statistics should be used. If, on the other hand, subjects are given an attitude score constructed by rating responses to various questions, the researcher would be justified in using parametric procedures.

Most statisticians seem to feel that statistical analysis is performed on the numbers yielded by the measures, not the measures themselves, and that the properties of interval scales actually belong to the number system (Nunnally, 1978; Roscoe, 1975). Additionally, there have been several studies in which various types of data have been subjected to different statistical analyses. These studies suggest that the distinction between ordinal and interval data is not particularly crucial in selecting an analysis method (McNemar, 1962).

Discrete and Continuous Variables

Two forms of variables are used in mass media investigations. A **discrete variable** includes only a finite set of values; it cannot be divided into subparts. For instance, the number of children in a family is a discrete variable because the unit is a person. It would not make much sense to talk about a family size of 2.24 because it is hard to conceptualize 0.24 of a person. Political affiliation, population, and sex are other discrete variables.

A **continuous variable** can take on any value (including fractions) and can be meaningfully broken into smaller subsections. Height is a continuous variable. If the measurement tool is sophisticated enough, it is possible to distinguish between one person 72.113 inches tall and another 72.114 inches tall. Time spent watching television is another example. It is perfectly meaningful to say that Person A spent 3.12115 hours viewing while Person B watched 3.12114 hours. The *average* number of children in a family is a continuous variable. In this regard, it may be perfectly legitimate to talk about 0.24 of a person.

When dealing with continuous variables, it is sometimes necessary to keep in mind the distinction between the variable and the measure of the variable. If a child's attitude toward television violence is measured by counting his or her positive responses to six questions, there are only seven possible scores: 0, 1, 2, 3, 4, 5, and 6. It is entirely likely, however, that the underlying variable is continuous even though the measure is discrete. In fact, even if a fractionalized scale were developed, it would still be limited to a finite number of scores. As a generalization, most of the measures in mass communication research tend to be discrete approximations of continuous variables. Both the level of measurement and the type of variable under consideration are important in developing useful measurement scales.

Scales and Indexes

Scales and indexes represent composite measures of variables, that is, measurements that are based on more than one item. Scales and indexes are generally used with complex variables that do not easily lend

Figure 3.1   Sample of Likert scale items

1. (positive item) "The President should be elected by direct popular vote."

	Score assigned
_____ strongly agree	5
_____ agree	4
_____ neutral	3
_____ disagree	2
_____ strongly disagree	1

2. (negative item) "Electing the President by direct popular vote would create more problems than it would solve."

	Score assigned
_____ strongly agree	1
_____ agree	2
_____ neutral	3
_____ disagree	4
_____ strongly disagree	5

(Notice that to maintain attitude measurement consistency, the scores are reversed for a negatively worded item.)

themselves to single-item or single-indicator measurement. Some items, such as newspaper circulation, can be adequately measured without scales and indexes. Others, such as attitude toward television news, generally require them.

Scales typically have formalized rules for developing the multiple indicators and assembling them into one composite value. Indexes generally do not have detailed rules. Otherwise, construction techniques are similar.

Perhaps the most commonly used scale in mass communication research is the Likert scale. A number of statements are drawn up with respect to a topic, and respondents can strongly agree, agree, be neutral, disagree, or strongly disagree with the statements. Each response option is weighted, and each subject's responses are added to produce a single score on the topic. Figure 3.1 contains an example of a Likert scale.

Another commonly used scaling procedure is the **semantic differential** technique. This general technique for measuring the meaning an item has for an individual was developed by Charles Osgood and his associates (Osgood, Suci, & Tannenbaum, 1957). To use the technique, a name or concept is placed at the top of a series of 7-point scales anchored by bipolar attitudes. Figure 3.2 shows an example

Figure 3.2 Sample form for applying the semantic differential technique

Time magazine

biased	_____:_____:_____:_____:_____:_____:_____ unbiased
trustworthy	_____:_____:_____:_____:_____:_____:_____ untrustworthy
valuable	_____:_____:_____:_____:_____:_____:_____ worthless
unfair	_____:_____:_____:_____:_____:_____:_____ fair
good	_____:_____:_____:_____:_____:_____:_____ bad

of this technique as used to measure attitudes toward *Time* magazine. The bipolar adjectives that typically "anchor" such evaluative scales are pleasant/unpleasant, valuable/worthless, honest/dishonest, nice/awful, clean/dirty, fair/unfair, and good/bad. It is recommended, however, that a unique set of anchoring adjectives be developed for each particular measurement situation. For example, Markham (1968), in his study of the credibility of television newscasters, used 13 variable sets, including deep/shallow, ordered/chaotic, annoying/pleasing, and clear/hazy. Robinson and Shaver (1969) present a collection of scales commonly used in social science research.

The best known index in mass communication research is probably the Violence Index, which is issued annually (see Gerbner et al., 1980). The following measures are incorporated in this index: (1) the percentage of programs in a sample that contain violence, (2) the frequency of violent acts per program, (3) the frequency of violent acts per hour, (4) the percentage of characters involved in violent actions, and (5) the percentage of characters involved in lethal violence.

Reliability and Validity

Developing any scale or index and using it without prior testing is poor research practice. At least one pilot study should be conducted for any newly developed scale or index to ensure its **reliability** and **validity**. To be useful, a measurement must possess these two related qualities.

A measure is *reliable* if it consistently gives the same answer at different points in time. Reliability in measurement is the same as reliability in any other context. For example, a reliable person is one who is dependable, stable, and consistent. His or her behavior will be the same tomorrow as it is today. On the other hand, an unreliable person is unstable and unpredictable. He or she may act one way today and another way tomorrow. Similarly, if measurements are consistent from one session to another, they are reliable, and some degree of faith can be placed in them. If they are unreliable, it is not a good idea to depend on them.

Figure 3.3 Illustration of "true" and "error" components of a scale

Measurement Instrument 1: Obtained Score = 50

True	Error
46	4

Measurement Instrument 2: Obtained Score = 50

True	Error
30	20

In understanding measurement reliability, it is helpful to think of a measure as containing two components. The first represents an individual's "true" score on the measuring instrument. The second represents random error and does not provide an accurate assessment of what is being measured. Error can slip into the measurement process from several sources. Perhaps a question has been worded ambiguously, or a person's pencil slipped as he or she was filling out a measuring instrument. Whatever the cause, all measurement is subject to some degree of random error. Figure 3.3 illustrates this concept. As is evident, Measurement Instrument 1 is highly reliable—the ratio of the true component of the score to the total score is high. Measurement Instrument 2, however, is unreliable—the ratio of the true component to the total is low.

A completely unreliable measurement measures nothing at all. If a measure is repeatedly given to individuals and each person's responses at a later session are unrelated to that individual's earlier responses, the measure is useless. If the responses are identical or nearly identical each time the measure is given, the measure is reliable—it at least measures something—although not necessarily what the researcher intended (this problem is discussed below).

The importance of reliability should be obvious now. Unreliable measures cannot be used to detect relationships between variables. When the measurement of a variable is unreliable, it is composed mainly of random error, and random error is seldom related to anything else.

Three general components of reliability can be identified: *intercoder reliability, stability,* and *equivalence.* Intercoder reliability (sometimes referred to as reproducibility) designates the degree to which a result can be achieved by other observers. Ideally, two individuals using the same operational measure and the same measuring instrument should end up with the same results. For example, if two researchers try to identify acts of violence in television content based on a given operational definition of "violence," the degree to which their results are consistent is a measure of intercoder reliability. Disagreements reflect a difference either in perception or in the way the original definition was interpreted.

Stability refers to the consistence of results or of a measure at different points in time. For example, suppose that a test designed to measure proofreading ability is administered during the first week of an editing class and again during the second week. The test possesses stability if the two results are consistent. Caution should be used whenever stability is used as a measure of reliability, since people and things can change over time. To use the previous example, it is entirely possible for a person to score higher the second time because some people might actually have improved their ability from week one to week two. In this case the measure is not really unstable; actual change has occurred.

Equivalence refers to the internal consistency of a measure. If separate items on a scale assign the same values to the concept being measured, the scale possesses equivalency. For instance, suppose a researcher had a 10-question scale designed to measure attitudes toward a certain newspaper. The total score of the first five questions should be equal to the total score of the last five. If this is so, then the researcher can conclude that the two parts of the scale are measuring the same underlying concept.

An assessment of reliability is necessary in all mass media research and should be reported along with other facets of the research as an aid in interpretation and evaluation. One commonly used statistic for assessing reliability takes the form of a correlation coefficient denoted as r_{xx}. Chapter 10 provides a more detailed examination of the correlation coefficient, but for now, we say only that r_{xx} is a number ranging from -1.00 to $+1.00$, used to gauge the strength of a relationship between two variables. When r_{xx} is high—that is, approaching ± 1.00—the relationship is strong. A negative number indicates a negative relationship (high scores on one variable are associated with low scores on the other), and a positive number indicates a positive relationship (a high score goes with another high score). In measuring reliability, a high, positive r_{xx} is desired. Another common reliability coefficient is *alpha* (sometimes referred to as Cronbach's alpha), which uses the analysis of variance approach (Chapter 10) to assess the general reliability of a measure.

One method that uses correlation coefficients to determine reliability is the *test–retest method*. This procedure measures the stability component of reliability. The same people are measured at two different points in time, and a coefficient between the two scores is computed. An r_{xx} that approaches $+1.00$ indicates that a person's score at

Time A was similar to his or her score at Time B, showing consistency over time. There are two limitations to the test–retest technique. First, the initial administration of the measure might affect scores on the second testing. If the measuring device is a questionnaire, a person might remember responses from session to session, thus falsely inflating reliability. Second, the concept measured may change from Time A to Time B, thus lowering the reliability estimate.

To overcome these two problems, two *equivalent forms* of the same measurement instrument are administered to the same subjects, and r_{xx} is computed between the two sets of scores. The two testing sessions are placed close together in time to reduce the chance that the property being measured will change greatly. The drawback to this technique is the difficulty of determining whether the two forms of the measure are in fact equivalent.

Another popular method of determining reliability is called the *split-half* technique. Only one administration of the measuring instrument is made, but the test is split into halves and scored separately. For example, if the test is in the form of a questionnaire, the even-numbered items might constitute one half and the odd-numbered items the other. A correlation coefficient is then computed between the two sets of scores. Since this coefficient is computed from a test that is only half as long as the final form, it is corrected by using the following formula:

$$r_{xx} = \frac{2(r_{oe})}{1 + r_{oe}}$$

where r_{oe} is the correlation between the odd and the even items. Both the equivalent forms and the split-half techniques measure the equivalence component of reliability.

In addition to being reliable, a measurement must be valid if it is to be of use in studying variables. A valid measuring device measures what it is supposed to measure. Or, to put it in familiar terms, determining validity requires an evaluation of the congruence between the operational definition of a variable and its conceptual or constitutive definition. Assessing validity requires some degree of judgment on the part of the researcher. In the following discussion of the major types of measurement validity, note that each one depends at least in part on the judgment of the researcher. Also, validity is almost never an all-or-none proposition; it is usually a matter of degree. A measurement rarely turns out to be totally valid or invalid. Typically it winds up somewhere in the middle.

There are four major types of validity, and each has corresponding techniques for evaluating the measurement method. They are: face validity, predictive validity, concurrent validity, and construct validity.

The simplest and most basic kind of validity, *face validity*, is achieved by examining the measurement device to see whether, on the

PART ONE ▪ THE RESEARCH PROCESS

face of it, it measures what it appears to measure. For example, a test designed to measure proofreading ability could include accounting problems, but this measurement would lack face validity. A test that asks people to read and correct certain paragraphs has more face validity as a measure of proofreading skill. Whether a measure possesses face validity depends to some degree on subjective judgment. To minimize subjectivity, the relevance of a given measurement should be independently judged by several experts.

Predictive validity is assessed by checking a measurement instrument against some future outcome. For example, scores on a test to predict whether a person will vote in an upcoming election can be checked against actual voting behavior. If the test scores allow the researcher to predict with a high degree of accuracy which people will actually vote and which will not, the test has predictive validity. Note that it is possible for a measure to have predictive validity and at the same time lack face validity. The sole factor in determining validity in the predictive method is the measurement's ability to correctly forecast future behavior. The concern is not what is being measured but whether the measurement instrument can predict something. Thus, a test to determine whether a person will become a successful mass communication researcher could conceivably consist of geometry problems. If it predicts the ultimate success of a researcher reasonably well, the test has predictive validity but little face validity. The biggest problem associated with predictive validity is determining the criteria against which test scores are to be checked. What, for example, constitutes a "successful mass communication researcher"? One who obtains an advanced degree? One who publishes research articles? One who writes a book?

Concurrent validity is closely related to predictive validity. In this method, however, the measuring instrument is checked against some present criterion. For example, it is possible to validate a test of proofreading ability by administering the test to a group of professional proofreaders and to a group of nonproofreaders. If the test discriminates well between the two groups, it can be said to have concurrent validity. Similarly, a test of aggression might discriminate between a group of children who are frequently detained after school for fighting and another group who have never been reprimanded for antisocial behavior.

The last form of validity, *construct validity*, is the most complex. In simplified form, construct validity involves relating a measuring instrument to some overall theoretic framework to ensure that the measurement is actually logically related to other concepts in the framework. Ideally, a researcher should be able to suggest various kinds of relationships between the property being measured and other variables. For construct validity to exist, the researcher must show that these relationships are in fact present. For example, an investigator might expect the frequency with which a person views a particular television

Figure 3.4 Relationship of reliability and validity

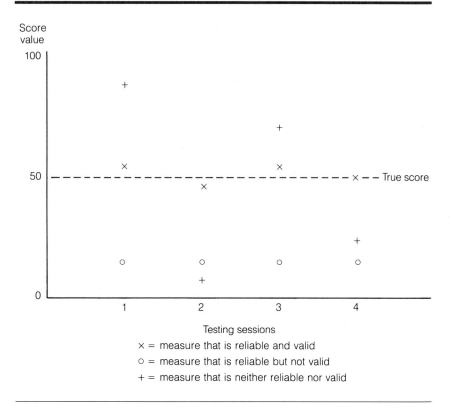

Score value

x = measure that is reliable and valid
o = measure that is reliable but not valid
+ = measure that is neither reliable nor valid

newscast to be influenced by his or her attitude toward that program. If the measure of attitudes correlates highly with frequency of viewing, there is some evidence for the validity of the attitude measure. By the same token, construct validity is evidenced if the measurement instrument under consideration does *not* relate to other variables when there is no theoretic reason to expect such a relationship. Thus, if an investigator finds a relationship between a measure and other variables that is predicted by a theory and fails to find other relationships that are not predicted by a theory, there is evidence for construct validity. For example, Milavsky and associates (1982) established the validity of their measure of respondent aggression by noting that, as expected, boys scored higher than girls and that high aggression scores were associated with high levels of parental punishment. In addition, aggression was negatively correlated with scores on a scale measuring prosocial behavior.

Before closing this discussion, it should be pointed out that reliability and validity are related. Reliability is necessary to establish validity, but it is not a sufficient condition—a reliable measure is not necessarily a valid one. Figure 3.4 demonstrates this relationship.

The x's represent a test that is both reliable and valid. The scores are consistent from session to session and lie close to the "true" value. The o's represent a measure that is reliable but not valid. The scores are stable from session to session but they are not close to the true score. The +'s represent a test that is neither valid nor reliable. Scores vary widely from session to session and are not close to the true score.

Summary

Understanding empirical research requires a basic knowledge of concepts and constructs, variables, and measurement. Concepts summarize related observations and express an abstract notion that has been formed by generalizing from particulars. Connections among concepts form propositions which, in turn, are used to build theories. Constructs consist of combinations of concepts and are also useful in building theories.

Variables are phenomena or events that take on one or more different values. Independent variables are manipulated by the researcher; dependent variables are what the researcher attempts to explain. All variables are related to the observable world by means of operational definitions.

Measurement is the assignment of numerals to objects, events, or properties according to certain rules. There are four levels of measurement: nominal, ordinal, interval, and ratio. To be useful, a measurement must be both reliable and valid.

Questions and Problems for Further Investigation

1. Provide operational definitions for the following items:
   a. Violence
   b. Artistic quality
   c. Programming appeal
   d. Sexual content
   e. Objectionable song lyrics
   Compare your definitions to those of others in the class. Would there be any difficulty in conducting a study using these definitions? Might you have demonstrated why so much controversy surrounds the topics, for example, of sex and violence on television?
2. What type of data (nominal, ordinal, interval, ratio) does each of the following concepts or measurements represent?

a. Baseball team standings
b. A test of listening comprehension
c. A. C. Nielsen's list of the top 10 television programs
d. Frequency of heads versus tails on coin flips
e. Baseball batting averages
f. A scale measuring intensity of attitudes toward violence
g. VHF channels 2–13
h. A scale for monitoring your weight over time
3. Try to develop a measurement technique that would examine each of the following concepts:
a. Newspaper reading
b. Aggressive tendencies
c. Brand loyalty (to purchase of products)
d. Television viewing

References and Suggested Readings

Atkin, C., & Block, M. (1983). Effectiveness of celebrity endorsers. *Journal of Advertising Research, 23*(1), 57–62.

Blankenburg, W. (1977). Nixon vs. the networks: Madison Avenue and Wall Street. *Journal of Broadcasting, 21*, 163–176.

Burgoon, J., & Burgoon, M. (1980). Predictors of newspaper readership. *Journalism Quarterly, 57*(4), 589–596.

Chadwick, B., Bahr, H., & Albrecht, S. (1984). *Social science research methods.* Englewood Cliffs, NJ: Prentice-Hall.

Davidson, B. (1981). Fact or fiction: Television docudramas. In R. P. Adler (Ed.), *Understanding television.* New York: Praeger.

Elliott, W., & Schenck-Hamlin, W. (1979). Film, politics and the press. *Journalism Quarterly, 56*(3), 546–553.

Elliott, W., & Slater, D. (1980). Exposure, experience and perceived TV reality for adolescents. *Journalism Quarterly, 57*(3), 409–414.

Farace, V., & Donohew, L. (1965). Communication in national social systems. *Journalism Quarterly, 42*, 253–261.

Filstead, W. (1970). *Qualitative methodology.* Chicago: Markham.

Gafke, R., & Leuthold, D. (1979). A caveat on *E&P* poll on newspaper endorsements. *Journalism Quarterly, 56*(2), 383–385.

Gantz, W. (1978). How uses and gratifications affect recall of television news. *Journalism Quarterly, 55*(4), 664–672.

Gerbner, G., et al. (1980). The mainstreaming of America: Violence profile No. 11. *Journal of Communication, 30*(3), 10–29.

Giffard, C. (1984). Developed and developing nations news in U.S. wire service files to Asia. *Journalism Quarterly, 61*(1), 14–19.

Guilford, J. P. (1954). *Psychometric methods.* New York: McGraw-Hill.

Haskins, J. & Kubas, L. (1979). Validation of a method for pretesting reader interest in newspaper content. *Journalism Quarterly, 56*(2), 269–276.

Heeter, C., et al. (1983). Cross-media coverage of local Hispanic American News. *Journal of Broadcasting, 27*(4), 395–403.

Henningham, J. (1984). Comparisons between three versions of the Professional Orientation Index. *Journalism Quarterly, 61*(2), 302–309.

Kerlinger, F. (1973). *Foundations of behavioral research* (2nd ed.). New York: Holt, Rinehart & Winston.

Kerlinger, F., & Pedhazur, E. (1973). *Multiple regression in behavioral research*. New York: Holt, Rinehart & Winston.

Markham, D. (1968). The dimensions of source credibility for television newscasters. *Journal of Communication, 18*(1), 57–64.

McNemar, Q. (1962). *Psychological statistics*. New York: John Wiley.

Milavsky, J., Kessler, R., Stipp, H., & Rubens, W. (1982). *Television and aggression*. New York: Academic Press.

Newcombe, H. (1979). *Television: The critical view*. New York: Oxford University Press.

Nunnally, J. (1978). *Psychometric theory*. New York: McGraw-Hill.

Osgood, C., Suci, G., & Tannenbaum, P. (1957). *The measurement of meaning*. Urbana: University of Illinois Press.

Robinson, J., & Shaver, P. (1969). *Measures of social psychological attitudes*. Ann Arbor, MI: Institute for Social Research.

Roscoe, J. (1975). *Fundamental research statistics for the behavioral sciences*. New York: Holt, Rinehart & Winston.

Rubin, A. (1983). Television uses and gratifications. *Journal of Broadcasting, 27*(1), 37–51.

Schwartz, H., & Jacobs, J. (1979). *Qualitative sociology*. New York: Free Press.

Thorburn, D. (1981). Television melodrama. In R. P. Adler (Ed.), *Understanding television*. New York: Praeger.

Webb, E., Campbell, D., Schwartz, E., & Sechrest, L. (1966). *Unobtrusive measures: Nonreactive research in the social sciences*. Skokie, IL: Rand McNally.

Williams, W., & Semlak, W. (1979). Campaign, '76: Agenda setting during the New Hampshire primary. *Journal of Broadcasting, 22*(4), 531–539.

Wilson, C. & Howard, D. (1978). Public perception of media accuracy. *Journalism Quarterly, 55*(1), 73–76.

C H A P T E R 4
Sampling

POPULATION AND SAMPLE

·

PROBABILITY AND NONPROBABILITY SAMPLES

·

SAMPLE SIZE

·

SAMPLING ERROR

·

SAMPLE WEIGHTING

·

SUMMARY

·

QUESTIONS AND PROBLEMS FOR FURTHER INVESTIGATION

·

REFERENCES AND SUGGESTED READINGS

This chapter describes the basics of the sampling methods that are widely used in mass media research. However, considering that sampling theory has become a distinct discipline in itself, there are some studies, such as nationwide surveys, that require a consultation of more technical discussions of sampling (for example, Blalock, 1972; Cochran, 1963; Kish, 1965; Raj, 1972).

Population and Sample

One goal of scientific research is to describe the nature of a **population**, that is, a group or class of subjects, variables, concepts, or phenomena (Walizer & Wienir, 1978). In some cases this is achieved through the investigation of an entire class or group, such as a study of prime time television programs during the week of September 10–16. The process of examining every member of such a population is called a **census**. In many situations, however, the chance of investigating an entire population is remote, if not nonexistent, due to time and resource constraints. The usual procedure in these instances is to select a **sample** from the population. A sample is a subset of the population that is taken to be representative of the entire population. An important word in this definition is *representative*. A sample that is not representative of the population, regardless of its size, is inadequate for testing purposes: the results cannot be generalized.

The sample selection process is illustrated using a Venn diagram (see Figure 4.1); the population is represented by the larger of the two spheres. A census would test or measure every element in the population (*A*); a sample would measure or test a segment of the population (*A*₁). Although in Figure 4.1 it might seem that the sample is drawn from only one portion of the population, it is actually selected from every portion. Assuming that a sample is chosen according to proper guidelines and is representative of the population, the results from a study using the sample can be generalized to the population. However, generalizing results must proceed with some caution because of the error that is inherent in all sample selection methods. Theoretically, when a population is studied, only **measurement error** (that is, inconsistencies produced by the instrument used) will be present. However, when a sample is drawn from the population, the procedure introduces the likelihood of **sampling error** (that is, the degree to which

Figure 4.1 A Venn diagram, as used in the process of sample selection

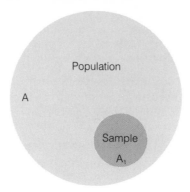

measurements of the units or subjects selected differ from those of the population as a whole). Because a sample does not provide the exact data that a population would, the potential error must be taken into account.

A classic example of sampling error occurred during the 1936 presidential campaign. *Literary Digest* had predicted, based on the results of a sample survey, that Alf Landon would beat Franklin D. Roosevelt. Although the *Digest* sample included more than a million voters, it was composed mainly of affluent Republicans. Consequently, it inaccurately represented the population of eligible voters in that election. The researchers who conducted the study had failed to consider the population **parameters** (characteristics) before selecting their sample. Of course FDR was reelected in 1936, and it may be no coincidence that the *Literary Digest* went out of business shortly thereafter.

Probability and Nonprobability Samples

A **probability sample** is selected according to mathematical guidelines whereby the chance for selection of each unit is known. A **nonprobability sample** does not follow the guidelines of mathematical probability. However, the most significant characteristic distinguishing the two types of samples is that probability sampling allows researchers to calculate the amount of sampling error present in a research study; nonprobability sampling does not.

In deciding whether to use a probability or a nonprobability sample, a researcher should consider four points.

1. *Cost versus value.* The sample should produce the greatest value for the least investment. If the cost of a probability sample is too high in relation to the type and quality of information collected, a nonprobability sample is a possible alternative.
2. *Time constraints.* In many cases researchers collecting preliminary information operate under time constraints imposed by sponsoring agencies, management directives, or publication guidelines. Since probability sampling is often time-consuming, a nonprobability sample may provide temporary relief.
3. *Purpose of the study.* Some research studies are not designed for generalization to the population, but rather to investigate variable relationships or to collect exploratory data for designing questionnaires or measurement instruments. A nonprobability sample is often appropriate in situations of these types.
4. *Amount of error allowed.* In preliminary or pilot studies, where error control is not a prime concern, a nonprobability sample is usually adequate.

Probability sampling generally incorporates some type of systematic selection procedure, such as a table of random numbers, to ensure that each unit has an equal chance of being selected. However, it does not always guarantee a representative sample from the population, even when systematic selection is followed. It is possible to randomly select 50 members of the student body at a university in order to determine the average height of all students enrolled and, by extraordinary coincidence, end up with 50 candidates for the basketball team. Such an event is unlikely, but it is possible, and this possibility underscores the need to replicate any study.

Types of Nonprobability Samples

Nonprobability sampling is frequently used in mass media research, particularly in the form of available samples, samples using volunteer subjects, and purposive samples. An **available sample** is a collection of readily accessible subjects for study, such as a group of students enrolled in an introductory mass media course. Although available samples can be helpful in collecting exploratory information and may produce useful data in some instances, the samples are problematic because they contain unknown quantities of error. Researchers need to consider the positive and negative qualities of available samples before using them in a research study.

Available samples are a subject of heated debate in many research fields. Critics argue that regardless of what results they may generate, available samples do not represent the population and therefore have no external validity. (This problem was discussed in Chapter 2.) Proponents of the available sample procedure claim that if a phenomenon, characteristic, or trait does in fact exist, it should exist in *any* sample. In addition, Raj (1972) has contested the very notion of sample representativeness:

> Some writers suggest the use of a "representative" sample as a safeguard against the hazards of sampling. This is an undefined term which appears to convey a great deal but which is unhelpful. If it means the sample should be a miniature of the population in every respect, we do not know how to select such a sample.

Available samples can be useful in pretesting questionnaires or other preliminary (pilot study) work. They often help eliminate potential problems in research procedures, testing, and methodology before the final research study is attempted.

Subjects who constitute a **volunteer sample** also form a non-probability sample, since the individuals are not selected mathematically. There is concern in all areas of research with regard to persons who willingly participate in research projects; these subjects differ greatly from nonvolunteers and may consequently produce erroneous research results. Rosenthal and Rosnow (1969) identified the characteristics of volunteer subjects on the basis of several studies and found that such subjects, in comparison with nonvolunteers, tend to exhibit higher educational levels, higher occupational status, greater need for approval, higher intelligence, and lower authoritarianism. They also seem to be more sociable, more "arousal-seeking," and more unconventional; they are more likely to be first children, and they are generally younger.

These characteristics mean that use of volunteer subjects may significantly bias the results of a research study and may lead to inaccurate estimates of various population parameters (Rosenthal & Rosnow, 1969). Also, available data seem to indicate that volunteers may more often than nonvolunteers provide data to support a researcher's hypothesis. In some cases volunteer subjects are necessary—for example, in comparison tests of products or services. However, volunteers should be used with caution because, as with available samples, there is an unknown quantity of error present in the data.

A **purposive sample** includes subjects selected on the basis of specific characteristics or qualities and eliminates those who fail to meet these criteria. Purposive samples are often used in advertising studies: researchers select subjects who use a particular type of product and ask them to compare it with a new product. A purposive sample is chosen with the knowledge that it is not representative of the general population; rather it attempts to represent a specific portion of the population. In a similar method, the **quota sample**, subjects are selected to meet a predetermined or known percentage. For example, a researcher interested in finding out how VCR owners differ in their use of television from non-VCR-owners may know that 10% of a particular population owns a VCR. The sample the researcher selected, therefore, would be comprised of 10% VCR owners and 90% non-VCR-owners (to reflect the population characteristics).

Another nonprobability sampling method is to select subjects haphazardly on the basis of appearance or convenience, or because they seem to meet certain requirements (the subjects *look* educated). Haphazard selection involves researcher subjectivity and introduces error. Some haphazard samples give the illusion of a probability sample; these must be carefully approached. For example, interviewing every tenth person who walks by in a shopping center is haphazard, since not everyone in the population has an equal chance of walking by that particular location. Some people live across town, some shop in other centers, and so on.

Types of Probability Samples

The most basic type of probability sampling is the simple **random sample**, where each subject or unit in the population has an equal chance of being selected. If a subject or unit is drawn from the population and removed from subsequent selections, the procedure is known as random sampling *without replacement*—the most widely used random sampling method. Random sampling *with replacement* involves returning the subject or unit into the population so that it has a chance of being chosen another time. Sampling with replacement is often used in more complicated research studies such as nationwide surveys (Raj, 1972).

Researchers usually use a table of random numbers to generate a simple random sample. For example, a researcher who wants to analyze 10 prime time television programs out of a total population of 100 programs to determine how the medium portrays elderly people can take a random sample from the 100 programs by numbering each show from 00 to 99 and then selecting 10 numbers from a table of random numbers, such as the brief listing in Table 4.1. First, a starting point in the table is selected at random. There is no specific way to choose a starting point; it is an arbitrary decision. The researcher then selects the remaining 9 numbers by going up, down, left, or right on the table—or even randomly throughout the table. For example, if it is decided to go down in the table from the starting point 44 until a sample of 10 has been drawn, the sample would include television programs numbered 44, 85, 46, 71, 17, 50, 66, 56, 03, and 49.

Simple random samples for use in telephone surveys are often obtained by a process called **random digit dialing**. One method involves randomly selecting four-digit numbers (usually generated by a computer or through the use of a random numbers table) and adding them to the three-digit exchange prefixes in the city in which the survey is conducted. A single four-digit series may be used once, or it may be added to all the prefixes.

Unfortunately, a large number of the telephone numbers

Table 4.1   Random Numbers

38	71	81	39	18	24	33	94	56	48	80	95	52	63	01	93	62
27	29	03	62	76	85	37	00	44	11	07	61	17	26	87	63	79
34	24	23	64	18	79	80	33	98	94	56	23	17	05	96	52	94
32	44	31	87	37	41	18	38	01	71	19	42	52	78	80	21	07
41	88	20	11	60	81	02	15	09	49	96	38	27	07	74	20	12
95	65	36	89	80	51	03	64	87	19	06	09	53	69	37	06	85
77	66	74	33	70	97	79	01	19	44	06	64	39	70	63	46	86
54	55	22	17	35	56	66	38	15	50	77	94	08	46	57	70	61
33	95	06	68	60	97	09	45	44	60	60	07	49	98	78	61	88
83	48	36	10	11	70	07	00	66	50	51	93	19	88	45	33	23
34	35	86	77	88	40	03	63	36	35	73	39	(44)	06	51	48	84
58	35	66	95	48	56	17	04	44	99	79	87	85	01	73	33	65
98	48	03	63	53	58	03	87	97	57	16	38	46	55	96	66	80
83	12	51	88	33	98	68	72	79	69	88	41	71	55	85	50	31
56	66	06	69	44	70	43	49	35	46	98	61	17	63	14	55	74
68	07	59	51	48	87	64	79	19	76	46	68	50	55	01	10	61
20	11	75	63	05	16	96	95	66	00	18	86	66	67	54	68	06
26	56	75	77	75	69	93	54	47	39	67	49	56	96	94	53	68
26	45	74	77	74	55	92	43	37	80	76	31	03	48	40	25	11
73	39	44	06	59	48	48	99	72	90	88	96	49	09	57	45	07
34	36	64	17	21	39	09	97	33	34	40	99	36	12	12	53	77
26	32	06	40	37	02	11	83	79	28	38	49	44	84	94	47	32
04	52	85	62	24	76	53	83	52	05	14	14	49	19	94	62	51
33	93	35	91	24	92	47	57	23	06	33	56	07	94	98	39	27
16	29	97	86	31	45	96	33	83	77	28	14	40	43	59	04	79

generated by this method of random digit dialing are invalid because some phones have been disconnected, because some numbers generated have not yet been assigned, and for other reasons. Therefore, it is advisable to produce at least three times the number of telephone numbers needed; if a sample of 100 is required, at least 300 numbers should be generated to allow for invalid numbers.

A second random digit dialing method that tends to decrease the occurrence of invalid numbers involves adding from one to three random digits to a telephone number selected from a phone directory or list of phone numbers. One first selects a number from a list of telephone numbers (a directory or list purchased from a supplier). Assume that the number 448-3047 was selected from the list. The researcher could simply add a predetermined number, say 6, to produce 448-3053; or a predetermined two-digit number, say 21, to achieve 448-3068; or even a three-digit number, say 112, to produce 448-3159. Each variation of the method helps to eliminate many of the invalid numbers produced in pure random number generation, since telephone companies tend to distribute telephone numbers in series, or blocks. In the example above, the block 30— is in use, and there is a good chance that random add-ons to this block will be residential telephone numbers.

As indicated above, random number generation is possible via a variety of methods. However, two rules are always applicable: (1)

SIMPLE RANDOM SAMPLE

Advantages

1. Detailed knowledge of the population is not required.
2. External validity may be statistically inferred.
3. A representative group is easily obtainable.
4. The possibility of classification error is eliminated.

Disadvantages

1. A list of the population must be compiled.
2. A representative sample may not result in all cases.
3. Sampling error tends to be high compared to other sampling procedures.
4. The procedure is expensive if several steps are involved.

---

each unit or subject in the population must have an equal chance of being selected, and (2) the selection procedure must be free from subjective intervention by the researcher. The purpose of random sampling is to reduce sampling error; violating random sampling rules only increases the chance of introducing such error into a study.

Similar in some ways to simple random sampling is a procedure called **systematic sampling**, in which every *n*th subject or unit is selected from a population. For example, to get a sample of 20 from a population of 100, or a **sampling rate** of 1/5, a researcher randomly selects a starting point and a **sampling interval**. Thus, if the number 11 is chosen, the sample will include the twenty subjects or items numbered 11, 16, 21, 26, and so on. To add further randomness to the process, the researcher may randomly select both the starting point and the interval. For example, an interval of 11 together with a starting point of 29 would generate the numbers 40, 51, 62, 73, and so on.

Systematic samples are frequently used in mass media research. They often save time, resources, and effort when compared to simple random samples. In fact, since the procedure so closely resembles a simple random sample, many researchers consider systematic sampling equal to the random procedure (Babbie, 1986). The method is widely used in selecting subjects from lists such as telephone directories, *Broadcasting/Cablecasting Yearbook*, and *Editor & Publisher*.

The degree of accuracy of systematic sampling depends on the adequacy of the **sampling frame**, or a complete list of members in the population. Telephone directories are inadequate sampling frames in most cases, since not all phone numbers are listed, and some people do not have telephones at all. However, lists that include all the members of a population have a high degree of precision. Before deciding

SYSTEMATIC SAMPLING

Advantages

1. Selection is easy.
2. Selection can be more accurate than in a simple random sample.
3. The procedure is generally inexpensive.

Disadvantages

1. A complete list of the population must be obtained.
2. Periodicity may bias the process.

---

to use systematic sampling, one should consider the goals and purpose of a study, as well as the availability of a comprehensive list of the population. If such a list is not available, systematic sampling is probably ill-advised.

One major problem associated with systematic sampling is that the procedure is susceptible to **periodicity**; that is, the arrangements or order of the items in the population list may bias the selection process. For example, consider the problem mentioned earlier of analyzing television programs to determine how the elderly are portrayed. Quite possibly, every tenth program listed may have been aired by ABC; the result would be a nonrepresentative sampling of the three networks. If periodicity is eliminated, systematic sampling can be an excellent sampling methodology.

A **stratified sample** is used when a researcher is interested in a particular characteristic, segment, or stratum of the population. Instead of selecting a sample from the population at large, the researcher identifies a significant variable, selects subjects who have this trait, and chooses a subsample from this group. The variable of interest might be age, sex, religion, education, income, or political affiliation. However, the more variables are added to the stratification list, the harder it becomes to identify subjects meeting the criteria. The term **incidence** is used to describe the frequency with which desired subjects can be found in the population. When several stratified variables are involved, the rate of incidence is low, and the time and expenses required for recruiting the sample increase.

Stratified sampling ensures that a sample is drawn from a homogeneous subset of the population, that is, from a population with similar characteristics. **Homogeneity** helps researchers to reduce sampling error. For example, consider a research study on subjects' attitudes toward two-way, interactive cable television. The investigator, knowing that cable subscribers tend to have higher achievement levels,

STRATIFIED SAMPLING

Advantages

1. Representativeness of relevant variables is ensured.
2. Comparisons can be made to other populations.
3. Selection is made from a homogeneous group.
4. Sampling error is reduced.

Disadvantages

1. A knowledge of the population prior to selection is required.
2. The procedure can be costly and time-consuming.
3. It can be difficult to find a sample if incidence is low.

---

may wish to stratify the population according to education. Before randomly selecting subjects, the researcher divides the population into three levels: grade school, high school, and college. Then, if it is determined that 10% of the population completed college, a random sample proportional to the population should contain 10% who meet this standard. As Babbie (1986, p. 161) noted:

> Stratified sampling ensures the proper representation of the stratification variables to enhance representation of other variables related to them. Taken as a whole, then, a stratified sample is likely to be more representative on a number of variables than a simple random sample.

The usual sampling procedure is to select one unit or subject at a time. But this requires the researcher to have a complete list of the population. In some cases there is no way to obtain such a list. One way to avoid this problem is to select the sample in groups or categories; this procedure is known as **cluster sampling**. For example, analyzing magazine readership habits of people in the state of Wisconsin would be time-consuming and complicated if individual subjects were randomly selected. With cluster sampling, one can divide the state into districts, counties, or zip code areas and select groups of people from these areas.

Cluster sampling creates two types of error: in addition to the error involved in defining the initial clusters, errors may arise in selecting from the clusters. For example, a zip code area may comprise mostly residents of a low socioeconomic status who are unrepresentative of the remainder of the state; if selected for analysis, such a group may confound the research results. To help control such error, it is best to use small areas or clusters, both to decrease the number of elements

CLUSTER SAMPLING

Advantages

1. Only part of the population need be enumerated.
2. Costs are reduced if clusters are well defined.
3. Estimates of cluster parameters are made and compared to the population.

Disadvantages

1. Sampling errors are likely.
2. Clusters may not be representative of the population.
3. Each subject or unit must be assigned to a specific cluster.

in each cluster and to maximize the number of clusters selected (Babbie, 1986).

In many nationwide studies, researchers use a form of cluster sampling called *multistage sampling*, in which individual households or persons are selected, not groups. Figure 4.2 demonstrates a four-stage sequence for a nationwide survey. First, a cluster of counties (or another specific geographic area) in the United States is selected. This cluster is narrowed by randomly selecting a county, district, or block group within the principal cluster. Next, individual blocks are selected within each area. Finally, a convention such as "the third household from the northeast corner" is established, and then the individual households in the sample can be identified by applying the selection formula in the stages just described.

In many cases researchers also need to randomly select an individual in a given household. In most cases researchers cannot count on being able to interview the person who happens to answer the telephone. Usually demographic quotas are established for a research study, which means that a certain percentage of all respondents must be of a certain sex or age. In this type of study, researchers determine which person in the household should answer the questionnaire by using a form of random numbers table, as illustrated in Table 4.2

To get a random selection of individuals in the selected households, the interviewer simply asks each person who answers the telephone, "How many people are there in your home who are age 12 or older?" If the first respondent answers "Five," the interviewer asks to speak to the fifth oldest (the youngest in this case) person in the home. Each time a call is completed, the interviewer checks off on the table the number representing the person questioned. If the next household called also had five family members, the interviewer would

Figure 4.2 Census tracts

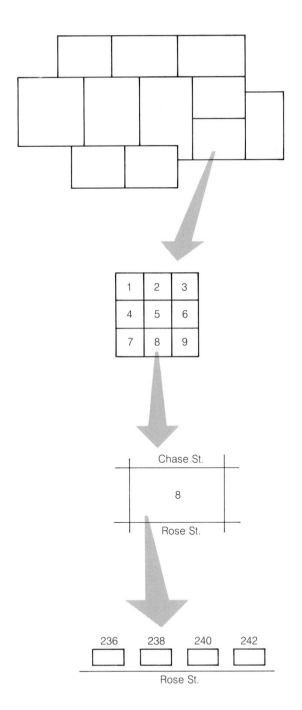

Table 4.2 Example of Matrix for Selecting Respondents at Random

	Number of people in household						
	1	2	3	4	5	6	7
Person to interview:	1	2	1	3	5	5	7
		1	3	4	3	2	6
			2	2	1	4	1
				1	2	6	4
					4	1	3
						3	2
							5

move to the next number in the "5" column and ask to talk to the third oldest person in the home.

The same table can be used to select respondents by sex. That is, the interviewer could ask, "How many males who are age 12 or older live in your home?" The interviewer could then ask for the "*n*th" oldest male, or female, according to the requirements of the survey.

Since the media are complex systems, researchers frequently encounter complicated sampling methods. These are known as *hybrid* situations. Consider some researchers attempting to determine the potential for videotext distribution of a local newspaper to cable subscribers. This problem requires investigating readers and nonreaders of the newspaper as well as cable subscribers and nonsubscribers. The research, therefore, requires random sampling from the following four groups:

Group A   Subscribers/Readers
Group B   Subscribers/Nonreaders
Group C   Nonsubscribers/Readers
Group D   Nonsubscribers/Nonreaders

The researchers must identify each subject as belonging to one of these four groups. If three variables were involved, sampling from eight groups would be required, and so on. In other words, researchers are often faced with very complicated sampling situations that involve numerous steps.

Sample Size

Determining an adequate sample size is one of the most controversial aspects of sampling. How large must a sample be to be representative of the population, or to provide the desired level of confidence in the results? Unfortunately, there is no simple answer. There are suggested sample sizes for various statistical procedures, but no single sample size formula or method is available for every research method or statistical procedure. For this reason, it is advisable to consult sampling texts for information concerning specific techniques (Cochran, 1963; Raj, 1972).

The few general principles that guide researchers in determining an acceptable sample size are not based on mathematical or statistical theory, but they should provide a starting point in most cases.

1. A primary consideration in determining sample size is the methodology to be used. In some cases, such as focus groups (see Chapter 7), a sample of 6–12 subjects is adequate if the subjects are representative of the population under study. Small samples are also adequate for pretesting measurement instruments, for pilot studies (to determine the practicality of a research project), and for studies designed for heuristic value.

2. Sample size is almost invariably controlled by cost and time. Although researchers may wish to use a sample of 1,000 for a survey, the economics of such a sample are usually restrictive. Private sector research using 1,000 subjects may cost more than $100,000. Research at any level is very expensive, and these costs have great influence on a project. The general rule is to use as large a sample as possible within the economic constraints of the study. If a small sample is forced on a researcher, the results must be interpreted accordingly—that is, with caution regarding generalization.

3. Multivariate studies (see Appendix 2) always require larger samples than univariate studies because they involve the analysis of multiple response data (several measurements on the same subject). One guideline recommended for multivariate studies is: 50 = very poor; 100 = poor; 200 = fair; 300 = good; 500 = very good; 1,000 = excellent (Comrey, 1973). Other researchers suggest using a sample of 100 *plus* 1 subject for each dependent variable in the analysis (Gorsuch, 1974).

4. Researchers should always select a larger sample than is actually required for a study, since attrition must be compensated for. Subjects drop out of research studies for one reason or another, and allowances must be made for this in planning the sample selection. Subject attrition is especially prevalent in panel studies, where the same group of subjects is tested or measured frequently over a long period of time. In most cases, researchers can expect from 10 to 25% of the sample to drop out of a study before it is completed.

5. Information about sample size is available in published research. Consulting the work of other researchers provides a base from which to start. If a survey is planned and similar research indicates that a representative sample of 400 has been used regularly with reliable results, a sample larger than 400 may be unnecessary.

6. Generally speaking, the larger the sample used, the better. However, a large unrepresentative sample is as meaningless as a small unrepresentative sample, so researchers should not consider numbers alone. Quality is always more important in sample selection than mere size.

Sampling Error

All research involves some degree of error. Research error is an additive process, That is, total error comprises sampling error plus measurement error plus **random** (unknown or uncontrollable) **error**.

In calculating sampling error, it must be recognized that measurements obtained from a sample differ to some degree from the measurements that would be obtained from the population. There are several ways to compute sampling error, but no single method is appropriate for all sample types or for all situations. In addition, error formulas vary in complexity. One error formula, designed for estimating audience sizes during certain time periods or for certain programs and for measuring cumulative audiences (see Chapter 14), uses the standard error of a percentage derived from a simple random sample. If the sample percent is designated as p, the size of the sample as n, and the estimated or **standard error** of the sample percentage as $SE(p)$, the formula is:

$$SE(p) = \sqrt{\frac{p(100 - p)}{n}}$$

Suppose a random sample of 500 households produces a **rating** (or estimate of the percentage of viewers; see Chapter 14) of 20 for a particular show. This means that 20% of those households were tuned in to that channel at that time. The formula can be used to calculate the standard error as follows:

$$SE(p) = \sqrt{\frac{20\,(80)}{500}}$$

$$= \sqrt{\frac{1,600}{500}}$$

$$= \sqrt{3.2}$$

$$= \pm\,1.78$$

That is, the rating of 20 computed in the survey is subject to an error of ± 1.78 points; the actual rating could be as low as 18.22 or as high as 21.78.

Standard error is directly related to sample size. The error figure improves as the sample size is increased, but in decreasing in-

Table 4.3 Finding Error Rate Using a Rating of 20

Sample size	Error	Lower limit	Upper limit
600	± 1.63	18.37	21.63
700	± 1.51	18.49	21.51
800	± 1.41	18.59	21.41
900	± 1.33	18.67	21.33
1,000	± 1.26	18.74	21.26
1,500	± 1.03	18.97	21.03

crements. Thus, an increase in sample size does not provide a big gain, as illustrated by Table 4.3. As can be seen, even with a sample of 1,500, the standard error is only .75 better than with a sample of 500 computed above. A researcher would need to determine whether the increase in time and expense caused by an additional 1,000 subjects would justify such a proportionally small increase in precision.

There are two important terms related to sampling error: **confidence interval** and **confidence level**. The confidence level, such as 95%, indicates that 95 times out of 100, a particular result will occur. A confidence interval (such as ± 1.0) relates to the amount a particular value found may vary. Table 4.4 shows the amount of error at the 95% confidence level for measurements that contain dichotomous variables (such as "yes/no"). For example, with a sample of 1,000 and a 30% "yes" response to a question, the probable error due to sample size alone is ± 2.9%. This means that we are 95% sure that our values for this particular question fall between 27.1 and 32.9%.

Sampling error is an important concept in all research areas because it provides an indication of the degree of accuracy of the research. Research studies published by large audience measurement firms such as Arbitron and A. C. Nielsen are required by the Electronic Media Ratings Council to include simplified charts to assist in determining sampling error. In addition, each company provides some type of explanation about error, such as the Arbitron statement contained in every ratings book:

> Arbitron estimates are subject to statistical variances associated with all surveys using a sample of the universe.... The accuracy of Arbitron estimates, data and reports and their statistical evaluators cannot be determined to any precise mathematical value or definition.

Statistical error due to sampling is found in all research studies. Researchers must pay specific attention to the potential sources of error in any study. Producing a study riddled with error is tantamount to never having conducted the study at all. If the magnitude of error were subject to accurate assessment, researchers could simply determine the source of error and correct it. Since this is not possible, however, they

Table 4.4 Sampling Error

Sample of:	1% or 99%	5% or 95%	10% or 90%	15% or 85%	20% or 80%	25% or 75%	30% or 70%	35% or 65%	40% or 60%	45% or 55%	50%
25	4.0	8.7	12.0	14.3	16.0	17.3	18.3	19.1	19.6	19.8	20.0
50	2.8	6.2	8.5	10.1	11.4	12.3	13.0	13.5	13.9	14.1	14.2
75	2.3	5.0	6.9	8.2	9.2	10.0	10.5	11.0	11.3	11.4	11.5
100	2.0	4.4	6.0	7.1	8.0	8.7	9.2	9.5	9.8	9.9	10.0
150	1.6	3.6	4.9	5.9	6.6	7.1	7.5	7.8	8.0	8.1	8.2
200	1.4	3.1	4.3	5.1	5.7	6.1	6.5	6.8	7.0	7.0	7.1
250	1.2	2.7	3.8	4.5	5.0	5.5	5.8	6.0	6.2	6.2	6.3
300	1.1	2.5	3.5	4.1	4.6	5.0	5.3	5.5	5.7	5.8	5.8
400	.99	2.2	3.0	3.6	4.0	4.3	4.6	4.8	4.9	5.0	5.0
500	.89	2.0	2.7	3.2	3.6	3.9	4.1	4.3	4.4	4.5	4.5
600	.81	1.8	2.5	2.9	3.3	3.6	3.8	3.9	4.0	4.1	4.1
800	.69	1.5	2.1	2.5	2.8	3.0	3.2	3.3	3.4	3.5	3.5
1000	.63	1.4	1.9	2.3	2.6	2.8	2.9	3.1	3.1	3.2	3.2
2000	.44	.96	1.3	1.6	1.8	1.9	2.0	2.1	2.2	2.2	2.2
5000	.28	.62	.85	1.0	1.1	1.2	1.3	1.4	1.4	1.4	1.4

Survey result is:

Source: A Broadcast Research Primer. Washington, DC: National Association of Broadcasters, 1976, p. 19. Reprinted by permission.

must accept error as part of the research process, attempt to reduce its effects to a minimum, and remember always to interpret their results with regard to its presence.

Sample Weighting

In an ideal study, the researcher will have enough subjects to represent the demographic, **psychographic** (why people behave in specific ways), and lifestyle characteristics of the population. The ideal sample, however, is rare, due to the time and budget constraints of most research. Instead of canceling a research project because of sampling inadequacies, most researchers utilize a statistical procedure known as **weighting**, or sample balancing. That is, when subject totals in given categories do not reach the necessary population percentages, subjects' responses are multiplied (weighted) to allow for the shortfall. A single subject's responses may be multiplied by 1.3, 1.7, 2.0, or any other figure to reach the predetermined required level.

Subject weighting is a controversial data manipulation technique, especially in the area of broadcast ratings. The major question is just how much one subject's responses can be weighted and still be representative. Weighting is discussed in greater detail in Chapter 14.

Summary

To make predictions about events, concepts, or phenomena, researchers must perform detailed, objective analyses. One procedure to use in such analyses is a census, in which every member of the population is studied. Conducting a census for each research project is impractical, however, and researchers must resort to alternative methods. The most widely used alternative is to select a random sample from the population, examine it, and make predictions from it that can be generalized to the population. There are several procedures for identifying the units that are to compose a random sample.

If the scientific procedure is to provide valid and useful results, researchers must pay close attention to the methods they use in selecting a sample. This chapter has described several types of samples commonly used in mass media research. Some are elementary and do not require a great deal of time or resources. Other sampling methods entail great expense and time. Researchers must decide whether costs and time are justified in relation to the results generated.

Sampling procedures must not be taken lightly in the process of scientific investigation. It makes no sense to develop a research design for testing a valuable hypothesis or research question and then nullify this effort by neglecting correct sampling procedures. These procedures must be continually scrutinized to ensure that the results of an analysis are not sample-specific; that is, results are not based on the type of sample used in the study.

Questions and Problems for Further Investigation

1. The use of available samples in research has long been a target for heated debate. Some researchers say that available samples are inaccurate representations of the population; others claim that if a concept or phenomenon exists, it should exist in an available sample as well as in a random sample. Which argument do you agree with? Explain your answer.

2. Many research studies use small samples. What are the advantages or disadvantages of this practice? Can any gain other than cost savings be realized by using a small sample in a research study?

3. What sampling technique might be appropriate for the following research projects?
   a. A pilot study to test whether people understand the directions to a telephone questionnaire.
   b. A study to determine who buys video cassette recorders.
   c. A study to determine the demographic makeup of the audience for a local television show.
   d. A content analysis of commercials during Saturday morning children's programs.
   e. A survey examining the differences between newspaper readership in high- and low-income households.

References and Suggested Readings

Babbie, E. R. (1986). *The practice of social research* (4th ed.). Belmont, CA: Wadsworth.

Blalock, H. M. (1972). *Social statistics*. New York: McGraw-Hill.

Cochran, W. G. (1963). *Sampling techniques*. New York: John Wiley.

Comrey, A. L. (1973). *A first course in factor analysis*. New York: Academic Press.

Fletcher, J. E. (Ed.). (1981). *Handbook of radio and TV broadcasting*. New York: Van Nostrand Reinhold.

Gorsuch, R. L. (1974). *Factor analysis*. Philadelphia: W. B. Saunders.

Kish, L. (1965). *Survey sampling*. New York: John Wiley.

Nunnally, J. C. (1978). *Psychometric theory*. New York: McGraw-Hill.

Raj, D. (1972). *The design of sample surveys*. New York: McGraw-Hill.

Rosenthal, R., & Rosnow, R. L. (1969). *Artifact in behavioral research*. New York: Academic Press.

Walizer, M. H., & Wienir, P. L. (1978). *Research methods and analysis*. New York: Harper & Row.

C H A P T E R 5

Laboratory Research and Experimental Design

The mass media are complicated phenomena. Not only are there a variety of media presenting information to audience members, the audience uses these media in a variety of ways. Some people use the media for information, others use them for entertainment or just to pass time, creating a variety of research opportunities for investigators. A single research approach cannot be used because there are simply too many different situations that need investigation. Some situations require that subjects be studied under controlled conditions; other situations require telephone or in-person interviews.

This chapter describes the laboratory method of research and its use in mass media investigations. The laboratory method is the oldest approach in mass media research and continues to provide a wealth of information for researchers and critics of the media.

Laboratory research has been a popular approach since the early 1900s, for at least two reasons. First, laboratory experiments follow a fairly simple format: the relationship between two types of variables is measured under closely observed and controlled conditions. Second, laboratory experiments are often valuable in determining causation, since variable manipulation is controlled by the researcher.

The laboratory approach has five basic uses in mass media research:

1. To investigate hypotheses and research questions under controlled conditions
2. To develop theories that can be tested in the field
3. To refine existing theories and research findings
4. To investigate problems in small steps
5. To ease replication, since conditions of the study are clearly specified

Controls

The fact that laboratory research is conducted under controlled conditions is particularly important. Researchers using this method have control over three areas of the project: the environment, the variables, and the subjects.

Environmental Control

Laboratory research allows investigators to isolate a testing situation from the competing influences of normal activity. Researchers are free to structure the experimental environment in almost any way. Lighting and temperature levels, proximity of subjects to measurement instruments, soundproofing, and nearly every other aspect of the experimental situation can be arranged and altered.

However, the environmental artificiality created in laboratory experiments has been a thorn in the side of laboratory research for years. Critics claim that the sterile and unnatural conditions created in the laboratory produce results that have little direct application to "real-world settings," where subjects are continually exposed to competing stimuli. Miller (1977) noted that critics of the laboratory method often resort to ambiguous and disjunctive arguments about the artificiality of the procedure, suggesting that contrasting the "real" world with the "unreal" world may, in fact, be merely a problem in semantics. The main point, he claimed, is that both laboratory and field methods investigate communication behavior, and if viewed in this way, it is meaningless to speak of behavior as "real" or "unreal": all behavior is real.

Miller also noted, however, that it is unsatisfactory and unscientific to dodge the problem of artificiality in laboratory procedures by including a disclaimer in a study indicating that the findings are applicable only to a particular audience, the environmental conditions of the analysis, and the period during which the study was conducted. Since external validity is a major goal of scientific research, a disclaimer of this nature is counterproductive. If researchers are not willing to expand their interests beyond the scope of a single analysis, such studies have only heuristic value; they make little or no contribution to the advancement of knowledge in mass media.

Laboratory studies can be particularly valuable as an initial phase of research. Problems can be defined, methods can be tested, and the worth of a study can be judged. The results of such studies are not necessarily invalid or irrelevant. For example, suppose researchers are interested in determining how television soap operas help college students solve communication problems—a question that has not been investigated. A preliminary laboratory study finds that a number of college students do use soap operas as models in their own communication encounters. Is this finding totally irrelevant? The answer is no. The researchers might conclude their preliminary study with the following statement:

> The purpose of this study was to conduct a preliminary analysis of the use of television soap operas in solving communication problems. The results indicated that 25% of the sample feel that soap operas do in fact help them solve communication problems in their

own lives. This leads to speculation that other samples, and other groups in the general population, may also share these attitudes. We suggest further research using other types of samples, different soap operas, and different research .designs. It is possible that a substantial number of viewers in the general population reflect the attitudes and behaviors of the subjects uncovered in the analysis.

This explanation neither totally supports nor totally discounts the findings of the hypothetical study. It states only that an attitude or behavior is present and that the same characteristics may quite likely be found in other samples using different research procedures.

Severe criticisms of the laboratory method (in reference to statistical analysis) may subside when more reliable measurements have been developed. In addition, not all laboratory experiments involve wiring subjects to machines or placing them in soundproof rooms; many more "natural" studies, such as measurement development (see Nunnally, 1978, for information on measurement development), are particularly suited to the laboratory approach.

Variable Control

Laboratory studies also allow researchers to control the number and types of independent and dependent variables selected and the way these variables are manipulated. Variable control strengthens internal validity and helps eliminate confounding influences. Appel, Weinstein, and Weinstein (1979), for example, were able to control almost every detail of their laboratory analysis of alpha brain wave activity while subjects viewed television commercials.

Control over Subject Selection

More than any other research method, the laboratory approach allows researchers to control subjects. This includes control over the selection process, assignment to the experimental or the control group, and exposure to the experimental treatment. Researchers can place limits on the number of subjects participating in a study and can choose specific types of subjects for exposure in varying degrees to the independent variable. For example, they may select subjects according to which medium they use for news information and vary each subject's exposure to commercials of different types to determine which is the most effective.

Control is important in experimentation because it allows researchers to rule out rival explanations of results. The laboratory method, although often criticized for its lack of external validity, does offer the benefits of control.

Experimental Design

Experimental design consists of the steps in the conduct of laboratory research. An experimental design does not have to be a complicated series of statements, diagrams, and figures; it may be as simple as:

Pretest → Experimental treatment → Posttest

Although other factors, such as variable and sample selection, control, and construction of a measurement instrument, enter into this design, the diagram does provide a legitimate starting point for research.

To facilitate the discussion of experimental design, the following notations are used to represent specific parts of a design (Campbell & Stanley, 1963):

- R   represents a random sample or random assignment.
- X   represents a treatment or manipulation of the independent variables so that the effects of these variables on the dependent variables can be measured.
- O   refers to a process of observation or measurement; it is usually followed by a numerical subscript indicating the number of the observation (O_1 = "observation 1").

A left-to-right listing of symbols, such as $R\ O_1\ X\ O_2$, represents the order of the experiment. In this case, subjects are randomly selected or assigned to groups (R) and then observed or measured (O_1). Next, some type of treatment or manipulation of the independent variable is performed (X), followed by a second observation or measurement (O_2). Each line in experimental notation refers to the experience of a single group. A design such as the following:

R O_1 X O_2

R O_1 O_2

indicates that the operations in the experiment are conducted simultaneously on two different groups. Notice that the control group does not receive the experimental treatment.

An alternative notation system that provides a number of more complex notational schemes was developed by Haskins (1981). Researchers interested in a more detailed approach to research design notation should consult this paper.

Basic Experimental Designs

Research designs are as unique and as varied as the questions and hypotheses they help answer. Designs of different types yield different types of information. If information about the effects of time is desired,

Figure 5.1   Pretest-posttest control group design

R O_1 X O_2

R O_1 O_2

---

a **repeated measures design** (several measurements on the same subjects) or a panel (long-term) design can be used. If information about the effects of experimental treatment *order* is desired, a procedure known as a *Latin Square* design is necessary because the order of presenting the independent variable is changed to help control error.

Each experimental design makes assumptions about the type of data the researcher wishes to collect, since different data require different research methods. Several questions need to be answered by the researcher before any type of design is constructed.

1. What is the purpose of the study?
2. What is to be measured or tested?
3. How many factors (independent variables) are involved?
4. How many levels of the factors (degrees of the independent variables) are involved?
5. What type of data is desired?
6. What is the easiest and most efficient way to collect the data?
7. What type of statistical analysis is appropriate for the data?
8. How much will the study cost?
9. How can these costs be trimmed?
10. What facilities are available for conducting the study?
11. What types of studies have been conducted in the area?
12. What benefits will be received from the results of the study?

The answer to each question has a bearing on the sequence of steps a study should follow. For example, if a limited budget is available for the study, a complicated, four-group research design must be excluded. Or, if previous studies have shown the "posttest only" design to be useful, another design may be unjustified.

Not all experimental designs are covered in this section; only the most widely used are considered. The sources listed at the end of the chapter provide more information about these and other designs.

Pretest-posttest control group.   The pretest-posttest control group design is a fundamental and widely used procedure in all research areas. The design controls many of the rival hypotheses generated by artifacts: the effects of maturation, testing, history, and other sources are controlled, because each group faces the same circumstances in the study. As shown in Figure 5.1, subjects are to be randomly selected or assigned, and each group is to be given a pretest. Only the first group, however, is to receive the experimental treatment. The difference be-

Figure 5.2 Posttest-only control group design

R   X O_1

R O_2

tween O_1 and O_2 for Group 1 is compared to the difference between O_1 and O_2 for Group 2. If a significant statistical difference is found, it is assumed that the experimental treatment was the primary cause.

Posttest-only control group. When researchers are hesitant to use a pretest because of the possibility of subject sensitization to the posttest, the design in Figure 5.1 can be altered to describe a posttest-only control group (Figure 5.2). Neither group has a pretest, but Group 1 is exposed to the treatment variable, followed by a posttest. The two groups are compared to determine if a statistical significance is present.

The posttest-only control group design is also widely used to control rival explanations. Both groups are equally affected by maturation, history, and so on. Also, both normally call for a **t-test,** a test to compare the significance between two groups, to determine whether a significant statistical difference is present.

Solomon four-group design. The Solomon four-group design (Figure 5.3) combines the first two designs and is useful if pretesting is considered to be a negative factor. Each alternative for pretesting and posttesting is accounted for in the design, which makes it attractive to researchers. The main drawback is that four separate groups are required—a luxury many researchers cannot afford.

The Solomon four-group design, in addition to controlling extraneous variables, considers the aspect of external validity, since effects and interaction of testing are determinable (two groups receive the pretest, and two do not). It allows for greater generalizability than the designs previously discussed.

Figure 5.3 Solomon four-group design

R O_1 X O_2

R O_3 O_4

R   X O_5

R O_6

Figure 5.4 2 × 2 factorial design

	Radio	No radio
Newspapers	I	II
No newspapers	III	IV

Factorial Studies

Research studies involving the simultaneous analysis of two or more independent variables are called **factorial designs,** and each independent variable is called a *factor.* The approach saves time, money, and resources and allows researchers to investigate the interaction between the independent variables. That is, in many instances, it is possible that two or more variables are *interdependent* in the effects they produce on the dependent variable, a relationship that could not be detected if two simple randomized designs were used.

The term *two-factor design* indicates that two independent variables are manipulated; a three-factor design includes three independent variables, and so on. (A one-factor design is a simple random design, because only one independent variable is involved.) A "factorial" design for a study must have at least two factors or independent variables.

Factors may also have two or more levels. Therefore, the term *2 × 2 factorial design* means "two independent variables, each with two levels." A 3 × 3 factorial design has three levels for each of the two independent variables. A 2 × 3 × 3 factorial design has three independent variables: the first has two levels, and the second and third have three levels each.

To demonstrate the concept of levels, imagine that a television station manager would like to study the success of a promotional campaign for a new movie-of-the-week series. The manager plans to advertise the new series on radio and in the newspaper. Subjects selected randomly are placed into one of the *cells* of the 2 × 2 factorial design in Figure 5.4. This allows for the testing of two levels of two independent variables, exposure to radio and exposure to newspapers.

Four groups are involved in the study: Group I receives exposure to both newspaper and radio materials; Group II is exposed only to newspaper; Group III is exposed only to the radio; and Group IV serves as a control group and receives no exposure to either radio or newspaper. After the groups have undergone the experimental

Figure 5.5 2 × 3 factorial design

	Radio	No radio
Full color newspaper ad	I	II
Black/white newspaper ad	III	IV
No newspaper	V	VI

treatment, the manager can administer a short questionnaire to determine which medium, or combination of media, worked most effectively.

A 2 × 3 factorial design, which adds a third level to the second independent variable, is shown in Figure 5.5. This design demonstrates how the manager might investigate the relative effectiveness of full color versus black and white newspaper advertisements while also measuring the impact of the exposure to radio materials.

Say the television station manager wants to include promotional advertisements on television as well as using radio and newspaper. The third factor produces a 2 × 2 × 2 factorial design. This three-factor design (see Figure 5.6) shows the eight possibilities of a 2 × 2 × 2 factorial study. Note that the subjects in Group I are exposed to newspaper, radio, and television announcements, while those in Group VIII are not exposed to any of the announcements.

The testing procedure in the three-factor design is similar to that of previous methods. Subjects in all eight cells would be given some type of measurement instrument, and differences between the groups would be tested for statistical significance.

Laboratory Research Example

An example from published literature is used here to illustrate the various facets of research design and the laboratory method. Cantor and Venus (1980) were interested in the effects of humor on the ability to recall radio commercials. It would have been possible to study this topic by conducting a survey or by launching a field experiment, but these researchers chose to investigate the problem under tightly controlled laboratory conditions. The authors were dissatisfied with the ambiguity of existing literature relating to humor and advertising and decided to investigate the problem using a broad research question:

Figure 5.6 2 × 2 × 2 factorial design

	Radio		No radio	
	TV	No TV	TV	No TV
Newspaper	I	II	III	IV
No newspaper	V	VI	VII	VIII

they tested the "effect of humor on the memorability and persuasiveness of a rigorously manipulated radio advertisement which was heard in a quasi-naturalistic setting."

Step 1: Experimental design. After reviewing the available literature in the field and defining their research question, Cantor and Venus designed a 2 × 2 × 2 factorial study (Figure 5.7).

Step 2: Sample selection and assignment. The authors recruited undergraduate students at the University of Wisconsin (59 male, 58 female) as subjects for the experiment and assigned them randomly to the four different exposure groups for each sex.

Step 3: Manipulation. The experiment was designed to make subjects believe they were involved in three separate studies; in reality, however, two of the experiments were fabricated to disguise the "real" experiment—listening to preproduced radio recordings. The recordings contained: (1) a serious commercial preceded by a humorous programming segment, (2) a humorous commercial preceded by a serious programming segment, (3) a serious commercial preceded by a serious programming segment, and (4) a humorous commercial preceded by a humorous programming segment. In all cases, the content of the commercial was the same; only the approach was changed. Additionally, Cantor and Venus studied the differences between male and female perceptions of the commercials.

This design demonstrates how variables can be manipulated in the laboratory approach. The researchers controlled when, how, and where subjects would be exposed to the commercials and program segments. The messages were also controlled, since they were produced specifically for the experiment.

Step 4: Gathering data. Cantor and Venus first escorted subjects individually into a cubicle, where they heard a radio message, then transferred them to another cubicle, where they were exposed to the

Figure 5.7 Design for the Cantor-Venus study

| | Serious commercial | | Humorous commercial | |
	Serious intro	Humorous intro	Serious intro	Humorous intro
Male				
Female				

experimental treatment. Finally, subjects were taken to another room to complete a survey and participate in an experiment of recall.

Step 5: Data analysis. The authors selected analysis of variance (see Chapter 12) as an appropriate statistic to analyze their data. The article must be read to fully understand the details of their analysis; basically, however, the presence or absence of humor in the commercials had no appreciable effect on attitudes toward the products advertised.

Summary

Mass media researchers have a number of research designs from which to choose when analyzing a given topic. The laboratory experiment has been a staple in mass media research for several decades. Although criticized by many researchers as being artificial, the method offers a number of advantages that make it particularly useful to some researchers. Of specific importance is the researcher's ability to control the experimental situation and to manipulate experimental treatments.

This chapter also described the process of experimental design, the researcher's blueprint for conducting an experiment. The experimental design provides the steps the researcher will follow to accept or reject a hypothesis or research question. Some experimental designs are simple and take very little time to perform; others involve many different groups and numerous treatments.

The laboratory research approach has shortcomings, as do all research procedures, but the method has proved efficient in many instances and will continue to be used by mass media researchers.

Questions and Problems for Further Investigation

1. Provide four research questions or hypotheses for any mass media area. Which of the designs described in this chapter is best suited to investigate the problems?

2. What are the advantages and/or disadvantages of each of the following experimental designs?

a.			X	O_1
				O_2
b.	R		X	O_1
c.	R	O_1	X	O_2
	R		X	O_3
d.	R	O_1	X	O_2

3. The Cantor–Venus laboratory study on the effect of humor on radio advertisements was described in this chapter. In the same issue of the *Journal of Broadcasting* (Volume 24:1), Krull and Husson (pp. 35–47) investigated children's perceptions of television. Read this study and compare the authors' approach to the laboratory methods used by Cantor and Venus.

References and Suggested Readings

Appel, V., Weinstein, S., & Weinstein, C. (1979). Brain activity and recall of TV advertising. *Journal of Advertising Research, 19*(4), 7–18.

Babbie, E. R. (1986). *The practice of social research* (4th ed.). Belmont, CA: Wadsworth.

Bruning, J. L., & Kintz, B. L. (1977). *Computational handbook of statistics.* Chicago: Scott, Foresman.

Campbell, D. T., & Stanley, J. C. (1963). *Experimental and quasi-experimental designs and research.* Skokie, IL: Rand McNally.

Cantor, J., & Venus, P. (1980). The effects of humor on recall of a radio advertisement. *Journal of Broadcasting, 24*(1), 13–22.

Cook, T. D., & Campbell, D. T. (1979). *Quasi-experimentation: Designs and analysis for field studies.* Skokie, IL: Rand McNally.

Haskins, J. B. (1968). *How to evaluate mass communication.* New York: Advertising Research Foundation.

Haskins, J. B. (1981). A precise notational system for planning and analysis. *Evaluation Review, 5*(1), 33–50.

Keppel, G. (1973). *Design and analysis: A researcher's handbook.* Englewood Cliffs, NJ: Prentice-Hall.

Miller, D. C. (1977). *Handbook of research design and social measurement* (3rd ed.). New York: David McKay.

Nunnally, J. C. (1978). *Psychometric theory.* New York: McGraw-Hill.

Roscoe, J. T. (1975). *Fundamantal research statistics for the behavioral sciences.* New York: Holt, Rinehart & Winston.

Rosenberg, M. J. (1965). When dissonance fails: On eliminating evaluation apprehension from attitude measurement. *Journal of Personality and Social Psychology, 1,* 28–42.

Rosenthal, R. (1969). *Experimenter effects in behavioral research.* New York: Appleton-Century-Crofts.

Rosenthal, R., & Rosnow, R. L. (1969). *Artifact in behavioral research.* New York: Academic Press.

Senter, R. J. (1969). *Analysis of data.* Chicago: Scott, Foresman.

Walizer, M. H., & Wienir, P. L. (1978). *Research methods and analysis: Searching for relationships.* New York: Harper & Row.

C H A P T E R 6

Survey Research

DESCRIPTIVE AND ANALYTICAL SURVEYS

ADVANTAGES AND DISADVANTAGES OF SURVEY RESEARCH

CONSTRUCTING QUESTIONS

QUESTIONNAIRE DESIGN

PILOT STUDIES

GATHERING SURVEY DATA

ACHIEVING A REASONABLE RESPONSE RATE

GENERAL PROBLEMS IN SURVEY RESEARCH

SUMMARY

QUESTIONS AND PROBLEMS FOR FURTHER INVESTIGATION

REFERENCES AND SUGGESTED READINGS

S urveys are now used in all areas of life. Businesses, consumer groups, politicians, and advertisers use them in their everyday decision-making processes. Some firms, such as Gallup and Harris, conduct public opinion surveys on a full-time basis.

The importance of survey research to the public at large is confirmed by the frequent reporting of survey results in the popular media. This is especially evident during campaign periods, when the public continually hears or reads about polls conducted to ascertain candidates' positions with the electorate.

The increased use of surveys has created changes in the way they are conducted and reported. More attention is now given to sample selection, questionnaire design, and error rates. This means that surveys require careful planning and execution; mass media studies using survey research must take into account a wide variety of decisions and problems. This chapter acquaints the beginning researcher with the basic steps of survey methodology.

Descriptive and Analytical Surveys

At least two major types of surveys are used by researchers: descriptive and analytical. A **descriptive survey** attempts to picture or document current conditions or attitudes, that is, to *describe* what exists at the moment. For example, the Department of Labor regularly conducts surveys on the amount of unemployment in the United States. Professional pollsters survey the electorate to learn its opinions of candidates or issues. Broadcast stations and networks continually survey their audiences to determine programming tastes, changing values, and lifestyle variations that might affect programming. In descriptive surveys of this type, researchers are interested in discovering the current situation in a given area.

Analytical surveys attempt to describe and explain *why* certain situations exist. In this approach two or more variables usually are examined to test research hypotheses. The results allow researchers to examine the interrelationships among variables and to draw explanatory inferences. For example, television station owners occasionally survey the market to determine how lifestyles affect viewing habits, or to determine whether viewers' lifestyles can be used to predict the success of syndicated programming. On a much broader scale, television networks conduct yearly surveys to determine how the public's tastes and desires are changing and how these attitudes relate to the perception viewers have of the three commercial networks.

Analytical and descriptive surveys are important to mass media researchers in both the academic and the private sector. Syndicated survey researchers such as Simmons and A. C. Nielsen provide media management with current audience data. In addition, custom research, designed by companies such as Frank N. Magid Associates, Surrey Consulting & Research, and Reymer-Gersin, allows broadcasters to investigate unique problems. Academicians, on the other hand, generally conduct theoretical rather than applied research.

Advantages and Disadvantages of Survey Research

Surveys have certain well-defined advantages. First, these instruments can be used to investigate problems in realistic settings. Newspaper reading, television viewing, and consumer behavior patterns can be examined where they happen, rather than in a laboratory or screening room under artificial conditions.

Second, the cost of surveys is reasonable considering the amount of information gathered. In addition, researchers can control expenses by selecting from four major types of surveys: mail, telephone, personal interview, and group administration.

A third advantage is that large amounts of data can be collected with relative ease from a variety of people. The survey technique allows the researcher to examine many variables (demographic and lifestyle information, attitudes, motives, intentions, and so on) and to use multivariate statistics (see Appendix 2) to analyze the data. Also, geographic boundaries do not limit most surveys.

Finally, data helpful to survey research already exist. Data archives, government documents, census materials, radio and television rating books, and voter registration lists can be used as *primary* sources (main sources of data) or as *secondary* sources (supportive data) of information. With archive data, it is possible to conduct an entire survey study without ever developing a questionnaire or contacting a single respondent.

Survey research is not a perfect research methodology. The technique also possesses several disadvantages. The first and most important is that independent variables cannot be manipulated as in laboratory experiments. Without control of independent variable variation, the researcher cannot be certain whether the relations between independent and dependent variables are causal or noncausal. That is, a survey may establish that A and B are related, but it is impossible to determine solely from the survey results that A causes B. Causality is difficult to establish because many intervening and extraneous variables are involved. Time series studies help correct this problem sometimes, but not always.

A second disadvantage is that the wording of questions and the placement of items within questionnaries can have biasing effects on survey results. Great care must be taken to assure that the data collected as well as the measurement process are reliable and valid. This problem is discussed later in the chapter.

Another potential disadvantage of survey research is its dependence on sampling techniques. If the sample is largely unrepresentative, the results will have little relevance to other situations, even though the sample size may be quite large (see Chapter 4).

Surveys do, however, produce reliable and useful information. They are especially useful for collecting information on audiences and readership; however, they are not particularly suited for testing causal hypotheses.

Constructing Questions

Two basic considerations apply to the construction of good survey questions: (1) the questions must clearly and unambiguously communicate the desired information to the respondent, and (2) the questions should be worded to allow accurate transmission of respondents' answers to researchers.

Questionnaire design depends on choice of data collection technique. Questions written for a **mail survey** must be easy to read and understand, since respondents are unable to obtain explanations. **Telephone surveys** cannot use questions with long lists of response options; the respondent may forget the first few responses by the time the last ones have been read. Questions written for **group administration** must be concise and easy for the respondents to answer. In a **personal interview** the interviewer must tread lightly with sensitive and personal questions, which his or her physical presence might make the respondent less willing to answer. (These procedures are discussed in greater detail later in this chapter.)

The design of a questionnaire must always reflect the basic purpose of the research. A complex research topic such as media use during a political campaign requires more detailed questions than does a survey to determine a favorite radio station or magazine. Nonetheless, there are several general guidelines to follow regarding wording of questions and question order and length.

Types of Questions

Surveys can consist of two basic types of questions, open-ended and close-ended. An **open-ended question** requires respondents to generate their own answers. For example:

What do you like most about your local newspaper?

_____

_____

What type of television program do you prefer?

_____

_____

What are the three most important problems in your community?

_____

_____

_____

Open-ended questions allow respondents freedom in answering questions and the chance to provide in-depth responses. Furthermore, they give researchers the opportunity to ask: "Why did you give that particular answer?" or "Could you explain your answer in more detail?" This flexibility to follow up on, or probe, certain questions enables the interviewers to gather information about the respondents' feelings and the motives behind their answers.

Also, open-ended questions allow for answers that researchers did not foresee in the construction of the questionnaire, answers that may suggest possible relationships with other answers or variables. For example, in response to the question, "What types of programs would you like to hear on radio?" the manager of a local radio station might expect to hear "news" and "weather" or "sports." However, a subject may give an unexpected response, such as "obituaries" (Fletcher & Wimmer, 1981). This will force the manager to reconsider his perceptions of some of the local radio listeners.

Finally, open-ended questions are particularly useful in pilot versions of major studies. Researchers may not know what types of responses to expect from subjects, so open-ended questions can be used to allow subjects to answer in any way they wish. From the list of responses provided by the subjects, the researchers can then select the most-often mentioned items and include them in multiple-choice or forced-choice questions. Using open-ended questions on a pilot study generally saves time and resources, since all possible responses are more likely to be included on the final measurement instrument; there would be no reason to reconduct the analysis for failure to include an adequate number of responses or response items.

The major disadvantage associated with open-ended questions is the amount of time needed to collect and analyze the data. Since subjects' responses are always varied, their content must be analyzed (see Chapter 8) before they can be tabulated. Content analysis allows common responses to be grouped into categories, making the question similar to a **forced-choice question** (see p.112).

In the case of **close-ended questions,** respondents are asked to select an answer from a list provided by the researcher. These questions are popular both because they provide greater uniformity of response and because the answers are easily quantifiable for computer analysis. Their chief disadvantage is that researchers may fail to include some important responses. Respondents may not have the opportunity to answer questions according to their own beliefs or feelings and sometimes comment that the "correct" responses were not available. One common technique is to include a response of "other" followed by a blank space. This provides subjects an opportunity to supply an answer not included among the choices devised by the researcher. Unfortunately, many repondents simply check "other" without writing in the preferred response. A pilot study can help determine which response alternatives to include.

General Observations

Before examining specific question types appropriate in survey research, some general do's and don'ts about writing questions are in order.

1. Make questions clear. This should go without saying, but many researchers become so closely associated with a problem that they can no longer put themselves in the respondents' position. What might be perfectly clear to researchers might not be nearly as clear to persons answering the question. For example, "What do you think of our company's rebate program?" might seem to be a perfectly sensible question to a researcher, but to respondents it might mean, "Is the monetary amount of the rebate too small?" "Is the rebate given on the wrong items?" "Does it take too long for the rebate to be paid?" or "Have the details of the program been poorly explained?" Questionnaire items must be phrased precisely so that respondents know what is being asked.

Making questions clear also requires avoiding difficult or specialized words, acronyms, and stilted language. In general, the level of vocabulary commonly found in newspapers or popular magazines is adequate for a survey. Questions should be phrased in everyday speech, and social science jargon and technical words should be eliminated. For example, "Would you consider buying a VHS or Beta system if it retailed for less than $150?" might be better phrased: "Would you buy a machine that could record and play back television programs if it cost less than $150?" The item, "Should the city council approve the construction of an interactive cable TV system?" assumes that respondents know what "interactive cable TV systems" are. A preferable option is: "An interactive cable television system is one in which viewers can send messages back to the cable company as well as receive normal television. Do you think the city council should approve such a system for this community?"

The clarity of a questionnaire item can be affected by double or hidden meanings in the words that are not apparent to investigators. For example, the question, "How many television shows do you think are a little too violent—most, some, few or none?" contains such a problem. Some respondents who feel that TV shows are extremely violent will answer "none" on the basis of the question's wording. These subjects reason that all shows are more than "a little too violent"; therefore, the most appropriate answer to the question is "none." Deleting the phrase "a little" from the question helps avoid this pitfall.

2. *Keep questions short.* To be precise and unambiguous, researchers sometimes write long and complicated items. However, respondents who are in a hurry to complete a questionnaire are unlikely to take the time to study the precise intent of the person who drafted the items. Short, concise items that will not be misunderstood are best.

3. *Include complete instructions.* Questionnaire instructions vary depending on the type of survey conducted. Mail surveys usually require the most specific instructions, since respondents are not able to ask questions about the survey. Respondents and interviewers should understand whether the correct response consists of circling, checking, placing in a specific order, or skipping an item. **Filter questions,** which are used to eliminate unwanted subjects, often require respondents or interviewers to skip one or more questions. This information should be clearly specified. For example:

Do you listen to FM radio?

    _____ YES   _____ NO
   (If yes, go to Q 2)   (If no, skip to Q 5)

A survey using this question might be designed to question only subjects who listen to FM radio. The filter question (or screener) immediately assesses whether the subject falls into this group. If the subject responds "no" the interviewer skips a certain number of related questions, or may terminate the interview immediately.

Some questionnaires require respondents to rank a list of items. In this case, the instructions must clearly describe which response represents the highest value:

Please rate the following magazines in order of importance to you. Place a "1" next to the magazine you prefer most, a "2" next to the magazine in second place, and so on up to "5."

_____ PLAYBOY
_____ BETTER HOMES AND GARDENS
_____ POPULAR SCIENCE
_____ READER'S DIGEST
_____ SCIENTIFIC AMERICAN

All questions should be tested in a pilot study to determine whether directions for answering questions are clear.

4. Remember the purposes of the research. It is important to include in a questionnaire only items that directly relate to what is being studied. For example, if the occupational level of the respondents is not relevant to the hypothesis, the questionnaire should not ask about it. Beginning researchers often add questions merely for the sake of developing a longer questionnaire. Keep in mind that parsimony in questionnaires is a paramount consideration.

5. Do not ask double-barreled questions. A **double-barreled question** is one that actually asks two or more questions. Whenever the word *and* appears in a question, the sentence structure should be examined to see whether more than one question is being asked. For example, "This product is mild on hands and gets out stubborn stains. Do you agree _____ or disagree _____ ?" Since a product that gets out stubborn stains might at the same time be highly irritating to the skin, a respondent could agree with the second part of the question while disagreeing with the first part. This question should be divided into two items.

6. Avoid biased words or terms. Consider the following item: "In your free time, would you rather read a book or just watch television?" The word *just* in this example injects a pro-book bias into the question because it implies that there is something less than desirable about watching television. In like manner, "Where did you hear the news about the president's new program?" is mildly biased against newspapers; the word *hear* suggests that "radio," "television," or "other people" is a more appropriate answer. Questionnaire items that start off with "Do you agree or disagree with so-and-so's proposal to . . ." almost always bias a survey. If the name "Adolf Hitler" is inserted for "so-and-so," the item becomes overwhelmingly negative. By inserting "the President," a potential for both positive and negative bias is created. Any time a specific person or source is mentioned in a question, the possibility of introducing bias arises.

7. Avoid leading questions. A **leading question** is one that suggests a certain response (either literally or by implication) or contains a hidden premise. For example, "Like most Americans, do you read a newspaper every day?" suggests that the respondent should answer in the affirmative or run the risk of being unlike most Americans. The question "Do you still use marijuana?" contains a hidden premise. This type of question is usually referred to as a *double bind*: regardless of how the respondent answers, an affirmative response to the hidden premise is implied—in this case, he or she has used marijuana at some point.

8. Do not use questions that ask for highly detailed information. The question "In the past 30 days, how many hours of television have you viewed with your family?" is unrealistic. Few respondents could answer such a question. A more realistic approach would be to ask, "How many hours did you spend watching television with your family yesterday?" A researcher who is interested in a 30-day period should ask respondents to keep a log or diary of family viewing habits.

9. Avoid potentially embarrassing questions unless absolutely necessary. Most surveys need to collect data of a confidential or personal nature, but an overly personal question may cause embarrassment and inhibit respondents from answering honestly. Two common areas with high potential for embarrassment are age and income. Many individuals are reluctant to tell their exact ages to strangers doing a survey. Instead of asking directly how old a respondent is, it is better to allow some degree of confidentiality by asking, "Now, about your age—are you in your 20s, 30s, 40s, 50s, 60s, . . . ?" Most respondents are willing to state what decade they fall in, and this information is usually adequate for statistical purposes. Interviewers might also say, "I'm going to read several age categories to you. Please stop me when I reach the category you're in."

Income may be handled in a similar manner. A straightforward, "What is your annual income?" often prompts the reply, "None of your business." It is more prudent to preface a reading of the following list with the question "Which of these categories includes your total annual income?"

_____ More than $30,000	_____ $4,000–$7,999
_____ $15,000–$29,999	_____ $2,000–$3,999
_____ $8,000–$14,999	_____ Under $2,000

These categories are broad enough to allow respondents some privacy but narrow enough for statistical analysis. Moreover, the bottom category, "Under $2,000," was made artificially low so that individuals who fall into the $2,000–$3,999 slot would not have to be embarrassed by giving the very lowest choice. The income classifications depend on the purpose of the questionnaire and the geographic and demographic distribution of the subjects. The $30,000 upper level in the example would be much too low in several parts of the country.

Other potentially sensitive areas include people's sex lives, drug use, religion, business practices, and trustworthiness. In all these areas, care should be taken to ensure respondents of confidentiality and even anonymity, when possible.

The simplest type of close-ended question is one that provides a *dichotomous response*, usually "agree/disagree" or "yes/no." For example:

In general, television commercials tell the truth . . .

> Television stations should editorialize.
>
> _____ AGREE
> _____ DISAGREE
> _____ NO OPINION

While such questions provide little sensitivity to different degrees of conviction, they are the easiest to tabulate of all question forms. Whether they provide enough sensitivity is a question the researcher must seriously consider.

The *multiple-choice* question allows respondents to choose an answer from several options. For example:

> In general, television commercials tell the truth . . .
>
> _____ ALL OF THE TIME
> _____ MOST OF THE TIME
> _____ SOME OF THE TIME
> _____ RARELY
> _____ NEVER

Multiple-choice questions should include all possible responses. A question that excludes any significant response usually creates problems. For example:

> What is your favorite television network?
>
> _____ ABC
> _____ CBS
> _____ NBC

Subjects who favor PBS (although not a *network* in the strictest sense of the word) cannot answer the question as presented.

Additionally, multiple-choice responses must be **mutually exclusive:** there should be only one response option per question for each respondent. For instance:

> How many years have you been working in newspapers?
>
> _____ LESS THAN ONE YEAR
> _____ ONE TO FIVE YEARS
> _____ FIVE TO TEN YEARS

Which blank should a person with exactly five years of experience check? One way to correct this problem is to reword the responses, such as:

How many years have you been working in newspapers?

    ____ LESS THAN ONE YEAR
    ____ ONE TO FIVE YEARS
    ____ SIX TO TEN YEARS

Rating scales are also widely used in mass media research (see Chapter 3). They can be arranged horizontally or vertically:

There are too many commercials on TV.

    ____ STRONGLY AGREE (translated as a "5" for analysis)
    ____ AGREE (translated as a "4")
    ____ NEUTRAL (translated as a "3")
    ____ DISAGREE (translated as a "2")
    ____ STRONGLY DISAGREE (translated as a "1")

What is your opinion of TV news?

FAIR ____ ____ ____ ____ ____ UNFAIR
    (5) (4) (3) (2) (1)

Semantic differential scales (see Chapter 3) are another form of rating scale and are frequently used to rate persons, concepts, or objects. These scales use bipolar adjectives with seven scale points:

How do you perceive the term *public television*?

```
          GOOD ___ ___ ___ ___ ___ ___ ___ BAD
         HAPPY ___ ___ ___ ___ ___ ___ ___ SAD
 UNINTERESTING ___ ___ ___ ___ ___ ___ ___ INTERESTING
          DULL ___ ___ ___ ___ ___ ___ ___ EXCITING
```

In many instances researchers are interested in the relative perception of several concepts or items. In such cases the *rank ordering* technique is appropriate:

Here are several common occupations. Please rank them in terms of their prestige. Put a "1" next to the profession that has the most prestige, a "2" next to the one with the second most, and so on.

    ____ POLICE OFFICER   ____ TV REPORTER
    ____ BANKER   ____ TEACHER
    ____ LAWYER   ____ DENTIST
    ____ POLITICIAN   ____ NEWSPAPER WRITER

Ranking of more than a dozen objects is not recommended because the process can become tedious and the discriminations exceedingly fine. Furthermore, ranking data imposes limitations on the statistical analyses that can be performed.

The **checklist** question is often used in pilot studies to refine questions for the final project. For example:

What things do you look for in a new television set? (Check as many as apply.)

_____ AUTOMATIC FINE TUNING	_____ CONSOLE MODEL
_____ REMOTE CONTROL	_____ PORTABLE
_____ LARGE SCREEN	_____ STEREO SOUND
_____ CABLE READY	_____ OTHER _____

The most frequently checked answers are later used to develop a multiple-choice question; the unchecked responses are dropped.

Forced-choice questions frequently are used in media studies designed to gather information about lifestyles and are always listed in pairs. Forced-choice questionnaires are usually very long—sometimes hundreds of questions—and repeat questions (in different form) on the same topic. The answers for each topic are analyzed for patterns. Then a respondent's interest in that topic is scored. A typical forced-choice questionnaire might contain the following pairs.

Select one statement from each of the following pairs of statements:

_____ I enjoy attending parties with my friends.
_____ I enjoy staying at home alone.

_____ Gun control is necessary to stop crime.
_____ Gun control can only increase crime.

_____ If I see an injured animal, I always try to help it.
_____ If I see an injured animal, I figure that nature will take care of it.

Respondents generally complain that neither of the responses to a forced-choice question is satisfactory, but they have to select one or the other. Through a series of questions on the same topic (violence, lifestyles, career goals), a pattern of behavior or attitude generally develops.

Fill-in-the-blank questions are used infrequently by survey researchers. However, some studies are particularly suited for fill-in-the-blank questions. In advertising copy testing, for example, they are often employed to test subjects' recall of a commercial. After seeing, hearing, or reading a commercial, subjects receive a script of the commercial in which a number of words have been randomly omitted (often every fifth or seventh word). Subjects are required to fill in the missing words to complete the commercial. Fill-in-the-blank questions can also be used in information tests. For example, "The senators from your state are _____ and _____ ." Or, "The headline story on the front page was about _____ ."

Tables, graphs, and figures are also used in survey research. Some ingenious questioning devices have been developed to help respondents more accurately describe how they think and feel. For example, the University of Michigan Survey Research Center developed

Figure 6.1 A "feeling thermometer," for recording a subject's degree of like or dislike

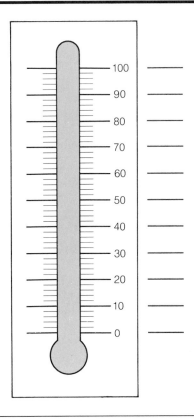

the **feeling thermometer**, on which subjects can rate an idea or object. The thermometer, which is patterned after a normal mercury thermometer, offers an easy way for subjects to rate their degree of like or dislike in terms of "hot" or "cold." For example:

> How would you rate the coverage your local newspaper provided on the recent school board campaign? (Place an "X" near the number on the thermometer in Figure 6.1 that most accurately reflects your feelings; "100 indicates strong approval, and "0" reflects strong disapproval.)

Some questionnaires designed for children use other methods to collect information. Since young children have difficulty in assigning numbers to values, one logical alternative is to use pictures. For example, the interviewer might read the question, "How do you feel about Saturday morning cartoons on television?" and present the faces in Figure 6.2 to elicit a response from a 5-year-old. Zillmann and Bryant (1975) present a similar approach in their "Yucky" scale.

Figure 6.2 A simple picture scale for use with young children

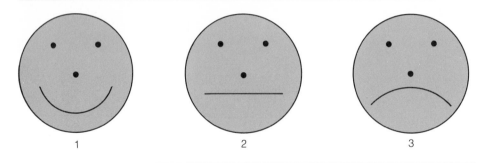

1   2   3

Questionnaire Design

The approach used in asking questions as well as the physical appearance of a questionnaire can affect the response rate. Time and effort invested in developing a good questionnaire always pay off with more usable data. The following section offers some useful suggestions.

Introduction

One way to increase response rate in any type of survey is to prepare a persuasive introduction to the survey. Backstrom and Hursh-Cesar (1981) suggest six principles for writing a successful introduction to a questionnaire; namely, the introduction should be short, realistically worded, nonthreatening, serious, neutral, and pleasant, but firm. It is important to convince respondents early on that the survey is a legitimate research project. It is also necessary to convince them that the survey is valuable and will help solve problems, whether theoretical or applied. In a telephone survey, it is wise to tell respondents how much time is needed to complete the interview: "This will take only about 3 minutes of your time. . . ." A mail survey introduction might similarly stress the brevity of the task: ". . . a one-page questionnaire is enclosed."

Regardless of the survey approach used, a well-constructed introduction usually generates higher response rates than a simple "Please answer the following questions. . . ."

Instructions

All instructions necessary to complete the questionnaire should be clearly stated for both respondents and interviewers. Procedural instructions for respondents are often highlighted using a different typeface or some graphic device, perhaps arrows or lines. The following is an example from a mail survey:

> Do you have a favorite radio station that you listen to most of the time?
>
> _____ YES   _____ NO
>   ↓
>
> If yes, can you remember the names of any of the disc jockeys or newscasters who work for that station? *WRITE THE NAMES BELOW.*
> _____
> _____
> _____

Fowler (1984) offers the following suggestions for putting together a self-administered questionnaire:

> *1.* The questionnaire must be self-explanatory.
> *2.* Questionnaires should be limited to close-ended items. Checking a box or circling an answer should be the only task required.
> *3.* The question forms should be few in number.
> *4.* The questionnaire should be typed and laid out to ensure a clear and uncluttered product.
> *5.* Instructions should be kept to a minimum. If people can be confused about what they are supposed to do, they will be.

When interviewers are used, as is the case with telephone and person-to-person surveys, it is imperative that they be supplied with an easy-to-follow questionnaire.

Procedural instructions for interviewers, on the other hand, are usually distinguished from the rest of the questionnaire by being typed in capital letters and often enclosed in boxes. For example:

> We'd like to start by asking you some things about television. First, what are your favorite TV shows?
>
> ┌───┐
> │ TAKE DOWN ALL NAMES OF TV SHOWS. PROBE WITH   │
> │ "ARE THERE ANY MORE?" TO GET AT LEAST THREE SHOWS.   │
> └───┘
>
> 1. _____   3. _____
>
> 2. _____   4. _____

In drafting copy to be read by interviewers, use parentheses to call attention to options, such as: "Does your (husband/wife) watch . . . ?" In addition, make sure that all the words that are to be spoken by the interviewer are written, including introductions, explanations, definitions, and transitions.

All instructions should be clear and simple. A confusing questionnaire impairs the effectiveness of the interviewer, lowers the number of respondents who complete the test, and, in the long run, increases costs.

Question Order

All surveys tend to flow better when the initial questions are simple and easy to answer. Researchers often include one or two "warm-up" questions not directly related to the study so that respondents become accustomed to the task of answering. Preliminary questions can also serve as motivational steps to create subject interest in the questionnaire. Demographic data, personal questions, and other sensitive items should be placed toward the end of the questionnaire to allow the interviewer to establish a rapport with each respondent. Subjects may still refuse to answer these questions, but at least the main body of data will have been collected.

The questionnaire should be organized in a logical sequence, proceeding from the general to the specific. Questions on similar topics should be grouped together, and the transitions between different question sections should be clear and logical.

Poor question order may bias a respondent's answers. For example, suppose that after several questions about the presence of violence in society, the respondent is asked to rank the major problems facing the country today from the following list:

____	WAR	____	HIGH PRICES
____	COMMUNISM	____	CORRUPT GOVERNMENT
____	VIOLENCE ON TV	____	POLLUTION

It is possible that violence on television might receive a higher ranking than it would if the ranking question had been asked before the series of questions on violence. Or, to take another example, suppose a public relations researcher is attempting to discover the public's attitudes toward a large oil company. If the questionnaire that began with attitudinal questions concerning oil spills and inflated profits asked respondents to rate certain oil companies, it is likely that the ratings of all the companies would be lower, due to general impressions created by the earlier questions.

There is no easy solution for the problem of question "contamination." Obviously, some questions have to be asked before others. Perhaps the best approach for researchers is to be sensitive to the problem and test for it in a pilot study. If they think that question order A, B, C may have biasing effects, they should test another version using the order C, B, A. Completely neutral positioning is not always possible, however, and when bias may enter because of how responses are ordered, the list of items should be rotated. The word (ROTATE) after a question indicates that the interviewer must alter the order of responses for each respondent.

Layout

The physical design of the questionnaire is another important factor in survey research. A badly typed, poorly reproduced questionnaire is not likely to attract many responses in a mail survey. Nor does a cramped questionnaire with 40 questions to a page help to instill respondents with a positive attitude. Response categories should be adequately spaced and presented in a nonconfusing manner. For example, the following format might lead to problems:

There are too many commercials on television.

DO YOU STRONGLY AGREE ＿＿ AGREE ＿＿ HAVE NO
OPINION ＿＿ DISAGREE ＿＿ STRONGLY DISAGREE ＿＿ ?

A more effective and less confusing method is to provide a vertical ordering of the response choices:

There are too many commercials on television.

＿＿ STRONGLY AGREE
＿＿ AGREE
＿＿ NO OPINION
＿＿ DISAGREE
＿＿ STRONGLY DISAGREE

Some researchers recommend avoiding blanks altogether because respondents and interviewers tend to make large check marks or X's that cover more than one blank, making interpretation difficult. If blanks are perceived as a problem, one can provide boxes to check or numbers to circle. In any case, the response form should be consistent throughout the questionnaire. Format changes generally create confusion for both respondents and interviewers.

Finally, each question must have enough space for answers. This is especially true for open-ended questions. Nothing is more discouraging to respondents and interviewers than to be confronted with a presentation like the following.

Why do you go to the movies?＿＿＿＿＿＿＿＿＿＿＿＿＿＿
Who are your favorite movie stars?＿＿＿＿＿＿＿＿＿＿＿＿
What are your favorite television shows?＿＿＿＿＿＿＿＿＿＿

If a research budget does not allow for a long questionnaire (created by adding extra space for answers), subjects should be invited to add further comments on the back of the survey or on another sheet of paper.

Questionnaire Length

An important consideration in questionnaire construction is length. Obviously, the researcher wants to keep the interview or mail survey short enough to encourage the respondents to complete it. On the other hand, the researcher must ask enough questions to cover the topic under investigation. Our discussion gives certain guidelines as to how long a questionnaire should be in each of the various survey data collection situations. These guidelines are simply that: guidelines. Hard and fast rules about length are not possible. The criteria for determining the appropriate length should include cost, context, and the limits of the respondents' ability and willingness to answer the questions.

The federal Office of Management and Budget (OMB) suggests that no survey should take more than one-half hour unless more time is needed for some compelling reason. Interestingly, there has been little empirical study of this topic. Yu and Cooper (1983) in a study of 497 response rates found a weak negative correlation ($r = -.06$) between response rate and number of items in a questionnaire. In another study (Sharp & Frankel, 1983), the investigators manipulated the length of the questionnaire, using a short version (25 minutes) and a long version (75 minutes). The percentage of completed interviews in both conditions was virtually the same. However, the subjects who participated in the long form were significantly more likely to have negative attitudes about the interview experience. In addition, twice as many respondents in the long-form condition were unwilling to be reinterviewed the next year. But among those whose presurvey opinions held that being interviewed was in general a beneficial thing, there was no difference between the short-form and long-form respondents in willingness to be reinterviewed. Among those who thought that in general surveys were of no value, the spread between the short- and long-form groups was much greater, with far more of those in the long-form group indicating no desire to be reinterviewed. Thus, the crucial variable was the respondents' own prior attitudes toward surveys. Among those favorably disposed, longer interviews were not nearly as burdensome. In sum, the issue is a complicated one, and length appears to be a variable that needs careful consideration in light of specific research goals and respondent populations.

Pilot Studies

Without a doubt, the best way to discover whether a research instrument is adequately designed is to pretest it. That is, conduct a pilot study to check for problems. Small samples can be invaluable for determining whether the study approach is correct and for refining questions. Areas of misunderstanding or confusion can be easily corrected without wasting time or money.

One of the first steps in pretesting occurs during the question-writing stage. One valuable technique is to bring together a focus group (Chapter 7) of 5–10 potential respondents and have them discuss the topics to be investigated. These discussions help the researcher select the proper phrasing and vocabulary in writing questions.

Pilot study results provide researchers with approaches to use in editing the questionnaire: to delete or rewrite questions, to change open-ended questions to close-ended questions (or vice versa), and to verify that all response options have been provided. A second run-through is recommended if several problems are uncovered in the first test. The pilot study should include a run-through for interviewers. A "dress rehearsal" of the full-scale project ensures that the interviewers fully understand what is being researched.

With a first draft of the questionnaire in hand, the researcher should send senior, experienced interviewers into the field to interview about 15–20 respondents. If possible, the pretest interviews should be tape recorded for later use in analysis and interviewer training.

If a self-administered questionnaire is being developed, other pretesting procedures are necessary. First of all, a group of potential respondents should be brought together and asked to fill out the questionnaire in private. When this has been done, the researcher should enter and conduct a discussion about the questionnaire to find out whether the instructions were clear, the questions understandable, the response categories complete, and so on. After revisions, the questionnaire should be mailed to a small sample of respondents. Included with the questionnaire should be a set of questions about the clarity and understandability of the questionnaire itself. Taken together, these two pretesting devices should identify any serious problems in questionnaire design.

Gathering Survey Data

After a questionnaire has been developed and one or more pilot studies have been conducted, the next step is to gather data from a sample of respondents. There are four basic methods for doing this: the mail survey, the telephone survey, the personal interview survey, and group administration. Researchers can also use variations and combinations of these four methods. Each procedure has definite advantages and disadvantages that must be considered before a choice is made. The remainder of this chapter highlights the characteristics of each method.

Mail Surveys

Mail surveys involve mailing self-administrable questionnaires to a sample of individuals. Stamped reply envelopes are enclosed to encourage respondents to mail completed questionnaires back to the researcher. Mail surveys are popular because they can secure a great deal of data with a minimum expenditure of time and money. At the outset, however, researchers should be aware that respondents are busy people with many demands on their time. Consequently, many people do not share the researcher's enthusiasm for questionnaires and often simply throw them away.

The general stages of a mail survey are discussed below. Even though the steps are listed in numerical sequence, many of these tasks are often accomplished in a different order or even simultaneously.

1. Select a sample. Sampling is generally done from a prepared frame (see Chapter 4) that contains the names and addresses of potential respondents. The most common sampling frame used is the **mailing list**, a compilation of names and addresses in narrowly defined groupings that commercial firms sometimes prepare (see accompanying boxed material).

2. Construct the questionnaire. As discussed earlier, mail survey questionnaires must be concise and specific, since no interviewer is present to alleviate misunderstandings, answer questions, or give directions.

3. Write a cover letter. A brief note explaining the purpose and importance of the questionnaire usually increases response rates.

4. Assemble the package. The questionnaires, cover letters, and return envelopes are stuffed into mailing envelopes. Researchers sometimes choose to use bulk mail with first-class return envelopes. An alternate method is to send questionnaires first class and use business reply envelopes for responses. This method allows researchers to pay postage only for the questionnaires actually returned. Postal options always depend on the research budget.

5. Mail the surveys.

6. Closely monitor the return rates.

7. Send follow-up mailings. The first follow-up should be sent 2 weeks after the initial mailing, and a second (if necessary) 2 weeks after the first. The follow-up letters can be sent to the entire sample or only the subjects who failed to answer.

8. Tabulate and analyze the data.

Advantages. Mail surveys cover a wide geographic area for a rather reasonable cost. They are often the only way to gather information from people who live in hard-to-reach areas of the country (or in other countries). Mail surveys also allow for selective sampling through the

OBTAINING SPECIALIZED LISTS

More than 50 firms specialize in providing mailing lists to advertisers and marketing research organizations. A few of the more prominent companies and some of the types of lists they provide are listed below.

R. R. Bowker Company
1180 Avenue of the Americas
New York, NY 10036
(Bookstores, colleges,
libraries, librarians,
audiovisual specialists)

Customized Mailing Lists
158–23 Grand Central Parkway
Jamaica Estates, NY 11432
(Business and professional
people, executives)

Dunhill International List Company
2430 W. Oakland Park Boulevard
Fort Lauderdale, FL 33311
(engineers, lawyers, physicians,
small business owners)

Market Development
Company
41 Kimler Drive
Hazlewood, MO 63043
(families with children,
newlyweds, high school
students)

Alvin B. Zeller, Inc.
475 Park Ave. S.
New York, NY 10016
(aircraft pilots,xylophone manufacturers,
botanists, career women,
turkey farmers, barber
school operators, and a
host of others)

use of specialized mailing lists. In addition to those mentioned, lists are available that include only people with annual incomes exceeding $50,000, or consumers who have bought a car within the past year, or subscribers to a particular magazine, or residents of a specific zip code area. If researchers need to collect information from a highly specialized audience, the mail technique can be quite attractive.

Another advantage of the mail survey is that it provides anonymity, so that subjects are more likely to answer sensitive questions candidly. Questionnaires can be completed at home or in the office, affording subjects a certain sense of privacy. People can answer questions at their own pace and have an opportunity to look up facts or check past information. Mail surveys also eliminate interviewer bias, since there is no personal contact.

Probably the biggest advantage of this method, however, is its relatively low cost. Mail surveys do not require a large staff of trained workers. The only costs are for printing, mailing lists, envelopes, and postage. If the cost per completed questionnaire were to be computed, it is likely that the mail survey would prove to be the most inexpensive of all the survey methods. At a minimum, it can be said that researchers who are willing to spend time, energy, and money in a mail survey can usually ensure an above-average return rate.

Disadvantages. First, mail questionnaires must be self-explanatory. There is no interviewer present to answer questions or to clear up misunderstandings. Mail surveys are also the slowest form of data collection. Returns start to trickle in around a week or so after the initial mailing and continue to arrive for several weeks thereafter. In fact, it may be months before some responses are returned. Many researchers simply set a cutoff date, after which returns are not included in the analysis.

Another problem with mail surveys is that researchers never know exactly who answers the questions. A survey sent to corporate executives, for example, may be completed by assistants. Furthermore, replies are often received only from people who are interested in the survey, and this injects bias into the results. Most researchers agree, however, that the biggest disadvantage of the mail survey is the typically low return rate. A typical survey (depending on the area and type of survey) will achieve a response rate of 20–40%. This low return casts doubt on the validity of the findings.

Increasing response rates. A number of procedures for improving return rates have been investigated by survey reseachers. There are no hard and fast guarantees, but the techniques mentioned below have been shown to increase response rates in some mail surveys.

1. Keep questions to a minimum. One study (Sewell & Shaw, 1968) found that while only 28% of the sample returned a three-page questionnaire, 50% returned a double postcard containing a single question. It would appear that up to a certain point, questionnaire length and response rate are negatively correlated (see above).

2. Use follow-ups. The most common follow-up procedure is to send a letter (or postcard) to each respondent about 2 weeks after the initial mailing. The letter thanks all those who have returned the questionnaire and urges those who have not returned it to do so. Occasionally, a second copy of the questionnaire is included with the follow-up letter. Using follow-up letters can produce an additional 10–20% return, and at least one study that used multiple follow-up requests reported a 50% increase. Of course, follow-up letters add to the total cost of the survey.

3. Use inducements. A small sum of money is the most common form of inducement used in survey research. It is not designed to pay individuals for their answers, but is rather an acknowledgment that someone has gone out of his or her way to answer the questions. To illustrate, one study utilized an inducement of 25¢; the response rate among those who received the money was 52%, compared with 19% among those who received no reward (Erdos, 1974).

    4. Include a cover letter. An introductory letter stressing the importance of the survey can increase returns. Although not as potent a factor as the other items mentioned above, a well-constructed cover letter might add 10% or more to the response rate.

    Other factors that have been shown to increase response rates include: having an important person or prestigious group sponsor the survey, using stamped envelopes rather than business reply envelopes, asking for objective rather than subjective information, and addressing cover letters to individuals by name, as opposed to "Dear Sir or Madam" (Miller, 1977).

Telephone Surveys

Telephone surveys and personal interviews employ trained members of a research team to ask questions verbally and record the responses. The respondents generally do not get a chance to see the actual questionnaire. Since telephone and personal interviewing techniques have certain similarities, much of what follows applies to personal interviews as well.

    Telephone surveys seem to fill a middle ground between mail surveys and personal interviews. They offer more control and higher response rates than most mail surveys but are limited in the types of questions that can be used. They are generally more expensive than mail surveys but less expensive than face-to-face interviews. Because of these factors, telephone surveys seem to represent a compromise between the other two techniques, and this may account for their growing popularity in mass media research.

    Interviewers are extremely important to both telephone and personal surveys. An interviewer ideally should function as a neutral medium through which the respondents' answers are communicated to the researcher. The interviewer's presence and manner of speaking should not influence respondents' answers in any way. Adequate training and instruction can minimize bias that the interviewer might inject into the data. For example, if he or she shows disdain or shock over an answer, it is unlikely that the respondent will continue to answer questions in a totally honest manner. Showing agreement with certain responses might prompt similar answers to other questions. Skipping questions, carelessly asking questions, and being impatient with the respondent might also cause problems. As an aid to minimizing interviewer bias, the National Association of Broadcasters has published the following recommendations to interviewers.*

---

*From *A Broadcast Research Primer*, 1976, pp. 37–38. Reprinted with permission.

1. Read the questions exactly as worded. Ask them in the exact order listed. Skip questions only when the instructions on the questionnaire tell you to. There are no exceptions to this.
2. Never suggest an answer, try to explain a question, or imply what kind of reply is wanted. Don't prompt in any way.
3. If a question is not understood, say, "Let me read it again," and repeat it slowly and clearly. If it is still not understood, report a "no answer."
4. Report answers and comments exactly as given, writing fully. If an answer seems vague or imcomplete, probe with neutral questions, such as, "Will you explain that?" or, "How do you mean that?" Sometimes just waiting a bit will tell the respondent you want more information.
5. Act interested, alert, and appreciative of the respondent's co-operation. But never comment on his or her replies. Never express approval, disapproval, or surprise. Even an "Oh" can cause a respondent to hesitate or refuse to answer further questions. Never talk up or down to a respondent.
6. Follow all instructions carefully, whether you agree with them or not.
7. Thank each respondent. Leave a good impression for the next interviewer.

A general procedure for conducting a telephone survey follows. Again, the steps are presented in numerical order, but it is possible to address many tasks simultaneously.

1. Select a sample. Telephone surveys require researchers to specify clearly the geographic area to be covered and to identify which persons will be interviewed in each household contacted. Many surveys are restricted to people over 18, heads of households, and so forth. The sampling procedure used depends on the purpose of the study (see Chapter 4).

2. Construct the questionnaire. Phone surveys require straightforward and uncomplicated response options. Ranking a long list of items is especially difficult over the telephone, and this task should be avoided. In addition, the length of the survey should not exceed 10 minutes for nonprofessional interviewers. Longer interviews require professionals who are capable of keeping people on the telephone.

3. Prepare an interviewer instruction manual. This document should cover the basic mechanics of the survey (what numbers to call, when to call, how to record times, and so on). It should also specify which household member to interview and should provide general guidelines on how to ask the questions and how to record the responses.

4. Train the interviewers. Interviewers need to practice going through the questionnaire to become familiar with all the items, response options, and instructions. It is best to train interviewers in a group using interview simulations that allow each person to practice asking questions. It is advisable to pretest interviewers as well as the questionnaire.

5. Collect the data. Data collection is most efficient when conducted from one central location (assuming enough telephone lines are available). Problems that develop are easier to remedy, and important questions raised by one interviewer can easily be communicated to the rest of the group. A central location also makes it easier for researchers to check (validate) the interviewers' work. The completion rate should also be monitored during this stage.

6. Make necessary callbacks. Additional calls (usually no more than two) should be made to respondents whose lines were busy or who did not answer during the first session. Callbacks done on a different day or night tend to have a greater chance of success in reaching someone willing to be interviewed.

Backstrom and Hursh-Cesar (1981) offer the following advice about callbacks.

> About 95% of all telephone interviews are successfully completed within three calls. However, we have rules for the number of callbacks to make if the first call results in a busy signal or a no answer. . . . We generally permit only three calls—one original and two callbacks—but if any of these calls produce busy signals or [future interview] appointments, we allow up to five calls total. . . .
>
> When the first call produces a busy signal, the rule is to wait one-half hour before calling again. If the first call produced a "no answer," wait 2 to 3 hours before calling again, assuming it will still be a reasonable hour to call. If evening calls produce no answer, call during the following day.

In addition, interviewers should keep track of the disposition or status of their sample numbers. Figure 6.3 contains a sample disposition sheet.

7. Verify the results. When all questionnaires have been completed, a small subsample of each interviewer's respondents should be called again to check that the information they provided was accurately recorded. Respondents should be told during the initial survey that they may receive an additional call at a later date. This tends to eliminate any confusion when subjects receive a second call. A typical procedure is to ask the subject's first name in the interview so that it can be used later. The interviewer should ask, "Was James called a few days ago and asked questions about television viewing?" The verification can begin from there, and need consist of only two or three of the original questions (preferably open-ended and sensitive questions, since interviewers are most likely to omit these).

8. Tabulate the data. Along with the normal data analysis, telephone researchers generally compute a response rate: how many completed interviews, how many refusals, how many no-answers, and how many disconnects.

Figure 6.3 Sample telephone interview disposition sheet

Phone number _____

Call #1 _____ #2 _____ #3 _____ #4 _____ #5 _____

     Date _____ Date _____ Date _____ Date _____ Date _____

     Time _____ Time _____ Time _____ Time _____ Time _____

Code

    1 Completed interview

    2 Busy

    3 No answer

    4 Refusal

    5 Appointment to call again

       (when _____)

    6 Nonworking number (out of order, disconnected, nonexistent)

    7 Nonresidential number

    8 Reached but respondent not available (out of town, hospital, etc.)

    9 Reached but not interviewed (ineligible household, speech or phys-
       ical problem, etc.)

Advantages. The cost of telephone surveys tends to be reasonable. The sampling involves minimal expense, and there are no elaborate transportation costs. Callbacks are simple and economical. Wide Area Telephone Service (WATS) enables researchers to conduct telephone surveys on a nationwide basis from any location.

      Compared to mail surveys, telephone surveys can include more detailed questions, and, as stated earlier, interviewers can clarify misunderstandings that might arise during the administration of the questionnaire.

      The nonresponse rate of a telephone survey is generally low, especially when multiple callbacks are employed. In addition, phone surveys are much faster than mail. A large staff of interviewers can collect the data from the designated sample in a relatively short time. In summary, phone surveys tend to be fast, easy, and relatively inexpensive.

Disadvantages. First of all, researchers must recognize that much of what is called survey "research" by telephone is not research at all, but an attempt to sell people something. Unfortunately, many companies disguise their sales pitch as a "survey," and this has made respondents suspicious and even prompts some to terminate an interview before it has gotten started. Additionally, visual questions are prohibited. A researcher cannot, for example, hold up a picture of a product and ask if the respondent remembers seeing it advertised. Finally, a potentially severe problem is that not everyone in a community is listed in the telephone directory, the most often used sampling frame. Not everyone has a phone, and many people have unlisted phone numbers; also, some numbers are listed incorrectly, and others are too new to be listed. These problems would not be serious if the people with no phones or unlisted numbers were just like those listed in the phone book. Unfortunately, researchers generally have no way of checking for such similarities or differences, so it is possible that a sample obtained from a telephone directory may be significantly different from the population. (See Chapter 4 concerning random digit dialing.)

Personal Interviews

Personal interviews generally involve having the interviewer visit the respondent at his or her home or place of work, although brief interviews are often collected in shopping centers (known as "intercepts"). There are two basic types of interviews, structured and unstructured. In a **structured interview,** standardized questions are asked in a predetermined order; relatively little freedom is given to interviewers. In an **unstructured interview,** broad questions are asked, which allows interviewers freedom in determining what further questions to ask to obtain the required information. Structured interviews are easy to tabulate and analyze but do not achieve the depth or expanse of unstructured interviews. Conversely, the unstructured type elicits more detail but takes a great deal of time to score and analyze.

The steps in constructing a personal interview survey are similar to those for a telephone survey. The list below discusses instances in which the personal interview differs substantially from the telephone method.

1. Select a sample. Drawing a sample for a personal interview survey is more complicated than for a telephone survey. Usually a multistage procedure must be used. A common technique is to obtain detailed maps of the sample area, number each block, pick blocks at random, and then randomly select dwelling units within blocks (see Figure 4.2).

2. Construct the questionnaire. Personal interviews are flexible: detailed questions are easy to ask, and the time taken to complete the survey can be greatly extended (many personal interviews last 30–60 minutes). Researchers can also make use of visual exhibits, lists, and photographs to ask questions, and respondents can be asked to sort items into categories (the *Q-sort technique)* or to point to their answers on printed cards. Respondents can have privacy and anonymity by marking ballots, which can be slipped into envelopes and sealed.

3. Prepare an interviewer instruction manual. This manual should include detailed instructions on what households to visit, who in the household to interview, what to do if a vacant dwelling falls into the sample, when to do the interviewing, how to dress and act during the interview period, how to record data, and so on.

  4. Train the interviewers. Training is important because the questionnaires are longer and more detailed. Interviewers should receive instruction on gaining access and establishing a rapport with subjects, administrative details (when to conduct the interviews, how long each will take, and how much the interviewers will be paid), and follow-up questions. Several practice sessions are necessary to ensure that the goal of the project is being met and that interviewers are following the established guidelines.

  5. Collect the data. This part of the survey is the sole reason many researchers give for preferring telephone or mail surveys. Interviewers' expenses for travel, food, and salary can be substantial (up to $100 per interview, or more for some types of private sector research; it is not uncommon for custom research companies to charge $1,000 per respondent). Data collection also takes longer, possibly several months. Researchers need to consider these points before deciding to conduct personal interviews.

  6. Make necessary callbacks. Each callback requires an interviewer to return to a household originally selected in the sample, and each callback takes longer (and costs more) than a phone survey callback.

  7. Verify the results. As with the phone survey, a subsample of each interviewer's completed questionnaires is selected and assigned to another staff member. This person returns to the households in question (or calls on the telephone) and reviews a few of the more pertinent items to check on the original interviewer's completeness and veracity.

  8. Tabulate the data. As with the phone survey, a completion rate should be computed, noting how many people refused to be interviewed, how many were not at home, and so forth.

Advantages. Many of the advantages of the personal interview technique have already been mentioned. It is the most flexible means of obtaining information, since the face-to-face situation lends itself easily to questioning in greater depth and detail. Furthermore, some information can be observed by the interviewer during the interview without adding to the length of the questionnaire. For example, what magazines were displayed in the home? Was the television or radio turned on? Did the respondent have an outside antenna? Additionally, the interviewers can develop a rapport with the respondents and may be able to get replies to sensitive questions that would remain unanswered in a mail or phone survey.

  The identity of the respondent is known or can be controlled in the personal interview survey. Whereas in a mail survey it is possible that all members of a family might confer on an answer, in a face-to-face interview, this can usually be avoided. Finally, once an interview has begun, it is harder for respondents to terminate the interview before all the questions have been asked. In a phone survey, all the subject needs to do is to hang up.

Disadvantages. The single largest drawback to the personal inter-view technique is cost. The transportation and labor costs generally make this the most expensive of all data collection methods. If respondents are spread out over a wide geographic area, the travel, food, and lodging costs for interviewers can quickly mount up. Additionally, in recent years people have become more and more reticent about letting strangers into their homes, even if these individuals have credentials from a reputable survey organization. It would appear that people are becoming more security conscious and more skeptical of individuals who represent themselves as "survey researchers." This trend may make it difficult to complete a large percentage of interviews.

Another major disadvantage is the problem of interviewer bias. The physical appearance, age, race, sex, dress, nonverbal behavior, and/or comments of the interviewer may prompt respondents to answer questions untruthfully. Moreover, the organization necessary for recruiting, training, and administering a field staff of interviewers is much greater than that required for other data collection procedures. If large numbers of interviewers are needed, it is usually necessary to employ field supervisors to coordinate their work, which in turn will make the survey even more expensive. Finally, of course, if personal interviewing is done during the day, most of the respondents will be persons not employed outside the home. If it is desirable to interview those with jobs outside the home, it will be necessary to schedule interviews on the weekends or during the evening. This requirement might make it more difficult to establish initial cooperation, driving costs even higher.

Group Administration

Another survey method combines features of the mail survey and the personal interview. The group-administered survey takes place when a group of respondents is gathered together and given individual copies of a questionnaire for self-administration or is asked to participate in a group interview, as explained below. For example, at the end of a sneak preview of a new movie, the audience might be asked to fill out a questionnaire about what parts of the film were liked best, whether the ending was believable, and so on. Students in a classroom filling out reports of their newspaper reading behavior constitute another example.

In the group interview technique, the interviewer reads the questions aloud and each respondent records responses on an answer form that is supplied. This technique can be particularly helpful with respondents who have only minimal reading skills. Additional interviewers are present in the room so that individual problems or questions can be resolved quickly. In the self-administered situation, the questionnaires are simply passed out and the respondents proceed at their own pace, much as in a mail survey. The respondents, of course, have the opportunity to ask questions of the research personnel in the room.

Advantages. The group administration technique has certain advantages. In the first place, a group-administered questionnaire can be longer than the typical questionnaire used in a mail survey. Since the respondents are usually assembled for the express purpose of completing the questionnaire, the response rates are almost always quite high. The opportunity for researchers to answer questions and handle problems that might arise generally means that fewer items are left blank or answered incorrectly. Finally, the group-administered survey is less costly than a face-to-face or telephone interview.

Disadvantages. On the negative side, if a group-administered survey leads to the perception that the study is sanctioned by some authority, suspicion or uneasiness on the part of respondents might result. For example, if a group of teachers is brought together to fill out a questionnaire, some might think that the survey has the approval of the local school administration and that the results will be made available to their superiors. Also, the group environment makes it possible for interaction among the respondents; this has the potential for making the situation more difficult for the researcher to control. Finally, not all surveys can use samples that can be tested together in a group. Surveys often require responses from a wide variety of people, and mixing respondents together may bias the results.

Achieving a Reasonable Response Rate

No matter what type of survey is conducted, it is virtually impossible to get a 100% response rate. Researchers have more control over the situation in some types of surveys (such as the personal interview) and less in others (such as the mail survey). But no matter what the situation, not all respondents will be available for interviews and not all will cooperate. Consequently, the researcher must try to achieve the highest response rate possible under the circumstances.

The term "response rate" refers to the percentage of subjects whose answers are sought and who actually complete the interview or the questionnaire. In mathematical terms, it is the number of people interviewed (or responding) divided by the number of people sampled. The denominator includes those who responded plus everybody in the study population who was chosen but did not respond. Sometimes a sample is "screened" to find suitable population members to be studied. The respondents or units screened out do not enter into the response rate calculation. For example, in a phone survey, disconnected numbers, nonresidential phones, and nonworking numbers are omitted in calculating response rates. To illustrate the calculation, suppose a mail survey drew an initial sample of 2,000 families and questionnaires were sent to each one. Of these, 200 were returned with no forwarding address, and 100 were returned with a note that the addressee was deceased. This leaves 1,700. If completed questionnaires are returned from 1,000 families, the response rate is 1,000/1,700 or about 59%.

What constitutes an acceptable response rate? Obviously, the higher the response rate the better, since as more respondents are sampled, it becomes less likely that response bias is present. But is there a minimum rate that should be achieved? Not everyone would agree on an answer to this question, but there are some helpful data available. Several studies have calculated the average response rates for surveys of various kinds. A comparison with these figures can at least tell a researcher if a given response rate is above or below the norm. For example, Dillman (1978) noted that response rates for face-to-face interviews have dropped sharply in recent years. In the 1960s, the average rate was 80–85%. More recently, the completion rates of general population samples interviewed by the face-to-face technique is about 60–65%. Yu and Cooper (1983) studied the completion rates reported in 93 social science journal articles from 1965 to 1981. They found the completion rate for personal interviews to be 82% and for telephone surveys about 72%. Mail surveys had an average completion rate of about 47%. (Note that many of the personal interviews included in this study were done in the 1960s and early 1970s. This should be kept in mind when comparing these figures to Dillman's data mentioned above.)

Regardless of how good the response rate, the researcher is responsible for examining any possible biases in response patterns. Were females more likely to respond than males? Older respondents more likely than younger ones? Whites more likely than nonwhites? A significant lack of response from a particular group might weaken the strength of any inferences from the data to the population under study. To be on the safe side, the researcher should attempt to gather from other sources information about the people who did not respond; by comparing such additional data with those from respondents, it should be possible to determine whether underrepresentation introduced any bias into the results.

Using common sense will help increase the response rate. In phone surveys, respondents should be called when they are likely to be at home and receptive to interviewing. Don't call when people are likely to be eating or asleep. In a face-to-face situation, the interviewer should be appropriately attired. In addition, the researcher should spend time tracking down some of the nonrespondents and asking them why they refused to be interviewed or did not fill out the questionnaire. Responses such as "The interviewer was insensitive and pushy," "The questionnaire was delivered with postage due," and "The survey sounded like a ploy to sell something" can be quite illuminating.

Along with common sense, certain elements of the research design can have a significant impact on response rates. Yu and Cooper (1983) in their survey of 93 published studies discovered the following.

1. Monetary incentives increased the response, with larger incentives being the most effective. Nonmonetary incentives (for example, ballpoint pens) were also helpful.
2. Preliminary notification, personalization of the questionnaire, follow-up letter, and assertive "foot-in-the-door" personal interview techniques all significantly increased the response rate.
3. Things that were not significantly related to an increased response rate were a cover letter, assurance of anonymity, and stating a deadline.
4. Stressing the social utility of the study and appealing to the respondent to help out the researcher did not affect response rates.

General Problems in Survey Research

Although surveys are valuable tools in mass communication research, there are problems present in any survey. Experience in survey research confirms the following points.

1. Subjects or respondents are often unable to recall information about themselves or their activities. This inability may be caused by memory failure, confusion about the questions asked on the questionnaire, or some other intervening factor. Questions that seem glaringly simple to researchers may create severe problems for respondents. With this in mind, survey researchers must accept the fact that not all respondents will be able or willing to provide the required information.

2. **Prestige bias**—due to the respondent's feelings of inadequacy or lack of knowledge about a particular topic or area—is a phenomenon present in any type of survey. That is, respondents will often provide a "prestigious" answer rather than admit that they don't know something. Prestige bias is particularly apparent in surveys that probe respondents' television viewing habits: a respondent is likely to report heavy viewing of public television rather than confess an addiction to situation comedies or soap operas on commercial television.

It is human nature not to want to feel "dumb" or "inferior," so answers that have the air of sophistication or education may be given.

3. Subjects may purposely deceive researchers by giving incorrect answers to a question. Almost nothing can be done about subjects who knowingly lie. A large enough sample may discount this type of response, however. At present, there are no acceptable and valid methods of determining whether a respondent's answers are truthful; the answers must be accepted as they are given.

4. Surveys are often complicated by the inability of respondents to explain their true feelings and beliefs, not because they don't have any, but because they can't put them into words. The question, "Why do you like to watch soap operas?" may be particularly difficult for some respondents. They may watch them every day but respond only "Because I like them." Probing respondents for further description may help, but not in every case.

Survey research can be an exciting process. Researchers must continually be aware of obstacles that may hinder data collection and deal with these problems immediately. The United States is the most surveyed country in the world, and many citizens now refuse to take part in any such enterprise. Researchers must convince the subjects that the study will be helpful in making a particular decision or in solving a particular problem.

The shape of survey research may be changing. Brighton (1981) suggests that the increasing difficulty and cost of arranging traditional face-to-face interviews at the homes of individual respondents will mean a greater emphasis on postal surveys, intercept surveys, and electronic data-gathering devices. In the telephone survey area, computer-assisted telephone interviewing (CATI) is becoming more prevalent. **CATI** uses video display terminals operated by interviewers to present questions and accept respondent answers, thus eliminating the need for the traditional pencil-and-paper questionnaires. The computer displays the proper questions in the proper order, eliminating the possibility of the interviewer making an error by asking the wrong questions or skipping the right ones. The respondent's answers are entered by the interviewer through the keyboard, making data coding much easier. Groves and Mathiowetz (1984) found that there was little difference in results from using CATI and non-CATI techniques. The response rates, reactions of the interviewers and respondents, and quality of data were virtually equivalent. CATI interviews tended to take slightly more time, but this was balanced by the presence of fewer interviewer errors due to skipping questions. As new software is developed in this area, it seems likely that a greater proportion of surveys will use the CATI technique. In addition, computer-generated, voice-synthesized surveys are being used in some areas. Public reaction to these devices is being examined.

Summary

Survey research is an important and useful method of data collection. The survey is also one of the most widely used methods of media research, primarily due to its flexibility. Surveys, however, involve a number of steps. Researchers must decide whether to use a descriptive or an analytical approach; define the purpose of the study; review the available literature in the area; select a survey approach, a questionnaire design, and a sample; analyze the data; and finally, decide whether to publish or disseminate the results. These steps are not necessarily taken in that order, but all must be considered before a survey is conducted.

To ensure that all the steps in the survey process are in harmony, researchers should conduct one or more pilot studies to detect any errors in the approach. Pilot studies save time, money, and frustration, since an error that could void an entire analysis sometimes is overlooked until this stage.

Questionnaire design is also a major step in any survey. In this chapter, examples have been provided to show how a question or interviewing approach may elicit a specific response. The goal in questionnaire design is to avoid bias in answers. Question wording, length, style, and order may affect a respondent's answers. Extreme care must be taken when questions are developed to ensure that they are neutral. To achieve a reasonable response rate, researchers should consider including an incentive, notifying survey subjects beforehand, and personalizing the questionnaire. Also, researchers should mention the response rate in their description of the survey.

Finally, researchers are charged with selecting a survey approach from among four basic types: mail, telephone, personal interview, and group administration. Each approach has advantages and disadvantages, which must be weighed before a decision is made. The type of survey will depend on the purpose of the study, the amount of time available to the researcher, and the funds available for the study. In the future, survey researchers may depend less on the face-to-face survey and more on computer-assisted telephone interviewing.

Questions and Problems for Further Investigation

1. Develop five questions or hypotheses that could be tested by survey research. What approaches could be used to collect data on these topics?
2. Nonresponse is a problem in all survey research. In addition, many people refuse to participate in surveys at all. Provide an

example of a cover letter for a survey on television viewing habits. Include comments that might help increase the response rate.

3. Define a target group and design questions to collect information on the following topics.
   a. Political party affiliation
   b. Attitudes toward television soap operas
   c. Attitudes toward newspaper editorials
   d. Attitudes toward the frequency of television commercials
   e. Public television viewing habits

4. Locate one or more survey studies in journals related to mass media research. Answer the following questions in relation to the article(s).
   a. What was the purpose of the survey?
   b. How were the data collected?
   c. What type of information was produced?
   d. Did the data answer a particular research question or hypothesis?
   e. Were any problems evident with the survey and its approach?

5. Design a survey to collect data on a topic of your choice. Be sure to address the following points.
   a. What is the purpose of the survey? What is its goal?
   b. What research questions or hypotheses will be tested?
   c. Are any operational definitions required?
   d. Develop at least 10 questions relevant to the problem.
   e. Describe the approach to be used to collect data.
   f. Design a cover letter or interview schedule for the study.
   g. Conduct a brief pilot study to test the questionnaire.

References and Suggested Readings

Babbie, E. R. (1973). *Survey research methods*. Belmont, CA: Wadsworth.

Backstrom, C., & Hursh-Cesar, G. (1981). *Survey research*. New York: John Wiley.

Beville, H. (1985). *Audience ratings*. Hillsdale, NJ: Lawrence Erlbaum.

Brighton, M. (1981). Data capture in the 1980s. *Communicare: Journal of Communication Science, 2*(1), 12–19.

Chaffee, S. H., & Choe, S. Y. (1980). Time of decision and media use during the Ford–Carter campaign. *Public Opinion Quarterly, 44*, 53–70.

Dillman, D. (1978). *Mail and telephone surveys*. New York: John Wiley.

Erdos, P. L. (1974). Data collection methods: Mail surveys. In R. Ferber (Ed.), *Handbook of marketing research*. New York: McGraw-Hill.

Fletcher, J. E., & Wimmer, R. D. (1981). *Focus group interviews in radio research*. Washington, DC: National Association of Broadcasters.

Fowler, F. (1984). *Survey research methods*. Beverly Hills, CA: Sage Publications.

Groves, R., & Mathiowetz, N. (1984). Computer-assisted telephone interviewing: Effects on interviewers and respondents. *Public Opinion Quarterly, 48*(1), 356–369.

Kerlinger, F. N. (1973). *Foundations of behavioral research* (2nd ed.). New York: Holt, Rinehart & Winston.

Miller, D. C. (1977). *Handbook of research design and social measurement.* New York: David McKay.

National Association of Broadcasters. (1976). *A broadcast research primer.* Washington, DC: NAB.

Oppenheim, A. N. (1966). *Questionnaire design and attitude measurement.* New York: Basic Books.

Poindexter, P. M. (1979). Daily newspaper non-readers: Why they don't read. *Journalism Quarterly, 56,* 764–770.

Rosenberg, M. (1968). *The logic of survey analysis.* New York: Basic Books.

Sewell, W., & Shaw, M. (1968). Increasing returns in mail surveys. *American Sociological Review, 33,* 193.

Sharp, L., & Frankel, J. (1983). Respondent burden: A test of some common assumptions. *Public Opinion Quarterly, 47*(1), 36–53.

Wakshlag, J. J., & Greenberg, B. S. (1979). Programming strategies and the popularity of television programs for children. *Journal of Communication, 6,* 58–68.

Walizer, M. H., & Wienir, P. L. (1978). *Research methods and analysis: Searching for relationships.* New York: Harper & Row.

Weisberg, H. F., & Bowen, B. D. (1977). *An introduction to survey research and data analysis.* New York: W. H. Freeman.

Wimmer, R. D. (1976). *A multivariate analysis of the uses and effects of the mass media in the 1968 presidential campaign.* Unpublished doctoral dissertation, Bowling Green University, Ohio.

Winkler, R. L., & Hays, W. L. (1975). *Statistics: Probability, inference and decision* (2nd ed.). New York: Holt, Rinehart & Winston.

Yu, J. & Cooper, H. (1983). A quantitative review of research design effects on response rates to questionnaires. *Journal of Marketing Research, 20*(1), 36–44.

Zillmann, D., & Bryant, J. (1975). Viewers' moral sanctions of retribution in the appreciation of dramatic presentations. *Journal of Experimental Social Psychology, 11,* 572–582.

C H A P T E R 7

Field Research and Related Research Methods

FIELD EXPERIMENTS

·

FIELD OBSERVATIONS

·

FOCUS GROUPS

·

CASE STUDIES

·

SUMMARY

·

QUESTIONS AND PROBLEMS FOR FURTHER INVESTIGATION

·

REFERENCES AND SUGGESTED READINGS

T he laboratory approach and the survey are not suitable for all research situations. This chapter discusses field experiments, field observations, focus groups, and case studies: alternatives for the investigation of problems in the field.

Field Experiments

Experiments conducted in a laboratory, as seen in Chapter 5, can be disadvantageous for many research studies because of certain problems they present: they are performed in controlled conditions that are unlike natural settings; they are generally considered to lack external validity; and they usually necessitate subject awareness of the testing situation. Because of these shortcomings, many researchers prefer to use field experiments (Haskins, 1968).

The exact difference between laboratory and field experiments has been a subject of debate for years, especially with regard to the "realism" of the situations involved (Redding, 1970). Many researchers consider field and laboratory experiments to be on opposite ends of the "realism" continuum. However, the main difference between the two approaches is the setting. As Westley (1981) pointed out:

> The laboratory experiment is carried out on the experimenter's own turf; the subjects come into the laboratory. In the field experiment, the experimenter goes to the subject's turf. In general, the physical controls available in the laboratory are greater than those found in the field. For that reason, statistical controls are often substituted for physical controls in the field.

The two approaches can also be distinguished by the presence or absence of rules and procedures to control the conditions and the subjects' awareness or unawareness of being subjects. If the researcher maintains tight control over the subjects' behavior and the subjects are placed in an environment they perceive to be radically different from their everyday life, the situation is probably better described as a laboratory experiment. On the other hand, if the subjects function primarily in their everyday social roles with little investigator interference or environmental restructuring, the case is probably closer to a field experiment. Basically, the difference between laboratory experiments and field experiments is one of degree (for a detailed discussion of this topic, see Redding, 1970).

Advantages of Field Experiments

The major advantage of field experiments is their external validity: since study conditions closely resemble natural settings, subjects usually provide a truer picture of their normal behavior and are not influenced by the experimental situation. For example, consider a laboratory study designed to test the effectiveness of two different versions of a television commercial. One group views Version A and the other views Version B. Both groups are then given a questionnaire to measure their willingness to purchase the advertised product. On the basis of these results, it may be concluded that Version B is more effective in selling the product. Although this may actually be the case, the validity of the experiment is questionable because the subjects knew they were being studied (see the discussion of demand characteristics in Chapter 2). Another problem is that answering a questionnaire cannot be equated to actually buying a product. Furthermore, viewing commercials in a laboratory setting is different from the normal viewing situation, in which competing stimuli (crying children, ringing telephones, and so on) are often present.

In a field experiment, these commercials might be tested by showing Version A in one market and Version B in a similar, but different, market. Actual sales of the product in both markets might then be monitored to determine which commercial was the more successful in persuading viewers to buy the product. As can be seen, the results of the field experiment have more relevance to reality, but the degree of control involved is markedly less than is the case in the laboratory experiment.

Some field studies possess the advantage of being nonreactive. **Reactivity** is the influence that a subject's awareness of being measured or observed has on his or her behavior. Laboratory subjects are almost always aware of being measured. Although this is also the case in some field experiments, many can be conducted without subjects' knowledge of their participation.

Field experiments are useful for studying complex social processes and situations. In their study of the effects of the arrival of television in an English community, Himmelweit, Oppenheim, and Vince (1958) recognized the advantages of the field experiment for examining such a complicated topic. Since television has an impact on several lifestyle variables, the researchers employed a wide range of analysis techniques, including diaries, personal interviews, direct observation, questionnaires, and teachers' ratings of students, to document this impact. A topic area as broad as this does not easily lend itself to laboratory research.

Field experiments can be inexpensive. Most studies require no special equipment or facilities. However, expenses increase rapidly with the size and scope of the study (Babbie, 1986).

Finally, the field experiment may be the only research option to use. For example, suppose a researcher is interested in examining patterns of communication at a television station before and after a change in management—a problem difficult if not impossible to simulate in a laboratory. The only practical option is to conduct the study in the field, that is, at the station.

Disadvantages of Field Experiments

The disadvantages of the field experiment are mostly practical ones. However, some research is impossible to conduct because of ethical considerations. The vexing question of the effects of television violence on young viewers provides a good example of this problem. Probably the most informative study that could be performed in this area would be a field experiment in which one group of children is required to watch violent television programs while another, similar group views only nonviolent programs. The subjects could be carefully observed over a number of years to check for any significant difference in the number of aggressive acts committed by the members of each group. However, the ethics involved in controlling the television viewing behavior of children and possibly encouraging aggressive acts, are extremely questionable. Therefore, scientists have resorted to laboratory and survey techniques to study this problem.

On a more practical level, field experiments often encounter external hindrances that cannot be anticipated. For example, a researcher may spend weeks planning a study to manipulate the media use of students in a summer camp, only to have the camp counselors or a group of parents scuttle the project because they do not want the children used as "guinea pigs." Also, it takes time for researchers to establish contacts, secure cooperation, and gain necessary permissions before beginning a field experiment. In many cases this phase of the process may take weeks or months to complete.

Finally, and perhaps most important, researchers cannot control all the intervening variables in a field experiment. The presence of these extraneous variables affects the precision of the experiment and the confidence the researchers have in its outcome.

Types of Field Experiments

There are two basic categories of field experiments: those in which the researcher manipulates the independent variable(s), and those in which independent variable manipulation occurs naturally as a result of other circumstances. To illustrate the first type, suppose that a researcher is interested in investigating the effects of not being able to read a newspaper. A possible approach would be to select two comparable samples and not allow one to read any newspapers for a period of time; the second sample (the control group) would continue to read the newspaper as usual. A comparison could then be made to determine whether abstinence from newspapers has any effect in other areas of life, such as interpersonal communication. In this example, reading the newspaper is the independent variable that has been manipulated.

The second type of field experiment involves passive manipulation of independent variables. Suppose a community with no cable television system is scheduled to be wired for cable in the near future. In an attempt to gauge the effects of cable on television viewing and other media use, a researcher might begin studying a large sample of television set owners in the community long before the cable service is available. A few months after it is introduced, the researcher could return to the original sample, sort out the households that subscribed to cable and those that did not, and proceed from there to determine the effects of the cable service. In this case, there is no control over the independent variable (cable service); the researcher is merely taking advantage of existing conditions.

Examples of Field Experiments

Tan (1977) was interested in what people would do in a week without television. He recruited a sample of 51 adults and paid each of them $4 a day not to watch television for an entire week. Before depriving these subjects of television, Tan requested that they watch television normally for a one-week period and keep a detailed diary of all their activities. At the start of the experimental week, Tan's assistants visited the subjects' homes and taped up the electrical plugs on their television sets to lessen temptation. Again, the subjects were requested to record their activities for the week. To maintain some control over the experiment, the assistants visited the subjects' homes periodically during the week to ensure that television was not being viewed.

One week later, the diaries completed during the week of deprivation were collected and the data compared to the week of normal television viewing. Tan discovered that when deprived of television, subjects turned more to radio and newspapers for entertainment and information. They also tended to engage in more social activities with their friends and family.

This study illustrates some of the strengths and weaknesses of field experiments. In the first place, they probably represent the only viable techinque available to investigate this particular topic. A survey (see Chapter 6) does not permit the researcher to control whether the subjects watch television, and it would be impossible in the United States to select a representative sample composed of people who do not own a television set. Nor would it be feasible to bring people into the laboratory for a whole week of television deprivation.

On the other hand, the ability of the field experimenter to control independent variables is not conclusively demonstrated here: Tan had no way to be sure that his sample actually avoided television for the entire week. Subjects could have watched at friends' homes or at local bars, or even at home by untaping the plugs. Moreover, Tan mentioned that several individuals who fell into the initial sample refused to go without television for only $4 per day. As a result, the nonprobability sample did not accurately reflect the general makeup of the community.

Field experiments are sometimes used to test the effectiveness of advertising campaigns. For example, Robertson et al. (1974) reported the results of a campaign designed to increase the use of auto safety belts. Six public service announcements were shown to households on one half of a dual cable system, while the households on the other half of the system served as a control group and were shown no messages. The researchers used traffic flow maps to select 14 observation sites likely to maximize the possibility of observing autos from the neighborhoods that were part of the message and no-message groups, respectively. Observing periods were arranged so that morning and afternoon traffic could be sampled.

The observers were strategically located to allow them to observe the drivers of the automobiles that passed their positions (some observers were in trees near key intersections). As a car approached, the driver's sex, apparent ethnic background, estimated age, and use of a safety belt were noted. The auto license number was recorded as the car drove away. With cooperation of the state department of motor vehicles, the license plate numbers were matched with the owners' names and addresses. These were then checked to see whether the person was or was not a subscriber to one of the dual cable systems. This process ultimately led to four different groups for analysis: Cable A households, where the messages were shown; Cable B households, the control group; noncable households in the same county; and out-of-county households. Observations were done before the safety belt campaign aired and for several months thereafter. The ads were scheduled so that an average TV viewer would see two or three messages per week.

The results of the observations revealed that the campaign had no measurable effect on safety belt use. Drivers in the half of the cable system that carried the messages were no more likely to use safety belts than were motorists in the control group or people not on the cable at all. In fact, the percentage of drivers using safety belts actually decreased during the time the announcements were aired.

This field experiment illustrates the considerable amounts of time, energy, and money that are necessary to conduct a study of this scope. Six different messages were produced, the cooperation of the cable system and the department of motor vehicles had to be secured, at least 14 observers were needed, and the data-gathering phase lasted for 9 months. The study also demonstrates some of the problems associated with field experiments. For example, the investigators could tell only that a person was or was not living in a household that was part of the cable system where the ads were shown; they had no way of knowing whether the driver had actually seen the announcements. Moreover, they had no way of knowing whether individuals in the control group had seen the messages while visiting friends or neighbors. Nor was it possible to assess the subjects' exposure to information about safety belt use in other media. Finally, motorists were observed only in their immediate neighborhoods. The study was not designed to observe safety belt use while driving on the highways.

Two rather ambitious field experiments were conducted by Milgram and Shotland (1973) with the cooperation of the CBS television network. The researchers arranged to have three different versions of the popular television series "Medical Center" constructed. One version depicted antisocial behavior that was punished (a jail sentence), another portrayed antisocial behavior that went unpunished, and a third contained prosocial (favorable) behavior. The antisocial behavior consisted of scenes of a distraught young man smashing a plastic charity collection box and pocketing the money.

In the first experiment, the researchers recruited subjects in two ways: ads placed in New York City newspapers promised a free transistor radio to anyone willing to view a one-hour television show; and business reply cards containing the same message were passed out to pedestrians near several subway stops. Subjects were asked to report to a special television theater to view the program; upon arrival, each person was randomly assigned to one of four groups, and each group was shown a different program (the three described above plus a different nonviolent show used as a control). After viewing the program (with no commercial interruptions) and completing a short questionnaire about it, the subjects were instructed to go to an office in a downtown building to receive their free radio.

The downtown office, monitored by hidden cameras, was part of the experiment. The office contained a plastic charity collection box with about $5 in it; a notice informed the subjects that no more transistor radios were available. Their behavior on reading the notice was to be the dependent variable: how many would emulate the antisocial act seen in the program and take the money from the charity box? Milgram and Shotland found no differences in antisocial behavior among the viewers of each group; no one broke into the charity box.

The second study tried to gauge the immediate effects of televised antisocial acts on viewers. Subjects were recruited from the streets of New York City's Times Square area and ushered into a room with a color television set and a plastic charity collection box containing $4.45. A hidden camera monitored the subjects' behavior, even though they were told that they would not be observed. Once again, no differences emerged between the groups.

These two studies also demonstrate several positive and negative aspects of field experiments. In the first place, Milgram and Shotland had to secure the cooperation of CBS to conduct this expensive study. Second, volunteer subjects were used, and it is reasonable to assume that the sample was unrepresentative of the general population. Third, in the first experiment, the researchers did not control for the amount of time that passed between viewing the program and arriving at the testing center. Some participants arrived 24 hours after watching "Medical Center," while others came several days later. Clearly, the subjects' experiences during this interval may have influenced their responses. Finally, Milgram and Shotland reported that the second experiment had to be terminated early because some of the subjects started resorting to behavior that the researchers could not control.

On the plus side, the first experiment clearly shows the potential of the field experiment to simulate natural conditions and to provide a nonreactive setting. Upon leaving the theater after seeing the program, subjects had no reason to believe that they would be participating in another phase of the research. Consequently, their behavior at the supposed gift center was probably genuine and not a reaction to the experimental situation.

The Milgram and Shotland studies also raise the important question of ethics in field experiments. Subjects were observed without their knowledge and apparently were never told about the real purpose of the study, nor even that they were involved in a research study. Does the use of a hidden camera constitute an invasion of privacy? Does the experimental situation constitute entrapment? How about the subjects who stole the money from the "charity" box? Have they committed a crime? Field experiments can sometimes pose difficult ethical considerations, and these points must be dealt with *before* the experiment is conducted, not afterward, when harm may already have been inflicted on the subjects (see Chapter 18).

Field Observations

Before 1980, field observation was rarely used in mass media research. Lowry (1979) reported that only 2–3% of the articles published in journalism and broadcasting journals had employed the technique. Recently, however, field observations have become more common in the research literature.

Field observation is useful for collecting data as well as for generating hypotheses and theories; it is more concerned with description and explanation than it is with measurement and quantification. There are two extremes of field observation, total observation and total participation. **Total observation** occurs when the observer assumes no role in the phenomenon being observed (subjects may or may not be aware that they are being studied). At the other extreme, **total participation** occurs when the observer becomes a full-fledged participant in the situation (subjects are usually unaware that a study is being conducted, although they may be told).

To illustrate the distinction between the two approaches, consider the example of a researcher who wishes to observe and analyze the dynamics of writing comedy for television. The researcher has two basic choices: to study television comedy writers in a passive role by merely watching them in action, or to participate directly in the process by joining a writing team. In the latter case, the researcher would probably want to be considered a fellow writer by the other members of the team (such arrangements might be made with the chief writer, who would be the only person to know the true identity of the researcher).

A combination of the two approaches, known as participant observation, occurs when a researcher is identified as such but still interacts with the other participants in the social or working situation. For example, a researcher who has been introduced as a mass media investigator might still participate in the creative writing process.

The choice of technique depends on the research problem. Total participation may affect subjects' behavior and also raises the ethical question of deception. On the other hand, the information gathered may be more valid if subjects are unaware of being scrutinized.

Some examples of field observation studies in mass media research include Geiber's (1956) classic study of gatekeeping (information flow) in the newsroom and Epstein's (1974) description of network news operations. Ravage (1977) was able to gain access to all meetings, production work, and postproduction operations of a network company in his study of television production. Similarly, Pekurny (1980) focused on the production of the NBC's "Saturday Night Live." He was given access to the blocking, rehearsal, and live broadcast phases of the program. Pekurny also functioned as a participant observer when he took part in discussions with writers about how to structure a joke and about the suitability of some material for broadcast.

Lull (1982) conducted a mass observation study of the TV viewing habits of more than 90 families. Observers spent 2 days with the families and then returned to conduct interviews with each person they observed. Note that by using the two data sources (observations and interviews) Lull was "triangulating" to gain additional perspective on his data. He found that the interview data were only partially supported by the observations. Observers noted that the father was the primary controller of the TV set, but the interviews suggested the father's influence was somewhat less.

Advantages of Field Observations

Field observation is not an appropriate technique for every research question, owing to the lack of control and quantification, but it does possess several unique advantages. For one thing, many mass media problems and questions cannot be studied using any other methodology. Field observation often helps the researcher to define basic background information necessary to frame a hypothesis and to isolate independent and dependent variables. For example, a researcher interested in how creative decisions in advertising are made could observe several decision-making sessions to see what actually transpires. Field observations often make excellent pilot studies in that they identify important variables and provide useful preliminary information. In addition, since the data are gathered firsthand, observation is not dependent on the subjects' ability or willingness to report their behavior. For example, young children may lack the reading or verbal skills necessary to respond to a questionnaire concerning their play behavior, but such data are easily gathered by the observational technique.

A field observation is not always used as a preliminary step to other approaches, however. In many cases it alone is the only appropriate approach, especially when quantification is difficult. Field observation is particularly suitable for a study of the gatekeeping process in a network television news department, because quantification of gatekeeping is rather tenuous.

Field observation may also provide access to groups that would otherwise be difficult to observe or examine. For example, a questionnaire sent to a group of producers of X-rated movies is not likely to have a high return rate. An observer, however, may be able to establish enough mutual trust with such a group to persuade them to respond to rigorous questioning.

Field observation is usually inexpensive. In most cases, writing materials or a small tape recorder will suffice. Expenses increase if the problem under study requires a large number of observers, extensive travel, or special equipment (such as video recording machines).

Perhaps the most noteworthy advantage of field observation is that the study takes place in the natural setting of the activity being observed and can thus provide data rich in detail and subtlety. Many mass media situations, such as a family watching television, are complex and are constantly subjected to intervening influences. Field observation, because of the opportunity for careful examination, allows observers to identify these otherwise unknown variables.

Disadvantages of Field Observations

On the negative side, field observation is a bad choice if the researcher is concerned with external validity. This difficulty is partly due to the potentially questionable representativeness of the observations made and partly to problems in sampling. Observing the television viewing behavior of a group of children at a day-care center can provide valuable insights into the social setting of television viewing, but it probably has little correlation to what preschoolers do in other places and under different circumstances.

Moreover, since field observation relies heavily on a researcher's perceptions and judgments as well as on preconceived notions about the material under study, experimenter bias may unavoidably favor specific preconceptions of results, while observations to the contrary are ignored or distorted. This, primarily, is why one observer is rarely used in a field observation study. Observations need to be *cross-validated* by second or third observers.

Finally, like field experiments, field observations suffer from the problem of reactivity. The very process of being observed may influence the behavior under study. Of course, reactivity can be a problem with other research methods, but it is most often mentioned as a criticism of field observation (Chadwick, Bahr, & Albrecht, 1984). Lull (1985), who provides some perspective on observer effects using data taken from an observational study of families' TV viewing behavior, found that the presence of an observer in the house did have some impact on family members. About 20% of parents and 25% of children reported that their overall behavior was affected by the presence of an observer. The majority of those who were affected thought that they became nicer or more polite and formal because of the observer's presence. When it came to differences in the key behavior under study, 87% said that the observer's presence had no effect on their TV viewing activity. Additionally, among those who reported an observer effect, there were no systematic differences in the distribution of changes. About the same number said that they watched more because of the observer as said they watched less. Obviously, additional studies of different groups in different settings are needed before this problem is fully understood, but Lull's data suggest that although reactivity is a problem with observational techniques, its impact may not be as drastic as some suggest.

In any case, at least two strategies are available to diminish the impact of selective perception and reactance. One is to use several observers to cross-validate the results. A second strategy has to do with the notion of triangulation—the supplementing of observational data by data gathered by other means (questionnaires, existing records, and so on). Accuracy is sought by using multiple data collection methods.

Field Observation Techniques

There are at least five stages in a typical field observation study: gaining access, sampling, collecting data, analyzing data, and exiting.

Gaining access. The first step in gaining access to a setting and/or group of people is to define the research goal. Is there a need to observe homes with school-age children, or to watch newspaper reporters as they perform their daily routines? Once the goal has been clearly articulated, the next step is to establish contact. Observation of a formal group (such as a film production crew) often requires permission from management and perhaps union officials. School systems and other bureaucracies usually have a special unit to handle requests from researchers and to assist them in obtaining necessary permissions.

Gaining permission to conduct field observation research requires persistence and public relations skills. Researchers must determine how much to disclose about the nature of the research. In most cases it is not necessary to provide a complete explanation of the hypothesis and procedures, unless there may be objections to sensitive areas. Researchers interested in observing which family member actually controls the television set might explain that they are studying patterns of family communication. Once the contact has been made, it is necessary to establish a rapport with the subject(s). Bogdan and Taylor (1975) suggested the following techniques for building rapport: establish common interests with the participants; start relationships slowly; if appropriate, participate in common events and activities; and do not disrupt participants' normal routines.

Sampling. Sampling in field observation is more ambiguous than in most other research approaches. In the first place, there is the problem of how many individuals or groups to observe. If the focus of the study is communication in the newsroom, how many newsrooms should be observed? If the topic is family viewing of television, how many families should be included? Unfortunately, there are no guidelines to help answer these questions. The reseach problem and the goals of the study are often used as indicators for sample size: if the results are intended for generalization to a population, one subject or group is probably inadequate.

Another problem is deciding what behavior episodes or segments to sample. The observer cannot be everywhere and see everything, so what is observed becomes a de facto sample of what is not observed. If an observer views one staff meeting in the newsroom, this meeting represents other, unobserved meetings; one conversation at the coffee machine is a sample of all such conversations. In many cases researchers cannot adhere closely to the principles of probability sampling, but they should keep in mind the general notion of representativeness.

Most field observations use purposive sampling: observers draw on their knowledge of the subject(s) under study and sample only from the behaviors or events that are relevant. In many cases, previous experience and study of the activity in question will suggest what needs to be examined. In a study of newsroom decision making, for example, researchers would want to observe staff meetings, since they are obviously an important part of the process. However, restricting the sampling to observations of staff meetings would be a mistake; many decisions are made at the water fountain, over lunch, and in the hallways. Experienced observers tend not to isolate a specific situation but rather to consider even the most insignificant situation for potential analysis. For most field observation, researchers need to spend some time simply getting the "feel" of the situation and absorbing the pertinent aspects of the environment before beginning a detailed analysis.

Collecting data. The traditional tools of data collection—the notebook and pen—have given way to radically new equipment in many cases, due to recent advances in electronics. For example, Bechtel, Achelpohl, and Akers (1972) installed television cameras in a small sample of households to document the families' television-viewing behavior. Two cameras, automatically activated when the television set was turned on, videotaped the scene in front of the set. However, while a camera is able to record more information than an observer with a notebook, Bechtel reported that problems in finding consenting families, maintaining the equipment, and interpreting tapes shot at low light levels made the project difficult.

Note taking in the total participant situation requires special attention. Continually scribbling away on a notepad is certain to draw attention and suspicion to the note taker and might expose the researcher's real purpose in a particular setting. In a situation of this type, it is advisable to make mental notes and transcribe them at the first opportunity. If the researcher is initially identified as such, the problem of note taking is somewhat alleviated. Nonetheless, it is not recommended that the observer spend all of his or her time furiously taking notes. Subjects are already aware of being observed, and conspicuous note taking could make them more uneasy. Brief notes jotted down during natural breaks in a situation attract a minimum of attention and can be expanded at a later time.

The field notes constitute the basic corpus of data in any field study. In them, the observers record not only what happened and what was said, but also personal impressions, feelings, and interpretations of what was observed. A general procedure is to separate personal opinions from the descriptive narrative by enclosing the former in brackets.

How much should be recorded? It is always better to record too much imformation than too little. An apparently irrelevant observation made during the first viewing session might become significant during the course of the project. If the material is sensitive, or if the researcher does not wish it known that research is taking place, the notes may be written in abbreviated form or in code.

Analyzing data. Quantitative data analysis procedures have only partial relevance to field observations due to the qualitative nature of field data. In field observation, data analysis consists primarily of filing and content analysis.

Constructing a filing system is an important step in observation. The purpose of the filing system is to arrange raw field data in an orderly format to enable systematic retrieval later (the precise filing categories are determined by the data). Using the hypothetical study of decision making in the newsroom, filing categories might include the headings "Relationships," "Interaction—Horizontal," "Interaction—Vertical," and "Disputes." An observation may be placed in more than one category. It is a good idea to make multiple copies of all notes, and periodic filing of notes throughout the observation period will save time and confusion later.

A rough content analysis is performed to search for consistent patterns once all the notes have been ascribed to their proper files. Perhaps most decisions in the newsroom are made in informal settings such as hallways rather than in formal settings such as conference rooms. Perhaps most decisions are made with little superior-subordinate consultation. At the same time, deviations from the norm should be investigated. Perhaps all reporters except one are typically asked their opinions on the newsworthiness of events. Why the exception?

The overall goal of data analysis in field observation is to arrive at a general understanding of the phenomenon under study. In this regard, the observer has the advantage of flexibility. In laboratory and other research approaches, investigators must at some point commit themselves to a particular design or questionnaire. If it subsequently turns out that a crucial variable was left out, there is little that can be done. In field observation, the researcher can analyze data during the course of the study and change the research design accordingly.

Exiting. A participant observer must also have a plan for leaving the setting or the group under study. Of course, if the participant is known to everyone, exiting will not be a problem. Exiting from a setting that participants regularly enter and leave also is not a problem. Exiting can be difficult, however, when participation is covert. In some instances, the group may have become dependent on the researcher in some way and the departure may have a negative effect on the group as a whole. In other cases, the sudden revelation that a group has been infiltrated or "taken in" by an outsider might be unpleasant or distressing to some. The researcher has an ethical obligation to do everything possible to prevent psychological, emotional, or physical injury to those being studied. Consequently, leaving the scene must be handled with diplomacy and tact.

Focus Groups

The **focus group,** or group interviewing, is a research strategy for understanding audience/consumer attitudes and behavior. From 6 to 12 people are interviewed simultaneously, with a moderator leading the respondents in a relatively free discussion about the focal topic. The identifying characteristic of the focus group is *controlled group discussion,* which is employed to gather preliminary information for a research project, to help develop questionnaire items for survey research, and to gather other preliminary qualitative data as a foundation for further study.

A brief guide for conducting focus groups is contained in Appendix 3.

Advantages of Focus Groups

The primary advantage of focus groups is that they allow the collection of preliminary information about a topic or phenomenon. Focus groups should never be used as the only research approach because the sample size is too small. Focus groups should be used only in pilot studies to detect ideas that will be investigated further using another research method, such as a telephone survey.

A second important advantage is that focus groups can be conducted very quickly. The major portion of time is spent recruiting the respondents. A good research company that specializes in recruiting for focus groups can usually recruit respondents in about 7–10 days, depending on the type of person required.

The cost of focus groups also makes the approach an attractive research method; most focus groups can be conducted for about $1,000–$2,000 per group, depending on the type of respondent required for the group, the part of the country in which the group is conducted, and the moderator or company used to conduct the group. When respondents are difficult to recruit, or the topic requires a specially trained moderator, a focus group may cost several thousand dollars. The price, however, is not excessive if the groups provide valuable data for future research studies.

Researchers also like focus groups because of the flexibility in question design and follow-up. In conventional surveys, interviewers work from a rigid series of questions and are instructed to follow explicit directions in asking the questions. A moderator in a focus group, on the other hand, works from a list of broad questions as well as more refined probe questions; hence, follow-up on important points raised by participants in the group is easy. The ability to clear up confusing responses from respondents makes focus groups valuable in the research process.

Most professional focus group moderators or research companies use a procedure known as an *extended focus group*, in which respondents are required to complete a written questionnaire before the start of the group. The pregroup questionnaire, which basically covers the material that will be discussed during the group session, serves to "force" the respondents to commit to a particular answer or position before entering the group session. This commitment eliminates one potential problem created by group dynamics, namely, the person who does not wish to offer an opinion because he or she is in a minority.

Finally, focus group responses are often more complete and less inhibited than those from individual interviews. One respondent's remarks tend to stimulate others to pursue lines of thinking that might not have been brought out in an individual situation. With a competent moderator, the discussion can have a beneficial snowball effect, as one respondent comments on the views of another. A skilled moderator can also detect the opinions and attitudes of those who are less articulate by noting facial expressions and other nonverbal behavior while others are speaking.

Disadvantages of Focus Groups

Focus group research is not totally free from complications; the approach is far from perfect. Some of the problems are discussed here, while others are included later in Appendix 3.

Some groups become dominated by a self-appointed group leader who monopolizes the conversation and attempts to impose his or her opinion on the other participants. Such a person usually draws the resentment of the other participants and may have an extremely adverse effect on the performance of the group. The moderator needs to control such situations tactfully before they get out of hand.

Gathering quantitative data is inappropriate for a focus group. If quantification is important, it is wise to supplement the focus group with other research tools that permit more specific questions to be addressed to a more representative sample. Many people unfamiliar with focus group research incorrectly assume that the method will answer questions of "how many" or "how much." Focus group research is intended to gather qualitative data to answer questions such as "why" or "how." Many times people who hire a person or company to conduct a focus group are disgruntled with the results because they expected exact numbers and percentages. Focus groups do not provide such information; the method is a complement to other research techniques and the results must be interpreted in that light.

As suggested above, focus groups depend heavily on the skills of the moderator, who must know when to probe for further information, when to stop respondents from discussing irrelevant topics, and how to get all respondents involved in the discussion. All these things must be accomplished with professionalism and care, since one sarcastic or inappropriate comment to a respondent may have a chilling effect on the group's performance.

There are other drawbacks, as well. The small focus group samples are composed of volunteers and do not necessarily represent the population from which they were drawn, the recording equipment or other physical characteristics of the location may inhibit respondents, and if the respondents are allowed to stray too far from the topic under consideration, the data produced may not be useful.

The Methodology of Focus Groups

There are eight basic steps in focus group research.

1. Defining the problem. This step is similar in all types of scientific research: a well-defined problem is established, either on the basis of some previous investigation or out of curiosity. For example, many television production companies that produce pilot programs for potential series will conduct 10–50 focus groups with target viewers to determine their reactions to each concept.

2. Selecting a sample. Because focus groups are small, researchers must define a narrow audience for the study. The type of sample depends on the purpose of the focus group: the sample might consist of housewives who use a particular type of laundry detergent, men aged 18–34 who listen to a certain type of music, or teenagers who purchase more than 10 record albums a year.

3. Determining the number of groups necessary. To help eliminate part of the problem of selecting a representative group, most researchers conduct two or more focus groups on the same topic. Results can then be compared to determine whether any similarities or differences exist; or, one group may be used as a basis for comparison to the other group. A focus group study using only one group is rare, since there is no way to know if the results are group-specific or characteristic of a wider audience.

4. Preparing the study mechanics. A more detailed description of the mechanical aspects of focus groups is in Appendix 3; suffice it to say here that this step includes arranging for the recruitment of respondents (by telephone or possibly by shopping center intercept), reserving the facilities at which the groups will be conducted, and deciding what type of recording (audio and/or video) will be used. The moderator must be selected and briefed about the purpose of the group. In addition, the researcher needs to determine the amount of money *(co-op)* each respondent will receive for participating. Respondents usually receive between \$10 and \$20 for attending, although professionals such as doctors and lawyers may require up to \$100 or more for co-op.

5. Preparing the focus group materials. Each aspect of a focus group must be planned in detail; nothing should be left to chance— in particular, the moderator must not be allowed to "wing it." The screener questionnaire is developed to produce the correct respondents; recordings and other materials the subjects will hear or see are prepared; any questionnaires the subjects will complete are produced (including the presession questionnaire); and a list of questions is developed for the presession questionnaire and the moderator's guide.

Generally a focus group session begins with some type of shared experience, so that the individuals have a common base from which to start the discussion. The members may listen to or view a tape or examine a new product, or they may simply be asked how they answered question 1 on the presession questionnaire.

The existence of a moderator's guide (see Appendix 3) does not mean that the moderator cannot ask questions not contained in the guide. Quite the opposite is true. The significant quality of a focus group is that it allows the moderator to probe comments that respondents make during the session. A professional moderator is often able to develop a line of questioning that no one thought about before the group began, and many times the questioning provides extremely important information. Professional moderators who have this skill receive very substantial fees for conducting focus groups.

6. Conducting the session. Focus groups may be conducted in a variety of settings, from professional conference rooms equipped with two-way mirrors to motel rooms rented for the occasion. In most situations, a professional conference room is used. Hotel and motel rooms are used when a focus facility is not located close by.

7. Analyzing the data and preparing a summary report. The written summary of focus group interviews depends on the needs of the study and the amount of time and money available. At one extreme, the moderator/researcher may simply write a brief synopsis of what was said and offer an interpretation of the subjects' responses. For a more elaborate content analysis, or a more complete description of what happened, the sessions can be transcribed so that the moderator/researcher can scan the comments and develop a category system, coding each comment into the appropriate category. For example, a researcher who notices that most respondents focus on the price of a new product can establish a content category labeled "Price," code all statements in the transcript referring to price, and arrange these statements under the general heading. The same technique is followed for other content categories. When the coding is completed, the researcher makes summary statements about the number, tone, and consistency of the comments that fall into each category. Needless to say, this approach requires some expenditure of time and money on the researcher's (or client's) part.

8. Determining the next step. Upon conclusion of the focus groups, one of three steps usually is taken: the results are used to prepare other research projects such as a telephone survey; it is decided that the groups did not provide the required information and that other groups must be conducted; and due to the nature of the information, the project is substantially changed, or even canceled.

Individual Focus Sessions

In the past few years, some researchers have begun to use a refinement of the standard focus group to eliminate some of the potential problems of group discussions (for example, a group leader who sways the answers of other respondents). In the method known as *individual focus sessions (IFS)*, researchers may interview 40 or more people separately. Each respondent is given a specific appointment time and is interviewed by the researcher. Each one-on-one interview generally lasts about 45 minutes.

The IFS approach is considered by many to be a valuable data collection method because it allows the researcher to probe very carefully each answer a respondent gives. The one-on-one interview eliminates the potential problem of group pressure and generally allows the shy respondent to provide more specific information.

Like any research approach, the IFS method has its drawbacks. First of all, a great deal of time is required to interview 40 or more people in a series of 45-minute sessions. Researcher fatigue is common because the process generally takes at least two days. Second, the method is more expensive—generally at least twice as costly as typical focus groups with 40 people. However, the value of the data collected in the IFS generally offsets the additional time and expense; the method allows researchers to gather a tremendous amount of information.

Case Studies

The **case study** method is another technique that is commonly referred to as qualitative research. Simply put, a case study uses as many data sources as possible to investigate systematically an individual, group, organization, or event. Case studies are performed when a researcher desires to understand or explain a phenomenon. Case studies are frequently used in medicine, anthropology, clinical psychology, management science, and history. Sigmund Freud wrote case studies of his patients; economists wrote case studies of the cable TV industry for the FCC; the list is endless.

On a more formal level, Yin (1984) defines a case study as an empirical inquiry that uses multiple sources of evidence to investigate a contemporary phenomenon within its real-life context in which the boundaries between the phenomenon and its context are not clearly evident. This definition highlights how a case study differs from other research strategies. For example, an experiment separates phenomenon from real-life context. The context is controlled by the laboratory environment. The survey technique tries to define the phenomenon under study narrowly enough to limit the number of variables to be examined. Case study research includes both single and multiple cases. Comparative case study research, frequently used in political science, is an example of the multiple case study technique.

The case study method is not synonymous with participant observation (where a researcher enters a group and takes part in its activities). In the first place, as Yin (1984) correctly points out, participant observation does not always result in case studies. Second, case studies may not necessarily include direct observations as a source of evidence. In fact, it is perfectly feasible for a researcher to do an exemplary case study by using just the telephone and the library. In short, the case study method is not recommended in all research situations. It does represent, however, another valuable addition to the researcher's stock of available tools.

Advantages of Case Studies

The case study method is most valuable when the researcher wants to obtain a wealth of information about the research topic. Case studies provide tremendous detail. Many times researchers want such detail when they don't know exactly what they are looking for. The case study is particularly advantageous to the researcher who is trying to find clues and ideas for further research (Simon, 1969). This is not to suggest, however, that case studies are to be used only at the exploratory stage of research. The method can also be used to gather descriptive and explanatory data.

The case study technique can suggest *why* something has occurred. For example, in many cities in the mid-1980s, cable companies asked to be released from certain promises made when negotiating for a franchise. To learn why this occurred, a multiple case study approach, examining several cities, could have been used. Other research techniques, such as the survey, might not be able to get at all the possible reasons behind this phenomenon. Ideally, case studies should be used in combination with theory to achieve maximum understanding.

The case study method also affords the researcher the ability to deal with a wide spectrum of evidence. Documents, historical artifacts, systematic interviews, direct observations, and even traditional surveys can all be incorporated into a case study. In fact, the more data sources that can be brought to bear in a case, the more likely it is that the study will be valid.

Disadvantages of Case Studies

There are three main criticisms. The first has to do with a general lack of scientific rigor in many case studies. Yin (1984) points out that "too many times, the case study investigator has been sloppy, and has allowed equivocal evidence or biased views to influence the . . . findings and conclusions" (p. 21). It is easy to do a sloppy case study; rigorous case studies require a good deal of time and effort.

The second criticism is that the case study is not easily open to generalization. If the main goal of the researcher is to make statistically based normative statements about the frequency of occurrence of a phenomenon in a defined population, some other method may be more appropriate. This is not to say that the results of all case studies are idiosyncratic and unique. In fact, if generalizing theoretic propositions is the main goal, the case study method is perfectly suited to the task.

Finally, like participant observation, case studies are likely to be time-consuming and may occasionally produce massive quantities of data that are hard to summarize. Consequently, fellow researchers are forced to wait years for the results of the research, which too often are poorly presented. Some authors, however, are experimenting with nontraditional methods of reporting to overcome this last criticism (see Peters & Waterman, 1982).

Doing a Case Study

The precise method of conducting a case study has not been as well documented as the more traditional techniques of the survey and the experiment. Nonetheless, there appear to be five distinct stages in carrying out a case study: design, pilot study, data collection, data analysis, and report writing.

Design. The first concern in a case study is what to ask. The case study is most appropriate for questions that begin with "how" or "why." A research question that is clear and precise will focus the remainder of the efforts in a case study. A second design concern is what to analyze. What exactly constitutes a "case"? In many instances, a case may be an individual, several individuals, or an event or events. If information is gathered about each relevant individual, the results are reported in the single or multiple case study format; in other instances, however, the precise boundaries of the case are harder to pinpoint. A case might be a specific decision, a particular organization at a certain point in time, a program, or some other discrete event. One rough guide for determining what to use as the unit of analysis is the available research literature. Since researchers want to compare their findings with the results of previous research, it is sometimes a good idea not to stray too far from what was done in past research.

Pilot study. Before the pilot study is conducted, the case study researcher must construct a study **protocol.** This document contains the procedures to be used in the study and also includes the data-gathering instrument or instruments. A good case study protocol contains the procedures necessary for gaining access to a particular person or organization and the methods for accessing records. It also contains the schedule of data collection and addresses the problems of logistics. For example, the protocol should note whether a copy machine will be available in the field to duplicate records, whether office space is available to the researchers, and what will be needed in the way of supplies. The protocol should also list the questions central to the inquiry and the possible sources of information to be tapped in answering these questions. If interviews are to be used in the case study, the protocol should contain the questions to be asked.

Once the protocol has been developed, the researcher is ready to go into the field for the pilot study. A pilot study is used to refine both the research design and the field procedures. Variables that were not foreseen during the design phase can crop up during the pilot study, and problems with the protocol or with study logistics can also be uncovered. The pilot study also allows the researchers to try different data-gathering approaches and to observe different activities from several trial perspectives. The results of the pilot study are used to revise and polish study protocol.

Data collection. At least five sources of data can be used in case studies. Documents, which represent a rich data source, may take the form of letters, memos, minutes, agendas, historical records, and so on. A second source of case study data is the interview. Most case study interviews are either *open-ended* or *focused*. An open-ended interview is highly flexible and can range over a wide variety of topics. Sometimes the respondent's answers will suggest a new line of questioning to the interviewer. Broad topic areas may be specified in advance, but the interviewer does not have a rigid format to follow. In a focused interview, the interviewer generally uses a set of predetermined questions or at least specific topic areas to be investigated. For example, Baldwin and Lewis (1972) used a focused technique in their study of Hollywood producers. Certain questions and topic areas covering television violence were included in every interview.

Observation and participant observation, respectively, are the third and fourth techniques that may be used. The same general comments made about these techniques earlier in this chapter apply to the case study method as well. The last source of evidence used in case studies is the physical artifact—a tool, a piece of furniture, or even a computer printout. Although artifacts are commonly used as a data source in anthropology and history, they are seldom used in mass media case study research. (They are, however, frequently used in legal research concerning the media.)

Most case study researchers recommend using multiple sources of data, thus affording triangulation of the phenomenon under study (Rubin, 1984). In addition, multiple sources help the case study researcher improve the reliability and validity of the study. Not surprisingly, a study of the case study method found that the ones that used multiple sources of evidence were rated higher than those relying on a single source (Yin, Bateman, & Moore, 1983).

Data analysis. Unlike more quantitative research techniques, there are no specific formulas or "cookbook" techniques to guide the researcher in analyzing the data. Consequently, this stage is probably the most difficult in the case study method. Although it is hard to generalize to all case study situations, Yin (1984) has suggested three broad analytic strategies: pattern matching, explanation building, and time series. In the pattern-matching strategy, an empirically based pattern is compared with a predicted pattern or several alternative predicted patterns. For instance, suppose a newspaper is about to institute a new management tool: a regular series of meetings between top management and reporters, excluding editors. Based on organizational theory, a researcher might predict certain outcomes, namely, more stress between editors and reporters, increased productivity, weakened supervisory links, and so on. If analysis of the case study data indicates that these results did in fact occur, some conclusions about the management change can be made. If the predicted pattern did not match the actual one, the initial study propositions would have to be questioned.

In the analysis strategy of explanation building, the researcher tries to construct an explanation about the case by making statements about the cause or causes of the phenomenon under study. This method can take several forms. Typically, however, an investigator drafts an initial theoretical statement about some process or outcome, compares the findings of an initial case study against the statement, revises the statement, analyzes a second comparable case, and repeats this process as many times as necessary. For example, to explain why some new communication technologies are failing, a researcher might suggest lack of managerial expertise as an initial proposition. But an investigator who examined the subscription television industry might find that lack of management expertise is only part of the problem—inadequate market research is also contributory. Armed with the revised version of the explanatory statement, the researcher would next examine the direct broadcast satellite industry to see whether this explanation needs to be further refined, and so on, until a full and satisfactory answer is achieved.

In the third analytic strategy, time series analysis, the investigator tries to compare a series of data points to some theoretic trend that was predicted before the research, or to some rival trend. If, for instance, several cities have experienced newspaper strikes, a case study investigator might generate predictions about the changes in information-seeking behaviors of residents in these communities and conduct a case study to see whether these predictions were supported.

Report writing. The case study report can take several forms. The report can follow the traditional research study format: problem, methods, findings, and discussion. Or it can use a nontraditional technique. Some case studies are best suited for a chronological arrangement, whereas cases studies that are comparative in nature can be reported from that perspective. No matter what form is chosen, the researcher must consider the intended audience of the report. A case study report written for policy makers would be done in a style different from one that was to be published in a scholarly journal.

Examples of Case Studies

Browne (1983) conducted a comparative case study of the newsroom practices at the Voice of America, the BBC, and Deutsche-Welle, three of the world's largest international radio stations. Browne's study illustrated how multiple sources of evidence are used in the case study technique. He interviewed 55 staff members of the three stations, sat in on editorial meetings, observed actual newsroom practices, and had access to corporate documents. He found that all three stations had common problems, particularly in their relationships with their foreign language services.

Woodside and Fleck (1979) used the case study approach to investigate how consumers made decisions about buying various brands of beer. They conducted a series of intensive unstructured interviews and surveys with two beer drinkers to generate hypotheses concerning the effects of advertising on consumer information processing. Each consumer was interviewed for about 5 hours, and each one also filled out lengthy questionnaires and participated in taste tests. The researchers used their results to develop a decision-making model to be tested in subsequent research.

Perhaps the most famous of all case studies is Woodward and Bernstein's book about Watergate, *All the President's Men* (1974). Using interviews and documents as their primary data base, the two reporters attempted to answer "how" and "why" questions: Why was there a cover-up, and how did it occur?

Summary

This chapter discusses four alternatives to laboratory and survey research: field experiments, field observations, focus groups, and case studies. *Field experiments* are carried out in natural settings. Their main advantage is their external validity; they are not influenced by the artificiality of the laboratory. On the other hand, their biggest drawback is the difficulty of maintaining control over contaminating influences. *Field observation* involves the study of a phenomenon under natural circumstances. The researcher may be a detached observer or a participant in the process under study. The main advantage of this technique is its flexibility; it can be used to develop hypotheses, to gather preliminary data, or to study groups that would otherwise be inaccessible. Its biggest disadvantage is the difficulty in achieving external validity.

The *focus group*, or group interviewing, is used to gather preliminary information for a research study or to gather qualitative data concerning a research question. The advantages of the focus group method are the ease of data collection and the depth of information that can be gathered. Among the disadvantages: the quality of information gathered during focus groups depends heavily on the group moderators' skill; focus groups can only complement other research because they provide qualitative not quantitative data. The *case study* method draws from as many data sources as possible to investigate an event. Case studies are particularly helpful when a researcher desires to explain or understand some phenomenon. Some problems with case studies are that they can lack scientific rigor, they can be time-consuming to conduct, and the data they provide can be difficult to generalize from and to summarize.

Questions and Problems for Further Investigation

1. Develop a research topic that would be appropriate for a study by:
   a. Field experiment
   b. Field observation
2. Suggest three specific research topics that would be best studied by the technique of total participation. Would any ethical problems be involved?
3. Select a research topic that is suitable for study using the focus group method, then assemble six or eight of your classmates or friends and conduct a sample interview. Select an appropriate method for analyzing the data.
4. Examine recent journals in the mass communication research field and identify instances where the case study method was

used. For each example, specify the sources of data used in the study, how the data were analyzed, and how the study was reported.

References and Suggested Readings

Babbie, E. R. (1986). *The practice of social research* (4th ed.). Belmont, CA: Wadsworth.

Baldwin, T., & Lewis, C. (1972). Violence in television: The industry looks at itself. In E. Rubinstein, G. Comstock, & J. Murray (Eds.), *Television and social behavior* (Vol. I). Washington, DC: U.S. Government Printing Office.

Bechtel, R., Achelpohl, C., & Akers, R. (1972). Correlates between observed behavior and questionnaire responses on television viewing. In E. Rubinstein, G. Comstock, & J. Murray (Eds.), *Television and social behavior* (Vol. IV). Washington, DC: U.S. Government Printing Office.

Bickman, L., & Hency, T. (1972). *Beyond the laboratory: Field research in social psychology.* New York: McGraw-Hill.

Bogdan, R., & Taylor, S. (1975). *Introduction to qualitative research methods.* New York: John Wiley.

Browne, D. (1983). The international newsroom. *Journal of Broadcasting, 27*(3), 205–231.

Calder, B. J. (1977). Focus groups and the nature of qualitative marketing research. *Journal of Marketing Research, 14,* 353–364.

Chadwick, B., Bahr, H., & Albrecht, S. (1984). *Social science research methods.* Englewood Cliffs, NJ: Prentice-Hall.

Cox, K. D., Higginbotham, J. B., & Burton, J. (1976). Applications of focus group interviewing in marketing. *Journal of Marketing, 40,* 77–80.

Elliot, S. C. (1980). Focus group research: A workbook for broadcasters. Washington, DC: National Association of Broadcasters.

Epstein, E. J. (1974). *News from nowhere.* New York: Vintage.

Fletcher, A., & Bowers, T. (1979). *Fundamentals of advertising research.* Columbus, OH: Grid.

Fletcher, J. E., & Wimmer, R. D. (1981). *Focus group interviews in radio research.* Washington, DC: National Association of Broadcasters.

Geiber, W. (1956). Across the desk: A study of 16 telegraph editors. *Journalism Quarterly, 33,* 423–432.

Haskins, J. B. (1968). *How to evaluate mass communications.* New York: Advertising Research Foundation.

Himmelweit, H., Oppenheim, A. N., & Vince, P. (1958). *Television and the child.* London: Oxford University Press.

Lowry, D. (1979). An evaluation of empirical studies reported in seven journals in the '70s. *Journalism Quarterly, 56,* 262–268.

Lull, J. (1982). How families select television programs. *Journal of Broadcasting, (26)* 4, 801–812.

Lull, J. (1985). Ethnographic studies of broadcast media audiences. In J. Dominick & J. Fletcher (Eds.), *Broadcasting research methods.* Boston: Allyn & Bacon.

Milgram, S., & Shotland, R. (1973). *Television and antisocial behavior: Field experiments.* New York: Academic Press.

Pekurny, R. (1980). The production process and environment of NBC's *Saturday Night Live. Journal of Broadcasting, 24,* 91–100.

Peters, T. J., & Waterman, R. (1982). *In search of excellence.* New York: Harper & Row.

Ravage, J. W. (1977). Not in the quality business: A case study of contemporary production. *Journal of Broadcasting, 21,* 47–60.

Redding, C. W. (1970). Research settings: Field studies. In P. Emmert & W. D. Brooks (Eds.), *Methods of research in communication.* Boston: Houghton Mifflin.

Reid, L. N., Soley, L. C., & Wimmer, R. D. (1981). Replication in advertising research: 1977, 1978, 1979. *Journal of Advertising, 10,* 3–13.

Reynolds, F. D., & Johnson, D. K. (1978). Validity of focus group findings. *Journal of Advertising Research, 18,* 21–24.

Robertson, L., et al. (1974). A controlled study of the effect of television messages of safety belt use. *American Journal of Public Health, 64,* 1074–1084.

Rubin, H. (1984). *Applied social research.* Columbus, OH: Charles E. Merrill.

Simon, J. (1969). *Basic research methods in social science.* New York: Random House.

Szybillo, G., & Berger, R. (1979). What advertising agencies think of focus groups. *Journal of Advertising Research, 19*(3), 29–33.

Tan, A. (1977). Why TV is missed: A functional analysis. *Journal of Broadcasting, 21,* 371–380.

Tull, D., & Hawkins, D. (1980). *Marketing research.* New York: Macmillan.

Westley, B. H. (1981). The controlled experiment. In G. H. Stempel & B. H. Westley (Eds.), *Research methods in mass communication.* Englewood Cliffs, NJ: Prentice-Hall.

Wimmer, R. D., & Reid, L. N. (1982). Researchers' response to replication requests. *Journalism Quarterly, 59*(2), 317–320.

Woodside, A., & Fleck, R. (1979). The case approach to understanding brand choice. *Journal of Advertising Research, 19*(2), 23–30.

Woodward, B., & Bernstein, C. (1974). *All the president's men.* New York: Simon & Schuster.

Yin, R. (1984). *Case study research.* Beverly Hills, CA: Sage Publications.

Yin, R., Bateman, P., & Moore, G. (1983). *Case studies and organizational innovation.* Washington, DC: Cosmos Corporation.

C H A P T E R 8

Content Analysis

DEFINITION OF CONTENT ANALYSIS

•

USES OF CONTENT ANALYSIS

•

LIMITATIONS OF CONTENT ANALYSIS

•

STEPS IN CONTENT ANALYSIS

•

RELIABILITY

•

VALIDITY

•

EXAMPLES OF CONTENT ANALYSIS

•

SUMMARY

•

QUESTIONS AND PROBLEMS FOR FURTHER INVESTIGATION

•

REFERENCES AND SUGGESTED READINGS

The chapters in Part 2 up to this point have concentrated on more general approaches used in mass media investigation. This chapter moves to content analysis, a specific research approach used frequently in all areas of the media. The method is popular with mass media researchers because it provides an efficient way to investigate the content of the media such as the number and types of commercials or advertisements in broadcasting or in the print media. Beginning researchers will find content analysis a valuable tool in answering many mass media questions.

Modern content analysis can be traced back to World War II, when allied intelligence units painstakingly monitored the number and types of popular songs played on European radio stations. By comparing the music played on German stations with that on other stations in occupied Europe, the allies were able to measure with some degree of success the changes in troop concentration on the continent. In the Pacific theater, communications between Japan and various island bases were carefully tabulated; an increase in message volume usually meant that some new operation involving that particular base was planned.

About this time, content analysis was used in attempts to verify the authorship of historical documents. These studies (see Yule, 1944) were primarily concerned with counting words in documents of questionable authenticity and comparing their frequencies with the same words in documents whose authors were known. These literary detective cases demonstrated the usefulness of quantification in content analysis.

After the war, content analysis was used by researchers studying propaganda in newspapers and radio. In 1952 Bernard Berelson published *Content Analysis in Communication Research*, which signaled that the technique had gained recognition as a tool for communication scholars.

Since that time, the method has achieved wide popularity. In 1968, Tannenbaum and Greenberg reported that content analysis of newspapers was the largest single category of master's theses in mass communication. A later publication (Comstock, 1975) listed more than 225 content analyses of television programming. Recent concern over the portrayal of violence on television and the treatment of women and minority groups in print and television advertising and in music videos has further popularized the content analysis technique among mass media researchers.

Definition of Content Analysis

Many definitions of content analysis exist. Walizer and Wienir (1978) have defined it as any systematic procedure devised to examine the content of recorded information, Krippendorf (1980) defined it as a research technique for making replicable and valid references from data to their context. Kerlinger's (1973) definition is fairly typical: content analysis is a method of studying and analyzing communication in a systematic, objective, and quantitative manner for the purpose of measuring variables.

Kerlinger's definition involves three concepts that require elaboration. First, content analysis is *systematic*. This means that the content to be analyzed is selected according to explicit and consistently applied rules: sample selection must follow proper procedures, and each item must have an equal chance of being included in the analysis. The evaluation process, also, must be systematic: all content under consideration is to be treated in exactly the same manner. There must be uniformity in the coding and analysis procedures, as well as in the length of time coders are exposed to the material. Systematic evaluation simply means that one and only one set of guidelines for evaluation is used throughout the study. Alternating procedures in an analysis is a sure way to confound the results.

Second, content analysis is *objective*. That is, the personal idiosyncrasies and biases of the investigator should not enter into the findings; if replicated by another researcher, the analysis should yield the same results. Operational definitions and rules for classification of variables should be explicit and comprehensive enough that other researchers who repeat the process will arrive at the same decisions. Unless a clear set of criteria and procedures are established that fully explain the sampling and categorization methods, the researcher does not meet the requirement of objectivity, and the reliability of the results may be called into question. Perfect objectivity is seldom achieved in a content analysis, however. The specification of the unit of analysis and the precise makeup and definition of relevant categories are areas in which individual researchers must exercise subjective choice. (Reliability is discussed at length later in the chapter.)

Third, content analysis is *quantitative*. The goal of content analysis is the accurate representation of a body of messages. Quantification is important in fulfilling that objective, since it aids researchers in the quest for precision. The statement "Seventy percent of all prime time programs contain at least one act of violence" is more precise than "Most shows are violent." Additionally, quantification allows researchers to summarize results and report them with greater parsimony. If measurements are to be made over intervals of time, comparisons of the numerical data from one time period to another can help to simplify and standardize the evaluation procedure. Finally, quantification gives researchers additional statistical tools to use that can aid in interpretation and analysis.

Uses of Content Analysis

Over the past decade the symbols and messages contained in the mass media have become increasingly popular research topics in both the academic and private sectors. The American Broadcasting Company conducts systematic comparative analyses of the three networks' evening newscasts to see how ABC's news coverage compares to that of its competitors. The national Parent-Teachers' Association has offered "do-it-yourself" training in rough forms of content analysis so that local members can monitor television violence levels in their viewing areas. Citizens' groups, such as the National Coalition on Television Violence, keep track of TV content. Public relations firms use content analysis to monitor the subject matter of company publications, and some labor unions now perform content analyses of the mass media to examine their own images.

Content analysis in the mass media often makes use of **medium variables,** the aspects of content that are unique to the medium under consideration. For example, in newspapers and magazines such variables include typography, layout, and makeup; in television, they include shot duration, editing pace, shot selection, scene location, and camera angle. A discussion of medium variables as they relate to television news is contained in Adams and Schreibman (1978).

Although it is difficult to classify and categorize studies as varied and diverse as those using content analysis, they are generally employed for one of five purposes. A discussion of these aims will help illustrate some of the ways in which this technique can be applied.

Describing Communication Content

Several recent studies have catalogued the characteristics of a given body of communication content at one or more points in time. These studies exemplify content analysis used in the traditional, descriptive manner: to identify what exists. For example, Katzman (1972) described the problems, events, characters, and conversations involved in one week of soap operas. In like manner, Adams and Ferber (1977) described the positions and party affiliations of guests on Sunday television interview programs. Other analyses of this type describe trends in content over time, such as the description of characters in three different seasons of prime time television by Greenberg, Simmons, Hogan, and Atkin (1980).

These descriptive studies can also be used to study societal change. For example, changing public opinion on various controversial issues could be gauged by means of a longitudinal study (see Chapter 9) of letters to the editor or newspaper editorials. Statements about what values are judged to be important by a society could be inferred by a study of the nonfiction books on the best-seller list at different points in time.

Chadwick, Bahr, and Albrecht (1984) suggest that content analysis is useful in the analysis of projective personality tests such as the Rorschach and the Thematic Apperception tests. Subjects' responses to these tests can be content analyzed for characteristics suggesting certain personality traits. For example, Attkisson, Handler, and Shrader (1969) used content analysis to assess the validity of the Draw-A-Man test in determining religious values. The size, position, and details of the drawings were compared with subjects' religious beliefs.

Testing Hypotheses of Message Characteristics

A number of analyses attempt to relate certain characteristics of the source of a given body of message content to characteristics of the messages that are produced. As Holsti (1969) pointed out, this category of content analysis has been used in many studies that test hypotheses of form: "If the source has characteristic A, then messages containing elements x and y will be produced; if the source has characteristic B, then messages with elements w and z will be produced." Merritt and Gross (1978), for example, found that female editors of women's life-style pages were more likely than male editors to use stories about the women's movement. A study of local television newscasts revealed that the "eyewitness" format broadcast more news in the violent and human interest categories (Dominick, Wurtzel, & Lometti 1975). Benze and Declercq (1985) analyzed 113 TV commercials by 23 male and 23 female political candidates. They found that ads for female candidates were less likely to stress strength and more likely to stress compassion.

Comparing Media Content to the "Real World"

Many content analyses may be described as "reality checks," in which the portrayal of a certain group, phenomenon, trait, or characteristic is assessed against a standard taken from actuality. The congruence of the media presentation and the situation that exists is then discussed. Probably the earliest study of this type was by Davis (1951), who found that crime coverage in Colorado newspapers bore no relationship to changes in state crime rates. DeFleur (1964) compared television's portrayal of the work world with job data taken from the U.S. census. More recently, the National Commission on the Causes and Prevention of Violence used content analysis data collected by Gerbner (1969) to compare the world of television violence with real-life violence. Lowry (1981) compared alcohol consumption patterns as shown on prime time TV with those in real life and concluded that TV portrays drinking as more prevalent than in real life and with fewer negative consequences.

Assessing the Image of Particular Groups in Society

An ever-growing number of content analyses have focused on exploring the media image of certain minority or otherwise notable groups. In many instances, these studies are conducted to assess changes in media policy toward these groups, to make inferences about the media's responsiveness to demands for "better" coverage, or to document social trends. For example, as part of a license renewal challenge, Hennessee and Nicholson (1972) performed an extensive analysis of the image presented of women by a New York television station. Mertz (1970) analyzed the portrayal of the elderly on network television, and Greenberg and Kahn (1970) examined changes in the portrayal of blacks in *Playboy* cartoons. More recently, Greenberg (1983) completed a lengthy content analysis of the image of Mexican-Americans in the mass media.

Establishing a Starting Point for Studies of Media Effects

The use of content analysis as a starting point for subsequent studies is relatively new. The best-known example is **cultivation analysis,** whereby the dominant message and themes in media content are documented by systematic procedures, and a separate study of the audience is conducted to see whether these messages are fostering similar attitudes among heavy media users. Gerbner, Gross, Signorielli, Morgan, and Jackson-Beeck (1979) discovered that heavy viewers of television tend to be more fearful of the world around them. In other words, television content—in this case, large doses of crime and violence—may cultivate attitudes more consistent with its messages than with reality. Other work that has used a similar framework includes DeFleur and DeFleur's (1967) study of the possible effects of occupational stereotypes in television programs and Dominick's (1973) study of the influence of television crime on the viewers' perception of actual crime.

A second example of this approach was summarized by Zillmann and Bryant (1983). These investigators examined the effects of the most common forms of humor used in educational TV programs.

Among other things, they found that for a child audience, humor that is unrelated to the educational message fosters superior information gain.

Limitations of Content Analysis

Content analysis alone cannot serve as a basis for making statements about the effects of content on an audience. A study of Saturday morning cartoon programs on television might reveal that 80% of these programs contain commercials for sugared cereal, but this finding alone does not allow researchers to claim that children who watch these programs will want to purchase sugared cereals. To make such an assertion, an additional study of the viewers would be necessary (as in cultivation analysis). Content analysis cannot serve as the sole basis for claims about media effects.

Also, the findings of a particular content analysis are limited to the framework of the categories and definitions used in that analysis. Different researchers may use varying definitions and category systems to measure a single concept. In mass media research, this problem is most evident in studies of televised violence. Some reseachers rule out comic or slapstick violence in their studies, while others consider it an important dimension. Obviously, great care must be exercised in comparing the results of different content analysis studies. Researchers who use different tools of measurement will naturally arrive at different conclusions.

Another potential limitation of content analysis is a lack of messages relevant to the research. There are many topics or characters that receive relatively little exposure in the mass media. For example, a study of how Asians are portrayed in U.S. television commercials would be difficult because characters of this ethnicity are rarely seen (of course, this fact in itself might be a significant finding). A researcher interested in such a topic must be prepared to examine a large body of media content to find sufficient quantities for analysis.

Finally, content analysis is frequently time-consuming and expensive. The task of examining and categorizing large volumes of content is often laborious and tedious. Plowing through 100 copies of the *New York Times* or 50 issues of *Newsweek* involves large chunks of time and a corresponding degree of patience. In addition, if television content is selected for analysis, some means of preserving the programs for detailed examination is necessary. Typically, researchers videotape programs for analysis, but this requires access to a recorder and large supplies of videotape, materials not all researchers can afford.

Steps in Content Analysis

In general, a content analysis is conducted in several discrete stages. Although the steps are listed here in sequence, they need not be followed in the order given. In fact, the initial stages of analysis can easily be combined. Nonetheless, the following steps may be used as a rough outline.

1. Formulate the research question or hypothesis.
2. Define the population in question.
3. Select an appropriate sample from the population.
4. Select and define a unit of analysis.
5. Construct the categories of content to be analyzed.
6. Establish a quantification system.
7. Train coders and conduct a pilot study.
8. Code the content according to established definitions.
9. Analyze the collected data.
10. Draw conclusions and search for indications.

Formulating a Research Question

One problem to avoid in content analysis is the "counting-for-the-sake-of-counting" syndrome. The ultimate goal of the analysis must be clearly articulated, to avoid aimless exercises in data collection that have little utility for mass media reseach. For example, by counting the punctuation marks that are used in the *New York Times* and *Esquire* it would be possible to generate a statement such as: "*Esquire* used 45% more commas, but 23% fewer semicolons than the *New York Times*." The value of such information for mass media theory or policy making, however, is dubious. Content analysis should not be conducted simply because the material exists and can be tabulated.

As with other methods of mass media research, content analyses should be guided by well-formulated research questions or hypotheses. A basic review of the literature is a required step. The sources for hypotheses are the same as for other areas of media research. It is possible to generate a research question based on existing theory, prior research, or practical problems, or as a response to changing social conditions. For example, a research question might ask whether the growing visibility of the women's movement has produced a change in the way women are depicted in advertisements. Or, a content analysis might be conducted to determine whether the public affairs programming of group-owned television stations differs from that of other stations. Well-defined research questions or hypotheses enable the development of accurate and sensitive content categories, which in turn helps to produce more valuable data.

Defining the Universe

This stage is not as grandiose as it sounds. To "define the universe" is to specify the boundaries of the body of content to be considered, which requires an appropriate operational definition of the relevant population. If researchers are interested in analyzing the content of popular songs, they must define what is meant by a "popular" song. All songs listed in *Billboard*'s "Hot 100" chart? The top 50 songs? The top 10? What time period will be considered? The past 6 months? This month? A researcher who intends to study the image of minority groups on television must define "television." Is it evening programming, or does it also include daytime shows? Will the study examine news content or confine itself to dramatic offerings? By now, the requirements should be clear. What is needed is a concise statement that spells out the parameters of the investigation; for example:

> This study considers TV commercials broadcast in prime time in the New York City area from September 1, 1986, to October 1, 1986.

Or:

> This study considers the news content on the front pages of the *Washington Post* and the *New York Times*, excluding Sundays, from January 1 to December 31 of the past year.

Selecting a Sample

Once the universe has been defined, a sample is selected. Although many of the guidelines and procedures discussed in Chapter 4 are applicable here, the sampling of content involves some special considerations. On one hand, some analyses are concerned with a relatively finite amount of data, and it may be possible to conduct a census of the content. Thus, Wurtzel (1975) was able to perform a census of 2 years of public access television programming in New York, and Wimmer and Haynes (1978) conducted a census of 7 years' worth of articles published in the *Journal of Broadcasting*. On the other hand, in the more typical situation, the researcher has such a vast amount of content available that a census is not practical. Thus, a sample must be drawn.

Most content analysis in mass media involves multistage sampling. This process typically involves two stages (although it may entail three). The first stage is usually to take a sampling of content sources. For example, a researcher interested in the treatment of the nuclear freeze movement by American newspapers would first need to sample from among the 1,650 or so newspapers published each day. The researcher may decide to focus primarily on the way big city dailies covered the story and opt to analyze only the leading circulation newspapers in the 10 largest American cities. To take another example, a researcher interested in the changing portrayal of the elderly in magazine advertisements would first need to sample from among the thousands of publications available. In this instance, the researcher might select only the top 10, 15, or 25 mass circulation magazines. Of course, it is also possible to sample randomly if the task of analyzing all the titles is too overwhelming. A further possibility is to use the technique of stratified sampling discussed in Chapter 4. For example, the researcher studying the nuclear freeze movement might wish to stratify the sample by circulation size and sample from within strata composed of big city papers, medium city papers, and small city papers. The magazine researcher might stratify by type of magazine: news, women's interests, men's interests, and so on. A researcher interested in television content might stratify by network or by program type.

When the sources have been identified, the dates can be selected. In many studies, the time period from which the issues are to be selected is determined by the goal of the project. If the goal is to assess the nature of Watergate news, then the sampling period is fairly well defined by the actual duration of the story. If the research question is directed toward changes in the image of NASA and the space program following the explosion of the space shuttle Challenger in January 1986, then content should be sampled before, at the time of, and after the disaster. But within this period, what editions of newspapers and magazines and which television programs will be selected for analysis? It would be a tremendous amount of work to analyze each copy of *Time, Newsweek,* and *U.S. News and World Report* over a 5-year period. It is possible to sample from within that time period and obtain a representative group of issues. A simple random sample of the calendar dates involved is one possibility: after a random start, every *n*th issue of a publication is selected for the sample. This method cannot be used without planning, however. For instance, if the goal is 50 edition dates, and an interval of 7 is used, the sample might include 50 Saturday editions (periodicity). Since news content is not randomly distributed over the days of the week, the sample will not be representative.

Another technique for sampling edition dates is to stratify by week of the month and by day of the week. A sampling rule that no more than two days from one week can be chosen is one way to ensure a balanced distribution across the month. Another procedure is to construct a *composite week* for each month in the sample. For example, a study might use a sample of one Monday, drawn at random from the four or five possible Mondays in the month, one Tuesday drawn from the available Tuesdays, and so on, until all weekdays have been included. How many edition dates should be selected? Obviously, this depends on the topic under study. If an investigator is trying to describe the portrayal of Mexican-Americans on prime time television, a large number of dates would have to be sampled to ensure a representative analysis. If there is an interest in analyzing the geographic sources of news stories, a smaller number of dates would be needed, since almost every story would be relevant. The number of dates should be a function of the incidence of the phenomenon in question: the lower the incidence, the more dates will have to be sampled.

There are some rough guidelines for sampling in the media. Stempel (1952) drew separate samples of 6, 12, 18, 24, and 48 issues of a newspaper and compared the average content of each of the sample sizes in a single subject category against the total for the entire year. He found that each of the five sample sizes was adequate and that increasing the sample beyond 12 issues did not significantly improve upon accuracy. In television, Gerbner and his associates (1977) demonstrated that at least for the purpose of measuring violent behavior, a sample of one week of fall programming and various sample dates drawn throughout the year will produce comparable results. As a general rule, however, the larger the sample the better—within reason, of course. If too few dates are selected for analysis, the possibility of an unrepresentative sample is increased. Larger samples, if chosen randomly, usually run less risk of being atypical.

Another problem to examine during the sampling phase relates to systematic bias in the content itself. For example, a study of the amount of sports news in a daily paper might yield inflated results if the sampling were done only in April, when three or more professional sports are simultaneously in season. A study of marriage announcements in the Sunday *New York Times* for the month of June from 1932 to 1942 revealed no announcement of a marriage in a synagogue (Hatch & Hatch, 1947). It was later pointed out that the month of June usually falls within a period during which traditional Jewish marriages are prohibited. Researchers familiar with their topics can generally detect and guard against this type of distortion.

Once the sources and the dates have been determined, there may be one further stage of sampling. A researcher might wish to confine his or her attention to a selection of content within an edition. For example, an analysis of the front page of a newspaper is valid for a study of general reporting trends but is probably inadequate for a study of social news coverage. Figure 8.1 provides an example of multistage sampling in content analysis.

Selecting the Unit of Analysis

The **unit of analysis** is the thing that is actually counted. It is the smallest element of a content analysis, but it is also one of the most important. In written content, the unit of analysis might be a single word or symbol, a theme (a single assertion about one subject), or an entire article or story. In television and film analyses, units of analysis can be characters, acts, or entire programs. Specific rules and defi-

Figure 8.1 Multistage sampling in a hypothetical content analysis study

Research Question: Have there been changes in the type of products advertised in men's magazines from 1975 to 1985?

Sampling Stage 1: Selection of Titles
Men's magazines are defined as those magazines whose circulation figures show that 80% or more of their readers are men. These magazines will be divided into two groups: large and medium circulation.

      Large circulation: reaches more than 1,000,000 men.

      Medium circulation: reaches between 500,000 and 999,999 men.

From all the magazines that fall into these two groups, three will be selected at random from each division, for a total of six titles.

Sampling Stage 2: Selection of Dates
Three issues from each year will be chosen at random from clusters of four months. One magazine will be selected from the January, February, March, April issues, etc. This procedure will be followed for each magazine, yielding a final sample of 30 issues per magazine, or 180 total issues.

Sampling Stage 3: Selection of Content
Every other display ad will be tabulated, regardless of size.

nitions are required for determining these units to allow for greater agreement between coders and fewer "judgment calls."

Certain units of analysis are simpler to count than others. It is easier to determine the number of stories on the "CBS Evening News" that deal with international news than the number of acts of violence in a week of network television because a "story" is a more readily distinguishable unit of analysis than an "act." The beginning and ending of a news story are fairly easy to see, but suppose that a researcher trying to catalog violent content was faced with a long fistfight between three characters? Is the whole sequence one act of violence, or is every blow considered an act? What if a fourth character joins in? Does it then become a different act?

Operational definitions of the unit of analysis should be clear-cut and thorough; the criteria for inclusion should be apparent and easily observed. These goals cannot be accomplished without effort and some trial and error. As a preliminary step, researchers must form a rough draft of a definition and then sample representative content to see whether problems exist. This procedure usually results in further refinement and modification of the operational definition. Table 8.1 presents typical operational definitions of units of analysis taken from mass media research.

Constructing Categories for Analysis

At the heart of any content analysis is the category system used to classify media content. The precise makeup of this system, of course, varies with the topic under study. As Berelson (1952) pointed out, "Particular studies have been productive to the extent that the categories

Table 8.1 Examples of Units of Analysis

Researchers	Title of study	Universe	Sample	Unit
Humphrey & Schuman (1984)	The portrayal of blacks in magazine advertisements, 1950–1982	General interest magazines in 1950 and 1980	Systematically selected issues of *Time* and *Ladies' Home Journal* in 1950 and 1980	All blacks depicted by photograph, cartoon, or realistic line drawings in magazine ads
Shaw (1984)	News about slavery from 1820–1860 in newspapers of South, North, and West	All newspapers published in North, South, and West from 1820–1860	Randomly selected stories from 67 daily and nondaily papers in different geographic regions	Any newspaper story dealing directly or indirectly with slavery
Greenberg, Simmons, Hogan, & Atkin (1980)	Three seasons of television characters	Network prime time fiction, 1975–1977	Composite week of prime time TV shows from 1975 to 1977	Each speaking character on TV
Baker & Walter (1975)	The press as a source of information about activities of a state legislature	U.S. daily newspapers	Eight Wyoming daily newspapers published from 1972 to 1973	All reports on the legislature longer than one sentence
Miller (1975)	The content of news photos: Women's and men's roles	U.S. daily newspapers	Randomly selected photos in the *Washington Post* and *Los Angeles Times* in 1974	Every person appearing in a news photo except individuals less than 13 years old, people in standing shots (columnists), people in crowd shots, and people appearing in photos in special sections

were clearly formulated and well-adapted to the problem and the content."

To be serviceable, all category systems should be mutually exclusive, exhaustive, and reliable. A category system is mutually exclusive if a unit of analysis can be placed in one and only one category. If the researcher discovers that certain units fall simultaneously into two different categories, the definitions of those categories must be revised. For example, suppose researchers attempted to describe the ethnic makeup of prime time television characters using the following category system: (1) black, (2) Jewish, (3) white, (4) American Indian, and (5) other. Obviously, a Jewish person would fall into two categories at once, thus violating the exclusivity rule. Or, to take another example, a researcher might start with the following categories in an attempt to describe the types of programming on network television: (1) situation comedies, (2) children's shows, (3) movies, (4) documentaries, (5) action/adventure programs, (6) quiz and talk shows, and (7) general drama. This list might look acceptable at first glance, but a program such as "Knight Rider" raises questions. Is it to be placed in the action/adventure category or in general drama? Definitions must have a high degree of specificity to handle problems such as this.

In addition to exclusivity, content analysis categories must have the property of **exhaustivity:** there must be an existing slot into which every unit of analysis can be placed. If investigators suddenly find a unit of analysis that does not logically fit into a predefined category, they have a problem with their category system. Taken as a whole, the category system should account for every unit of analysis. Achieving exhaustivity usually is not a great problem in mass media content analysis. If one or two unusual instances are detected, a category labeled "other" or "miscellaneous" usually solves the problem. (If too many items fall into this category, however, a reexamination of the original category definitions is called for; a study with 10% or more of its content in the "other" category is probably overlooking some relevant content characteristic.) An additional way to assure exhaustivity is to dichotomize or trichotomize the content: attempts at problem solving might be defined as aggressive and nonaggressive; statements might be placed in positive, neutral, and negative categories. The most practical way to determine whether a proposed categorization system is exhaustive is to pretest it on a sample of content. If unanticipated items appear, the original scheme requires changes before the primary analysis can begin.

The categorization system should also be reliable; that is, different coders should agree in the great majority of instances about the proper category for each unit of analysis. This agreement is usually quantified in content analysis and is called **intercoder reliability.** Precise category definitions generally increase reliability, while sloppily defined categories tend to lower it. Pretesting the category system for reliability is highly recommended before beginning to process the main body of content. Reliability is crucial in content analysis, as discussed in more detail later in this chapter.

The question of how many categories to include may arise in constructing category systems. Common sense, pretesting, and practice with the coding system are valuable guides to aid the researcher in steering between the two extremes: developing a system with too few categories (so that essential differences are obscured) and defining too many categories (so that only a small percentage falls into each, thus limiting generalizations). As an illustration of too few categories, consider Wurtzel's (1975) study of programming on public access television. One of the preliminary categories was labeled "informational," and the data indicated that more than 70% of the content fell into this classification. As a result, Wurtzel subdivided the category into seven informational headings (ethnic, community, health, consumer, etc.). An example of the opposite extreme is the attempt made by Dominick, Richman, and Wurtzel (1979) to describe the types of problems encountered by characters in prime time television shows popular with children. They originally developed seven categories, including problems that dealt with romance, problems between friends, and other emotional problems arising out of relationships (with siblings, co-workers, or others). Preliminary analysis, however, indicated that only a small fraction of problems fell into the "friendship" and "other emotional" slots. Consequently, these three categories were combined into a single classification labeled "problems dealing with romance, sentiment, and other emotions." As a general rule, many researchers suggest that too many initial categories are preferable to too few, since it is usually easier to combine several categories than it is to subdivide a large one after the units have been coded.

Establishing a Quantification System

Quantification in content analysis can involve all four of the levels of data measurement discussed in Chapter 3, although usually only nominal, interval, and ratio data are used. At the nominal level, researchers simply count the frequency of occurrence of the units in each category. Gantz, Gartenberg, and Rainbow (1980) employed nominal measurement to determine the percentage of elderly people appearing in different categories of magazine advertisements: 14% in "corporate image" advertisements, 12% liquor, 11% travel, and so on. The topics of conversation on daytime television, the themes of newspaper editorials, and the occupation of prime time television characters can all be quantified by means of nominal measurement.

At the interval level, it is possible to develop scales for coders to use to rate certain attributes of characters or situations. For example, in a study dealing with the images of women in commercials, each character might be rated by coders on several scales, such as:

```
independent  _____ : _____ : _____ : _____ : _____  dependent
  dominant   _____ : _____ : _____ : _____ : _____  submissive
```

Scales such as these add depth and texture to a content analysis and are perhaps more interesting than the surface data obtained through nominal measurement. However, rating scales inject subjectivity into the analysis and may lower intercoder reliability unless careful training is undertaken. Chang (1975), for example, constructed an interval scale based on the degree of liking movie critics had for certain films.

Ratio level measurements in mass media research generally are applied to space and time. In the print media, column-inch measurements are used to analyze editorials, advertisements, and stories about particular events or phenomena. In television and radio, ratio level measurements are made concerning time: the number of commercial minutes, the types of programs on the air, the amount of the program day devoted to programs of various types, and so on.

Coding the Content

Placing a unit of analysis into a content category is called **coding.** It is the most time-consuming and least glamorous part of a content analysis. Individuals who do the coding are called *coders.* The number of coders involved in a content analysis is typically small; a brief examination of a sampling of recent content analyses indicates that typically two to six coders are used.

Careful training of coders, which usually results in a more reliable analysis, is an integral task in any content analysis. Although the investigator may have a firm grasp of the operational definitions and the category schemes, coders may not share this close knowledge. Consequently, they must become thoroughly familiar with the study's mechanics and peculiarities. To this end, researchers should plan several lengthy training sessions in which sample content is examined and coded. These sessions are used to revise definitions, clarify category boundaries, and revamp coding sheets until the coders are comfortable with the materials and procedure.

When this stage has been reached, a pilot study is done to check intercoder reliability. The pilot study should be conducted with a fresh set of coders who are given some initial training to impart familiarity with the instructions and methods of the study. Some would argue that fresh coders are to be preferred for this task because intercoder reliability between coders who have worked for long periods of time developing the coding scheme might be artificially high. As Lorr and McNair (1966) suggest, "Interrater agreement for a new set of judges given a reasonable but practical amount of training . . . would represent a more realistic index of reliability."

To facilitate coding, standardized sheets are usually used (Figure 8.2). These sheets allow coders to classify the data by simply

Figure 8.2 Sample form of standardized coding sheet

Coder Initials _____   Program Code _____

   PROBLEM-SOLVING ATTEMPT DESCRIPTION SHEET

1. Program code number   01   02   03   04   06   07

2. Name of character attempting solution _____
   (NOTE: ANSWER QUESTIONS 3-8 ONLY IF INFORMATION HAS NOT BEEN PREVI-
   OUSLY RECORDED ON CHARACTER DESCRIPTION SHEET)

3. Is character   4. Is character   5. Is character
   _____ hero   _____ human   _____ male
   _____ villain   _____ animal   _____ female
                            _____ other (specify)

6. Is character   7. Does character have magical or
   _____ kid (2–11)   unrealistic powers?
   _____ teen (12–19)   _____ yes _____ no
   _____ young adult (20–49)
   _____ mature adult (50 +)

---

placing check marks or slashes in predetermined spaces. If data are to be tabulated by hand, the coding sheets should be constructed to allow for rapid tabulation. Some studies code data on 4 inch × 6 inch index cards, with information recorded across the top of the card. This enables researchers to sort the information quickly into categories. Templates are available to speed the measurement of newspaper space. Researchers who work with television generally videotape the programs and allow coders to stop and start the tape at their own pace while coding data. If a tape machine is not available, the coding procedure has to be simplified, since the coders have no opportunity for a second look.

When a computer is used in tabulating data, the data are usually transferred directly to computer coding sheets or perhaps mark-sense forms or optical scan sheets (answer sheets scored by computer). These forms save time and reduce data errors.

Computers are useful not only in the data tabulation phase of a content analysis, but also in the actual coding process. Computers will perform with unerring accuracy any coding task in which the classification rules are unambiguous. Computers can do simple tasks such as recognizing words or even syllables as they occur in a sample of text, with extreme speed. Wilhoit and Sherrill (1968), for example, instructed a computer to recognize the names of U.S. senators as they appeared in wire service copy. Of course the drawback to this approach is that the body of copy to be scanned must be in computer-readable form. In many instances, transcribing the original copy into the necessary format would require far more effort than counting the data manually. This situation may change, however, with the advent of teletext or viewdata systems, which supply copy that is already machine-readable, or with the arrival of high-speed scanning devices. In any case, the use of computers in content analysis is now widely accepted. For more information, consult Gerbner, Holsti, Krippendorf, Paisley, and Stone (1969) or Krippendorf (1980).

Television content can be coded with computer assistance by using event recorders that tabulate frequency and duration data. Coders push a series of buttons corresponding to the appropriate unit of analysis and their responses are electronically recorded. Bryant, Hezel, and Zillmann (1979) used such an arrangement to code humorous events in children's educational TV programs.

Analyzing the Data

The descriptive statistics discussed in Chapter 10–12 and in Appendix 2 such as percentages, means, modes, and medians, are appropriate for content analysis. If hypothesis tests are planned, common inferential statistics (results are generalized to the population) are acceptable. The chi-square test is the most commonly used, since content analysis data tend to be nominal in form; however, if the data meet the requirements of interval or ratio levels, a t-test, ANOVA, or Pearson's r may be appropriate. Other statistical analyses are discussed by Krippendorf (1980), such as discriminant analysis, cluster analysis, and contextual analysis.

Interpreting the Results

If an investigator is testing specific hypotheses concerning the relationships between variables, the interpretation will be fairly evident. However, if the study is descriptive, questions about the meaning or importance of the results may arise. Researchers are often faced with a "fully/only" dilemma. Suppose, for example, that a content analysis of children's television programs reveals that 30% of the commercials were for snacks and candy. What is the researcher to conclude? Is this a high or a low amount? Should the researcher report, "*Fully* 30% of the commercials fell into this category," or should the same percentage be presented as: "*Only* 30% of the commercials fell into this category"? Clearly, the investigator needs some benchmark for comparison. Thirty percent may indeed be a high figure when compared to commercials for other products or for those shown during adult programs.

In a study done by one of the authors, the amount of network news time devoted to the various states was tabulated. It was determined that California and New York receive 19 and 18%, respectively, of non-Washington, DC, national news coverage. By themselves, these numbers are interesting, but their significance is somewhat unclear. In an attempt to aid interpretation, each state's relative news time was compared to its population, and an "attention index" was created by subtracting the ratio of each state's population to the national population from its percentage of news coverage. This provided a listing of states that were either "over-covered" or "under-covered" (Dominick, 1977).

Reliability

The concept of reliability is crucial to content analysis. If a content analysis is to be objective, its measures and procedures must be reliable. Reliability is present when repeated measurement of the same material result in similar decisions or conclusions. If the results fail to achieve reliability, something is amiss with the coders, the coding instructions, the category definitions, the unit of analysis, or some combination of these. To achieve acceptable levels of reliability the following steps are recommended.

1. Define category boundaries with maximum detail. A group of vague or ambiguously defined categories makes reliability extremely difficult to achieve. Examples of units of analysis and a brief explanation for each are necessary for coders to fully understand the procedure.

2. Train the coders. Training sessions in using the coding instrument and the category system conducted before the data are collected can help to eliminate methodological problems. During these sessions, the group as a whole should code sample material; afterward, they should discuss the results as well as the purpose of the study. Disagreements should be analyzed as they occur. The end result of the training sessions is a "bible" of detailed instructions and coding examples, and each coder should receive a copy.

3. Conduct a pilot study. Select a subsample of the content universe under consideration and let independent coders categorize it. These data are useful for two reasons: poorly defined categories can be detected, and chronically dissenting coders can be identified. To illustrate these problems, consider Tables 8.2 and 8.3.

In Table 8.2, the definitions for Categories I and IV appear satisfactory. All four coders placed Units 1, 3, 7, and 11 in the first category; in Category IV, Item 14 is classified consistently by three of the four coders and Items 4 and 9 by all four coders. The confusion apparently lies in the boundaries between Categories II and III. Two coders put Items 2, 6, and 13 in Category II and two placed them in Category III. The definitions of these two categories require reexamination and perhaps revision because of this ambiguity.

Table 8.2 Detecting Poorly Defined Categories from Pilot Study Data *

	Categories			
Coders	I	II	III	IV
A	1,3,7,11	2,5,6,8,12,13	10	4,9,14
B	1,3,7,11	5,8,10,12	2,6,13	4,9,14
C	1,3,7,11	2,8,12,13	5,6,10	4,9,14
D	1,3,7,11	5,6	2,8,10,12,13,14	4,9

* Arabic numerals refer to items.

Table 8.3 illustrates the problem of the chronic disagreer. Coders A and B agree seven times out of eight. Coders B and C, however, agree only two times out of eight, and coders A and C agree only once. Obviously, Coder C is going to be a problem. As a rule, the investigator would carefully reexplain to this coder the rules used in categorization and examine the reasons for his or her consistent deviation. If the problem persists, however, it may be necessary to dismiss the coder from the analysis.

Assuming that the initial test of reliability yields satisfactory results, the main body of data is coded. When the coding is complete, it is recommended that a subsample of the data, probably between 10% and 25%, be reanalyzed by independent coders to calculate an overall intercoder reliability coefficient.

Intercoder reliability can be calculated by several methods. Holsti (1969) reported a formula for determining the reliability of nominal data in terms of percentage of agreement:

$$\text{Reliability} = \frac{2M}{N_1 + N_2}$$

where M is the number of coding decisions on which two coders agree,

Table 8.3 Identifying a Chronic Dissenter from Pilot Study Data *

		Coders		
Items	A	B	C	
1	I	I	II	
2	III	III	I	
3	II	II	II	
4	IV	IV	III	
5	I	II	II	
6	IV	IV	I	
7	I	I	III	
8	II	II	I	

* Roman numerals refer to categories.

and N_1 and N_2 refer to the total number of coding decisions by the first and second coder, respectively. Thus, if two coders judge a sub-sample of 50 units and agree on 35 of them, the calculation is:

$$\text{Reliability} = \frac{2(35)}{50 + 50} = .70$$

This method is straightforward and easy to apply, but it is criticized because it does not take into account the occurrence of some coder agreement strictly by chance, an amount that is a function of the number of categories in the analysis. For example, a two-category system should obtain 50% reliability simply by chance; a five-category system would generate a 20% agreement by chance; and so on. To take this into account, Scott (1955) developed the *pi* index, which corrects for the number of categories used and also for the probable frequency of use.

$$\text{pi} = \frac{\% \text{ observed agreement} - \% \text{ expected agreement}}{1 - \% \text{ expected agreement}}$$

A hypothetical example will demonstrate the use of this index. Suppose that two coders are assigning magazine advertisements to the six categories shown and obtain the following distribution.

Category	Percent of All Ads
1 Prestige appeal	30%
2 Economic appeal	20%
3 Affiliation appeal	20%
4 Fear appeal	15%
5 Utilitarian appeal	10%
6 Other appeal	5%

First, the percentage of expected agreement must be calculated. This is the sum of the squared percentages of all categories. Thus, % expected agreement = $(.3)^2 + (.2)^2 + (.2)^2 (.15)^2 + (.1)^2 + (.05)^2 = .20$. If the coders agree on 90% of their classifications (% observed agreement), *pi* can be calculated as follows:

$$\text{pi} = \frac{.90 - .20}{1 - .20} = .875$$

Fless (1971) extended this notion to cases of the same content seen simultaneously by a number of coders.

Estimating reliability with interval data requires certain care. Several studies have used the correlation method called the Pearson *r*, a method that investigates the relationship between two items. The Pearson *r* can range from -1.00 to $+1.00$. In estimating reliability in content analysis, however, if this measure has a high value, it may

Table 8.4 False Equivalence as a Reliability Measure When *r* Is Used

	Situation I				Situation II	
Items	Coder 1	Coder 2		Items	Coder 1	Coder 2
1	1	1		1	1	4
2	2	2		2	2	5
3	3	3		3	3	6
4	3	3		4	3	6
5	4	4		5	4	7
6	5	5		6	5	8
7	6	6		7	6	9
8	6	6		8	6	9
9	7	7		9	7	10
10	7	7		10	7	10
	$r = 1.00$				$r = 1.00$	

indicate either that the coders were in agreement or that their ratings were associated in some systematic manner.

For example, suppose an interval scale ranging from 1 to 10 is used to score the degree of favorability of a news item to some person or topic (a score of "1" represents very positive; "10" represents very negative). Assume that two coders are independently scoring the same 10 items. Table 8.4 illustrates two possible outcomes. In Situation I, the coders agree on every item, and *r* equals 1.00. In Situation II, the coders disagree on every item by three scale positions, yet *r* still equals 1.00. Clearly, the uses of this estimate are not equally reliable in the two situations.

Krippendorf (1980) circumvents this dilemma by presenting what might be termed an "all-purpose reliability measure," *alpha*, which can be used for nominal, ordinal, interval, and ratio scales and for more than one coder. Although somewhat difficult to calculate, *alpha* is the equivalent of Scott's *pi* at the nominal level with two coders and represents an improvement over *r* in the interval situation.

What is an acceptable level of intercoder reliability? This depends on the research context and the type of information coded. In some instances little coder judgment is needed to place units into categories (e.g., counting the number of words per sentence in a newspaper story or tabulating the number of times a network correspondent contributes a story to the evening news), and coding becomes a mechanical or clerical task. In this context, one would expect a fairly high degree of reliability, perhaps approaching 100%, since coder disagreements would probably be the result of carelessness or fatigue. If, however, a certain amount of interpretation is involved, reliability estimates are typically lower. In general, the greater the amount of judgmental leeway given to coders, the lower the reliability coefficients will be. As a rule of thumb, most published content analyses typically report a minimum reliability coefficient of about 90% or above when using Holsti's formula, and about .75 or above when using *pi* or *alpha*.

Note that the discussion above assumed that at least two independent coders categorized the same content. In some situations, however, *intracoder* reliability might also be assessed. These circumstances occur most frequently when only a few coders are used because extensive training must be employed to ensure the detection of subtle message elements. To test intracoder reliability, the same individual codes a set of data twice, at different times, and the reliability statistics are computed using the two sets of results.

Validity

In addition to being reliable, a content analysis must yield valid results. As indicated in Chapter 3, validity is usually defined as the degree to which an instrument actually measures what it sets out to measure. This raises special concerns in content analysis. In the first place, validity is intimately connected with the procedures used in the analysis. If the sampling design is faulty, if categories overlap, or if reliability is low, the results of the study probably possess little validity.

Additionally, the adequacy of the definitions used in a content analysis bears directly on the question of validity. For example, a great deal of content analysis has focused on the depiction of televised violence; different investigators have offered different definitions of what constitutes a violent act. The question of validity emerges when one tries to decide whether each of the various definitions actually encompasses what one might logically refer to as violence. The continuing debate between Gerbner and the television networks vividly illustrates this problem. The definition of violence propounded by Gerbner and his associates in 1977 includes accidents, acts of nature, or violence that might occur in a fantasy or a humorous setting. However, network analysts do not consider these phenomena to be acts of violence (Blank, 1977). Both Gerbner and the networks offer arguments in support of their decisions. Which analysis is the more valid? The answer depends in part on the plausibility of the rationale that underlies the definitions.

This discussion relates closely to a technique traditionally called *face validity*. This validation technique assumes that an instrument adequately measures what it purports to measure if the categories are rigidly and satisfactorily defined and if the procedures of the analysis have been adequately conducted. Most descriptive content analyses usually rely on face validity, but other techniques are available.

The use of *concurrent validity* in content analysis is exemplified in a study by Clarke and Blankenburg (1972). These investigators attempted a longitudinal study of violence in television shows dating back to 1952. Unfortunately, few copies of the early programs were available, and the authors were forced to use program summaries in *TV Guide.* To establish that such summaries would indeed disclose the presence of violence, the authors compared the results of a subsample of programs coded from these synopses to the results obtained from a direct viewing of the same programs. The results were sufficiently related to convince the authors that their measurement technique was valid. However, this method of checking validity is only as good as the criterion measurement: if the direct viewing technique is itself invalid, there is little value in showing that synopsis coding is related to it.

Only a few studies have attempted to document *construct validity.* One instance involves the use of "sensationalism" in news stories. This construct has been measured by semantic differentials and factor analysis (see Appendix 2), in an attempt to isolate its underlying dimensions, and related to relevant message characteristics (Tannenbaum, 1962; Tannenbaum & Lynch, 1960). Another technique that investigators occasionally use is *predictive validity.* For example, certain content attributes from wire stories might allow a researcher to predict which items will be carried by a newspaper and which will not.

In summary, several different methods to assess validity are used in content analysis. The most common is face validity, which is appropriate for some studies. It is recommended, however, that the content analyst also examine other methods to establish the validity of a given study.

Examples of Content Analysis

Table 8.5, which summarizes four recent content analyses, lists the purpose of the analysis, the sample, the unit of analysis, illustrative categories, and the type of statistic used for each study.

Summary

Content analysis is a popular technique in mass media research. Many of the steps involved in laboratory and survey studies are also found in content analysis; in particular, sampling procedures need to be objective and detailed, and operational definitions are mandatory. Coders must be carefully trained to ensure accurate data. Interpreting a content analysis, however, requires more caution: no claims about the impact of the content can be drawn from an analysis of the message in the absence of study that examines the audience. In the future, the computer will become an integral part of many content analyses.

Table 8.5 Examples of Content Analysis Studies

Researchers	Purpose of study	Sample	Units of analysis	Representative categories	Statistic
Breed & Defoe (1981)	To examine the motives, contents, and outcomes of episodes of drinking behavior on television	225 episodes of 30 prime time situation comedies and dramas	Behaviors in a scene that portrayed alcohol consumption	Consequences of drinking: strained relationships, danger to self, harm to self, and so on	Chi-square
Bush, Hair, & Bush (1983)	To examine the uses of animation in adult-oriented and child-oriented TV advertising	36 hours of TV content from the three major networks and three cable networks during the fall of 1975	All advertisements in the sample	Level of animation: totally animated, mixed, nonanimated	Chi-square
Greenberg & Atkin (1983)	To describe driving behavior as portrayed on TV	One week of prime time programming in each of four consecutive years beginning in 1975	All driving scenes lasting at least 5 seconds, excluding the opening credits	Driving acts: quick braking, quick acceleration, stunt driving, speeding, and so on	Frequencies; percentages
Sparkes (1978)	To describe the flow of news between the United States and Canada	Two composite weeks of issues from 10 Canadian papers and 29 U.S. papers drawn from the first 6 months of 1975	All news items in each issue of each paper	Sources of news: staff, AP, UPI, Reuters, etc.	Percentages; r correlation

Questions and Problems for Further Investigation

1. Define a unit of analysis that could be used in a content analysis of:
   a. Problem-solving on television
   b. News emphasis in a daily and a weekly newspaper
   c. Changes in the values expressed by popular songs
   d. The role of women in editorial cartoons
2. Using the topics in Question 1, define a sample selection procedure that would be appropriate for each.
3. Generate two content analyses that could be used as preliminary tests for an audience study.
4. Conduct a brief content analysis of one of the topics listed below. (Train a second individual in the use of the category system that you develop and have this person independently code a subsample of the content.)
   a. Similarities and differences between local newscasts on two television stations
   b. Changes in the subject matter of movies from 1970 to 1980
   c. The treatment of the elderly on network television
5. Using the topic selected in Question 4, compute a reliability coefficient for the items that were scored by both coders.

References and Suggested Readings

Adams, W., & Ferber, P. (1977). Television interview shows: The politics of visibility. *Journal of Broadcasting 21*, 141–151.

Adams, W., & Schreibman, F. (1978). *Television network news: Issues in content research*. Washington, DC: George Washington University.

Attkisson, C., Handler, L., & Shrader, R. (1969). The use of figure drawing to assess religious values. *Journal of Psychology, 71*, 27–31.

Baker, K., & Walter, B. (1975). The press as a source of information about activities of a state legislature. *Journalism Quarterly, 52*, 735–740.

Benze, J., & Declercq, E. (1985). Content of television political spot ads for female candidates. *Journalism Quarterly, 62*(2), 278–283.

Berelson, B. (1952). *Content analysis in communication research*. New York: Free Press.

Blank, D. (1977). The Gerbner violence profile. *Journal of Broadcasting, 21*, 273–279.

Breed, W., & Defoe, J. (1981). The portrayal of the drinking process on prime time television. *Journal of Communication, 31*, 58–67.

Bryant, J., Hezel, R., & Zillmann, D. (1979). Humor in children's educational television. *Communication Education, 28*(4), 49–59.

Bush, A., Hair, J., & Bush, R. (1983). A content analysis of animation in television advertising. *Journal of Advertising, 12*(4), 20–26.

Chadwick, B., Bahr, H., & Albrecht, S. (1984). *Social science research methods.* Englewood Cliffs, NJ: Prentice-Hall.

Chang, W. (1975). A typology study of movie critics. *Journalism Quarterly, 52*(4), 721–725.

Clarke, D., & Blankenburg, W. (1972). Trends in violent content in selected mass media. In G. Comstock & E. Rubinstein (Eds.), *Television and social behavior: Media content and control.* Washington, DC: U.S. Government Printing Office.

Comstock, G. (1975). *Television and human behavior: The key studies.* Santa Monica, CA: Rand Corporation.

Davis, F. (1951). Crime news in Colorado newspapers. *American Journal of Sociology, 57,* 325–330.

DeFleur, M. (1964). Occupational roles as portrayed on television. *Public Opinion Quarterly, 28,* 57–74.

DeFleur, M., & DeFleur, L. (1967). The relative contribution of television as a learning source for children's occupational knowledge. *American Sociological Review, 32,* 777–789.

Dominick, J. (1973). Crime and law enforcement on prime time television. *Public Opinion Quarterly, 37,* 241–250.

Dominick, J. (1977). Geographic bias in national TV news. *Journal of Communication, 27,* 94–99.

Dominick, J., Richman, S., & Wurtzel, A. (1979). Problem-solving in TV shows popular with children: Assertion vs. aggression. *Journalism Quarterly, 56,* 455–463.

Dominick, J., Wurtzel, A., & Lometti, G. (1975). Television journalism vs. show business: A content analysis of eyewitness news. *Journalism Quarterly, 52,* 213–218.

Fless, J. L. (1971). Measuring nominal scale agreement among many raters. *Psychological Bulletin, 76,* 378–382.

Gantz, W., Gartenberg, H., & Rainbow, C. (1980). Approaching invisibility: The portrayal of the elderly in magazine advertisements. *Journal of Communication, 30,* 56–60.

Gerbner, G. (1969). The television world of violence. In D. Lange, R. Baker, & S. Ball (Eds.), *Mass media and violence.* Washington, DC: U.S. Government Printing Office.

Gerbner, G. Gross, L., Jackson-Beeck, M., Jeffries-Fox, S., & Signorielli, N. (1977). One more time: An analysis of the CBS "Final Comments on the Violence Profile." *Journal of Broadcasting, 21,* 297–304.

Gerbner, G., Gross, L., Signorielli, N., Morgan, M., & Jackson-Beeck, M. (1979). The demonstration of power: Violence Profile No. 10. *Journal of Communication, 29,* 177–198.

Gerbner, G., Holsti, O., Krippendorf, K., Paisley, W., & Stone, P. (1969). *The analysis of communication content.* New York: John Wiley.

Greenberg, B. (1983). *Mexican–Americans and the mass media.* Norwood, NJ: Ablex Publishers.

Greenberg, B., & Atkin, C. (1983). The portrayal of driving on television. *Journal of Communication, 33*(2), 44–55.

Greenberg, B., & Kahn, S. (1970). Blacks in *Playboy* cartoons. *Journalism Quarterly, 47,* 557–560.

Greenberg, B., Simmons, K., Hogan, L., & Atkin, C. (1980). Three seasons of television characters: A demographic analysis. *Journal of Broadcasting, 24,* 49–60.

Hatch, D., & Hatch, M. (1947). Criteria of social status as derived from marriage announcements in the *New York Times. American Sociological Review, 12,* 396–403.

Hennessee, J., & Nicholson, J. (1972, May 28). NOW Says: TV commercials insult women. *New York Times Magazine,* pp. 12–14.

Holsti, O. (1969). *Content analysis for the social sciences and humanities.* Reading, MA: Addison-Wesley.

Humphrey, R., & Schuman, H. (1984). The portrayal of blacks in magazine advertisements, 1950–1982. *Public Opinion Quarterly, 48,* 551–563.

Katzman, N. (1972). Television soap operas. *Public Opinion Quarterly, 36,* 200–212.

Kerlinger, F. (1973). *Foundations of behavioral research* (2nd ed.). New York: Holt, Rinehart & Winston.

Krippendorf, K. (1980). *Content analysis: An introduction to its methodology.* Beverly Hills, CA: Sage Publications.

Lorr, M., & McNair, D. (1966). Methods relating to evaluation of therapeutic outcome. In L. Gottschalk & A. Auerbach (Eds.), *Methods of research in psychotherapy.* Englewood Cliffs, NJ: Prentice-Hall.

Lowry, D. (1981). Alcohol consumption patterns and consequences on prime time network TV. *Journalism Quarterly, 58*(1), 3–9.

Merritt, S., & Gross, H. (1978). Women's page lifestyle editors: Does sex make a difference? *Journalism Quarterly, 55,* 508–514.

Mertz, R. (1970). Analysis of the portrayal of older Americans in commercial television programming. Paper presented to the International Communication Association, Minneapolis, MN.

Miller, S. (1975). The content of news photos: Women's and men's roles. *Journalism Quarterly, 52,* 70–75.

Scott, W. (1955). Reliability of content analysis: The case of nominal scale coding. *Public Opinion Quarterly, 17,* 321–325.

Shaw, D. (1984). News about slavery from 1820–60 in newspapers of South, North, and West. *Journalism Quarterly, 61,* 483–492.

Sparkes, V. (1978). The flow of news between Canada and the United States. *Journalism Quarterly, 55,* 260–268.

Stempel, G. (1952). Sample size for classifying subject matter in dailies. *Journalism Quarterly, 29,* 333–334.

Tannenbaum, P. (1962). Sensationalism: Some objective message correlates. *Journalism Quarterly, 39,* 317–323.

Tannenbaum, P., & Greenberg, B. (1968). Mass communication. *Annual Review of Psychology, 19,* 351–386.

Tannenbaum, P., & Lynch, M. (1960). Sensationalism: The concept and its measurement. *Journalism Quarterly, 37,* 381–392.

Walizer, M. H., & Wienir, P. L. (1978). *Research methods and analysis.* New York: Harper & Row.

Wilhoit, G., & Sherrill, K. (1968). Wire service visibility of U.S. senators. *Journalism Quarterly, 45,* 42–48.

Wimmer, R., & Haynes, R. (1978). Statistical analyses in the *Journal of Broadcasting. Journal of Broadcasting, 22,* 241–248.

Wurtzel, A. (1975). Public access cable television: Programming. *Journal of Communication, 25,* 15–21.

Yule, G. (1944). *The statistical study of literary vocabulary.* Cambridge, England: Cambridge University Press.

Zillmann, D., & Bryant, J. (1983). Uses and effects of humor in educational ventures. In P. McGhee and J. Goldstein (Eds.), *Handbook of humor research* (Vol. II). New York: Springer-Verlag.

Longitudinal Research

In **cross-sectional research** data are collected from a representative sample at only one point in time. Most of the research discussed to this point has been cross sectional. **Longitudinal research** involves the collection of data at different points in time. Although longitudinal investigations appear relatively infrequently in mass communication research, several longitudinal studies have been among the most influential and provocative in the field. For example, of the 11 studies Lowery and DeFleur (1983) consider to be milestones in the evolution of mass communication research, 3 represent the longitudinal approach: Lazarsfeld, Berelson, and Gaudet, *The People's Choice* (1944), which introduced the two-step flow model; Katz and Lazarsfeld, *Personal Influence* (1955), which examined the role of opinion leaders; and the Surgeon General's Report on Television and Social Behavior, particularly as used in the study by Lefkowitz et al. (1972), which found evidence suggesting that viewing violence on television caused subsequent aggressive behavior. Other longitudinal studies also figure prominently in the field, including the elaborate panel study done for NBC by Milavsky et al. (1982), discussed in greater detail below, and the studies of mass media in elections as summarized by Peterson (1980). Thus, although not widely used, the longitudinal design can produce results that are both theoretically and socially important.

Development

Longitudinal studies have a long history in the behavioral sciences; in psychology in particular, they have been used to trace the development of children and the clinical progress of patients. In medicine, longitudinal studies have been widely used to study the impact of disease and treatment methods. The pioneering work in political science was done by sociologists studying the 1924 election campaign. Somewhat later, Newcomb (1943) conducted repeated interviews of Bennington College students from 1935 to 1939 to examine the impact of a liberal college environment on respondents who came from conservative families.

In the mass communication area, the first major longitudinal study was that of Lazarsfeld, Berelson, and Gaudet (1944) during the 1940 presidential election. Lazarsfeld pioneered the use of the panel technique in which the same individuals are interviewed several times. Lazarsfeld also developed the use of the 16-fold table, one of the earliest statistical techniques to attempt to derive causation from longitudinal survey data. Another form of longitudinal research, **trend studies** (in which different people are asked the same question at different points in time) began showing up in mass media research in the 1960s. One of the most publicized trend studies was the continuing survey of media credibility done by the Roper organization. Other trend studies by Gallup and Harris, among others, also gained notoriety during this time.

More recently, the notion of cohort analysis, a method of research developed by demographers, has achieved some popularity. **Cohort analysis** involves the study of specific populations, usually all those born during a given period, as they change over time. The other significant developments in the longitudinal area have taken place in analysis methods as more sophisticated techniques for analyzing longitudinal data were developed. **Cross-lagged correlation** was widely discussed during the 1960s and 1970s. Path analysis was used to chart causal directions in panel data and log–linear models were also shown to have relevance in longitudinal studies. LISREL (LInear Structural RELations), a model developed by Joreskog (1973), is another statistical technique that has broad application in longitudinal analysis.

Types of Longitudinal Studies

The three main types of longitudinal studies are the trend study, the cohort analysis, and the panel study. Each will be discussed in turn.

Trend Studies

The trend study is probably the most common longitudinal study in mass media research. Recall that a trend study samples different groups of people drawn at different times from the same population. Trend studies are common around presidential election time. Suppose that 3 months before an election a sample of adults is drawn; 57% report that they intend to vote for Candidate A and 43% for Candidate B. A month later a different sample, drawn from the same population, shows a change: 55% report that they are going to vote for A and 45% for B. This is a simple example of a trend study. Trend studies provide information about net changes. In the example, we know that in the period under consideration, Candidate A lost 2% of his support. We don't know how many people changed from B to A or from A to B, nor do we know how many stayed with their original choice. We only know that the net result was a 2-point loss for A. To determine both the gross and the net change, a panel study would be necessary.

Trend studies are valuable in describing long-term changes in a population. Both university and commercial research firms have asked some of the same questions on many national and statewide surveys. For example, in the United States, a question about satisfaction with the president's performance has been asked hundreds of times dating back to the administration of Harry Truman. *Public Opinion Quarterly* has a regular section entitled "The Polls," which allows researchers to construct trend data on selected topics. In recent issues, the following trend data have appeared: (1) a 25-year sampling of attitudes toward Israel and the Arab nations, (2) data spanning 46 years of attitudes toward the death penalty, and (3) 20-year trend data about attitudes toward the Soviet Union. Of specific interest in the field of mass communication research are the trend data on changing patterns in media credibility, compiled for more than three decades by the Roper organization for the Television Information Office. The Violence Index constructed by George Gerbner and his associates (Gerbner et al., 1979) is another well-known trend study.

Trend studies can be based on a comparison of survey data originally constructed for other purposes. Of course, in utilizing such data, the researcher needs to recognize any differences in question wording, context, sampling, or analysis techniques that might differ from one survey to the next. Hyman (1972) provides extensive guidance on the secondary analysis of survey data. The growing movement to preserve data archives and the ability of microcomputer networks that make retrieval and sharing much easier suggest that this technique will gain in popularity. Secondary analysis saves time, money, and personnel; it also makes it possible to understand long-term change. In fact, mass media researchers might want to consider what socially significant data concerning media behaviors should be collected and archived at regular intervals. Economists have developed regular trend indicators to gauge the health of the economy, but mass communication scholars have developed almost no analogous social indicator of media or audience conduct.

Cohort Analysis

To the Romans, a "cohort" was one of the 10 divisions of a military legion. For research purposes, a *cohort* is any group of individuals who are linked in some way or who have experienced the same significant life event within a given period of time. Usually the "significant life event" is birth, in which case the group is termed a birth cohort. There are, however, many other kinds of cohorts, including marriage (for example, all those married between 1975 and 1984), divorce (for example, all those divorced between 1980 and 1985), educational (the

Table 9.1 Percentage Who Regularly Read News Magazines

	Year		
Age	1980	1984	1988
18–21	15	12	10
22–25	34	32	28
26–29	48	44	35

class of 1982), and others (all those who attended college during the Vietnam era).

Any study in which there are measures of some characteristic of one or more cohorts at two or more points in time is a cohort analysis. Cohort analysis attempts to identify a *cohort effect*: Are changes in the dependent variable due to aging or are they present because the sample members belong to the same cohort? To illustrate, suppose that 50% of college seniors reported that they regularly read news magazines, whereas only 10% of college freshmen in the same survey made this report. How might the difference be accounted for? One possible explanation is that freshmen change their reading habits as they progress through college. Another is that this year's freshman class is composed of people with reading habits different from those who were enrolled 3 years ago.

There are two ways to distinguish between these explanations. One way involves questioning the same students during their freshman year and again during their senior year and comparing their second set of responses to those of a group of current freshmen. (This is the familiar panel design, which is discussed in detail below.) Or, a researcher can take two samples of the student population, at Time 1 and Time 2. Each survey has different participants—the same people are not questioned again as in a panel study—but each sample represents the same group of people at different points in their college career. Although we have no direct information about which individuals changed their habits over time, we do have information on how the cohort of people who entered college at Time 1 had changed by the time they became seniors. If 15% of the freshmen at Time 1 read news magazines and if 40% of the seniors at Time 2 read them, we can deduce that students change their reading habits as they progress through college.

Typically, a cohort analysis involves data in more than one cohort, and a standard table for presenting the data from multiple cohorts was proposed by Glenn (1977). Table 9.1 is such a table. It displays news magazine readership for a number of birth cohorts. Note that the column variable (read down) is age, and the row variable (read across) is the year of data collection. Because the interval between any two periods of measurement (that is, surveys) corresponds to the age

Table 9.2 Cohort Table Showing Pure Age Effects

Age	Year		
	1980	1984	1988
18–21	15	15	15
22–25	20	20	20
26–29	25	25	25
Average	20	20	20

class intervals, cohorts can be followed over time. When the intervals are not equal, the progress of cohorts cannot be followed with precision.

Three different types of comparisons can be made from such a table. Reading down a single column is analogous to a cross-sectional study and represents comparisons among different age cohorts at one point in time (intercohort differences). Trends at each age level that occur when cohorts replace one another can be seen by reading across the rows. Third, reading diagonally toward the right reveals changes in a single cohort from one point in time to another (an intracohort study). Thus Table 9.1 suggests that news magazine reading increases with age (reading down each column). In each successive time period, the percentage of younger readers has diminished (reading across the rows), and the increase in reading percentage as each cohort ages is about the same (reading diagonally to the right).

The variations in the percentages in the table can be categorized into three different kinds of effects (for the moment we will assume that there is no variation due to sampling error or to changing composition in each cohort as it ages). First, there are the influences produced by the sheer fact of maturation or growing older, called age effects. Second, there are the influences associated with members in a certain birth cohort (cohort effects), and finally there are the influences associated with each particular time period (period effects).

To recognize these various influences at work, examine the hypothetical data in Tables 9.2, 9.3, and 9.4. Again, let us assume that the dependent variable is the percentage of the sample who regularly read a news magazine. Table 9.2 demonstrates a "pure" age effect. Note that the rows are identical, and the columns show the same pattern of variation. Apparently it doesn't matter when a person was born or in which period he or she lived. As the individual gets older, news magazine readership increases. For ease of illustration, Table 9.2 illustrates a linear effect, but this is not necessarily the only effect possible. For example, readership might increase from the first age interval to the next and increase from the second to the third.

Table 9.3 demonstrates a "pure" period effect. There is no variation by age at any period—the columns are identical, and the var-

Table 9.3 Cohort Table Showing Period Effects

	Year		
Age	1980	1984	1988
18–21	15	20	25
22–25	15	20	25
26–29	15	20	25
Average	15	20	25

iations from one period to the next are identical. Furthermore, the change in each cohort (read diagonally to the right) is the same as the average change in the total population. The data in this table suggest that year of birth and maturation have little to do with news magazine reading. In this hypothetical case, the time period seems to be most important. Knowing when the survey was done enables the researcher to predict the variation in news magazine reading.

A "pure" cohort effect is illustrated in Table 9.4. Here the cohort diagonals are constant and the variation from younger to older respondents is in the opposite direction from the variation from earlier to later survey periods. In this table, the key variable seems to be date of birth. Among those who were born between 1959 and 1962, news magazine readership was 15% regardless of their age or when they were surveyed.

Of course in actual data, these pure patterns rarely occur. Nonetheless an examination of Tables 9.2, 9.3, and 9.4 can help develop a sensitivity to the patterns one can detect in analyzing cohort data. In addition, the tables illustrate the logic behind the analysis. Glenn (1977) and Mason et al. (1973) also present tables showing pure effects.

Although cohort analysis is an appealing and useful technique, it is not without its disadvantages. In the first place, the specific effects of age, cohort, and period are difficult to untangle through purely statistical analysis of a standard cohort table. In survey data, much of the variation in percentages among cells is due to sampling

Table 9.4 Cohort Table Showing Pure Cohort Effect

	Year		
Age	1980	1984	1988
18–21	15	10	5
22–25	20	15	10
26–29	25	20	15
Average	20	15	10

variability. As of this writing, there are no uniformly accepted tests of significance appropriate to a cohort table that allow researchers to estimate that the probability that the observed differences are due to chance. Moreover, as a cohort grows older, many of its members die. If the remaining cohort members differ in regard to the variable under study, the variation in the cohort table may simply reflect this change. Finally, as Glenn (1977) points out, no matter how a cohort table is examined, two of the basic effects—namely, age, cohort, and period— are confounded. Age and cohort effects are confounded in the columns, age and period effects in the diagonals, and cohort and period effects in each row. Even the patterns of variations in the "pure" cohort Tables 9.2, 9.3, and 9.4 could be explained by a combination of influences.

Several authors have developed techniques to try to sort out these effects. Two of the most useful are Palmore's (1978) triad method and the constrained multiple regression model (Rentz, Reynolds, & Stout, 1983). If the researcher is willing to make certain assumptions, these methods can provide some tentative evidence about the probable influences of age, period, and cohort. Moreover, in many cases there is only one likely or plausible situation explanation for the variation. Nonetheless, a researcher should exercise caution in attributing causation to any variable in a cohort analysis. Theory and evidence from outside sources should also be utilized in any interpretation.

A second disadvantage of the technique is sample mortality. If a long time period is involved or if the specific sample group is hard to reach, the researcher may have some empty cells in the cohort table or some that contain too few members for meaningful analysis.

Cohort analysis is widely used in advertising and marketing research. For example, Rentz, Reynolds, and Stout (1983) conducted a cohort analysis of consumers born in four time periods: 1931–1940, 1941–1950, 1951–1960, and 1961–1970. Soft drink consumption was the dependent variable. Multiple regression analysis was employed to help separate the three possible sources of variation. The results indicated a large cohort effect suggesting that soft drink consumption will not decrease as successive cohorts age. Cohort analysis is also useful in the study of public opinion. Cassell (1977) conducted a cohort analysis of political party identification of Southern whites. The data indicated that both younger and older cohorts showed some movement from Democratic affiliation to the independent position.

Panel Studies

The measurement of the same sample of respondents at different points in time represents the panel design. Unlike trend studies, **panel studies** can reveal information about both net and gross changes in the dependent variable. For example, a study of voting intentions might reveal that between Time 1 and Time 2, 20% of the panel switched from Candidate A to Candidate B and 20% switched from Candidate B to Candidate A. Whereas a trend study would show only a net change of zero, the panel study would show a high degree of volatility in voting intention as the gross changes simply canceled each other out.

Similar to trend and cohort studies, panel studies can make use of mail questionnaires, telephone interviews, or personal interviews. Television networks, advertising agencies, and marketing research firms use panel studies to track changes in consumer behavior. Panel studies can reveal shifting attitudes and patterns of behavior that might go unnoticed with other research approaches; thus trends, new ideas, fads, and buying habits are among the variables investigated. For a panel study on the effectiveness of political commercials, for example, all members of the panel would be interviewed periodically during a campaign to determine if and when each respondent makes a voting decision.

Depending on the purpose of the study, researchers can use either a *continuous panel*, consisting of members who report specific attitudes or behavior patterns on a regular basis, or an *interval panel*, whose members agree to complete a certain number of measurement instruments (usually questionnaires) only when the information is needed. Panel studies produce data suitable for sophisticated statistical analysis and enable researchers to predict cause-and-effect relationships (see below).

Panel data are particularly useful in answering questions about the dynamics of change. For example, under what conditions do voters change political party affiliation? What are the respective roles of mass media and friends in changing political attitudes? Moreover, repeated contacts with the respondents may help reduce suspicions, so that later interviews yield more information than the initial encounters. Of course, the other side to this benefit is the sensitization effect, discussed below.

Finally, panel studies help solve the problems normally encountered when defining a theory on the basis of a one-shot case study. Since the research progresses over a period of time, the researcher can allow for the influences of competing stimuli on the subject.

On the negative side, panel members are often difficult to recruit because of unwillingness to fill out questionnaires or submit to interviews several times. The number of initial refusals in a panel study fluctuates depending on the amount of time required, the prestige of the organization directing the study, and the presence or absence of some type of compensation. One analysis of the refusal rates in twelve marketing panel studies found a range of 15–80%, with a median of about 40% (Carman, 1974).

Once the sample has been secured, the problem of mortality emerges. Some panel members will drop out for one reason or another. Since the strength of panel studies lies in interviewing the same people at different times, this advantage diminishes as the sample size decreases. Another serious problem is that respondents often become sensitized to measurement instruments after repeated interviewing, thus making the sample atypical (see Chapter 4). For example, panelists who know in advance that they will be interviewed about public television watching might alter their viewing patterns to include more PBS programs (or fewer). Respondent error is always a problem in situations that depend on self-administered measurement instruments. If panelists are asked to keep a diary over a certain period of time, some may not fill it out until immediately before it is due. And, of course, panel studies require much time and can be quite expensive.

Perhaps the most famous example of the panel technique in mass media research is the collection of national television audience data by the A. C. Nielsen Company. Nielsen's sample consists of about 1,800 households spread across the United States. These homes are wired with a mechanical device called an **audimeter** that records when the television set is turned on and the channel that is tuned in. Strictly speaking, the Nielsen sample is a panel of TV sets rather than people. To collect information on viewers, Nielsen supplements this technique with diaries (Chapter 14 includes a discussion of people meters, a device that may eliminate diaries in broadcast audience measurement). Twenty percent of the Nielsen sample is replaced every year. Other panels are maintained by such commercial research organizations as Market Facts, Inc., National Family Opinion, Inc., and the Home Testing Institute.

Outside the marketing area, the best-known recent panel study was carried out with the support of the National Broadcasting Company (Milavsky et al., 1982). The overall purpose of this study was to isolate any possible causal influence of the viewing of violence on television on aggression among young people. Three panel studies were conducted, with the most ambitious involving boys aged 7–12. In brief, the methodology in the boys' study involved collecting data on aggression, TV viewing, and a host of sociological variables on six different occasions from children in Minneapolis, Minnesota, and Fort Worth, Texas. About 1,200 boys participated in the study. The time lags between each wave of data collection were deliberately varied so that the effects of TV viewing could be analyzed over different durations. Thus, there was a 5-month lag between the first and second waves, a 4-month lag between Waves 2 and 3, and a 3-month lag between Waves 3 and 4. The lag between Waves 1 and 6 constituted the longest time lapse (3 years). As is the case in all panel studies, the NBC study suffered from attrition. The particular design, however, magnified the effects of attrition. When a respondent left the sixth grade, he left the panel. Consequently, only a small number of children were available for the analysis of long-term effects. In fact, only 58 boys had valid aggression and TV viewing data in all six waves. The year-to-year losses reported by the NBC team illustrate the impact of year-to-year attrition on a sample of this age group. About 7% of the sample was lost in the first year, approximately 37% in the first two years, and 63% over all three years.

   The study also illustrates how a panel design influences the statistical analysis. The most powerful statistical test would have incorporated data from all six waves and simultaneously examined all the possible causal relationships. This was impossible, however, because due to the initial study design and subsequent attrition, the sample size fell below minimum standards. Instead, the investigators worked with each of the 15 possible wave pairs in the sample. The main statistical tests used the analytical technique of partial regression coefficients to remove the impact of earlier aggression levels. In effect, the researchers sought to determine whether TV viewing at an earlier time added to the predictability of aggression at a later time, once the aggression levels present before the test began had been statistically discounted. After looking at all the resulting coefficients for all the possible wave pairs, the investigators concluded that there was no consistently statistically significant relationship between watching violent TV programs and later aggression. Nonetheless, they did find a large number of small but consistently positive coefficients that suggested the possibility of a weak relationship that might not have been detected by conventional statistical methods. Upon further analysis, however, the researchers concluded that these associations were due to chance.

   Since their initial publication, the NBC data have been the topic of at least two reanalyses and reinterpretations (Cook, Kendizierski, & Thomas, 1983; Kenny, 1984). Concerns were raised over various aspects of the methodology and the appropriateness of conventional standards of statistical significance in light of small samples and skewed aggression measures. It is likely that more reanalyses will follow. Nonetheless, this study has value for anyone interested in longitudinal research. Many of the problems involved in panel studies and the compromises involved in doing a 3-year study are discussed in great detail.

Special Panel Designs

Panel data can be expensive to obtain. Moreover, analysis cannot begin until at least two waves of data are available. For many panel studies, this may take years. Researchers who have limited time and resources might consider one of the alternatives discussed below.

   Schulsinger, Mednick, and Knop (1981) outline a research design called a **retrospective panel**. In this method, the respondent is asked to recall facts or attitudes about education, occupations, events, situations, and so on, from the past. These recalled factors are then compared with a later measure of the same variable, thus producing an "instant" longitudinal design. Belson (1978) used a variation of this design in his study of the effects of exposure to violent TV shows on the aggressive behavior of teenage boys when he asked his respondents to recall when they first started watching certain violent TV programs.

With this technique, obviously there will be problems. Many people have faulty memories; some will deliberately misrepresent the past; and others will try to give a socially desirable response. Only a few research studies have examined the extent to which retrospective panel data might be misleading. Powers, Goudy, and Keith (1978) reanalyzed data from a 1964 study of adult men. In 1974 all the original respondents who could be located were reinterviewed and asked about their answers to the 1964 survey. In most instances, the recall responses presented respondents in a more favorable light than did their original answers. Interestingly enough, using the 1974 recall data produced virtually the same pattern of correlations as using the 1964 data, suggesting that recall data might be used, albeit with caution, in correlational studies. In 1974 Norlen (1977) reinterviewed about 4,700 persons originally questioned in 1968. Of those reinterviewed, 464 had originally reported that they had written a letter to the editor of a newspaper or magazine, but in 1974 about a third of this group denied ever having written to a newspaper or magazine. Clearly, the savings in time and money accrued by using retrospective data must be weighted against possible losses in accuracy.

A **follow-back panel** selects a cross-sectional sample in the present and uses archival data from an earlier point in time to create the longitudinal dimension of the study. The advantages of such a technique are clearly seen. Changes that occurred over a great many years can be analyzed in a short time period. This design is also useful in studying rare populations, since the researcher can assemble a sample from baseline investigations conducted earlier, probably at great expense. The disadvantages are also obvious. The follow-back panel depends on archival data, and many of the variables that interest mass media researchers are not contained in archives. In addition, the resulting sample in a follow-back design may not represent all possible entities. For example, a follow-back study of the managerial practices of small radio stations will not represent stations that went out of business and no longer exist.

A **catch-up panel** involves the selection of a cross-sectional study done in the past and locating all possible units of analysis for observation in the present. The catch-up design is particularly attractive if the researcher has a rich source of baseline data in the archive. Of course, this is usually not the case, since most data sources lack enough identifying information to allow the investigator to track down the respondents. When the appropriate data exist, however, the catch-up study can be highly useful. In effect, Lefkowitz et al. (1972) used a catch-up technique in their study of TV watching and child aggression. After a lapse of 10 years, the investigators tracked down 735 of 875

Figure 9.1 Comparison of retrospective, follow-back, and catch-up techniques

Retrospective
  Step 1: Select current sample.
  Step 2: Interview sample about past recollections concerning topic of interest.
  Step 3: Collect current data on topic of interest.
  Step 4: Compare data.

Follow-back
  Step 1: Select current sample.
  Step 2: Collect current data on topic of interest.
  Step 3: Locate archival data on sample regarding topic of interest.
  Step 4: Compare data.

Catch-up Panel
  Step 1: Locate archival data on topic of interest.
  Step 2: Select current sample by locating as many respondents as possible for whom data exist in the archive.
  Step 3: Collect current data on topic of interest.
  Step 4: Compare data.

youths who had participated in a survey of mental health factors when they were in the third grade. These individuals were recontacted and asked questions similar to those they had answered as young children. Another problem associated with the catch-up panel involves comparability of measures. If the earlier study was not constructed to be part of a longitudinal design, the original measurement instruments will have to be modified. For example, a study of 10-year-olds might have used teacher ratings to measure aggressiveness; such a measure would not be appropriate to 20-year-olds, however. Finally, the researcher in the catch-up situation is confined to the variables measured in the original study. In the intervening time, new variables might have been identified as important, but if those variables were not measured during the original survey, they are unavailable to the researcher. Figure 9.1 shows the similarities and differences in these three techniques.

Analyzing Causation in Panel Data

The panel design provides an opportunity for the researcher to make statements about the causal ordering among different variables, and this is a major advantage. Cross-sectional surveys, for which the data are collected at a single point in time, generate only correlational information. A cross-sectional survey allows the researcher to say that variables *A* and *B* are related. Only if the time order between *A* and *B* is evident can statements of cause be inferred. For example, a person's education typically is acquired before occupational status. Thus, the statement that education is a cause of occupational status (all other things equal) can be inferred. If there is no distinguishable temporal sequence in the data (as is the case with viewing of violence on TV and aggressive behavior), causal statements are conjectural. In a panel study, however, the variables are measured across time, making causal inferences more defensible.

There are many statistical techniques available for determining a causal sequence in panel data. A detailed listing and explanation of the computations involved is beyond the scope of this book. Nonetheless, some of the following references will be helpful to readers who desire more detailed information. Kessler and Greenberg (1981) discuss common methods for analyzing panel data measured at the interval level. Markus (1979) gives computational methods for data measured at the interval level and also discusses ways to analyze dichotomous panel data, including the increasingly popular log–linear technique. Asher (1976) provides a detailed discussion of path analysis. McCullough (1978) compares four methods of analysis for panel data: Lazarsfeld's 16-fold table, Coleman's mathematical model, cross-lagged panel correlation, and path analysis. Finally, the most mathematically sophisticated technique, linear structural equations, or LISREL, is discussed in Joreskog (1973), Long (1976), and Wheaton et al. (1977). Since it appears that the LISREL method has much to recommend it (the LISREL technique was used in the NBC panel study discussed above), researchers who intend to do panel studies should be familiar with its assumptions and techniques.

Longitudinal Design in Experiments

Although the preceding discussion was concerned with survey research, experimental research has a longitudinal dimension that should not be overlooked. Many research designs are based on a single exposure to a message, with the dependent variable measured almost immediately afterward. This procedure might be appropriate in many circumstances, but a longitudinal treatment design may be necessary to measure subtle, cumulative media effects. Furthermore, delayed assessment is essential to determine the duration of the impact of certain media effects (for example, How long does it take a persuasive effect to decay?). Bryant, Carveth, and Brown (1981) illustrated the importance of the longitudinal design to the experimental approach. In investigating TV viewing and anxiety, they divided their subjects into groups and assigned to each a menu of TV shows that could be watched. Over a 6-week period, one group was assigned a light viewing schedule, while a second was directed to watch a large number of shows that depicted a clear triumph of justice. A third group was assigned to view a large number of shows in which justice did not triumph. One of the dependent variables was also measured over time. The investigators obtained voluntary viewing data by having students fill out diaries for another 3 weeks. The results of this study indicated that the cumulative exposure to TV shows in which justice does not prevail seemed to make some viewers more anxious, thus offering some support to Gerbner's cultivation hypothesis.

A study by Zillmann and Bryant (1982) also showed the importance of the longitudinal dimension in assessing the cumulative effects of continued exposure. One experimental group watched nearly 5 hours of pornographic films over a 6-week period. A second group saw about 2.5 hours over the same period, while a control group saw nonerotic films. Those exposed to the larger dose of pornography showed less compassion toward women as rape victims and toward women in general. Clearly, the longitudinal design can be of great value in experimental research.

Summary

Longitudinal research involves the collection of data at different points in time. There are three different types of longitudinal study: trend, cohort, and panel. A trend study asks the same questions of different groups of people at different points in time. A cohort study measures some characteristic of a sample whose members share some significant life event (usually time of birth) at two or more points in time. In a panel study the same respondents are measured at least twice. One of the advantages of the panel design is that it allows the researcher to make statements about the causal ordering of the study variables, and several different statistical methods are available for this task.

Questions and Problems for Further Investigation

1. Search recent issues of scholarly journals for examples of longitudinal studies. Which of the three designs discussed in this chapter was used? Try to find additional longitudinal studies done by commercial research firms. What design was most used?

2. What are some mass communication variables that would be best studied using the cohort method?

3. What are some possible measures of media or audience characteristics that might be regularly made and stored in a data archive for secondary trend analysis?

4. How might a panel study make use of laboratory techniques?

References and Suggested Readings

Asher, H. (1976). *Causal modeling.* Beverly Hills, CA: Sage Publications.

Belson, W. (1978). *Television violence and the adolescent boy.* Hampshire, England: Saxon House.

Bryant, J., Carveth, R., & Brown, D. (1981). Television viewing and anxiety. *Journal of Communication, 31*(1), 106–119.

Carman, J. (1974). Consumer panels. In R. Ferber (Ed.), *Handbook of marketing research.* New York: McGraw-Hill.

Cassell, C. (1977). Cohort analysis of party identification among Southern whites, 1952–72. *Public Opinion Quarterly, 41*(1), 28–33.

Cook, T., Kendizierski, D., & Thomas, S. (1983). The implicit assumptions of television research. *Public Opinion Quarterly, 47*(2), 161–201.

Gerbner, G., et al. (1979). The demonstration of power: Violence Profile No. 10. *Journal of Communication, 29*(3), 177–196.

Glenn, N. (1977). *Cohort analysis.* Beverly Hills, CA: Sage Publications.

Hyman, H. (1972). *Secondary analysis of sample surveys.* New York: John Wiley.

Joreskog, K. (1973). A general method for estimating a linear structural equation system. In A. Goldberger & O. Duncan (Eds.), *Structural equations models in the social sciences.* New York: Seminar Press.

Katz, E., & Lazarsfeld, P. (1955). *Personal influence.* New York: Free Press.

Kenny, D., et al. (1984). The NBC study and television violence. *Journal of Communication, 34*(1), 176–188.

Kessler, R., & Greenberg, D. (1981). *Linear panel analysis.* New York: Academic Press.

Lazarsfeld, P., Berelson, B., & Gaudet, H. (1944). *The people's choice.* New York: Columbia University Press.

Lefkowitz, M., et al. (1972). Television violence and child aggression. In E. Rubinstein, G. Comstock, & J. Murray (Eds.), *Television and adolescent aggressiveness.* Washington, DC: U.S. Government Printing Office.

Long, J. (1976). Estimation and hypothesis testing in linear models containing measurement error. *Sociological Methods and Research, 5,* 157–206.

Lowery, S., & DeFleur, M. (1983). *Milestones in mass communication research.* New York: Longman.

McCullough, B. (1978). Effects of variables using panel data. *Public Opinion Quarterly, 42*(2), 199–220.

Markus, G. (1979). *Analyzing panel data.* Beverly Hills, CA: Sage Publications.

Mason, K., et al. (1973, April). Some methodological issues in cohort analysis of archival data. *American Sociological Review,* pp. 242–258.

Milavsky, J., et al. (1982). *Television and aggression.* New York: Academic Press.

Newcomb, T. (1943). *Personality and social change.* New York: Dryden.

Norlen, V. (1977). Response errors in the answers to retrospective questions. *Statistik Tidskrift, 4,* 331–341.

Palmore, E. (1978). When can age, period and cohort effects be separated? *Social Forces, 57,* 282–295.

Peterson, T. (1980). *The mass media election.* New York: Praeger.

Powers, E., Goudy, W., & Keith, P. (1978). Congruence between panel and recall data in longitudinal research. *Public Opinion Quarterly, 42*(3), 380–389.

Rentz, J., Reynolds, F., & Stout, R. (1983, February). Analyzing changing consumption patterns with cohort analysis. *Journal of Marketing Research, 20,* 12–20.

Schulsinger, F., Mednick, S., & Knop, J. (1981). *Longitudinal research.* Boston: Nijhoff Publishing.

Wheaton, B., et al. (1977). Assessing reliability and stability in panel models. In D. Heise (Ed.), *Sociological methodology, 1977.* San Francisco: Jossey-Bass.

Zillmann, D., & Bryant, J. (1982). Pornography, sexual callousness and the trivialization of rape. *Journal of Communication, 32*(4), 10–21.

C H A P T E R 1 0

Introduction to Statistics

DESCRIPTIVE STATISTICS

∎

INFERENTIAL STATISTICS

∎

DATA TRANSFORMATION

∎

SUMMARY

∎

QUESTIONS AND PROBLEMS FOR FURTHER INVESTIGATION

∎

REFERENCES AND SUGGESTED READINGS

S tatistics provide mathematical methods for organizing, summarizing, and analyzing data that have been collected and measured. Statistics cannot perform miracles, however. If a research question is misdirected, poorly phrased, or ambiguous, or if a study uses sloppy measurement and design, a statistical technique cannot magically salvage the project. Statistics can produce valid results only if the data variables they comprise have been established scientifically.

Part 3 focuses on the statistical procedures used by mass media researchers. This chapter provides an introduction to the two types of research statistics: descriptive and inferential.

Descriptive Statistics

Descriptive statistics are intended to reduce data sets to allow for easier interpretation. If you asked 100 people how long they listened to radio yesterday and recorded all 100 answers at random on a sheet of paper, you would be hard pressed to draw conclusions from a simple examination of that paper. Analysis of the data would be facilitated if they were organized in some fashion. In this regard, descriptive statistics can be useful.

During the course of a research study, investigators typically collect data that are the results of measurements or observations of the people or items in the sample. These data usually have little meaning or usefulness until they are displayed or summarized using one of the techniques of descriptive statistics. Mass media researchers use two primary methods to make their data more manageable: data distribution and summary statistics.

Data Distribution

One way researchers can display their data is by distributing it in tables or graphs. A **distribution** is simply a collection of numbers. Table 10.1 is a hypothetical distribution of the responses of 20 people to the question, "How many hours did you listen to the radio yesterday?" It would be difficult, however, for the investigator to draw any conclusions or make any generalizations from this collection of unordered scores.

Table 10.1 Distribution of Responses to "How Many Hours Did You Listen to the Radio Yesterday?"

Respondent	Hours listened	Respondent	Hours listened
A	0.0	K	0.0
B	2.5	L	2.0
C	1.0	M	1.0
D	2.0	N	3.0
E	0.0	O	0.5
F	0.5	P	0.5
G	1.0	Q	1.0
H	1.0	R	1.0
I	1.5	S	1.0
J	0.5	T	0.0

As a preliminary step toward making these numbers more manageable, the data may be arranged in a **frequency distribution**, that is, a table of each possible score, ordered according to magnitude, and its actual frequency of occurrence. Table 10.2 presents the data from the hypothetical survey in a frequency distribution.

Now the data begin to show a pattern. Note that the typical frequency distribution table consists of two columns. The first, on the left, contains all the values of the variable under study, and the second, on the right, shows the number of occurrences of each value. The sum of the frequency column is the number (N) of persons or items that make up the distribution.

A frequency distribution can also be constructed using grouped intervals, each of which contains several score levels. Table 10.3 shows the data from the radio listening survey with the scores grouped together in intervals. This table is a more compact frequency distribution than Table 10.2, but the scores have lost their individual identity.

Other columns can be included in frequency distribution tables. For example, the data can be transformed into proportions or percentages. To obtain the percentage of a response, simply divide the frequency of the response by N, or the total number of responses in

Table 10.2 Frequency Distribution of Responses to "How Many Hours Did You Listen to the Radio Yesterday?"

Hours	Frequency
0.0	4
0.5	4
1.0	7
1.5	1
2.0	2
2.5	1
3.0	1

Table 10.3 Frequency Distribution of Radio Listening Scores Grouped in Intervals

Hours	Frequency
0.00–0.50	8
0.51–1.50	8
1.51–3.00	4

the distribution. Percentages allow comparisons to be made between frequency distributions that are based on different values of N.

Some frequency distributions give the cumulative frequency (cf); this column is constructed by adding the number of scores in one interval to the number of scores in the intervals above it. Table 10.4 displays the frequency distribution from Table 10.2 with the addition of a percentage column, a cumulative frequency column, and a column showing cumulative frequency as a percentage of N.

Sometimes it is desirable to present data in graph form. The graphs described below contain the same amount of information as frequency distributions. Graphs usually consist of two perpendicular lines, the *x-axis* (horizontal) and the *y-axis* (vertical). Over the years, statisticians have developed certain conventions regarding graphic format. One common convention is to list the scores along the *x*-axis and the frequency or relative frequency along the *y*-axis. Thus, the height of a line or bar indicates the frequency of a score.

One common form of graph is the **histogram**, or bar chart, in which frequencies are represented by vertical bars. Figure 10.1 is a histogram constructed from the data in Table 10.1. Note that the scores across the *x*-axis are actually the midpoints of half-hour intervals: the first category extends from 0 to 0.2499 hour, the second from 0.25 to 0.7499 hour, and so on.

If a line is drawn from the midpoint of each interval at its peak along the *y*-axis to each adjacent midpoint/peak, the resulting graph is called a **frequency polygon**. Figure 10.2 shows a frequency polygon superimposed onto the histogram from Figure 10.1. As can be seen, the two figures display the same information.

Table 10.4 Frequency Distribution of Radio Listening Scores

Hours	Frequency	Percentage	cf	cf Percentage of N
0.0	4	20	4	20
0.5	4	20	8	40
1.0	7	35	15	75
1.5	1	5	16	80
2.0	2	10	18	90
2.5	1	5	19	95
3.0	1	5	20	100
	$N = 20$	100%		

Figure 10.1 Histogram of radio listening scores

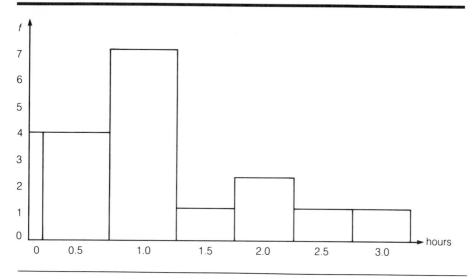

A **frequency curve** is similar to a frequency polygon except that points are connected by a continuous, unbroken curve instead of by lines. Such a curve assumes that any irregularities shown in a frequency polygon are simply due to chance and that the variable being

Figure 10.2 Frequency polygon of radio listening scores imposed on the histogram of the same scores

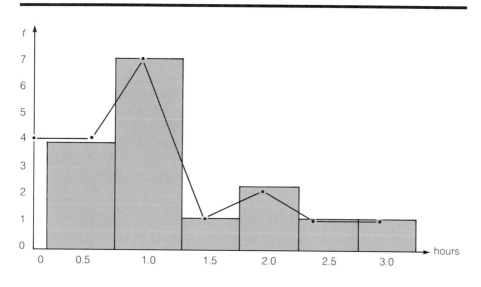

Figure 10.3 Frequency curve (shaded) of radio listening scores imposed on the frequency polygon of the same scores

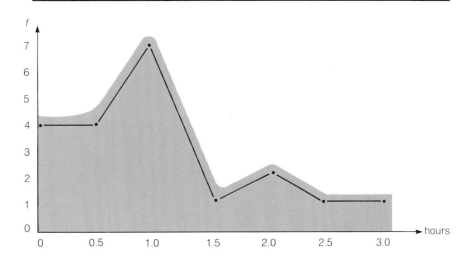

studied is distributed continuously over the population. Figure 10.3 superimposes a frequency curve onto the frequency polygon shown in Figure 10.2.

Frequency curves are described in relation to the **normal curve**, a symmetrical bell curve whose properties are discussed more fully later in this chapter. Figure 10.4 illustrates the normal curve and shows the ways in which a frequency curve can deviate from it. These patterns of deviation are referred to as skewness and kurtosis.

Skewness refers to the concentration of scores around a particular point on the *x*-axis. If this concentration lies toward the low end of the scale, with the tail of the curve trailing off to the right, the curve is *positively skewed* (or skewed to the right). If the tail of the curve trails off to the left, it is said to be *negatively skewed*. If the halves of the curve are identical, the curve is *symmetrical*.

Kurtosis refers to the peakedness of a frequency distribution, or the height of the curve along the *y*-axis. A *leptokurtic* distribution occurs when a large number of scores are clustered around the center of the distribution; in a *platykurtic* distribution, scores are spread over a wide area. A *mesokurtic* distribution is close to a normal distribution but usually has two or more areas with a high concentration of scores.

A normal distribution is free from skewness and kurtosis. If researchers find that a frequency curve deviates excessively from the normal curve, they may have to manipulate or transform the data to achieve a more normal distribution (transformation is discussed briefly at the end of this chapter).

Figure 10.4 Skewness, kurtosis, and the normal curve

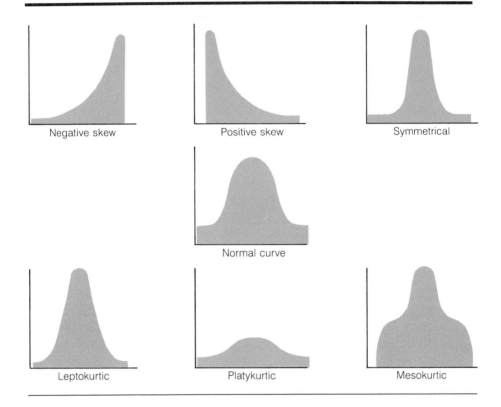

Summary Statistics

The data in Table 10.1 can be condensed still further through the use of **summary statistics**. These statistics help make data more manageable by measuring two basic tendencies of distributions: central tendency and dispersion or variability.

 Central tendency statistics answer the question, What is a typical score? They provide information about the grouping of the numbers in a distribution by calculating a single number that is characteristic of the entire distribution. Exactly what constitutes a "typical" score depends on the level of measurement and the purpose for which the data will be used.

 For every distribution, three types of characteristic numbers can be identified. One is the **mode** (Mo), or the score or scores occurring most frequently. Calculation is not necessary to determine the mode; it is found by inspecting the distribution. For the data in Table 10.1, the mode is 1.0. Although easy to determine, the mode has some serious drawbacks as a descriptive statistic. It focuses attention on only one possible score and can thus camouflage important facts about the

Table 10.5 The Mode as a Potentially Misleading Statistic

Score	f
70	2
35–69	0
34	1
33	1
32	1
31	1
30	1
29	1
28	1
27	1
26	1

data when considered in isolation. This is illustrated by the data in Table 10.5: the mode is 70, but the most striking feature about the numbers is the way they cluster around 30.

A second characteristic score is the **median** (Mdn), which is the midpoint of a distribution: half the scores lie above it, and half lie below it. If the distribution has an odd number of scores, the median is the middle score; if there is an even number, the median is a hypothetical score halfway between the two middle scores. To determine the median, one must order the scores from smallest to largest and locate the midpoint by inspection. For example, here are nine scores:

$$0 \quad 2 \quad 2 \quad 5 \quad ⑥ \quad 17 \quad 18 \quad 19 \quad 67$$

The median score is 6, since there are four scores above this number and four below it. Now consider these numbers:

$$0 \quad 2 \quad 2 \quad 5 \quad 6 \underset{\underset{11.5}{\uparrow}}{\quad} 17 \quad 18 \quad 19 \quad 67 \quad 75$$

No score neatly bisects this distribution; to determine the median, the two middle scores must be added and divided by 2:

$$\text{Mdn} = \frac{6 + 17}{2} = 11.5$$

When many scores in the distribution are the same, computing the median becomes a bit more complicated. Roscoe (1975) should be consulted for precise directions.

The third type of central tendency statistic is the **mean**. The mean is probably the most familiar summary statistic; it represents the average of a set of scores. Mathematically speaking, the mean is defined as the sum of all scores divided by N, or the total number of scores. Since the mean is widely used in both descriptive and inferential statistics, it is described here in greater detail.

Table 10.6 Calculation of Mean from Frequency Distribution

Hours	f	fx
0.0	4	0.0
0.5	4	2.0
1.0	7	7.0
1.5	1	1.5
2.0	2	4.0
2.5	1	2.5
3.0	1	3.0
	$N = 20$	$\Sigma fX = 20$

$$\overline{X} = \frac{20}{20} = 1.00$$

As a first step, some basic statistical notation is required:

X = any score in a series of scores
$\overline{X}$ = the mean (read "X-bar"; M is also commonly used to denote the mean)
Σ = the sum (symbol is Greek capital letter **sigma**)
N = the total number of scores in a distribution

Using these symbols, the formula for the calculation of the mean is:

$$\overline{X} = \frac{\Sigma X}{N}$$

This equation indicates that the mean is the sum of all scores (ΣX) divided by the number of scores (N). Using the data in Table 10.1:

$$\overline{X} = \frac{20}{20}$$
$$= 1.00$$

If the data are contained in a frequency distribution, a slightly different formula is used to calculate the mean:

$$\overline{X} = \frac{\Sigma fX}{N}$$

In this case, X represents the midpoint of any given interval, and f is the frequency of that interval. Table 10.6 uses this formula to calculate the mean of the frequency distribution in Table 10.2.

Unlike the mode and the median, the mean takes into account all the values in the distribution, making it especially sensitive to extreme scores or "outliers." Extreme scores draw the mean in their direction. For example, suppose Table 10.1 contained another response, from Respondent U, who reported 12 hours of radio listening. The new mean would then be approximately 1.52 hours, an increase of more than 50% due to the addition of a single large score.

The mean may be thought of as the score that would be assigned to each individual if the total were to be evenly distributed among all members of the sample. It is also the only measure of central tendency that can be defined algebraically. As will be seen later, this allows the mean to be used in a wide range of situations. It also suggests that the data used to calculate the mean should be at the interval or ratio level (see Chapter 3).

In deciding which of the three measures of central tendency to report for a given set of data, the researcher must consider two main factors. First of all, the level of measurement used may determine the choice: if the data are at the nominal level, only the mode is meaningful; with ordinal data, either the mode or the median may be used. All three measures are appropriate for interval and ratio data, however, and a researcher may find it desirable to report more than one.

Second, the purpose of the statistic is important. If the ultimate goal is to describe a set of data, the measure that is most typical of the distribution should be used. To illustrate, suppose the scores on a statistics exam were 100, 100, 100, 100, 0, and 0. To say that the mean grade was 67 does not accurately portray the distribution; the mode would provide a more characteristic description.

The second type of descriptive statistics is used to measure **dispersion**, or variation. Measures of central tendency determine the typical score of a distribution; dispersion measures describe the way in which the scores are spread out about this central point. Dispersion measures can be particularly valuable when comparing different distributions. For example, suppose the average grades for two classes in research methods are exactly the same; however, one class has several excellent students and many poor students, while in the other class, all students are just about average. A measure of dispersion must be employed to reflect this difference. In many cases, an adequate description of a data set can be achieved by simply reporting a measure of central tendency (usually the mean) and an index of dispersion.

There are three measures of variation or dispersion; the simplest, **range** (R), is the difference between the highest and lowest scores in a distribution of scores. The formula used to calculate the range is:

$$R = X_{hi} - X_{lo}$$

where X_{hi} = the highest score and X_{lo} = the lowest score. The range is sometimes reported simply as "the scores ranged from 20 to 40."

Since the range uses only two scores out of the entire distribution, it is not particularly descriptive of the data set. Additionally, the range often increases with sample size, since larger samples tend to include more extreme values. For these reasons, the range is seldom used in mass media research as the sole measure of dispersion.

Table 10.7 Calculation of Variance: X = Score

X	$\overline{X}$	$X - \overline{X}$	$(X - \overline{X})^2$
0.0	1.00	−1.00	1.00
0.0	1.00	−1.00	1.00
0.0	1.00	−1.00	1.00
0.0	1.00	−1.00	1.00
0.5	1.00	−0.5	.25
0.5	1.00	−0.5	.25
0.5	1.00	−0.5	.25
0.5	1.00	−0.5	.25
1.0	1.00	0	0
1.0	1.00	0	0
1.0	1.00	0	0
1.0	1.00	0	0
1.0	1.00	0	0
1.0	1.00	0	0
1.0	1.00	0	0
1.5	1.00	0.5	.25
2.0	1.00	1.00	1.00
2.0	1.00	1.00	1.00
2.5	1.00	1.50	2.25
3.0	1.00	2.00	4.00

$$S^2 = \frac{\Sigma(X - \overline{X})^2}{N} = \frac{13.5}{20} = 0.675$$

A second measure, **variance**, provides a mathematical index of the degree to which scores deviate from, or are at variance with, the mean. A small variance indicates that most of the scores in the distribution lie fairly close to the mean; a large variance represents scores that are widely scattered. Thus, variance is directly proportional to the degree of dispersion.

To compute the variance of a distribution, the mean is subtracted from each score; these *deviation scores* are then squared, and the squares are summed and divided by N. The formula for variance (usually symbolized as S^2, although many textbooks use a different notation) is:

$$S^2 = \frac{\Sigma(X - \overline{X})^2}{N}$$

(In many texts, the expression $(X - \overline{X})^2$ is symbolized by x^2.) The numerator in this formula, $\Sigma(X - \overline{X})^2$, is called the *sum of squares*. Although this quantity is usually not reported as a descriptive statistic, the sum of squares is used in the calculation of several other statistics. An example using this variance formula is found in Table 10.7.

Table 10.8 Calculation of Variance Using an Alternate Formula: X = Score

X	X^2
0.0	0
0.0	0
0.0	0
0.0	0
0.5	0.25
0.5	0.25
0.5	0.25
0.5	0.25
1.0	1.00
1.0	1.00
1.0	1.00
1.0	1.00
1.0	1.00
1.0	1.00
1.0	1.00
1.5	2.25
2.0	4.00
2.0	4.00
2.5	6.25
3.0	9.00
	ΣX^2 = 33.50

$$S^2 = \frac{\Sigma X^2}{N} - \overline{X}^2 = \frac{33.50}{20} - (1.00)^2 = 1.675 - 1.00 = 0.675$$

This equation may not be the most convenient formula for calculating variance, especially if N is large. A simpler, equivalent formula is:

$$S^2 = \frac{\Sigma X^2}{N} - \overline{X}^2$$

The expression ΣX^2 indicates that one should square each score and sum the squared scores. (Note that this is not the same as $(\Sigma X)^2$, which means to sum all the scores and then square the sum.) An example of this formula is shown in Table 10.8, using the data from Table 10.7. Not surprisingly, S^2 is the same in both cases.

Variance is a commonly used and highly valuable measure of dispersion. In fact, it is at the heart of one powerful technique, analysis of variance (see Chapter 12), which is widely used in inferential statistics. However, variance does have one minor inconvenience: it is expressed in terms of squared deviations from the mean rather than in terms of the original measurements. To obtain a measure of dispersion that is calibrated in the same units as the original data, it is necessary to take the square root of the variance. This quantity, called the **standard deviation**, is the third type of dispersion measure.

To illustrate, a variance for the distribution of family income of $90,000 would be interpreted as 90,000 "squared dollars." Since "squared dollars" is a confusing concept to work with, a researcher would probably choose to report the standard deviation, 300 "regular dollars" (300 = $\sqrt{90,000}$). Usually symbolized as S (or SD), standard deviation is computed using either of the formulas shown below:

$$S = \sqrt{\frac{\Sigma(X - \overline{X})^2}{N}}$$

$$S = \sqrt{\frac{\Sigma X^2}{N} - \overline{X}^2}$$

Note that these two equations correspond to the respective variance formulas described above.

Standard deviation represents a given distance of the scores from the mean of a distribution. This figure can be especially useful in describing the results of standardized tests. For example, modern intelligence tests are constructed to yield a mean of 100 and a standard deviation of 15. A person with a score of 115 falls one standard deviation above the mean; a person with a score of 85 falls one standard deviation below the mean.

The notions of variance and standard deviation are easier to understand if they are visualized. Figure 10.5 contains two pairs of frequency curves. Which curve in each pair would have the larger S^2 and S?

By determining the mean and the standard deviation, it is possible to derive **standard scores** (z) for any distribution of data. Standard scores are commonly used in psychology, education, and sociology, as well as in mass media research, to allow comparison of observations obtained by different methods (see Table 10.9).

A standard or "z" score indicates the placement of any score with respect to the mean, in terms of standard deviations above or below the mean. It can be calculated as follows:

$$z = \frac{X - \overline{X}}{S}$$

To illustrate, suppose that two roommates are in different sections of a research course. On a particular day each section is given a different exam. The first roommate scores a 40, and the second scores a 70. Surprisingly, the first roommate receives an A, while the second receives a C. To understand how the professor arrived at these marks, one must examine each student's standard score. It could be that the mean in the first roommate's class was 20 with a standard deviation of 5, while the mean in the second roommate's class was 72, also with a

Figure 10.5 Variance as seen in frequency curves

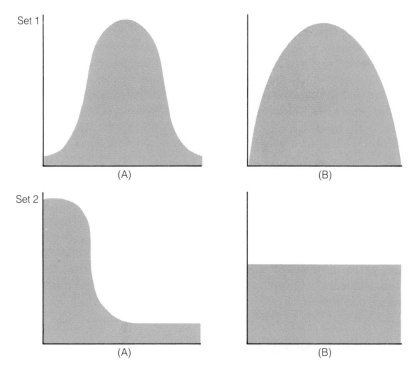

Set 1

(A)

(B)

Set 2

(A)

(B)

Which curve in each set represents the distribution with the larger S^2 and S?

Answers: Set 1 (B); Set 2 (A)

standard deviation of 5. Thus, the z score of Roommate 1 is 4.00, while Roommate 2's score is only -0.40. Clearly, with respect to the average grade in his or her section, Roommate 1 did extremely well. In fact, the z score indicates a score that is four standard deviations above average. On the other hand, Roommate 2's score was slightly below average; seen in this light, the C seems justified.

Table 10.9 Raw and Standard Scores and the Mean $(\overline{X})$ and Standard Deviation (S) for Each Set

Raw score	z score
2	-1.34
4	-0.45
6	0.45
8	1.34
$\overline{X} = 5$	$\overline{X} = 0$
$S = 2.24$	$S = 1.00$

When any collection of raw scores is transformed into z scores, the resulting distribution possesses certain characteristics. Any score below the mean becomes a negative z score, while any score above the mean is positive. The mean of a distribution of z scores is 0, which is also the z score assigned to a person whose raw score equals the mean. The variance and the standard deviation of a z-score distribution are both 1.00 (see Table 10.9). Standard scores are expressed in units of the standard deviation; thus, a z score of 3.00 means that the score is three standard deviation units above the mean.

Standard scores are used frequently in media research because they allow researchers to directly compare the performance of different subjects on tests using different measurements (assuming the distributions have similar shapes). They can literally be used to compare apples and oranges. Assume for a moment that the apple harvest for a certain year was 24 bushels per acre, compared to an average annual yield of 22 bushels per acre with a standard deviation of 10. During the same year, the orange crop yielded 18 bushels per acre, compared to an average of 16 bushels with a standard deviation of 8. Was it a better year for apples or oranges? The standard score formula reveals a z score of .20 for apples and .25 for oranges. Relatively speaking, oranges had a better year.

The Normal Curve

An important tool in statistical analysis is the normal curve. Standard scores not only enable comparisons to be made between dissimilar measurements, but, when used in connection with the normal curve, they also allow statements to be made regarding the frequency of occurrence of certain variables. Figure 10.6 shows an example of the familiar normal curve. The curve is symmetrical and achieves maximum height at its mean, which is also its median and its mode. Also note that the curve in Figure 10.6 is calibrated in standard score units. When the curve is expressed in this way, it is called a *standard normal curve* and possesses all of the properties of a z-score distribution.

Statisticians have studied the normal curve closely to be able to describe its properties. The most important of these is the fact that a fixed proportion of the area below the curve lies between the mean and any unit of standard deviation. The area under a certain segment of the curve is representative of the frequency of the scores that fall therein. From Figure 10.7, which portrays the areas contained under the normal curve between several key standard deviation units, it can be determined that roughly 68% of the total area, hence of the scores, lies within $+1$ and -1 standard deviation from the mean; about 95% lies within $+2$ and -2 standard deviations, and so forth. This knowledge, together with the presence of a normal distribution, allows researchers to make useful predictive statements. For example, suppose

Figure 10.6 The normal curve

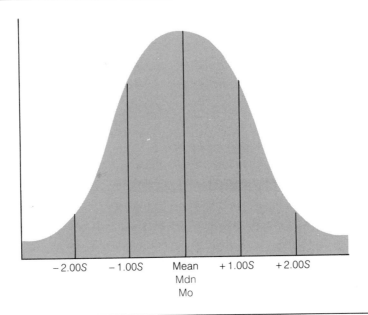

−2.00S   −1.00S   Mean   +1.00S   +2.00S
Mdn
Mo

that television viewing is normally distributed with a mean of 2 hours per day and a standard deviation of 0.5 hour. What proportion of the population watches between 2 and 2.5 hours of TV? First, the raw scores are changed to standard scores:

$$\frac{2-2}{0.5} = 0 \quad \text{and} \quad \frac{2.5-2}{0.5} = 1.00$$

Figure 10.7 shows that approximately 34% of the area below the curve is contained between the mean and one standard deviation. Thus, 34% of the population watches between 2 and 2.5 hours of television daily.

The same data can be used to find the proportion of the population that watches more than 3 hours of television per day. Again, the first step is to translate the raw figures into z scores. In this case, 3 hours corresponds to a z score of 2.00. A glance at Figure 10.7 shows that approximately 98% of the area under the curve falls below a score of 2.00 (50% in the left half of the curve plus about 48% from the mean to the 2.00 mark). Thus, only 2% of the population views more than 3 hours of television daily.

Table 3 in Appendix 1 contains all the areas under the normal curve between the mean of the curve and some specified distance. To use this table, we match the row and the column represented by some standard score. For example, let's assume that the standard score of a normally distributed variable is 1.79. In Table 3 first find the row labeled 1.7. Next find the column labeled .09. At the intersection of

Figure 10.7 Areas under the normal curve

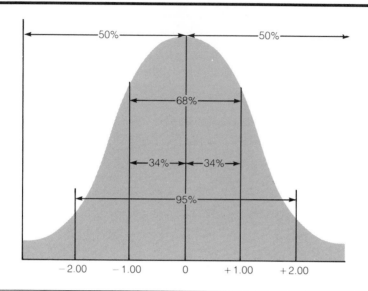

the 1.7 row and .09 column is the number .4633. The area between the mean of the curve (the midpoint) and a standard score of 1.79 is .4633 or roughly 46%. To take another example, what is the distance from the midpoint of the curve to the standard score of −1.32? According to Table 3, 40.66% of the curve lies between these two values. Note that the area is always positive even though the standard score was expressed as a negative value.

To make this exercise more meaningful, let's go back to our example of the two roommates. Let's assume that the scores were normally distributed in the class that had a mean of 72 and a standard deviation of 5.0. The instructor decided to assign C's to 50% of the class. What numerical scores would receive these grades? To begin, remember that "50% of the grades" actually means "25% above the mean and 25% below the mean." What standard deviation unit corresponds to this distance? To answer this question, it is necessary to reverse the process performed above. Specifically, the first thing that we must do is examine the *body* of Table 3 in Appendix 1 for the value .2500. Unfortunately, it does not appear. There are, however, two numbers bracketing it, .2486 and .2517. Since .2486 is a little closer to .2500, let's use it as our area. Examining the row and column that intersect at .2486, we find that it corresponds to 0.67 standard deviation unit. Now we can quickly calculate the scores that receive C's. First we find the upper limit of the C range by taking the mean (72) and adding to it 0.67 × 5 or 3.35. This yields 75.35, which represents the quarter of the area above the mean. To get the lower limit of the range, we take the mean (72) and subtract from it 0.67×5, or $72 - 3.35$. This gives us 68.65. After rounding, we find that all students who scored 69–75 would receive the C grade.

The normal curve is important because many of the variables mass media researchers encounter are distributed in a normal manner, or normally enough that minor departures can be overlooked. Furthermore, the normal curve is an example of a probability distribution which becomes important in inferential statistics (see Chapter 12). Finally, many of the more advanced statistics discussed in later chapters assume normal distribution of the variable(s) under consideration.

Basic Correlational Statistics

The discussion up to this point has dealt with analysis of a single variable. In many situations, however, two different pieces of data must be examined simultaneously to determine whether a relationship exists between them, that is, to discover whether the variables are covariant. For example, a researcher might hypothesize an association between the number of pictures on the front page of a newspaper and the total number of copies of the paper sold at newsstands. If the observations reveal that the more pictures there are, the more papers are sold, a relationship can be said to exist between the two variables. Numerical expressions of the degree to which two variables change in relation with one another are called *measures of association* or *correlation*.

When making two different measurements of the same person, it is common to designate one measure as the X *variable* and the other as the Y *variable*. For example, in determining whether a relationship exists between the size of a subject's family and the frequency with which that person reads a newspaper, the measure of family size could be the X variable and the measure of newspaper reading the Y variable. Note that each subject in the group under study must be measured for both variables.

Figure 10.8 contains hypothetical data collected from a study of eight subjects. The Y variable is the number of times per week the newspaper is read; the X variable is the number of persons in the household. The scores are plotted on a **scattergram**, a graphic technique for portraying a relationship between two or more variables. The two scores per subject are shown on the scattergram. As indicated, family size and newspaper reading increase together. This is an example of a *positive relationship*.

An *inverse* (or *negative*) *relationship* exists when one variable increases while the other decreases. Sometimes the relationship between two variables is positive up to a point and then becomes inverse (or vice versa). When this happens, the relationship is said to be *curvilinear*. When there is no tendency for a high score on one variable to be

Figure 10.8 Scattergram of family size and newspaper reading scores

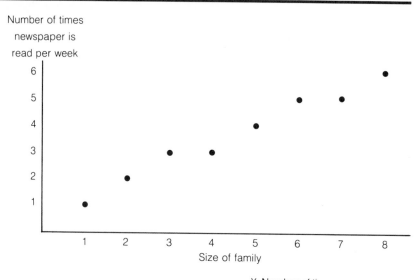

Subject	X: Family size	Y: Number of times newspaper is read per week
A	1	1
B	2	2
C	3	3
D	4	3
E	5	4
F	6	5
G	7	5
H	8	6

associated with a high or low score on another variable, the two are said to be *uncorrelated*. Figure 10.9 illustrates these relationships.

There are many statistics available to measure the degree of relationship between two variables, but the most commonly used is the Pearson product–moment correlation, commonly symbolized as r. It varies between -1.00 and $+1.00$. A correlation coefficient of $+1.00$ indicates a perfect positive correlation: X and Y are completely co-variant. A Pearson r of -1.00 indicates a perfect relationship in the negative direction. The lowest value that the Pearson r can achieve is 0.00. This represents absolutely no relationship between two variables. Thus, the Pearson r contains two pieces of information: (1) an estimate of the strength of the relationship, as indicated by the number, and (2) a statement about the direction of the relationship, as shown by the sign. Keep in mind that the strength of the relationship depends solely on the number; strength of relationship must be interpreted in terms

Figure 10.9 Scattergrams of various possible relationships

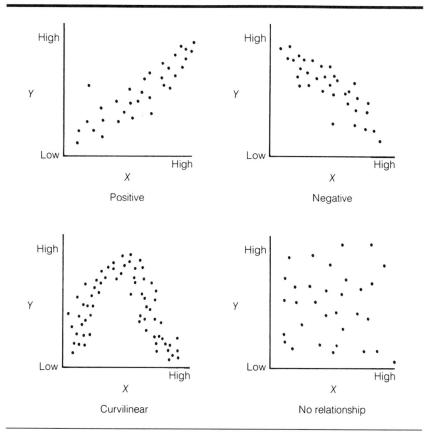

of absolute value. A correlation of − .83 is a stronger relationship than one of + .23.

The formula for calculating *r* looks foreboding; actually, however, it includes only one new expression:

$$r = \frac{N\Sigma XY - \Sigma X \Sigma Y}{\sqrt{[N\Sigma X^2 - (\Sigma X)^2][N\Sigma Y^2 - (\Sigma Y)^2]}}$$

Where *X* and *Y* stand for the original scores, *N* is the number of pairs of scores, and Σ again is the summation symbol. The only new term is Σ*XY*, which stands for the sum of the products of each *X* and *Y*. To find this quantity, simply multiply each *X* variable by its corresponding *Y* variable and add the results. Table 10.10 demonstrates a computation of *r*. (The use of a calculator or computer is recommended when *N* is large, since the calculation of *r* can be tedious when many observations are involved.)

A correlation coefficient is a pure number—it is not expressed in feet, inches, or pounds, nor is it a proportion or percent.

Table 10.10 Calculation of r

Subject	X	X^2	Y	Y^2	XY
A	1	1	1	1	1
B	2	4	2	4	4
C	3	9	3	9	9
D	4	16	3	9	12
E	4	16	4	16	16
F	5	25	5	25	25
G	6	36	5	25	30
H	8	64	6	36	48
$N = 8$	$\Sigma X = 33$	$\Sigma X^2 = 171$	$\Sigma Y = 29$	$\Sigma Y^2 = 125$	$\Sigma XY = 145$

$(\Sigma X)^2 = 1{,}089$

$(\Sigma Y)^2 = 841$

$$r = \frac{(8)(145) - (33)(29)}{\sqrt{[(8)(171) - 1089][(8)(125) - 841]}}$$

$$= \frac{203}{\sqrt{(279)(159)}} = \frac{203}{(16.7)(12.6)}$$

$$= \frac{203}{210.62} = .964$$

r formula:

$$\frac{N\Sigma XY - \Sigma X\Sigma Y}{\sqrt{[N\Sigma X^2 - (\Sigma X)^2][N\Sigma Y^2 - (\Sigma Y)^2]}}$$

The Pearson r is independent of the size and units of measurement of the original data (in fact, the original scores do not have to be expressed in the same units). Because of its abstract nature, r must be interpreted with care. In particular, it is not as easy as it sounds to determine whether a correlation is large or small. Some writers have suggested various adjectives to describe certain ranges of r. For example, an r between .40 and .70 might be called a "moderate" or "substantial" relationship, while an r of .71 to .90 might be termed "very high." These labels are helpful, but they may lead to confusion. The best advice is to consider the nature of the study. For example, an r of .70 between frequency of viewing television violence and frequency of arrest for violent crimes would be more than substantial; it would be phenomenal. Conversely, a correlation of .70 between two coders' timings of the length of news stories on the evening news is low enough to call the reliability of the study into question.

Additionally, correlation does not in itself imply causation. Newspaper reading and income might be strongly related, but this does not mean that earning a high salary "causes" people to read the newspaper. Correlation is just one factor in determining causality. Furthermore, a large r does not necessarily mean that the two sets of correlated scores are equal. For example, the time spent reading a newspaper might have a correlation of .90 with the time spent viewing television news. This does not mean that people spend the same amount of time reading a newspaper as they do watching news. The Pearson r measures only covariation of the variables; it says nothing about magnitude.

Perhaps the best way to interpret r is in terms of the **coefficient of determination**, or the proportion of the total variation of one measure that can be determined by the other. This is calculated by squaring the Pearson r to arrive at a ratio of the two variances: the denominator of this ratio is the total variance of one of the variables, while the numerator is the part of the total variance that can be attributed to the other variable. For example, if $r = .40$, then $r^2 = .16$. One variable explains 16% of the variation in the other. Or, to put it another way, 16% of the information necessary to make a perfect prediction from one variable to another is known. Obviously, if $r = 1.00$, then $r^2 = 100\%$; one variable allows perfect predictability of the other. The quantity $1 - r^2$ is usually called the **coefficient of nondetermination** because it represents that proportion of the variance left unaccounted for or unexplained.

Suppose that a correlation of .30 is found between a child's aggression and the amount of television violence the child views. This would mean that 9% of the total variance in aggression is accounted for by television violence. The other 91% of the variation is unexplained (except to the extent that it is not accounted for by the television variable). Note that the coefficient of determination is not measured on an equal interval scale: .80 is twice as large as .40, but this does not mean that an r of .80 represents twice as great a relationship between two variables as an r of .40. In fact, the r of .40 explains 16% of the variance, while the r of .80 explains 64%—four times as much.

The Pearson r can be computed between any two sets of scores. For the statistic to be a valid description of the relationship, however, several assumptions must be made: (1) that the data represent interval or ratio measurements; (2) that the relationship between X and Y is a linear one, not curvilinear; (3) that the distributions of the X and Y variables are symmetrical and comparable. (Pearson's r can also be used as an inferential statistic. When this is the case, it is necessary to assume that X and Y come from normally distributed populations with similar variances.) If these assumptions cannot validly be made, the researcher must use another kind of correlation coefficient, such as Spearman's rho or Kendall's W. For a thorough discussion of these and other correlation coefficients, the reader should consult Siegel (1956) or Nunnally (1978).

Figure 10.10 Perfect linear correlation

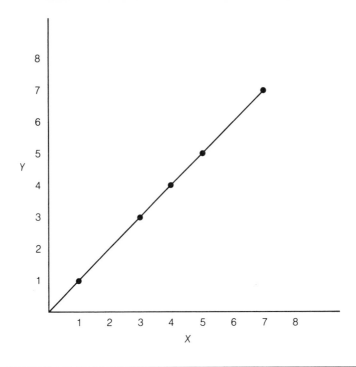

Simple Linear Regression

Simple correlation requires the measurement of the relationship between two variables. Simple linear regression is used to determine the degree to which one variable changes with a given change in another variable. Thus, linear regression is a way of using the association between two variables as a method of prediction. Let's take the simplest case to illustrate the logic behind this technique. Suppose two variables are perfectly related ($r = 1.00$). Knowledge of a person's score on one variable will allow the researcher to determine the score on the other. Figure 10.10 is a scattergram that portrays such a situation. Note that all the points lie on a straight line, the regression line. Unfortunately, relationships are never this simple, and scattergrams more often resemble the one portrayed in Figure 10.11a. Obviously, no single line can be drawn straight through all the points in the scattergram. It is possible, however, to mathematically construct a line that best represents all the observations in the figure. This line will come the closest to all the dots, although it might not pass through any of them. Mathematicians have worked out a technique to calculate such a line. This procedure, known as the "least squares" technique, yields a line that is

Figure 10.11 (a) Scattergram of X and Y; (b) scattergram with regression line

(a)

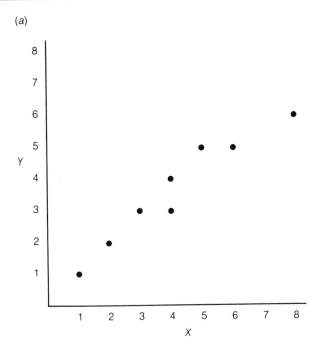

(b)

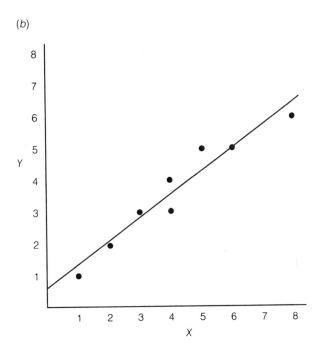

the best summary description of the relationship between two variables, X and Y. Figure 10.11b shows the best fitting line drawn through the data of Figure 10.11a.

At this point it is necessary to review some basic analytical geometry. Recall that the general equation for a line is $Y = a + bX$, where Y is the variable we are trying to predict and X is the variable we are predicting from. Furthermore, a represents the point at which the line crosses the y-axis (the vertical axis) and b is a measure of the slope (or steepness) of the line. In other words, b indicates how much Y changes for each change in X. Depending on the relationship between X and Y, slope can be positive or negative. To illustrate, Figure 10.10 shows that every time X increases one unit, so does Y. In addition, the a value is zero, since the line crosses the vertical axis at the origin.

Strictly speaking, the equation for a regression line is a little different from the general equation for a line, since the Y in the regression equation does not represent the actual variable Y but rather a predicted Y. Hence, the Y in the regression equation is usually symbolized $\hat{Y}$. Thus, the regression equation is written $\hat{Y} = a + bX$.

Now let's put this general equation into more concrete terms. Pretend that we have data on the relationship between years of education and number of minutes spent looking at the newspaper per day. The regression equation is:

$$\text{Minutes reading newspaper} = 2 + 3 \text{ (education)}$$

What can we deduce from this? In the first place, the a value tells us that a person with no formal education spends 2 minutes per day looking at the newspaper. The b value indicates that time spent with the newspaper increases 3 minutes with each additional year of education. What would be the prediction for someone with 10 years of education? Substituting, we have $\hat{Y} = 2 + 3(10) = 32$ minutes spent with the newspaper each day.

To take an additional example, consider the hypothetical regression equation predicting hours of TV viewed daily from a person's IQ score: $\hat{Y} = 5 - .01(\text{IQ})$. How many hours of TV would be viewed daily by someone with an IQ of 100?

$$\hat{Y} = 5 - (.01)(100) = 5 - 1 = 4 \text{ hours}$$

Thus, according to this equation, TV viewing per day decreases 0.01 hour for every point of IQ.

The arithmetical calculation of the regression equation is straightforward. First to find b, the slope of the line:

$$b = \frac{N\Sigma XY - (\Sigma X)(\Sigma Y)}{N\Sigma X^2 - (\Sigma X)^2}$$

Note that the numerator is exactly the same as that for the r coefficient and the denominator corresponds to the first expression in the denominator of the r formula. Thus, calculation of b is easily determined once the quantities necessary for r have been determined. To illustrate, using the data from Table 10.10:

$$b = \frac{8\,(145) - (33)\,(29)}{[8\,(171) - 1{,}089]} = \frac{203}{279} = 0.73$$

The value of the Y intercept (a) is found by the following:

$$a = \overline{Y} - b\overline{X}$$

Again, using the data in Table 10.10 and the foregoing calculation of b:

$$
\begin{aligned}
a &= 3.63 - (0.73)\,(4.125) \\
&= 3.63 - 3.01 \\
&= 0.62
\end{aligned}
$$

The completed regression equation is: $\hat{Y} = 0.62 + 0.73X$.

Of course, as the name suggests, simple linear regression assumes that the relationship between X and Y is linear. If an examination of the scattergram suggests a curvilinear relationship, other regression techniques are necessary. The notion of regression is extended in Chapter 12 to the situation of multiple predictor variables being used to predict the value of a single criterion variable.

Inferential Statistics

As seen in Chapter 4, researchers are not generally content to obtain results that apply only to the sample studied. They are interested in results that can be generalized to the population from which the sample was drawn. The statistics used to determine the degree of generalizability are called **inferential statistics**, and they represent the most widely used of all mass media research techniques.

To discuss the basics of inferential statistics, it is necessary to introduce some new symbols to differentiate those statistics that indicate population parameters, or characteristics, from those used to describe a sample:

Characteristic	Sample Statistic	Population Parameter
Average	$\overline{X}$ (or M)	μ (mu)
Variance	S^2	σ^2 (sigma squared)
Standard deviation	S (or SD)	σ (sigma)

It is also necessary to distinguish between three different types of distribution. A **sample distribution** is the distribution of some characteristic measured in the individuals or other units of analysis that were part of a sample. If a random sample of 1,500 college students were asked how many movies they attended in the last month, the resulting distribution of the variable "number of movies attended" would be a sample distribution, with a mean $(\overline{X})$ and variance (S^2). It is theoretically possible (though not practical) to ask the same question of every college student in the United States. This would create a **population distribution** with a mean (μ) and variance (σ^2). Ordinarily, the precise shape of the population distribution and the values of μ and σ^2 are unknown and are estimated from the sample. This estimate is called a **sampling distribution**.

In any sample drawn from a specified population, the mean of the sample, $\overline{X}$, will probably differ somewhat from the population mean, μ. For example, suppose that the average number of movies seen by each college student in the United States during the past month was exactly 3.8. It is unlikely that a random sample of 10 students from this population would produce a mean of exactly 3.8. The amount that the sample mean differs from μ is called *sampling error* (see Chapter 4). If more random samples of 10 were selected from this population, the values calculated for X that are close to the population mean would become more numerous than the values of X that are greatly different from μ. If this process were duplicated an infinite number of times and each mean placed on a frequency curve, the curve would form a sampling distribution.

Once the sampling distribution has been identified, statements about the *probability* of occurrence of certain values are possible. There are many ways to define the concept of probability. Stated simply, the probability that an event will occur is equal to the relative frequency of occurrence of that event in the population under consideration (Roscoe, 1975). To illustrate, suppose a large urn contains 1,000 table tennis balls, of which 700 are red and 300 white. The probability of drawing a red ball at random is 700/1,000, or 70%. It is also possible to calculate probability when the relative frequency of occurrence of an event is determined theoretically. For example, what is the probability of randomly guessing the answer to a true/false question? One out of two, or 50%. What is the probability of guessing the right answer on a four-item multiple-choice question? One out of four, or 25%. Probabilities can range from zero (no chance) to one (a sure thing). The sum of all the probable events in a population must equal 1.00, which is also the sum of the probabilities that an event will and will not occur. For instance, when a coin is tossed, the probability of its landing face up ("heads") is .50 and the probability of its not landing face up ("tails") is .50 (.50 + .50 = 1.00).

There are two important rules of probability. The "addition rule" states that the probability that any one of a set of mutually exclusive events will occur is the sum of the probabilities of the separate events. (Two events are mutually exclusive if the occurrence of one precludes the other. In the table tennis ball example, the color of the ball is either red or white; it cannot be both.) To illustrate the addition rule, consider a population in which 20% of the people read no magazines per month, 40% read only one, 20% read two, 10% read three, and 10% read four. What is the probability of selecting at random a person who reads at least two magazines per month? The answer is .40 (.20 + .10 + .10), the sum of the probabilities of the separate events.

The "multiplication rule" states that the probability of a combination of independent events occurring is the product of the separate probabilities of the events. (Two events are independent when the occurrence of one has no effect on the other. For example, getting "tails" on a flip of a coin has no impact on the next flip.) To illustrate the multiplication rule, calculate the probability that an unprepared student will correctly guess the right answers to the first four questions on a true/false test. The answer is the product of the probabilities of each event: .5 (chance of guessing right on Question 1) times .5 (chance of guessing right on Question 2) times .5 (chance of guessing right on Question 3) times .5 (chance of guessing right on Question 4) = .0625.

The notion of probability is important in inferential statistics because sampling distributions are a type of probability distribution. When the concept of probability is understood, a formal definition of "sampling distribution" is possible. A sampling distribution is *a probability distribution of all possible values of a statistic that would occur if all possible samples of a fixed size from a given population were taken*. For each outcome, the sampling distribution determines the probability of occurrence. For example, assume that a population consists of six college students. Their film viewing for the last month was as follows:

Student	Number of Films Seen
A	1
B	2
C	3
D	3
E	4
F	5

$$\mu = \frac{1 + 2 + 3 + 3 + 4 + 5}{6} = 3.00$$

Suppose a study is made using a sample of two ($N = 2$) from this population. As is evident, there is a limit to the number of combinations that can be generated, assuming that sampling is done without replacement. Table 10.11 shows the possible outcomes.

The mean of this sampling distribution is equal to μ, the mean of the population. The likelihood of drawing a sample whose mean is 2.0 or 1.5 or any other value is found simply by reading the figure in the far right-hand column.

Table 10.11 Generating a Sampling Distribution Population = (1,2,3,3,4,5) N = 2

$\overline{X}$	Number of possible sample combinations producing this $\overline{X}$	Probability of occurrence
1.5	2 (1,2) (2,1)	2/30 or .07
2.0	4 (1,3) (1,3) (3,1) (3,1)	4/30 or .13
2.5	6 (1,4) (2,3) (2,3) (3,2) (3,2) (4,1)	6/30 or .20
3.0	6 (1,5) (2,4) (3,3) (3,3) (4,2) (5,1)	6/30 or .20
3.5	6 (2,5) (3,4) (3,4) (4,3) (4,3) (5,2)	6/30 or .20
4.0	4 (3,5) (3,5) (5,3) (5,3)	4/30 or .13
4.5	2 (4,5) (5,4)	2/30 or .07
		1.00

Total number of possible sample combinations = 30

Table 10.11 is an example of a sampling distribution determined by empirical means. Many sampling distributions, however, are not derived by mathematical calculations but are determined theoretically. For example, sampling distributions often take the form of a normal curve. When this is the case, the researcher can make use of everything that is known about the properties of the normal curve. This can be illustrated by a hypothetical example using dichotomous data, or data with only two possible values. (This type of data is chosen because it makes the mathematics less complicated. The same logic applies to continuous data, but the computations are elaborate.) Consider the case of a television rating firm attempting to estimate from the results of a sample the total number of people in the population who saw a given program. One sample of 100 people might produce an estimate of 40%, a second an estimate of 42%, and a third an estimate of 39%. If, after a large number of samples have been taken, the results are expressed as a sampling distribution, probability theory predicts that it would have the shape of the normal curve with a mean equal to μ. This distribution is shown in Figure 10.12. Interestingly enough, if a person draws samples of size N repeatedly from a given population, the sampling distribution of the means of these samples, assuming N is large enough, will almost always be normal. This holds even if the population itself is not normally distributed. Furthermore, the mean of the sampling distribution will equal the population mean—the parameter.

In earlier discussions of the normal curve, the horizontal divisions along the base of the curve were expressed in terms of standard deviation units. With sampling distributions, this unit is called the *standard error* (*SE*) and serves as a criterion for determining the probable accuracy of an estimate. As is the case with the normal curve, roughly 68% of the sample will fall within ± 1 standard error of the population mean, and about 95% will fall within ± 2 standard errors.

Figure 10.12 Hypothetical sampling distribution

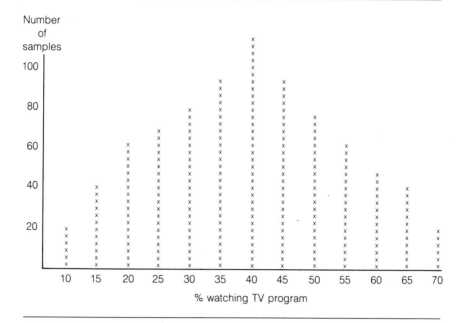

In most actual research studies, a sampling distribution is not generated by taking large numbers of samples and computing the probable outcome of each, and the standard error is not computed by taking the standard deviation of a sampling distribution of means. Instead, a researcher takes only one sample and uses it to estimate the population mean and the standard error. The process of inference from only one sample works in the following way: the sample mean is used as the best estimate of the population mean, and the standard error is calculated from the sample data. Suppose that in the foregoing example, 40 out of a sample of 100 people were watching a particular program. The mean, in this case symbolized as p because the data are dichotomous, is 40% (dichotomous data require this unique formula). The standard error in this dichotomous situation is calculated by the formula:

$$SE = \sqrt{\frac{pq}{N}}$$

where p = the proportion viewing, $q = 1 - p$, and N = the number in the sample. In the example, the standard error is $[(.6)(.4)/100]^{1/2}$ or .048. This means that about 68% of all possible samples will give estimates of 35.2–44.8%, and 95% will give estimates of 30.4–49.6%. There is only a .025 chance of getting a sample mean of less than 30.4%.

Instead of calculating the chances of a given sample mean falling two standard errors or more from the population mean, we could just as easily compute the chances of the population mean falling two or more standard errors from a given sample mean. In fact, the two procedures are mirror images. It is just as probable that the sample mean will be two standard errors above the population mean as it is that the population mean will be two standard errors below the sample mean. This fact allows the researcher to construct *confidence intervals* (*CI*) from the results of one sample. There is a specified probability that the parameter will lie within a predetermined confidence interval. The most common confidence interval is the .95 level, which is expressed by the following formula:

$$.95CI = p \pm 1.96SE$$

where p is the proportion obtained in the sample, SE is the standard error, and 1.96 is the specific value to use for encompassing exactly 95% of the scores in a normal distribution.

As an example, consider that a television ratings firm sampled 400 people and found that 20% of the sample were watching a certain program. What is the .95 confidence interval estimate for the population mean? The standard error is equal to the square root of [(.20)(.80)]/400, or .02. Inserting this value into the formula above yields a confidence interval of .20 $\pm$ (2)(.02), or .16–.24. In other words, there is a .95 chance that the population average lies between 16 and 24%. There is also a 5% chance of error, that is, that μ lies outside this interval. If this 5% chance is too great a risk, it is possible to compute a .99 confidence interval estimate by substituting 2.58 for 2 in the formula (in the normal curve, 99% of all scores fall within $\pm$ 2.58 standard errors of the mean). For a discussion of confidence intervals using continuous data, the reader should consult Hays (1973).

The concept of sampling distribution is important to statistical inference. Confidence intervals represent only one way in which sampling distributions are used in inferential statistics. They are also an important feature of *hypothesis testing*, in which the probability of a specified sample result is determined under assumed population conditions (see Chapter 11).

Data Transformation

Most statistical procedures are based on the assumption that the data are normally distributed. Although many statistical procedures are "robust" or conservative in their requirement of normally distributed data, in some instances the results of studies using data that show a high degree of skewness or kurtosis may be invalid. The data used for any study should be checked for normality, a procedure accomplished very easily with most canned computer programs (see Chapter 17).

Most abnormal distributions are caused by outliers. When such anomalies arise, researchers can attempt to transform the data to achieve normality. Basically, transformation involves performing some type of mathematical adjustment to *each score* to try and bring the outliers closer to the group mean. This may take the form of multiplying or dividing each score by a certain number, or even taking the square root or log of the scores. It makes no difference what procedure is used (although some methods are more powerful than others), as long as the same method is employed for all the data.

There are a variety of transformation methods from which to choose, depending on the type of distribution found in the data. Rummel (1970) describes these procedures in great detail.

Summary

This chapter has introduced some of the more common descriptive and inferential statistics used by mass media researchers. Little attempt has been made to explain the mathematical derivations of the formulas and principles presented; rather, the emphasis here (as throughout the book) has been placed on understanding the reasoning behind these statistics and their applications. Unless researchers understand the logic underlying such concepts as "mean," "standard deviation," and "standard error," the statistics themselves will be of little value.

Questions and Problems for Further Investigation

1. Find the mean, variance, and standard deviation for the following frequency distribution:

   X f
   0 5
   1 2
   2 2
   3 1
   4 0

2. From a regular deck of playing cards, what is the probability of randomly drawing an ace? An ace *or* a nine? A spade *or* a face card?

3. Assume that scores on the Miller Analogies Test are normally distributed in the population with a μ of 50 and a population standard deviation of 5. What is the probability that:

a. Someone picked at random will have a score between 50 and 55?

b. Someone picked at random will score two standard deviations above the mean?

c. Someone picked at random will have a score of 58 or higher?

4. Assume a population of scores consisting of the following: 2, 4, 5, 5, 7, and 9. Generate the sampling distribution of the mean if $N = 2$ (sampling without replacement).

5. Calculate r between the following set of scores:

X	Y
1	8
1	6
3	5
2	4
2	3
4	5
5	2
7	3

References and Suggested Readings

Blalock, H. M. (1972). *Social statistics.* New York: McGraw-Hill.

Champion, D. J. (1981). *Basic statistics for social research.* Boston: Houghton Mifflin.

Hays, W. L. (1973). *Statistics for the social sciences.* New York: Holt, Rinehart & Winston.

Nunnally, J. (1978). *Psychometric theory.* New York: McGraw-Hill.

Roscoe, J. T. (1975). *Fundamental research statistics for the behavioral sciences.* New York: Holt, Rinehart & Winston.

Rummel, R. J. (1970). *Factor analysis.* Chicago: Northwestern University Press.

Siegel, S. (1956). *Nonparametric statistics for the behavioral sciences.* New York: McGraw-Hill.

Williams, F. (1979). *Reasoning with statistics.* New York: Holt, Rinehart & Winston.

C H A P T E R   1 1

Hypothesis Testing

RESEARCH QUESTIONS AND HYPOTHESES

·

TESTING HYPOTHESES FOR STATISTICAL SIGNIFICANCE

·

SUMMARY

·

QUESTIONS AND PROBLEMS FOR FURTHER INVESTIGATION

·

REFERENCES AND SUGGESTED READINGS

I t is a rare occurrence for a scientist to begin a research study without a problem or question to test. This is similar to holding a cross-country running race without telling the runners where to start. Both situations need an initial step: for the cross-country race, a starting line is required; the research study needs a statement or question to test. This chapter describes the procedures of developing research questions and the steps involved in testing them.

Research Questions and Hypotheses

Mass media research utilizes a variety of approaches to help answer questions. Some research is informal and seeks to solve relatively simple problems; some is based on theory and requires formally worded questions. All researchers, however, must start with some tentative generalization regarding a relationship between two or more variables. These generalizations may take two forms: *research questions* and *statistical hypotheses*. The two are identical except for the aspect of prediction: hypotheses predict an experimental outcome; research questions do not.

Research Questions

Research questions are often used in problem- or policy-oriented studies where researchers are not specifically interested in testing the statistical significance of their findings. For instance, researchers analyzing television program preferences or newspaper circulation probably would be concerned only with discovering general indications, not with gathering data for statistical testing. However, research questions can be tested for statistical significance. They are not merely weak hypotheses; they are valuable tools for many types of research.

Research questions are frequently used in areas that have been studied only marginally, or not at all. Studies of this nature are classified as *exploratory research* because investigators have no idea what may be found. They do not have enough prior information to make predictions. Exploratory research is intended to search for data *indications* rather than to attempt to determine *causality* (Tukey, 1962). The goal is to gather preliminary data, to be able to refine research questions and possibly to develop hypotheses.

Research questions may be stated as simple questions about the relationship between two or more variables, or about the components of a phenomenon. For example, researchers might ask "How does the content of political spot ads for female candidates differ from the content of ads for male candidates?" (Benze & Declerq, 1985) or "How do television and radio programs influence children's creativity as measured by a standardized test?" (Runco & Pezdek, 1984). Slater and Thompson (1984) posed several research questions about the attitudes of parents concerning warning statements that precede some television shows: "Do parents indicate that they frequently see the warning statements?" "Do the warnings influence parents' decisions about the suitability of a program for their child's viewing?" "Do parents advocate the imposition of a movie-type rating system for TV programs?"

In countless situations, however, researchers develop studies on the basis of existing theory and are thus able to attempt predictions about the outcome of the work. Brody (1984) hypothesized that access to the diverse offerings of cable television will produce a decline in borrowing books from the library. His data revealed support for this hypothesis in one cable market but not in another. Stroman and Seltzer (1985) hypothesized that persons relying on the newspaper for most of their news about crime would differ from those who rely on television news in their perceptions of the causes of crime. The hypothesis was supported by the data: TV news viewers said that flaws in the court system were a major contributing factor to crime, whereas newspaper readers cited poverty as a main cause.

To facilitate the discussion of research testing, the remainder of this chapter uses only the word *hypothesis*. But recall that research questions and hypotheses are identical except for the absence of the element of prediction in the former.

Purpose of Hypotheses

Hypotheses offer researchers a variety of benefits. First, they *provide direction* for a study. As indicated at the opening of the chapter, research begun without hypotheses offers no starting point; there is no indication of the sequence of steps to follow. Hypothesis development is usually the culmination of a rigorous literature review and emerges as a natural step in the research process. Without hypotheses, research would lack focus and clarity.

A second benefit of hypotheses is that they *eliminate trial-and-error research*, that is, the haphazard investigation of a topic in the hope of finding something significant. Hypothesis development requires researchers to isolate a specific area for study. Trial-and-error research is time-consuming and wasteful. The development of hypotheses eliminates this waste.

Hypotheses also *help rule out intervening and confounding variables*. Since hypotheses focus research to precise testable statements, other variables, whether relevant or not, are excluded. For instance, researchers interested in determining how the media are used to provide consumer information must develop a specific hypothesis stating what media are included, what products are being tested for what specific demographic groups, and so on. Through this process of narrowing, extraneous and intervening variables are eliminated or controlled. This does not mean that hypotheses eliminate all error in research; nothing can do that. Error in some form is present in every study (see Chapter 3).

Finally, hypotheses *allow for quantification of variables.* As stated in Chapter 3, any concept or phenomenon is capable of quantification if put into an adequate operational definition. All terms used in hypotheses must have an operational definition. For example, to test the hypothesis "there is a significant difference between recall of television commercials for subjects exposed to low-frequency and high-frequency broadcasts," researchers would need operational definitions of "recall," "low-frequency," and "high-frequency." Words incapable of quantification cannot be included in a hypothesis.

In addition, some concepts have a variety of definitions. One example of this is "violence." The complaint of many researchers is not that violence is incapable of quantification, but rather that it is capable of being operationally defined in more than one way. Therefore, before comparing the results of studies of media violence, it is necessary to consider the definition of "violence" used in each study. Contradictory results may be due to the definitions used, not to the presence or absence of violence (see *Journal of Broadcasting, 21*(3), 1977, for several articles on violence).

Criteria for Good Hypotheses

A useful hypothesis should possess at least four essential characteristics: it should be compatible with current knowledge in the area; it should follow logical consistency; it should be in its most parsimonious form; and it should be testable.

That hypotheses must be in harmony with current knowledge is obvious. If available literature strongly suggests one point of view, researchers who develop hypotheses that oppose this knowledge without basis only slow the development of the area. For example, it has been demonstrated beyond a doubt that most people get their news information from television. It would be rather ludicrous for a researcher to develop a hypothesis suggesting that this is not true. There is simply too much evidence to the contrary.

The criterion of logical consistency means that if a hypothesis suggests that $A = B$ and $B = C$, then A must also be equal to C. That is, if reading the *New York Times* implies a knowledge of current events, and a knowledge of current events means greater participation in social activities, then readers of the *New York Times* should exhibit greater participation in social activities.

It should come as no surprise that hypotheses must be in their most parsimonious form. The concept of "the simpler, the better" (Occam's razor) is stressed throughout this book. A hypothesis such as, "Intellectual and psychomotor creativity possessed by an individual positively coincides with the level of intelligence of the individual as indicated by standardized evaluative procedures measuring intelligence" is not exactly parsimonious. Stated simply, the same hypothesis could read: "Psychomotor ability and IQ are positively related."

Developing an untestable hypothesis is clearly unproductive. Research is complicated enough without attempting to develop hypotheses that can add nothing to existing knowledge. For example, the hypothesis "High school students with no exposure to television in their lifetime will develop paranoid tendencies after viewing television for 48 hours" cannot be tested. Where would researchers find a sample of high school students who have never seen television? Additionally, it is important to avoid value-laden concepts that are difficult or impossible to operationalize, such as: "Watching television is morally degrading."

The Null Hypothesis

The **null hypothesis** (also called the "alternative hypothesis" and the "hypothesis of no difference") asserts that the statistical differences or relationships being analyzed are due to chance or random error. The null hypothesis (H_0) is the logical alternative to the research hypothesis (H_1). For example, the hypothesis "The level of attention paid to radio commercials is positively related to the amount of recall of the commercial" has its logical alternative, "The level of attention paid to radio commercials is not related to the amount of recall of the commercial."

In practice, researchers rarely state the null hypothesis. Since every research hypothesis does have its logical alternative, stating the null form is redundant (Williams, 1979). However, the null hypothesis is always present and plays an important role in the rationale underlying hypothesis testing.

Testing Hypotheses for Statistical Significance

In hypothesis testing, or significance testing, the researcher either rejects or accepts the null hypothesis. That is, if H_0 is accepted (supported), it is assumed that H_1 is rejected; and if H_0 is rejected, H_1 must be accepted.

To determine the statistical significance of a research study, the researcher must set a **probability level,** or significance level, against which the null hypothesis can be tested. If the results of the study indicate a probability lower than this level, the researcher can reject the null hypothesis. If the research outcome has a high probability, the researcher must support (or, more precisely, fail to reject) the null hypothesis. In reality, since the null hypothesis is not generally stated, acceptance and rejection apply to the research hypothesis, not to the null hypothesis.

The probability level is expressed by a lowercase letter p (indicating probability), followed by a "less than" or "less than or equal to" sign, and then a value. For example, "$p \leq .01$" means that the null hypothesis is being tested at the .01 level of significance and that the results will be considered statistically significant if the probability is equal to or lower than this level. A .05 level of significance indicates that the researcher has a 5% chance of making a wrong decision about rejecting the null hypothesis (or accepting the research hypothesis). Establishing a level of significance depends on the amount of error researchers are willing to accept (in addition to other factors peculiar to the particular research study). The question of error is discussed in greater detail later in the chapter.

It is common practice in behavioral research studies to set the probability level at .01 or .05, which means that either once or five times out of 100, the results of the study are based on random error or chance. There is no logical reason for using these figures; the practice has been followed for many years, basically because Sir Ronald A. Fisher, who developed the concept of significance testing, formulated tables based on the areas under the normal curve defined by these points. In many research areas, however, the trend is to set the significance level according to the purpose of the study rather than by general convention. Some studies use .10 or .20 depending on the goals of the research. In exploratory research especially, more liberal levels are generally used; these are made more restrictive as further information is gathered.

In a theoretical sampling distribution, the proportion of the area in which the null hypothesis is rejected is called the **region of rejection.** This area is defined by the level of significance chosen by the researcher. If the .05 level of significance is used, then 5% of the sampling distribution becomes the critical region. Conversely, the null hypothesis is retained in the region between the two rejection values (or levels).

As Figure 11.1 shows, the regions of rejection are located in the tails or outer edges of the sampling distribution. The terms "one-tail testing" and "two-tail testing" refer to the type of prediction made in a research study. A one-tail test predicts that the results will fall in only one direction—either positive or negative. This approach is more stringent than the two-tail test, which predicts results in both directions.

Figure 11.1 The regions of rejection for $p \leq .05$ (two-tailed)

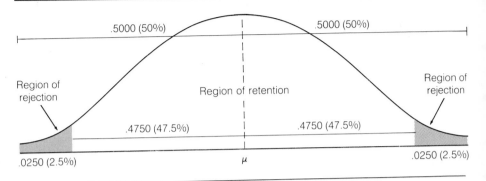

Two-tail tests are generally used when little information is available about the research area. One-tail tests are used when researchers have more knowledge of the area and are able to more accurately predict the outcome of the study.

Consider, for example, a study of the math competency of a group of subjects who receive a special type of learning treatment, possibly a series of television programs on mathematics. The hypothesis is that the group, after viewing the programs, will have scores on a standardized math test significantly different from those of the remainder of the population, which has not seen the programs. The level of significance is set at .05, indicating that for the null hypothesis to be rejected, the sample's mean test score must fall outside the boundaries in the normal distribution that are specified by the statement, "$p \leq .05$." These boundaries, or values, are determined by a simple computation. First, the critical values of the boundaries are found by consulting the normal distribution table (see Areas Under the Normal Curve, Appendix 1, Table 3).

In Figure 11.1, the area from the middle of the distribution, or μ, the hypothesized mean (denoted by a dotted line), to the end of the tails is 50%. At the .05 level, using a two-tailed test, there is a 2.5% (.0250) area of rejection tucked into each tail. Consequently, the area from the middle of the distribution to the region of rejection is equal to 47.5% (50% − 2.5% = 47.5%). It follows that the corresponding z values that will define the region of rejection are those that cut off 47.5% (.4750) of the area from μ to each end of the tail. To find this z value, use Table 3 of Appendix 1 (Areas Under the Normal Curve). This table provides a list of the proportions of various areas under the curve as measured from the midpoint of the curve out toward the tails. The far left column displays the first two digits of the z value. The row across the top of the table contains the third digit. For example, find the 1.0 row in the left-hand column. Next, find the entry under the .08 column in this row. The tabled entry is .3599. This means that 35.99% of the curve is found between the midpoint and a z value of

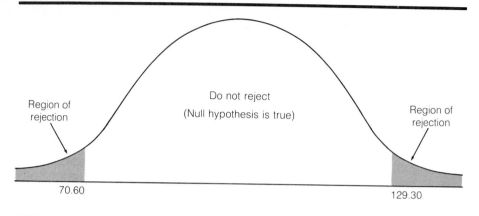

Figure 11.2 Regions of rejection for math test

Region of rejection

Do not reject
(Null hypothesis is true)

Region of rejection

70.60

129.30

1.08. Of course, another 35.99% lies in the other direction, from the midpoint to a z value of − 1.08. In our current example, it is necessary to work backwards. We know the areas under the curve that we want to define (.4750 to the left and right of μ) and need to find the z values. An examination of the body of Table 3 shows that .4750 corresponds to a z value of ± 1.96.

These values are then used to determine the region of rejection:

$$-1.96 \; \alpha_m + \mu = \text{lower boundary}$$
$$+1.96 \; \alpha_m + \mu = \text{upper boundary}$$

where α_m = the standard deviation of the distribution and μ = the population mean. Assume that the population mean for math competency is 100 and the standard deviation is 15. Thus, the sample group must achieve a mean math competency score either lower than 70.60 or higher than 129.40 for the research study to be considered significant:

$$-1.96(15) + 100 = 70.60$$
$$+1.96(15) + 100 = 129.40$$

If a research study produces a number between 70.60 and 129.40, the null hypothesis cannot be rejected; the instructional television programs had no significant effect on math levels. Using the normal distribution to demonstrate these boundaries, the area of rejection is illustrated in Figure 11.2.

Error

As with all steps in the research process, testing for statistical significance involves error. Two types of error particularly relevant

Figure 11.3 Type I and Type II errors

	Reject H_0	Accept H_0
H_0 is true	Type I error	Correct
H_0 is false	Correct	Type II error

to hypothesis testing are known as **Type I error** and **Type II error.** Type I error is the rejection of a null hypothesis that should be accepted, and Type II error is the acceptance of a null hypothesis that should be rejected. These error types are represented in Figure 11.3.

The probability of making a Type I error is equal to the established level of significance and is therefore under the direct control of the researcher. That is, to reduce the probability of Type I error, the researcher can simply set the level of significance closer to zero.

Type II error, often signified by the symbol β, is a bit more difficult to conceptualize. The researcher does not have direct control over Type II error; instead, Type II error is controlled, although indirectly, by the design of the experiment. In addition, the level of Type II error is inversely proportional to the level of Type I error: as Type I error decreases, Type II error increases, and vice versa. The potential magnitude of Type II error depends in part on the probability level and in part on which of the possible alternative hypotheses actually is true. Figure 11.4 shows the inverse relationship between the two types of error.

As mentioned earlier, most research studies do not state the null hypothesis, since it is generally assumed. There is a way to depict Type I and Type II errors without considering the null hypothesis, however, and this approach may help to demonstrate the relationship between Type I and Type II errors.

As Figure 11.5 demonstrates, the research hypothesis is used to describe Type I and Type II errors instead of the null hypothesis. To use the table, start at the desired row on the left side and then read the column entry that completes the hypothesis to be tested. For example: "Significant difference found where none exists = Type I error."

Figure 11.4 Inverse relationship between errors of Type I and Type II

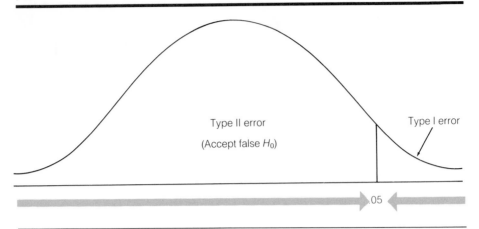

One final way to explain Type I and Type II errors is by using a hypothetical example. Consider a research study to determine the effects of a short-term public relations campaign promoting the use of safety belts in automobiles. Suppose that the effort was highly successful and indeed changed the behavior of a majority of the subjects exposed to the campaign (this information is of course unknown to the researcher). If the researcher finds that a significant effect was created by the campaign, the conclusion is a correct one; if the researcher does not find a significant effect, he or she has committed a Type II error. On the other hand, if the campaign actually had no effect, but the researcher concludes that the campaign was successful, he or she has committed a Type I error.

Figure 11.5 Use of the research hypothesis to distinguish between errors of Type I and Type II

	Where one exists	Where none exists
Significant difference found	Correct	Type I error
No significant difference found	Type II error	Correct

The Importance of Significance

The concept of significance testing causes problems for many people. The main reason for this is that too many researchers overemphasize the importance of significance. When researchers find that the results of a study are nonsignificant, it is not uncommon to "talk around" the results—to de-emphasize the finding that the results were not significant. But there is really no need to follow this course of action.

There is no difference in value between a study that finds significant results and a study that does not. Both studies provide valuable information. Discovering that some variables are not significant is just as important as determining what variables are significant. The nonsignificant study can save time for other researchers working in the same area by ruling out worthless variables. Nonsignificant research is important in collecting information about a theory or concept.

Also, there is nothing wrong with the idea of proposing a null hypothesis as the research hypothesis. For example, a researcher could formulate the following hypothesis: "There is no significant difference in comprehension of program content between a group of adults (age 18–49) with normal hearing that views a television program with closed-captioned phrases and a similar group that views the same program without captions." A scientific research study does not always have to test for significant relationships; it can also test for nonsignificance. However, sloppy research techniques and faulty measurement procedures can add to the error variance in a study and contribute to the failure to reject a hypothesis of no difference as well as jeopardize the entire study. This is a danger in using a null hypothesis as a substantive hypothesis.

Power

The concept of **power** is intimately related to Type I and Type II errors. Power refers to the probability of rejecting the null hypothesis when an alternative is true. In other words, power indicates the probability that a statistical test of a null hypothesis will result in the conclusion that the phenomenon under study actually exists (Cohen, 1969).

Statistical power is a function of three parameters: probability level, sample size, and effects size. As we know, the probability level is under the direct control of the researcher and predetermines the probability of committing a Type I error. Sample size refers to the number of subjects utilized in an experiment. The most difficult concept is *effects size*. Basically, the effects size is the degree to which the null hypothesis is rejected; this can be stated either in general terms (such as *any* nonzero value) or in exact terms (such as .40). That is, when a null hypothesis is false, it is false to some degree; researchers can state that the null hypothesis is false and leave it at that, or they can specify exactly how false it is. The larger the effects size, the greater the degree to which the phenomenon under study is present (Cohen, 1969). However, researchers seldom know the exact value of effects size. When such precision is lacking, researchers can use one of three alternatives.

1. Estimate the effects size, based on knowledge in the area of investigation or indications from previous studies in the area, or simply state the size as "small," "medium," or "large." (Cohen describes these values in greater detail.)
2. Assume an effects size of "medium."
3. Select a series of effects sizes and experiment.

When the probability level, sample size, and effects size are known, researchers can consult power tables (published in statistics books) to determine the level of power present in their study.

A determination of power is important for two reasons. First and most important, if a low power level prevents researchers from attaining statistical significance, a Type II error may result. If the power of the statistical test is increased, however, the results may be made significant.

Second, a high power level may help in interpretation of research results. If an experiment just barely reaches the significance level but has high power, researchers can place more faith in the results. Without power figures, the researchers would have to be more hesitant in their interpretations.

Consideration of statistical power should be a step in all research studies. Although power is only an approximation, computation of the value helps control Type II error. In addition, as power increases, there is no direct effect on Type I error; power acts independently of Type I error. Since the mid-1970s, researchers have paid closer attention to statistical power.

Chase and Tucker (1975) conducted power analyses on articles published in nine communications journals. The authors found that 82% of the 46 articles analyzed had an average power for medium effects of less than .80 (the recommended minimum power value). In addition, more than half the articles had an average power of less than .50, which suggests a significant increase in the probability of Type II error.

Summary

Hypothesis development in scientific research is important because the process refines and focuses a research question. Rarely will a scientist begin a research study without a hypothesis in some form. This chapter served to introduce the process of developing hypotheses and to illustrate how they are tested and examined by mass media researchers. The chapters that follow describe various methods researchers use to test hypotheses and research questions.

Questions and Problems for Further Investigation

1. Develop three research questions and three hypotheses in any mass media area which could be investigated or tested.
2. What is your opinion about using very conservative levels of significance (.10 or greater) in exploratory research?
3. Conduct a brief review of published research in mass media. What percentage of the studies report the results of a power analysis calculation?
4. Explain the relationship between Type I and Type II errors.
5. Under what circumstances might a researcher use a probability level of .001?
6. If a researcher's significance level is set at $\alpha = .02$ and the results of the experiment indicate that the null hypothesis cannot be rejected, what is the probability of a Type I error?

References and Suggested Readings

Benze, J., & Declerq, E. (1985). Content of television spot ads for female candidates. *Journalism Quarterly, 62*(2), 278–283.

Brody, E. (1984). Impact of cable television on library borrowing. *Journalism Quarterly, 61*(3), 686–688.

Chase, L. J., & Tucker, R. K. (1975). A power-analytic examination of contemporary communication research. *Speech Monographs, 42*, 29–41.

Cohen, J. (1969). *Statistical power analysis for the behavioral sciences.* New York: Academic Press.

Doolittle, J. C. (1979). News media use by older adults. *Journalism Quarterly, 56*(2), 311–317.

Holly, S. (1979). Women in management of weeklies. *Journalism Quarterly, 56*(4), 810–815.

Joslyn, R. A. (1981). The impact of campaign spot advertising on voting decisions. *Human Communication Research, 7*(4), 347–360.

Roscoe, J. T. (1975). *Fundamental research statistics for the behavioral sciences.* New York: Holt, Rinehart & Winston.

Runco, M., & Pezdek, K. (1984). The effects of TV and radio on children's creativity. *Human Communication Research, 11*(1), 109–120.

Ryan, M. (1979). Reports, inferences and judgments in news coverage of social issues. *Journalism Quarterly, (56)*3, 497–503.

Slater, D., & Thompson, T. (1984). Attitudes of parents concerning televised warning statements. *Journalism Quarterly, 61*(4), 853–859.

Stroman C., & Seltzer, R. (1985). Media use and perception of crime. *Journalism Quarterly, 62*(2), 340–345.

Tukey, J. W. (1962). The future of data analysis. *Annals of Mathematical Statistics, 33*, 1–67.

Williams, F. (1979). *Reasoning with statistics.* (2nd ed). New York: Holt, Rinehart & Winston.

Inferential Statistics

HISTORY OF SMALL-SAMPLE STATISTICS

·

NONPARAMETRIC STATISTICS

·

PARAMETRIC STATISTICS

·

SUMMARY

·

QUESTIONS AND PROBLEMS FOR FURTHER INVESTIGATION

·

REFERENCES AND SUGGESTED READINGS

Researchers often wish to do more than merely describe a sample; they want to use their results to make inferences about the population from which the sample has been taken. This chapter describes some of the basic inferential statistical methods used in mass media research and indicates ways in which these methods may help answer questions.

History of Small-Sample Statistics

Samples were being employed in scientific research as long ago as 1627, when Sir Francis Bacon published an account of tests he had conducted measuring wheat seed growth in various forms of fertilizer. In 1763 Arthur Young began a series of experiments to discover the most profitable method of farming; and in 1849 James Johnston published a book called *Experimental Agriculture,* in which he provided advice on scientific research (Cochran, 1976).

One of the best-known investigators of the early twentieth century was William S. Gossett, who in 1908 attempted to quantify experimental results in a paper entitled "The Probable Error of the Mean." Under the pen name "Student," Gossett published the results of small-sample investigations he had conducted while working in a Dublin brewery. The *t*-distribution statistics Gossett developed were not widely accepted at the time; in fact, it was more than 15 years before other researchers began to take an interest in his work. The *t*-test, however, as will be seen, is now one of the most widely used statistical procedures in all areas of research.

Sir Ronald Fisher provided a stepping stone from early work in statistics and sampling procedures to modern statistical inference techniques. It was Fisher who developed the concept of probability and established the use of the .01 and .05 levels of probability testing (see Chapter 11). Until Fisher, statistical methods were not generally perceived as practical in areas other than agriculture, for which they were originally developed.

Nonparametric Statistics

Statistical methods are divided into two broad categories: **parametric** and **nonparametric.** Recall from Chapter 3 that a parameter is a population value such as the mean or variance. This definition describes the two broad categories of statistics: parametric statistics make assumptions about population parameters; nonparametric statistics make no such assumptions.

Another difference between the two categories is that nonparametric statistics are appropriate for nominal and ordinal data and parametric statistics are appropriate for interval and ratio data (see Chapter 3 for discussions of data forms). These two differences focus on one main point: parametric statistics are normally used to infer results from a sample to the population from which the sample was drawn; nonparametric statistics are generally not used for such inferences. However, the differences between nonparametric and parametric statistics have been questioned during the past several years, and many researchers no longer consider the two categories to be distinctly different. Some statisticians and researchers argue that both methods can be used successfully with any type of data (see Roscoe, 1975).

Chi-Square Goodness of Fit

It is often desirable in mass media research to compare the *observed* frequencies of a phenomenon with the frequencies that might be *expected* or hypothesized. For example, a researcher who wanted to determine whether the sales of television sets by four manufacturers in the current year are the same as sales for the previous year might advance the following hypothesis. "Television set sales of four major manufacturers are significantly different this year from those of the previous year."

Suppose the previous year's television set sales were distributed as follows:

Manufacturer	Percent of Sales
RCA	22
Sony	36
Quasar	19
Zenith	23

From these data, the investigator can calculate the expected frequencies (using a sample of 1,000) for each manufacturer's sales by multiplying the percentage of each sale by 1,000. The expected frequencies are:

Manufacturer	Expected Frequency
RCA	220
Sony	360
Quasar	190
Zenith	230

Next, the researcher surveys a random sample of 1,000

households known to have purchased one of the four manufacturers' television sets during the current year. Assume the data from this survey indicate the following distribution:

Manufacturer	Expected Frequency	Observed Frequency
RCA	220	180
Sony	360	330
Quasar	190	220
Zenith	230	270

The researcher now must interpret these data in a way that permits a statement of whether the change in frequency is actually *significant*. This can be done by reducing the data to a **chi-square statistic** and performing a test known as the chi-square "goodness of fit" test.

A chi-square (x^2) is simply a value showing the relationship between expected and observed frequencies. It is computed by means of the following formula:

$$x^2 = \sum \frac{(O_i - E_i)^2}{E_i}$$

where O_i = the observed frequencies and E_i = the expected frequencies. This means that the difference between each expected and observed frequency must be squared and then divided by the expected frequency. The sum of the quotients is the chi-square for those frequencies. For the frequency distribution above, chi-square is calculated as follows:

$$x^2 = \sum \frac{(O_1 - E_1)^2}{E_1}$$

$$= \frac{(O_1 - E_1)^2}{E_1} + \frac{(O_2 - E_2)^2}{E_2} + \frac{(O_3 - E_3)^2}{E_3} + \frac{(O_4 - E_4)^2}{E_4}$$

$$= \frac{(180 - 220)^2}{220} + \frac{(330 - 360)^2}{360} + \frac{(220 - 190)^2}{190} + \frac{(270 - 230)^2}{230}$$

$$= \frac{(-40)^2}{220} + \frac{(-30)^2}{360} + \frac{(30)^2}{190} + \frac{(40)^2}{230}$$

$$= \frac{1,600}{220} + \frac{900}{360} + \frac{900}{190} + \frac{1,600}{230}$$

$$= 7.27 + 2.50 + 4.73 + 6.95$$

$$= 21.45$$

Once the value of chi-square is known, the goodness of fit test can be performed to determine whether this value represents a significant difference in frequencies. To do this, the researcher must know two more values: the first is the probability level, which must be predetermined by the researcher; the second, called *degrees of freedom (df)*, is the number of scores in any particular test that are free to vary in value. For example, if one has three unknown values $(x, y,$ and $z)$ such that $x + y + z = 10$, there are two degrees of freedom: any two of the three variables may be assigned any value without affecting the total, but the value of the third will then be predetermined. Thus, if $x = 2$ and $y = 5$, z must be 3. In the goodness of fit test, degrees of freedom are expressed in terms of $K - 1$, where K is the number of categories. In the case of the television sales study, $K = 4$, and $df = 4 - 1 = 3$.

Next, the researcher must consult a chi-square table (see Appendix 1, Table 4). These tables are arranged by probability level and degrees of freedom. A portion of the chi-square table relevant to the hypothetical study has been adapted here to show how the table is used:

df	Probability			
	.10	.05	.01	.001
1	2.706	3.841	6.635	10.827
2	4.605	5.991	9.210	13.815
3	6.251	7.815	11.345	16.266
4	7.779	9.488	13.277	18.467

If the calculated chi-square value equals or exceeds the value found in the table, the differences in frequency are considered to be statistically significant at the predetermined alpha level; if the calculated value is smaller, the results are considered to be nonsignificant.

In the television sales example, suppose the researcher finds a chi-square value of 21.45, with a degree of freedom of 3 and has established a probability level of .05. The chi-square table shows a value of 7.815 at this level when $df = 3$. Since 21.45 is greater than 7.815, the frequency difference is significant, and the hypothesis is accepted or supported: television set sales of the four manufacturers are significantly different in the current year from sales in the previous year.

The chi-square goodness of fit test can be used in a variety of ways to measure changes—for example, in studies of audience perceptions of advertising messages over time, in planning changes in television programming, or in analyzing the results of public relations campaigns. Idsvoog and Hoyt (1977) used a chi-square test to analyze the professionalism and performance of television journalists. The authors were attempting to determine whether "professionalism" was related to several other characteristics, including the desire to look for employment, educational level, and job satisfaction. The results indi-

Media Most Used for New Product Information

	Radio	Newspapers	Television	
Male	3	26	71	100
Female	18	31	61	110
	21	57	132	

Sex

cated that journalists classified on the basis of questionnaire responses differed significantly from those classified as "medium" or "low" professionals.

There are limitations to the use of the goodness of fit test, however. Since this is a nonparametric statistical procedure, the variables must be measured at the nominal or ordinal level. The categories must be mutually exclusive, and each observation in each category must be independent from all others. Additionally, because the chi-square distribution square is sharply skewed (see Chapter 10) for small samples, Type II error may occur: small samples may not produce significant results in cases that could have yielded significant results if a larger sample had been used. To avoid this problem, most researchers suggest that each category contain at least five observations.

As an alternative to the chi-square goodness of fit test, many researchers prefer the Kolomogorov–Smirnov test, which is considered to be more powerful than the chi-square approach. In addition, a minimum number of expected frequencies in each cell is not required, as in the chi-square test (see Winkler & Hays, 1975, for more information about the Kolomogorov–Smirnov test).

Contingency Table Analysis

Another nonparametric statistical test that is often used in mass media research is the contingency table analysis, frequently called **cross-tabulation** or simply **crosstabs**. Crosstab analysis is basically an extension of the goodness of fit test, the primary difference being that two or more variables can be tested simultaneously. Consider a study to determine the relationship between a person's sex and his or her media usage habits in regard to obtaining information on new products. Suppose the researcher selects a random sample of 210 adults and obtains the information displayed in Figure 12.1.

The next step is to calculate the expected frequencies for each cell. This procedure is similar to that used in the goodness of fit test, but it involves a slightly more detailed formula:

$$E_{ij} = \frac{R_i C_j}{N}$$

where E_{ij} = expected frequency for cell in row i, column j; R_i = sum of frequencies in row i; C_j = sum of frequencies in column j; and N = sum of frequencies for all cells. Using this formula, the researcher in the hypothetical example can calculate the expected frequencies as follows:

$$\text{Male/radio} = \frac{100 \times 21}{210} = \frac{2,100}{210} = 10$$

$$\text{Female/radio} = \frac{110 \times 21}{210} = \frac{2,310}{210} = 11$$

and so forth. Each expected frequency is placed in a small square in the upper right-hand corner of the appropriate cell, as illustrated in Figure 12.2.

After the expected frequencies have been calculated, the investigator must compute the chi-square, using the following formula:

$$\chi^2 = \sum \frac{(O_{ij} - E_{ij})^2}{E_{ij}}$$

Using the same example:

$$\chi^2 = \frac{(3 - 10)^2}{10} + \frac{(26 - 27)^2}{27} + \frac{(71 - 63)^2}{63}$$

$$+ \frac{(18 - 11)^2}{11} + \frac{(31 - 30)^2}{30} + \frac{(61 - 69)^2}{69}$$

$$= \frac{49}{10} + \frac{1}{27} + \frac{64}{63} + \frac{49}{11} + \frac{1}{30} + \frac{64}{69}$$

$$= 4.90 + 0.04 + 1.01 + 4.45 + 0.03 + 0.92$$

$$= 11.35$$

To determine statistical significance, the researcher must now consult the chi-square table. In a crosstab analysis, the degrees of freedom are expressed as $(R - 1)(C - 1)$, where R is the number of

Figure 12.2 Random sample of media users showing expected frequencies

Media Most Used for New Product Information

	Radio	Newspapers	Television	
Male	10 / 3	27 / 26	63 / 71	100
Female	11 / 18	30 / 31	69 / 61	110
	21	57	132	

rows and C the number of columns. Assuming that $p \leq .05$, the chi-square value is listed in Table 4 of Appendix 1 as 5.991, which is lower than the calculated value of 11.35. Thus, there is a significant relationship between the sex of the respondent and the media used to acquire new product information. The test indicates that the two variables are somehow related, but it does not tell exactly how. To find this out, it is necessary to go back and examine the original crosstab data (Figure 12.1). Looking at the distribution, it is easy to see that females use radio more and television less than do males.

In the case of a 2 × 2 crosstab (where $df = 1$), computational effort is saved when the corresponding cells are represented by the letters A, B, C, and D, such as:

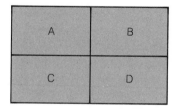

The following formula can then be used to compute the chi-square:

$$\chi^2 = \frac{N(AD - BC)^2}{(A + B)(C + D)(A + C)(B + D)}$$

Crosstab analysis has become a widely used statistical technique in mass media research, especially since the development of computer programs such as the Statistical Package for the Social Sciences (SPSS-X). In addition to chi-square, various other statistics can be used in crosstabs to determine whether the variables are statistically independent; alternatively, the data can be summarized by a variety of measures of association (see Nie et al., 1975).

Parametric Statistics

The nonparametric statistical procedures discussed above are used primarily with nominal and ordinal data; as a rule, results are not intended to be generalized to the population. The sections that follow discuss parametric statistical methods intended for use with higher level data (interval and ratio); their results are intended to be generalized to the population from which the sample was drawn. The most basic parametric statistic is the *t*-test, a procedure widely used in all areas of mass media research.

The *t*-Test

In many research studies, two groups of subjects are tested: one group receives some type of treatment, and the other serves as the control. After the treatment has been administered, both groups are tested, and the results are compared to determine whether a statistically significant difference exists between the groups. That is, did the treatment have an effect on the results of the test? In cases such as this, the mean score for each group is compared through the use of a *t*-test, as described in Chapter 5.

The *t*-test is the most elementary method for comparing two groups' mean scores. A variety of *t*-test alternatives are available, depending on the problem under consideration and the situation of a particular research study. Variations of the *t*-test are available for testing independent groups, related groups, and cases in which the population mean is either known or unknown (Champion, 1981; Roscoe, 1975).

The *t*-test assumes that the variables in the populations from which the samples are drawn are normally distributed (see Chapter 10). The test also assumes that the populations have homogeneity of variance, that is, that they deviate equally from the mean.

The basic formula for the *t*-test is relatively simple. The numerator of the formula is the difference between the sample mean and the hypothesized population mean, and the denominator is the estimate of the standard error of the mean (S_m):

$$t = \frac{\overline{X} - \mu}{S_m}$$

where

$$S_m = \sqrt{\frac{SS}{n - 1}} \quad \text{and} \quad SS = \Sigma(X - \overline{X})^2$$

One of the more popular forms of the *t*-test is the test for independent groups or means. This procedure is used in studying two independent groups for differences (the type of study described at the beginning of this section). The formula for the independent t-test is:

$$t = \frac{\overline{X}_1 - \overline{X}_2}{S_{\overline{x}_1 - \overline{x}_2}}$$

where $\overline{X}_1$ = the mean for Group 1, $\overline{X}_2$ = the mean for Group 2, and $S_{\overline{x}_1 - \overline{x}_2}$ = the standard error for the groups. The standard error is an important part of the t-test formula and is computed as follows:

$$S_{\overline{x}_1 - \overline{x}_2} = \sqrt{\left(\frac{SS_1 + SS_2}{n_1 + n_2 - 2}\right)\left(\frac{1}{n_1} + \frac{1}{n_2}\right)}$$

where SS_1 = the sum of squares for Group 1, SS_2 = the sum of squares for Group 2, N_1 = the sample size for Group 1, and N_2 = the sample size for Group 2.

To illustrate a t-test, imagine a research problem to determine the recall of two groups of subjects with regard to a television commercial for a new household cleaner. One group consists of 10 males and the other consists of 10 females. Each group views the commercial once and then completes a 15-item questionnaire. The hypothesis predicts a significant difference between the recall scores of males and females. The following data are collected.

Female Recall Scores			Male Recall Scores		
X	x	x^2 (SS)	X	x	x^2(SS)
4	−4	16	2	−4	16
4	−4	16	3	−3	9
5	−3	9	4	−2	4
7	−1	1	4	−2	4
7	−1	1	4	−2	4
8	0	0	6	0	0
9	1	1	6	0	0
9	1	1	8	2	4
12	4	16	10	4	16
15	7	49	13	7	49
80		110	60		106
$\overline{X} = 8$			$\overline{X} = 6$		

Using the t-test formula, the next step is to compute the standard error for the groups by using the previous formula:

$$S_{\overline{x}_1 - \overline{x}_2} = \sqrt{\left(\frac{110 + 106}{10 + 10 - 2}\right)\left(\frac{1}{10} + \frac{1}{10}\right)}$$

$$= 1.55$$

Table 12.1 Portion of the *t*-Distribution Table for the Two-tailed Test

	Probability			
n	.10	.05	.01	.001
1	6.314	12.706	63.657	636.619
2	2.920	4.303	9.925	31.598
•				
•				
•				
17	1.740	2.110	2.898	3.965
18	1.734	2.101	2.878	3.992
19	1.729	2.093	2.861	3.883
•				
•				
•				

The researcher then substitutes this standard error value in the *t*-test formula:

$$t = \frac{8 - 6}{1.55}$$
$$= 1.29$$

To determine whether the *t* value of 1.29 is statistically significant, a *t*-distribution table is consulted. The *t*-distribution is a family of curves closely resembling the normal curve. The portion of the *t*-distribution table relevant to the sample problem is reproduced in Table 12.1. Again, to interpret the table, two values are required: degrees of freedom and level of probability (for a complete *t*-distribution table see Appendix 1, Table 2).

For purposes of the *t*-test, degrees of freedom are equal to $N_1 + N_2 - 2$, where N_1 and N_2 represent the sizes of the respective groups. In the example of advertising recall, $df = 18$ ($10 + 10 - 2$). If the problem is tested at the .05 level of significance, a *t* value of 2.101 is required for the study to be considered statistically significant. However, since the sample problem is a "two-tailed test" (the hypothesis predicts only a difference between the two groups, not that one particular group will have the higher mean score), the required values are actually $t \leq -2.101$ *and* $t \geq 2.101$. The conclusion of the hypothetical problem is that there is no significant difference between the recall scores of the female group and the recall scores of the male group, since *t* does not equal or exceed these values.

There are numerous examples of the *t*-test in mass media research that demonstrate the versatility of the method. For example, Garramone (1985) investigated political advertising by exploring the roles of the commercial sponsor (the source of the message), and the rebuttal commercial (a message that charges as false the claims of another commercial). Among six separate hypotheses that were tested, Garramone predicted that:

H_1 Viewers of a negative political commercial will perceive an independent sponsor as more trustworthy than a candidate sponsor.

H_2 Viewers of an independent commercial opposing a candidate will demonstrate:
  a. a more negative perception of the target's image
  b. a lesser likelihood of voting for the target than viewers of a candidate commercial.

H_3 Viewers of an independent commercial opposing a candidate will demonstrate:
  a. a more positive perception of the target's opponent
  b. a greater likelihood of voting for the target's opponent than viewers of a candidate commercial.

Among other findings, Garramone concluded that:

The first hypothesis . . . was not supported. [However], hypotheses 2 and 3 . . . were supported. Viewers of an independent commercial opposing a candidate demonstrated a more negative perception of the target's image, $t(110) = 2.41$, $p \leq .01$, and a lesser likelihood of voting for the target, $t(110) = 1.83$, $p \leq .05$, than did viewers of a candidate commercial. Also as predicted, viewers of an independent commercial demonstrated a more positive perception of the target's opponent, $t(110) = 1.89$, $p \leq .05$, and a greater likelihood of voting for the target's opponent, $t(110) = 2.45$, $p \leq .01$, than did viewers of a candidate commercial.

Analysis of Variance

In many situations, researchers must investigate differences between more than two groups of subjects. In addition, researchers sometimes want to measure the effects of different degrees or levels of an independent variable. A t-test in these cases would not be adequate; what is required is an **analysis of variance** (ANOVA).

ANOVA is essentially an extension of the t-test. In fact, the two-sample ANOVA is mathematically equivalent to the t-test. The advantage of ANOVA, however, is that it can also be used in factorial designs, that is, research involving simultaneous analysis of two or more independent variables or factors. An ANOVA is classified according to the number of factors involved in the analysis: a *one-way* ANOVA investigates one independent variable, a *two-way* ANOVA investigates two independent variables, and so on. Also, several levels of any independent variable may be analyzed. Thus, a 2×2 ANOVA studies two independent variables, each with two levels.

ANOVA is a versatile statistic that is widely used in mass media research. The name of the statistic is somewhat misleading, however, because the most common form of ANOVA tests for significant differences between two or more group means and has nothing to do with the analysis of differences of variance. Additionally, ANOVA breaks down the total variability of a set of data into its component *sources of variation;* that is, it "explains" the variation in a set of scores on one or more independent variables.

An ANOVA identifies or explains two types of variance: systematic and error. **Systematic variance** in data is attributable to a known factor that predictably increases or decreases all the scores it influences. One such factor commonly identified in mass media research is sex: often an increase or decrease in a given score can be predicted simply by determining whether a subject is male or female. **Error variance** in data is created by an unknown factor that most likely has not been examined or controlled in the study. A primary goal of all research is to eliminate or control as much error variance as possible (a task that is generally easier to accomplish in the laboratory—see Chapter 5).

The ANOVA model assumes: (1) that each sample is normally distributed, (2) that variances for each group are equal, (3) that the subjects are randomly selected from the population, and (4) that the scores are statistically independent: they have no concomitant relationship with any other variable or score.

The ANOVA procedure begins with the selection of two or more random samples. Samples may be from the same or different populations. Each group is subjected to different experimental treatments, followed by some type of test or measurement. The scores from the measurements are then used to calculate a ratio of variance, known as the F ratio (F).

To understand this calculation, it is necessary to examine in greater detail the procedure known as sum of squares (discussed briefly in Chapter 10). In the sum of squares procedure, raw scores or deviation scores are squared and summed, to eliminate the need for dealing with negative numbers. The squaring process does not change the meaning of the data as long as the same procedure is used on all the data; it simply converts the data into a more easily interpreted set of scores.

In ANOVA, sums of squares are computed *between groups* (of subjects), *within groups* (of subjects), and *in total* (the sum of the between and within figures). The sums of squares between groups and within groups are divided by their respective degrees of freedom (as will be illustrated) to obtain a *mean square:* mean squares between (MS_b) and mean squares within (MS_w). The F ratio is then calculated using the following formula:

$$F = \frac{MS_b}{MS_w}$$

where $MS_b df = K - 1$, $MS_w df = N - K$, K = the number of groups, and N = the total sample. The F ratio derived from the data is then compared to the value in the F-distribution table (Table 5 in Appendix 1) that corresponds to the appropriate degrees of freedom and the desired probability level. If the calculated value equals or exceeds the tabled value, the ANOVA is considered to be statistically significant. The F table is similar to the t table and the chi-square table except that two different degrees of freedom are used, one for the numerator of the F ratio and one for the denominator.

The ANOVA statistic can be demonstrated by using an example from advertising. Suppose that three groups of five subjects each are randomly selected to determine the credibility of a newspaper advertisement for a new laundry detergent. The groups are exposed to versions of the advertisement that reflect varying degrees of design complexity: easy, medium, and difficult. The subjects are then asked to rate the advertisement on a scale of 1 to 10, with 10 indicating believable and 1 indicating not believable. The null hypothesis is advanced: "There is no significant difference in credibility among the three versions of the ad."

To test this hypothesis, the researchers must first calculate the three sums of squares: total, within, and between. The formulas for sums of squares *(SS)* are:

$$\text{Total}_{ss} = \Sigma X^2 - \frac{(\Sigma X)^2}{N}$$

$$\text{Within}_{ss} = \Sigma X^2 - \frac{\Sigma (\Sigma X)^2}{N}$$

$$\text{Between}_{ss} = T_{ss} - W_{ss}$$

The scores for the three groups furnish the following data.

Group A (Easy)		Group B (Medium)		Group C (Difficult)	
X	X^2	X	X^2	X	X^2
1	1	4	16	6	36
2	4	5	25	7	49
4	16	6	36	7	49
4	16	6	36	8	64
5	25	8	64	10	100
16	62	29	177	38	298

$$\Sigma X = 83 \ (16 + 29 + 38)$$
$$\Sigma X^2 = 537 \ (62 + 177 + 298)$$

Figure 12.3 Values for one-way ANOVA example

Sources of variation	df	Sums of squares	Mean square	F
Between groups	2 $(K-1)$	49	24.50	10.19
Within groups	12 $(N-K)$	28.8	2.4	xxxx
Total	14 $(N-1)$	77.8	xxxx	

By inserting the figures so obtained in the formulas, the researchers are able to calculate the sums of squares as follows:

$$T_{ss} = \Sigma X^2 - \frac{(\Sigma X)^2}{N} = 537 - \frac{(83)^2}{15} = 537 - 459.2 = 77.8$$

$$W_{ss} = \Sigma X^2 - \frac{\Sigma(\Sigma X)^2}{N} = 537 - \frac{16^2}{5} - \frac{29^2}{5} - \frac{38^2}{5}$$

$$= 537 - 508.2 = 28.8$$

$$B_{ss} = T_{ss} - W_{ss} = 77.8 - 28.8 = 49$$

With this information, the research team can deduce the mean squares between and within groups (SS/df), which can then be divided (MS_b/MS_w) to obtain the value of the F ratio. These results are displayed in Figure 12.3.

Assuming a significance level of .05, the F-distribution data (Table 5, Appendix 1) for degrees of freedom of 2 and 12 indicate that the F ratio must be 3.89 or greater to show statistical significance. Since the calculated value of 10.2 is greater than 3.89, a significant difference in credibility among the three types of advertisements does exist, and the researchers must reject the null hypothesis.

Two-Way ANOVA

Researchers must often examine more than one independent variable in a study. For example, if the researchers in the preceding example had wished to investigate simultaneously a second independent variable, product knowledge, at the same time, they could have used a two-way ANOVA. In a two-way ANOVA, the researchers gather the data and organize them in table form, as with the one-way ANOVA, but the two-way table has both rows *and* columns, where each row and column

Figure 12.4 Two-way ANOVA table

	Group A (Easy)	Group B (Medium)	Group C (Hard)
No product knowledge	$X_{111}, X_{112} \cdots$	$X_{121}, X_{122} \cdots$	$X_{131}, X_{132} \cdots$
High product knowledge	$X_{211}, X_{212} \cdots$	$X_{221}, X_{222} \cdots$	$X_{311}, X_{321} \cdots$

X represents a dependent measurement score.

The subscripts identify the subject who received that score.

For example:

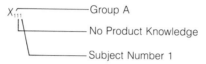

X_{111} ———— Group A

———— No Product Knowledge

———— Subject Number 1

represents an independent variable. The dependent variable score, represented by the letter X, for each subject is entered into each cell of the table. This procedure is demonstrated in Figure 12.4.

The two-way ANOVA can save time and resources, since studies for each independent variable are being conducted simultaneously. In addition, it enables researchers to calculate two types of independent variable effects on the dependent variable: main effects and interactions (one-way ANOVA tests only for main effects). A **main effect** is simply the influence of an independent variable on the dependent variable. **Interaction** refers to the concomitant influence of two or more independent variables on the single dependent variable. For example, it may be found that a subject's educational background has no effect on media used for entertainment, but education and socioeconomic status may interact to create a significant effect.

The main effects plus interaction in a two-way ANOVA create a summary table slightly different from that shown for the one-way ANOVA, as illustrated by comparing Figures 12.3 and 12.4.

Instead of computing only one F ratio as in one-way ANOVA, a two-way ANOVA will compute four F ratios, each of which is tested for statistical significance on the F distribution table. "Between Columns" (a main effect) represents the test of the independent variable levels located in the columns of a two-way ANOVA (from the preceding example, this would be a test for the differences between groups "easy," "medium," and "hard"). "Between Rows" is another main effects test; it represents the significance between levels of the independent

Figure 12.5 Multiple regression model

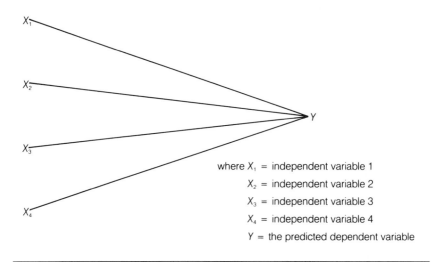

where X_1 = independent variable 1
X_2 = independent variable 2
X_3 = independent variable 3
X_4 = independent variable 4
Y = the predicted dependent variable

variable identified in the rows of the two-way ANOVA (product knowledge and no product knowledge). The "Interaction" section is the test for interaction between both independent variables in the study, and "Within Cells" tests for significant differences between each cell in the study to determine how each individual group performed in the analysis. F ratios are not computed for the "Total," which accounts for the Xs in the mean square and F columns.

Multiple Regression

Multiple regression, an extension of linear regression (discussed in Chapter 10), is another parametric technique used to analyze the relationship between two or more independent variables and a single dependent (criterion) variable. Although similar in some ways to an analysis of variance, multiple regression serves basically to *predict* the dependent variable, using information derived from an analysis of the independent variables.

In any research problem, the dependent variable is considered to be affected by a variety of independent variables. The primary goal of multiple regression is to develop a formula that accounts for, or explains, as much variance in the dependent variable as possible. It is widely used by researchers to predict success in college, sales levels, and so on. These dependent variables are predicted on the basis of *weighted linear combinations* of independent variables. A simple model of multiple regression is shown in Figure 12.5.

Linear combinations of variables play an important role in higher level statistics. To understand the concept of a weighted linear combination, consider the following methods of classroom grading. One instructor determines each student's final grade by his or her performance on five exams: the scores on these exams are summed and averaged to obtain each final grade. A student might receive the following scores for the five exams: B (3.0); D+ (1.5); B (3.0); B+ (3.5); and A (4.0); thus the final grade would be a B (15/5 = 3.0). This grade is the dependent variable determined by the linear combination of five exam scores (the independent variables). No test is considered more important than another; hence, the linear combination is not said to be weighted (except in the sense that all the scores are "weighted" equally).

The second instructor also determines the final grades by students' performances on five exams; however, the first exam counts 30%, the last exam 40%, and the remaining three exams 10% each in the determination. A student with the same five scores as above would thus receive a final grade of 3.3. Again, the scores represent a linear combination, but it is a weighted linear combination: the first and last exam contribute more to the final grade than do the other tests.

The second "grading system" above is used in multiple regression: the independent variables are weighted and summed to permit a prediction of a dependent variable. The weight of each variable in a linear combination is referred to as its **beta weight.**

A multiple regression formula may involve any number of independent variables, depending on the complexity of the dependent variable. A simple formula of this type might look as follows (hypothetical values are used):

$$\hat{Y} = 0.89X_1 + 2.5X_2 - 3$$

where $\hat{Y}$ = the predicted score or variable, X_1 = independent variable 1, and X_2 = independent variable 2. The number 3 in the formula, a constant subtracted from each subject's scores, is derived as part of the multiple regression formula. All formulas produced by multiple regression analyses represent a line in space; that is, the dependent variable is interpreted as a linear combination, or line, of independent variables. The slope of this line is determined by the beta weights (also known as *regression coefficients*) assigned to the variables (see Cohen & Cohen, 1975; Thorndike, 1978). The goal of the researcher is to derive a formula for a line that coincides as nearly as possible with the *true* line (a mathematically determined line that represents a perfect prediction) of the dependent variable: the closer the computed line comes to the true line, the more accurate the prediction will be.

The basic computational procedure involved in multiple regression to predict a line is known as the principle of least squares. This procedure, shown in Figure 12.6, bears discussion. The multiple regression problem begins by gathering data for the independent variables. The computer projects the values for these variables (repre-

Figure 12.6 Principle of least squares

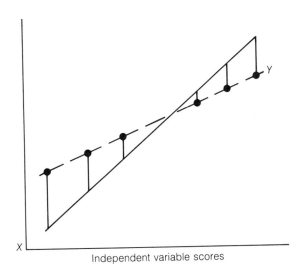

Independent variable scores

sented by dots in Figure 12.6) onto a graph and determines the line equation for the plotted data points such that the line passes through, or near, the greatest number of points. This computed line is then compared to the true, or perfect, line to determine the accuracy of the predicted line developed from the data. The closer the computed line to the true line, the more accurate the prediction.

The solid line in Figure 12.6 represents the true value; the broken line is plotted according to the multiple regression equation. Obviously, the independent variables (the broken lines) do not fall directly on the solid line, but rather are located at various distances from it. The principle of least squares requires that these distances be measured and the resulting values squared (to eliminate negative values) and then summed, as the two lines approach coincidence. Thus, the principle provides a measure of the predictive value of a multiple regression formula: the smaller the sum of squares, the higher the accuracy with which the formula predicts the dependent variable. As Kerlinger and Pedhazur (1973) noted:

> In any prediction of one variable from other variables there are errors of prediction. All scientific data are fallible. The data of the behavioral sciences are considerably more fallible than most data of the natural sciences. This really means that errors of prediction are larger and more conspicuous in analysis. In a word, error variance is larger. The principle of least squares tells us, in effect, to so analyze the data that the squared errors of prediction are minimized.

Table 12.2 Drew and Reeves' Multiple Regression Table

Predictor variables	Beta weights
Like program	.15**
Credibility	.10*
Informational content	.39***
Like story	.25***
Multiple R	.546
R^2	.298

*$p < .05$
**$p < .01$
***$p < .001$

Another important value that must be calculated in a multiple regression analysis is the *coefficient of correlation (R)*, which represents the product-moment correlation (see Chapter 10) between the predicted $\hat{Y}$ score and the weighted linear combination of the X scores. The square of this coefficient (R^2) indicates the proportion of variance in the dependent variable that is accounted for by the predictor variables. The higher the R^2 (i.e., the closer the figure is to 1.00), the more accurate the prediction is considered to be.

Drew and Reeves (1980) conducted a multiple regression analysis to determine what factors affect the way children learn from television news stories. They defined the dependent variable, "learning," in terms of performance on a 10-point questionnaire regarding a news program the children watched in an experimental setting. The selection of independent variables was based on the results of previous studies; they decided to measure: (1) whether the children liked the program, (2) whether the children liked the particular news story, (3) the credibility of the program, and (4) the informational content of the particular story.

The results, shown in Table 12.2, indicate that all the independent variables were statistically significant in their relation to learning. As the beta weights show, "informational content" seems to be the best predictor of learning, while "credibility" accounts for the least amount of variance. The multiple R of .546 could be considered highly significant; however, since it means that only 30% ($.546^2$) of the variance in the dependent variable was accounted for by the four predictor variables, this value may not substantially explain the variance.

Partial Correlation

Partial correlation is a method researchers use when they believe that a confounding or spurious variable may affect the relationship between the independent variables and the dependent variable: if such an in-

Figure 12.7 Basic product purchase study design

	Liquid detergent users	Powdered detergent users
Straight sell		
Hard sell		

fluence is perceived, they can "partial out" or control the confounding variable. For example, consider a study of the relationship between exposure to television commercials and the purchase of the advertised products. The researchers select two commercials for a liquid laundry detergent (a "straight" version, with no special video or audio effects, and a "hard sell" version that does use special effects) and show them to two groups of subjects: people who use only powdered detergent and people who use only liquid detergent. The study design is shown in Figure 12.7.

If the results show a very low correlation, indicating that any prediction made on the basis of these two variables would be very tenuous, the researchers should suspect the presence of a confounding variable. An examination might reveal, for example, that the technicians had problems adjusting the color definition of the recording equipment; instead of its natural blue color, the detergent appeared dingy brown on the television screen. The study could be repeated to control (statistically eliminated) for this variable by filming new commercials with the color controls properly adjusted. The design for the new study is shown in Figure 12.8.

The partial correlation statistical procedure would enable the researchers to determine the influence of the controlled variable. Using the new statistical method, the correlation might increase from the original study.

Cutler and Danowski (1981) used partial correlation in their study of older persons' use of television. The authors found it necessary, on the basis of suggestions from previous analyses, to control for sex and education when determining the correlation between political interest and television use. When these variables were partialed out (controlled), they found that media use varied with the subject's age and when the media were used during the campaign.

Figure 12.8 Product purchase study design incorporating partial correlation analysis

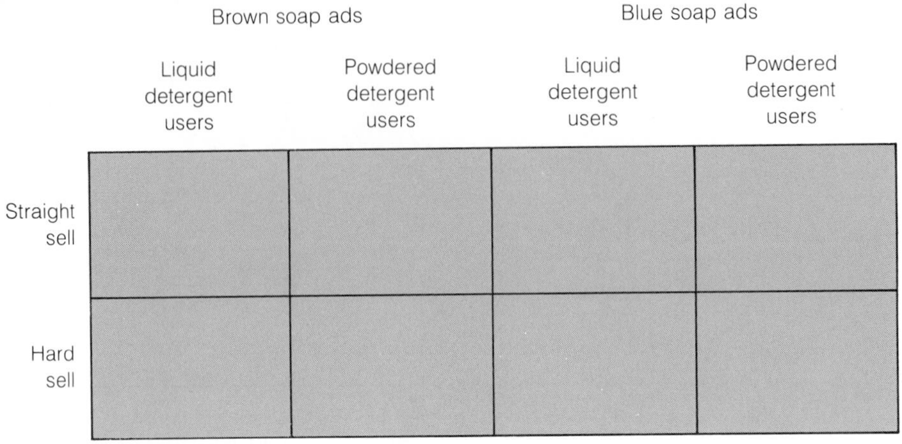

Summary

Mass media research has made great strides in terms of both number of research studies completed and types of statistical method used. This chapter has introduced some of the more widely used inferential statistical procedures involving one dependent variable and one or more independent variables. The information is intended to help beginning researchers in reading and analyzing published research.

The emphasis in this chapter is on *using* statistical methods rather than on the statistics themselves. The basic formula for each statistic is briefly outlined so that beginning researchers can understand how the data are derived; the goal, however, has been to convey a knowledge of how and when to use each procedure. It is important that researchers be able to determine not only what the problem or research question is, but also which statistical method most accurately fits the requirements of a particular research study.

Questions and Problems for Further Investigation

1. Design a mass media study for which a chi-square analysis is appropriate.

2. In the chi-square example of television set sales, assume that the observed sales frequencies are 210 (RCA), 350 (Sony), 200 (Quasar), and 240 (Zenith). What is the chi-square value? Is it significant?
3. What are the advantages of using an ANOVA over conducting several separate *t*-tests of the same phenomena?
4. How could multiple regression be used to predict a subject's television viewing, radio listening, and newspaper reading behavior?
5. The *t*-test is frequently used in natural science investigations. In the early years of mass media research, the *t*-test was also considered a staple research tool. During the past several years, however, this practice has changed: researchers no longer seem to rely on the *t*-test. Why do you think this is true?

References and Suggested Readings

Atwood, L. E., & Sanders, K. R. (1976). Information sources and voting in a primary and general election. *Journal of Broadcasting, 20,* 291–301.

Champion, D. J. (1981). *Basic statistics for social research.* New York: Macmillan.

Cochran, W. G. (1976). Early development of techniques in comparative experimentation. In D. B. Owen (Ed.), *On the history of statistics and probability.* New York: Marcel Dekker.

Cohen, J., & Cohen, P. (1975). *Applied multiple regression/correlation analysis for the behavioral sciences.* Hillsdale, N.J.:Lawrence Erlbaum.

Cutler, N. E., & Danowski, J. A. (1981). Process gratification in aging cohorts. *Journalism Quarterly, 57,* 269–276.

Drew, D., & Reeves, B. (1980). Learning from a television news story. *Communication Research, 7,* 121–135.

Garramone, G. (1985). Effects of negative political advertising: The roles of sponsor and rebuttal. *Journal of Broadcasting & Electronic Media, 29,* 147–159.

Genova, B. K. L., & Greenberg, B. S. (1979). Interests in news and the knowledge gap. *Public Opinion Quarterly, 43,* 79–91.

Idsvoog, K. A., & Hoyt, J. L. (1977). Professionalism and performance of television journalists. *Journal of Broadcasting, 21,* 97–109.

Jeffres, L. (1978). Cable TV and viewer selectivity. *Journal of Broadcasting, 22,* 167–178.

Kerlinger, F. N., & Pedhazur, E. J. (1973). *Multiple regression in behavioral research.* New York: Holt, Rinehart & Winston.

Krull, R., & Husson, W. (1980). Children's anticipatory attention to the TV screen. *Journal of Broadcasting, 24,* 35–48.

Metallinos, N., & Tiemens, R. (1977). Asymmetry of the screen: The effect of left versus right placement of television images. *Journal of Broadcasting, 21,* 21–34.

Nie, N. H., et al. (1975). *Statistical package for the social sciences.* New York: McGraw-Hill.

Presser, S., & Schuman, H. (1980). The measurement of a middle position in attitude surveys. *Public Opinion Quarterly, 44,* 70–85.

Reeves, B., & Miller, M. (1977). A multidimensional measure of children's identification with television characters. *Journal of Broadcasting, 22,* 71–86.

Roscoe, J. T. (1975). *Fundamental research statistics for the behavioral sciences.* New York: Holt, Rinehart & Winston.

Thorndike, R. M. (1978). *Correlation procedures for research.* New York: Gardner Press.

Wakshlag, J., & Greenberg, B. S. (1979). Programming strategies and the popularity of television programs for children. *Human Communication Research, 6,* 58–68.

Winer, B. J. (1971). *Statistical principles in experimental design.* New York: McGraw-Hill.

Winkler, R., & Hays, W. (1975). *Statistics: Probability, inference, and decision.* New York: Holt, Rinehart & Winston.

Research Applications

Research in the Print Media

Methodologies used to study the print media are similar to those employed in most areas of research; academic and commercial research organizations often employ content analysis, experiments, focus groups, and surveys, among other procedures, to study newspapers and magazines. Print media research, however, tends to be more narrowly focused and more oriented toward practical application than is the case in other fields. This chapter provides a brief overview of the most common types of studies in newspaper and magazine research, with a special emphasis on the research most likely to be conducted by advertiser-supported publications.

This chapter does not attempt to deal with *basic market studies* and *advertising exposure studies*. A basic market study provides a statistical portrait of the potential readers of a newspaper or magazine in terms of their demographic or psychographic characteristics. This market research technique is described more fully by Ferber (1974). Advertising exposure studies (also called reader traffic studies) are conducted to determine which advertisements are noticed or read by a publication's audience. For more information on these studies see Chapter 15.

Background

Research dealing with magazines and newspapers was one of the first areas of mass communication research to be developed. The initial interest in such research came from colleges and universities. In 1924 the *Journalism Bulletin* was first published by the Association of American Schools and Departments of Journalism. The first issue contained an article by William Bleyer entitled "Research Problems and Newspaper Analysis," which presented a list of possible research topics in journalism. Among them were the effects of form and typography on the ease and rapidity of newspaper reading, the effects of newspaper content on circulation, and the analysis of newspaper content. Bleyer's article was remarkably accurate in predicting the types of studies that would characterize newspaper and magazine research in the coming years.

Much of the content of early print media research was qualitative. The first volume of *Journalism Quarterly*, founded in 1928 to succeed the *Journalism Bulletin*, contained articles on press law, history, international comparisons, and ethics. Soon, however, quantitative research began to make its appearance in this academic journal: an article published in March of 1930 surveyed the research interests of those currently working in the newspaper and magazine field and found the most prevalent type of study to be the survey of reader interest in newspaper content. The June 1930 issue contained an article by Ralph Nafziger, "A Reader Interest Survey of Madison, Wisconsin," which served as the prototype for hundreds of future research studies.

The 1930s also saw the publication of many studies designed to assess the results of print media advertising. This led to studies in applied research, and several publications began sponsoring their own readership surveys. By and large, however, the results of these studies were considered proprietary.

As the techniques of quantitative research became more widely known and adopted, newspaper and magazine research became more empirical. The growth of this trend was first recognized by Wilbur Schramm (1957) in an article in *Public Opinion Quarterly* that reviewed 20 years of research as reported in *Journalism Quarterly*. Schramm found that only 10% of the 101 articles published between 1937 and 1941 concerned quantitative analyses. By 1952–1956, nearly half the 143 articles published were quantitative, a fivefold increase in only 15 years. The reasons for this growth, according to Schramm, were the growing availability of basic data, the development of more sophisticated research tools, and the increase in institutional support for research.

By 1960, newspapers and magazines were competing with television as well as radio for audience attention and advertiser investment. This situation greatly spurred the growth of private sector research. The Bureau of Advertising of the American Newspaper Publishers Association (now called the Newspaper Advertising Bureau) began conducting studies on all aspects of the press and its audience. In the 1970s, it founded the News Research Center, which reports the results of research to editors. The Magazine Publishers Association also began to sponsor survey research at about this same time. The continuing interests of academics in print media research led to the creation of the *Newspaper Research Journal* in 1979, a publication devoted entirely to research that has practical implications for newspaper management.

In 1976 the Newspaper Readership Project was instituted to study the problems of declining circulation and sagging readership. One major part of the 6-year, $5-million study was sponsoring research into newspaper reading habits. A news research center was set up at Syracuse University to abstract and synthesize the results of more than 300 private and published studies. The Newspaper Advertising Bureau produced dozens of research reports and conducted extensive focus group studies. In addition, regional workshops were held across the country to explain to editors the uses and limitations of research. By the time the Readership Project ended, most editors had accepted research as a necessary tool of the trade. In fact, research activity in the newspaper business is growing rapidly. Once the exclusive province of big-city papers, research is now conducted by dailies in many medium and small markets. Private research companies serving newspapers have shown steady growth, and syndicated research has become important in establishing key demographic characteristics of newspaper readers.

Ruth (1984) noted that newspaper research is used in almost all departments. In circulation, for example, researchers are studying ways to reduce subscriber "churn" or turnover. In advertising, computerized data bases portray typical readers that would-be advertisers might find attractive. In the editorial department, newspapers are using readership studies to find out what people want from their newspapers.

Print media research is conducted by universities, colleges, in-house research organizations, professional associations, and commercial research firms, and Stempel (1985) forecasts that print media research will continue to grow. He predicts that the emphasis will shift from studies concerned primarily with marketing to studies that examine the editorial products and help editors satisfy readers' needs. In any case, it is likely that research will play an important role in the newspaper and magazine industries for many years to come.

Types of Print Media Research

Newspaper and magazine researchers conduct four basic types of study: readership studies, circulation studies, studies of typography and makeup, and readability studies. Most of their research falls into the first category; circulation studies rank second but are far less numerous, while relatively few studies fall into the last two categories.

Readership Research

Many readership studies were done in the United States in the years immediately preceding and following World War II. The George Gallup organization was a pioneer in the development of the methodology of these studies, namely, a personal interview in which respondents were shown a copy of a newspaper and asked to identify the articles they had read. The most complete survey of newspaper readership was undertaken by the American Newspaper Publishers Association (ANPA), whose *Continuing Studies of Newspapers* involved more than 50,000 interviews with readers of 130 daily newspapers between 1939 and 1950 (Swanson, 1955).

Readership research became important to management during the 1960s and 1970s, as circulation rates in metropolitan areas began to level off or decline. Concerned with holding the interests of their readers, editors and publishers began more than ever to depend on surveys for the detailed audience information they needed to shape the content of a publication.

Today, research into newspaper readership is composed primarily of studies of five types: reader profiles, item-selection studies, reader–nonreader studies, uses and gratifications studies, and editor–reader comparisons. A **reader profile** provides a demographic summary of the readers of a particular publication. For example, a profile of the audience of a travel-oriented magazine might disclose that the majority of the readers earn more than $40,000 a year, are 25–34 years old, hold college degrees, possess six credit cards, and travel at least three times a year. This information can be used to focus the publication, prepare advertising promotions, and increase subscriptions.

Such information is particularly helpful when launching a new publication. For example, when *USA Today* debuted, a reader profile showed that 29% of its readers had annual incomes exceeding $35,000, 67% reported attending college, 32% were 18–29, and 26% had taken six or more round-trip plane trips in the past year. Obviously, such numbers would be of interest to both advertisers and editors.

Because there may be significant differences in the nature and extent of newspaper reading among individuals who have the same demographic characteristics, researchers recently have turned to psychographic and lifestyle segmentation studies to construct reader profiles. Both procedures go beyond the traditional demographic portrait and describe readers in terms of what they think or how they live. Psychographic studies usually ask readers to indicate their level of agreement or disagreement with a large number of attitudinal statements. Subsequently, patterns of response are analyzed to see how they correlate or cluster together. People who show high levels of agreement with questions that cluster together can be described with labels that summarize the substance of the questions. For example, people who tend to agree with statements such as "I like to think I'm a swinger," "I'm a night person," and "Sex outside marriage can be a healthy thing" might be called "Progressives." On the other hand, people who agree with items such as "Women's lib has gone too far," "Young people have too much freedom," and "The good old days were better" might be labeled "Traditionalists."

Lifestyle segmentation research takes basically the same approach. Respondents are asked a battery of questions concerning activities, hobbies, interests, and attitudes. Again, the results are analyzed to see what items cluster together. Groups of individuals who share the same attitudes and activities are extracted and labeled. To illustrate, Guzda (1984) reported on a lifestyle segmentation study that resulted in the following group labels: Young Busy Mothers, Mrs. Traditionalist,

Ladder Climbers, Senior Solid Conservatives, Mid-Life Upscalers, and Winter Affluents. Both psychographic and lifestyle segmentation studies are designed to provide management with additional insights about editorial aims, target audiences, and circulation goals. Moreover, they give advertisers a multidimensional portrait of the publication's readers.

A second type of newspaper readership study, the **item-selection study**, is used to determine who reads specific parts of the paper. The readership of a particular item is usually measured by means of **aided recall**, whereby the interviewer shows a copy of the paper to the respondent to find out which stories the respondent remembers. In one variation on this technique the interviewer preselects items for which readership data are to be gathered and asks subjects about those items only.

Because of the expense involved in conducting personal interviews, some researchers now use phone interviews to collect readership data. Calls are made on the same day the issue of the paper is published. The interviewer asks the respondent to bring a copy of the paper to the phone, and together they go over each page, with the respondent identifying the items he or she has read. Although this method saves money, it excludes from study readers who do not happen to have a copy of the paper handy.

Another money-saving technique is to mail respondents a self-administered readership survey. Hvistendahl (1977) described two variations of this type of study. In the "whole copy" method, a sample of respondents receives an entire copy of the previous day's paper in the mail, along with a set of instructions and a questionnaire. The instructions direct the respondents to go through the newspaper and mark each item they have read by drawing a line through it. A return envelope with postage prepaid is provided. In the "clipping" method, the procedure is identical except that respondents are mailed clippings of certain items rather than the whole paper. To save postage fees, the clippings are pasted up on pages, reduced 25%, and reproduced by offset. Hvistendahl reported a 67% return rate using this method with only one follow-up postcard. He noted that the whole copy and clipping methods produced roughly equivalent results, although readership scores on some items tended to be slightly higher when clippings were used. A comparison of the results of these self-administered surveys with the results of personal interviews also indicated a basic equivalence.

Recently Stamm, Jackson, and Jacoubovitch (1980) suggested a more detailed method of item-selection analysis, which they called a tracking study. They supplied their respondents with a selection of colored pencils and asked them to identify which parts of an article (headline, text, photo, outline) they had read, using a different colored pencil each time they began a new *reading episode* (defined as a stream of uninterrupted reading). The results showed a wide degree of variability in the readership of the elements that made up an item: for one story, 27% of the subjects had read the headline, 32% the text, and 36% the outline. There was also variation in the length and type of articles read per reading episode.

The unit of analysis in an item-selection study is a specific news article (such as the story on page 1 dealing with a fire) or a specific content category (such as crime news, sports, obituaries). The readership of items or categories is then related to certain audience demographic or psychographic characteristics. For example, Larkin and Hecht (1979) found that readers of nonmetropolitan daily papers read news about local events the most and news about national events the least. Schwartz, Moore, and Krekel (1979) constructed a psychographic profile of frequent newspaper readers that placed each reader into one of four categories—young optimists, traditional conservatives, progressive conservatives, and grim independents—on the basis of which sections of the paper they tended to read. Young optimists, for example, were heavy readers of astrology columns, housing ads, and the classified section; in contrast, grim independents were heavy consumers of sports and business news. In another readership study, Lynn and Bennett (1980) divided their sample according to residence in urban, rural, or farming areas. Their survey found that there was little difference in the type of news content read by farm and rural dwellers, but that urban residents were more likely to read letters to the editor, society items, and local news.

More recently, the trend in item-selection studies has been toward comprehensive surveys that encompass many newspaper markets. For example, the Newspaper Research Council sponsored a national survey examining selection patterns for approximately 80,000 newspaper items. The study, "Three-quarters of U.S. Adults Read Dailies" (1984) found that item readership nationwide was characterized by a high degree of diversity. In a second study Burgoon, Burgoon, and Wilkinson (1983) surveyed approximately 6,500 adults in 10 newspaper markets to identify clusters of items and topics that interested readers. Respondents were asked how often they typically read items dealing with about 30 topics normally found in the newspaper. Natural disasters/tragedies and stories about the national economy were the most read.

The third type of newspaper readership research is called the **reader–nonreader study**. This type of study can be conducted via personal, telephone, or mail interviews with minor modifications. It is difficult, however, to establish an operational definition for the term "nonreader." In some studies, a nonreader is determined by a "no" answer to the question "Do you generally read a newspaper?" Others have used the more specific question "Have you read a newspaper yesterday or today?" (the rationale being that respondents are more likely to admit they haven't read a paper today or yesterday than that they never read one). A third form of this question uses multiple response categories. Respondents are asked, "How often do you read a daily paper?" and are given five choices of response: "very often," "often," "sometimes," "seldom," and "never." Nonreaders are defined as those who check the "never" response or, in some studies, "seldom" or "never." Obviously, the form of the question has an impact on how many people are classified as nonreaders. The largest percentage of nonreaders generally occurs when researchers ask, "Have you read a newspaper today or yesterday?" (Penrose, Weaver, Cole, & Shaw, 1974); the smallest number is obtained by requiring a "never" response to the multiple response question (Sobal & Jackson-Beeck, 1981).

Once the nonreaders have been identified, researchers typically attempt to describe them by means of traditional demographic variables. For example, Penrose and others (1974) found nonreading to be related to low education, low income, and residence in a nonurban area. Sobal and Jackson-Beeck (1981) reported that nonreaders tend to be older, to have less education and lower incomes, and to have more often been widowed or divorced than readers. And Bogart (1981) concluded that nonreaders are less likely to have voted in the last presidential election and to believe that their opinions had an impact on local government.

Several nonreader studies have attempted to identify the reasons for not reading the newspaper. The data for these subjects have generally been collected by asking nonreaders to tell the interviewer in their own words why they don't read. Responses are analyzed, and the most frequent reasons reported. Poindexter (1978) found that the three reasons named most often by nonreaders were lack of time, preference for another news medium (especially TV), and cost. Bogart (1981) identified four reasons: depressing news, cost, lack of interest, and inability to spend sufficient time at home.

More recent studies in this area have broadened their focus to include variables that go beyond the control of the newspaper. Chaffee and Choe (1981) in a longitudinal study found that changes in marital status, residence, and employment all had an impact on newspaper readership. Similarly, Einseidel and Kang (1983) found that reading habits are accounted for, at least in part, by civic attitudes. Finally, Grotta and Babbili (1984) questioned the traditional dichotomous division that classifies people as subscribers *or* nonsubscribers. Their study suggested that subscribership is really a continuous variable, exemplified by hard-core subscribers at the positive end of the range through marginal and potential subscribers to the hard-core nonsubscribers at the other extreme.

The **uses and gratifications study** is used to study all media content. In the newspaper area, it is used to determine the motives that lead to newspaper reading and the personal and psychological rewards that result from it. The methodology of the uses and gratifications study is straightforward: respondents are given a list of possible uses and gratifications and are asked whether any of these are the motives behind their reading. For example, a reader might be presented with the following item.

> Here is a list of some things people have said about why they read the newspaper. How much do you agree or disagree with each statement?
>
> 1. I read the newspaper because it is entertaining.
> 2. I read the newspaper because I want to kill time.
> 3. I read the newspaper to keep up to date with what's going on around me.
> 4. I read the newspaper to relax and to relieve tension.
> 5. I read the newspaper so I can find out what other people are saying about things that are important to me.

The responses are summed and an average score for each motivation item is calculated.

Several studies have taken this approach to explain readership. For example, McCombs (1979) found three primary psychological motivations for reading newspapers: the need to keep up to date, the need for information, and the need for fun. Reading for information seemed to be the strongest factor. Similarly, Weaver, Wilhoit, and Reide (1979) found that the three motivations most common in explaining general media use are the need to keep tabs on what is going on around one, the need to be entertained, and the need to kill time. The authors also noted differences among demographic groups as to which of these needs were best met by the newspaper. For example, young males, young females, and middle-aged males were most likely to say they used a newspaper to satisfy their need to keep tabs on things, but they preferred other forms of media for entertainment and killing time. A study done in Hawaii (Blood, Keir, & Kang, 1983) reinforced these conclusions. The two factors that were the best predictors of readership were "use in daily living" and "fun to read." In addition, gratifications from reading the newspaper seemed to differ across ethnic groups.

In the final area of newspaper readership research, **editor–reader comparisons**, a group of editors is questioned about a certain topic, and their answers are compared to those of their readers to see whether there is any correspondence between the two groups. Bogart (1981) presented two examples of such research. In one study, a group of several hundred editors was asked to rate 23 attributes of a high-quality newspaper. The editors ranked "high ratio of staff-written copy to wire service copy" first; "high amount of nonadvertising content" second; and "high ratio of news interpretations . . . to spot news reports" third. When a sample of readers ranked the same list, the editors' three top attributes were ranked seventh, eleventh, and twelfth, respectively. The readers rated "presence of an action line column" first, "high ratio of sports and feature news to total news" second, and "presence of a news summary" and "high number of letters to the editor per issue" as a tie for third. In short, there was little congruence between the two groups in their perceptions of the attributes of a high-quality newspaper.

In a related study, Bogart gave readers an opportunity to design their own newspaper. Interviewers presented a sample of readers with 34 subjects and asked how much space they would give to each in a paper tailor-made to their own interests. Major categories of news were omitted from the listings because they were topics over which editors have little control. When the results were tabulated, the contents of a sample of newspapers were analyzed to see whether the space allocations made by editors matched the public's preferences. The resulting data indicated that readers wanted more of certain content than they are getting (consumer news; health, nutritional, and medical advice; home maintenance; travel) and that they were getting more of some topics than they desired (sports news; human interest stories; school news; crossword puzzles; astrology).

Two recent studies indicate that this technique has been broadened to include journalist–reader comparisons as well as editor–reader matchups. Ogan and Lafky (1983) asked editors, reporters, and the general public to rank the most important news stories from the preceding year. These orderings were compared to the list of the top 10 stories compiled by the Associated Press and United Press International. The results demonstrated that local news stories seemed less important to readers than to professionals but, in general, consumers and newspaper staffers agreed on significant issues. Burgoon, Bernstein, and Burgoon (1983) asked 1,118 journalists (publishers, editors, reporters, and photographers) and 6,112 adults to assign rank order to statements describing the functions of a newspaper. Both the readers and the professionals agreed that the most important functions of a newspaper were to provide a timely account of significant events and to explain how important events and issues relate to the local community. There was one notable disagreement: readers ranked the watchdog function of the press much lower than did journalists.

Magazine readership surveys are fundamentally similar to those conducted for newspapers but tend to differ in the particulars. Some magazine research is done by personal interview; the respondent is shown a copy of the magazine under study and is asked to rate each article on a 4-point scale ("read all," "read most," "read some," or "didn't read"). The mail survey technique, also frequently used, involves sending a second copy of the magazine to a subscriber shortly after the regular copy has been mailed; instructions on how to mark the survey copy to show readership are included. For example, the respondents might be instructed to mark with a check the articles that they scanned, to draw an "X" through articles read in their entirety, and to underline titles of articles that were only partly read.

Many magazines maintain *reader panels* of 25–30 people who are selected to participate for a predetermined period. All feature articles appearing in each issue of the magazine are sent to these panel members, who rate each article on a number of scales, including interest, ease of readership, and usefulness. Over time, a set of guidelines for evaluating the success of an article is drawn up, and future articles can be measured against that standard. The primary advantage of this form of panel survey is that it can provide information about audience reactions at a modest cost.

Another procedure that is peculiar to magazine research is the **item pretest** (Haskins, 1960). A random sample of magazine readers is shown an article title, a byline, and a brief description of the content of the story. Respondents are asked to rate the idea on a scale from 0 to 100, where "100" represents "would certainly read this article" and "0" represents "would not read this article." The average ratings of the proposed articles are tabulated as a guide for editorial decisions. Note that this technique can be used in personal interviews or with a mail survey with little variation in approach. Haskins also reported a positive correlation between scores obtained using this technique and those determined by postpublication readership surveys.

Other magazine research involves item-selection and editor–reader comparisons. For example, *Glamour* surveys reader response to every issue. Questionnaires are mailed to readers asking them about the articles, the cover, and the respondents' general reading habits. *Travel & Leisure* follows a similar system. The McGraw-Hill magazine group spends approximately $250,000 a year on readership research. *Good Housekeeping* takes a random survey of its subscribers each month to determine what stories were enjoyed and what recipes were tried. Harcourt Brace Jovanovich does both pretesting and posttesting in their health care journals. The company sends the titles of 15 articles printed on a single sheet of paper to 400 or 500 physicians. The respondents are asked to rate each article as having high, moderate, or low interest value. Carlson (1984) summarized some typical questions used in many magazine surveys:

1. Did you find the cover to be
   ____ interesting
   ____ fairly interesting
   ____ slightly interesting
   ____ not interesting
2. What do you like most in this issue? The least?
3. Which regular features are most helpful to you?
4. What do you do with your copy when you finish it?
   ____ save it
   ____ clip and save some articles
   ____ pass it along to another reader
   ____ throw it out

Savvy uses editor–reader comparison research to test staff members' knowledge of their audience. The magazine sends surveys to about 500 readers a month and asks them to list the four best and four worst articles in the previous issue. Editors are asked the same thing. *Savvy* gives a monetary reward to the editors who come the closest to the readers' ranking.

In addition to traditional readership studies, many magazines are conducting focus groups. Harcourt Brace Jovanovich depends particularly on focus groups to help fine-tune the content of new publications. *Farmer* uses focus group sessions for reader reaction to headlines, graphics, and general editorial feedback. Other magazines have started using focus groups as supplements to their monthly questionnaires.

Circulation Studies

The term **circulation research** is applied to two different forms of newspaper and magazine study. One form attempts to measure circulation in terms of the overall characteristics of a particular market, for example, to determine the proportion of households in a given market that are reached by a particular newspaper or the circulation pattern of a magazine among certain demographic groups or in specific geographic areas. Tillinghast (1981), who analyzed changes in newspaper circulation in four regions of the country, found that the greatest decrease had occurred in the East and the South. He also reported that the degree of urbanization in a region was positively related to circulation. Nunn (1979) studied the relationship between circulation and separate editorial management for the morning and evening editions of certain newspapers. He found that papers with different editors for the morning and evening editions had a higher circulation ratio than papers that used the same editor for both editions; this difference was most pronounced in large metropolitan markets. In a study of 69 Canadian daily newspaper markets, Alperstein (1980) discovered that newspaper circulation was positively related to the proportion of reading households within the newspaper's home city. In addition, daily newspaper circulation was found to be inversely related to weekly newspaper circulation. Stone (1978) provides a review of other market characteristics that have been employed in analyzing newspaper circulation.

Some researchers have used computer models with this form of circulation research. *Playboy*, for example, collected data for 52 issues of its publication on number of copies sold, cover price, current unemployment statistics, dollars spent on promotion, number of days on sale, editors' estimates of the cover, number of full-page displays, and several other variables. These figures were subjected to a regression analysis to determine how each factor was related to total sales. Interestingly, the number of copies distributed, the number of days an issue was on sale, and the cover rating proved to be good predictors, but the amount of money spent on promotion was found to have little impact on sales. This kind of analysis is generally limited to large publication companies because of the expense involved in data collection and using the computer for data storage and analysis.

The other type of circulation research uses the individual reader as the unit of analysis to measure the effects of certain aspects of delivery and pricing systems on reader behavior. For example, McCombs, Mullins, and Weaver (1974) studied why people cancel their subscriptions to newspapers. They found that the primary reasons had less to do with content than with circulation problems, such as irregular delivery and delivery in unreadable condition. Magazine publishers often conduct this type of circulation research by drawing samples of subscribers in different states and checking on the delivery dates of their publication and its physical condition when received. Other publications contact subscribers who don't renew to determine what can be done to prevent cancellations. In recent years, several newspapers have researched the effects of price increases on their circulation. Studies have even been conducted to ascertain why some people don't pay their subscription bills promptly. In short, this form of circulation research investigates the effect on readership or subscription rates of variables that are unrelated to a publication's content.

The recent trend in circulation research has been the identification of other market level or market structure variables that have an impact on circulation. Stone and Trotter (1981) found that the number of households in the local community and measures of broadcast media availability were the two best predictors of circulation. Blankenburg (1981) analyzed market structure variables and determined that county population and distance from the point of publication were strong predictors of circulation. Hale (1983) concluded from a regression analysis of Sunday newspaper sales in all 50 states that degree of urbanization, population density, and affluence were key predictors of circulation. In sum, it appears from these studies that many factors outside the control of the newspaper publisher will have an impact on circulation.

Typography and Makeup

Another type of study that is unique to print media research measures the effects of news design elements, specifically typeface and page makeup, on readership and reader preferences. By means of this approach, researchers have tested the effects of dozens of different typography and makeup elements, including: amount of white space, presence of paragraph headlines, size and style of type, variations in column width, and use of vertical or horizontal page makeup.

The experimental method (Chapter 5) is used most often in typography and makeup studies. Subjects are typically assigned to one or more treatment groups, exposed to an experimental stimulus (typically in the form of a mock newspaper or magazine page), and asked to rate what they have seen according to a series of dependent variable measures.

Among dependent variables that have been rated by subjects are the informative value of a publication, interest in reading a publication, the "image" of a page, recall of textual material, readability, and general preference for a particular page. A common practice is to measure these variables by means of a semantic differential rating scale. For example, Siskind (1979) used a nine-point, 20-item differential scale with such adjective pairs as "informative/uninformative," "unpleasant/pleasant," "easy/difficult," "clear/unclear," "messy/neat," "bold/timid," and "passive/active." She obtained a general reader preference score by having subjects rate a newspaper page and summing their responses to all 20 items. Other studies have measured reader interest by using the rating scale technique or the 0–100 "feeling thermometer" (Figure 6.1). Comprehension and recall are typically measured by a series of true/false or multiple-choice questions on the content that is being evaluated.

Haskins and Flynne (1974) conducted a typical design study to test the effects of different typefaces on perceived attractiveness of and reader interest in the women's section of a newspaper. They hypothesized that some typefaces would be perceived as more "feminine" than others and that headlines in such typefaces would create more reader interest in the page. The authors showed an experimental copy of a newspaper prepared specially for the study to a sample of 150 female heads of households: one subsample saw a paper with headlines in the women's section printed in Garamond Italic (a typeface experts had rated as being "feminine"), while a second group saw the same page with Spartan Black headlines (considered to be a more "masculine" typeface). A third group served as a control and saw only the headline copy typed on individual white cards. The subjects were asked to evaluate each article for reading interest. Additionally, each woman was shown a sample of 10 typefaces and asked to rate them on a semantic differential scale with 16 adjective pairs.

The researchers discovered that typeface had no impact on reader interest scores. In fact, the scores were about the same for the printed headlines as they were for those typed on white cards. Analysis of the typeface ratings revealed that readers were able to differentiate between typefaces; Garamond Italic was rated as the second most "feminine" typeface while Spartan Black was rated most "masculine," thus confirming the judgment of the expert raters.

Studies of page layout have been used to help magazine editors make decisions about the mechanics of editing and makeup. Click and Baird (1979) have provided a summary of the more pertinent research in this area. A few of their conclusions are listed here to illustrate the types of independent variables that have been studied.

1. Large illustrations attract more readers than small ones.

2. Unusually shaped pictures irritate readers.
3. A small amount of text and a large picture on the opening pages of an article increases readership.
4. Readers do not like to read type set in italics.
5. For titles, readers prefer simple, familiar typefaces.
6. Readers and graphic designers seldom agree about what constitutes superior type design.
7. Roman type can be read more quickly than other typefaces.

Recent technological and makeup innovations have sparked renewed research interest in this area. In particular, the advent of *USA Today* with its ground-breaking illustrations and use of color has prompted several studies. Two studies by Geraci (1984a, 1984b) compared the photographs, drawings, and other illustrations used by *USA Today* with those in traditional papers. Click and Stempel (1982) used seven front page formats ranging from a modular page with a four-color halftone (the format favored by *USA Today*) to a traditional format with no color. Respondents were shown a slide of each page for 15 seconds and were asked to rate the page using 20 semantic differential scales. The results indicated that readers preferred modular pages and color. Solow, Fielder, and Ruben (1982) wanted to determine whether newspaper readers perceived any differences between the traditional letterpress printing technique and the newer offset process. Two sets of identical pages were prepared; one was printed offset, the other was reproduced by the letterpress technique. Respondents rated each sample on five dimensions including quality of printing, realism of photographs, and ease of reading. Printing style preferences were not clear-cut, but offset printing did seem to be slightly favored over letterpress.

Readability

Simply defined, **readability** is the sum total of all the elements and their interactions that affect the success of a piece of printed material. "Success" is measured by the extent to which readers understand the piece, are able to read it at an optimum speed, and find it interesting (Dale & Chall, 1948).

Several formulas have been developed to objectively determine the readability of text. One of the best known is the **Flesch** (1948) **reading ease formula**, which requires the researcher to systematically select 100 words from the text, determine the total number of syllables in those words (wl), determine the average number of words per sentence (sl), and compute the following equation:

$$\text{Reading ease} = 206.835 - 0.846wl - 1.015\,sl$$

The score is compared to a chart that provides a description of style (such as "very easy") or a school grade level for the potential audience.

Another measure of readability is the **Fog Index**, which was developed by Gunning (1952). To compute the Fog Index, researchers must systematically select samples of 100 words each, determine the mean sentence length by dividing the number of words by the number of sentences, count the number of words with three or more syllables, add the mean sentence length to the number of words with three or more syllables, and multiply this sum by 0.4. Like the Flesch index, the Gunning formula suggests the educational level required for understanding a text. The chief advantages of the Fog Index are that the syllable count and the overall calculations are simpler to perform.

McLaughlin (1969) proposed a third readability index called **SMOG Grading** (for Simple Measure of Gobbledygook). The SMOG Grading is quick and easy to calculate: the researcher merely selects 10 consecutive sentences near the beginning of the text, 10 from the middle, and 10 from the end, counts every word of three or more syllables, and takes the square root of the total. The number thus obtained represents the reading grade that a person must have reached to understand the text. McLaughlin's index can be quickly calculated using a small, easily measured sample. Although the procedure is related to that for the Fog Index, it appears that the SMOG grade is generally lower.

Taylor (1953) developed yet another method for measuring readability called the **Cloze procedure**. This technique departs from the formulas listed above in that it does not require an actual count of words or syllables. Instead, the researcher chooses a passage of about 250–300 words, deletes every fifth word from a random starting point and replaces it with a blank, gives the passage to subjects and asks them to fill in the blanks with what they think are the correct words, and counts the number of times the blanks are replaced with the correct words. The number of correct words or the percentage of correct replacement constitutes the readability score for that passage. The paragraph below is a sample of what a passage might look like after it has been prepared for the Cloze procedure:

> The main stronghold of the far left ＿＿ to be the large ＿＿ centers of north Italy. ＿＿ is significant, however, that ＿＿ largest relative increase in ＿＿ leftist vote occurred in ＿＿ areas where most of ＿＿ landless peasants live—in ＿＿ and south Italy and ＿＿ Sicily and Sardinia. The ＿＿ had concentrated much of ＿＿ efforts on winning the ＿＿ of those peasants.

Nestvold (1972) found that Cloze procedure scores were highly correlated with readers' own evaluations of content difficulty. The Cloze procedure was also found to be a better predictor of such evaluations than several other common readability tests.

Although they are not used extensively in print media research, readability studies can provide valuable information. For example, Fowler and Smith (1979), using samples from 1904, 1933, and

1965, found that text from magazines had remained constant in readability while text from newspapers had fluctuated. For all years studied, magazines were easier to read than newspapers. Hoskins (1973) analyzed the readability levels of Associated Press and United Press International wire copy and found that both services scored in the "difficult" range; the Flesch indexes indicated that a 13th- to 16th-grade education was necessary for comprehension.

Fowler and Smith (1982) analyzed delayed-reward content (national affairs, science, medicine, business, and economy) and immediate-reward content (sports, people, newsmakers, and movies) in *Time* and *Newsweek*. In general, delayed-reward items were found to be more difficult to read than immediate-reward items. Smith (1984) also found differences in readability among categories of newspaper content, with features and entertainment more readable than national–international or state and local news. Smith also noted that three popular readability formulas did not assign the same level of reading difficulty to his sample of stories.

Print Media Research: An Overview

In 1977 ANPA began to compile, review, and index research studies and private reports dealing with newspaper readership and circulation. The first summary of the project was reported by McCombs (1977) and updated by Poindexter (1979). The research literature was categorized according to 16 major dependent variables that have been studied by newspaper researchers. The most frequent research method was item selection, followed by reader–nonreader studies and studies measuring the amount read in the newspaper. Table 13.1 lists the dependent variables identified in the ANPA summary.

Readers who are interested in pursuing newspaper research studies can make use of the ANPA computerized bibliography service, which indexes the past 35 years of readership studies. The index contains six pieces of information about each study: independent variables, dependent variables, date of publication, source of the study, whether the report was public or confidential, and whether the study was a major or a minor one. Researchers can request either a bibliography of relevant studies or a set of abstracts. The computerized bibliography is housed at the ANPA News Research Center at Reston, Virginia. A nominal charge for this service covers the cost of computer time used in making the search.

The amount and type of research done in the magazine industry is tabulated by *Folio* magazine. Specifically, *Folio*'s surveys are designed to determine how many and what kinds of magazines use research, what types of research they use, how valuable it is to them,

Table 13.1 Newspaper Research Interest: Focal Questions

Type of study	Total number of research findings, 1950–1979
Item selection	179
Reader–nonreader	75
Amount read	34
Selection of particular paper	33
Frequency of reading	31
Selecting newspaper over other media	31
Selecting newspaper or TV for news	30
Subscribing versus nonsubscribing	23
Circulation penetration	22
Other studies	96

Source: Paula Poindexter, *Newspaper Readership and Circulation: An Update, 1977–79*, American Newspaper Publishers Association, ANPA News Research Report, No. 22, September 28, 1979. Reprinted by permission.

and how much they spend on it. The results of a recent survey conducted by Love (1981) included the following observations:

1. Business magazines conduct research more often than consumer magazines: 70% of all business magazines responding to the survey conducted research, compared to 60% of consumer magazines.
2. The income of a magazine is related to its research effort: virtually all magazines with annual incomes exceeding $2 million conducted research.
3. Among the magazines that conducted research, the median annual amount spent was about $8,000.
4. About one-third of the magazines who reported doing research have an in-house research department; the remainder hire commercial firms to conduct their studies.

Folio's survey also revealed that the mail survey was the research method most often used by magazines; about 72% of the studies conducted by magazines that did research employed this method. Telephone interviews placed a distant second, accounting for only 7% of the studies, and the remaining 21% were performed using in-person interviews, panel studies, and focus groups. The type of test that was conducted most often was the market study. Table 13.2 shows all the types of research projects conducted by magazines.

Summary

Magazine and newspaper research began in the 1920s and for much of its early existence was qualitative in nature. Typical research studies

Table 13.2 Types of Research Projects Conducted by Magazines (Rank Order)

Project type	Total (%)
Market studies	57
Reader profile/demographic surveys	55
Surveys for editorial articles and features	54
Editorial effectiveness	44
Buying influence	36
Competitive publication analysis	34
Circulation profiling	32
Competitive readership studies	19
Product ownership and usage	17
Brand awareness/preference	15
Acquisition/launch analysis/appraisals	12
Advertiser/agency perception of media	11
Reader traffic studies	5
Syndicated readership	2

Source: Barbara Love, ""Folio Survey of Magazine Research," *Folio*, February 1981, pp. 54–61. Reprinted by permission.

dealt with law, history, and international press comparisons. During the 1930s and 1940s, readership surveys and studies of the effectiveness of print media advertising were frequently done by private firms. By the 1950s, quantitative research techniques became common in print media research. The continuing competition with television and radio for advertisers and audiences during the past three decades has spurred the growth of private sector research. Professional associations have started their own research operations.

Research in the print media encompasses readership studies, circulation studies, studies of typography and makeup, and readability studies. Readership research is the most extensive area; it serves to determine who reads a publication, what items are read, and what gratifications the readers get from their choices. Circulation studies examine the penetration levels of newspapers and magazines in various markets as well as various aspects of the delivery and pricing systems. Typography and makeup are studied to determine the impact of different newspaper and magazine design elements on readership and item preferences. Readability studies investigate the textual elements that affect comprehension of a message.

Questions and Problems for Further Investigation

1. Assume you are the editor of an afternoon newspaper faced with a declining circulation. What types of research projects might you conduct to help increase your readership?

2. Now suppose you have decided to publish a new magazine about women's sports. What types of research would you conduct before starting publication? Why?
3. Conduct a pilot uses and gratifications study of 15–20 people to determine why they read the local daily newspaper.
4. Using any 5 pages from this chapter as a sample, calculate the Flesch reading ease formula, the Gunning Fog Index, and McLaughlin's SMOG Grading.

References and Suggested Readings

Alperstein, G. (1980). *The influence of local information on daily newspaper household penetration in Canada.* (ANPA News Research Report No. 26). Reston, VA: ANPA News Research Center.

Blankenburg, W. (1981). Structural determination of circulation. *Journalism Quarterly, 58*(4), 543–551.

Bleyer, W. (1924). Research problems and newspaper analysis. *Journalism Bulletin, 1*(1), 17–22.

Blood, R., Keir, G., & Kang, N. (1983). Newspaper use and gratification in Hawaii. *Newspaper Research Journal, 4*(4), 43–52.

Bogart, L. (1981). *Press and public.* Hillsdale, NJ: Lawrence Erlbaum.

Burgoon, J., Bernstein, J., & Burgoon, M. (1983). Public and journalist perceptions of newspaper functions. *Newspaper Research Journal, 5*(1), 77–85.

Burgoon, J., Burgoon, M., & Wilkinson, M. (1983). Dimensions of content readership in ten newspaper markets. *Journalism Quarterly, 60*(1), 74–80.

Carlson, W. (1984, September). Researching readers' needs. *Folio,* pp. 63–64.

Chaffee, S., & Choe, S. (1981). Newspaper reading in longitudinal perspective. *Journalism Quarterly, 58*(2), 201–211.

Click, J. W., & Baird, R. (1979). *Magazine editing and production.* Dubuque, IA: William C. Brown.

Click, J., & Stempel, G. (1982). *Reader response to front pages with modular format and color.* (ANPA News Research Report No. 35). Reston, VA: ANPA News Research Center.

Dale, E., & Chall, J. S. (1948). A formula for predicting readability. *Education Research Journal, 27*(1), 11–20.

Einseidel, E., & Kang, N. (1983). Civic attitudes among non-readers and non-subscribers. *Newspaper Research Journal, 4*(4), 37–42.

Ferber, R. (1974). *Handbook of marketing research.* New York: McGraw-Hill.

Flesch, R. (1948). A new readability yardstick. *Journal of Applied Psychology, 32*(2), 221–233.

Fowler, G., & Smith, E. (1979). Readability of newspapers and magazines over time. *Newspaper Research Journal, 1*(1), 3–8.

Fowler, G., & Smith, E. (1982). Readability of delayed and immediate reward content in *Time* and *Newsweek. Journalism Quarterly, 59*(3), 431–434.

Geraci, P. (1984a). Comparison of graphic design and illustration use in three Washington, DC newspapers. *Newspaper Research Journal, 5*(2), 29–40.

Geraci, P. (1984b). Newspaper illustration and readership: Is *USA Today* on target? *Journalism Quarterly, 61*(2), 409–413.

Grotta, G., & Babbili, A. (1984). Daily newspaper subscribing behavior. *Newspaper Research Journal, 5*(2), 3–8.

Gunning, R. (1952). *The technique of clear writing.* New York: McGraw-Hill.

Guzda, M. (1984, June 9). Lifestyle segmentation. *Editor & Publisher*, p. 16.

Hale, D. (1983). Sunday newspaper circulation related to characteristics of the 50 states. *Newspaper Research Journal, 5*(1), 53–62.

Haskins, J. (1960). Pretesting editorial items and ideas for reader interest. *Journalism Quarterly, 37*(1), 224–230.

Haskins, J., & Flynne, L. (1974). Effects of headline typeface variation on reader interest. *Journalism Quarterly, 51*(4), 677–682.

Hoskins, R. (1973). A readability study of AP and UPI wire copy. *Journalism Quarterly, 50*(2), 360–362.

Hvistendahl, J. K. (1977). Self-administered readership surveys: Whole copy vs. clipping method. *Journalism Quarterly, 54*(2), 350–356.

Larkin, E., & Hecht, T. (1979). Research assistance for the non-metro newspaper, 1979. *Newspaper Research Journal*, prototype edition, pp. 62–66.

Love, B. (1981, February). *Folio* survey of magazine research. *Folio*, pp. 54–61.

Lynn, J., & Bennett, E. (1980). Newspaper readership patterns in non-metropolitan communities. *Newspaper Research Journal, 1*(4), 18–24.

McCombs, M. (1977). *Newspaper readership and circulation.* (ANPA News Research Report No. 3). Reston, VA: ANPA News Research Bureau.

McCombs, M. (1979). *Using readership research.* Washington, DC: National Newspaper Foundation Community Journalism Textbook Project.

McCombs, M., Mullins, L. E., & Weaver, D. (1974). *Why people subscribe and cancel: A stop–start survey of three daily newspapers.* (ANPA News Research Bulletin No. 3). Reston, VA: ANPA News Research Center.

McLaughlin, H. (1969). SMOG Grading: A New Readability Formula. *Journal of Reading, 22*(4), 639–646.

Nafziger, R. (1930). Reader-interest survey of Madison, Wisconsin. *Journalism Quarterly, 7*(2), 128–141.

Nestvold, K. (1972). Cloze procedure correlation with perceived readability. *Journalism Quarterly, 49*(3), 592–594.

Nunn, C. (1979). *Newspapers with separate editorial managements have higher household penetration.* (ANPA News Research Report No. 17). Reston, VA: ANPA News Research Center.

Ogan, C., & Lafky, S. (1983). 1981's most important events as seen by reporters, editors, wire services, and media consumers. *Newspaper Research Journal, 5*(1), 63–76.

Penrose, J., Weaver, D., Cole, R. & Shaw, D. (1974). The newspaper non-reader ten years later. *Journalism Quarterly, 51*(4), 631–639.

Poindexter, P. (1978). *Non-readers, Why they don't read.* (ANPA News Research Report No. 9). Reston, VA: ANPA News Research Center.

Poindexter, P. (1979). *Newspaper readership and circulation: An update, 1977–79.* (ANPA News Research Report No. 22). Reston, VA: ANPA News Research Center.

Ruth, M. (1984, October). Newspaper research. *presstime*, pp. 8–10.

Schramm, W. (1957). Twenty years of journalism research. *Public Opinion Quarterly, 21*(1), 91–108.

Schwartz, S., Moore, R., & Krekel, T. (1979). Life style and the daily paper: A psychographic profile of Midwestern readers. *Newspaper Research Journal, 1*(1), 9–18.

Siskind, T. (1979). The effect of newspaper design on reader preference. *Journalism Quarterly, 56*(1), 54–62.

Smith, R. (1984). How consistently do readability tests measure the difficulty of newswriting? *Newspaper Research Journal, 5*(4), 1–8.

Sobal, J., & Jackson-Beeck, M. (1981). Newspaper nonreaders: A national profile. *Journalism Quarterly, 58*(1), 9–13.

Solow, N., Fielder, V., & Ruben, J. (1982). Newspaper readers' perceptions of differences between letterflex and offset printing. *Newspaper Research Journal, 3*(4), 54–60.

Stamm, K., Jackson, K. & Jacoubovitch, D. (1980). Exploring new options in newspaper readership methods. *Newspaper Research Journal, 1*(2), 63–74.

Stempel, G. (1985, January). News research. *presstime*, p. 28.

Stone, G. (1978). *Literature review: Using community characteristics to predict newspaper circulation.* (ANPA News Research Report No. 14). Reston, VA: ANPA News Research Center.

Stone, G., & Trotter, E. (1981). Community traits and predictions of circulation. *Journalism Quarterly, 58*(3), 460–463.

Swanson, C. (1955). What they read in 130 daily newspapers. *Journalism Quarterly, 32*(3), 411–421.

Taylor, W. (1953). Cloze procedure: A new tool for measuring readability. *Journalism Quarterly, 30*(4), 415–433.

Three-Quarters of U.S. adults read dailies. (1984, June). *presstime*, p. 38.

Tillinghast, W. (1981). Declining newspaper readership: Impact of region and urbanization. *Journalism Quarterly, 58*(1), 14–23.

Weaver, D., Wilhoit, C., & Reide, P. (1979). *Personal needs and media use.* (ANPA News Research Report No. 21). Reston, VA: ANPA News Research Center.

C　H　A　P　T　E　R　　1　4

Research in the Electronic Media

BACKGROUND

■

RATINGS RESEARCH

■

NONRATINGS RESEARCH

■

THE FUTURE OF ELECTRONIC MEDIA RESEARCH

■

SUMMARY

■

QUESTIONS AND PROBLEMS FOR FURTHER INVESTIGATION

■

REFERENCES AND SUGGESTED READINGS

During the past decade research in the electronic media has expanded at a phenomenal rate. The 1985 *Broadcasting/Cablecasting Yearbook* lists no fewer than 110 companies and individuals involved in some type of electronic media research (this represents an increase from about 80 companies in 1982). And the data are not complete: hundreds of college and university professors and private citizens also conduct studies of the electronic media. Add to this the in-house research conducted by stations and networks, and it is easy to see why broadcasting and cable research is now a multimillion-dollar business.

Electronic media research is changing continually, due to advancements in technology as well as improved research methodologies. This chapter introduces some of the more widely used research procedures in this area.

Background

Although broadcasting is relatively young compared to other mass media, the amount and sophistication of broadcasting research have grown rapidly. During the initial years of broadcasting (the 1920s), there was little or no concern for audience research. The broadcasters were experimenters and hobbyists who were interested mainly in making sure that their signal was being sent and received. The potential popularity of radio was unknown, and there was no reason to be concerned with audience size at that time.

This situation changed rapidly during the 1930s as radio became a popular mass medium. When broadcast stations began to attract large audiences, concern emerged over how radio would be financed. Eventually it was decided that advertising (as opposed to government financing or taxes on sales of equipment) was the most viable alternative. The acceptance of advertising on radio was the first step in the development of electronic media research.

Advertisers, not broadcasters, were the initiators of broadcast research. Once commercials began to be heard on the air, advertisers naturally wondered how many listeners were exposed to their messages and just how effective the messages were. Broadcasters were thus compelled to provide empirical evidence of the size and characteristics of their audience. This situation still exists—advertisers continually want more information about the people who hear and see their commercial announcements.

In addition to desiring information about audience size, advertisers became interested in why people behave the way they do. This led to the development of the research area known as *psychographics*. But because psychographic data are rather vague, they were not adequate predictors of audience behavior; advertisers wanted more information. Research procedures were designed to study *lifestyle* patterns and how they affect media use and buying behavior. Such information is valuable in designing advertising campaigns: if advertisers understand the lifestyle patterns of the people who purchase their products, they can design commercials to match these lifestyles.

Electronic media research studies today fall into two main categories: *ratings* and *nonratings* research. The remainder of this chapter is devoted to discussion of these two areas of research.

Ratings Research

When radio first became popular and advertisers began to see its potential for attracting customers, they were faced with the problem of documenting audience size. The print media were able to collect circulation figures, but broadcasters had no equivalent "hard" information—merely estimates. The early attempts at audience measurement failed to provide adequate data. Volunteer mail from listeners was the first source of data, but it is a well-known axiom of research that volunteers do not represent the general audience. Advertisers and broadcasters quickly realized that further information was urgently needed.

Since 1929, when the Crosley Radio Company conducted one of the first radio surveys, the bulk of ratings information for broadcast stations has come to be provided by two companies: A. C. Nielsen and Arbitron. A third company, Birch Radio, has made great strides in broadcast ratings during the early 1980s and promises to offer formidable competition to Arbitron. The A. C. Nielsen Company, purchased by Dun and Bradstreet in 1984, is one of the world's largest market research corporations, with offices in several countries. The Arbitron Ratings Company (often referred to as ARB) is a subsidiary of the Control Data Corporation. Birch Radio, the product of former radio programmer Tom Birch, is based in Miami and conducts local market radio ratings.

The Nielsen Company collects several different types of ratings data for the broadcasting industry, including the National Television Index (NTI), the only *network* television ratings service in the country. Nielsen's National Station Index (NSI) provides local television market ratings, and the National Audience Composition (NAC) sample uses a diary approach to provide information about the people who watch television. These approaches are combined four times a year to produce **sweeps,** or simultaneous surveys of every market in the country. Arbitron also conducts television sweeps at the same time as Nielsen. These rating periods—February, May, July, and November—produce the year's most important ratings surveys. Although other surveys are conducted, much of the advertising rate setting is based on these four books, or sets of results. The great significance to broadcasting executives of the results of the sweeps is the reason for the frequency of blockbuster movies and special programming aired during these four periods; the networks and stations attempt to get the highest audience numbers possible.

Nielsen also has 12 metered markets, in which ratings data are collected by electronic meters (discussed later). The Nielsen-metered markets are New York, Chicago, Los Angeles, Philadelphia, San Francisco, Washington, DC, Detroit, Boston, Dallas, Houston, Miami, and Denver (Atlanta is scheduled for meters in August 1986). In addition to the data collected for the NTI and NSI reports, the metered markets also provide **overnights,** which are preliminary ratings data gathered to give network and station executives, program producers, advertising agencies, and others an indication of the performance of the previous night's programs. Because the sample sizes involved in overnights are small (usually only 200–300), the actual ratings for the programs do not appear until several days later when sample data are added to increase statistical reliability.

The Arbitron Ratings Company provides ratings for both local market radio and television; the company does not currently provide network ratings information. Arbitron uses diaries to collect radio estimates and both diaries and meters for television estimates; the company also produces overnights in its 11 metered markets (currently the same markets as Nielsen excluding Denver). Arbitron is the largest ratings company in the United States that collects radio audience listening estimates. The only network radio ratings are gathered by Statistical Research, Inc., which is hired by networks to produce a RADAR report (Radio's All-Dimension Audience Research).

Broadcast ratings create controversy in many areas: viewers complain that "good" shows are canceled; producers, actors, and other artists complain that *numbers* are no judge of artistic quality (they are not intended to be); and advertisers often balk at the lack of reliable information. Although there may be merit to many of these complaints, one basic fact remains: until further refinements are made, ratings as they currently exist will remain the primary decision-making tool in programming and advertising.

Since ratings will continue to be used for some time, it is important to understand several basic points about them. First, ratings are only approximations or estimates of audience size. They do not measure either the quality of programs or opinions about the programs. Second, all ratings are not equally dependable: different companies produce different ratings figures for the same market during the same time period.

The key point to remember when discussing or using ratings is that the figures are riddled with error. The data must be interpreted in light of several limitations (which are always printed in the last few pages of every ratings book). Individuals who depend on ratings as though they were "facts" are misusing the data.

Ratings Methodology

The research methodologies used by Nielsen, Arbitron, and Birch are complex; a detailed description of any one procedure would fill a small textbook. The data for ratings surveys are gathered by three basic methods: electronic recordings, diaries, and telephone interviews. Each method involves a slightly different sample selection procedure, and each has specific advantages and disadvantages.

Broadcast ratings provide a classic example of the need to sample the population. With about 85 million television households in the United States, it would be impossible for any ratings company to conduct a census of media use. The companies naturally resort to sampling to produce data that can be generalized to the population.

Nielsen's national sample for the NTI and NAC are selected using national census data and involve a procedure known as *multistage area probability sampling*, which ensures that the sample reflects actual population distributions. That is, if Los Angeles accounts for 10% of the television households in the United States, Los Angeles households should compose 10% of the sample as well. Nielsen uses four stages in sampling: selection of counties in the country, selection of block groups within the counties, selection of certain blocks within the groups, and selection of individual households within the blocks. Twenty percent of the NTI sample of approximately 1,800 households is reportedly replaced each year, as are one-third of the approximately 2,500 households in the NAC sample.

To obtain samples for producing broadcast listening and viewing estimates, Arbitron, Nielsen, and Birch use recruitment by telephone, which includes calls to both listed and unlisted telephone numbers. Although all the ratings companies begin sample selection from telephone directories, each firm uses a statistical procedure to ensure the inclusion of unlisted telephone numbers, thus eliminating the bias that would be created if only persons or households listed in telephone directories were asked to participate in broadcast audience estimates (see Chapter 4). Nielsen calls its procedure a Total Telephone Frame; Arbitron and Birch use the terms Expanded Sample Frame and Randomization of Last Digits, respectively.

Target sample sizes for local audience measurements vary from market to market. Each ratings service uses a formula to establish a minimum sample size required for a specific level of statistical efficiency, but there is no guarantee that this number of subjects will actually be produced. Although many people may agree to participate in an audience survey, there is no way to force them all to complete the diaries they are given. Additionally, completed diaries are often rejected because they are illegible or obviously inaccurate. The companies are often lucky to get a 50% response rate in their local measurements.

In addition, since participation by minority groups in audience surveys is generally lower than for the remainder of the population, Arbitron and Nielsen make an extra effort to collect data from these groups by contacting households by telephone or in person to assist them in completing the diary. (These methods are generally used in high-density Hispanic and black areas; otherwise, return rates could be too low to provide any type of audience estimates.) In such cases where the return (or in-tab) rate is low, statistical weighting or sample balancing is used to compensate for the shortfall; this topic is discussed later.

Perhaps the best-known method of gathering ratings data from a sample is by means of electronic ratings-gathering instruments, in particular the Nielsen *audimeter*, which was introduced in 1936 to record radio usage on a moving roll of paper. Today's audimeter, the storage instantaneous audimeter (SIA), is a sophisticated device that automatically records the time each set in a household is turned on or off, the broadcasting station, how long each set stays on a channel, and all channel switchings. At least twice a day, each household in the NTI sample is called by the central computer, located in Dunedin, Florida, which retrieves the stored data and stores them for computation of the National Television Index. All the data collection is done automatically and does not require participation by persons in the NTI households. The ratings results thus obtained from approximately 1,800 households are reported in trade journals and newspapers throughout the country.

The Arbitron Ratings Company collects metered data via its television meter (TVM), a sensing device very similar to the Nielsen SIA. The TVM records the on/off condition of the set and the channel to which the set is tuned. However, no information is collected about the number of people watching, nor is there any demographic information about the viewers. Arbitron retrieves the household meter data nightly via a direct telephone line attached to the TVM.

For the second major form of data collection, subjects are asked to record in diaries the channels they watch or the stations they listen to, the time periods, and the number of people viewing or listening to each program. Arbitron uses diaries for both television and radio. Nielsen gives diaries to the 2,500 households in its NAC sample

Figure 14.1 (a) Instructions for using the Arbitron Television Ratings Diary; (b) a sample diary page

(a)

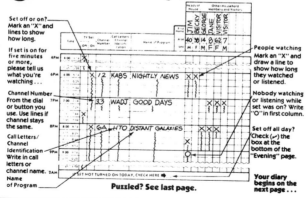

Figure 14.1 *(continued)*

(b)

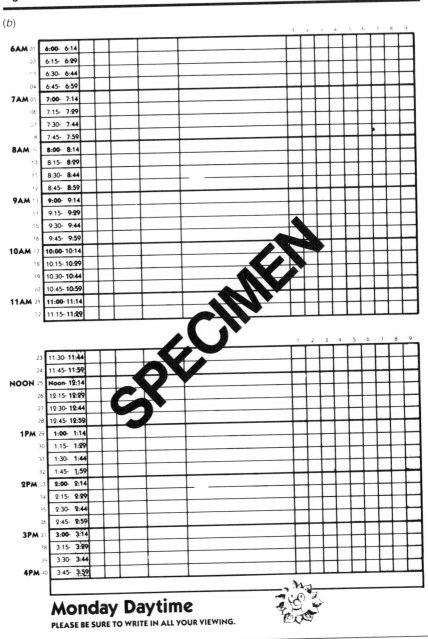

Monday Daytime
PLEASE BE SURE TO WRITE IN ALL YOUR VIEWING.

to supplement the information gathered from the SIA households, since the audimeter cannot record the number of people watching each set. An example of an Arbitron television diary is shown in Figure 14.1; a radio diary sample is shown in Figure 14.2.

Figure 14.2 (*a*) Instructions for using the Arbtiron Radio Ratings Diary; (*b*) a sample diary page

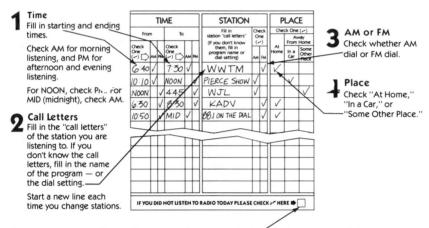

(a)

This is your Arbitron Ratings diary. Please fill it in yourself. Throughout the seven days of the survey, beginning on Thursday, please keep this diary with you . . .

. . . at home

. . . in your car

. . . at work

. . . or wherever you go

Each time you listen to radio (whether you yourself turn it on or not), please fill in the following information:

1 Time
Fill in starting and ending times.

Check AM for morning listening, and PM for afternoon and evening listening.

For NOON, check PM for MID (midnight), check AM.

2 Call Letters
Fill in the "call letters" of the station you are listening to. If you don't know the call letters, fill in the name of the program — or the dial setting.

Start a new line each time you change stations.

3 AM or FM
Check whether AM dial or FM dial.

4 Place
Check "At Home," "In a Car," or "Some Other Place."

On days when you do not listen to radio, check the box at the bottom of the page.

Important: Many stations broadcast on both AM and FM. For this Arbitron Ratings survey, it is important to correctly identify whether you are listening on AM or FM (even though the station may use the same call letters and broadcast the same thing on the air).

To keep your Arbitron Ratings diary from getting mixed up with others in your household — please fill in your initials (or first name) here . . .

The third major type of data collection is by telephone. Birch Radio collects data only in this manner, using a telephone recall methodology. Respondents to the Birch Radio survey are asked to report the previous day's listening activity from 6 A.M. to midnight, along with start and stop times for each listening time period.

Nielsen and Arbitron also use the telephone to conduct a variety of special studies, allowing clients to request almost any type of survey research project. One of the most frequent types of custom work is the **telephone coincidental**. This procedure measures the size of the medium's audience at a given time—the survey coincides with actual

Figure 14.2 (*continued*)

(b)

Please start recording your listening on the date shown on the front cover.

Thursday

TIME						STATION			PLACE			
From			To			Fill in station "call letters" (If you don't know them, fill in program name or dial setting)	Check One (✓)		Check One (✓)			
Check One (✓) ⇨	AM	PM	Check One (✓) ⇨	AM	PM		AM	FM	At Home	In a Car	Away From Home — Some Other Place	

IF YOU DID NOT LISTEN TO RADIO TODAY PLEASE CHECK ☑ HERE ➡ ☐

Each time you listen to the radio, please be sure to use a new line, and write in the station "call letters."

---

viewing or listening. Basically, the method involves selecting a sample of households at random and calling these numbers during the viewing or listening period of interest. Individuals are simply asked what they are watching or listening to at that moment. This method avoids the necessity of trying to recall information from the previous day. Coincidentals are fairly inexpensive (generally only a few hundred dollars) and are frequently used by station management to receive immediate feedback about the success of special programming. In most cases, coincidental data are used for advertising sales purposes. The Cable-television Advertising Bureau (CAB) in New York has prepared a detailed document called "Telephone Coincidental Guidelines."

Interpreting the Ratings

To explain the ratings interpretation process and its terminology, consider the following hypothetical analysis. (This example uses television networks, but the procedures are the same for radio ratings. In addition, the example has been simplified by using only three commercial television networks; local market ratings books will always include many more stations). Assume that Nielsen has collected the following data for a certain *daypart* (time of day) on network television:

Network	Households Viewing
ABC	396
CBS	360
NBC	322
Not watching	722
	1,800

Recall that Nielsen's NTI sample includes about 1,800 households in the United States and the data collected from them are generalized to the *total* population of about 85 million television households.

Rating. An *audience rating* is the percentage of people or households in a population with television or radio tuned to a specific station or network. Thus, the rating is expressed as the station or network's audience divided by the total number of television households in the population:

$$\frac{\text{People or households}}{\text{Population}} = \text{Rating}$$

For example, ABC's rating using the hypothetical data is computed as:

$$\frac{396}{1,800} = 0.22 \text{ or } 22\%$$

This indicates that approximately 22% of the sample of 1,800 households was tuned to ABC at the time of the survey. (Note that although ratings and related statistical values are percentages, the decimal points are eliminated when the data are reported to ease reading.)

The combined ratings of all the networks or stations during a specific time period provide an estimate of the total number of *homes using television* (HUT). Since radio ratings deal with persons rather than households, however, the term *persons using radio* (PUR) is used. The HUT or PUR can be found either by adding together the households or persons using radio or television, or by computing the total rating and multiplying times the sample (or population when generalized).

The total rating in the sample data is 59.9, which is computed as follows:

$$\text{ABC} \quad \frac{396}{1,800} = 0.22 \text{ or } 22\%$$

$$\text{CBS} \quad \frac{360}{1,800} = 0.20 \text{ or } 20\%$$

$$\text{NBC} \quad \frac{322}{1,800} = 0.179 \text{ or } 17.9\%$$

$$\text{HUT} = 1,078 \quad \text{Total rating} = 59.9\%$$

In other words, about 59.9% of all households (HH) with television were watching one of the three networks at the time of the survey. As mentioned, the HUT can also be computed by multiplying the total rating times the sample size: $0.599 \times 1,800 = 1,078$. The same formula is used to project to the population. The population HUT is computed as follows: 0.599×85 million $= 50.915$ million households.

Stations, networks, and advertisers naturally wish to know the estimated number of households in the HUT tuned to specific channels. The data from the sample of 1,800 households are again generalized to find a rough estimate of the households viewing for each network (or station):

Network rating	×	Population	=	Population HH estimate
ABC: 0.22	×	85 million	=	18,700,000
CBS: 0.20	×	85 million	=	17,000,000
NBC: 0.179	×	85 million	=	15,215,000

Share. A **share** of the audience is the percentage of the HUT or PUR that is tuned to a specific channel or network. It is determined by dividing the number of households or persons tuned to a channel or network by the number of households or person using their sets:

$$\frac{\text{People or households}}{\text{HUT or PUR}} = \text{Share}$$

In the example, the sample HUT is 1,078 ($396 + 360 + 322$), or 59.9% of 1,800. The audience share for ABC would thus be:

$$\frac{396}{1,078} = 0.367 \text{ or } 36.7\%$$

That is, of the households in the sample whose television sets were turned on at the time of the survey, 36.7% were tuned to ABC (people may not have been *watching* the set in the case of electronic data gathering). The shares for CBS and NBC are computed in the same manner: CBS share = 360/1,078 or 33.4%; NBC share = 322/1,078 or 29.9%.

Shares are also used to estimate the number of households in the population viewing a station or network. The example demonstrating how to compute households is considered a "rough" estimate. However, there is often need for a more "exact" method for computing households. This is achieved by multiplying the share times the HUT or PUR. The exact households estimates for each network are computed as follows (rough estimates are for comparison):

Network share	×	HUT	=	HH in population (exact)	(Rough estimate)
ABC: 36.7	×	50.915		18,685,805	18,700,000
CBS: 33.4	×	50.915		17,005,610	17,000,000
NBC: 29.9	×	50.915		15,223,585	15,215,000
				50,915,000	50,915,000

Cost per thousand (CPM). Stations, networks, and advertisers need to be able to assess the efficiency of advertising on radio and television, to be able to determine which advertising "buy" is the most cost effective. One common way to express advertising efficiency is in terms of **cost per thousand (CPM),** or what it costs an advertiser to reach 1,000 households or persons. The CPM provides no information about the effectiveness of a commercial message, only a dollar estimate of its reach. It is computed according to the following formula:

$$CPM = \frac{\text{Cost of advertisement}}{\text{Audience size (in thousands)}}$$

Using the hypothetical television survey, assume that a single 30-second commercial on ABC costs $110,000. The CPM for such a commercial would be:

$$\text{ABC CPM} = \frac{\$130,000}{18,685.805 \text{ M}} = \$6.96$$

Computing the CPM in the same manner for CBS and NBC, we find: CBS = $7.64 and NBC = $8.54.

The CPM is regularly used when buying commercial time. Advertisers and stations or networks often negotiate an advertising contract using CPM figures; the advertiser might agree to pay $7.75 per thousand households. In some cases, no negotiation is involved; a station or network simply offers a program to advertisers at a specified CPM.

The CPM is seldom the only criterion used in purchasing commercial time. Other information, such as audience demographics and type of program on which the advertisement will be aired, is considered before a contract is signed. An advertiser may be willing to pay a higher CPM to a network or station that is reaching a more desirable audience for its product. Cost per thousand should be used as the sole purchasing criterion only when all else is equal: demographics, programming, advertising strategy, and so on.

Related ratings concepts. Although ratings and shares are important in audience research, a number of other computations can be performed with the data. In addition, ratings, shares, and other figures are computed for a variety of survey areas and are split into several demographic categories. For an additional fee, ratings companies will also provide "custom" information such as ratings according to zip code areas.

A **metro survey area** (MSA) generally corresponds to the Consolidated Metropolitan Statistical Areas (CMSA) for the country, as defined by the U.S. Office of Management and Budget. In other words, the MSA generally includes the town, county, or other designated area closest to the station's transmitter. The **area of dominant influence** (ADI), another area for which ratings data are gathered, defines each television or radio market in exclusive terms. Each county in the United States belongs to one and only one ADI, and rankings are determined by the number of television households in the ADI. Radio ratings use the ADIs established from television households; they are not computed separately. (Nielsen uses the term "designated market area," or DMA, instead of ADI.)

The **total survey area** (TSA) includes the ADI and MSA as well as some other areas the market's stations reach (known as *adjacent ADIs*). Broadcasters are most interested in TSA data because they represent the largest number of households or persons. In reality, however, advertising agencies look at ADI/DMA figures when purchasing commercial time for television stations, and metro figures when purchasing radio time. The TSA is infrequently used in the sale or purchase of advertising time; it serves primarily to determine the reach of the station, or the total number of people or households that listened to or watched a station or channel. Nielsen's equivalent to Arbitron's ADI is the NSI area.

Ratings books contain information about the TSA/NSI, ADI/DMA, and the MSA. Each area is important to stations and advertisers for various reasons, depending on the type of product or service being advertised and the goals of the advertising campaign. For instance, a new business placing a large number of spots on several local stations may be interested in reaching as many people in the trading area as possible. In this case, the advertising agency or individual client may ask for TSA/NSI numbers only, disregarding the ADI/DMA and metro.

A sample page from an Arbitron television ratings book is shown in Figure 14.3. The page is taken from the "daypart" section of the book; thus the numbers represent averages of the programming that aired during the listed times. For example, under the first listing for "Mon–Fri 6:00P–7:30P", station WSB received a 17 rating and a

Figure 14.3 Sample page from an Arbitron ratings book

Daypart Audience Estimates Summary

DAYPART AND STATION	ADI TV HH RTG	ADI TV HH SHR	NOV 84	JUL 84	MAY 84	FEB 84	METRO TV HH RTG	METRO TV HH SHR	TV HH	PERS TOT 2+	PERS 18+	PERS 18-49	PERS 12-24	PERS 12-34	PERS 18-34	W TOT 18+	W 18-49	W 12-24	W 18-34	W 25-49	W 25-54	WKG WMN 18+	M TOT 18+	M 18-49	M 18-34	M 25-49	M 25-54	TEENS 12-17
col	5	6	58	59	60	61	8	9	11	12	13	14	15	16	17	18	19	20	21	22	23	24	25	26	27	28	29	30
MON-FRI 6:00P-7:30P																												
WSB	17	26	24	27	24	29	18	29	200	328	289	184	52	113	94	162	99	31	49	78	85	48	127	84	45	72	81	19
WAGA	18	28	27	27	25	27	16	25	211	376	341	166	45	102	87	189	87	22	46	72	86	56	152	79	42	64	74	15
WXIA	14	22	22	20	23	19	15	23	169	277	259	124	28	60	50	142	64	14	27	54	70	35	117	59	23	51	66	10
WTBS	5	8	8	10	13	8	5	8	112	226	144	125	69	123	95	79	70	36	54	47	49	32	64	55	41	37	40	28
WATL	2	3	3	2	4	5	2	3	20	35	26	18	6	14	11	16	11	4	8	9	10	6	11	7	4	6	6	2
WGNX	6	10	9	7	5	6	7	12	79	161	75	67	49	75	45	46	41	28	28	31	32	18	29	26	17	16	17	30
• WVEU									4	6	3	3	1	2	1	2	2		1	2	2	1	2	1		1		1
WGTV		1							6	8	4					4	2		1	2	2		4	2	1	2	2	
WPBA									2	2	1					1			1	2	2	1	1	1		1	1	
HUT/TOT	64		55	52	51	62	63		803	1419	1147	692	250	492	386	641	376	135	214	295	336	198	507	314	173	250	288	105
6:00P-8:00P																												
WSB	16	25	24	27	23	28	18	28	193	314	276	178	51	113	94	156	98	31	51	77	84	46	120	80	44	69	76	19
WAGA	16	25	24	25	23	26	14	23	192	342	308	150	41	92	77	173	80	20	41	66	79	51	136	70	36	58	67	15
WXIA	16	24	24	20	24	20	16	26	191	329	295	148	42	83	66	165	79	22	35	66	83	44	130	69	30	57	72	17
WTBS	5	8	9	11	13	8	5	8	113	234	148	127	68	123	96	83	72	37	55	49	51	33	65	56	41	38	41	28
WATL	2	3	3	2	4	5	2	4	24	42	33	21	7	15	12	20	13	4	8	11	12	7	13	8	4	7	8	3
WGNX	6	10	9	7	6	6	7	11	77	157	78	69	46	75	48	46	41	26	29	31	31	18	32	28	19	19	20	27
• WVEU									4	5	3	4	1	2	1	2	2		1	1	2	1	4	2	1	2	1	1
WGTV		1							5	8	4					4	2		1	2	2		2	2		2		
WPBA									3	4	4	2				1			1	2	2	1	1	1				
HUT/TOT	64		55	52	50	63	63		802	1435	1153	702	256	506	397	651	386	140	221	303	344	203	504	315	175	252	288	110
7:00P-7:30P																												
WSB	15	24	21	26	21	25	17	26	186	304	267	164	46	103	85	147	87	27	45	70	76	43	120	77	39	67	74	18
WAGA	14	22	23	24	21	25	13	20	172	295	270	125	31	74	62	150	66	16	31	55	65	45	120	59	31	51	59	12
WXIA	12	19	19	17	21	17	9	14	119	263	164	139	70	130	101	95	80	40	59	57	59	39	69	56	44	41	44	29
WTBS	6	9	13	14	17	9	6	9	37	67	55	32	9	21	17	32	20	7	12	17	20	10	22	12	5	10	12	5
WATL	3	5	4	3	5	6	4	6								2	1			1	1		2	2	1	2	2	
WGNX	9	14	12	6	8	9	10	16	106	220	106	95	67	106	66	65	58	37	39	42	44	28	37	27	25	26	39	1
• WVEU									3	6	3	2	1	2	1	2	2		1	1	2	1	2	1		1		
WGTV		1							3	4	4	3		2	2	2	1		1	2	2		2	2	1	2	2	
WPBA									4	4	4	2				1				1	1		2	2		2	1	
HUT/TOT	63		56	51	47	61	63		781	1416	1112	673	245	489	377	623	370	137	210	293	331	198	489	304	164	248	281	112
7:30P-8:00P																												
WSB	14	22	22	28	21	27	16	24	170	275	235	163	49	113	93	137	95	29	54	75	81	42	98	68	39	58	63	20
WAGA	11	17	16	18	17	22	10	15	134	240	211	103	30	61	47	123	58	15	26	48	56	38	88	45	21	39	46	14
WXIA	21	32	31	22	20	22	11	34	257	485	404	221	81	151	114	235	124	44	62	102	122	70	169	97	52	75	91	37
WTBS	5	8	11	13	15	10	5	9	114	260	160	134	65	125	97	92	77	39	57	55	58	38	68	57	40	41	45	28
WATL	3	5	4	3	5	6	4	6	36	65	54	31	9	19	15	32	19	6	10	17	20	9	22	12	5	10	11	4
WGNX	6	9	8	6	6	6	6	10	71	145	87	76	36	73	57	46	41	19	32	30	31	19	22	15	9	14	16	1
• WVEU									3	4	3	2	1	2	1		2		1	2	2		2	3	2	2	2	
WGTV		1	1						4	7	6	4		3	3	4	2		2	2	2		3	2	2	2	2	
WPBA							1	1	7	9	9	4		1	1	5	1			1	1		2	1	1	3	3	
HUT/TOT	65		56	51	50	63	64		796	1490	1169	738	271	548	428	675	418	152	244	331	372	220	496	320	184	255	290	120
8:00P-11:00P																												
WSB	17	27	25	28	25	28	18	28	207	366	309	215	78	156	129	181	123	44	73	94	103	60	128	93	56	71	79	28
WAGA	19	30	31	18	23	32	19	30	230	421	352	230	85	171	135	206	132	48	77	102	115	72	145	98	57	78	86	36
WXIA	17	26	26	18	21	23	18	28	200	376	302	220	79	166	134	169	122	40	76	97	105	62	132	99	58	77	86	32
WTBS	2	3	4	18	15	4	2	4	53	86	76	48	14	32	28	31	18	5	10	15	17	9	44	30	18	23	25	4
WATL	2	2	2	3	3	3	2	3	17	28	25	17	5	12	11	11	7	2	5	6	7	3	14	10	6	8	9	1
WGNX	2	4	5	6	6	6	6	10	31	51	44	29	9	22	18	23	15	5	9	12	13	9	22	15	9	14	14	3
• WVEU									4	6	5	1				2	1		1			1	4	3	1	3		
WGTV	1	2	2	2	2	2	1	2	17	25	23	13	2	6	5	12	7	1	3	6	7	4	11	6	2	6	7	1
WPBA	1	1					1	1	5	9	9	5		2	4	2			1	1	1		2	1		2		
HUT/TOT	64		61	56	57	66	64		765	1368	1146	782	273	570	464	639	427	145	255	335	371	221	505	357	208	280	315	106
11:00P-11:30P																												
WSB	13	30	29	33	30	32	14	32	153	245	228	151	45	96	86	123	78	23	42	59	64	31	105	74	44	57	64	10
WAGA	15	35	32	25	30	35	15	34	180	285	270	155	37	98	89	156	89	20	52	73	81	50	113	86	51	53	64	9
WXIA	11	25	24	18	22	22	11	25	131	211	200	117	31	69	62	114	66	18	35	50	58	32	86	51	27	43	50	7
WTBS	1	2	3	11		1	1	1	20	30	27	19	4	13	11	13	8	1	5	7	8	3	14	10	6	8	9	1
WATL	1	1			3	2	1	1	9	8	6	2	3	2		5	4	1	1	2	3	1	3	2	1	2		
WGNX	1	3	5	6	7	2	2	3	18	26	23	20	6	16	15	12	11	3	8	8	8	5	12	10	7	8	8	1
• WVEU				2					4	5	6	4	3	3	2	4	3	2		1	1	1	2	1		1		
WGTV	1								3	5	3	2				2	1		1	1	2		2	1		1	1	
WPBA									1	1	1	1																
HUT/TOT	44		36	41	38	40	45		516	815	765	474	128	299	268	429	260	68	146	201	225	122	335	215	122	172	198	28

ATLANTA   3   FEBRUARY 1985 DAYPART SUMMARY

* ESTIMATES EXCLUDE QTR-HRS STATION WAS NOT ON AIR
■ SHARE/HUT TRENDS NOT AVAILABLE
+ COMBINED PARENT/SATELLITE

26 share. These numbers represent the average audience estimates for all programs aired during the 1.5-hour time period for the entire 4-week ratings sweep.

Reading a ratings book is relatively simple. As mentioned earlier, all decimal points are deleted, but also notice that all numbers have been rounded to the nearest whole number. (All ratings and shares are rounded to the nearest whole number.) The top of the page indicates the section of the book, in this case "Daypart Audience Estimates Summary." A **daypart** is a segment of a broadcast day, such as "prime time" (8:00 P.M.–11:00 P.M. EST).

To use the summary, first refer to the column headings for the identification of the numbered columns. For example, Column 5 shows the rating for the 4-week sweep, Column 6 shows the station's share. Columns 58–61 contain the ratings the station received for the same time period for the four preceding ratings books. Columns 11–30 contain the TSA information in thousands; WSB television had an average of 184,000 adults aged 18–49 in the audience for the "6:00P–7:30P" daypart (see Column 14). The right-hand portion of the daypart section (not shown) contains additional information about the ADI and TSA. Every ratings book has a detailed glossary that defines every term used in the book. Some of the more widely used terms are discussed below.

The **average quarter-hour** (AQH) is an estimate of the number of persons or households tuned to a specific channel for at least 5 minutes during a 15-minute time segment. These estimates are provided for the TSA/NSI, ADI/DMA, and MSA in all ratings books. Stations are obviously interested in obtaining high AQH figures in all demographic areas, since these figures indicate how long an audience is tuned in, and thus how "loyal" the audience is to the station.

The **cume** (cumulative audience) or **reach** is an estimate of the number of persons who listened to or viewed at least 5 minutes within a given daypart. The cume is also referred to as the "unduplicated audience." For example, a person who watches a soap opera at least 5 minutes a day Monday through Friday would be counted only once in a cume rating, whereas his or her viewing would be "duplicated" five times in determining average quarter-hours.

The **gross rating points** (GRPs) are a total of a station's ratings during two or more dayparts and represent the size of the gross audience. Advertising purchases are often made on the basis of GRPs. For example, a radio advertiser who purchases 10 commercials on a station may wish to know the gross audience they will reach. Using hypothetical data, the GRP is calculated as shown in Table 14.1. The gross rating point indicates that about 32.4% of the listening audience will be exposed to the ten commercials.

A useful figure for radio stations is the **audience turnover**, or the number of times the audience changes during a given daypart. A high turnover is not always a negative factor in advertising sales; some stations naturally have high turnover (such as "Top 40" stations, whose audiences comprise mainly younger people who tend to change

Table 14.1 Calculation of GRP for Five Dayparts

Daypart	Number of spots		Station rating		GRP (%)
M–F, 6A.M.–9A.M.	2	×	3.1	=	6.2
M–F, 12P.M.–3P.M.	2	×	2.9	=	5.8
M–F, 1P.M.–6P.M.	2	×	3.6	=	7.2
Sat, 6A.M.–9A.M.	2	×	2.5	=	5.0
Sun, 3P.M.–6P.M.	2	×	4.1	=	8.2
	10				32.4

stations frequently). A high turnover factor simply means that an advertiser will need to run more spots to reach the station's audience. Usually such stations compensate by charging less for commercial spots than stations with low turnovers.

Turnover is computed by dividing a station's cume audience by its average persons total (both these figures are reported in ratings books). Consider three stations in the Monday–Friday, 3:00–6:00 P.M. daypart, as shown in Table 14.2. In this market, an advertiser on Station C would need to run more commercials to reach all listeners than one who uses Station A. However, Station C, in addition to having a larger audience, may have the demographic audience most suitable for the advertiser's product.

Although information on ratings and shares is computed the same way for radio and television audience measurements, the information is presented very differently in the respective media. Radio books are divided into several sections: share trends, men, women, adults, teens, dayparts average and cume, and several others. Each section contains a variety of information for different dayparts and for different demographic groups. A sample page from an Arbitron radio book is shown in Figure 14.4. This page is from the "adults" section of the book and includes data only for listeners over the age of 18, as well as various age categories that divide the adult 18–64 audience. The "adults" section of the radio book is actually the combined numbers from the "men" and "women" sections.

The first step in reading a radio book is to determine the type of numbers reported on the page. In Figure 14.4, the upper right-hand corner indicates that the data are for the period Monday–Sunday, 6:00 A.M.–midnight (that is, the whole week). The top center of the page identifies the numbers reported as "Average Quarter-Hour and

Table 14.2 Computation of Turnover for Three Stations

Station	Cume audience		Average persons		Turnover
A	2,900	÷	850	=	3.4
B	1,750	÷	420	=	4.2
C	960	÷	190	=	5.1

Figure 14.4 Sample AQH and cume data

Average Quarter-Hour and Cume Listening Estimates

PHILADELPHIA
WINTER 1985

MONDAY-SUNDAY
6:00AM-MIDNIGHT

Column groupings: ADULTS 18+, ADULTS 18-34, ADULTS 18-49, ADULTS 25-49, ADULTS 25-54, ADULTS 35-54

For each group: TOTAL AREA (AVG PERS (00), CUME PERS (00)), METRO SURVEY AREA (AVG PERS (00), CUME PERS (00), AVG PERS RTG, AVG PERS SHR)

STATION CALL LETTERS: KYW, WCAU, WCAU FM, *WCOJ, WDAS, WDAS FM, WEAZ, WFIL, *WFLN, WFLN FM, WHAT, WIOQ, WIP, WMSZ, WMGK, WMMR, WPEN, *WPGR, WSNI, WUSL, WWDB, WXTU, WYSP, WZGO, WZZD, WBYO, WFMZ, WJBR FM, WPST, WNBC

Footnote Symbols   (*) means audience estimates adjusted for actual broadcast schedule

ARBITRON RATINGS

Copyright 1985 Arbitron Ratings Company

Cume Listening Estimates." The top left-hand corner displays the market and the rating period reported.

Refer to KYW, the first station listed in the left-hand column, to determine how to read the page. Many of the numbers reported on this page, as well as on several other pages in a radio book, are listed in 100s (designated by (00) at the top of the column). Always refer to the top of a column to determine whether the data are truncated or shortened by "00." In the first block of columns, "Adults 18+," an average of 70,000 adults 18+ (in the TSA) listened to KYW during each quarter-hour of the total week; during the week, an estimated 1,243,400 people tuned in to KYW for at least 5 minutes in a quarter-hour during the total week (listed as "Cume Pers"). The same two figures are then reported for the metro—KYW's metro "average quarter-hour adults 18+" was 62,400, with a cume audience of 1,066,800. These data gave KYW and "adults 18+" average quarter-hour rating of 1.8 and a share of 8.6.

The audience share is the most important figure in radio because ratings tend to be small (in comparison to television). In Figure 14.4, KYW's 8.6 was the highest share for "Adults 18+." However, high shares may not always be beneficial. For example, even though KYW does have a high 18+ share, the shares for the other demographic categories show that much of the 18+ audience consists of adults 35–64, as indicated by the 9.8 share. This high number (in relation to the 35–64 shares for the other stations, and KYW's other demographic shares) indicates an older skewing audience—an audience that would be hard to sell to advertisers primarily interested in younger consumers.

If you were an advertiser interested in an audience in the 18–34 range, which station would you probably contact to purchase advertising? A "guess" of WMMR is on target, since the station received a 17.1 share of the demographic group. Yet, most advertisers would not blindly purchase spots on WMMR without finding out something about the station's format. The station does have a high 18–34 share, but the format may not be suitable to all types of product or service. For example, MTV might not wish to advertise on WMMR if the station aired a country format.

There are two hash lines dividing Figure 14.4, one after WZZD and one after WPST. These lines separate the location of the stations into those that are "home to the Arbitron metro area" and those "outside the Arbitron metro area but home to the Philadelphia ADI," respectively. The third section lists any station that is "outside the Arbitron metro area and the ADI."

The bottom line of all Arbitron radio pages shows the totals for each of the columns presented. In Philadelphia, there was an average of 729,400 adults 18+ listening to radio each quarter-hour of the total week, with a total cume audience of 3,399,000 (about 3.4 million adults 18+ tuned to a radio station for at least 5 minutes during the total week). An important point about the bottom line reported on each page is that all the numbers shown above the total line do not always add to the total number.

The total numbers at the bottom of the page include radio listening to stations in the home market as well as to stations that do not fall into one of the three divisions on the Arbitron page (listening to a station far away from home). In addition, Arbitron includes on the bottom total listening line all illegible entries made in radio diaries or entries that cannot be attributed to any station in the market or a nearby market. For example, a person who records having listened to radio at a given time may fail to identify the station in any way—through call letters, dial setting, or description of the program heard. All these unattributed entries are included as "listening" and are added to the bottom line total. Incidentally, the same procedure is used in television ratings books; people may be watching or using their sets, but not necessarily to view the stations in the ADI/DMA—the television use is recorded, but none of the stations in the market gets credit for the use.

In early 1985 Arbitron began testing a new printing layout for its radio ratings books and planned to introduce the "new look" with the fall 1986 survey period. Readers interested in radio ratings are urged to contact the nearest Arbitron office to receive a copy of the new format. The new books will contain no new formulas; the changes are basically cosmetic.

Adjusting for Unrepresentative Samples

Since ratings are computed using samples from the population, there is always a certain amount of error associated with the data. This error, designated by the notation σ, is known as standard error (introduced in Chapter 4). Standard error must always be considered before interpreting ratings, to determine whether a certain sex/age group has been undersampled or oversampled.

There are numerous approaches to calculating standard error. One of the simpler methods is:

$$SE(p) = \sqrt{\frac{p(100 - p)}{n}}$$

where p = sample percentage or rating, n = sample size, and SE = standard error. For example, suppose a random sample of 1,200 households produces a rating of 20. The standard error can be expressed as follows:

$$SE(p) = \sqrt{\frac{20(100 - 20)}{1,200}}$$

$$= \sqrt{\frac{20(80)}{1,200}}$$

$$= \sqrt{1.33}$$

$$= \pm\ 1.15$$

The rating of 20 has a standard error of ± 1.15 points, which means the rating actually ranges from 18.85 to 21.15. Standard error formulas are included in all ratings books; Arbitron has simplified the procedure by publishing tables in the back of each book.

Weighting is another procedure used by ratings companies to adjust for samples that are not representative of the population. In some situations a particular sex/age group cannot be adequately sampled, and it becomes imperative that a correction be made.

Assume that population estimates for an ADI/DMA indicate that there are 41,500 men aged 18–34 and that this group accounts for 8.3% of the population over the age of 12. The researchers distribute diaries to a sample of the ADI/DMA population of which 950 are returned and usable (known as *in-tab* diaries). They would expect about 79 of these to be from men aged 18–34 (8.3% of 950). However, they find that only 63 of the diaries are from this demographic group—16 short of the anticipated number. The data must be weighted to adjust for this deficiency. The weighting formula is:

$$\text{Weight}_{\text{sex/group}} = \frac{\text{Group share of population}}{\text{Group share of sample}}$$

In the example, the weighting for men age 18–34 is calculated as:

$$\text{Weight}_{\text{MSA men, 18-34}} = \frac{0.083}{0.066}$$
$$= 1.25$$

This figure must be multiplied by the number of persons in the group that each diary would normally represent. That is, instead of representing 525 men (41,500 ÷ 79), each diary would represent 656 men (525 × 1.25). The ideal weighting value is 1.00, indicating that the group was adequately represented in the sample. On occasion, a group may be oversampled, in which case the weighting value will be a number less than 1.00

Recent Developments in Ratings Research

The measurement of audiences for broadcasting and cable is on the verge of many sweeping changes. The next 5–10 years should be very exciting. In radio, the controversy over the use of diaries versus the telephone should continue. There are critics of both systems; however, no one has developed a satisfactory answer to improve the current methods. Any changes made in radio measurement are likely to be refinements of the current methodologies, not a total overhaul of the system. It also seems unlikely (at present) that electronic data collection will be tried again in radio, since the medium is so mobile.

The most dramatic changes in the near future will be related to television and cable audience measurement. The major focus of the changes in television research relates to a concept known as "single-source data"—the ability to collect ratings data, demographic data, and even household member purchasing behavior at one time.

The key to achieving single-source data hinges on the development and acceptance of **people meters** in the household. Traditional television meters tell only whether the television set is on or off, and the channel to which the set is tuned; there are no data about *who* is watching. Such information must be obtained by pooling TV meter data with information from households in the diary samples used by Arbitron and Nielsen. People meters attempt to simplify this data collection task by requiring each person in the household, as well as all visitors, to push a specific button on a mechanical unit that records the viewing. Each person in the home is assigned a button on the meter. The meter instantaneously records information about how many people in the household are watching, and the identity of each viewer. The data from each night's viewing is collected via computer. This specific information is valuable for advertisers and their agencies, who now can more accurately target their advertising messages.

The A. C. Nielsen Company and Arbitron have made great strides in the development of people meters in the United States. In late 1985, Nielsen announced a very ambitious schedule for installing people meters in households across the country. The plan calls for a completed meter system by late 1988. The concept depends on whether validation of the system meets Nielsen's standards; however, it seems likely that people meters will be the system of the future.

The single-source data concept has been expanded by Arbitron in a system called ScanAmerica, a method to collect household purchasing data related directly to television viewing in the household. When purchases are made and brought into the home, a household member passes a scanning wand over the Universal Product Code (UPC) lines on the items and the information is stored in Arbitron's RD-100 people meter for later retrieval. This method, if accepted by consumers involved in the surveys, will provide specific data about television viewing behavior (exposure to commercials) and product purchases (effect of exposure to commercials).

In addition to Arbitron and Nielsen, a company from Great Britain, AGB Research, is participating in the development of people meters in the United States. In fact, AGB provided the impetus for the other two companies to get involved in people meters. AGB has installed people meters in several countries and has offered to provide the service to America. During the next several years the three companies will "battle" to determine which system, or systems, will be accepted by U.S. advertisers. It is highly likely that two systems, and possibly all three, will survive testing and experimentation. In that case, the marketplace will determine which service, or services, exists.

In theory, people meters are quite simple—when a person begins or stops watching television, he or she pushes a button to document the behavior. The button may be located on a hand-held device or enclosed in a small box mounted on top of the television set. In practice, however, several significant questions need to be answered before people meters can be considered a viable alternative for single-source data collection. For example: Does the physical action of pushing a button significantly interfere with normal viewing behavior of viewers? Since viewers will be required to push their buttons a number of times during viewing (and are reminded to do so by a flashing light or audio tone), will they change their viewing habits? Will they be truthful and consistent in their button pushing behavior?

There is also a question about motivation to continue in the sample. People who complete diaries are asked to do so for only one week. Current Nielsen and Arbitron meter households, whose participation in documenting viewing behavior consists solely in permitting installation of the metering device, are involved for up to 5 years. A major concern is whether household members in a people meter household will continue the button pushing procedure for such a long time. If not, sample turnover will be very high and the quality of sample selection may deteriorate.

Even with these and countless other questions about the reliability and validity of people meters, the research companies are convinced they can produce a valid and reliable system. The question is not whether the people meters can be developed, but how long it will take the three companies to get such a system on-line. Advertisers and broadcasters will have people meters; they will have a ScanAmerica type of system; they will have single-source data. The next step is to wait and see how each company approaches the same problems.

Qualitative audience ratings for television may also become significant in the near future. At present, only Television Audience Assessment, Inc. (TAA), of Cambridge, Massachusetts, is involved in this experimental area, but there are indications that the data may prove to be very useful to broadcast programmers. As the company states in its executive summary:

> Although Americans are watching more television than ever before, they are also watching more channels . . . with sets on for so much longer every day than they once were, television programs must now compete with other demands on people's time and attention. . . . Industry executives need more detailed consumer information. They need to know whether viewers are involved with and are enjoying what they see, whether they find a program worth planning ahead to watch, whether they will set aside other activities to pay attention to it, and whether they will remain in the room throughout the program and its commercial breaks.

To provide the answers to these and other questions, TAA developed a new form of audience "ratings" that provide information on programs in two specific areas: the Program Appeal Index measures the overall entertainment value of a program, and the Program Impact Index measures the degree of intellectual and emotional stimulation a program provides for its viewers. Both indexes use a 0–100 scale to assess the program's effects on viewers (Television Audience Assessment, 1983).

Although the TAA has completed several tests of the new qualitative system, the "broadcast jury" has yet to determine whether the new methodology and information will be useful.

Nonratings Research

Although audience ratings are the most visible research data used in broadcasting, broadcasters, production companies, advertisers, and broadcast consultants use numerous other methodologies. Ratings yield estimates of audience size and composition. Nonratings research provides information about what the audience likes and dislikes, analyses of different types of programming, demographic and lifestyle information about the audience, and much more. All these data are intended to furnish decision makers in the industry with information they can use to eliminate some of the guesswork.

Nonratings research cannot solve all the problems broadcasters face, but it can be used to support decision making. This section describes some of the nonratings research that is conducted in the electronic media.

Program Testing

Research has become an accepted step in the development and production of programs and commercials. It is now common practice to test these productions in each of the following stages: initial idea or plan, rough cut, and postproduction. A variety of research approaches can be used in each of these stages, depending on the purpose of the study, how much time is allowed for testing, and what types of decisions will be made with the results. A research director must determine what the decision makers will need to know and design an analysis to provide that information.

Since major programs and commercials are very expensive to produce, producers and directors are interested in gathering preliminary reactions to a planned project. It would be ludicrous to spend thousands or millions of dollars on a project that would have little audience appeal.

Although most program testing is conducted by major networks, large advertising agencies, and production companies, there is an increasing interest in this area of research at the local level. Stations now test promotional campaigns, prime time access scheduling, the acceptability of locally produced commercials, and various programming strategies.

One way to collect preliminary data is to show subjects a short statement summarizing a program or commercial and ask them for their opinions about the idea and their willingness to watch the program or buy the product on the basis of the description. The results may provide some indication about the potential success of a show or commercial.

However, program descriptions cannot demonstrate the characters and their relationships to other characters in the program. This can be done only through the program dialogue and the characters' on-screen performance. For example, the NBC-TV program "The Cosby Show" might have been described as follows:

> *The Cosby Show*: A comedy series about the Cliff Huxtable family. Huxtable (Cosby), an obstetrician, and his wife, an attorney, have five children. Each week the program concerns the problems, experiences, and human emotions the Huxtable family faces—with Cosby as ringleader of this typical, yet very comical, middle-class American family.

To many people this statement might seem to describe the type of show generally referred to as a "bomb." However, the indescribable on-screen relationship between Cosby and the other cast members, as well as good story lines, made "The Cosby Show" a hit in 1985. If producers relied totally on program descriptions in testing situations, many successful shows would never have reached the air.

If an idea tests well in the preliminary stages (or if the producer or advertiser wishes to go ahead with the project regardless of what the research indicates), a model or simulation is produced. These media "hardware" items are referred to as *rough cuts, storyboards, photomatics, animatics,* or *executions.* The **rough cut** is a simplistic production that usually uses amateur actors, little or no editing, and makeshift sets. The other models are photographs, pictures, or drawings of major scenes designed to give the basic idea of a program or commercial to anyone who looks at them.

Rough cuts or models are tested by companies such as Burke Marketing Research. They do not involve a great deal of production expense, which is especially important if the tests show a lack of acceptance or understanding of the product. The tests provide information about the script, characterizations, character relationships, settings, cinematic approach, and overall appeal. They seldom identify the causes when a program or commercial is found to be unacceptable to the test audience; rather, they provide an overall indication that something is wrong.

When the final product is available, postproduction research can be conducted. Finished products are tested in experimental theaters, in shopping centers (where mobile vans are used to show commercials or programs), at subjects' homes in cities where cable systems provide test channels, or via telephone, in the case of radio commercials. Results from postproduction research often indicate that, for example, the ending of a program is unacceptable and must be reedited or reshot. Many problems that were not foreseen during production may be encountered in postproduction research, and the data usually provide producers with an initial audience reaction to the finished, or partially finished, product.

One of the better known experimental theaters used for testing television programs and commercials and theatrical films is run by Audience Studies Incorporated (ASI). The ASI Preview House in Hollywood, California, has a capacity of 400, and each seat contains a dial with which the viewer rates the material presented. The responses, from "very good" to "very dull," are recorded by a computer in the back of the theater. The data are then displayed in a graph form that enables researchers to determine whether the material contains any problem areas when compared to similar material tested previously. Preview House begins each testing session with a "Mr. Magoo" cartoon that serves as a baseline for comparison for further testing and also allows the audience to learn to operate the dials. For this reason, the results of these tests are referred to as "Magoos." Although Preview House is often criticized for its methodology, sample selection, and quality of data, most broadcast and film executives seem to think that its research provides at least an indication of audience likes and dislikes.

BehaviorScan is an approach to testing commercials as well as new consumer products that operates on cable television systems. It offers the capability to cut in commercials (that is, to replace a regularly scheduled commercial with a test spot) in certain target households. The other households on the cable system view the regular spot. Some time after the airing of the test commercial to the target households, follow-up research is conducted to determine the success of the commercial or the response to a new consumer product.

Nielsen has a similar system called Testsight that began test marketing in Sioux City, South Dakota, in late 1984. A microprocessor called a telemeter is attached to test panel television sets and allows commercials to be cut into normal over-the-air television programs. The telemeter also records viewing activity, much like the standard Nielsen meter. Both BehaviorScan, a system of Chicago-based Information Resources, Inc., and Testsight give test panel households plastic identification cards for use when making purchases at supermarkets or drug stores. The card electronically credits the products purchased by the household members, taking advantage of the UPC bars used in the identification of retail items. The purchasing behavior is then related to television viewing behavior (similar to Arbitron's ScanAmerica).

Music Research

Music is one of the most important elements in a music radio station's programming schedule. To provide listeners with music they like to hear and to eliminate songs that people are tired of hearing (known as burn-out), radio programmers engage in a variety of research procedures.

In two widely used methods, auditorium testing and **call-out research**, listeners are asked their opinions about established music selections the station is playing or is thinking about adding to the playlist (music tests are not suitable for newly released recordings). Both procedures have the same purpose: to provide the program director and/or music director with information about the types of songs that are liked and disliked. The information eliminates the "gut feeling" approach that many radio personnel use in selecting music for their station.

Both methods involve playing short segments, or hooks, of a number of recordings for the sample of people. A **hook** is a 5–15 second representative sample of the recording—enough for a person to identify a song that is already familiar and produce a positive or negative opinion. Music research supplies decision makers with information about what songs listeners do and do not like; the purpose is *not* to advise the program director and/or music director how frequently a song should appear in the station's rotation of songs (that is, how often a song should be played). Many researchers do conduct music tests and from the results of the test suggest to station management a very specific playlist and rotation scheme. This, however, is an incorrect use of music research. The data provide only an indication of what songs the sample of listeners do and do not like; the results do not tell how often the people wish to hear a particular song.

Auditorium testing. In this method between 75 and 100 people are invited to a large room or hall, often a hotel conference room. Subjects are invited to the test because they meet specific requirements determined by the radio station and/or the research company (for example, people between the ages of 25 and 40 who listen to soft rock stations in the client's market). The recruiting of subjects for auditorium testing is generally conducted by a field service company that specializes in recruiting people for focus groups or other similar research projects. Respondents are generally paid $20 for their cooperation.

The auditorium setting itself—namely, a comfortable location away from distractions at home—enables researchers to test several hundred hooks in one 60–90 minute session. Usually between 200 and 400 hooks are tested although some companies routinely test up to 600 hooks in a single session. However, after 300 songs, subject fatigue becomes evident by explicit physical behavior (looking around the room, fidgeting, talking to neighbors), and statistical reliability decreases (standard deviations for song rating grow progressively larger as the number of tested hooks increases). There is definite evidence that summary scores for hooks after the 300 limit are not reliable.

Several types of measurement scales are appropriate for use in music research. For example, respondents can be asked to rate a hook on a 5- or 7-point scale where 1 represents "don't like" and 5 or 7 represents "like a lot." A feeling thermometer might also be used to rate selections, with 0 indicating an unfavorable response and 100 a very positive response. Scores for each hook are tabulated to determine those that appealed most to the listeners. A variety of statistical procedures are used in analyzing music test research. The methods of analysis vary among research companies and researchers.

Music testing is designed to test only selections that have been heard for some time. It cannot be used on new releases because people cannot be expected to rate an unfamiliar recording on the basis of a 5–15 second hook.

Call-out research. The purpose of call-out research is the same as for auditorium testing; only the procedure for collecting the data is changed. Instead of inviting people to a large hall or ballroom, randomly selected subjects are called on the telephone. Subjects are given the same rating instructions as in the auditorium test; they listen to the hook and provide a verbal response to the researcher making the telephone call.

The major limitation to call-out research is that the number of testable hooks is limited to a maximum of about 20, since subject fatigue sets in very quickly over the telephone. Further problems include the distractions that are often present in the home, and the frequently poor quality of sound transmission created by the telephone equipment (the auditorium setting allows subjects to hear the hooks in quality stereo sound).

Even with such limitations, call-out research is used by many radio stations throughout the country. Since call-out research is fairly inexpensive when compared to the auditorium method, the research can be conducted on a continual basis to track the performance of songs in a particular market. Auditorium research, which can cost from $10,000–$100,000 to test approximately 800 songs, is generally conducted only once or twice per year.

News and Programming Consultants

Several private research and consulting firms conduct news and programming research for radio and television stations. Some of the largest are Frank N. Magid Associates, Coleman Research, Surrey Consulting & Research, and The Research Group. Although each of these firms specializes in specific areas of broadcasting and uses different research procedures, they have a common goal: to provide broadcast management with data to be used in decision making.

Consultants supply custom research for broadcasters; they perform studies of news formats and their popularity, news personalities, programming formats in radio, and program scheduling in both radio and television, as well as individual research studies developed by management. Data are collected in a variety of ways. Usually a company will settle on one or two basic methods such as telephone interviews, focus groups, in-person interviews, or intercepts.

Custom research is not conducted solely by large companies; a number of highly qualified individuals also provide research to broadcasters. Usually these consultants work in the industry for several years before branching out into research. There are also a number of college and university professors who conduct research on a variety of topics.

Performer Q

Producers and directors in broadcasting naturally desire an indication of the popularity of various performers and entertainers. A basic question in the planning stage of any program is "What performer or group of performers should be used to give the show the greatest appeal?" Not unreasonably, producers prefer using the most popular and likable performers in the industry to taking a chance on an unknown entertainer.

Marketing Evaluations, Inc., of Port Washington, New York, meets the demand for information about performers, entertainers, and personalities. The company conducts nationwide telephone surveys using three panels of about 1,250 households and interviewing about 5,400 people 6 years of age and older. The surveys are divided into three sections, Performer Q, Target Audience Rankings, and Demographic Profiles. The Performer Q portion of the analysis provides Familiarity and Appeal scores for more than 1,000 different personalities. The Target Audience Rankings provide a rank-order list of all personalities for several different target audiences, such as women 18–49. The target rank tells producers and directors which personalities appeal to specific demographic groups. In the third section, each personality is listed according to eight demographic profiles of the survey respondents. This section indicates the types of people that do and do not like the personalities in the survey.

Focus Groups

The focus group, discussed in Chapter 7, is a standard procedure in electronic media research, probably due to its versatility. Focus groups are used to develop questionnaires for further research and to provide preliminary information on a variety of topics, such as format and programming changes, personalities, station images, and lifestyle characteristics of the audience. Data in the last category are particularly useful when the focus group consists of a specific demographic segment.

Miscellaneous Research

Broadcast stations are unique and require different types of research. Research conducted by and for stations includes the following.

1. Station image. It is important for a station's management to know how the public perceives the station and its services; hence, "station image" has been mentioned throughout this chapter. Public misperception of management's purpose can create a decrease in audience size and, consequently, in advertising revenue. For example, suppose a radio station that has aired "Top 40" music for 10 years switches to a country format. It is important that the audience and advertisers be aware of this change and have a chance to voice their opinions. This can be accomplished through a station image study, in which respondents to telephone calls are asked questions such as: "What type of music does radio station WAAA play?" "What types of people do you think listen to WAAA radio?" and "Did you know that WAAA now plays country music?" If the research reveals that few people are aware of the change in format, management can develop a new promotion strategy. Or, the station might find that the current promotional efforts have been successful and should not be changed.

Station image studies are conducted periodically by most larger stations to maintain current information on how the audience perceives each station in the market. If station managers are to provide the services that listeners and viewers want, they must keep up to date with audience trends and social changes.

2. Advertiser (account) analysis. To increase the value of their service to advertisers, many stations administer questionnaires to local business executives. Some typical questions include: "When did your business open?" "How many people own this business?" "How much do you invest in advertising per year?" "When are advertising purchase decisions made?" and "What do you expect from your advertising?" Information obtained from client questionnaires is used to help write more effective advertising copy, to develop better advertising proposals, and to allow the sales staff to know more about each client. Generally, the questionnaires are administered before a business becomes an advertiser on the station, but they can also be used for advertisers who have done business with the station for several years.

3. Account executive research. Radio and television station managers throughout the country conduct surveys of advertising agency personnel, usually buyers, to determine how their sales executives are perceived. It is vitally important to know how the sales people are received by the buyers. The results of the survey indicate which sales people are performing very well and which ones may need additional help. Many times a survey discloses that a problem between a sales executive and a buyer is purely a personality difference, and the station can easily correct the problem by assigning another sales person to the advertising agency.

4. Sales research. In an effort to increase sales, many stations themselves conduct research for local clients. For example, a station may conduct a "banking image" study of all banks in the area to determine how residents perceive each bank and the service it provides. The results from such a study are then used in an advertising proposal for the banks in the area. If it is discovered that First National Bank's 24-hour automatic teller service is not well understood by local residents, for example, the station might develop an advertising proposal to concentrate on this point.

5. Diversification analyses. The goals of any business are to expand and to achieve higher profits. In an effort to reach these goals, most larger stations, partnerships, and companies engage in a variety of studies to determine where investments should be made. Should other stations be purchased? What other types of activity should the business invest in? Such studies are used for forecasting and represent a major portion of the research undertaken by larger stations and companies. The changes in broadcast ownership rules made by the FCC have significantly increased the level of acquisition research conducted by individuals, group owners, and other large companies in the broadcasting industry.

The Future of Electronic
Media Research

Trying to predict the future is no simple task. Certain trends in electronic media research are clear, but long-range predictions must be tenuous because the media change so rapidly. This section discusses some significant topics that have or will have an affect in the research area.

The change in broadcast ownership rules from the Rule of Sevens (where one person or group could own 7 AM, 7 FM, and 7 TV stations), to the Rule of Twelves has changed the course of broadcasting. With individuals and groups able to own almost twice as many stations (although the limit in television is restricted to 12 stations or coverage of 25% of the television audience in the United States, with a 50% reduction given to any UHF station), broadcast researchers became very active in acquisition research. The goal is to find and analyze stations for sale and determine if the station would be a beneficial addition to the company or group.

The research related to television meters and people meters has only begun. With such a large amount of revenue and pride at stake for the "winner," Arbitron, Nielsen, and AGB Research will surely be involved in hundreds and hundreds of types of research projects. And after people meters do become a reality, there will surely be hundreds of other studies conducted by researchers throughout the country to determine whether the methodology does in fact produce the data it is intended to produce.

In addition, assuming that more than one people meter methodology is accepted, there will no doubt be countless studies to determine why the results from the two (or possibly three) methods do not agree. This has been a problem with the current Arbitron and Nielsen meters and will surely remain when the more complicated systems are used.

The high degree of audience segmentation created in radio during the 1980s has in turn created extreme competition for radio listeners. Not even the most established stations in the country can continue to rely on tried-and-true methods of the past. Radio listeners are fickle and change their tastes and demands very quickly. Radio managers need to be able to respond with equal speed to keep up with trends and new directions. Their responses have been, and will continue to be (even with more regularity), guided by audience research. For anyone involved in broadcast research, the recent increase in the importance and the sophistication of radio research has been easy to see, and there is no indication that research will become less important in the years to come. Station image studies, music research, personality testing, and general marketing analyses have become commonplace even for radio stations in small markets throughout the country.

Television offers an even more confusing picture than radio. The decade of the 1970s provided the stepping-stone to the future of television as new technologies paved the way for what was and is to come: direct broadcast satellite transmission; multitiered cable television operations; video games; videotape recorders; videodiscs; television component systems; multiple-use television sets that double as security systems, telephone extensions, and so forth; and multiple-screen sets, which allow viewing of several channels simultaneously.

All these developments lead to the same conclusion about the future of research in the electronic media: there will be a need for information about how people are using the new technologies. How is conventional television use changing? What effects do all these new devices have on consumers? Specific questions that will need research include the following.

1. What effect do cable systems that offer 50 or more channels have on consumers' utilization of television? What do people watch? Why do they select specific channels?

2. What kinds of programming will fill these 50+ channels? Can cable companies afford all these channels? What is the dollar limit that subscribers can be charged for premium (or basic) services?

3. To what degree are audiences segmented by the new technologies? Will advertisers be willing to sponsor programs aimed at a narrowly defined audience? What will happen to commercial network advertising when such a variety of choices becomes available?

4. How do videotape and videodisc households differ in their use of television from homes without such devices?

5. Does active participation in the documentation of viewing affect the normal viewing habits of individuals? Do viewers become tired of pushing buttons, and if so, how does this relate to their viewing habits and the validity and reliability of the data collected?

6. How do video cassette recorders and hand-held remote control devices affect audience "zipping" (fast forwarding past commercials in the case of recorders) and "zapping" (switching to another channel when a commercial begins)? There has been some research conducted on these topics, but more data are required to determine the full extent and effects of zipping and zapping.

7. Initial research studies indicate that the addition of stereo to AM radio has not significantly increased the desire to choose the AM band over the FM band. AM radio broadcasters had hoped that stereo would be the factor that brought the band back to parity with FM. If stereo AM radio does, in fact, provide no additional benefits for listeners, what can AM radio broadcasters do to increase their market share? What type of unique service should AM radio provide to more adequately compete with FM? Also, how will stereo television affect sales, viewership, and production?

8. What long-term effects might result from the changing ownership patterns of the television networks? What, if any, effects on consumers are directly attributable to the rule change that allows individuals or groups to own more than 12 television stations and 24 radio stations? Are there effects in news or programming?

9. How will the increased popularity of various pay services such as HBO and Showtime affect network television? Will the networks attempt to decrease the importance of theatrical movies in their schedules in favor of specials of other types?

10. How do music channels such as MTV affect the promotion, sales, and distribution of records in the United States? How has viewing MTV affected the viewing of other types of television programming? Is there an age at which individuals no longer have an interest in music video channels, or has this programming become a standard offering that may continue for many years? Do people who watch MTV "grow out of" the format and watch other types of music video format?

The list could continue for several pages. The main point is that many questions need investigation. The electronic media can be a literal gold mine for researchers in search of questions.

In addition to the variety of questions that need investigation, researchers will need to develop new methodologies. Although the same procedures used today will be adequate for many of the questions of the future, the need for new research methods is clear. How will audience measurements be conducted when viewers (and listeners) can select from so many channels? What methods are appropriate to help advertisers make better judgments in purchasing advertising slots? What type of media mix in advertising is the most efficient? Again, the list is almost endless. But the future of electronic media research seems clear: new methodologies will be required to answer new research questions.

Summary

This chapter has introduced some of the more common methodologies used in broadcast research. Ratings are the most visible form of research used in broadcasting as well as the most influential in the decision-making process. However, nonratings approaches such as focus groups, music research, image studies, and program testing are all used frequently to collect data. The importance of research is fueled by an ever-increasing desire by management to learn more about broadcast audiences and their uses of the media.

The phenomenon of audience fragmentation has become evident during the past several years. All media now attract smaller, much more narrowly defined groups of people. This competition for viewers and listeners has created a need for research data. Broadcast owners and managers realize now that they can no longer rely on gut feelings when making programming, sales, and marketing decisions. The discussions in this chapter have been designed to emphasize the importance of research in all areas of broadcasting.

Questions and Problems for Further Investigation

1. Assume that a local television market has three stations: Channel 2, Channel 7, and Channel 9. There are 200,000 television

households in the market. A ratings company samples 1,200 households at random and finds that 25% of the sample is watching Channel 2, 15% Channel 7, and 10% Channel 9.

   a. Calculate each station's share of the audience.

   b. Project the total number of households in the population watching each channel.

   c. Calculate the CPM for a $1,000, 30-second spot on Channel 2.

   d. Calculate the standard error involved in Channel 2's rating.

2. What are the major data-gathering problems associated with: (a) electronic records, (b) diaries, and (c) telephone coincidentals?

3. Examine a recent Arbitron market radio ratings book. Select a station and a daypart and compute that station's: (a) AQH, (b) cume, and (c) turnover.

4. Perform your own music call-out research. Edit several 15-second selections of new recordings on a reel or cassette and ask people to rate them on a 7-point scale. Compute means and standard deviations for the results. What can you conclude?

5. Several questions relevant to modern broadcasting trends are listed at the end of the chapter. What type or types of research methods could be used to try to answer these questions?

References and Suggested Readings

Advertising Research Foundation. (1985). *Electronic media and research technologies: Vol. III*. New York: Advertising Research Foundation.

Arbitron. (1985). *Description of methodology*. Arbitron Ratings Company. (Manuals are available for both radio and television).

Beville, H. M. (1985). *Audience ratings*. Hillsdale, NJ: Lawrence Erlbaum Associates.

Cabletelevision Advertising Bureau. *Telephone coincidental guidelines*. New York: Cabletelevision Advertising Bureau.

Fletcher, J. E. (Ed.). (1981). *Handbook of radio and TV broadcasting*. New York: Van Nostrand Reinhold.

Naples, M. (1984). Electronic media research: An update and a look at the future. *Journal of Advertising Research, 24*(4), 39–48.

Nielsen, A. C. (1985). *Reference supplement 1984–85*. Chicago: A. C. Nielsen Company.

Television Audience Assessment. (1983). *The audience rates television (Executive summary)*. Cambridge, MA: Television Audience Assessment.

Webster, J.G. (1984). *People meters*. Washington, DC: National Association of Broadcasters.

C H A P T E R   1 5

Research in Advertising and Public Relations

For many years, research was not widely used in advertising and public relations; decisions were made on a more or less intuitive basis. However, with increased competition, mass markets, and mounting costs, more and more advertisers and public relations specialists have come to rely on research as a basic management tool.

Much of the research in advertising and public relations is **applied research**, which attempts to solve a specific problem and is not concerned with theorizing or generalizing to other situations. Advertising and public relations researchers want to answer questions such as: "Should a certain product be packaged in blue or red?" "Is *Cosmopolitan* a better advertising buy than *Vogue*?" and "Should a company stress its minority hiring program in a planned publicity campaign?"

Advertising and public relations research does not involve any special techniques; the methods discussed earlier—laboratory, survey, field research, and content analysis—are in common use. They have been adapted, however, to provide specific types of information that meet the needs of these industries.

This chapter discusses the more common areas of advertising and public relations research and the types of studies they entail. In describing these research studies, the primary aim is to convey the facts the reader must know to understand the methods and to use them intelligently. A significant portion of the research in these areas involves market studies conducted by commercial research firms; these studies form the basis for much of the more specific research that follows in either the academic or the private sector. The importance of market research notwithstanding, this chapter does not have the space required to treat this topic. Readers who desire additional information about market research techniques should consult Tull and Hawkins (1980) and Ferber (1974).

There are three functional research areas in advertising: copy research, media research, and campaign assessment research. Each is discussed in turn, and the syndicated research available in each case is described as appropriate.

Copy Testing

Everyone who does advertising research agrees that the term "copy testing" is misleading. The word "copy" implies that only the words in the ad are tested. This, of course, is not the case: every element in an ad (layout, narration, music, illustration, size, length, etc.) is a possible variable in copy testing. Leckenby (1984) has suggested that "advertising stimulus measurement and research" (ASMAR) be substituted for "copy testing," but the new term has not gained wide usage. Likewise, the term **message research** is a less frequently used synonym. Thus we will continue to use the traditional term, despite its shortcomings.

Copy testing refers to that research that helps develop effective advertisements and determines which of several advertisements is the most effective. Copy testing takes place at every stage of the advertising process. Before a campaign starts, it is used to determine what to stress and what to avoid. Once the content of the ad has been established, tests must be performed to ascertain the most effective way to structure these ideas. For example, in studying the illustration copy of a proposed magazine spread, a researcher might show to two or more groups of subjects an illustration of the product photographed from different angles. The headline might be evaluated by having potential users rate the typefaces used in several versions of the ad. The copy might be tested for readability and recall. In all cases, the aim is to determine whether the variable tested significantly affects the recall of the ad.

In TV, a rough cut of an entire commercial might be produced. The rough cut is a filmed or taped version of the ad in which amateur actors are used, locations are simplified, and the editing and narration lack the smoothness characteristic of broadcast (final cut) commercials. In this way, variations in the ad can be tested without incurring great expense.

The final phase of copy testing, which occurs after the finished commercials have appeared, serves to determine whether the campaign is having the desired effects. Any negative or unintended effects can be corrected before serious damage is done to a company's sales or reputation. This type of copy testing requires precisely defined goals. Some campaigns, for example, are designed to draw customers away from competitors; others are conducted for the purpose of retaining a company's present customers. Still others are intended to enhance the image of a firm and may not be concerned with consumers' purchase preferences. As will be discussed later, this type of copy testing blends in with campaign assessment research.

There are several different ways to categorize copy testing methods. Perhaps the most useful, summarized by Leckenby and Wedding (1982), suggests that there are appropriate copy testing methods for each of the three dimensions of impact in the persuasion process. Although, as represented in Table 15.1, the model seems to suggest a linear process starting with the cognitive dimension (knowing) through the affective dimension (feeling) to the conative dimension (doing), it is not necessary for the steps to take place in this order. In any event,

Table 15.1 Typology of Copy Testing Effects

Dimension of impact	Typical dependent Variables	Professional firms conducting research that exemplifies area
Cognitive	Exposure Awareness Recognition Comprehension Recall	Burke Marketing Research (DAR) Gallup & Robinson (MIRS) Starch INRA Hooper
Affective	Attitude change Liking/disliking Involvement	Audits & Surveys Mapes & Ross Various firms (physiological measures)
Conative	Intention to buy Purchase behavior	AdTel Nielsen (Testsight) ASI (pre/post intention to buy)

the model does serve as a convenient guide for discussing copy research testing methods.

The Cognitive Dimension

Turning first to the cognitive dimension, the key dependent variables are attention, awareness, exposure, comprehension, and recall. One measurement technique that taps these variables is used primarily by the print media: subjects are shown a copy of a newspaper or magazine and are asked which advertisements they remember seeing or reading. The results are used to tabulate a "reader traffic score" for each ad. This method is prone to criticism, however, because some respondents confuse the advertisements or the publications in which they were seen, and some try to please the interviewer by reporting that they saw more than they actually did. To control this problem, researchers often make use of aided recall techniques; for instance, they might also show the respondent a list of advertisers, some of whose advertisements actually appeared in the publication and some whose did not.

For obvious reasons, this type of **recall study** is not entirely suitable for radio and television commercials; a more commonly used method in such cases is the telephone survey. Two variations of this approach are sometimes used. In *aided recall*, the interviewer mentions a general class of product and asks whether the respondent remembers an ad for a specific brand. A typical question might be "Have you seen any ads for soft drinks lately?" In the *unaided recall technique*, researchers ask a general question such as "Have you seen any ads that interested you lately?" Obviously, it is harder for the consumer to respond to the second type of question. Only truly memorable ads score high on this form of measurement.

Perhaps a better understanding can be gained by examining the several research companies that offer syndicated services in this area. For example, Burke Marketing Research offers day-after recall (DAR) testing to measure the effectiveness of TV commercials.

Burke has the capacity to test recall of commercials by consumers in more than 30 cities, although typically only three to five are used in a single test. On the day after the commercial is run, the Burke interviewers conduct a telephone survey to obtain a sample of about 200 people, all of whom have watched the program that contained the commercial. These individuals are asked whether they remember seeing the commercial and, if so, what details they can remember about it. Over the years, Burke has compiled data on numerous commercials and has computed average scores for recall; the scores (called "Burkes") of the commercials that the firm now tests can be considered in light of these norms, thus providing the advertiser with a benchmark for comparison.

Another method of posttesting television commercials is provided by Gallup & Robinson. Like Burke, Gallup & Robinson measure the percentages of respondents who remember seeing the commercial and of those who can remember specific points. Additionally, they provide a score indicating the degree of favorable attitude toward the product, based on positive statements made by the subjects during the interview.

Gallup & Robinson also conducts pretests and posttests of magazine advertisements. Their Magazine Impact Research Service (MIRS) measures recall of advertisements appearing in general-interest magazines. Copies of a particular issue containing the advertisement under study are mailed to approximately 150 readers. (In the case of a pretest, the MIRS binds the proposed advertisement into each magazine.) The day after delivery of the magazines, respondents are telephoned and asked which advertisements they noticed in the magazine and what details they can remember about them. These results are reported to the advertiser.

One of the best-known professional research firms is the Starch Message Report Service, which conducts posttest recall and recognition research. Starch INRA Hooper, Inc. routinely measures advertising readership in more than 100 magazines and newspapers. Using a sample of approximately 300 people, Starch interviewers take a copy of the periodical under study to respondents' homes. If a subject has already looked through that particular publication, he or she is questioned at length. The interviewer shows the respondent an advertisement and asks whether he or she has seen or read any part of it. If the answer is no, the interviewer moves on to another advertisement; if the answer is yes, more questions are asked to determine how much was read. This procedure continues until the respondent has been questioned about every advertisement in that issue up to 100 (at which point the interview is terminated to avoid subject fatigue). Starch places each respondent into one of four categories for each advertisement:

1. *Nonreader* (did not recall seeing the advertisement)
2. *Noted reader* (remembered seeing the advertisement)
3. *Associated reader* (not only saw the advertisement but also read some part of it that clearly indicated the brand name)
4. *Read most reader* (read more than half the written material in the advertisement)

The Starch organization reports the findings of its recall studies in a novel manner. Advertisers are given a copy of the magazine in which readership scores printed on yellow stickers have been attached to each advertisement. Figure 15.1 is an example of a "Starched" advertisement.

The Starch Message Report provides a measurement of recognition only; for an indication of an advertisement's success in getting its message across, advertisers can request a Starch Reader Impression Study. Such studies also involve in-depth interviews with readers; those who have seen an advertisement in a particular newspaper or magazine are asked a series of detailed questions about it, such as:

1. "In your own words, what did this ad tell you about the product?"
2. "What did the pictures tell you?"
3. "What did the written material tell you?"

The responses are subjected to content analysis, and the results are summarized for clients. Additionally, Starch reports the percentage of favorable and unfavorable comments about each advertisement.

Another company that conducts message research is the Advertising Index, which provides posttest data on brand awareness and advertising effectiveness. The Index collects these data through telephone interviews with respondents selected at random from particular geographic areas. The interviews are lengthy and include questions designed to test such variables as usage of certain products, brands of products recently purchased, and effectiveness of specific advertisements. For example, one measure of effectiveness, known as "top-of-mind awareness," is based on responses to the question: "When you think of (*a product*), what brand first comes to mind?" Questions regarding advertisement recall are also asked, to permit comparisons of the purchasing behavior of subjects who remember seeing a particular advertisement with that of those who do not. The Index performs such studies for both print and electronic media advertising campaigns.

The Affective Dimension

The affective dimension usually involves research into whether a consumer's attitudes toward a particular product have changed because of

Figure 15.1 A "Starched" ad

Poetry etched in a morning sky.
This is Georgia.

STARCH AD-AS-A-WHOLE

Noted % W 52 | Associated % W 42 | Read Most % W 13

STARCH Seen % W 51

STARCH Read Some % W 18

And it's just a fleeting glimpse of Georgia's lavish natural beauty. Here, on a sun-drenched coast, wind-shaped live oaks line wide, sandy beaches. And resorts offer endless diversions.

There's year 'round golfing to challenge every handicap. Great fishing in "Lunker Country." Camping in state parks. And canoeing on unspoiled rivers.

Throughout the coastal plain, the past unfolds before you. As you visit historic plantations and gardens in Thomasville, "city of roses." Or the Springer

Opera House, a restored Victorian theater in Columbus.

On a tour of Savannah, Georgia's original capital, you'll wind your way down cobblestone streets. Past ornate fountains and wrought-iron fences.

Then you'll be captivated by Georgia's Golden Isles—Jekyll, St. Simons and Sea Island. Here

STARCH Signature % W 41

orgia

) TIME. OR A LIFETIME.
reau of Industry & Trade
t Division, Box 1776
Atlanta, Georgia 30301
Dept. SL-763
Please send me "Georgia Days,"
your free vacation guide.

STARCH Read % W 12

Name

Address

City, State, Zip

you'll visit the sple_____ of Millionaires' Villa_____

Mail the coupon a_____ gia become your have_____ friendly place wher_____

spend your days gathering seashells. Watching craftsmen demonstrate long-forgotten skills in Westville, a recreated nineteenth century village. Or gliding back thousands of years in a primitive wilderness, the mysterious Okefenokee Swamp.

It's all here. All awaiting you in sunny, uncrowded Georgia.

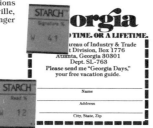

Source: Starch INRA Hooper, Inc. Readership Report of *Southern Living*, April 1977, p. 77. Reprinted by permission.

exposure to an ad or a campaign. The two techniques used most often to measure attitude change are the semantic differential and the rating scale (see Chapter 7). For these measurements to be most useful, it is necessary to accomplish three things. First, a picture of the consumer's attitudes before exposure to the ad should be obtained. Second, the consumer must be exposed to the ad or ads under examination, and third, the attitudes must be remeasured after exposure. To diminish the difficulties associated with achieving all three of these goals in testing television ads, many researchers prefer a **forced-exposure** method. In this technique, respondents are invited to a theater for a special screening of a TV program. Before viewing the program, they are asked to fill out questionnaires concerning their attitudes toward several different products, one of which is of interest to the researchers. Next, everyone watches the TV show, which contains one or more commercials for the product under investigation as well as ads for other products. When the show is over, all respondents again fill out the questionnaire concerning product attitudes. Change in evaluation is the key variable of interest. The same basic method can be used in testing attitudes toward print ads except that the testing is done individually, in each respondent's home. Typically, a consumer is interviewed about product attitudes, a copy of a magazine that includes the test ad (or ads) is left at the house, and the respondent is asked to read or look through the publication before the next interview. A short time later, the interviewer calls back the respondent and asks whether the magazine has been read. If it has, product attitudes are once again measured.

Many research companies offer services designed to measure attitudes. In the TV area, Audits & Surveys uses a cable TV system with on-air exposure to measure the attitudes toward their test ads. Viewers are telephoned and requested to watch a particular cable TV channel at a particular time. Twenty-four hours after the commercial was aired, the respondents are called back and their attitudes measured. Mapes & Ross also uses on-air exposure to measure the affective dimension. Respondents are recruited and urged to watch a TV program soon to be aired over a local UHF station. Before exposure, respondents are asked to use a 10-point scale in assigning attitudinal ratings to several brands. After viewing, respondents are called back and reasked the attitude questions. In magazine measurement, Gallup & Robinson construct a special issue of a magazine containing the ads under consideration. Respondents are randomly selected from the phone book, visited at home, and given a copy of the magazine. The next day, to establish readership, respondents are asked questions about the magazine's contents. The interviewer next reads a list of products and asks whether the magazine contained ads for each product. Each time that a respondent remembers seeing a product ad, the interviewer asks for a description of the ad, as well as the respondent's attitudes toward the product after reading the ad.

Another facet of research that involves the affective dimension uses physiological measurement. Two tests are commonly used in this area. In the *pupillometer test*, a tiny camera, focused on the subject's eye, measures the amount of pupil dilation that occurs while the person is looking at an ad. Changes in pupil diameter are recorded, because findings from psychophysiology suggest that people tend to respond to appealing stimuli with dilation (enlargement) of their pupils. Conversely, when unappealing, disagreeable stimuli are shown, the pupil narrows. The second test measures galvanic skin response, or *GSR* (that is, changes in the electrical conductance of the surface of the skin). A change in GSR rating while the subject is looking at an ad is taken to signify emotional involvement or arousal.

The Conative Dimension

The conative dimension deals with actual consumer behavior and, in many instances, it is the most pertinent of all dependent variables. The two main categories of behavior that are usually measured are buying predisposition and actual purchase behavior. In the first category, the usual design is to gather precampaign predisposition data and reinterview the subjects after the advertising has been in place. Subjects are typically asked a question along these lines: "If you were going shopping tomorrow to buy breakfast cereal, which brand would you buy?" This might be followed by: "Would you consider buying any other brands?" and "Are there any cereals you would definitely not buy?" (The last question is included to determine whether the advertising campaign has had any negative effects.) Additionally, some researchers (Haskins, 1976) suggest using a buying intention scale and instructing respondents to check the one position on the scale that best fits their intention. Such a scale might look like this:

_____ I'll definitely buy this cereal as soon as I can.
_____ I'll probably buy this cereal sometime.
_____ I might buy this cereal, but I don't know when.
_____ I'll probably never buy this cereal.
_____ I wouldn't eat this cereal even if somebody gave it to me.

The scale allows advertisers to see how consumers' buying preferences change during and after the campaign.

Perhaps the most reliable methods of posttesting are those that measure actual sales, direct response, and other easily quantifiable behavior patterns. Direct response, for example, might be measured by counting the number of redeemable coupons returned or the number of requests for free samples. The BehaviorScan and Testsight systems (see Chapter 14) can also be used to measure consumer purchases. Actual sales figures can be obtained in many ways. It is possible to measure sales indirectly, by asking a question such as "What brand of breakfast cereal did you most recently purchase?" However, the findings would be subject to error due to faulty recall, courtesy bias, and so forth; for this reason, more direct methods are generally preferred. If enough time and money are available, direct observation of people's selections in the cereal aisles at a sample of supermarkets can be a useful source of data. Store audits that list the total number of boxes sold at predetermined times are another possibility. Last, and possibly most expensive, is the household audit technique, whereby an interviewer visits the homes of a sample of consumers and actually inspects their kitchen cupboards to see what brands of cereals are there. In addition to the audit, a traditional questionnaire is used to gather further information about the respondent's feelings toward the commercials.

Advertising research literature provides many good examples of posttest studies. Becknell and McIsaac (1963) evaluated the effects of a television advertising campaign: they found that the commercials increased the total cookware market by 21% and doubled the sales of the product advertised. Hoofnagle (1963) conducted a field experiment to test the impact of an advertising campaign for lamb. By monitoring purchases of lamb in a sample of supermarkets, Hoofnagle was able to show that a program of cooperative advertising raised sales by 26%. Some years later, Bogart, Tolley, and Orenstein (1970) conducted a posttest of 31 separate newspaper advertisements for several different products. They compared the purchasing behavior of subjects who had seen the advertisements with the behavior of a control group that had not. On balance, the advertisements were found to be effective.

Many professional research firms conduct surveys that deal with purchasing behavior. One such firm, the AdTel Company, a subsidiary of Burke, uses special cable television facilities to test the effectiveness of commercials. The AdTel cable system, which is operated in three separate communities, is designed to carry two signals per channel, so that a household can receive either the A signal or the B signal. The households in these communities are grouped according to key demographic variables, and one group is connected to the A signal and the other to the B signal (the subscribers themselves do not know which channel they are receiving). The A households receive one version of the commercial being tested, while the B group receives either a different version or no commercial. About 1,000 families in each group keep diaries about the products and services that they purchase. The effectiveness of a commercial or campaign is judged by examining the purchasing behavior of the families in each group, as reflected in their diary entries. Measurement bias is eliminated because the families do not realize the connection between the diary and their television viewing. The AdTel system also has the advantage of measuring actual purchasing behavior as the dependent variable.

A. C. Nielsen's new Testsight system, mentioned in Chapter 14, uses advanced computer technology to monitor the viewing behavior of 2,500 households. The research company can also electronically cut in test commercials without viewers being aware that something different is being inserted. A tiny device attached to the TV set allows the set to accept these test commercials and to store viewing data for later retrieval. At the supermarket, members of Nielsen's sample present an ID card, and through the use of the UPC all their purchases are electronically recorded and tabulated. Thus, clients are able to monitor actual buying behavior changes in response to test commercials.

In the print area, ASI-Market Research, Inc., uses a less expensive technique that measures pseudo-purchase behavior. A test magazine containing the client's ad is left at the house. The respondent is asked to read the magazine, is told there will be a prize for participation, and is asked which brands would be preferred if he or she is a grand prize winner. After the test ads have been looked at, the respondent is again asked about prize preferences. Changes in pre- and postexposure scores are carefully noted.

Media Research

The two key terms in media research are **reach** and **frequency**. Reach is the total number of households that will be exposed to a message in a particular medium at least once over a certain period of time (usually 4 weeks). Reach can be thought of as the cumulative audience and is usually expressed as a percentage of the total universe of households that have been exposed. For example, if 25 of a possible 100 households are exposed to a message, the reach is 25%. Frequency refers to the number of exposures to the same message that each household receives. Of course, not every household in the sample will receive exactly the same number of messages. Consequently, advertisers prefer to use the average frequency of exposure, expressed by the formula:

$$\frac{\text{Total exposures for all households}}{\text{Reach}} = \text{Average frequency}$$

Thus, if the total number of exposures for a sample of households is 400 and the reach is 25, the average frequency is 16. In other words, the "average" household was exposed 16 times. Notice that if the reach were 80%, the frequency would be 5. As reach increases, average frequency drops. (Maximizing both reach and frequency would require an unlimited budget, something most advertisers lack.)

A concept closely related to reach and frequency is gross rating points (GRPs), introduced in Chapter 14. GRPs are useful when it comes to deciding between two media alternatives. For example, suppose Program A has a reach of 30% and an average frequency of 2.5 while Program B has a reach of 45% and a frequency of 1.25. Which program offers a better reach–frequency relationship? First, determine the GRPs of each program using the following formula:

$$\text{GRPs} = \text{Reach} \times \text{Average frequency}$$

For A:

$$\text{GRPs} = 30 \times 2.5 = 75.00$$

For B:

$$\text{GRPs} = 45 \times 1.25 = 56.25$$

Program A scores better in the reach–frequency combination, and this would probably be a factor in deciding which was the better buy.

Media research falls into three general categories: studies of the size and composition of an audience of a particular medium or media (reach studies), studies of the relative efficiency of advertising exposures provided by various combinations of media (reach and frequency studies), and studies of the advertising activities of competitors.

Audience Size and Composition

Analyses of audiences are probably the most commonly used advertising studies in print and electronic media research. Since advertisers spend large amounts of money in the print and electronic media, they have an understandable interest in the audiences for those messages. In most cases, audience information is gathered using techniques that are compromises between the practical and the ideal.

The audience size of a newspaper or magazine is commonly measured in terms of the number of copies distributed per issue. This number, which is called the publication's **circulation**, includes all copies delivered to subscribers as well as those bought at newsstands or from other sellers. Because a publication's advertising rate is directly determined by its circulation, the print media have developed a standardized method of measuring circulation and have instituted an organization, the Audit Bureau of Circulation (ABC), to verify that a publication actually distributes the number of copies per issue that it claims. (The specific procedures used by the ABC are discussed later in this chapter.)

Circulation figures are used to compute the CPMs of various publications. For example, suppose Newspaper X charges $1,800 for an advertisement and has an ABC-verified circulation of 180,000; Newspaper Y, with a circulation of 300,000, charges $2,700 for the same size space. Table 15.2 shows that Newspaper Y is the more efficient advertising vehicle.

Note that this method considers only the number of circulated copies of a newspaper or magazine. This information is useful,

Table 15.2 Determining Advertising Efficiency from Ad Cost and Circulation Data

	Newspaper X	Newspaper Y
Ad cost	$1,800	$2,700
Circulation	180,000	300,000
Cost per thousand circulated copies	$\dfrac{\$1,800}{180} = \$10.00$	$\dfrac{\$2,700}{300} = \$9.00$

but it does not necessarily indicate the total number of readers of the publication. To estimate the total audience, the circulation figure must be multiplied by the average number of readers of each copy of an issue. This information is obtained by performing audience surveys.

A preliminary step in conducting such surveys is to operationally define the concept *magazine reader* or *newspaper reader*. There are many possible definitions, but the one most commonly used is fairly liberal: a *reader* is a person who has read or at least looked through an issue.

Three techniques are used to measure readership. The most rigorous is the unaided recall method, in which respondents are asked whether they have read any newspapers or magazines in the past month (or other time period). If the answer is yes, subjects are asked to specify the magazines or newspapers they read. When a publication is named, the interviewer attempts to verify reading by asking questions about the contents of that publication. The reliability of the unaided recall method is open to question (as has been discussed) because of the difficulty respondents often have in recalling specific content.

A second technique involves aided recall. In this method, the interviewer names several publications and asks whether the respondent has read any of them lately. Each time the respondent claims to have read a publication, the interviewer asks whether he or she remembers seeing the most recent copy. The interviewer may jog a respondent's memory by describing the front page or the cover. Finally, the respondent is asked to recall anything that was seen or read in that particular issue. (In a variation on this process, **masked recall**, respondents are shown the front page or the cover of a publication with the name blacked out and are asked whether they remember reading that particular issue. Those who respond in the affirmative are asked to recall any items they have seen or read.)

The third technique, called the **recognition** method, entails showing respondents the logo or cover of a publication. For each publication the respondent has seen or read, the interviewer produces a copy and the respondent leafs through it to identify the articles or stories he or she recognizes. All respondents who definitely remember reading the publication are counted in its audience. To check the accuracy of the respondent's memory, dummy articles may be inserted into the interviewer's copy of the publication; respondents who claim

Table 15.3 Determining Ad Efficiency from an Extended Data Base

	Newspaper X	Newspaper Y
Ad cost	$1,800	$2,700
Circulation	180,000	300,000
CPM	$10.00	$9.00
Number of people	630,000	540,000
who read the issue	(3.5 readers per copy)	(1.8 readers per copy)
Revised CPM	$2.86	$5.00

to have read the dummy items may thus be eliminated from the sample or given less weight in the analysis. Many advertising researchers consider the recognition technique to be the most accurate predictor of readership scores.

Once the total audience for each magazine or newspaper has been tabulated, the advertiser can determine which publication is the most efficient buy. For example, returning to the example of Table 15.2, suppose that Newspaper X and Newspaper Y have the audience figures given in Table 15.3. On the basis of these figures, Newspaper X is seen to be the more efficient choice.

Another variable to be considered in determining the advertising efficiency (or **media efficiency**) of a newspaper or magazine is the number of times a person reads each issue. For example, imagine two newspapers or magazines that have exactly the same number of readers per issue. Publication A consists primarily of pictures and contains little text; people tend to read it once and not look at it again. Publication B, on the other hand, contains several lengthy and interesting articles; people pick it up several times. Publication B would seem to be a more efficient advertising vehicle, since it provides several possible exposures to an advertisement for the same cost as Publication A. Unfortunately, a practical and reliable method for measuring the number of exposures per issue has yet to be developed.

Perhaps the most important gauge for advertising efficiency is the composition of the audience. It matters little if an advertisement for farm equipment is seen by 100,000 people if only a few of them are in the market for such products. To evaluate the number of potential customers in the audience, an advertiser must first conduct a survey to determine certain demographic characteristics of the people who tend to purchase a particular product. For example, potential customers for beer might be typically described as males between the ages of 18 and 49; those for fast-food restaurants might be households in which the primary wage earner is between 18 and 35 and there are at least two children under 12. These demographic characteristics of the "typical consumer" are then compared with the characteristics of a publication's audience (also determined by a survey) to tabulate the potential buying audience for the product. The cost of reaching this audience is also expressed in CPM units, as shown in Table 15.4. An examination

Table 15.4 Calculation of Ad Efficiency Incorporating Demographic Survey Results

	Newspaper X	Newspaper Y
Ad cost	$1,800	$2,700
Circulation	180,000	300,000
CPM	$10.00	$9.00
Number of people who read average issue	630,000	540,000
Number of potential beer drinkers	150,000	220,000
Number of potential fast food customers	300,000	200,000
CPM (beer drinkers)	$12.00	$12.27
CPM (fast food customers)	$ 6.00	$13.50

of these figures indicates that Newspaper X is slightly more efficient as a vehicle for reaching potential beer customers and much more efficient in reaching fast-food restaurant patrons.

Determining audience size and composition in the electronic media poses special problems for advertising researchers, due to the ephemeral nature of radio and television broadcasts. For a detailed discussion of the techniques involved in this type of audience or ratings research, the reader is referred to Chapter 14.

Frequency of Exposure in Media Schedules

An advertiser working within a strict budget to promote a product or service may be limited to the use of a single vehicle or medium. Often, however, an advertising campaign is conducted via several advertising vehicles simultaneously. But which combination of vehicles and/or media will provide the greatest reach and frequency for the advertiser's product? A substantial amount of recent media research has been devoted to this question, much of it concentrated on the development of mathematical models of advertising media and their audiences. The mathematical derivations of these models are beyond the scope of this book. However, the material that follows describes in simplified form the concepts underlying two computerized models: stepwise analysis and decision calculus. Readers who wish to pursue these topics in more rigorous detail should consult Aaker and Myers (1975) and Moran (1963).

Stepwise analysis is called an iterative model because the same basic series of instructions to the computer is repeated over and over again with slight modifications until a predetermined best or optimum solution is reached. The Young & Rubicam agency pioneered development in this area with their stepwise "high-assay" model. Stepwise analysis constructs a media schedule in increments, initially choosing a particular vehicle on the basis of the lowest cost per potential customer reached. After this selection has been made, all the remaining media vehicles are reevaluated to determine whether the optimum advertising exposure rate has been achieved. If not, the second most efficient vehicle is chosen and the process repeated until the optimum exposure rate is reached. This method is called the "high-assay" model because it is analogous to gold mining. The easiest-to-get gold is mined first, followed by less accessible ore. In like manner, the consumers who are the easiest to reach are first targeted, followed by those consumers who are harder to find and more costly to reach.

Decision calculus models make use of an **objective function**, a mathematical statement that provides a quantitative value for a given media combination (also known as a schedule). This value represents the schedule's effectiveness in providing advertising exposure. The advertising researcher determines which schedule offers the maximum exposure for a given product by calculating the objective functions of various media schedules.

Calculations of objective function are based on values generated by studies of audience size and composition for each vehicle or medium. In addition, a schedule's objective function value takes into account such variables as the probability that the advertisement will be forgotten, the total cost of the media schedule compared with the advertiser's budget, and the "media option source effect"—that is, the relative impact of exposure in a particular advertising vehicle (for example, an advertisement for men's clothes is likely to have more impact in *Gentlemen's Quarterly* than in *True Detective*).

Two computer media models are frequently used to calculate objective functions. MEDIAC (Little & Lodish, 1969), which is designed to maximize sales in a particular market segment by allowing a product's market potential within that segment to be included as an additional variable, calculates the probability that a given person within a market segment will be exposed to an advertisement. This probability depends on such factors as the size of the advertisement, the use of color, and the characteristics of the media vehicle used to deliver the message. It is assumed that exposure to one or more advertisements will affect a person's willingness to buy the advertised product. The advertiser provides MEDIAC with data on the probable sales response to different levels of exposure within all relevant segments of the market; MEDIAC computes the probable sales response for each market segment and totals the response for the entire audience for any given schedule.

A second computer model, called ADMOD (Aaker, 1975), is designed to maximize favorable attitude changes among consumers toward the advertised product. ADMOD evaluates a media schedule by examining its likely impact on each individual in samples drawn from the market population. This impact is calculated by taking into account the number and source of exposures for each individual and the effect of these exposures on the probability of obtaining the desired attitude change. The results are then projected to the population. A unique ADMOD feature allows the researcher to include certain data about different message strategies that might be employed. As media schedules increase in complexity and become more expensive, it is expected that computer models such as MEDIAC and ADMOD will be used more widely.

The increased use of microcomputers in advertising agencies has facilitated the computation of the best reach and frequency combinations for the media dollar. The MEDIAC model is available from the Telmar Communications Corporation in an interactive mode. In addition, Telmar and Interactive Market Systems have developed Micronet and Mediapak, two similar software packages designed to calculate reach and frequency data. Current syndicated research data bases are standard with both programs. As new generations of software come on the market, the microcomputer probably will become the media planner's best friend.

Competitors' Activities

It is often helpful to advertisers to know the media choices of their competitors. This information can help the advertiser to avoid making the mistakes of less successful competitors and to imitate the strategies of the more successful. Moreover, an advertiser seeking to promote a new product who knows that the three leading competitors are using basically the same media mix might feel that their consensus is worthy of consideration.

An advertiser can collect data on competitors' activity either by setting up a special research team or by subscribing to the services of a syndicated research company. Since the job of monitoring the media activity of a large number of firms advertising in several media is so difficult, most advertisers rely on the syndicated service. Such services gather data by direct observation, that is, by tabulating the advertisements that appear in a given medium. For magazines, television, and radio, the complete population of advertisements is studied. For newspapers, samples are observed and the results generalized. In addition to information about frequency of advertisements, cost figures are helpful; these estimates are obtained from the published rate cards of the various media vehicles.

Advertisers also find it helpful to know *what* competitors are saying. To acquire this information, many advertising agencies conduct systematic content analyses of the messages in a sample of the competitors' advertisements. The results often provide insight into the persuasive themes, strategies, and goals of competitors' advertising. It is because of such studies that many commercials tend to look and sound alike: successful commercial approaches are often mimicked.

Media Research by Private Firms

As mentioned earlier, the Audit Bureau of Circulation (ABC) supplies advertisers with data on the circulation figures of newspapers and magazines. As of 1980, ABC measured the circulation of about 75% of all print media vehicles in the United States and Canada. ABC requires publishers to submit a detailed report of their circulation every 6 months; it verifies these reports by sending field workers to conduct an audit at each publication. The auditors typically examine records of the publications' press runs, newsprint bills, or other invoices for paper, as well as transcripts of circulation records and other related files.

The ABC audit results, as well as overall circulation data, coverage maps, press times, and market data, are published in an annual report and distributed to ABC members and advertisers. ABC now reports data on audience size for certain selected newspapers. Called the "Newspaper Audience Research Data Bank," this report consists of a collection of audience surveys conducted by newspapers in the top 100 markets.

Verified Audit Circulation (VAC) is another organization that audits the circulation of newspapers and magazines. While ABC measures only paid circulation, VAC tabulates both free and paid circulation figures. (Free circulation publications are given away; shoppers' bulletins and magazines for airline passengers are examples.) VAC uses procedures somewhat similar to those of ABC in its newspaper audits, whereas magazine audits are conducted by counting the names on a publication's subscriber list and mailing questionnaires to a sample of subscribers.

The Simmons Market Research Bureau provides comprehensive feedback about magazine readership. This service selects a large random sample of readers and shows them illustrations of the titles of about 70 magazines to determine which ones they have recently read or looked through. Subjects are shown stripped-down versions of the publications they identified, and readership is verified by further questioning. At the same time, data are gathered about the ownership, purchase, and use of a wide variety of products and services. This information is tabulated by Simmons and released in a series of detailed reports on the demographic makeup and purchasing behavior of each magazine's audience. Using these data, advertisers can determine the cost of reaching potential buyers of their products or services. A portion of a Simmons Report is reproduced in Table 15.5.

Mediamark Research, Inc. (MRI) uses a recent-reading technique to produce audience estimates for magazines and product usage data. More than 25,000 persons are interviewed nationwide about their magazine reading. Additionally, all respondents are given a questionnaire that asks about product usage behavior. Results are summarized in MRI's Magazine Total Audience Report. The Three Sigma Company

Table 15.5 Example of Simmons Report

	Total U.S. '000	Broadminded				Creative				Dominating				Efficient			
		A '000	B % Down	C Across %	D Index	A '000	B % Down	C Across %	D Index	A '000	B % Down	C Across %	D Index	A '000	B % Down	C Across %	D Index
Total Adults	158437	61916	100.0	39.1	100	43842	100.0	27.7	100	61408	100.0	38.8	100	49042	100.0	31.0	100
Magazines																	
Quintile 1	31799	14393	23.2	45.3	116	10510	24.0	33.1	119	14280	23.3	44.9	116	10764	21.9	33.9	109
Quintile 2	32954	13592	22.0	41.2	106	9897	22.6	30.0	109	13319	21.7	40.4	104	10637	21.7	32.3	104
Quintile 3	26611	10309	16.6	38.7	99	7394	16.9	27.8	100	9856	16.1	37.0	96	8672	17.7	32.6	105
Quintile 4	31322	11819	19.1	37.7	97	8254	18.8	26.4	95	11811	19.2	37.7	97	9632	19.6	30.8	99
Quintile 5	35752	11802	19.1	33.0	84	7787	17.8	21.8	79	12143	19.8	34.0	88	9337	19.0	26.1	84
Newspapers Weekday																	
Tercile 1	25455	10839	17.5	42.6	109	7254	16.5	28.5	103	10383	16.9	40.8	105	8790	17.9	34.5	112
Tercile 2	67522	26639	43.0	39.5	101	18433	42.0	27.3	99	25971	42.3	38.5	99	21484	43.8	31.8	103
Tercile 3	65460	24438	39.5	37.3	96	18154	41.4	27.7	100	25054	40.8	38.3	99	18768	38.3	28.7	93
TV-Prime Time																	
Quintile 1	31001	12033	19.4	38.8	99	8352	19.1	26.9	97	11273	18.4	36.4	94	9665	19.7	31.2	101
Quintile 2	31417	12330	19.9	39.2	100	8180	18.7	26.0	94	12493	20.3	39.8	103	9407	19.2	29.9	97
Quintile 3	32124	12750	20.6	39.7	102	9311	21.2	29.0	105	13299	21.7	41.4	107	10445	21.3	32.5	105
Quintile 4	32131	12493	20.2	38.9	99	9088	20.7	28.3	102	12431	20.2	38.7	100	10018	20.4	31.2	101
Quintile 5	31764	12309	19.9	38.8	99	8912	20.3	28.1	101	11912	19.4	37.5	97	9507	19.4	29.9	97
TV-Daytime																	
Tercile 1	45111	17747	28.7	39.3	101	11262	25.7	25.0	90	16297	26.5	36.1	93	13056	26.6	28.9	94
Tercile 2	45241	17258	27.9	38.1	98	12093	27.6	26.7	97	17441	28.4	38.6	99	13426	27.4	29.7	96
Tercile 3	68084	26911	43.5	39.5	101	20488	46.7	30.1	109	27671	45.1	40.6	105	22560	46.0	33.1	107
TV Total																	
Quintile 1	31204	12203	19.7	39.1	100	7668	17.5	24.6	89	11474	18.7	36.8	95	8928	18.2	28.6	92
Quintile 2	31981	11953	19.3	37.4	96	8306	18.9	26.0	94	12352	20.1	38.6	100	9512	19.4	29.7	96
Quintile 3	31816	13041	21.1	41.0	105	9066	20.7	28.5	103	11970	19.5	37.6	97	10421	21.2	32.8	106
Quintile 4	31404	12396	20.0	39.5	101	9662	22.0	30.8	111	12702	20.7	40.4	104	10062	20.5	32.0	104
Quintile 5	32033	13223	20.6	38.5	98	9140	20.8	28.3	103	12911	21.0	40.3	104	10121	20.6	31.6	102

Source: Simmons Market Research Bureau, *1980 Study of Media & Markets*, Volume M-5, pp. 0368, 0369. Reprinted by permission.

produces a syndicated study of major market newspapers. All interviews are conducted over the phone, from samples drawn in approximately 35 markets using a random digit method, and interviewers are instructed to make six calls per household to complete the interview. The readership information in the Three Sigma studies is based only on data from respondents who reported reading a particular newspaper on the day before the interview. The Three Sigma reports contain both reach and frequency data. For example, advertisers can determine that an ad will reach 46% of the adults in the market if it appears in one issue of the newspaper and 73% if it appears five times.

Three companies—Arbitron, A. C. Nielsen, and Birch Radio—supply broadcast audience data for advertisers. Arbitron and Birch measure radio listening in about 200 markets across the United States, while Arbitron and Nielsen provide audience estimates for local television markets. (Chapter 14 gives more information on the methods employed by these two companies and others.)

Private research firms are also available to provide advertisers with information about their competitors' advertising campaigns.

Data about magazine advertising are collected by *Leading National Advertisers* (LNA), in cooperation with the Publishers Information Bureau (PIB). The publishers of magazines that belong to the PIB mark all paid advertising in each issue and send the marked copies to LNA, where trained coders record detailed information about each advertisement. This information is recorded in a report sent to LNA subscribers. The data are arranged according to product type and brand name. By scanning the LNA reports, it is possible to determine which magazines competitors are using, the size of the advertisements they purchase, when they appear, and their approximate cost.

Information about advertising activity in newspapers is supplied by Media Records. Since it is impossible to examine every newspaper in the country, Media Records concentrates on about 225 newspapers published in approximately 75 urban areas. During a specified time period, coders measure the size of every advertisement appearing in each issue of these papers and also estimate costs. The data from this sample are used to project estimates for the top 125 market areas. Media Records publishes this information in its "Bluebooks," which provide data on advertising activity for all comparable products and services.

The most comprehensive information about advertisers' activities and expenditures is provided by Broadcast Advertiser Reports (BAR). This organization collects data on commercials appearing on network radio and television as well as on local television stations. Advertising activity on network radio is measured by recording all network programs on audio tape. The tapes are played back for coders, who record programs, lengths of commercials, sponsors, brand names, and other details. BAR estimates the cost of each commercial by referring to the network's published rate card. Totals are computed for each brand, and the results are published in BAR's quarterly Network Radio Reports. The reports allow an advertiser to determine competitors' schedules and expenditures.

BAR uses basically the same technique to compile its weekly Network Television Reports. Network programs are recorded and all commercials coded according to brand, length, and program. Rate cards are used to estimate costs. The report also contains a daily log of advertising, indexed by product type, and a total of the week's advertising costs per product.

BAR monitors advertising on local television stations by sampling approximately 275 stations located in the top 75 television markets. In the two top markets, New York and Los Angeles, measurements are made every week. In the other 73 markets, BAR selects one week per month for analysis, during which all station programming is recorded or videotaped, and this sample is used to make projections for the entire month. BAR issues two summary reports: a local market report for each city and a cumulative report covering all 75 markets. The types of data and the format are similar to those used for the network summaries.

Local radio advertising is not monitored by BAR. The only data available for advertisers in this area are provided by Radio Expenditure Reports (RER), a firm that sends questionnaires to about 800 stations in the top 150 markets. Each station is asked to provide an estimate of its advertising revenue generated from regional and national commercials. RER tabulates the data and projects a national figure for all such radio advertising. An RER report tells an advertiser how much a competitor spent for radio spots during a certain time period, but it does not show when or on what stations the competitor advertised.

Campaign Assessment Research

Leckenby (1984) argues that the purpose of campaign assessment research is ". . . to understand the overall response of the consumer to an integrated and executed advertising campaign which itself was the result of copy [and] media . . . research conducted previously." Campaign assessment research builds on copy and media research, but its research strategies are generally different from those used in the other areas. In general, there are two kinds of assessment research. The *pretest/posttest method* takes measurements before and after the campaign, while **tracking studies** assess the impact of the campaign by measuring effects at several points during the progress of the campaign. Both techniques can be used to examine a wide range of dependent variables: brand name awareness, attitudes toward advertised brands, reported purchase intentions, actual purchases, awareness of advertising. The major advantage of a tracking study is that it provides important feedback to the advertiser while the campaign is still in progress. This feedback might ultimately lead to changes in the creative or media strategy.

Pretest/posttest studies typically use personal interviews for data collection. At times, the same people are interviewed before the campaign starts and again after its close (a panel study), or two different groups are chosen and asked the same questions (a trend study; see Chapter 9). In any case, changes before and after the campaign are examined to gauge advertising effects. Winters (1983) reports several pretest/posttest studies done for a major oil company. In one study, a pretest showed that about 80% of the sample agreed that a particular oil company made too much profit. Five months later a posttest revealed that the percentage had dropped slightly among those who had seen an oil company newspaper ad but had remained the same among those who had not seen the ad. Additionally, the study disclosed that people who saw both print and TV ads showed less attitude change than those who saw only the TV ads, suggesting that the print ad might have had a dampening effect.

Tracking studies also rely on personal or telephone interviews as their main data collection devices. Technological developments including split cable systems (such as AdTel) and the UPC scanner have allowed researchers to track advertising and sales volume in a way not thought possible a few years ago. In addition, cable and scanners have permitted greater precision in media planning as well. Leckenby (1984) reports the results of a tracking study done for an instant coffee brand. It was determined that most of the TV commercials for the instant coffee were being seen by people who were regular coffee drinkers and, consequently, not good prospects. In response to this, the advertiser decided to shift the ads to reach more instant coffee drinkers. The cable and scanner data allowed researchers to identify the times of day when a high proportion of instant coffee buyers were watching TV, and with this information it was easy to reschedule the ads in more favorable slots.

Tracking studies are tremendously useful but they are not without drawbacks. Perhaps the biggest problem is cost. Tracking studies typically require large samples; in fact, a sample of less than 1,500 cases per year is unusual. If detailed analysis of subgroups is needed, the sample size must be much larger. Furthermore, if the product is a national one, test markets across the country might be necessary to present a complete picture of the results. Finally, the use of sophisticated research methods, such as split cable and scanner, makes the research even more expensive. For those who can afford it, however, the tracking study provides continuous measurement of the effects of a campaign and an opportunity to fine-tune the copy and the media schedule.

Public Relations Research

Much like advertising, public relations has become more research-oriented in recent years. As a leading text points out (Cutlip, Center, & Broom, 1985):

> For years, executives and practitioners alike bought the popular myth that public relations deals with intangibles that cannot be measured. With each passing day it becomes increasingly difficult to sell that position to results-oriented management.... Even though it will not answer all the questions or sway all decisions, methodical systematic research is the foundation of effective public relations.

Today techniques such as survey research, content analysis, and focus groups are widely employed in this field. Public relations researchers, however, use these methods for a highly specific reason: to improve communication with various publics.

Uses of Public Relations Research

The most common use of research in public relations is to gather data on audience attitudes and opinions. Such surveys are often conducted before, during, and after a public relations campaign. They may be custom-designed by the researcher or provided by professional research organizations. The Opinion Research Corporation, Roper Public Opinion Research Center, and Louis Harris and Associates are three well-known organizations that supply data to public relations practitioners.

Public relations research is also used as a means of surveillance. Specific types of survey and content research, discussed in more detail below, serve as early warning systems to identify public relations problems before they have a chance to occur. Many companies and organizations have public relations departments that systematically scan the environment to keep abreast of changes in society that might cause short-term or long-term problems.

Another common use of research by public relations departments is to secure management support for their own functions, policies, recommendations, and so forth. In many organizations, the marketing, financial, and production departments are the ones that can most effectively influence the decision-making process. This is partly because these departments typically rely on factual data and evidence to support their points of view. If a public relations department wishes to argue for a different course of action, it will naturally take advantage of the research methods at its disposal to provide a factual basis for this argument.

Finally, public relations research is often conducted to evaluate the effectiveness of a planned communication program. The pretest/posttest arrangement, discussed previously, is equally appropriate to gauging the results of a public relations campaign.

Types of Public Relations Research

As pointed out by Cutlip, Center, and Broom (1985), informal or exploratory methods are still widely used in public relations research despite the availability of highly developed social science methods. The major problem associated with these informal techniques lies in the selection of respondents. The representativeness of the samples is often questionable. In any event, these methods can be useful provided the researcher recognizes and appreciates their weaknesses. Some of the more common informal methods used in public relations research are personal contacts, expert opinion, focus groups, community forums, call-in telephone lines, mail analysis, and examination of media content.

The more formal methods of research provide objective and systematic information from representative samples. These methods include the familiar survey, tracking study, content analysis, secondary analysis of existing data, and panel studies.

There are five major categories of public relations research: (1) environmental monitoring programs, (2) public relations audits, (3) communication audits, (4) social audits, and (5) evaluation research. The first four were identified by Lerbinger (1977) nearly a decade ago.

Researchers use **environmental monitoring programs** to observe trends in public opinion and social events that may have a significant impact on an organization. Generally, two phases are involved. The "early warning" phase, an attempt to identify emerging issues, often takes the form of a systematic content analysis of publications likely to herald new developments. For example, one corporation has conducted a content analysis of scholarly journals in the fields of economics, politics, and science; another company sponsors a continuing analysis of trade and general newspapers. An alternate method is to perform panel studies of community leaders or other influential and knowledgeable citizens. These individuals are surveyed regularly with regard to the ideas they perceive to be important, and the interviews are analyzed to pick out new topics of interest.

The second phase of environmental monitoring consists of tracking public opinion on major issues. Typically this involves either a longitudinal panel study, in which the same respondents are interviewed several times during a specified interval, or a cross-sectional public opinion poll, in which a random sample is surveyed only once. One good example of the latter type of monitoring is seen in the efforts of the Television Information Office. Since 1959, this organization has commissioned the Roper organization to survey public attitudes con-

Figure 15.2 A semantic differential scale for eliciting perceptions of electric companies

The Ideal Electric Company

good   ____:____:____:____:____:____:____   bad

unconcerned   ____:____:____:____:____:____:____   concerned

responsive   ____:____:____:____:____:____:____   unresponsive

cold   ____:____:____:____:____:____:____   warm

big   ____:____:____:____:____:____:____   small

cerning the credibility of television and other media. These data give a clear picture of how public opinion has fluctuated over the years.

The **public relations audit**, as the name suggests, is a comprehensive study of the public relations position of an organization. Such studies are used to measure a company's standing both internally (in the eyes of its employees) and externally (with regard to the opinions of customers, stockholders, community leaders, and so on). In short, as summarized by Simon (1980), the public relations audit is a "research tool used specifically to describe, measure and assess an organization's public relations activities and to provide guidelines for future public relations programming."

The first step in a public relations audit is to list the segments of the public that are most important to the organization. This is generally accomplished through personal interviews with key management personnel in each department and by a content analysis of the company's external communications. The second step is to determine how the organization is viewed by each of these audiences. This involves conducting a corporate image study, that is, a survey of audience samples. The questions are designed to measure familiarity with the organization (can the respondents recognize the company logo? identify a product it manufactures? remember the president's name?) as well as attitudes and perceptions toward it.

Ratings scales are often used. For example, respondents might be asked to rank their perceptions of the ideal electric company on a 7-point scale for a series of adjective pairs as shown in Figure 15.2. Later, the respondents would rate a specific electric company on the same scales. The average score for each item would be tabulated, and the means connected by a zigzag line to form a composite profile. Thus, in Figure 15.3, the ideal electric company's profile is represented by a broken line and the actual electric company's standing by a solid line. By comparing the two lines, public relations researchers can readily identify the areas in which a company falls short of the ideal. Corporate image studies can also be conducted before the beginning of a public relations campaign and again at the conclusion of the campaign to evaluate its effectiveness.

Figure 15.3 Profiles of ideal (broken line) and actual (solid line) electric companies resulting from ratings study

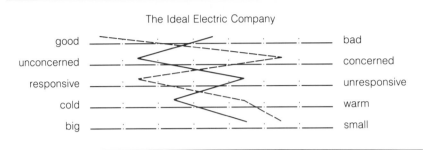

The Ideal Electric Company

good		bad
unconcerned		concerned
responsive		unresponsive
cold		warm
big		small

The **communication audit** resembles a public relations audit but has narrower goals; it concerns the internal and external means of communication used by an organization, rather than the company's entire public relations program. The three research techniques generally used in conducting such an audit are readership surveys, content analyses, and readability studies. Readership studies are designed to measure how many people read certain publications (such as employee newsletters or annual reports) and/or remember the messages they contain. The results are used to improve the content, appearance, and method of distribution of the publications. Content analyses reveal how the media are handling news and other information about and from the organization; they may be conducted in-house or by private firms that provide computerized studies of press coverage. Readability studies help a company gauge the ease with which its employee publications and press releases can be read. An internal audit would also include an analysis of channels of communication within the organization.

A **social audit** is a small-scale environmental monitoring program designed to measure an organization's social performance, that is, how well it is living up to its public responsibilities. The audit provides feedback on such company-sponsored social action programs as minority hiring, environmental cleanup, and employee safety. This is the newest form of public relations research and also the most challenging. Researchers are currently studying such questions as what activities to audit, how to collect data, and how to measure the effects of the programs. Nevertheless, several large companies, including General Motors and Celanese, have already conducted lengthy social audits.

A fifth major category of public relations research has recently achieved prominence and needs to be added to Lerbinger's list: evaluation research. **Evaluation research** refers to the process of judging the effectiveness of program planning, implementation, and impact. Rossi and Freeman (1982) have outlined some basic questions that occur at each of these stages. Some samples are given.

1. *Planning.* What is the extent of the target problem? How do the costs of the program relate to the potential benefits?
2. *Implementation.* Is the program reaching the target population or target area?
3. *Impact.* Is the program effective in achieving its intended goals? Is the program having some effects that were not intended?

The specific research methods used at each of these three levels have been mentioned in other chapters. For example, at the planning stage, content analysis (see Chapter 8) is used to determine how closely program efforts coincide with the actual plan. Readability tests (see Chapter 13) are frequently used to see whether the messages can be read and understood by the target group. During the implementation stage, content analysis is used again to count the number of messages that are placed in the media. Next, the number of people actually exposed to the message is determined by the methods of audience research mentioned earlier in this chapter. Circulation figures and audience estimates from the Audit Bureau of Circulation, Simmons Market Research Bureau, Nielsen, and Arbitron are helpful in measuring exposure.

At the impact level, public relations researchers are interested in the same three levels of effect that are mentioned in the discussion of copy research: cognitive, affective, conative. At the cognitive level, researchers attempt to find out how much people learned from the public relations campaign. At the affective level, measures of changes in attitudes, opinions, or perceptions are used quite frequently. Finally, behavioral change, the conative level, is an important way to gauge public relations impact. Obviously, the techniques used in advertising campaign effectiveness studies—pretest/posttest and tracking studies—can be applied in measuring the impact dimension of public relations campaigns.

Larson and Massetti-Miller (1984) provide an example of the use of evaluation research in a public relations campaign. The researchers were interested in assessing the impact of a public education program designed to promote recycling and to increase public awareness about the problems associated with illegal dumping of garbage. A survey was conducted before the campaign began to measure existing public attitudes and behavior patterns. The public education program ran for 9 months and included public service announcements, news releases, public service programming, posters, brochures, and a speakers' bureau. At the end of the campaign, another telephone survey was conducted among residents. The data revealed that attitudes toward littering showed no significant shift after the campaign. An information measure, the percentage of people who knew where a recycling center was located, also showed no change, nor was there any change in the behavioral measure, namely, the number of people who reported recycling.

At first glance, the campaign appeared to have had little impact, but subsequent analyses showed that once the campaign was over, people who had been recycling waste before the campaign showed a significant change in the importance they attached to the problems of illegal dumping. Thus, the real impact was reinforcement of the attitudes held by people already active in the desired behavior.

Several top public relations companies have recently started their own research companies. For example, Ruder Finn & Rotman has the largest wholly owned primary research facility. The division employs about 35 research professionals and a staff of 100–150 interviewers. Projects typically cost a client between $10,000 and $150,000. Hill & Knowlton's research section, Group Attitudes Corporation, employs about a dozen professionals who design, supervise, and analyze projects. The field work is contracted to outside research companies. Individual projects at Group Attitudes typically cost between $5,000 and $50,000. Carl Byoir & Associates, the public relations division of Foote, Cone & Belding, started its research operation in 1983. Known as Public Attitudes, the company employs three full-time professional researchers. Much of Public Attitudes' work consists of surveys designed for press consumption. One recent example was a survey done for Honeywell, Inc., profiling the attitudes of knowledge industry workers toward office automation.

Summary

There are three main areas of advertising research: copy testing, media research, and campaign assessment research. Copy testing consists of studies that examine the advertisement or commercial itself. The three main dimensions of impact examined by copy testing are cognitive (knowing), affective (feeling), and conative (doing). Media research helps determine which advertising vehicles are the most efficient and what type of media schedule will have the greatest impact. Campaign assessment studies examine the overall response of consumers to a complete campaign. The two main types of campaign assessment research are the pretest/posttest and the tracking study. Many private firms specialize in supplying copy, media, and assessment data to advertisers.

Research in public relations involves monitoring relevant developments and trends, studying the public relations position of an organization, examining the messages produced by an organization, measuring how well an organization is living up to its social responsibilities, and evaluating public relations campaigns.

Questions and Problems for Further Investigation

1. Assume you have developed a new diet soft drink and are ready to market it. Develop a research study for identifying the elements and topics that should be stressed in your advertising.
2. A full-page advertisement costs $16,000 in Magazine A and $26,000 in Magazine B. Magazine A has a circulation of 100,000 and 2.5 readers per copy, while Magazine B has a circulation of 150,000 and 1.8 readers per copy. In terms of CPM readers, which magazine is the most efficient advertising vehicle?
3. Select a sample of newspaper and magazine advertisements for two different airlines. Conduct a content analysis of the themes or major selling points in each advertisement. What similarities and differences are there?
4. Assume you are the public relations director for a major automobile manufacturer. How would you go about conducting an environmental monitoring study?
5. How would you assess the public relations impact of an information campaign designed to persuade people to conserve water?

References and Suggested Readings

Aaker, D. (1975, February). ADMOD, an advertising decision model. *Journal of Marketing Research, 12,* 37–45.

Aaker, D., & Myers, J. (1975). *Advertising management.* Englewood Cliffs, NJ: Prentice-Hall.

Anderson, R., & Barry, T. (1979). *Advertising management: Text and cases.* Columbus, OH: Charles E. Merrill.

Aronoff, C. (1975). Credibility of public relations for journalists. *Public Relations Review, 1*(2), 43–54.

Becknell, J., & McIsaac, R. (1963). Test marketing cookware coated with Teflon. *Journal of Advertising Research, 3*(3), 2–8.

Bogart, L., Tolley, S., & Orenstein, F. (1970). What one little ad can do. *Journal of Advertising Research, 10*(4), 3–15.

Bowes, J., & Stamm, K. (1975). Evaluating communication with public agencies. *Public Relations Review, 1*(1), 23–27.

Corley, L. (1970). How to isolate product attributes. *Journal of Advertising Research, 10*(4), 41–46.

Cutlip, S., Center, A., & Broom, G. (1985). *Effective public relations* (6th ed.). Englewood Cliffs, NJ: Prentice-Hall.

Dirksen, C., Kroeger, A., & Nicosia, F. (1977). *Advertising principles, problems and cases.* Homewood, IL: Richard D. Irwin.

Ferber, R. (Ed.). (1974). *Handbook of marketing research.* New York: McGraw-Hill.

Fletcher, A., & Bowers, T. (1979). *Fundamentals of advertising research*. Columbus, OH: Grid Publishing.

Friedman, H., Termini, S., & Washington, R. (1976). The effectiveness of advertising using four types of endorsers. *Journal of Advertising, 5*(3), 22–24.

Haskins, J. (1976). *An introduction to advertising research*. Knoxville, TN: Communication Research Center.

Hoofnagle, W. (1963). The effectiveness of advertising for farm products. *Journal of Advertising Research, 3*(4), 2–6.

LaChance, C., Chestnut, R., & Lubitt, A. (1977). The decorative female model. *Journal of Advertising, 6*(4), 11–14.

Larson, M., & Massetti-Miller, K. (1984). Measuring change after a public education campaign. *Public Relations Review, 10*(4), 23–32.

Leckenby, J. (1984). Current issues in the measurement of advertising effectiveness. Paper presented to the International Advertising Association, Tokyo, Japan.

Leckenby, J., & Wedding, N. (1982). *Advertising management*. Columbus, OH: Grid Publishing.

Lerbinger, O. (1977). Corporate use of research in public relations. *Public Relations Review, 3*(4), 11–20.

Little, J., & Lodish, L. (1969, January–February). A media planning calculus. *Operations Research*, pp. 1–35.

Moran, W. (1963, July). Practical media decisions and the computer. *Journal of Marketing*, pp. 26–30.

Myers, J. (1970). Finding determinants of buying attitudes. *Journal of Advertising Research, 10*(6), 9–13.

Rossi, P., & Freeman, H. (1982). *Evaluation: A systematic approach*. Beverly Hills, CA: Sage Publications.

Roy, R., & Nicolich, M. (1980). PLANNER: A media market position model. *Journal of Advertising Research, 20*(2), 61–68.

Simon, R. (1980). *Public relations: Concepts and practices*. Columbus, OH: Grid Publishing.

Tull, D., & Hawkins, D. (1980). *Marketing research* (2nd ed.). New York: Macmillan.

Winters, L. (1983). Comparing pretesting and posttesting of corporate advertising. *Journal of Advertising Research, 23*(1), 33–38.

Research in Media Effects

ANTISOCIAL AND PROSOCIAL EFFECTS OF MEDIA CONTENT
•
USES AND GRATIFICATIONS
•
AGENDA SETTING BY THE MEDIA
•
CULTIVATION OF PERCEPTIONS OF SOCIAL REALITY
•
ADVERTISING AND THE SOCIALIZATION OF CHILDREN
•
SUMMARY
•
QUESTIONS AND PROBLEMS FOR FURTHER INVESTIGATION
•
REFERENCES AND SUGGESTED READINGS

The preceding three chapters focused on research conducted in a professional or industry setting. However, a great deal of mass media research is conducted at colleges and universities. As mentioned in Chapter 1, there are several differences between research in the academic and the private sectors. To summarize briefly:

1. Academic research tends to be more theoretical in nature; private sector research is generally more applied.
2. The data used in academic research are public, while much industry research is based on proprietary data.
3. Private sector research topics are often determined by top management; academic researchers have more freedom in their choice of topics.
4. Projects in private sector research usually cost more to conduct than academic investigations.

The two research settings also have some things in common:

1. Many research techniques and approaches used in the private sector emerged from academic research.
2. Industry and academic researchers use the same basic research methodologies and approaches.
3. The goal of research is often the same in both settings—to explain and predict audience and consumer behavior.

This chapter describes some of the more popular types of research carried out by academic investigators and shows how this work relates to private sector research.

Obviously, not every type of scholarly research used in colleges and universities can be covered in one chapter. What follows is not an exhaustive survey, but rather an illustrative overview of the history, methods, and theoretical development of five research areas: (1) the antisocial and prosocial effects of specific media content, (2) uses and gratifications, (3) agenda setting, (4) cultivation of perceptions of social reality, and (5) advertising and the socialization of children.

Antisocial and Prosocial Effects of Media Content

The study of the *antisocial* effects of viewing television and motion pictures is one of the most heavily researched areas in all mass media.

Comstock, Chaffee and Katzman (1978) reported that empirical studies focusing on this topic outweighed work in all other problem areas by four to one, and this emphasis is still apparent almost a decade later. The impact of *prosocial* content is a newer area and grew out of the recognition that the same principles underlying the learning of anti-social activities ought to apply to more positive behavior. Applied and academic researchers share an interest in this area: all the major networks have sponsored such research, and the effects of antisocial and prosocial content have been popular topics on college and university campuses for the past 30 years. Not surprisingly, there has been a certain amount of friction between academic researchers and industry executives.

History

Concern over the social impact of the mass media was evident as far back as the 1920s when many critics charged that motion pictures had a negative influence on children. In 1928 the Motion Picture Research Council, with support from the Payne Fund, a private philanthropic organization, sponsored a series of 13 studies on aspects of the movies' influence on children. After examination of film content, information gain, attitude change, and influence on behavior, it was concluded that the movies were potent sources of information, attitudes, and behavior for children. Furthermore, many of the things that children learned had antisocial overtones. In the early 1950s, another medium, the comic book, was chastised for its alleged harmful effects (Wertham, 1954).

In 1960, Joseph Klapper summarized what was then known about the social impact of mass communication (Klapper, 1960). In contrast to many researchers, Klapper downplayed the potential harmful effects of the media. He concluded that the media function most often to reinforce an individual's existing attitudes and predispositions. Klapper's viewpoint, which came to be known as the "minimal effects" position, was influential in the development of a theory of media effects.

In the late 1950s and early 1960s, concern over the antisocial impact of the media shifted to television. Experiments on college campuses by Bandura and Berkowitz (summarized in Comstock, 1975) showed that aggressive behavior could be learned by viewing violent media content and that a stimulation effect was more probable than a cathartic (or cleansing) effect. Senate subcommittees examined possible links between viewing of violence on television and juvenile delinquency, and in 1965 one subcommittee concluded that televised crime and violence were related to antisocial behaviors among juvenile viewers. The civil unrest and assassinations in the middle 1960s prompted the formation of the National Commission on the Causes and Prevention of Violence, chaired by Milton Eisenhower. The full staff report of the Eisenhower Commission, which concluded that television violence taught the viewer how to engage in violence, made a series of recommendations about reducing the impact of television violence.

Just 3 years after the publication of the Eisenhower Commission report came the release of a multivolume report sponsored by the Surgeon General's Scientific Advisory Committee on Television and Social Behavior. In *Television and Growing Up* the committee cautiously summarized their research evidence by stating:

> There is a convergence of fairly substantial evidence on short-run causation of aggression among children by viewing violence . . . and the much less certain evidence from field studies that . . . violence viewing precedes some long-run manifestation of aggressive behavior. This convergence . . . constitutes some preliminary evidence of a causal relationship.

The committee tempered this conclusion, however, by noting that in accord with the reinforcement notion, ". . . any sequence by which viewing television violence causes aggressive behavior is most likely applicable only to some children who are predisposed in that direction" (Surgeon General's Scientific Advisory Committee, 1972).

At about the same time, the three television networks were also sponsoring research in this area. CBS commissioned two studies: a field experiment that found no link between television viewing and subsequent imitation of antisocial behavior (Milgram & Shotland, 1973) and a longitudinal study in Great Britain that found an association between viewing of violence on television and committing antisocial acts such a property damage and hurting others (Belson, 1978). ABC sponsored a series of studies by two mental health consultants who concluded that television contributed only a tiny amount to the stimulation of aggression in children (Heller & Polsky, 1976). NBC began a large-scale panel study, but results were not released until 1983 (see below).

In addition to television violence, the potential antisocial impact of pornography was under scrutiny. The Commission on Obscenity and Pornography, however, reported that this material was not a factor in determining antisocial behavior (Commission on Obscenity and Pornography, 1970). The commission's conclusions were somewhat controversial in political circles, but in general they supported the findings of other researchers in human sexuality (Tan, 1981). Subsequent efforts in this area were primarily directed toward examining links between pornography and aggression.

The early 1970s saw extensive research into the social effects of the mass media. In contrast to violence and pornography, the prosocial effect of television was investigated, as well. One stimulus for this research was the success of the television series "Sesame Street." A substantial research effort went into the preparation and evaluation of these children's programs. It was found that the series was helpful in preparing young children for school but not very successful in narrowing the information gap between advantaged and disadvantaged children (Minton, 1975). Other studies by both academic and industry researchers showed the prosocial impact of other programs. For example, the series "Fat Albert and the Cosby Kids" was found to be helpful in teaching prosocial lessons to children (CBS Broadcast Group, 1974).

Studies of these topics continued between 1975 and 1985, although there were far fewer than in the early 1970s. An update to the 1972 Surgeon General's Report, issued in 1982, reflected a broader research focus than the original document; it incorporated investigations of socialization, mental health, and perceptions of social reality. Nonetheless, its conclusions were even stronger than those of its predecessor: ". . . the consensus among most of the research community is that violence on television does lead to aggressive behavior" (National Institute of Mental Health, 1982). Other researchers, notably Wurtzel and Lometti (1984) and Bear (1984), argue that the report does not support the conclusion of a causal relationship, while Chaffee (1984) and Murray (1984), among others, contend that the conclusions are valid.

Not long after the Surgeon General's report was updated, the results of the NBC panel study begun in the early 1970s were published (Milavsky, Kessler, Stipp, & Rubens, 1983). This panel study, which used state-of-the-art statistical analyses, found a nonsignificant relationship between television violence viewing during the early phases of the study and subsequent aggression. The NBC data have been reexamined by others, and at least one article suggests that the data from this survey do show a slight relationship between violence viewing and aggression among at least one demographic subgroup—middle-class girls (Cook, Kendzierski, & Thomas, 1983). Clearly, the controversy has not abated, and the topic remains popular among academic researchers. As a rough indication, for the early to mid-1980s, *Communication Abstracts* listed an average of approximately 10 studies per year about the effects of television violence.

On the other hand, the antisocial effects of pornography averaged only three mentions per year for 1983–1985 in *Communication Abstracts*. Many of these studies have examined the association between exposure to pornography and sexual abuse of women (Silbert & Pines, 1984).

After a flurry of studies in the late 1970s, research interest in the prosocial effects of media exposure seemed to subside. Sprafkin and Rubinstein (1979) reported a correlational study in which the viewing of prosocial television programs accounted for only 1% of the variance in an index of prosocial behavior exhibited in school. The apparent lack of a strong relationship between these two variables, coupled with the absence of general agreement on a definition of "prosocial content," might have discouraged researchers from selecting this area. In any case, an average of only one study per year appears in the 1980–1985 editions of *Communication Abstracts.*

Methods

Researchers studying the effects of mass media have used most of the techniques discussed in this book: content analysis, laboratory experiments, surveys, field experiments, observations, and panels. Given the wide variety of methods used, it is not possible to describe a "typical" approach. Instead, this section focuses on four separate studies using different methods as illustrations of some of the research strategies.

The experimental method. A common design to study the antisocial impact of the media consists of showing one group of subjects violent media content, while a control group sees nonviolent content. This was the approach used by Berkowitz and Bandura in their early work. The dependent variable, aggression, is measured immediately after exposure—either by a pencil-and-paper test or by a mechanical device like the one described below. For example, Liebert and Baron (1972) divided children into two groups. The first group saw a 3.5-minute segment from a television show depicting a chase, two fist fights, two shootings, and a knifing. Children in the control group saw a segment of similar length in which athletes competed in track and field events. After viewing, the children were taken one at a time into another room that contained an apparatus with two buttons, one labeled "Help" and the other labeled "Hurt." An experimenter explained to the children that wires from the device were connected to a game in an adjacent room. The subjects were told that in the adjacent room, another child was starting to play a game (there was, in fact, no other child). At various times, by pressing the appropriate buttons, each child would be given a chance to help the unseen child win the game or to hurt the second child. The results showed that children who had seen the violent segment were significantly more likely than the control group to press the "Hurt" button.

   Of course, there are many variations on this basic design. To list just a few, the type of violent content shown to the subjects can be manipulated (for example, cartoon vs. live violence, entertainment vs. newscast violence, justified vs. unjustified violence). Also, some subjects may be frustrated before exposure. The degree of association between the media violence and the subsequent testing situation may be high or low. Subjects can watch alone or with others who praise or condemn the media violence. Media exposure can be a one-time event or manipulated over time. For a thorough summary of this research through the early 1970s, see Comstock, Chaffee, and Katzman (1978).

   Experimental studies examining the impact of media exposure on prosocial behavior have used essentially the same approach.

Subjects see a televised segment that is either prosocial or neutral and the dependent variable is then assessed. The operational definitions of prosocial behavior have shown wide variation. Studies have examined cooperative behaviors, sharing, kindness, altruism, friendliness, creativity, and absence of stereotyping.

Almost any behavior with a positive social value seems to be a candidate for study, as exemplified by the experiment by Baran, Chase, and Courtright (1979). Third graders were assigned to one of three treatment conditions. One group saw a condensed version of a segment of "The Waltons" demonstrating prosocial behavior. The second group saw a program portraying noncooperative behavior, and the third group saw no program. After answering a few written questions dealing with the program, each subject left the viewing room only to encounter a confederate of the experimenter who passed the doorway and dropped an armload of books. There were two dependent measures: whether the subject attempted to retrieve the books, and the amount of time that elapsed until the subject began to help. The group that saw the cooperative content was found to be more likely to help, and their responses were quicker than those of the control group. Interestingly, there was no difference in helping behavior or in duration between the group seeing "The Waltons" and the group seeing the noncooperative content.

The survey approach. Most such studies have used questionnaires incorporating measures of media exposure (viewing of television violence or exposure to pornography) and a pencil-and-paper measure of antisocial behavior or attitudes. In addition, many recent studies have included measures of demographic and sociographic variables that mediate the exposure–antisocial behavior relationship. Results are usually expressed as a series of correlations.

A survey by McLeod, Atkin, and Chaffee (1972) illustrates this approach. Their questionnaire contained measures of violence viewing, aggression, and family environment. Viewing was tabulated by giving respondents a list of 65 prime time television programs with a scale measuring how often each was viewed. An index of overall violence viewing was obtained by using independent ratings of the violence level of each show and multiplying it by the frequency of viewing. Aggression was measured by seven scales. One measured respondents' approval of manifest physical aggression (sample item: "Whoever insults me or my family is looking for a fight."). Another examined approval of aggression ("It's all right to hurt an enemy if you are mad at him."). Respondents indicated their degree of agreement with each of the items composing the separate scales. Family environment was measured by asking about parental control over television, parental emphasis on nonaggression punishment (such as withdrawal of privileges), and other variables. The researchers found a moderate positive relationship between the respondents' level of violence viewing and their self-reports of aggression. Family environment showed no consistent association with either of the two variables.

Sprafkin and Rubinstein (1979) used the survey method to examine the relationship between television viewing and prosocial behavior. They used basically the same approach as McLeod, Atkin, and Chaffee (1972), except that their viewing measure was designed to assess exposure to television programs established as prosocial by prior content analysis. Their measure of prosocial behaviors was based on peer nominations of persons who reflected 12 prosocial behaviors, including helping, sharing, rule-following, staying out of fights, and niceness. The researchers found that when the influence of the child's gender, the parents' educational level, and the child's academic level were statistically controlled, exposure to prosocial television explained only 1% of the variance in prosocial behaviors.

Field experiments. The imaginative and elaborate fieldwork used to study the antisocial effects of the media by Milgram and Shotland (1973) was discussed in Chapter 7. More recently, Parke, Berkowitz, and Leyens (1977) conducted a field experiment in a minimum-security penal institution for juveniles. The researchers exposed groups to unedited feature-length films that were either aggressive or nonaggressive. On the day after the last film was shown, in the context of a bogus learning experiment, the boys were told they had a chance to hurt a confederate of the experimenters who had insulted one group of boys and had been neutral to the other. The results on an electric shock measure similar to the one described previously revealed that the most aggressive of all the experimental groups were the boys who had seen the aggressive films and who had been insulted. In addition to this laboratory measure, the investigators collected observational data on the boys' aggressive interpersonal behavior in their everyday environment. These data showed that boys who saw the violent movies were more interpersonally aggressive. However, there was no apparent cumulative effect of movies on aggression. The boys who watched the diet of aggressive films were just as aggressive after the first film as after the last. As yet, there have been no large-scale field experiments to study prosocial behavior.

Panel studies. Primarily because of the time and expense involved in panel studies, this analysis mode is seldom used to examine the media in relation to antisocial effects. The two studies most relevant to the present topic, mentioned in Chapter 9, are reviewed briefly here. Lefkowitz, Eron, Waldner, and Huesmann (1972), using a catch-up panel design, reinterviewed 427 of 875 youthful subjects 10 years after they had participated in a study of mental health. Measures of television viewing and aggression had been administered to these subjects when they were in the third grade, and data on the two variables were gathered again a decade later. Slightly different methods were used to measure television viewing on the two time occasions. Viewing in the third grade was established on the basis of mothers' reports of their children's three favorite television shows. Ten years later, respondents rated their own frequency of viewing. The data were subjected to cross-lagged correlations and path analysis. The results supported the hypothesis that aggression in later life was caused in part by television viewing during early years. However the panel study by Milavsky et al. (1983), sponsored by NBC and discussed in Chapter 9, found no evidence of such a relationship.

The difference between the results of these studies might be due to several factors. The Milavsky study did not vary its measure of "violent television viewing" throughout its duration. In addition, the NBC researchers used LISREL (linear structural equations), a more powerful statistical technique, which was not available at the time of the Lefkowitz study. Finally, the Lefkowitz measures were taken 10 years apart; the maximum time lag in the NBC study was 3 years.

Summary. Experiments and surveys have been the most popular research strategies used to study the impact of media on antisocial and prosocial behavior. The more elaborate techniques of field experiments and panel studies have been used infrequently. Interestingly, as pointed out by Andison (1977), the method employed to study this topic is related to the strength and direction of the results. Laboratory experiments have shown a stronger positive relation between viewing media violence and aggression than have the other techniques.

Theoretical Developments

One of the earliest theoretical considerations in the debate over the impact of media violence was the controversy of catharsis versus stimulation. The *catharsis* approach suggests that viewing fantasy expressions of hostility reduces aggression because a person who watches filmed or televised violence is purged of his or her aggressive urges. This theory has some obvious attraction for industry executives, since it carries the implication that presenting violent television shows is a prosocial action. The stimulation theory argues the opposite: viewing violence prompts more aggression on the part of the viewer. The research findings in this area indicated little support for the catharsis position. A few studies did find a lessening of aggressive behavior after viewing violent content, but these results apparently were an artifact of the research design. The overwhelming majority of studies found evidence of a stimulation effect.

Since these early studies, many of the experiments and surveys have used social learning as their conceptual basis. As spelled out by Bandura (1977), the theory explains how people learn from direct experience or from observation (or modeling). Some of the key elements in this theory are attention, retention, motor reproduction, and motivations. According to Bandura, attention to an event is influenced by characteristics of the event and by characteristics of the observer. For example, repeated observation of an event by a person who has been paying close attention should increase learning. "Retention" refers to how well an individual remembers behaviors that have been observed. "Motor reproduction" is the actual behavioral enactment of the observed event. For example, some people can accurately imitate a behavior after merely observing it, while others need to experiment. The motivational component of the theory depends on the reinforcement or punishment that accompanies performance of the observed behavior.

Applied to the effects area, social learning theory predicts that antisocial or prosocial acts can be learned by watching films or television. The model further suggests that viewing repeated antisocial acts would make people more likely to perform these acts in real life. Yet another prediction involves *desensitization*, to account for the suggestion that people who are heavily exposed to violence and antisocial acts become less anxious about the consequences.

Bandura (1977) summarized much of the research concerning social learning theory. In brief, some of the key findings in laboratory and field experiments suggest that children can easily perform new acts of aggression after a single exposure to them on television or in films. The similarity between the circumstances of the observed antisocial acts and the postobservation circumstances will be important in determining whether the act is performed. If a model is positively reinforced for performing antisocial acts, the observed acts will be more frequently performed in real life. Likewise, when children were promised rewards for performing antisocial acts, more antisocial behavior was exhibited. Other factors that facilitated the performance of antisocial acts included the degree to which the media behavior is perceived to be real, the emotional arousal of the subjects, and the presence of cues in the postobservation environment that elicit antisocial behavior. Finally, as predicted by the theory, desensitization to violence can occur through repeated exposure to violent acts.

More recently, much research has continued to refine and reformulate some of the elements in social learning theory. For example, the arousal hypothesis (Tannenbaum & Zillmann, 1975) suggests that for a portrayal to have a demonstrable effect, increased arousal may be necessary. According to this model, if an angered person is exposed to an arousing stimulus, such as a pornographic film, and is placed in a situation to which aggression is a possible response, the person will become more aggressive ("excitation transfer" is the term used by the researchers). Zillmann, Hoyt, and Day (1979) offer some support for this model. Interestingly, it appears that subjects in a high state of arousal from seeing a violent film will perform more prosocial acts than nonaroused subjects. Like aggressive behavior, prosocial behavior seems facilitated by media-induced arousal (Mueller, Donnerstein, & Hallam, 1983).

Other research has shown that social learning theory can be applied to the study of the effects of viewing pornography. Zillmann and Bryant (1982) showed that heavy exposure to pornographic films apparently desensitized subjects to the seriousness of rape and led to decreased compassion for women as rape victims. A similar finding was obtained by Linz, Donnerstein, and Penrod (1984). Men who viewed five movies depicting erotic situations involving violence toward women perceived the films as less violent and less degrading to women than did a control group not exposed to the films. In sum, social learning theory appears to be a promising framework for integrating many of the findings in this area.

Uses and Gratifications

History

The *uses and gratifications* approach has its roots in the 1940s when researchers became interested in why people engaged in various forms of media behavior, such as radio listening or newspaper reading. These early studies were primarily descriptive, seeking to classify the responses of audience members into meaningful categories. For example, Herzog (1944) identified three types of gratification associated with listening to radio soap operas: emotional release, wishful thinking, and obtaining advice. Berelson (1949) took advantage of a New York newspaper strike to ask people why they read the paper. The responses were placed in five major categories: reading for information, reading for social prestige, reading for escape, reading as a tool for daily living, and reading for a social context. These early studies had little theoretical coherence; in fact, many were inspired by the practical needs of newspaper publishers and radio broadcasters to know the motivations of their audience in order to serve them more efficiently. (Chapter 13 notes that the uses and gratifications approach is still one of the major types of research performed by those interested in understanding newspaper readership.)

The next step in the development of this research began during the late 1950s and continued into the 1960s. In this phase the emphasis was on identifying and operationalizing the many social and psychological variables that were presumed to be the antecedents of different patterns of consumption and gratification. For example, Schramm, Lyle, and Parker (1961), in their extensive study, found that children's use of television was influenced by individual mental ability and relationships with parents and peers, among other things. Gerson

(1966) concluded that race was important in predicting how adolescents used the media. Greenberg and Dominick (1969) found that race and social class predicted how teenagers used television as an informal source of learning. These studies and many more conducted during this period reflected a shift from the traditional effects model of mass media research to the functional perspective.

According to Windahl (1981), a primary difference between the traditional effects approach and the uses and gratifications approach is that a media effects researcher usually examines mass communication from the perspective of the communicator, while the uses and gratifications researcher uses the audience member as a point of departure. Windahl argues for a synthesis of the two approaches, believing that it is more beneficial to emphasize their similarities than to stress their differences. He has coined the term *conseffects* of media content and use to categorize observations that are partly results of content use in itself (a viewpoint commonly adopted by effects researchers) and partly results of content mediated by use (a viewpoint adopted by many uses and gratifications researchers).

Windahl's perspective serves to link the earlier uses and gratifications approach to the third phase in its development. Recently, uses and gratifications research has become more conceptual and theoretical as investigators have offered their data in explanation of the connections between audience motives, media gratifications, and outcomes. As Rubin (1985) noted: ". . . several typologies of mass media motives and functions have been formulated to conceptualize the seeking of gratifications as variables that intervene before media effects." For example, Greenberg (1974) ascertained that a positive disposition to aggression characterized children who used television for arousal purposes. Rubin (1979) found a significant positive correlation between viewing television to learn something and the perceived reality of television content: those using television as a learning device thought television content was more true to life. And deBock (1980) noted that people who experienced the most frustration at being deprived of a newspaper during a strike were those who used the newspaper for information and those who viewed newspaper reading as a ritual. These and many other recent studies have revealed that a variety of audience gratifications are related to a wide range of media effects. These "uses and effects" studies (Rubin, 1985) have bridged the gap between the traditional effects approach and the uses and gratifications perspective.

Methods

Uses and gratifications researchers have relied heavily on the survey method to collect their data. As a first step, researchers have conducted focus groups or have asked respondents to write essays about their reasons for media consumption. Close-ended Likert-type scales based on what was said in the focus group or written in the essays are then constructed. The close-ended measures are typically subjected to multivariate statistical techniques such as factor analysis (see Appendix 2), which identifies various dimensions of gratifications.

Greenberg's (1974) study of British children and adolescents illustrates the usual approach to gathering uses and gratifications data. As a first step, British youngsters wrote essays entitled "Why I Like to Watch Television." These anonymous works were subjected to content analysis and eight general reasons for watching television were identified: passing time, diversion, learning about things, learning about myself, arousal, relaxation, companionship, and habit. Three or four statements were constructed that best appeared to reflect each of these eight reasons. This resulted in a list of 31 items. For example, "I watch television when I'm bored," ". . . because it's a habit," ". . . because it relaxes me," and ". . . because it's most like a real friend." Respondents could indicate that each reason was "a lot," "a little," "not much," or "not at all" like their reason for viewing. After the instrument had been administered to the sample, the data were factor analyzed. Eight separate factors (or functions) appeared: learning, habit, arousal, companionship, relaxation, forgetting, passing time, and boredom. Note that the eight factors derived from the statistical analysis are slightly different from the content analysis of the essays.

Each child or adolescent was given a score on each of the eight dimensions. A score of "4" meant that the child thought the reason was "a lot" like his or hers, while a score of "1" indicated "not at all" like the individual's reason. This analysis revealed that "habit" was the most endorsed reason and "forgetting" the least. In addition, when the average scores per factor were analyzed by age, it was found that each of the eight motives was more strongly present for younger children than for the others. Finally, each of the factor scores was correlated with measures of media use, aggressive attitudes, television attitudes, and demographic variables.

Note that the technique above assumes that the audience is aware of its reasons and can report them when asked. The method also assumes that the pencil-and-paper test is a valid and reliable measurement scale. Other assumptions include: an active audience with goal-directed media behavior; expectations for media use that are produced from individual predispositions, social interaction, and environmental factors; and media selection initiated by the individual. Some researchers (see Becker, 1980) suggest that reliability and validity checks should be built into the uses and gratifications approach. For an example of how this has been accomplished, see Rubin (1985).

The experimental method has not been widely used in uses and gratifications research. When it has been chosen, investigators typically manipulated the subjects' motivations and measured differences in their media consumption. To illustrate, Bryant and Zillmann (1984) placed their subjects in either a state of boredom or a state of stress and then gave them a choice between watching a relaxing or a stimulating television program. Stressed subjects watched more tranquil programs while bored subjects opted for the exciting fare. McLeod and Becker (1981) had their subjects sit in a lounge area that contained public affairs magazines. One group of subjects was told that they would soon be tested about the current situation in Pakistan. A second group was told they would be required to write an essay on U.S. military aid to Pakistan, while a control group was given no specific instructions. As expected, subjects in the test and essay conditions made greater use of the magazines than did the control group. The two test groups also differed in the type of information they remembered from the periodicals. Experiments such as these two indicate that different cognitive or affective states facilitate the use of media for various reasons, as predicted by the uses and gratifications rationale.

Theoretical Developments

As mentioned above, researchers in the academic sector are interested in developing theory concerning the topics they investigate. This tendency is well illustrated in the history of uses and gratifications research. Whereas early studies tended to be descriptive, later scholars have attempted to integrate research findings into a more theoretical context.

In an early explanation of the uses and gratifications process, Rosengren (1974) suggested that certain basic needs interact with personal characteristics and the social environment of the individual to produce perceived problems and perceived solutions. The problems and solutions constitute different motives for gratification behavior that can come from using the media or from other activities. Together the media use or other behaviors produce gratification (or nongratification) that has an impact on the individual or society, thereby starting the process anew. After reviewing the results of approximately 100 uses and gratifications studies, Palmgreen (1984) stated that "a rather complex theoretical structure . . . has begun to emerge." He proposed an integrative gratifications model that suggested a multivariate approach (see Appendix 2).

The gratifications sought by the audience form the central concept in the model. There are, however, many antecedent variables such as media structure, media technology, social circumstances, psychological variables, needs, values, and beliefs that all relate to the particular gratification pattern used by the audience. Additionally, the consequences of the gratifications relate directly to media and nonmedia consumption behaviors and perceived gratifications that are obtained. As Palmgreen admits, this model suffers from lack of parsimony and needs strengthening in several areas, but it does represent an increase in our understanding of the mass media process. Further refinements in the model will come from surveys and experiments designed to test specific hypotheses derived from well-articulated theoretical rationales and from carefully designed descriptive studies. For example, Levy and Windahl (1984) examined the assumption of an active audience in the uses and gratifications approach. They derived a typology of audience activity and prepared a model that linked activity to various uses and gratifications, thus clarifying further one of the important postulates in the uses and gratifications process.

The uses and gratifications approach also illustrates the difference in emphasis between academic and applied research objectives. Newspaper publishers and broadcasting executives, who want guidance in attracting readers, viewers, and listeners, seem to be particularly interested in determining what specific content is best suited to fulfilling the needs of the audience. College and university researchers are interested not only in content characteristics, they want to develop theories that explain and predict the media consumption of the public based on sociological, psychological and structural variables.

Agenda Setting by the Media

Agenda setting theory proposes that "the public agenda—or what kinds of things people discuss, think, and worry about (and sometimes ultimately press for legislation about)—is powerfully shaped and directed by what the news media choose to publicize" (Larson, 1986). This means that if the news media decide to give the most time and space to coverage of racial protests in South Africa, this issue will become the most important item on the audience's agenda. If the news media devote the second most amount of coverage to unemployment, audiences, too, will rate unemployment as the second most important issue to them, and so on. Agenda setting research examines the relationship between media priorities and audience priorities in the relative importance of news topics.

History

The notion of agenda setting by the media can be traced to Walter Lippmann (1922), who suggested the media were responsible for the "pictures in our heads." Forty years later, Cohen (1963) further articulated the idea when he argued that the media may not always be successful in telling people what to think, but they are usually successful in telling them what to think about. Lang and Lang (1966) reinforced this notion by observing, "The mass media force attention to certain issues. . . . They are constantly presenting objects, suggesting what individuals in the mass should think about, know about, have feelings about."

The first empirical test of agenda setting came in 1972, when McCombs and Shaw (1972) reported the results of a study done during the 1968 presidential election. They found strong support for the agenda setting hypothesis. There were strong relationships between the emphasis placed on different campaign issues by the media and the judgments of voters regarding the importance of various campaign topics. This study inspired a host of others, many of them concerned with agenda setting as it occurred during political campaigns. For example, Tipton, Haney, and Baseheart (1975) used cross-lagged correlation (see Chapter 9) to analyze the impact of the media on agenda setting during statewide elections. Patterson and McClure (1976) studied the impact of television news and television commercials on agenda setting in the 1972 election. They concluded that television news had minimal impact on public awareness of issues, but that television advertising accounted for a rise in the audience's awareness of candidates' positions on issues.

Lately, agenda setting research has enjoyed increased popularity. *Communication Abstracts* has listed an average of 7.5 articles per year on agenda setting from 1978 to 1985. The more recent articles signal a shift away from the political campaign approach. In the years 1978–1981, about 30% of the agenda setting articles were analyses of political campaigns. From 1982 to 1985, about 15% were of this type. In short, the agenda setting technique is now being used in a variety of areas: history, advertising, foreign news, and medical news. In addition, increased attention is being paid to the methods involved (Roberts & Bachen, 1981), to the time dimension (Eyal, Winter, & DeGeorge, 1981), and to theory building (Williams, 1985).

Method

The typical agenda setting study involves several of the approaches discussed in earlier chapters. Content analysis (see Chapter 8) is used to define the media agenda, and surveys (Chapter 6) are used to collect data on the audience agenda. In addition, since determination of the media agenda and surveying of the audience are not done simultaneously, a longitudinal dimension (Chapter 9) is present as well.

Measuring the media agenda. Several techniques have been used to establish the media agenda. The most common method involves grouping coverage topics into broad categories and measuring the amount of time or space devoted to each category. The operational definitions of these categories are important considerations because the more broadly a topic area is defined, the easier it is to demonstrate an agenda setting effect. Ideally, the content analysis should include all media, including television, radio, newspaper, and magazines. Unfortunately, this is too large a task for most researchers to handle comfortably, and most studies have been confined to one or two media, usually television and the daily newspaper. For example, Williams and Semlak (1978a) tabulated total air time for each topic mentioned in the three television network newscasts for a 19-day period. The topics were rank ordered according to their total time. At the same time, the newspaper agenda was constructed by measuring the total column inches devoted to each topic on the front and editorial pages of the local newspaper. McLeod, Becker, and Byrnes (1974) content analyzed local newspapers for a 6-week period, totaling the number of inches devoted to each topic, including headlines and pertinent pictures on the front and editorial pages. Among other things, they found that the front and editorial pages adequately represented the entire newspaper in their topical areas.

Other content-analytic approaches have included counting the number of articles that have appeared in major news magazines over a number of years. Funkhouser (1973) used the *Readers' Guide to Periodical Literature* to identify the major topics on the agenda of news magazines from 1960 to 1970. Williams and Semlak (1978b) analyzed the agenda-setting impact of the visual dimension in a television newscast. They categorized stories according to their use of chromakey, sound on film, rear-screen projection, and videotape. They found that static visuals (such as chromakey, where two pictures are electronically combined) had an impact on setting personal agendas.

Measuring public agendas. The public agenda has been constructed in at least four ways. First, respondents have been asked an open-ended question such as, "What do you feel is the most important political issue to you personally?" or, "What is the most important political issue in your community?" The phrasing of this question can elicit either the respondent's intrapersonal agenda (as in the first example) or interpersonal agenda (the second example). A second method asks respondents to rate in importance the issues in a list compiled by the researcher. The third technique is a variation of this approach. Respondents are given a list of topics selected by the researcher and asked to rank order them according to perceived importance. The fourth technique uses the paired-comparisons method. In this approach, each issue on a preselected list is paired with every other issue and the respondent is asked to consider each pair and to identify the more important issue. When all the responses have been tabulated, the issues are ordered from the most to the least important.

As with all measurement, each technique has its associated advantages and disadvantages. The open-ended method gives respondents great freedom in nominating issues, but it favors those people who are better able to verbalize their thoughts. The closed-ended ranking and rating techniques make sure that all respondents have a common vocabulary, but they assume each respondent is aware of all the public issues listed and restrict the respondent from expressing a personal point of view. The paired-comparisons method provides interval data, which allows for more sophisticated statistical techniques, but it takes longer to complete than the other methods, and this might be a problem in some forms of survey research.

There are three important time frames used in collecting the data for agenda setting research: (1) the duration of the media agenda measurement period, (2) the time lag between measuring the media agenda and measuring the personal agenda, and (3) the duration of the audience agenda measurement. Unfortunately, there is little in the way of research or theory to guide the investigator in this area. To illustrate, Mullins (1977) studied media content for a week to determine the media agenda, while Gormley (1975) gathered media data for 4.5 months. Similarly, the time lag between media agenda measurement and audience agenda measurement has varied from no time at all (McLeod et al., 1974) to a lag of 5 months (Gormley, 1975).

Not surprisingly, the duration of the measurement period for audience agendas also has shown wide variation. Hilker (1976) collected a public agenda measure in a single day, while McLeod et al. (1974) took 4 weeks. Eyal et al. (1981) suggested that methodological studies should be carried out to determine the optimal effect span or peak association period between the media emphasis and public emphasis. Winter and Eyal (1981), in an example of one of these methodological studies, found an optimal effect span of 6 weeks for agenda setting on the civil rights issue. Other variables that appear to be important in considering the proper longitudinal dimension for agenda setting studies are the nature of the issues and the media under study. It is conceivable that the electronic media and the print media influence the public agenda at different rates and that some issues take longer than others to show an agenda setting effect. Further study of the methods used in agenda setting should provide further information on these complicated topics.

Theoretical Developments

The construction of a theory of agenda setting is still at a formative level. In spite of the problems in method and time span mentioned above, the findings in agenda setting are consistent enough to permit some first steps toward theory building. To begin, the longitudinality of agenda setting has permitted some tentative causal statements. Most of this research has supported the interpretation that the media's agenda causes the public agenda; the rival causal hypothesis—that the public agenda establishes the media agenda—has not received much support (Behr & Iyengar, 1985; Roberts & Bachen, 1981). Thus, much of the recent research has attempted to specify the audience-related and media-related events that condition the agenda setting effect.

It is apparent that solving the problem will be a complicated task. Williams (1985), for example, posited eight antecedent variables that should have an impact on audience agendas during a political campaign. Four of these variables (voter interest, voter activity, political involvement, and civic activity) have been linked to agenda setting (Williams & Semlak, 1978a). In addition, several studies have suggested that a person's "need for orientation" should be a predictor of agenda holding. (Note that such an approach incorporates uses and gratifications thinking.) For example, Weaver (1977) found a positive correlation between the need for orientation and a greater acceptance of media agendas.

These antecedent variables define the media scanning behavior of the individual (McCombs, 1981). Important variables at this stage of the process include media use (see Weaver, 1977) and the use of interpersonal communication (Winter, 1981). Other influences on the individual's agenda setting behavior include the duration and obtrusiveness of the issues themselves and the specifics of media coverage (Winter, 1981). Finally, Lang and Lang (1981) suggest that the potential of the topic to affect many or few in the audience (called "issue threshold") has a bearing on agenda building. Further research is needed to identify and further refine these concepts.

Cultivation of Perceptions of Social Reality

How do the media affect audience perceptions of the real world? The basic assumption underlying the "cultivation" or "enculturation" approach is that repeated exposures to consistent media portrayals and themes will influence our perceptions of these items in the direction of the media portrayals. In effect, learning from the media environment is generalized, sometimes incorrectly, to the social environment.

As was the case with agenda setting research, most of the enculturation research has been conducted by investigators in the academic sector. Industry researchers are aware of this work and sometimes question its accuracy or meaning (Wurtzel & Lometti, 1984), but they seldom conduct it or sponsor it themselves.

History

Some of the early research studies indicated that media portrayals of certain topics could have an impact on audience perceptions, particularly if the media were the main information sources. Siegel (1958) found that children's role expectations about a taxi driver could be influenced by hearing a radio program about the character. DeFleur and DeFleur (1967) found that television had a homogenizing effect on children's perceptions of occupations commonly shown on television. On a more general level, Greenberg and Dominick (1969) discovered that lower-class teenagers were more likely than middle-class youngsters to believe that the middle-class world commonly portrayed on television programs was true to life.

The more recent research on viewer perceptions of social reality stems from the Cultural Indicators project of George Gerbner and his associates. Since 1968, they have collected data on the content of television and have analyzed the impact of heavy exposure on the audience. Some of the many variables that have been content analyzed include the demographic portraits of perpetrators and victims of television violence, the prevalence of violent acts, the types of violence portrayed, and the contexts of violence. The basic hypothesis of cultivation analysis is that the more time one spends living in the world of television, the more likely one is to report conceptions of social reality that can be traced to television portrayals (Gross & Morgan, 1985).

To test this hypothesis, Gerbner and his associates have analyzed data from adults, adolescents, and children in cities across the United States. The first cultivation data were reported a decade ago (Gerbner & Gross, 1976). Using data collected by the National Opinion Research Center (NORC), Gerbner found that heavy television viewers scored higher on a "mean world" index than did light viewers. (Sample items from this index included: "Do you think people try to take advantage of you?" and "You can't be too careful in dealing with people [agree/disagree].") Data from both adult and child NORC samples showed that heavy viewers were more suspicious and distrustful. Subsequent studies reinforced these findings and found that heavy television viewers were more likely to overestimate the prevalence of violence in society and their own chances of being involved in violence (Gerbner et al., 1978). In sum, their perceptions of reality were cultivated by television.

Not all researchers have accepted the cultivation hypothesis. In particular, Hughes (1980) and Hirsch (1980) reanalyzed the NORC data using simultaneous rather than individual controls for demographic variables and were unable to replicate Gerbner's findings. Gerbner responded by introducing *resonance* and *mainstreaming,* two new concepts to help explain inconsistencies in the results (Gerbner, Gross, Morgan, & Signorielli, 1980). When the media reinforce what is seen in real life, thus giving an audience member a "double dose," the resulting increase in the cultivation effect is attributed to "resonance." Mainstreaming is a leveling effect. Differences in perceptions of reality usually caused by demographic and social factors are washed out by heavy viewing, resulting in a common viewpoint. These concepts refine and further elaborate the cultivation hypothesis but they have not satisfied all the critics of this approach.

More recently, the study of the cultivation hypothesis has been characterized by four major trends. First is the attempt to find patterns of causation in the data (Doob & MacDonald, 1979; Gerbner et al., 1980). Second, some researchers are looking for the cultivation effect in areas other than crime and violence. Beurkel-Rothfuss and Mayes (1981), for example, found some evidence of a cultivation effect among college students who were heavy viewers of soap operas. Third, several studies have been designed to isolate important variables that affect the cultivation process. Slater and Elliot (1982) found that perceptions of program realism constituted an important variable. Similarly, Rouner (1984) found that active television viewers (those who take the initiative in seeking out media content) were less likely to show a cultivation effect. Although the nature of the cultivation hypothesis makes the work difficult, laboratory research has begun to address this topic. To illustrate, Tamborini, Zillmann, and Bryant (1985) found that exposure to programs about crime influenced some, but not all, of their subjects' perceptions about real-life crime. This effect, however, was transitory.

Method

There are two discrete steps in performing a cultivation analysis. First, descriptions of the media world are obtained from periodic content analyses of large blocks of media content. The result of this content analysis is the identification of the messages of the television world. These messages represent consistent patterns in portrayal of specific issues, policies, and topics that are often at odds with their occurrence in real life. The identification of the consistent portrayals is followed by the construction of a set of questions designed to detect a cultivation effect. Each question poses two alternatives. One alternative is more consistent with the world as seen on television, while the other is more in line with the real world. For example, according to the content analyses performed by Gerbner et al. (1977), about 60% of television homicides are committed by strangers. In real life, according to government statistics, only 16% of homicides occur between strangers. The question based on this discrepancy was, "Does fatal violence occur between strangers or between relatives and acquaintances?" The response "strangers" was considered to be the television answer. Another question was, "What percentage of all males who have jobs work in law enforcement and crime detection? Is it 1% or 5%?" According to census data, 1% of males in real life have such jobs, compared to 12% in television programs. Thus, 5% is the television answer.

The second step involves surveying audiences with regard to television exposure, dividing the sample into heavy and light viewers (4 hours of viewing a day is usually the dividing line) and comparing their answers to the questions differentiating the television world from the real world. In addition, data are often collected on possible control variables such as gender, age, and socioeconomic status. The basic statistical procedure consists of correlational analysis between the amount of television viewing and scores on an index reflecting the number of television answers to the comparison questions. Also, partial correlation is used to remove the effects of the control variables. Alternatively, sometimes the cultivation differential (CD) is reported. The CD is the percentage of heavy viewers minus the percentage of light viewers who gave the television answer. For example, if 73% of the heavy viewers gave the television answer to the question about violence being committed between strangers or acquaintances compared to 62% of the light viewers, the CD would be 11%. Laboratory experiments use the same general approach, but they usually manipulate the subjects' experience with the television world by showing an experimental group one or more preselected programs.

Theoretical Developments

What does the research tell us about cultivation? After an extensive literature review in which 48 studies were examined, Hawkins and Pingree (1981) concluded that there was evidence for a link between viewing and beliefs regardless of the kind of social reality in question. Was this link real or spurious? The authors concluded that the answer to this question did, in fact, depend on the type of belief under study. Relationships between viewing and demographic aspects of social reality held up under rigorous controls. Correlations between viewing and value-system measures (for example, "Are you [the respondent] afraid to go out at night?") were less robust, and the findings have been mixed. As far as causality was concerned, the authors concluded that most of the evidence went in one direction, namely, that television causes social reality to be interpreted in certain ways.

How does this process take place? Research in this area is so recent that there has been relatively little systematic effort to build a theory of the media's influence on social perception. As Tan (1981) suggested, the principles of social learning theory can be applied to this area, since learning from watching a television program is being generalized to a new situation. Nonetheless, there has been little effort to interpret the results of cultivation research in this context. This may be partly because researchers have not specified all the intervening variables that might affect cultivation.

At a general level, there are probably three class of variables that might influence the way the mass media shape a person's social perceptions: individual differences, situational variables, and content differences (most cultivation studies are based on measures of total television viewing, but as Hawkins & Pingree, 1981, noted, differences in content in patterns of action and characterization might temper the cultivation impact).

The work of Slater and Elliot (1982) and Rouner (1984) suggests two individual difference variables that have not been taken into account in most cultivation studies: active viewing and perceived realism of the program. Respondents' apprehension toward a certain topic (Wakshlag, Vial, & Tamborini, 1983), IQ, and involvement (Hawkins & Pingree, 1981) also may be important.

Situational variables include the viewer's own experience with the situation as portrayed on television. Doob and MacDonald (1979) noted that television viewing and increased levels of fear were related only in the high-crime urban areas in their sample. In addition, at least two studies show that the social situation of the audience member makes a difference in television's influence. Rothschild (1979) found that certain peer group characteristics could inhibit or even reverse cultivation relationships for television viewing and several areas of social perception. Gross and Morgan (1985) found that another situational variable, family context, had an impact on some cultivation relationships.

Hawkins and Pingree (1981) offered the following summary:

> The theory that has directed the research needs to be changed. TV's influence on individual constructions of reality can no longer be described as direct but must be viewed as a complex process. We need to modify the theory to recognize the conditional nature of TV's influence. Under some circumstances, TV does seem to contribute to the construction of reality, but in others, it doesn't.

Advertising and the Socialization of Children

The concern over the impact of advertising on children stems from the sheer magnitude of their exposure to such communications. By the time a child reaches high school, he or she has been exposed to approximately 350,000 commercial messages. Not surprisingly, this area has drawn research attention from both academic and applied researchers. There is a large body of applied research in which small samples of children were exposed to commercials to determine comprehensibility and persuasiveness (Griffin, 1976). Many of these studies are proprietary and not open for review. In the academic sector, the research has been conducted for two purposes: to develop theory concerning children and consumer socialization, and to provide guidelines for public policy. In fact, both the Federal Trade Commission (FTC) and the Federal Communications Commission have undertaken inquiries into the impact of advertising on children, and academic research played a key part in the deliberations of both agencies.

History

Concern over the effects of television advertising on children can be traced to the 1960s when the National Association of Broadcasters adopted guidelines concerning toy advertising. It was not until the 1970s, however, that this issue gained wide national attention. Action for Children's Television (ACT), a group of concerned parents, petitioned the Federal Communications Commission in 1970 for a new set of rules concerning children's television. Among other things, ACT requested a ban on commercials on children's programs. At about the same time, members on the Council on Children, Media and Merchandising appeared before Congress to complain about the advertising of high-sugar cereals on television.

This public concern was quickly followed by research into the effects of advertising directed at children. First to appear were content analyses of Saturday morning commercials (Winick, Williamson, & Chuzmir, 1973). The first behavioral studies were included as part of the Surgeon General's report on television and social behavior (Ward, 1972). A few additional studies appeared over the next few years, but research interest did not significantly increase until regulatory agencies used the results of existing studies to formulate new policy. The FTC, for example, cited research findings to support its prohibition of the use of premium offers in advertising.

The number of studies examining the socialization impact of television advertising increased markedly in the mid-1970s. A review of the literature of the period summarized 21 key studies in the area and reported that most were done between 1974 and 1976 (Adler et al., 1977). The main findings of these studies indicated that age was a crucial variable in determining children's understanding of television advertising. Young children (ages 3–5) had trouble separating the commercial messages from the program content. Older children (ages 6–8) could better identify commercials as distinct from the program but did not understand the selling motive behind their presentation. In 1978, in a report on children and television advertising, the FTC called for the banning of all commercials directed at children too young to understand their intent. In making this recommendation, the FTC used the results of many research studies that examined the age variable and its relationship to the understanding of commercials.

On the other hand, defenders of children's advertising have suggested that it helps the child become a better consumer because it contributes to general economic understanding and knowledge of different products. Research into these claims conducted in the late 1970s turned out to be inconclusive (Ward, 1980).

The shift toward deregulation of the media during the early 1980s de-emphasized the policy-making aspects of this research. Research interest in children's advertising leveled off during this period.

Many of the more recent studies have been concerned with developmental influences on children's understanding of commercials and their relation to Piaget's theory of cognitive development.

In 1984 the question of regulating ads directed at young people surfaced again when congressional hearings were held concerning the impact of liquor commercials on adolescent drinking behavior. The research evidence in this area suggested that young people who were heavily exposed to liquor and beer ads drank more frequently or reported that they expected to start drinking sooner than did those who were not as heavily exposed (Atkin, Hocking, & Block, 1984). There was no immediate federal action as a result of the hearings, but broadcasters and advertisers promised to present messages that would promote the responsible use of alcohol.

Method

The most popular methods used to study this topic have been the survey and the laboratory experiment. Of the 26 key studies reviewed by Adler et al. (1980), half were surveys and half were done in the laboratory. Accordingly, this section examines several illustrative experiments and surveys.

The three dependent variables that have been examined by much of the research are: (1) conditions concerning the identification and function of television advertising, (2) the impact of advertising on product preferences, and (3) the impact of advertising on the parent–child relationship. The survey technique has been widely used to study the first of these variables. Ward, Reale, and Levinson (1972) conducted a survey of 67 children, ranging in age from 5 to 12 years, concerning their knowledge of television commercials. Each child was asked a series of 16 questions and the answers were transcribed. The responses were content analyzed and placed in categories according to the degree of awareness exhibited by the child. For example, children were asked, "What is a commercial?" Those whose answers showed confused perceptions and low discrimination between commercials and program were categorized as having "low awareness." Answers from "medium-awareness" children showed an understanding of the advertising content and some information about product. "High-awareness" children gave answers characterized by an understanding of the sponsor concept and the motive of the seller. The results of this analysis showed that more than 50% of those 5–7 years old, but only about 13% of those 8–12 years old were in the low-awareness category, suggesting that understanding increases with age.

In a related study, Ward, Levinson, and Wackman (1972) used unobtrusive techniques to study children's attention to television commercials. Mothers were trained to record information about their children's normal viewing behaviors. Using code sheets, they noted whether the child was paying full attention, partial attention, or not watching commercials and programs. Analysis of the resulting data indicated a tendency for all children to exhibit a drop in attention when a commercial was shown, but the youngest group (5–7 years) showed the smallest drop. The researchers suggested that this more stable attention pattern among the youngest children demonstrated the difficulty they have in differentiating between program and commercial. Wartella and Ettema (1974), however, in a more controlled situation with trained observers, found an increase in attention among their youngest age group (nursery children) when the commercials came on. This observation suggested that the discrepancy in findings with the study by Ward et al. might be due to the visual complexity of the ads that were shown in the respective investigations.

The second dependent variable, advertising impact, has been studied using both experimental and survey techniques. Experimental studies that contrast children exposed to television commercials with those not so exposed demonstrate some of the dimensions of this impact. Goldberg and Gorn (1978) showed one group of children commercials for a new toy, while a control group saw no commercials. To examine the ability of commercials to enhance the value of the toy in comparison with the value of being with peers, children were asked to choose between playing with a "nice" child without the advertised toy or with a "not so nice" child with the toy. Almost twice as many children in the control group chose to play with the nice child without the toy; those who saw the commercial more often opted to play with the other child who had the toy.

In a related experiment, Goldberg, Gorn, and Gibson (1978) showed different groups of children: (1) a television show with ads for products high in sugar content, (2) a television show with public service announcements stressing a balanced diet, or (3) an entire program stressing the value of eating a balanced diet. The children were then given a chance to select various snacks and breakfast foods that varied in nutritional value. The group that saw the entire program on a balanced diet selected only a few items that were low in nutrition. The group that saw the ads for the sugared products selected the least nutritional foods. More recently, Kohn and Smart (1984) showed college students a videotape edited into three different versions. One program had nine beer commercials, the second had four such commercials, and the third had none. Subjects could choose beer and other refreshments while watching. Exposure to the first few beer commercials increased consumption, but continued exposure had no further effects.

The survey method investigates impact by correlating respondents' consumption patterns with exposure to ads. For example, Atkin, Reeves, and Gibson (1979) measured preferences in food brands among children 5–12 years old. There was a strong positive relationship between viewing television commercials for the food item and liking the food item. Atkin, Hocking, and Block (1984) sampled teenagers in four different regions of the country. They measured exposure to liquor advertising in several ways. In one method respondents were shown specimen ads and asked how often they remembered seeing the commercial messages represented. Alcohol consumption was measured by asking how many different brands of liquor the respondent had drunk, or how much beer and wine were consumed in a typical week. A regression analysis showed that advertising exposure was the strongest correlate of liquor drinking and ranked second behind peer influence in predicting beer drinking. Advertising exposure showed little relation to wine drinking.

The survey approach has also been used in studying the impact of advertising on parent–child relationships. To illustrate, Atkin (1975) found that children heavily exposed to Saturday morning commercials argued more with their parents when requests for an advertised product were turned down than did light viewers. Ward and Wackman (1972) asked a sample of 109 mothers of children 5–12 years old to report the number of times their children asked them to buy an advertised product, and to estimate the number of times these requests resulted in conflicts. The two variables were significantly related.

Researchers have also relied upon the experimental approach. In the study by Goldberg and Gorn (1978), children were asked how a hypothetical child would respond if his/her parents denied his/her request to purchase a particular toy. A significantly greater proportion of children who saw ads for the toy reported that they would express rejection toward their parents than did those who did not see the ads. Galst and White (1976) allowed children in a nursery school setting to regulate their own viewing of commercials. Subsequently, trained observers followed the children and their mothers to the supermarket and recorded each time a child tried to influence a purchase. There was a significant relationship between viewing television commercials and the number of purchase attempts made at the store.

In sum, both laboratory and survey studies of young consumers have demonstrated that age is an important factor in understanding the purpose of commercials, that ads do have an influence on product desirability, and that television commercials can be a source of friction in the parent–child relationship.

Theoretical Developments

Two main theoretical perspectives have been associated with research dealing with advertising and young people. Predictions from the first, *social learning theory,* suggest that behaviors observed in the media, such as eating certain foods or playing with certain toys, will be imitated by observers, resulting in more consumption of advertised products. In addition, investigators expect to be able to discern conditions that facilitate the social learning process, or inhibit it.

As the foregoing discussion of research methods and results indicates, the main predictions of this theory are substantiated. Watching television commercials for various products apparently leads to children's preferences for and consumption of the advertised products. Additionally, such factors as the presence of a celebrity endorser of the product (Atkin & Block, 1983) or specific audiovisual techniques (Meringoff & Lesser, 1980) can facilitate modeling. On the other hand, alerting the child audience to the persuasive intent of a commercial message seems to inhibit its effects (Sprafkin, Swift, & Hess, 1983). Further research that more accurately defines other contingent influences will make social learning theory more valuable as a predictive tool.

The other theoretical formulation is the *cognitive development theory* associated with Swiss psychologist Jean Piaget. This theory posits that children go through stages of development, one following another in a set pattern, but the age at which a child reaches any given stage depends on the individual. Thus these developmental stages are correlated with, but not synonymous with, the chronological age of the child. Piaget postulated four major stages in cognitive development: (1) the sensorimotor stage, characterized by the child defining his or her environment by behavior (grasping, sucking, etc.) without symbolic representation of objects; (2) the preoperational stage, during which the child develops some reasoning ability; (3) the concrete operations stage, characterized by the use of basic logical operations; and (4) the formal operations stage, in which the child achieves adultlike thought patterns such as abstract thought and hypothetical reasoning.

Much of the research in children's consumer socialization is devoted to applying this developmental mode to the comprehension of television messages. For example, Tada (1969) found that young children (those in the pre-formal operations stage) did not understand the various editing and production techniques used in an instructional film. Noble (1975) reported that preschool children had difficulty in understanding that television programs are "make believe" and that the characters seen on television are actors. Wartella (1980) sums up the results of many of the studies looking at advertising and children. She reported that the development of an understanding of the differences between programs and commercials begins at about age 4, and by kindergarten, most children are able to distinguish between them. Higher level understanding of the functional differences between programs and commercials occurs between kindergarten and third grade.

Recent research has been directed at modifying and refining Piaget's formulations. For example, the theory suggests that the four stages of development are fixed and unchanging, but some evidence suggests that there may be variation. In contrast to the findings of the studies summarized by Adler et al. (1977), as well as his own earlier work with associates (1972), Ward (1980) reported that some kindergarten children could identify the selling purpose of advertising and displayed other consumer-related skills beyond what would be expected from the cognitive stage typically observed in 5-year-olds. Soldow (1983) found greater cognitive ability than predicted by Piaget's theory among his subjects in a test of product recall. On the other hand, Acker and Tiemens (1981) found that logical operations concerning television images occurred among elementary school children at a later age than predicted. In addition, there is evidence that children can be taught to acquire some cognitive abilities earlier than the theory's guidelines predict (Wackman, Wartella, & Ward, 1979). It is likely that much of the future research in this area will further refine cognitive development theory.

Summary

Academic research and private sector research possess similarities and differences. They share common techniques and try to predict and explain behavior, but academic research differs from private sector research in that the former is public, more theoretical in nature, is generally determined more by the individual researcher than by management, and usually costs less than private sector research. Five main research areas that exemplify mass media effects research are: (1) research dealing with the prosocial and antisocial impact of specific media content, (2) uses and gratifications, (3) agenda setting, (4) perceptions of social reality, and (5) advertising and the socialization of children. Each of these areas is typified by its own research history, method, and theoretical formulations.

Questions and Problems for Further Investigation

1. List some topics in addition to those mentioned in this chapter that might interest both private sector and academic researchers.
2. Would it be possible to study agenda setting using the experimental technique? If yes, how might this be done?
3. Assume that as a consultant for a large metropolitan newspaper, you are designing a uses and gratifications study of newspaper reading. What variables would you include in the analysis? If you were instead an academic researcher interested in the same question, how might your investigation differ from the private sector study?
4. List some perceptions of social reality, in addition to those discussed in the chapter, that might be cultivated by heavy media exposure.

References and Suggested Readings

Acker, S., & Tiemens, R. (1981). Children's perception of changes in size of TV images. *Human Communication Research, 7*(4), 340–346.

Adler, R., et al. (1977). *Research on the effects of television advertising on children.* Washington, DC: U.S. Government Printing Office.

Adler, R., Lesser, G., Meringoff, L., Robertson, T., Rossiter, J., & Ward, S. (1980). *The effects of television advertising on children.* Lexington, MA: Lexington Books.

Andison, F. (1977). TV violence and viewer aggression: A cumulation of study results, 1956–76. *Public Opinion Quarterly, 41*(3), 314–331.

Atkin, C. (1975). *Effects on TV advertising on children* (Tech. Rep.). East Lansing: Michigan State University.

Atkin, C., & Block, M. (1983). Effectiveness of celebrity endorsers. *Journal of Advertising Research, 23*(1), 57–62.

Atkin, C., Hocking, J., & Block, M. (1984). Teenage drinking: Does advertising make a difference? *Journal of Communication, 34*(2), 157–167.

Atkin, C., Reeves, B., & Gibson, W. (1979). Effects of television food advertising on children. Paper presented to the Association for Education in Journalism, Houston.

Bandura, A. (1977). *Social learning theory.* Englewood Cliffs, NJ: Prentice-Hall.

Baran, S., Chase, L., & Courtright, J. (1979). Television drama as a facilitator of prosocial behavior. *Journal of Broadcasting, 23*(3), 277–284.

Bear, A. (1984). The myth of television violence. *Media Information Australia, 33*, 5–10.

Becker, L. (1980). Measurement of gratifications. In G. Wilhoit & H. deBock (Eds.), *Mass communication review yearbook* (Vol. I). Beverly Hills, CA: Sage Publications.

Behr, R., & Iyengar, S. (1985). TV news, real-world clues and changes in the public agenda. *Public Opinion Quarterly, 49*(1), 38–57.

Belson, W. (1978). *Television violence and the adolescent boy.* Hampshire, England: Saxon House.

Berelson, B. (1949). What missing the newspaper means. In P. Lazarsfeld & F. Stanton (Eds.), *Communication research, 1948–49.* New York: Harper & Row.

Beurkel-Rothfuss, N., & Mayes, S. (1981). Soap opera viewing and the cultivation effect. *Journal of Communication, 31*(3), 108–115.

Bryant, J., & Zillmann, D. (1984). Using television to alleviate boredom and stress. *Journal of Broadcasting, 28*(1), 1–20.

CBS Broadcast Group. (1974). Fat Albert and the Cosby kids. New York: CBS Office of Social Research.

Chaffee, S. (1984). Defending the indefensible. *Society, 21*(6), 30–35.

Cohen, B. (1963). *The press, the public and foreign policy.* Princeton, NJ: Princeton University Press.

Commission on Obscenity and Pornography. (1970). *The report of the commission on obscenity and pornography.* Washington, DC: U.S. Government Printing Office.

Comstock, G. (1975). *Television and human behavior: The key studies.* Santa Monica, CA: Rand Corporation.

Comstock, G., Chaffee, S., & Katzman, N. (1978). *Television and human behavior.* New York: Columbia University Press.

Cook, T., Kendzierski, D., & Thomas, S. (1983). The implicit assumptions of television research. *Public Opinion Quarterly, 47*(2), 161–201.

deBock, H. (1980). Gratification frustration during a newspaper strike and a TV blackout. *Journalism Quarterly, 57*(1), 61–66.

DeFleur, M., & DeFleur, L. (1967). The relative contribution of television as a learning source for children's occupational knowledge. *American Sociological Review, 32*, 777–789.

Doob, A, & MacDonald, G. (1979). Television viewing and fear of victimization. *Journal of Personality and Social Psychology, 37*(2), 170–179.

Eyal, C., Winter, J., & DeGeorge, W. (1981).The concept of time frame in agenda setting. In G. Wilhoit & H. deBock (Eds.), *Mass communication review yearbook* (Vol. II). Beverly Hills, CA: Sage Publications.

Funkhouser, G. (1973). Trends in media coverage of the issues of the 1960s. *Journalism Quarterly, 50*(3), 533–538.

Galst, J., & White, M. (1976). The unhealthy persuader: The reinforcing value of television and children's purchase influence attempts at the supermarket. *Child Development, 47*(4), 1089–1096.

Gerbner, G., et al. (1977). TV violence profile No. 8. *Journal of Communication, 27*(2), 171–180.

Gerbner, G., et al. (1978). Cultural indicators: Violence Profile No. 9. *Journal of Communication, 28*(3), 176–207.

Gerbner, G., & Gross, L. (1976). Living with television: The Violence Profile. *Journal of Communication, 26*(2), 173–179.

Gerbner, G., Gross, L., Morgan, M., & Signorielli, N. (1980). The mainstreaming of America. *Journal of Communication, 30*(3), 10–29.

Gerson, W. (1966). Mass media socialization behavior: Negro-white differences. *Social Forces, 45*, 40–50.

Goldberg, M., & Gorn, C. (1978). Some unintended consequences of TV advertising to children. *Journal of Consumer Research, 5*(1), 22–29.

Goldberg, M., Gorn, G., & Gibson, W. (1978). TV messages for snack and breakfast foods. *Journal of Consumer Research, 5*(1), 48–54.

Gormley, W. (1975). Newspaper agendas and political elites. *Journalism Quarterly, 52*(2), 304–308.

Greenberg, B. (1974). Gratifications of television viewing and their correlates for British children. In J. Blumler & E. Katz (Eds.), *The uses of mass communication.* Beverly Hills, CA: Sage Publications.

Greenberg, B., & Dominick, J. (1969). Racial and social class differences in teenagers' use of television. *Journal of Broadcasting, 13*(4), 331–344.

Griffin, E. (1976).What's fair to children? *Journal of Advertising, 5*(2), 14–18.

Gross, L., & Morgan, M. (1985). Television and enculturation. In J. Dominick & J. Fletcher (Eds.), *Broadcasting research methods.* Boston: Allyn & Bacon.

Hawkins, R., & Pingree, S. (1981). Using television to construct social reality. *Journal of Broadcasting, 25*(4), 347–364.

Heller, M., & Polsky, S. (1976). *Studies in violence and television.* New York: American Broadcasting Company.

Herzog, H. (1944). What do we really know about daytime serial listeners? In P. Lazarsfeld & F. Stanton (Eds.), *Radio research, 1942–43.* New York: Duell, Sloan & Pearce.

Hilker, A. (1976, November 10). Agenda-setting influence in an off-year election. *ANPA Research Bulletin*, pp. 7–10.

Hirsch, P. (1980). The "scary world" of the non-viewer and other anomalies. *Communication Research, 7*, 403–456.

Hughes, M. (1980). The fruits of cultivation analysis: A re-examination of some effects of television viewing. *Public Opinion Quarterly, 44*(3), 287–302.

Klapper, J. (1960). *The effects of mass communication.* Glencoe, IL: Free Press.

Kohn, P., & Smart, R. (1984). The impact of TV advertising on alcohol consumption. *Journal of Studies on Alcohol, 45*(4), 295–301.

Lang, G., & Lang, K. (1981). Watergate: An examination of the agenda-building process. In G. Wilhoit and H. deBock (Eds.), *Mass communication review yearbook*, pp. 447–468.

Lang, K., & Lang, G. (1966). The mass media and voting. In B. Berelson & M. Janowitz (Eds.), *Reader in public opinion and communication.* New York: Free Press.

Larson, C. U. (1986). *Persuasion* (4th ed.). Belmont, CA: Wadsworth.

Lefkowitz, M., Eron, L., Waldner, L., & Huesmann, L. (1972). Television violence and child aggression. In G. Comstock & E. Rubinstein (Eds.), *Television and social behavior: Vol. III. Television and adolescent aggressiveness.* Washington, DC: U.S. Government Printing Office.

Levy, M., & Windahl, S. (1984). Audience activity and gratifications. *Communication Research, 11*, 51–78.

Liebert, R., & Baron, R. (1972). Short-term effects of televised aggression on children's aggressive behavior. In J. Murray, E. Rubinstein, & G. Comstock (Eds.), *Television and social behavior: Vol. II. Television and social learning.* Washington, DC: U.S. Government Printing Office.

Linz, D., Donnerstein, D., & Penrod, S. (1984). The effects of multiple exposure to film violence against women. *Journal of Communication, 34*(3), 130–147.

Lippmann, W. (1922). *Public opinion.* New York: Macmillan. (Reprint, 1965). New York: Free Press.

McCombs, M. (1981). The agenda setting approach. In D. Nimmo & K. Sanders (Eds.), *Handbook of political communication.* Beverly Hills, CA: Sage Publications.

McCombs, M., & Shaw, D. (1972). The agenda-setting function of mass media. *Public Opinion Quarterly, 36*(2), 176–187.

McLeod, J., Atkin, C., & Chaffee, S. (1972). Adolescents, parents and television use. In G. Comstock & E. Rubinstein (Eds.), *Television and social behavior: Vol. III. Television and adolescent aggressiveness.* Washington, DC: U.S. Government Printing Office.

McLeod, J., & Becker, L. (1981). The uses and gratifications approach. In D. Nimmo & K. Sanders (Eds.), *Handbook of political communication.* Beverly Hills, CA: Sage Publications.

McLeod, J., Becker, L., & Byrnes, J. (1974). Another look at the agenda setting function of the press. *Communication Research, 1*(2), 131–166.

Meringoff, L., & Lesser, G. (1980). The influence of format and audiovisual techniques on children's perceptions of commercial messages. In R. Adler et al. (Eds.), *The effects of television advertising on children.* Lexington, MA: Lexington Books.

Milavsky, J., Kessler, R., Stipp, H., & Rubens, W. (1983). *Television and aggression.* New York: Academic Press.

Milgram, S., & Shotland, R. (1973). *Television and antisocial behavior.* New York: Academic Press.

Minton, J. (1975). The impact of "Sesame Street" on readiness. *Sociology of Education, 48*(2), 141–155.

Mueller, C., Donnerstein, E., & Hallam, J. (1983). Violent films and prosocial behavior. *Personality and Social Psychology Bulletin, 9*, 183–189.

Mullins, E. (1977). Agenda setting and the younger voter. In D. Shaw & M. McCombs (Eds.), *The Emergence of American Political Issues.* St. Paul, MN: West.

Murray, J. (1984). A soft response to hard attacks on research. *Media Information Australia (33)*, 11–16.

National Institute of Mental Health. (1982). *Television and behavior: Ten years of scientific progress and implications for the 1980s.* Washington, DC: U.S. Government Printing Office.

Noble, G. (1975). *Children in front of the small screen.* Beverly Hills, CA: Sage Publications.

Palmgreen, P. (1984). Uses and gratifications: A theoretical perspective. In R. Bostrom (Ed.), *Communication yearbook 8.* Beverly Hills, CA: Sage Publications.

Parke, R., Berkowitz, L., & Leyens, J. (1977). Some effects of violent and non-violent movies on the behavior of juvenile delinquents. *Advances in Experimental Social Psychology, 16*, 135–172.

Patterson, T. & McClure, R. (1976). *The unseeing eye.* New York: G. P. Putnam's.

Roberts, D., & Bachen, C. (1981). Mass communication effects. In M. Rosen-zweig & L. Porter (Eds.), *Annual Review of Psychology.* Palo Alto, CA: Annual Reviews.

Rosengren, K. (1974). Uses and gratifications: A paradigm outlined. In J. Blumler & E. Katz (Eds.), *The uses of mass communication.* Beverly Hills, CA: Sage Publications.

Rothschild, W. (1979). *Group as mediating factor in the cultivation process among young children.* Unpublished M. A. thesis, University of Pennsylvania, Philadelphia.

Rouner, D. (1984). Active television viewing and the cultivation hypothesis. *Journalism Quarterly, 61*(1), 168–174.

Rubin, A. (1979). Television use by children and adolescents. *Human Communication Research, 5*(2), 109–120.

Rubin, A. (1985). Uses and gratifications: Quasi-functional analysis. In J. Dominick & J. Fletcher (Eds.), *Broadcasting research methods.* Boston: Allyn & Bacon.

Schramm, W., Lyle, J., & Parker, E. (1961). *Television in the lives of our children.* Stanford, CA: Stanford University Press.

Siegel, A. (1958). The influence of violence in the mass media upon children's role expectations. *Child Development, 29*, 35–56.

Silbert, M., & Pines, A. (1984). Pornography and sexual abuse of women. *Sex Roles, 10* (11/12), 857–858.

Slater, D., & Elliot, W. (1982). Television influence on social reality. *Quarterly Journal of Speech, 68*(1), 69–79.

Soldow, G. (1983). The processing of information in the young consumer. *Journal of Advertising Research, 12*(3), 4–14.

Sprafkin, J., & Rubinstein, E. (1979). Children's television viewing habits and prosocial behavior. *Journal of Broadcasting, 23*(7), 265–276.

Sprafkin, J., Swift, C., & Hess, R. (1983). *Rx television: Enhancing the preventative impact of TV.* New York: Haworth Press.

Surgeon General's Scientific Advisory Committee on Television and Social Behavior. (1972). *Television and social behavior. Television and growing up* (summary report). Washington, DC: U.S. Government Printing Office.

Tada, T. (1969). Image cognition: A developmental approach. *Studies in Broadcasting, 7,* 105–174.

Tamborini, R., Zillmann, D., & Bryant, J. (1985). Fear and victimization. In R. Bostrom (Ed.), *Communication yearbook 8.* Beverly Hills, CA: Sage Publications.

Tan, A. (1981). *Mass communication theories and research.* Columbus, OH: Grid Publications.

Tannenbaum, P., & Zillmann, D. (1975). Emotional arousal in the facilitation of aggression through communication. In L. Berkowitz (Ed.), *Advances in experimental social psychology.* New York: Academic Press.

Tipton, L., Haney, R., & Baseheart, J. (1975). Media agenda setting in city and state election campaigns. *Journalism Quarterly 52*(1), 15–22.

Wackman, D., Wartella, E., & Ward, S. (1979). *Children's information processing of television advertising.* Washington, DC: National Science Foundation.

Wakshlag, J., Vial, V., & Tamborini, R. (1983). Selecting crime drama and apprehension about crime. *Human Communication Research, 10*(2), 227–241.

Ward, S. (1972). Effects of television advertising on children and adolescents. In E. Rubinstein, G. Comstock, & J. Murray (Eds.), *Television and social behavior: Vol. IV. Television in day-to-day life: Patterns of exposure.* Washington, DC: U.S. Government Printing Office.

Ward, S. (1980). The effects of television advertising on consumer socialization. In R. Adler et al. (Eds.), *The effects of television advertising on children.* Lexington, MA: Lexington Books.

Ward, S., Levinson, D., & Wackman, D. (1972). Children's attention to television advertising. In E. Rubinstein, G. Comstock, & J. Murray (Eds.), *Television and social behavior: Vol. IV. Television in day-to-day life: Patterns of exposure.* Washington, DC: U.S. Government Printing Office.

Ward, S., Reale, G., & Levinson, D. (1972). Children's perceptions, explanations, and judgments of television advertising. In E. Rubinstein, G. Comstock, & J. Murray (Eds.), *Television and social behavior: Vol. IV. Television in day-to-day life: Patterns of exposure.* Washington, DC: U.S. Government Printing Office.

Ward, S., & Wackman, D. (1972). Television advertising and intrafamily influence. In E. Rubinstein, G. Comstock, & J. Murray (Eds.), *Television and social behavior: Vol. IV. Television in day-to-day life: Patterns of exposure.* Washington, DC: U.S. Government Printing Office.

Wartella, E. (1980). Children and television: The development of the child's understanding of the medium. In G. Wilhoit & H. deBock (Eds.), *Mass communication review yearbook.* Beverly Hills, CA: Sage Publications.

Wartella, E., & Ettema, J. (1974). A cognitive developmental study of children's attention to television commercials. *Communication Research, 1*(1), 46–49.

Weaver, D. (1977). Political issues and voter need for orientation. In M. McCombs & D. Shaw (Eds.), *The emergence of American political issues.* St. Paul, MN: West.

Wertham, F. (1954). *The seduction of the innocent.* New York: Holt, Rinehart & Winston.

Williams, W. (1985). Agenda setting research. In J. Dominick & J. Fletcher (Eds.), *Broadcasting research methods.* Boston: Allyn & Bacon.

Williams, W., & Semlak, W. (1978a). Campaign '76: Agenda setting during the New Hampshire primary. *Journal of Broadcasting, 22*(4), 531–540.

Williams, W., & Semlak, W. (1978b). Structural effects of TV coverage on political agendas. *Journal of Communication, 28*(1), 114–119.

Windahl, S. (1981). Uses and gratifications at the crossroads. In G. Wilhoit & H. deBock (Eds.), *Mass communication review yearbook.* Beverly Hills, CA: Sage Publications.

Winick, C., Williamson, L., & Chuzmir, S. (1973). *Children's television commercials: A content analysis.* New York: Praeger.

Winter, J. (1981). Contingent conditions in the agenda setting process. In G. Wilhoit & H. deBock (Eds.), *Mass communication review yearbook.* Beverly Hills, CA: Sage Publications.

Winter, J., & Eyal, C. (1981). Agenda setting for the civil rights issue. *Public Opinion Quarterly, 45*(3), 376–383.

Wurtzel, A., & Lometti, G. (1984). Researching TV violence. *Society, 21*(6), 22–30.

Zillmann, D., & Bryant, J. (1982). Pornography, sexual callousness, and the trivialization of rape. *Journal of Communication, 32*(4), 10–21.

Zillmann, D., Hoyt, J., & Day, K. (1979). Strength and duration of the effect of violent and erotic communication on subsequent aggressive behavior. *Communication Research, 1,* 286–306.

C H A P T E R   1 7

The Computer as a
Research Tool

COMPUTER SYSTEMS
·
THE DEVELOPMENT OF THE MICROCOMPUTER
·
COMPUTER BASICS
·
USING THE COMPUTER IN MASS MEDIA RESEARCH
·
THE ORIGINAL FORM OF COMPUTER ANALYSIS
·
USING A COMPUTER
·
FURTHER SUGGESTIONS FOR OPERATORS
·
SUMMARY
·
QUESTIONS AND PROBLEMS FOR FURTHER INVESTIGATION
·
REFERENCES AND SUGGESTED READINGS

Data analysis in mass media research would be all but impossible today without computers. Researchers rely on computers for simple and complex problems, as well as for retrieving and analyzing ratings information in broadcast research. During the early 1980s, mass media researchers became even more closely tied to computers with the introduction of microcomputers (micros or personal computers). The mass media research field has been literally reshaped in less than 5 years.

That mass media research has become dependent on computers may seem odd to many "old-time" media researchers who recall predictions that "high-speed computers will one day make it possible to analyze complex research problems quickly." Today, however, the predictions of just a few years ago are reality, and ongoing technological developments continue to make computers one of the most fascinating areas of research.

The development of **microcomputers** has changed forever the role of computers in mass media research. It is now possible to conduct even the most sophisticated research using a computer that costs less than $3,000. Thus, an understanding of microcomputers is extremely important for anyone interested in mass media research. From now on, finding a job in media research (or any type of research) will be extremely difficult for a person without a working knowledge of microcomputers. Whereas only a few years ago classified ads for media research positions read "Computer experience helpful," computer literacy is now a requirement. Experience with micros is especially sought after.

This chapter, which serves as an introduction to computers, with an emphasis on micros, does *not* explain every aspect of computers in detail. Numerous magazines and periodicals are devoted solely to the topic of technological innovations in computers. With that in mind, we offer this suggestion. The discussion of computers in this chapter relates to the field as of mid-1985. However, computer technology changes at a dramatic rate, and readers interested in mass media research should keep an eye on a few of the following magazines and periodicals, which discuss computer use and technological innovations. These are a few of the many publications that can serve as sources of information about the use of computers and related technological developments:

- PC Magazine
- PC World

- PC Tech Journal
- Computer Graphics World
- InfoWorld
- Systems & Software
- Personal Computing
- PC Week

Computer Systems

Computer systems come in three basic types, or configurations.

1. Batch processing. The user is required to "log on" to the batch system by way of a "dumb" terminal or microcomputer, that is, a terminal that is not capable of performing calculations on its own. This terminal, which can be located either on site or at a remote location, merely acts as an input device; it must rely on the *mainframe* "host" to perform the necessary calculations. The mainframe itself is a large computer system, but the microcomputer can run programs independent of the mainframe

In the batch configuration, the user inputs a job into the mainframe and results are either displayed immediately on a video screen or provided in hard copy form (that is, print). Most colleges and universities in the United States use some form of batch processing, although stand-alone personal computers are also commonly used.

2. Time sharing. This process is similar to batch processing in that the user communicates with a mainframe computer via a dumb terminal or microcomputer. In a time-sharing system, however, several users have simultaneous access to the large mainframe computer. Not only can users take advantage of the sophistication of the mainframe, they also benefit in many cases from using large **data bases**—computer files of data for individuals to use. Because the computer is large, it is able to handle several different applications at once, making the best use of the system. In many time-sharing systems the user can *download*, or copy data from the mainframe to the remote computer system, then sign off the system and manipulate the data at a convenient time. Nielsen, Arbitron, and Birch Radio all have time-sharing systems that permit their customers to access ratings data.

3. Stand-alone. The stand-alone computer system, which operates independently from a mainframe, can be used to perform almost any task of calculation or word processing without the necessity of communicating with an outside system; it can be used in the batch and time-sharing configurations, as well. The personal computer has become the most important addition to mass media research because researchers are no longer tied to a mainframe and can even purchase a micro system without a great investment.

The Development of the Microcomputer

Up until about the late 1950s, the only type of computer available to the public was the large mainframe, which often required several people to operate. IBM, Univac, Honeywell, and several other companies provided the "monster" machines primarily to the large companies and academic institutions that could afford them. In the late 1950s, however, Digital Equipment Corporation and Hewlett Packard provided the first minicomputers to the general public. Although these devices, too, were quite expensive (about $30,000), the new technology provided an incentive for the larger hardware manufacturers to develop computers for the home.

The force behind the development of the personal computer came from technological advancements. Engineers first replaced the old vacuum tubes with transitors. But it was in 1974 that the real breakthrough happened: Intel introduced the 8080 microprocessor (MPU), a tiny chip of silicon that contained the equivalent of several thousand transistors. The first machine to use the Intel 8080 chip was the Altair; sales of this computer kit, designed by Ed Roberts, began in 1975.

In 1975 Steve Jobs and Steve Wozniak introduced the Apple I computer, followed by the Apple II in 1977. Then in 1978 Radio Shack brought out the now standard 5¼-inch disk drives (discussed later) and began marketing its own computers in 1979. Apple III was introduced in 1980, along with pesonal computers from Hewlett Packard, Epson, Digital Research, and others. The IBM PC appeared in 1981, and by then the major computer companies were hustling to develop faster, more portable systems. The highly competitive personal computer market forces all vendors to produce technologically sophisticated systems. Apple, IBM, Radio Shack, Compaq, and many other companies strive for the largest market share. All the competition means that the newest computer equipment existing at this moment (even as you read this sentence) will no longer be state of the art in just a few months.

Computer Basics

In the following section, we discuss the elementary aspects of computers to introduce those of you who do not yet have computer experience. To use computers, most media researchers need not know more about how computers function than is presented here—just as one needn't know how a car engine works to drive a car.

Hardware

The term **hardware** designates all the computer's physical equipment. A basic computer system consists of the central processing unit, or CPU (the main body of the computer); memory (the way the computer stores data); and **peripheral** components (which are attached to the CPU): the keyboard, for input, and the monitor and printer, for output. Other peripherals include modems and networks.

Input. An input device is any external device used to enter data into the computer. In the earliest computers, data had to be input via computer cards (discussed later in this chapter). However, the data card information could be transferred to a disk or tape for easier manipulation.

Today, the most common input device is the standard keyboard, and the input operation can be viewed on a monitor. In the early 1980s, however, the Mouse Systems Corporation designed the "mouse." This has become the generic term for small, box-type external devices that allow the user to point to any portion of the monitor by pushing a button (or one of two or more buttons) on the mouse. The mouse is especially handy in graphics work because the user merely touches the mouse to point to information on the monitor that is to be included in the graphic.

The newest type of input device, the **optical character reader (OCR),** represents an application of a technological system that has existed for quite some time. The OCR scans pages of text, digitizes the copy, and converts the resulting numbers into ASCII characters (described below) that can be analyzed by any type of software. The earliest form of OCR was developed for supermarkets to read bar codes from packages. Data entry other than bar codes, however, is much more complicated. The current OCRs can read only printed material, but readers that can also scan handwritten documents are not far in the future.

An input-related device is the terminal emulator. This piece of equipment is either a software package or a printed circuit board added to the computer to allow the machine to function as a dumb terminal.

Central processing unit. The **central processing unit (CPU),** or the heart of the computer, decides the order in which computations are to be made, determines where information is to be stored, sends information to the peripheral devices, and controls the operation of the entire system. The CPUs for the early mainframe computers generally took up several rooms. Silicon chip technology has reduced the CPU to incredibly small sizes. However, a CPU can still be very large (taking up the greater portion of a 10 foot × 10 foot room), such as the Cray

2, a supercomputer capable of performing hundreds of millions of calculations per second. In a microcomputer, the main body, which often houses the **disk drives** (the devices that read information from computer disks), also houses the CPU chip(s).

CPUs are differentiated by the number of **bits** that are processed at a time. Microcomputers process information using a language code called **ASCII,** short for **American Standard Code for Information Interchange.** (Mainframe IBM computers use another language called EBCDIC, short for Extended Binary Coded Decimal Interchange Code, a system somewhat more complex than ASCII). Each letter or character, such as the letter "b" or number "4," is called a **byte.** Each byte is made up of seven bits (the eighth bit is used only for special characters or instructions, and is generally a zero for all other characters). The computer's CPU stores data, or reads it, one location at a time. Therefore, only eight bits of data are removed during a single access cycle. Some computers are 8-bit systems, which access or remove from memory 8 bits per cycle. **Bit processing** for most personal computers is done with 8-bit systems, although the current trend is to 16-bit machines. The development of the 32-bit system is not far in the future.

Memory. A computer's size is judged by its capacity to store data. The **random access memory** or **RAM,** sometimes called the computer's *main memory*, stores information in units called bytes. A byte consists of 8 **bits,** or *b*inary dig*it*s, the 0s and 1s that are used in the actual encoding of data. The computer's size is stated by the number of bytes it can store in RAM. For example, a computer may be capable of storing 64,000 bytes of data, or possibly 320,000 bytes. Since these numbers are large, a shorthand form is used for brevity—1,000 bytes is shortened to 1K, where "K" stands for "kilo," the scientific prefix for "thousand." Thus a 64,000-byte capacity is shortened to 64K. Most personal computers can be fitted with additional hardware called *expansion boards*, which permit an increase in the RAM capacity of a machine, usually in increments of 64K.

A computer's permanent memory—memory that cannot be altered or changed in any way—is called the **read only memory,** or **ROM.** For example, when an IBM PC is turned on, the machine will automatically load, or boot, the programming language that is permanently stored in the machine's ROM, namely IBM BASIC.

On the other hand, the **programmable read only memory,** or **PROM,** contains information that is permanently stored but can be reprogrammed if necessary. A PROM is used to store information that is likely to be used in the same way time and time again. For example, cable television systems use PROMs in their channel converters to provide customers with pay services such as HBO or Showtime. Customers who wish to receive a pay service bring their channel converter to the cable system for insertion of a PROM for the particular service. The

PROM will only decode one pay service, that is, its job is always the same. If another service is desired, a different PROM must be inserted in the converter, or the cable system might reprogram the PROM to receive another service.

Buffer. Computers are incredibly fast devices. In most cases the computer works faster than the equipment attached to it—the peripheral devices. For example, the computer sends information to the printer much faster than the printer can produce hard copy. To solve this problem, most computers include a **buffer,** which is simply a block of memory in which the computer stores data until they can be processed by the peripheral. Thus "excess" data outputted to a printer are stored in a print buffer, allowing the user to continue with an additional task while the printer is completing the job. Print buffers can be almost any size, from a few thousand bytes to several million.

Combination board. Designed to save space in the computer, the *combination board* is simply a printed circuit board that contains a variety of integrated circuits capable of performing a variety of functions. The boards include memory expansion chips, graphics capability chips, and other chips to expand the available functions of the computer. Examples of combination boards include the Quadboard II and Megaplus.

Storage. A computer's RAM is only a temporary storage device. When the machine is turned off, the contents of the RAM are erased. To make a permanent record of the information, the data must be stored externally. The most popular data storage devices rely on some type of magnetic medium, a storage process very similar to the familiar audio and video tapes used for entertainment. A more recent form of storage device is the bubble memory system, which stores data in a liquid medium.

Floppy disks and **hard disks** are typical storage devices. Both of these disks are run by disk drives, the physical unit that rotates the disk so the head (similar to an audiotape head) can read data from the disk. Floppy disks are made in a variety of sizes from microdisks to the larger 8-inch disk. The most common is the 5¼-inch *double sided/double density* disk, which has a total storage capacity of about 360K. The floppy disks for the IBM AT are capable of storing up to about 1.2 million bytes of data. A hard disk, on the other hand, may store several million bytes. The scientific prefix for "million" is "mega," abbreviated "M" or "Mb"; thus a 20-megabyte hard (20M or 20Mb) disk can store up to 20 million bytes of data. Hard disks can be fixed (that is, the disk remains permanently in the disk storage unit) or removable (for users who have large amounts of data that cannot fit on one hard disk).

Before a disk can be used in a computer, it must be **formatted** to the *disk operating system* (*DOS*) of the machine. That is, the disk has to be made ready for the computer's DOS. Formatting, or initialization, is a simple procedure described in every computer manual and takes about 60 seconds to complete for each disk. Because the DOS of a computer varies from manufacturer to manufacturer, disks cannot be readily interchanged from one machine to another.

Regardless of the storage medium used, there should be at least one spare, or backup, copy of any important data. If data stored in only one place are accidentally erased, it is usually impossible to recover the information. There are many "horror stories" of computer users who failed to make a backup of information and lost many important, unreplicable data. The most basic rule in using a computer is to make a backup of all important data. It is interesting to see how quickly computer users learn to back up important data after an important document has been accidentally erased.

Output. Users can view what is entered into the computer as well as the results of any calculations or word-processing operations on a television-type screen called a **monitor,** or CRT (cathode ray tube). Monitors are available in a variety of sizes and may display data in monochrome (white, green, or amber) or in color. In most cases, a color monitor and a graphics adapter (a printed circuit board added to the computer) are necessary if the computer is to be used to generate colored graphs and other graphics. Color monitors are also known as RGBs, for red-green-blue.

A **printer** is a computer controlled "typewriter"; upon command from the user, it generates the results of the computations or word-processing data entered into the CPU. There are a wide variety of printers, from very simple and inexpensive dot-matrix printers, to letter-quality daisy wheel printers, to the highly sophisticated laser devices such as the Hewlett Packard LaserJet.

Some computer users also prefer to have a plotter as an additional piece of basic equipment. Plotters are used to produce quality artwork such as bar graphs and architectural renderings, which the typical printer cannot produce.

Modems and networks. The term **modem** is a contracted form of two words: *mo*dulate-*dem*odulate, which describe the function of the device. This small piece of equipment allows for communication between two computers via telephone lines.When modems have built-in auto-dial and auto-answering capabilities, computers can "communicate" without human intervention. That is, one computer can be instructed to send or receive information at a specific time of day without further instructions from an operator. When data are sent from one computer to another, the modem translates the electrical signals into signals that can be sent over telephone lines. When data are received, the modem translates the information back into electrical signals the computer can understand.

Not all modems are external, however. Some personal computers have a built-in **acoustic modem** or *coupler,* which allows the user to place a telephone receiver into two rubber cradles for transmission and receiving.

Modems send information in different speeds, known as a *baud rate*, which is the number of signal elements or *bits* transmitted from one computer to another. One baud is typically equivalent to one bit per second (bps), so a 300-baud modem sends or receives data at 300 bits per second, or about 30 characters per second. Modems are available to send up to 2400 baud, a rate that will surely increase in the future.

Many research departments and other facilities that use computers often need to share hardware and software. This need created the *local area network* or *LAN*. The LAN allows several different users to perform independent tasks while sharing the same equipment. For example, three microcomputers (nodes) may be joined together (both physically by wires and by software designed for the LAN), permitting one user to input data while another prints data and the third uses a plotter. In other words, any PC on the network system can use any peripheral or the files from any disk drive. A common use of the LAN is to connect several PCs to a hard disk and a printer, so that all units can use the services of both pieces of equipment.

Software

Computer **software** is any type of ready-to-use computer program for mathematical computations or word processing, for producing graphics or spreadsheets, or for sending communications (messages or data) from one point to another. Consumers do not need a knowledge of computer programming to operate most general purpose software programs. Most companies strive to produce software that is simple to use and understand (although there are varying definitions of "user friendly").

Software is available for tasks as simple as checkbook balancing to very sophisticated statistical analysis packages. The *integrated* software package, developed in 1984, has changed the software business. This type of package, which generally includes three separate program capabilities—word processing, spreadsheet or data base management, and graphics—eliminates the need to change programs to accomplish the different tasks. Data are easily transferred from one program to another within the package. Three popular integrated packages are SuperCalc 3 (Release 2), Symphony, and Framework.

There are thousands of types of software available for mainframes and personal computers, but not all software can be used on all machines. Thus software written for one type of machine may not be compatible, or usable, on another machine. If the instructions for a piece of software are written for a Compaq computer and say "compatible with the IBM-PC," the software will run on both personal computers. On the other hand, incompatibility may limit the usefulness of some material.

Computer software may be written in one of many different languages such as BASIC, Pascal, or COBOL. When a piece of software is written, the programmer must know which computer will be used to execute the program because each system uses somewhat different operating commands to perform calculations and word processing.

Using the Computer in Mass Media Research

The versatile computer is used not only for data analysis but also for word processing when preparing reports, and for routine record keeping and file maintenance. In fact, the conventional typewriter has become extinct in many research departments because it is so slow and limited in its functions.

This section summarizes some of the primary uses of microcomputers in mass media research. As might be expected, a complete list of possible uses for the personal computer cannot be included because new software is constantly being developed.

Fortunately, mass media researchers do not have to program their own software for data analysis or word processing. Nearly any conceivable piece of software already exists or is planned for introduction very quickly. The primary task of the researcher is to decide which software is the most appropriate for the job at hand. Researchers sometimes need unique programs for specific jobs, but this is a rare occurrence; seldom is programming expertise required of a researcher.

The sections that follow describe some of the principal types of software used by media researchers in conjunction with a personal computer.

Data Analysis

The most popular general-utility statistical package for mainframe computers is the Statistical Package for the Social Sciences (SPSS-X). The SPSS-X program has been used since the early 1970s, and the creators of the package have continuously updated the material as methodologies have changed. In 1985, SPSS-PC was introduced for personal computers. Media researchers who do not have access to microcomputers probably will use the mainframe SPSS-X package for most data analysis. However, there are other good general-utility packages available, such as SAS.

When personal computers became popular, researchers naturally demanded to have packages similar to SPSS-X available for their stand-alone systems. But software for statistical data analysis on personal computers was the slowest to develop because the early machines did not have enough memory to enable complex calculations. Once the bigger and faster machines were introduced, statistical software began to appear at a very rapid rate. The most recent packages—such as SPSS-PC and the Wolonick StatPac—include the ability to conduct both univariate and multivariate analyses.

In a review of statistical packages for microcomputers, Fridlund (1985) noted that performing complex statistical analyses on mainframe computers was often very slow and difficult. However, he suggests:

> Times have changed. The mainframe approach has given way to statistical packages that will run on personal computers, adding convenience and features that let you concentrate on the data and not the computer.

Nearly all statistical software packages are menu driven; that is, the instructions for operating the program are shown on the screen in stages: the user follows one instruction; then the next instruction, or set of choices, is displayed. In many cases the programs enable the researcher to accomplish a complicated task by entering only one or two pieces of information.

Statistical software is available in a variety of levels, and it is important to verify how much memory is needed to run a given statistical package. In most cases the programs require a minimum of 256K, with most suggesting up to 512K storage.

Word Processing

Statistical software opened the door to many researchers who did not have access to a mainframe computer. Research became a much simpler task. But the introduction of word-processing software has provided researchers with a tremendous amount of flexibility in preparing questionnaires and other measurement instruments as well as in writing the final research report.

It's very easy for researchers to get excited about the statistical software available for personal computers, but perhaps the word-processing capability is even more important in the daily routine of the mass media analyst. Word processing provides the freedom to write and edit a document without having to retype the entire text; sentences, paragraphs, or pages can be moved with ease. And most word-processing software includes some type of spell checking program that cuts down on proofreading time.

Word processing is possible either by using a dedicated word processor (computer designed solely for word processing) or with a personal computer and software designed for the system. Both types work very well.

One particularly strong advantage of word-processing systems is their filing capability. Users can store hundreds of documents, limited only by the capacity of the storage device, and can have the computer search for any documents on file. The time saved in searching filing cabinets alone makes word-processing extremely helpful for any researcher. With word processing readily available to anyone who has access to a personal computer, it makes very little sense to produce material on a standard typewriter.

Spreadsheets

Spreadsheet software is probably the most versatile tool available for personal computers. The more sophisticated packages not only can be used to produce tabular data, but also word-processing and graphics capabilities. In addition, nearly any type of statistical procedure can be performed on a spreadsheet. The only requirement for the researcher is to input the exact procedural steps. However, this can be done quite simply by an experienced spreadsheet user.

Researchers without much experience with microcomputers should select a spreadsheet package as their first purchase. Spreadsheets are extraordinarily flexible and versatile.

Graphics

Many media researchers use the graphics capabilities in spreadsheet software; however, for more professional looking artwork, a graphics package is required. As with other types of software, graphics packages have become very sophisticated and allow users to develop many styles of graphic presentation. In addition, several packages allow the user to go from computer to high-resolution photographic slide with just a touch of a button. Many large research departments have the expensive systems necessary to produce high-quality graphics.

Data Management

Data management systems are popular with researchers who need to account for large amounts of data and to be able to sort or find specific pieces of information very quickly. Quite simply, a data management package is very similar to a card catalog in a library.

Many researchers feel that data management programs are unnecessary because spreadsheets can be used for the same purpose. The more sophisticated spreadsheets can store several hundred thousand bytes of information on one sheet, and the programs include very simple procedures to locate specific pieces of information.

Microcomputers and Broadcast Audience Ratings

Access to a variety of data bases via time sharing is no novelty to mass media researchers. Broadcast researchers have been able to access Nielsen and Arbitron data through dumb terminals for many years. Now, however, several independent companies purchase Arbitron, Nielsen, and Birch data tapes and make them available to media researchers for use on personal computers.

The availability of data for further analysis has changed the type of research that can be produced. With the present ratings software, researchers are able to quickly produce a wide variety of charts, graphs, and tables that are used for advertising sales.

Arbitron has made additional strides in the use of microcomputers by offering to radio stations monthly ratings ("monthlies"), available only by microcomputer. This is the first step in Arbitron's planned elimination of hard copy ratings books. In the near future, the company will have rating information available only through microcomputer; any part of the book, or the whole survey, may be requested.

The Original Form of Computer Analysis

Even though microcomputers have become the most popular computer in the media research field, many researchers in both public and private sectors still use the old method of computer analysis—data input by computer cards for use in a mainframe computer. Computer card analysis is not obsolete for two main reasons: replacing card equipment is very expensive, and cards provide protection for the data—they cannot be purged (erased) by another researcher, and they can take rougher treatment than disks and tape.

This section provides a brief overview of the computer card system for researchers who may still encounter the process.

Computer Cards

Computer cards are pieces of heavy paper, measuring 3¼ inches × 7⅜ inches. Each card contains 80 columns in which holes (representing numbers, letters, or characters) are punched by means of a keypunch machine. Each column on the card represents only a single data entry—one letter, character, or number. There are also 12 positions, or rows, on each card; the lower 10 positions correspond to the numbers 0 through 9, and the top pair are used for characters or letters.

Although computer cards are fairly resilient, they must be handled carefully. Any change in the card's original form ("do not fold, spindle, or mutilate") makes it impossible for the card reader to interpret the punched information. Cards can be ruined by damage that is invisible to the naked eye. Even exposure to high humidity will alter the size of the punched holes as well as the size of the card itself. The computer card has been replaced by data entry via terminals, or data stored on disks and tape.

The Keypunch Machine

A keypunch machine is similar to a standard typewriter (or a common computer keyboard), and the process of using the machine can be learned as easily. Unlike a typewriter, however, a keypunch machine perforates cards with patterns of holes that represent the data (although the data are also printed along the top of the card for the convenience of the researcher or keypunch operator). Another difference between keypunch machines and typewriters is that the former use only capital letters; the shift key, known as the "numerical" key, is depressed to produce numbers and special characters.

Keypunch machines vary according to manufacturer, and details concerning their operation are not described here. The same basic procedure is followed with all models, however. The cards are inserted in the upper right-hand portion of the machine, released individually into the central portion of the machine, punched, and stored in the upper left-hand portion of the machine when punching is completed.

The Card Reader

The high-speed card reader is used to input the information into the computer; the device electronically "reads" the holes punched in each card. The card reader is simple to operate: cards are placed in a loading area, and a key is pushed to begin the reading process. Card readers can process several thousand cards per minute.

Running a Program

Although the computer card system takes a bit more time than input by terminal or microcomputer, it is quite simple to run a program. The deck of computer cards produced by the researcher includes all the necessary instructions for the computer to conduct the analysis. The first few cards in a deck give the control statements, telling the computer what statistical package or other type of program is desired. The remaining cards include the specific type of statistical analysis desired and the data cards. The entire deck is fed into the card reader, and the researcher need only wait for the hard copy printout.

Using a Computer

The experience a person can acquire from using a computer obviously depends on the facilities available. Most colleges and universities offer students a chance to learn to use some type of computer equipment. Some of the larger computer companies have developed special purchase plans that enable institutions and students to buy microcomputers at a very low cost. These plans have made it easy for students to gain practical experience with the machines. However, freedom of access to computers varies among schools.

Accordingly, the first step in using a computer is to learn the basic rules and procedures of the computer center in which it is located. This can be done by talking to people who have used the facilities before or to members of the computer center staff. An introduction to the computer facility is necessary to acquaint the student with the equipment.

The second step for the beginning computer operator should be to select an easy program and use it to analyze a simple problem. Data for such an exercise can be found in most elementary statistics books. It is important to read the manual for the selected program. The manual explains what type of statistics can be run and how to enter the data.

Beginners should not worry about the quality of the analyses they conduct in early computer runs. The idea is to learn the basic procedures, not to produce significant results. One must start by analyzing relatively simple hypotheses to gain the experience necessary to tackle more meaningful and complex issues.

The third step is to use the computer often to keep abreast of program changes and innovations. The SPSS-X and SPSS-PC programs, for example, are constantly updated with releases of new subprograms, alterations to existing subprograms, and changes in all procedures. These will go unnoticed unless the computer is used regularly.

The introduction of microcomputers has also created the interest in computer clubs. These organizations are excellent for novice computer operators and should be considered seriously by anyone interested in learning how to use a computer. Most clubs have informational meetings and make available to their members a wide variety of software.

Further Suggestions for Operators

Experience is important in using any type of electronic equipment, and computers are no exception. One can read books and listen to lectures about how to operate computers, but there is no substitute for actually sitting down and using one. Researchers who use the computer often quickly learn shortcuts for many procedures. They also learn to avoid minor problems that can arise in, for example, data entry. The following list of suggestions, which addresses some of the basic problems the beginning operator may encounter, may facilitate using the computer.

1. Don't be afraid to try any type of computer. Unless you physically abuse the equipment, nothing can break. Many beginning users have a fear of destroying expensive equipment. It won't happen.

2. During your initial uses of a computer, be sure that any information you are using, or any software you are trying, has a backup. Accidental erasure of material is always possible; a backup will solve any problem.

3. Read the program (or user's) manual before attempting to use any program. Although some manuals are written in very difficult language, most of them provide answers to the beginning user's questions. Many software companies also provide an 800 telephone number to use if problems are not answered in the manual.

4. Never assume that the data have been entered correctly. Before running a program, double-check all entries. Entry errors are very common, and a great deal of time and money can be saved if everything on the screen is carefully proofread before hitting the "run" button.

5. Handle data disks and tapes with care. These storage media contain magnetic information and can be damaged quite easily by, for example, the pressure of a pen or pencil. Therefore, never write on the protective cover of a floppy disk. The labels included with all floppy disks should be filled out before placing them on the disk, not after. Also, keep disks and tapes away from the sun and all other sources of heat, all liquids, telephones (a ringing telephone bell creates electromagnetic energy that may erase or obliterate data), small children, animals, food, and all magnetic devices. (Keeping storage devices away from sources of magnetism means, among other things, not placing a disk or tape on top of a monitor.)

6. Always make a backup of important data or information.

7. When computer cards are used, either keypunch the questionnaire number on the card or number all the cards in the deck with a pencil or felt-tip marker—a small number in the upper right-hand corner will suffice. This will save a great deal of time and frustration if the deck is accidentally dropped. Also, if data cards will be used several times, store the data on tape or disk: cards tend to wear out after several passes through the card reader.

8. Try more than one type of software to determine which works best in given situations.

9. Ask questions. Thousands of people use computers, and nearly all are willing to help someone learn. Don't be afraid to ask.

Summary

This chapter has introduced the basics of computers, especially micros. Computer use and the associated technology change very quickly. Within the past 5 years the microcomputer has drastically altered the media research field. Although researchers still use mainframe computers, they now have the flexibility to use micros, which often makes a project much easier and faster.

It is important to keep up to date with the computer field. This does not mean that all people interested in media research need to become computer experts. In fact, just the opposite is true. The difference that exists between statisticians and data analysts also is present in the computer field: there are developers and users. Nearly every type of media research position falls into the users category, however. Other people will develop the hardware and software. The researcher's task is merely to learn how to use these items.

Questions and Problems for Further Investigation

The list of questions and problems for further investigation in a chapter on computers could be several hundred pages long. However, since some people are just beginning to use the machines, while others have used them for several years, we offer brief but separate sets of exercises.

Beginners: Make every effort to read the periodicals listed at the beginning of this chapter. Many individual issues contain valuable introductory articles. If you haven't used a microcomputer, try to get access to one at a college or university or other computing center. Begin by running a few simple software packages to get the feel of the machine and what it can do. And be sure to ask questions. There are bound to be a few "hackers" nearby who will be more than happy to help you learn. Joining a local PC users' club is also extremely helpful in learning about the basics of microcomputers.

Experienced users: The development of integrated software packages has made it possible for users to combine several sophisticated programs in one system. Experiment with these packages to determine what they can do. Although user's manuals offer a variety of suggestions, there always seem to be other uses not mentioned. For example, the user's manual may not state that the original spreadsheet software is easily adaptable for word processing.

References and Suggested Readings

Fridlund, A. J. (1985, February 11). Taking the numbers bull by the horns. *InfoWorld, 12,* pp. 42–50.

Rubin, R. B., Rubin, A. M., & Piele, L. J. (1987). *Communication research: Strategies and sources.* Belmont, CA: Wadsworth.

C   H   A   P   T   E   R   1 8

Research Reporting, Ethics, and Financial Support

RESEARCH REPORTS
■
RESEARCH ETHICS
■
FINDING SUPPORT FOR MASS MEDIA RESEARCH
■
SUMMARY
■
QUESTIONS AND PROBLEMS FOR FURTHER INVESTIGATION
■
REFERENCES AND SUGGESTED READINGS

C hapters 13–16 discussed mass media research from the planning stages of a study to the selection of the most appropriate statistical methods for testing purposes. Chapter 17 introduced the computer as a research tool. This chapter focuses on three other areas that are not part of the research process itself but are nevertheless vital to the execution of any research project: reporting, ethics, and financial support.

Research Reports

The first step in writing any research report is to identify the intended readers. This is an important decision because the organization, style, and even the mode of presentation depend on the target audience. In mass media research, there are typically two types of audiences and two types of research reports:

1. Reports aimed at colleagues and intended for publication in scholarly and professional journals or for presentation at a convention
2. Reports aimed at decision makers and intended for in-house use only

The format, length, style, and organization of a published report will have to conform to the guidelines of the journal in which it appears. Since colleagues are the target audience for such reports and papers, the writer must pay close attention to the theory underlying the research, the methods used, and the techniques of analysis. In the second instance, there is more flexibility. Some decision makers prefer to be briefed orally by the researcher. In such cases the verbal presentation might be supplemented by a written summary, handouts, visual aids, and, on request, a detailed report. In other circumstances, the researcher might prepare a written report with a short executive summary, confining most of the technical material to appendixes. No matter what the situation or audience, the primary goal in all research reports is accuracy.

The Need for Accurate Reporting Procedures

Researchers need to report research accurately for two reasons. First, a clear explanation of the investigator's methods provides an opportunity for readers to more completely understand the project. Researchers should keep in mind that in most cases, a reader's knowledge of a given project is based solely on the information contained in the report. Since readers do not instinctively understand each procedure used in a study, these details must be supplied. Second, an accurate report provides the necessary information for those who wish to replicate the study. As Rummel (1970) suggested:

> Enough information must be included or filed somewhere in public archives to enable reproduction of the study without the necessity of personal contact with the investigator. This is to ensure that a study is always replicable regardless of the decades or generations that may pass.

Rummel has even argued that researchers should be able to replicate a published study from the information contained therein. Realistically speaking, however, this is not always possible. Mass media journals have limited space, and journal editors do not have the luxury of printing all raw data, tables, and graphs generated by a study; they are forced to eliminate some essential information. Therefore, Rummel's alternative—**data archives**—is very important. Unfortunately, the mass media field has yet to establish its own data archive service for researchers to use.

The conclusion, then, is that individual researchers must take full responsibility for accurately reporting and storing their own research data. To facilitate this task, the following subsections describe the important elements of research that should be included in a published study. The lists may appear long in some cases, but in reality, most of the information can be contained in a few short sentences. At any rate, it is better to include too much information than too little.

The Mechanics of Writing a Research Report

Beginning researchers may find the writing style used for research reports awkward or unaesthetic, but there is a definite purpose behind the rules governing scientific writing: clarity. Every effort must be made to avoid ambiguity.

Given the wide variety of approaches to research, it stands to reason that the possible approaches to writing a research report are equally varied. However, most research reports include only five basic sections or chapters: an introduction, a review of literature and/or a justification, a description of methodologies, a presentation of results, and a summary or conclusion. This format is used both in articles for professional publication and in management summaries.

The introductory section should alert the reader to what is to follow. Broadly speaking, it should identify the research problem or question under investigation as well as offer a brief rationale for the research. The potential significance or importance of the study should be noted, too. As the name implies, the literature review section briefly recapitulates work done in the field. This review is not meant to be exhaustive; the writer should summarize the major points of the directly relevant research studies. The literature review, however, is more than a simple cataloguing of research studies. It must also contain analysis and synthesis. The writer must discuss the relevance of the cited studies to the current project. What theoretic development can be seen in past work? What major conclusions were drawn? What common problems cropped up in past research? How do the answers to these questions relate to the current study? The ultimate aim of this section is to show how your study evolved out of past efforts and how the prior research provided justification for your study.

The methods section describes the approach used to confront the research problem. Some of the topics that are usually mentioned in this section are as follows.

1. Variables used in the analysis. This includes a description of both independent and dependent variables, explaining how the variables were selected for the study, what marker variables, if any (see Chapter 3) were included, and how extraneous variables were controlled. Each variable also requires some justification for its use—variables cannot be added without reason. The mean and the standard deviation for each variable should be reported when necessary.

2. Sample size. The researcher should state the number of subjects or units of study and also explain how these entities were selected. Additionally, any departure from normal randomization must be described in detail.

3. Sample characteristics. The sample should also be described in terms of its demographic, lifestyle, or other descriptor characteristics. When human subjects are used, at least their age and sex should be indicated.

4. Methodology. Every research report requires a description of the methods used to collect and analyze data. The amount of methodological description to be included depends on the audience; articles written for journals, for instance, must contain more detailed information than reports prepared in private sector research.

5. Data manipulation. Often the collected data are not normally distributed, and researchers must use data transformation to achieve an approximation of normality. If such a procedure is used, a full explanation should be given.

The results section contains the findings of the research. All relevant data are presented, as well as the results of any appropriate statistical tests. Tables, charts, graphs, and other data displays should be presented in their most parsimonious form. The last section of the research report might contain a summary of the project and a general discussion of the implications of the study. In addition, this section usually includes a consideration of the limitations of the research, a statement of the contributions the study makes to current knowledge, and an interpretation of the theoretical and/or social significance of the findings. The researcher should also describe the relationship of the current findings to previous research, pointing out similarities and differences. If the research involved hypothesis testing, the researcher should state directly whether each hypothesis was or was not supported. Questions raised in the introductory section should be addressed as well. The final section usually ends with a discussion of future research directions.

Since the writing requirements for journal articles and business or government reports vary in several ways, the following guidelines are divided into two sections.

There are nine principal guidelines for writing for scholarly journals.

1. Avoid using first personal pronouns: I, me, my, we, and so on. Research reports are almost always written in third person ("Subjects were selected randomly." "Subject A told the researcher, . . ." etc.). First personal pronouns should be used only when the article is a commentary.

2. When submitting a paper for professional publication, place each table, graph, chart, and figure on a separate page. This is done because if the article is accepted, these pages will be typeset by one department of the printing company and the text by another. (In management reports, tables, graphs, and other displays are included in the text unless they are too large, in which case they should be placed on separate pages.)

3. Read the authors' guidelines published by each journal. They provide specific rules concerning acceptable writing style, footnote and bibliography formats, the number of copies to submit, and so forth. A researcher who fails to follow these guidelines may decrease the chance that his or her report will be accepted for publication—or at least substantially delay the process while alterations are made.

4. Be stylistically consistent with regard to tables, charts, graphs, section headings, and so forth. Tables, for example, should follow the same format and should be numbered consecutively.

5. Clearly label all displays with meaningful titles. Each table, graph, chart, or figure caption should accurately describe the material presented and its contribution to the report.

6. Keep language and descriptions as simple as possible by avoiding unnecessary and overly complex words, phrases, and terms. The goal of scientific writing is to explain findings clearly, simply, and accurately.

7. Where possible, use the active rather than passive voice. For example, "The researchers found that . . ." is preferable to "It was found by the researchers that . . . ." Writing in the active voice makes reading more pleasant and also requires fewer words.

8. Proofread the manuscript carefully. Even researchers who are meticulous in their scientific approach can make errors in compiling a manuscript. All manuscripts, whether intended for publication or for management review, should be proofread several times to check for accuracy.

9. Miscellaneous considerations:

    a. Avoid phrases or references that could be interpreted as sexist or racist.

    b. Check all data for accuracy. Even one misplaced digit may affect the results of a study.

    c. Use acceptable grammar; avoid slang.

    d. Provide acknowledgments whenever another researcher's work is included in the report.

    e. Include footnotes to indicate where further information or assistance can be obtained.

Guidelines for writing a report for business or government decision makers include the following.

1. Provide an executive summary at the beginning of the report. Since busy decision makers may not read anything else in the report, great care must be taken in constructing this section. Some useful hints are:

    a. Get right to the point and state conclusions quickly.

    b. Keep the language simple and concise. Don't use jargon, clichés, or overly technical terms.

    c. Be brief. Keep the summary to no more than a page—surely no more than two pages. Anything else ceases to be a summary.

2. Place detailed and complicated discussions of methods in a technical appendix. Summarize the procedures in the body of the report.

3. Use clearly defined and easily understood quantitative analysis techniques. Most decision makers are not familiar with complicated statistical procedures. Keep the basic analysis simple. If it becomes necessary to use advanced statistical procedures, explain in the body of the report what was done and what the results mean. Include another technical appendix that describes the statistical technique in detail.

4. Use graphs and charts wherever appropriate to make numerical findings more understandable and meaningful. Never let tabular material stand alone; to ensure that its importance is not overlooked, mention or explain each such item.

5. Decision makers like research that provides answers to their questions. Put the conclusions reached by the investigators and, if appropriate, recommendations for action, in the last section of the report.

Research Ethics

The majority of mass communication research involves observations of human beings—asking them questions or examining what they have done. Since human beings have certain rights, the researcher must ensure that the rights of the participants in a project are not violated. This requires a consideration of ethics: distinguishing right from wrong and the proper from the improper. Unfortunately, there are no universal definitions for these terms. Instead, a series of guidelines, broad generalizations, and suggestions has been endorsed or at least tacitly accepted by most in the research profession. These guidelines will not provide an answer to every ethical question that may arise, but they can help make researchers more sensitive to the issues.

Before discussing these specific guidelines, we list some hypothetical research situations that involve ethics.

1. A researcher at a large university hands questionnaires to the students in his or her introductory mass media course and tells them that if they do not complete the forms, they will lose points toward their grade in the course.

2. A researcher is conducting a mail survey about attendance at X-rated motion pictures. The questionnaire states that responses will be anonymous. Unknown to the respondents, however, each return envelope is marked with a code that enables the researcher to identify the sender.

3. A researcher recruits subjects for an experiment by stating that participants will be asked to watch "a few scenes from some current movies." Those who decide to participate are shown several scenes of bloody and graphic violence.

4. A researcher shows one group of children a violent television show and another group a nonviolent program. After viewing, the children are sent to a public playground, where they are told to play with the children who are already there. The researcher records each instance of violent behavior exhibited by the young subjects.

5. Subjects in an experiment are told to submit a sample of their newswriting to an executive of a large newspaper. They are led to believe that whoever submits the best work will be offered a job at the paper. In fact, the "executive" is a confederate in the experiment and severely criticizes everyone's work.

These examples of ethically flawed study designs should be kept in mind while reading the following guidelines to ethics in mass media research.

General Ethical Principles

General ethical principles are difficult to construct in the research area. There are, however, at least four principles from the study of ethics that have relevance. First, is the principle of autonomy or the principle of self-determination. Basic to this concept is the demand that the researcher respect the rights, values, and decisions of other people. The reasons for a person's action should be respected and the actions not interfered with. This principle is exemplified by the use of informed consent in the research procedure. A second ethical principle important to social science research is that of nonmaleficence. In short, it is wrong to intentionally inflict harm on another. A third ethical principle—beneficence—is usually considered in tandem with nonmaleficence. Beneficence stipulates a positive obligation to remove existing harms and to confer benefits on others. These two principles operate together, and often the researcher must weigh the harmful risks of research against its possible benefits (for example, increase in knowledge, refinement of theory).

A fourth ethical principle that is sometimes relevant to social science is the principle of justice. At its general level, this principle holds that people who are equal in relevant respects should be treated equally. In the research context, this principle should be applied when new programs or policies are being evaluated. The positive results of such research should be shared with all. It would be unethical, for example, to deny the benefit of a new teaching procedure to children because they were originally chosen to be in the control group rather than the group that received the experimental procedure. Benefits should be shared with all who are qualified.

Although it is difficult to generalize, it is clear that mass media researchers must follow some set of rules to fulfill their ethical obligations to their subjects and respondents. Cook (1976), discussing the laboratory approach, offers one such code of behavior.

1. Do not involve people in research without their knowledge or consent.
2. Do not coerce people to participate.
3. Do not withhold from the participant the true nature of the research.
4. Do not actively lie to the participant about the nature of the research.
5. Do not lead the participant to commit acts that diminish his or her self-respect.
6. Do not violate the right to self-determination.

7. Do not expose the participant to physical or mental stress.
8. Do not invade the privacy of the participant.
9. Do not withhold benefits from participants in control groups.
10. Do not fail to treat research participants fairly and to show them consideration and respect.

Voluntary Participation and Informed Consent

An individual is entitled to decline to participate in any research project or to terminate participation at any time. Participation in an experiment, survey, or focus group is always voluntary, and any form of coercion is unacceptable. Researchers who are in a position of authority over subjects (as in Situation 1 above) should be especially sensitive to *implied* coercion: even though the researcher might tell the class that failure to participate will not affect their grades, many students may not believe this. In such a situation, it would be advisable to keep the questionnaires anonymous and to have the person in authority be absent from the room while the survey is administered.

Voluntary participation is a less pressing ethical issue in mail and telephone surveys, since respondents are free to hang up the phone or to throw away the questionnaire. Nonetheless, a researcher should not attempt to induce subjects to participate by misrepresenting the organization sponsoring the research or by exaggerating its purpose or importance. For example, phone interviewers should not be instructed to identify themselves as representatives of the "Department of Information" to mislead people into thinking the survey is government-sponsored. Likewise, mail questionnaires should not be constructed to mimic census forms, tax returns, social security questionnaires, or other official government forms.

Closely related to voluntary participation is the notion of *informed consent*. For people to volunteer for a research project, they need to know enough about the project to make an intelligent choice. Researchers have the responsibility to inform potential subjects or respondents of all features of the project that can reasonably be expected to influence participation. Respondents should understand that an interview may take as long as 45 minutes, or that a second interview is required, or that upon completing a mail questionnaire, they may be singled out for a telephone interview.

In an experiment, informed consent means that potential subjects must be warned of any possible discomfort or unpleasantness that might be involved. Subjects should be told if they are to receive or administer electric shocks, be subjected to unpleasant audio or visual stimuli, or undergo any procedure that may cause concern. Any unusual measurement techniques that may be used also must be described. Researchers have an obligation to answer candidly and truthfully, as far as possible, all the participant's questions about the research.

Experiments that involve deception (see the following subsection) cause special problems with regard to obtaining informed consent. If deception is absolutely necessary to conduct an experiment, is the experimenter obligated to inform subjects that they may be deceived during the upcoming experiment? Will such a disclosure affect participation in the experiment? Will it also affect the experimental results? Should one compromise by telling all potential subjects that deception will be involved for some participants but not for others?

A second problem is deciding exactly how much information about a research project must be disclosed in seeking to achieve informed consent. Is it enough to explain that the experiment involves rating commercials, or is it necessary to add that the experiment is designed to test whether subjects with high IQs prefer different commercials from those with low IQs? Obviously, in some situations the researcher cannot reveal everything about the project for fear of contaminating the results. For example, if the goal of the research is to examine the influence of peer pressure on commercial evaluations, alerting the subjects to this facet of the investigation might change their behavior in the experiment.

Problems might occur in research examining the impact of mass media in nonliterate communities, for example, if the research subjects did not comprehend what they were told regarding the proposed investigation. Even in literate societies, many people fail to understand the implications for confidentiality of the storage of survey data on computer disks or tape. Moreover, an investigator might not have realized in advance that some subjects would find part of an experiment or survey emotionally disturbing. Since it is impossible for informed consent to apply to all situations, the American Psychological Association has suggested that researchers have a responsibility to continue their attention to subjects' welfare after the completion of data collection.

Research findings provide some indication of what research participants should be told. Epstein, Suedefeld, and Silverstein (1973) found that subjects wanted a general description of the experiment and what was expected of them; they wanted to know whether danger was involved, how long the experiment would last, and the experiment's purpose. As far as informed consent and survey participation are concerned, Sobal (1984) found wide variation among researchers about what to tell respondents in the survey introduction. Almost all introductions identified the research organization and the interviewer by name and described the research topic. Less frequently mentioned in introductions were the sponsor of the research and guarantees of confidentiality or anonymity. Few survey introductions mentioned the length of the survey or that participation was voluntary.

Finally, one must consider the form of the consent to be obtained. Written consent is a requirement in certain government-sponsored research programs and may also be required by many university research review committees, as discussed below in connection with guidelines promulgated by the federal government. In several generally recognized situations, however, signed forms are regarded as impractical. These include telephone surveys, mail surveys, personal interviews, and cases in which the signed form itself might represent an occasion for breach of confidentiality. For example, a respondent who has been promised anonymity as an inducement to participate in a face-to-face interview might be suspicious if asked to sign a consent form after the interview. In these circumstances, the fact that respondent agreed to participate is taken as implied consent.

Concealment and Deception

Concealment and deception techniques are encountered most frequently in experimental research. Concealment is the withholding of certain information from the subjects; deception is deliberately providing false information. Both practices raise ethical problems. The difficulty in obtaining consent has already been mentioned. A second problem derives from the general feeling that it is wrong for experimenters to lie or otherwise to deceive subjects.

Many critics argue that deception transforms a subject from a human being into a manipulated object and is therefore demeaning to the participant. Moreover, once subjects have been deceived, they are likely to expect to be deceived again in other research projects. At least two research studies seem to suggest that this concern is valid. Stricker and Messick (1967) reported finding a high incidence of suspicion among subjects of high school age after having been deceived. Fillenbaum (1966) found that about one third to one half of subjects were suspicious at the beginning of an experiment after deception in a prior research experience.

On the other hand, some researchers argue that certain studies could not be conducted at all without the use of deception. They claim that the harm done to those who are deceived is outweighed by the benefits of the research to scientific knowledge. The same arguments can be used both for and against concealment. In general, however, concealment is a somewhat less worrisome ethical problem, provided enough information is given to subjects to allow informed consent and all the subjects' questions are answered candidly.

Obviously, deception is not a technique that should be used indiscriminately. Kelman (1967) suggested that before the investigator settles on deception as an experimental tactic, three questions should be examined:

1. How significant is the proposed study?
2. Are alternative procedures available that would provide the same information?

3. How severe is the deception? (It is one thing to tell subjects that the experimentally constructed message they are reading was taken from the *New York Times*; it is another to report that the test a subject has just completed was designed to measure latent suicidal tendencies.)

When an experiment is concluded, especially one involving concealment or deception, it is the responsibility of the investigator to "debrief" subjects. Debriefing should be thorough enough to remove any lasting effects that might have been created by the experimental manipulation or by any other aspect of the experiment. Subjects' questions should be answered and the potential value of the experiment stressed.

Another set of criteria was put forth by Elms (1982), who suggested five necessary and sufficient conditions under which deception can be considered ethically justified in social science research.

1. When there is no other feasible way to obtain the desired information
2. When the likely benefits substantially outweigh the likely harms
3. When subjects are given the option to withdraw at any time without penalty
4. When any physical or psychological harm to subjects is temporary
5. When subjects are debriefed as to all substantial deception and the research procedures are made available for public review

Together the suggestions of Kelman and Elms offer researchers good advice for the planning stages of investigations.

Protection of Privacy

The problem of protecting the privacy of participants usually occurs more often in survey research than in laboratory studies. Subjects have a right to know whether their privacy will be maintained and who will have access to the information they provide. There are two ways to guarantee privacy: by assuring anonymity and by assuring confidentiality. A promise of anonymity is a guarantee that a given respondent cannot possibly be linked to any particular response. In many research projects anonymity is an advantage, since it encourages respondents to be honest and candid in their answers. Strictly speaking, personal and telephone interviews cannot be anonymous because the researcher can link a given questionnaire to a specific person, household, or telephone number. In such instances, the researcher should promise confidentiality; that is, the respondents should be assured that even though as individuals they can be identified, their names will never be publicly associated with the information they provide. A researcher should never use "anonymous" in a way that is or seems to be synonymous with "confidential."

Additionally, respondents should be told who *will* have access to the information they provide. The researcher's responsibility for assuring confidentiality does not end once the data have been analyzed and the study concluded. Questionnaires that identify persons by name should not be stored in public places, nor should other investigators be given permission to examine confidential data unless all identifying marks have been obliterated.

Federal Regulations Concerning Research

Federal concern with protecting the rights of human subjects who participate in biomedical and social science research funded by the government is not new. In 1971 the Department of Health, Education, and Welfare drafted rules for obtaining informed consent from research participants. The basic elements of informed consent were as follows.

1. A fair explanation of the procedures to be followed
2. A description of the attendant discomfort and risks
3. A description of the benefits
4. A disclosure of the appropriate procedures (for example, medical treatments) that would be advantageous to the subject
5. An effort to answer any questions concerning the procedures
6. An instruction that the subject is free to withdraw consent and discontinue participation at any time

The federal policy required full documentation of informed consent procedures. In addition, the government set up a system of institutional review boards (IRBs) to safeguard the rights of human subjects. As of 1983, there were more than 550 IRBs at medical schools, colleges and universities, hospitals, and other institutions. At most universities, IRBs have become part of the permanent bureaucracy. They have regular meetings and have developed standardized forms that must accompany research proposals that involve human subjects or respondents.

Regulations concerning informed consent and its documentation have been a particularly controversial aspect of the IRB system. Social scientists who use the survey method for most of their research believe that their studies should not be regulated under the same rules that apply to biomedical studies. Survey researchers argue that their studies typically involve little risk to respondents and that procuring signed consent forms is impractical and expensive. Moreover, many social scientists fear that obtaining consent forms would restrict the validity of their findings by greatly diminishing the subject populations available for research.

The possible impact of the federal guidelines prompted several research studies designed to test their effects. For example, Lueptow et al. (1977) compared before and after response rates from surveys of high school students. After the federal rules took effect, about 70% of the students over 18 volunteered for a study, compared to virtually 100% before the guidelines. Among students under 18, for whom parental consent was needed, about 42% agreed to participate, effectively halving the pool of available subjects. The researchers also found that the reduced participation rate had little impact on measures of grade point and intelligence. A more recent study by Kearney et al. (1983) asked parents to sign forms consenting to the completion by their children of a questionnaire on alcohol and drug use. The resulting sample was about half the size of the available population, and it overrepresented white students and underrepresented blacks and Asian-Americans. Thus the sensitivity of the material in the questionnaire might have a bearing on the makeup of the participating sample.

A study by Singer (1977) shed additional light on this topic. The degree of informed consent was varied in a series of face-to-face interviews. Specifically, the variables that were manipulated included signing a consent form, assurance of confidentiality, and amount of information provided about the survey. Asking respondents to sign consent forms reduced the response rate. On the other hand, the promise of confidentiality reduced nonresponse of several items. Neither the confidentiality assurance nor the signature affected the quality of the data.

In a second study (Singer & Frankel, 1982), the interviews were done over the telephone. Two variables were manipulated to affect the degree of informed consent. Half the respondents were given a vague description of the survey as a study of leisure time, while the other half got a fuller description: they were told that some of the questions dealt with alcohol use and sex. The other variable had to do with revealing the purpose of the interview. Half the respondents were told nothing, while the other half heard a detailed description of the goals of the study. Neither of the factors varied in the experiment significantly affected overall response rate or response rates to individual items. Nor did there seem to be any impact on the quality of the data. Thus it appears that more complete disclosure did not hamper the research.

In the midst of this methodological research, the Department of Health and Human Services (successor to the Department of Health, Education, and Welfare) softened the regulations concerning social science research. In 1981 the department exempted from coverage (1) research in educational settings about new instructional techniques, (2) research involving the use of education tests (if anonymous), (3) survey and interview research and observational research in public places, provided the subjects are not identified and sensitive information is not collected, and (4) studies using existing public data. Additionally, signed consent forms are no longer needed when the research presents only a minimal risk of harm to subjects and involves no procedures for which written consent is normally required outside the research context. This means that no signed consent forms are necessary in the interview situation, since a person usually does not seek written consent before asking a question. Although the statements above apparently exempt most nonexperimental social science research from federal regulation, IRBs at many institutions still review all research proposals that involve human subjects and some IRBs may be following the old HEW standards. Indeed, some IRBs might have regulations more stringent than the federal guidelines. Thus, these regulations may still be important even though much social science research seems to be exempt. As a practical matter, a researcher should always build a little more time into the research schedule to accommodate IRB procedures.

Ethics in Data Analysis and Reporting

Researchers are also responsible for maintaining professional standards in the analysis and reporting of their data. The ethical guidelines in this area are less controversial and more clear-cut. One cardinal rule is that researchers have a moral and ethical obligation to refrain from tampering with data: questionnaire responses and experimental observations may not be fabricated, altered, or discarded. Similarly, researchers are expected to maintain reasonable care in processing the data to guard against needless errors that might affect the results.

Researchers should never conceal information that might influence the interpretation of their findings. For example, if 2 weeks elapsed between the testing of the experimental group and the testing of the control group, this delay should be reported so that other researchers can discount the effects of history and maturation on the results. Every research report should contain a full and complete description of method, and particularly of any departure from standard procedures.

Since science is a public activity, researchers have an ethical obligation to share their findings and methods with other researchers. All questionnaires, experimental materials, measurement instruments, instructions to subjects, and other relevant items should be made available to those who wish to examine them.

Finally, all investigators are under an ethical obligation to draw conclusions from their data that are consistent with those data. Interpretations should not be stretched or distorted to fit a personal point of view or a favorite theory, or to gain or maintain a client's favor. Nor should researchers attribute greater significance or credibility to their data than they justify. For example, when analyzing correlation coefficients obtained from a large sample, it is possible to achieve statistical significance with an r of only, for example, .10. It would be perfectly acceptable to report a statistically significant result in this case, but the investigator should also mention that the predictive utility of the correlation was not large, and specifically, that it explained only 1% of the total variation. In short, researchers should report results with candor and honesty.

A Professional Code of Ethics

Formalized codes of ethics have yet to be developed by all professional associations involved in mass media research. One organization that has developed its own ethical code is the American Association for Public Opinion Research. The code is reproduced below.

American Association for Public Opinion Research

Code of Professional Ethics and Practices

I. Principles of Professional Practice in the Conduct of our Work

  A. We shall exercise due care in gathering and processing data, taking all reasonable steps to assure the accuracy of results.

  B. We shall exercise due care in the development of research designs and in the analysis of data.

    1. We shall recommend and employ only research tools and methods of analysis which, in our professional judgment, are well suited to the research problem at hand.

    2. We shall not select research tools and methods of analysis because of their capacity to yield a misleading conclusion.

    3. We shall not knowingly make interpretations of research results, nor shall we tacitly permit interpretations, which are inconsistent with the data available.

    4. We shall not knowingly imply that interpretations should be accorded greater confidence than the data actually warrant.

  C. We shall describe our findings and methods accurately and in appropriate detail in all research reports.

II. Principles of Professional Responsibility in our Dealings with People

  A. The Public

    1. We shall cooperate with legally authorized representatives of the public by describing the methods used in our studies.

    2. When we become aware of the appearance in public of serious distortions of our research we shall publicly disclose what is required to correct the distortions.

  B. Clients and Sponsors

    1. When undertaking work for a private client we shall hold confidential all proprietary information obtained about the client's business affairs and about the findings of research conducted for the client, except when the dissemination of the information is expressly authorized by the client or becomes necessary under terms of Section II-A-2.

    2. We shall be mindful of the limitations of our techniques and facilities and shall accept only those research assignments which can be accomplished within these limitations.

C. The Profession

    1. We shall not cite our membership in the Association as evidence of professional competence, since the Association does not so certify any persons or organizations.

    2. We recognize our responsibility to contribute to the science of public opinion research and to disseminate as freely as possible the ideas and findings which emerge from our research.

D. The Respondent

    1. We shall not lie to survey respondents or use practices and methods which abuse, coerce, or humiliate them.

    2. Unless the respondent waives confidentiality for specified uses we shall hold as privileged and confidential all information that tends to identify a respondent with his or her responses. We shall also not disclose the names of respondents for nonresearch purposes.

Reprinted by permission of the American Association for Public Opinion Research.

Finding Support for Mass Media Research

Research costs money. Finding a source for research funds is a problem that confronts both quantitative and qualitative researchers in all fields of mass communication. This section mentions some organizations that have supported mass communication research projects. A researcher in need of funding should contact these organizations for details about the types of studies they support and the amount of funds available, as well as instructions for preparing research proposals.

University or college researchers should determine whether the institution has a program of research grants for individual faculty members. Many colleges award such grants, often on a competitive basis, for research in mass communication. Typically these grants are modest in size—usually under $5,000—but they are among the easiest to apply for and to administer. In many cases grants are available for student research, as well.

Several philanthropic foundations sponsor mass media research. Among the better known are the Ford Foundation, the John and Mary Markle Foundation, the Kellogg Foundation, and the Alfred P. Sloan Foundation. The amounts these organizations give to support research range from about $5,000 to as much as $150,000. Competition is stiff, and the researcher should be certain that his or her research area is one for which these foundations provide funding. As an alternative, there may be smaller foundations located near the researcher's base of operations that could be investigated.

Certain departments of the federal government sponsor mass communication research (although as of 1986, many were expecting budget cuts). Among the departments that have been active in supporting media research are the National Institute of Mental Health, the National Science Foundation, and the National Endowment for the Humanities. Other funding agencies can be identified by looking through the *Federal Grant Register*. Applying for a government grant tends to be complicated, and there are many guidelines and regulations. In addition, there is the usual problem of government red tape. Nonetheless, these agencies have been known to make sizable grants to investigators.

Many professional media associations sponsor continuing programs to support research relevant to their particular field. In radio and television, the National Association of Broadcasters awards annual grants for research in broadcasting. The competition is keen: approximately half a dozen grants of $5,000 are made each year to professors and students interested in broadcasting research. In the print media, ANPA sponsors research having to do with readership and circulation. The Frank E. Gannett Newspaper Foundation also provides research funding, and the Magazine Publishers Association (MPA) sponsors magazine-related research.

The American Academy of Advertising sponsors an annual competition to award a $1,500 grant to a new faculty member (one who has been teaching less than 5 years) to conduct research studies in the field of advertising. The American Association of Advertising Agencies has also funded research projects. Similarly, the Foundation for Research in Education and Public Relations has a program of small grants ($1,000–$3,000) to support research in public relations.

Many researchers have obtained money to finance their research by working with the media industry. The three television networks have research departments that are willing to examine proposals from outside investigators that might be of interest to them. Occasionally, they will even sponsor a research program themselves. The American Broadcasting Company in the mid-1970s funded five separate research projects submitted by academic researchers, providing $20,000 for each. The Columbia Broadcasting System recently sponsored a lengthy audience survey conducted among British youngsters. In addition, the larger group owners in broadcasting have research departments that might be approached. The Corporation for Public Broadcasting, for example, has sponsored several audience studies relating to their programs. Similarly, large newspaper chains are potential funding sources. In the public relations field, many researchers have obtained support by contacting the professional organization of the industry they are studying or by working with a private company or corporation.

Industry support can be a mixed blessing. On the one hand, working with industry backing makes it easier for a researcher to enlist the cooperation of people or organizations within that industry and also facilitates obtaining data about the inner workings of the industry. On the other hand, many media industries are interested in limited research areas that may not have much theoretical attraction for the researcher. A company may specify the focus of the study and the variables to be examined. Therefore, when approaching a media organization or any other private company for support, it is wise to determine in advance what control, if any, the private organization will have over the design, execution, and subsequent publicizing of the project.

Finally, most colleges and universities have an Office of Contracts and Grants (or some similar title) that can be of great help to researchers. In addition to aiding the researcher with the bureaucratic requirements necessary for a grant application, this office can offer valuable assistance in other areas. For example, this office might offer computerized searches for sponsoring agencies, information about current grants, budget advice, preparation of abstracts, and even word-processing services. Researchers in the academic setting should take advantage of this resource.

Summary

Writing a research report is naturally an important step in the scientific process, since the report places the research study in the public domain for consideration and confirmation. Beginning researchers generally find the process much easier after they have completed one or two studies. A key to successful writing is to follow the guidelines developed by journal editors, or styles developed by individual companies or businesses. The same basic five-part format is used for all reports.

Ethical considerations in conducting research should not be overlooked. Nearly every research study has the potential of affecting subjects in some way, either psychologically or physically. Researchers dealing with human subjects must take great care to ensure that all precautions are taken to alleviate any potential harm to subjects. This includes carefully planning a study as well as debriefing subjects upon completion of a project.

The final part of Chapter 18 describes financing research projects. This topic is relevant to all researchers, since lack of funds often cancels good research projects. The chapter describes a variety of sources that provide financial assistance; none should be overlooked.

Questions and Problems for Further Investigation

1. Read an article in a recent academic journal of mass media research. See how well the authors follow the reporting guidelines discussed in this chapter.
2. Using the five examples on page 432, provide, if possible, an alternate way of conducting the study that would be ethically acceptable.

References and Suggested Readings

Alwitt, L. F., Anderson, D. R., Lorch, E. P., & Levin, S. R. (1980). Preschool children's visual attention to attributes of television. *Human Communication Research, 7*, 52–67.

Beauchamp, T., et al. (Eds.). (1982). *Ethical issues in social science research*. Baltimore: Johns Hopkins University Press.

Bower, R., & de Gasparis, P. (1978). *Ethics in social research*. New York: Praeger.

Cook, S. (1976). Ethical issues in the conduct of research in social relations. In C. Sellitz, L. Wrightsman, & S. Cook (Eds.), *Research methods in social relations*. New York: Holt, Rinehart & Winston.

Elms, A. (1982). Keeping deception honest. In T. Beauchamp et al. (Eds.), *Ethical issues in social science research*. Baltimore: Johns Hopkins University Press.

Epstein, Y., Suedefeld, P., & Silverstein, S. (1973). The experimental contract. *American Psychologist, 28*, 212–221.

Fillenbaum, S. (1966). Prior deception and subsequent experimental performance. *Journal of Personality and Social Psychology, 4*, 532–537.

Kearney, K., et al. (1983). Sample bias resulting from a requirement for written parental consent. *Public Opinion Quarterly, 47*(1), 96–102.

Kelman, H. (1967). Human use of human subjects: The problem of deception in social psychological experiments. *Psychological Bulletin, 67*, 1–11.

Kelman, H. (1982). Ethical issues in different social science methods. In T. Beauchamp et al. (Eds.), *Ethical issues in social science research*. Baltimore: Johns Hopkins University Press.

Lueptow, L., et al. (1977). The impact of informed consent regulations on response rate and response bias. *Sociological Methods and Research, 6*(2), 182–203.

Rummel, R. J. (1970). *Applied factor analysis*. Evanston, IL: Northwestern University Press.

Singer, E. (1977). Informed consent: Consequences for response rate and response quality in social surveys. Paper presented at the American Sociological Association, San Francisco.

Singer, E., & Frankel, M. (1982). Informed consent procedures in telephone interviews. *American Sociological Review, 47*, 416–427.

Sobal, J. (1984). The content of survey introductions and the provision of informed consent. *Public Opinion Quarterly, 48*(4), 788–793.

Stricker, L., & Messick, J. (1967). The true deceiver. *Psychological Bulletin, 68,* 13–20.

Wimmer, R. D., & Reid, L. N. (1982). Willingness of communciation researchers to respond to replication requests. *Journalism Quarterly, 59,* 317–319.

A P P E N D I X E S

1 TABLES

·

2 MULTIVARIATE STATISTICS

·

3 BRIEF GUIDE FOR CONDUCTING FOCUS GROUPS

A P P E N D I X   1

Tables

Table 1 Random Numbers

```
0 8 9 5 6 4 4 8 9 4 0 7 5 9 7 0 4 5 3 1 2 7 8 6 6
8 2 4 4 8 8 0 2 6 5 5 0 3 5 9 1 3 8 6 8 8 3 1 8 5
3 1 2 3 7 6 4 1 1 4 3 5 2 7 4 9 3 2 7 5 5 4 7 6 2
2 3 8 1 8 6 6 1 0 8 4 1 0 5 0 4 8 5 3 7 8 7 6 5 7
0 0 4 3 6 5 5 2 3 5 2 4 3 3 9 3 2 5 2 0 8 4 6 2 1
1 2 8 9 7 5 8 9 7 8 6 7 4 0 4 0 4 9 7 8 5 0 2 9 8
9 8 4 6 9 9 0 8 0 2 3 2 8 0 5 4 5 0 6 7 6 2 3 9 8
0 7 3 6 9 5 1 6 3 8 0 5 9 0 0 2 0 9 3 6 8 8 2 4 3
2 2 3 9 5 7 9 4 0 6 7 3 6 9 6 4 1 7 3 6 5 1 8 2 6
4 9 5 6 9 3 1 4 7 8 1 5 6 7 2 2 4 6 3 6 5 4 2 1 2
4 0 6 6 8 5 4 3 7 8 3 2 6 8 1 2 2 7 0 6 5 3 5 8 4
6 3 3 2 0 3 9 7 0 2 3 6 9 5 3 4 1 6 1 8 3 9 4 3 3
0 6 1 8 4 2 1 8 6 7 5 4 1 9 0 3 2 4 1 5 7 7 4 0 8
2 2 4 2 9 6 8 5 8 2 6 1 0 7 6 1 7 9 2 0 9 2 8 7 8
8 3 2 3 0 7 4 3 5 8 9 0 8 0 5 8 8 7 1 3 6 0 1 3 9
2 3 1 8 2 3 1 0 9 0 0 8 9 1 2 0 3 7 0 2 0 1 8 1 7
0 8 7 3 4 4 5 1 8 7 4 5 1 9 9 0 3 2 2 3 1 2 6 4 6
5 8 5 6 7 6 1 0 1 6 7 0 2 1 9 1 6 3 2 0 1 1 5 5 9
6 1 1 0 5 1 3 6 7 7 7 8 2 4 5 9 3 0 7 6 7 9 1 1 6
5 3 6 1 2 7 2 6 2 7 3 3 6 8 2 6 5 5 8 4 2 4 2 1 8
8 7 3 9 5 1 1 8 4 1 8 5 6 6 0 6 9 2 2 6 8 2 5 8 5
2 9 1 9 9 5 6 1 8 6 6 4 0 5 0 0 8 8 2 5 9 2 0 1 2
8 1 0 2 1 7 2 0 2 7 6 8 4 8 0 2 6 2 8 0 8 3 6 0 7
9 7 1 5 5 7 4 6 1 5 6 5 9 9 2 2 7 1 2 7 0 0 5 0 9
6 3 7 9 8 8 7 4 9 5 0 3 3 0 3 7 0 7 5 8 1 2 8 3 1
9 4 2 2 1 3 2 0 5 6 0 6 0 9 0 9 3 1 7 8 1 2 3 1 1
5 2 8 5 1 0 2 4 6 0 8 3 4 2 9 0 2 4 0 5 2 7 8 8 8
7 9 7 1 3 7 2 4 6 3 8 4 0 2 5 5 4 6 1 6 5 4 6 3 0
0 1 5 0 6 5 1 1 8 0 9 4 1 1 2 6 1 4 2 0 8 6 3 1 0
5 8 1 7 4 7 5 6 2 1 9 3 7 4 0 4 6 4 6 9 6 7 5 0 6
2 5 0 7 5 1 6 0 4 0 4 1 9 4 9 8 3 6 3 8 0 0 1 7 9
8 8 3 7 8 1 4 6 3 8 0 5 6 4 4 3 5 0 6 9 5 5 0 6 0
4 3 1 8 7 3 4 1 7 1 6 1 5 2 7 9 4 0 2 9 9 6 8 7 6
9 1 4 7 7 4 3 7 4 2 5 5 0 2 1 1 1 4 0 6 4 7 5 9 6
8 6 0 8 2 9 3 4 3 4 7 6 9 6 1 8 2 3 3 8 3 4 6 8 3
3 3 0 6 2 3 8 7 4 3 8 3 1 1 5 9 7 4 4 4 9 7 6 0 9
1 8 2 0 2 9 8 8 0 1 6 8 0 7 5 6 0 8 3 9 2 1 1 2 0
4 7 4 1 1 8 5 9 6 9 7 7 8 0 8 0 8 5 7 2 6 9 4 6 7
7 2 8 1 1 0 4 0 5 0 0 8 2 5 7 4 9 4 0 6 9 7 1 8 0
8 4 0 0 8 1 8 7 1 5 0 1 3 7 3 1 1 4 1 9 7 1 7 8 5
1 5 0 5 3 1 9 7 5 0 3 7 6 3 4 7 2 2 0 5 0 0 7 5 1
6 8 5 1 2 4 1 0 4 6 2 5 9 9 3 2 5 6 0 1 2 0 6 7 7
7 6 5 5 4 6 1 9 1 1 7 9 9 9 6 6 7 1 3 7 7 4 8 8 2
7 8 2 4 2 1 6 4 3 9 7 2 6 6 5 7 0 1 2 8 9 7 1 4 5
9 0 3 3 8 1 3 5 1 4 2 8 7 7 0 3 5 8 0 8 4 2 6 6 4
5 5 4 8 6 5 6 8 0 3 2 0 4 8 4 5 6 6 5 4 7 1 3 1 2
0 6 4 9 7 7 9 8 0 6 4 0 9 2 4 7 8 2 5 1 7 2 3 5 2
6 0 6 7 8 0 8 7 6 8 5 0 1 3 4 3 0 4 7 0 5 2 4 1 3
1 6 3 6 4 9 6 5 3 5 5 3 0 3 3 8 3 7 9 1 1 5 8 2 2
2 1 5 9 7 1 2 6 4 4 5 0 2 1 4 5 1 1 7 0 4 0 1 3 0
```

Table 1 Random Numbers (*continued*)

5	0	3	9	1	8	3	8	9	5	5	6	7	3	0	6	7	9	7	1	4	9	2	3	3
3	5	8	1	8	1	6	3	4	7	0	6	7	7	8	9	6	2	0	8	5	0	4	3	7
7	0	6	4	0	6	9	0	5	9	3	3	7	7	1	1	4	4	3	8	0	6	2	1	8
1	0	4	9	2	7	8	1	6	4	4	9	3	2	9	6	7	3	2	4	2	6	4	9	6
7	7	7	0	3	2	5	7	9	3	0	5	6	6	5	8	7	6	2	8	5	2	5	3	8
3	1	4	2	0	1	2	3	5	8	0	4	9	9	9	5	6	4	8	6	4	3	5	0	8
8	7	9	8	4	6	4	1	7	0	8	6	0	0	6	1	7	0	9	0	2	9	8	4	2
5	0	6	9	7	6	4	6	4	9	6	6	0	5	3	2	7	9	2	4	4	4	0	6	5
0	9	7	6	2	3	7	3	6	5	7	7	4	8	5	9	4	9	6	6	0	9	5	6	3
1	1	2	9	9	4	6	0	0	6	3	7	1	3	1	9	1	2	6	6	0	8	7	5	2
9	5	5	5	1	9	7	5	9	0	3	2	1	5	6	1	1	1	2	8	3	5	9	5	5
5	6	2	2	6	5	2	0	4	0	5	8	1	8	6	1	2	3	9	0	3	4	3	0	3
3	0	8	5	5	8	7	5	1	7	1	0	7	0	2	7	4	9	9	5	4	9	3	4	6
1	9	4	1	2	5	8	1	2	4	4	9	7	5	9	7	5	8	8	6	2	2	2	4	0
1	6	0	1	7	5	6	9	4	1	7	3	2	2	6	5	1	4	5	9	8	9	9	2	4
9	4	3	4	6	5	3	2	3	0	8	5	6	6	1	1	0	6	6	6	9	6	0	1	1
3	8	5	2	2	5	3	1	3	4	8	8	2	8	7	5	4	6	4	6	4	0	3	3	4
6	5	9	8	7	5	1	5	0	1	3	1	3	5	7	1	1	7	6	6	6	6	8	4	5
9	9	7	6	9	8	8	7	0	6	1	5	7	9	7	1	5	9	7	9	2	6	7	1	1
3	2	8	0	3	7	7	6	8	3	1	2	6	3	0	8	1	4	8	6	1	2	6	6	8
8	9	9	2	9	7	7	4	2	3	3	5	9	2	3	5	8	6	7	3	0	6	4	9	9
5	2	2	0	3	2	8	7	3	4	1	2	6	8	9	6	8	9	4	1	7	6	8	2	9
9	3	7	1	9	8	3	6	0	2	8	6	3	5	3	0	1	6	1	3	3	8	3	4	8
0	6	7	9	9	0	3	7	7	2	6	0	7	7	1	1	8	1	2	9	9	7	8	0	6
6	5	3	1	0	4	2	4	5	1	4	9	5	3	9	0	2	2	4	5	9	9	9	0	0
4	1	8	9	1	7	4	3	6	4	4	6	6	6	0	7	6	3	2	5	8	2	0	6	8
4	5	4	7	1	1	4	5	0	4	7	9	4	0	6	1	2	1	9	4	9	9	0	2	3
2	5	4	3	3	6	3	1	4	0	9	3	7	9	1	1	8	8	1	8	0	3	1	9	5
4	3	6	4	0	1	7	8	2	0	4	9	5	9	7	9	0	3	3	7	2	9	9	4	0
2	3	8	5	4	4	3	3	0	6	1	0	7	3	5	3	1	3	2	0	6	0	9	1	7
1	6	4	8	7	9	9	9	1	3	1	0	8	6	7	5	6	9	0	3	1	6	8	2	0
4	8	1	6	3	4	5	0	2	7	5	7	0	8	3	2	4	8	5	3	2	9	6	8	1
4	2	1	9	4	6	2	3	0	1	1	6	1	0	7	2	2	3	4	8	7	9	1	4	6
4	0	7	6	5	4	2	9	5	3	3	9	0	6	3	0	2	5	4	9	5	3	6	0	8
8	4	9	3	0	8	2	8	4	0	4	5	6	9	0	6	8	1	1	4	6	7	4	8	1
1	7	6	3	8	1	4	6	2	2	9	4	5	0	3	5	7	0	0	2	4	1	7	1	2
5	6	4	6	9	0	1	5	1	5	5	0	3	1	4	5	1	2	7	0	2	4	9	9	6
0	3	6	0	7	1	4	8	0	3	5	4	8	8	0	4	0	6	7	3	3	1	1	7	4
6	7	2	9	0	4	2	9	2	6	4	6	4	6	4	6	9	4	6	2	3	9	4	8	8
0	3	1	4	5	9	5	0	8	2	6	5	0	8	5	8	0	7	5	0	9	5	3	1	5
7	3	0	9	3	6	1	9	3	1	3	9	8	3	9	7	7	6	6	5	3	0	2	6	8
8	6	7	9	6	6	8	3	4	0	5	9	5	1	7	8	0	1	0	8	9	7	1	4	6
4	9	5	8	6	8	0	4	4	4	5	6	7	4	8	1	7	1	4	9	2	9	5	1	9
6	0	3	9	9	5	8	4	4	1	5	4	0	6	8	6	0	2	0	0	1	8	8	8	0
4	1	0	5	3	6	3	5	0	6	4	0	0	1	2	1	8	2	9	5	4	8	7	2	5
5	2	7	9	6	5	7	4	5	1	3	3	8	8	4	4	0	4	1	8	9	1	1	6	5
3	4	6	1	2	1	8	7	4	7	6	3	3	5	0	0	7	9	1	6	4	0	7	4	6
8	2	2	0	8	8	8	7	3	8	3	1	5	8	4	9	5	1	9	1	7	9	7	9	9
4	8	7	0	7	8	9	4	3	0	9	2	3	5	4	7	2	1	4	6	6	8	6	3	2
9	0	4	3	8	0	1	5	7	6	7	1	6	3	0	5	7	3	7	1	0	9	5	6	6

Table 1 Random Numbers (*continued*)

```
8 2 8 9 7 9 6 9 7 9 0 8 2 9 8 1 5 6 9 3 2 9 2 3 3
9 4 6 9 2 6 8 4 4 7 8 3 5 1 0 1 3 9 9 2 9 0 4 0 8
5 6 7 4 2 7 4 1 2 7 3 1 5 8 3 1 0 7 3 8 7 5 2 5 1
8 0 9 9 8 3 2 9 7 5 5 8 0 5 2 1 3 4 2 3 8 6 8 3 6
6 7 0 3 7 9 8 8 2 0 9 1 0 6 0 7 2 4 5 1 3 3 5 1 0
8 1 3 0 0 8 3 4 8 8 3 4 8 9 9 2 0 4 3 9 6 7 6 5 7
1 7 6 2 5 8 6 2 6 6 8 0 8 3 9 8 8 7 4 2 1 3 3 3 2
9 9 7 1 7 5 9 1 3 2 4 6 0 5 9 0 7 3 8 2 3 5 4 7 1
0 4 6 4 0 1 7 9 9 3 6 8 1 5 3 7 1 1 9 5 1 0 1 4 8
9 7 8 2 1 2 9 7 2 0 6 4 2 5 2 7 0 8 1 1 9 7 7 7 0
2 4 6 4 6 3 6 7 5 2 0 0 5 4 7 3 3 4 1 0 7 4 4 0 9
8 5 4 5 4 7 7 4 0 0 5 0 6 4 2 8 8 0 8 0 9 9 0 5 8
5 8 6 7 6 6 4 7 0 1 4 9 9 5 7 2 1 4 1 1 9 7 7 3 5
1 3 8 1 4 7 0 7 4 8 8 4 4 0 1 2 5 1 4 8 1 7 7 3 2
4 1 5 9 7 9 5 6 6 7 4 5 6 1 8 8 8 2 8 9 0 0 9 2 5
9 5 4 7 0 6 8 1 2 1 4 0 4 5 8 3 1 6 0 1 9 7 5 6 0
3 7 2 7 4 1 4 8 3 6 4 1 6 1 9 0 4 1 3 2 6 8 9 2 5
9 7 1 8 1 0 8 3 6 0 1 7 5 0 6 3 2 7 9 2 5 6 2 9 9
9 9 9 9 1 9 4 2 6 9 5 8 5 6 8 3 9 8 6 9 9 6 8 2 5
9 3 0 1 8 1 5 8 8 1 1 4 4 6 6 4 1 0 9 6 6 7 5 5 8
7 9 4 6 8 9 0 6 6 9 5 4 3 1 9 5 1 9 5 6 2 8 2 7 4
3 5 5 4 5 2 5 2 2 1 4 8 2 0 9 1 8 4 3 5 0 3 2 6 5
6 7 2 1 9 0 5 4 3 3 9 8 9 0 1 2 6 6 1 3 0 4 5 4 1
4 0 5 3 9 2 6 3 2 2 0 4 2 0 9 1 0 0 8 8 8 0 2 8 1
2 1 5 7 3 7 3 6 2 8 9 3 2 8 7 9 6 7 9 5 1 9 5 5 4
8 2 9 1 7 6 5 0 5 7 4 2 4 7 5 1 4 2 8 4 0 2 0 4 5
0 4 9 2 5 9 9 8 7 4 7 3 2 2 1 7 7 1 9 5 1 4 4 9 4
3 8 6 7 5 6 1 5 3 0 9 0 8 4 0 4 6 7 2 2 6 8 4 3 5
7 1 8 8 3 6 3 7 4 3 6 3 3 0 1 3 4 9 7 3 8 9 2 3 6
2 3 0 4 7 4 6 9 9 9 8 7 4 4 2 8 1 4 4 4 0 0 6 0 8
8 6 4 4 0 7 1 2 9 6 3 1 3 4 9 1 6 2 9 3 7 6 1 1 0
0 5 5 4 6 7 7 9 6 9 0 2 5 5 3 5 8 5 1 2 9 6 9 3 9
5 7 4 3 2 8 8 4 4 2 0 8 9 6 3 0 5 1 1 2 7 3 7 8 0
8 3 2 7 1 2 7 0 2 9 1 1 7 1 5 4 8 1 9 1 2 5 0 5 3
3 1 2 1 0 7 7 3 0 4 7 1 3 8 9 3 8 7 2 7 5 1 4 8 9
0 7 9 7 0 6 4 5 3 0 5 8 2 7 3 7 3 0 6 2 4 3 3 9 1
9 0 3 4 4 3 1 8 2 1 0 4 5 9 7 2 9 0 5 5 4 7 1 5 9
1 5 7 9 2 9 5 2 8 9 1 8 6 4 2 3 4 0 6 1 4 1 7 9 9
7 3 8 2 7 8 4 7 5 9 3 4 2 9 9 4 8 3 1 1 6 5 1 5 6
2 4 0 4 4 0 4 5 0 7 6 4 9 2 0 5 3 9 2 8 1 1 8 0 2
2 9 9 9 6 6 8 0 6 9 4 0 8 4 2 4 0 4 6 0 2 1 2 2 4
5 8 2 2 2 1 7 7 2 5 9 4 2 1 7 2 1 7 7 9 3 3 5 9 8
7 3 7 4 3 6 3 0 9 9 1 6 3 9 2 3 0 2 6 8 9 8 9 0 7
8 8 9 7 6 2 9 9 0 1 2 0 0 1 0 2 4 7 8 9 6 6 9 7 8
1 4 0 9 6 1 0 9 8 7 0 5 8 0 6 5 8 0 5 0 1 9 3 0 1
1 6 4 2 4 7 6 7 7 3 5 9 3 2 2 9 2 7 8 6 3 7 7 8 1
1 2 9 8 1 2 5 7 7 9 6 8 4 4 0 6 3 3 1 1 6 7 2 5 8
5 7 7 5 3 5 5 5 6 7 9 4 3 1 5 7 2 7 6 9 7 6 1 0 3
2 4 7 9 1 7 2 8 3 4 4 1 1 1 3 0 6 9 1 4 8 8 7 5 6
0 2 5 9 4 0 8 2 5 6 0 4 7 1 6 3 6 5 5 6 1 1 6 7 6
```

Table 1 Random Numbers (*continued*)

```
8  9  0  8  8  8  7  4  1  9  9  9  5  5  1  8  2  1  3  7  5  7  8  7  1
1  1  0  4  2  7  2  3  9  9  5  7  5  0  9  5  3  9  6  8  6  7  4  9  0
0  0  6  6  6  3  1  5  6  3  8  9  7  2  9  0  9  8  4  9  4  2  5  0  0
2  8  5  9  9  3  5  2  5  2  1  1  7  4  0  7  9  0  1  4  9  1  9  8  9
7  5  8  0  7  9  4  5  7  9  3  2  0  7  6  3  2  6  3  6  0  9  7  8  5
2  8  1  2  4  9  9  2  0  1  9  7  9  7  2  0  8  1  4  9  2  8  6  5  9
1  6  5  9  5  2  6  8  5  8  1  8  0  6  1  2  2  7  1  0  8  6  1  9  9
3  8  0  2  2  2  0  4  5  5  5  4  5  6  9  9  1  4  2  6  7  3  9  3  5
7  0  7  8  2  1  9  6  3  1  1  8  1  1  7  8  1  6  0  3  9  6  7  1  0
9  5  9  2  6  6  6  7  4  1  9  5  1  9  8  4  2  7  9  3  8  5  5  0  8
9  9  3  7  7  0  5  3  1  2  2  4  7  0  2  2  4  0  2  1  4  5  2  6  9
2  8  6  7  5  0  2  8  7  0  4  2  5  4  1  5  3  3  7  0  7  8  8  0  8
5  8  4  6  5  0  3  6  4  5  2  4  7  9  6  7  7  3  1  5  9  7  7  4  2
2  7  9  4  0  0  1  7  0  7  2  0  0  5  1  8  6  4  9  7  9  7  0  4  8
3  2  0  4  1  5  9  2  4  0  8  3  9  0  6  9  8  3  7  7  2  6  0  6  8
9  4  4  2  4  3  1  3  1  3  0  2  2  8  2  7  5  6  8  5  3  2  9  9  9
1  4  7  7  0  3  1  3  3  5  9  6  5  1  6  4  0  6  9  7  3  9  2  1  6
2  7  4  6  7  2  6  2  7  2  5  1  3  8  7  7  8  2  1  9  2  5  0  9  0
5  3  2  1  6  4  9  4  4  6  2  5  3  3  3  5  2  5  4  9  5  7  4  4  6
6  0  9  6  4  0  0  9  3  2  7  7  6  6  7  9  7  8  1  8  0  4  1  8  1
6  8  6  5  0  5  3  4  2  3  3  7  5  7  7  9  7  4  7  0  5  6  5  1  3
7  2  1  3  4  1  7  8  1  8  4  4  1  6  6  6  2  5  6  6  2  0  4  1  9
7  5  9  1  3  2  7  1  2  6  3  1  3  3  1  2  9  0  9  8  9  8  6  9  8
8  7  7  6  8  8  8  1  6  8  6  1  8  8  6  1  7  5  6  8  6  4  3  6  9
0  4  6  4  6  1  9  6  1  4  5  9  1  1  3  6  1  4  5  7  0  8  2  5  4
9  6  8  6  1  6  3  0  3  7  0  4  9  8  8  7  7  6  8  1  7  1  5  0  8
7  6  9  7  0  9  8  7  1  2  0  9  0  3  8  5  3  9  3  7  4  1  1  5  7
3  2  7  0  9  2  7  5  8  0  4  7  8  1  4  2  4  0  0  9  6  5  9  2  5
4  2  6  8  9  1  9  0  4  2  1  3  4  3  2  0  6  7  4  7  1  3  9  7  9
6  8  6  5  1  4  1  3  0  6  7  0  9  5  2  8  7  0  9  3  8  5  1  3  5
6  3  5  7  2  0  2  8  6  3  3  8  5  3  1  0  4  6  6  3  1  7  9  9  7
7  3  7  7  3  4  5  2  3  6  2  3  6  5  5  3  9  2  1  7  0  6  4  2  0
6  0  1  2  5  0  2  9  4  9  8  3  5  9  5  7  4  5  2  8  4  7  6  6  4
2  6  6  8  6  5  0  7  7  5  5  4  9  1  2  0  3  4  8  9  6  4  9  8  9
3  6  8  7  2  9  9  2  7  5  6  0  9  0  6  5  8  8  2  8  3  4  7  4  0
4  2  5  5  7  2  6  5  9  4  3  8  7  5  6  5  3  6  3  4  3  8  5  4  7
3  2  3  1  1  5  6  5  8  3  9  6  2  2  0  2  9  0  9  3  1  1  3  1  4
0  2  3  6  6  9  4  4  6  6  0  9  9  7  4  0  1  3  2  5  6  9  4  5  1
6  5  6  9  4  1  6  8  8  6  7  0  0  6  0  8  8  3  9  7  8  4  1  7  6
7  3  1  3  9  1  2  0  7  1  5  2  1  2  0  7  0  1  7  8  6  4  6  6  3
3  5  2  5  5  9  9  0  1  5  3  2  1  7  0  1  9  3  6  3  3  4  5  0  9
2  7  6  2  3  9  6  7  5  3  6  1  5  0  2  0  3  2  9  1  6  2  1  4  6
7  8  9  1  3  0  3  0  0  2  8  5  5  4  3  8  9  6  8  2  2  1  8  8  1
1  1  0  8  2  7  9  9  8  5  5  1  9  0  7  1  2  5  7  6  8  5  8  2  8
9  6  3  9  6  2  1  1  1  0  3  2  1  7  5  0  6  9  0  6  2  0  9  5  1
1  0  3  2  4  6  1  9  9  8  8  6  5  7  6  9  8  9  1  2  4  9  1  3  5
2  3  7  1  5  7  2  5  8  1  1  7  6  6  4  9  1  3  0  3  5  2  6  3  3
2  3  6  4  7  5  3  4  7  7  7  6  4  3  5  9  6  3  8  7  8  0  1  3  2
9  3  6  1  5  4  4  5  3  3  5  4  1  5  2  3  4  6  4  5  3  7  6  9  2
0  4  0  4  6  7  0  2  9  4  3  5  9  9  7  4  9  0  6  8  7  5  9  3  6
```

Table 1 Random Numbers (*continued*)

```
9 3 6 4 8 6 5 9 2 6 4 5 1 6 9 9 0 8 6 7 4 5 7 2 8
1 1 5 8 8 6 9 0 3 3 6 8 4 1 8 1 3 9 0 8 3 4 5 6 5
7 2 8 1 8 8 3 7 4 4 3 5 0 2 1 3 1 9 9 1 1 1 7 0 0
1 8 4 9 4 8 6 2 6 5 1 7 6 9 5 8 8 2 8 4 0 6 2 7 8
2 7 3 0 6 1 3 6 4 1 9 2 4 5 4 4 9 5 4 7 1 4 2 0 0
2 1 0 3 9 9 3 2 8 0 0 3 4 6 2 9 2 5 5 9 6 5 0 7 8
5 1 2 1 7 3 1 5 7 1 5 8 7 7 5 7 9 8 0 8 5 3 2 5 8
2 5 3 5 4 8 4 5 2 5 7 7 2 8 7 1 8 2 3 9 3 1 5 9 9
0 6 1 5 3 1 9 8 0 4 3 2 0 1 4 5 4 2 9 8 2 9 1 5 5
4 7 0 9 2 7 5 8 6 1 5 4 0 9 9 7 3 9 6 5 5 4 0 1 4
4 6 1 4 8 5 7 1 9 7 0 9 4 2 8 0 1 3 6 4 0 4 9 7 2
8 5 2 7 5 0 5 6 6 3 3 3 1 8 1 6 7 3 2 4 9 6 6 8 9
1 9 5 1 2 4 1 4 7 2 9 8 7 7 4 9 5 1 2 8 6 7 0 0 7
1 1 7 5 2 6 4 7 5 9 2 9 2 7 0 9 3 3 1 6 2 1 0 8 2
6 0 4 0 7 7 9 9 5 0 3 8 6 9 8 9 1 2 5 2 6 3 3 6 5
4 2 8 8 4 2 2 6 5 9 7 6 4 5 2 4 4 4 7 2 3 3 8 0 1
6 3 1 3 5 0 4 8 3 4 1 7 2 9 0 6 3 3 5 0 4 0 4 5 1
4 9 9 6 2 8 3 1 8 4 8 1 1 0 9 4 6 4 2 1 5 9 4 8 6
5 5 8 5 7 3 5 3 1 0 8 9 8 0 1 0 6 2 1 6 9 7 3 5 1
0 8 3 6 4 9 7 5 6 2 8 7 3 8 9 0 2 2 0 0 4 9 9 0 9
5 6 2 1 3 3 7 4 0 7 1 9 3 8 7 6 5 8 9 0 8 3 7 1 4
6 7 6 6 5 2 7 1 5 0 1 5 8 3 1 5 3 5 5 2 2 4 2 5 4
1 0 2 9 2 0 9 5 4 1 6 9 6 8 4 0 2 6 5 3 2 2 1 3 9
9 7 3 0 4 1 8 8 6 5 9 3 9 1 2 2 0 7 2 3 8 9 9 7 8
3 6 6 7 1 6 5 6 6 9 6 7 8 6 2 1 4 1 1 0 8 8 5 4 0
2 4 3 9 7 6 0 0 6 2 8 4 3 4 4 1 1 5 9 3 7 9 4 8 3
0 4 7 0 4 1 0 7 2 9 6 4 5 2 7 2 9 8 3 4 5 6 8 8 2
6 0 5 9 1 1 1 4 4 6 9 7 8 8 6 3 6 7 6 0 5 1 0 5 5
1 1 5 1 6 6 0 5 1 5 6 0 7 5 2 7 3 7 2 4 8 6 2 5 4
3 4 2 3 2 5 9 4 7 1 7 8 4 1 3 8 8 5 3 7 6 8 8 6 4
8 3 3 6 5 8 0 5 9 6 6 1 3 4 5 4 2 8 3 9 5 0 8 9 1
9 2 1 2 4 7 6 5 9 3 6 0 5 0 7 5 3 7 9 3 8 5 1 7 6
2 6 6 8 4 7 5 4 7 0 8 4 2 6 8 3 1 4 5 9 8 7 5 0 6
6 6 4 6 5 8 8 5 9 8 5 9 4 6 5 2 4 0 7 1 4 1 8 7 0
1 1 6 5 4 5 4 0 4 1 7 2 1 5 7 5 8 5 7 4 4 8 2 6 2
3 0 8 3 7 1 3 1 9 0 7 7 5 2 2 7 6 3 9 9 9 0 3 8 6
8 0 2 6 1 8 5 9 3 1 7 9 4 7 5 5 4 9 6 4 6 1 6 0 1
4 5 2 7 5 1 0 6 4 2 1 6 2 4 9 1 8 3 1 8 8 2 7 4 1
0 5 6 1 3 8 3 9 8 3 6 9 4 9 1 5 2 5 6 5 8 4 5 1 9
7 4 1 5 0 4 4 3 4 8 7 4 8 7 4 5 1 3 9 2 4 1 2 2 5
7 4 5 7 0 9 8 3 4 9 7 8 1 3 2 2 8 3 7 3 8 5 2 6 1
5 8 8 2 4 5 4 9 5 6 5 5 0 1 7 6 3 6 1 6 6 5 6 8 9
1 4 9 9 2 0 5 4 1 2 6 4 3 8 4 3 4 3 2 4 4 2 9 5 6
2 3 5 4 3 3 6 9 2 8 2 1 1 5 5 0 7 1 4 5 0 5 6 3 0
9 6 1 5 9 9 1 2 9 2 5 3 9 9 4 1 6 2 3 4 0 8 8 6 9
0 7 2 9 3 7 5 5 5 0 5 7 3 3 6 8 6 2 7 2 1 5 0 0 3
6 2 8 1 5 1 1 4 8 2 9 5 5 6 5 2 0 6 7 3 3 9 2 2 2
2 7 8 8 9 0 4 1 4 6 9 7 5 4 9 2 4 4 0 6 9 5 4 4 4
4 3 3 9 1 2 1 3 6 3 4 3 4 8 8 6 9 3 2 3 3 4 7 1 2
8 8 0 5 2 2 8 0 8 5 3 0 3 7 4 9 6 0 1 8 5 3 8 6 4
```

Table 2 Distribution of *t*

	Level of significance for one-tailed test					
	.10	.05	.025	.01	.005	.0005
df	Level of significance for two-tailed test					
	.20	.10	.05	.02	.01	.001
1	3.078	6.314	12.706	31.821	63.657	636.619
2	1.886	2.920	4.303	6.965	9.925	31.598
3	1.638	2.353	3.182	4.541	5.841	12.941
4	1.533	2.132	2.776	3.747	4.604	8.610
5	1.476	2.015	2.571	3.365	4.032	6.859
6	1.440	1.943	2.447	3.143	3.707	5.959
7	1.415	1.895	2.365	2.998	3.499	5.405
8	1.397	1.860	2.306	2.896	3.355	5.041
9	1.383	1.833	2.262	2.821	3.250	4.781
10	1.372	1.812	2.228	2.764	3.169	4.587
11	1.363	1.796	2.201	2.718	3.106	4.437
12	1.356	1.782	2.179	2.681	3.055	4.318
13	1.350	1.771	2.160	2.650	3.012	4.221
14	1.345	1.761	2.145	2.624	2.977	4.140
15	1.341	1.753	2.131	2.602	2.947	4.073
16	1.337	1.746	2.120	2.583	2.921	4.015
17	1.333	1.740	2.110	2.567	2.898	3.965
18	1.330	1.734	2.101	2.552	2.878	3.992
19	1.328	1.729	2.093	2.539	2.861	3.883
20	1.325	1.725	2.086	2.528	2.845	3.850
21	1.323	1.721	2.080	2.518	2.831	3.819
22	1.321	1.717	2.074	2.508	2.819	3.792
23	1.319	1.714	2.069	2.500	2.807	3.767
24	1.318	1.711	2.064	2.492	2.797	3.745
25	1.316	1.708	2.060	2.485	2.787	3.725
26	1.315	1.706	2.056	2.479	2.779	3.707
27	1.314	1.703	2.052	2.473	2.771	3.690
28	1.313	1.701	2.048	2.467	2.763	3.674
29	1.311	1.699	2.045	2.462	2.756	3.659
30	1.310	1.697	2.042	2.457	2.750	3.646
40	1.303	1.684	2.021	2.423	2.704	3.551
60	1.296	1.671	2.000	2.390	2.660	3.460
120	1.289	1.658	1.980	2.358	2.617	3.373
∞	1.282	1.645	1.960	2.326	2.576	3.291

Table abridged from Table III of Fisher and Yates, *Statistical Tables for Biological, Agricultural, and Medical Research*, published by Longman Group Ltd., London (previously published by Oliver and Boyd Ltd., Edinburgh), by permission of the authors and publishers.

Table 3 Areas Under the Normal Curve: Proportion of Area Under the Normal Curve Between the Mean and a z Distance from the Mean

$\dfrac{x}{\sigma}$ or z	.00	.01	.02	.03	.04	.05	.06	.07	.08	.09
.0	.0000	.0040	.0080	.0120	.0160	.0199	.0239	.0279	.0319	.0359
.1	.0398	.0438	.0478	.0517	.0557	.0596	.0636	.0675	.0714	.0753
.2	.0793	.0832	.0871	.0910	.0948	.0987	.1026	.1064	.1103	.1141
.3	.1179	.1217	.1255	.1293	.1331	.1368	.1406	.1443	.1480	.1517
.4	.1554	.1591	.1628	.1664	.1700	.1736	.1772	.1808	.1844	.1879
.5	.1915	.1950	.1985	.2019	.2054	.2088	.2123	.2157	.2190	.2224
.6	.2257	.2291	.2324	.2357	.2389	.2422	.2454	.2486	.2517	.2549
.7	.2580	.2611	.2642	.2673	.2704	.2734	.2764	.2794	.2823	.2852
.8	.2881	.2910	.2939	.2967	.2995	.3023	.3051	.3078	.3106	.3133
.9	.3159	.3186	.3212	.3238	.3264	.3289	.3315	.3340	.3365	.3389
1.0	.3413	.3438	.3461	.3485	.3508	.3531	.3554	.3577	.3599	.3621
1.1	.3643	.3665	.3686	.3708	.3729	.3749	.3770	.3790	.3810	.3830
1.2	.3849	.3869	.3888	.3907	.3925	.3944	.3962	.3980	.3997	.4015
1.3	.4032	.4049	.4066	.4082	.4099	.4115	.4131	.4147	.4162	.4177
1.4	.4192	.4207	.4222	.4236	.4251	.4265	.4279	.4292	.4306	.4319
1.5	.4332	.4345	.4357	.4370	.4382	.4394	.4406	.4418	.4429	.4441
1.6	.4452	.4463	.4474	.4484	.4495	.4505	.4515	.4525	.4535	.4545
1.7	.4554	.4564	.4573	.4582	.4591	.4599	.4608	.4616	.4625	.4633
1.8	.4641	.4649	.4656	.4664	.4671	.4678	.4686	.4693	.4699	.4706
1.9	.4713	.4719	.4726	.4732	.4738	.4744	.4750	.4756	.4761	.4767
2.0	.4772	.4778	.4783	.4788	.4793	.4798	.4803	.4808	.4812	.4817
2.1	.4821	.4826	.4830	.4834	.4838	.4842	.4846	.4850	.4854	.4857
2.2	.4861	.4864	.4868	.4871	.4875	.4878	.4881	.4884	.4887	.4890
2.3	.4893	.4896	.4898	.4901	.4904	.4906	.4909	.4911	.4913	.4916
2.4	.4918	.4920	.4922	.4925	.4927	.4929	.4931	.4932	.4934	.4936
2.5	.4938	.4940	.4941	.4943	.4945	.4946	.4948	.4949	.4951	.4952
2.6	.4953	.4955	.4956	.4957	.4959	.4960	.4961	.4962	.4963	.4964
2.7	.4965	.4966	.4967	.4968	.4969	.4970	.4971	.4972	.4973	.4974
2.8	.4974	.4975	.4976	.4977	.4977	.4978	.4979	.4979	.4980	.4981
2.9	.4981	.4982	.4982	.4983	.4984	.4984	.4985	.4985	.4986	.4986
3.0	.4987	.4987	.4987	.4988	.4988	.4989	.4989	.4989	.4990	.4990
3.1	.4990	.4991	.4991	.4991	.4992	.4992	.4992	.4992	.4993	.4993
3.2	.4993	.4993	.4994	.4994	.4994	.4994	.4994	.4995	.4995	.4995
3.3	.4995	.4995	.4995	.4996	.4996	.4996	.4996	.4996	.4996	.4997
3.4	.4997	.4997	.4997	.4997	.4997	.4997	.4997	.4997	.4997	.4998
3.5	.4998									
4.0	.49997									
4.5	.499997									
5.0	.4999997									

Table 4 Distribution of Chi-Square

df	Probability					
	.20	.10	.05	.02	.01	.001
1	1.642	2.706	3.841	5.412	6.635	10.827
2	3.219	4.605	5.991	7.824	9.210	13.815
3	4.642	6.251	7.815	9.837	11.345	16.266
4	5.989	7.779	9.488	11.668	13.277	18.467
5	7.289	9.236	11.070	13.388	15.086	20.515
6	8.558	10.645	12.592	15.033	16.812	22.457
7	9.803	12.017	14.067	16.622	18.475	24.322
8	11.030	13.362	15.507	18.168	20.090	26.125
9	12.242	14.684	16.919	19.679	21.666	27.877
10	13.442	15.987	18.307	21.161	23.209	29.588
11	14.631	17.275	19.675	22.618	24.725	31.264
12	15.812	18.549	21.026	24.054	26.217	32.909
13	16.985	19.812	22.362	25.472	27.688	34.528
14	18.151	21.064	23.685	26.873	29.141	36.123
15	19.311	22.307	24.996	28.259	30.578	37.697
16	20.465	23.542	26.296	29.633	32.000	39.252
17	21.615	24.769	27.587	30.995	33.409	40.790
18	22.760	25.989	28.869	32.346	34.805	42.312
19	23.900	27.204	30.144	33.687	36.191	43.820
20	25.038	28.412	31.410	35.020	37.566	45.315
21	26.171	29.615	32.671	36.343	38.932	46.797
22	27.301	30.813	33.924	37.659	40.289	48.268
23	28.429	32.007	35.172	38.968	41.638	49.728
24	29.553	33.196	36.415	40.270	42.980	51.179
25	30.675	34.382	37.652	41.566	44.314	52.620

Table 4 Distribution of Chi-Square (*continued*)

df			Probability			
	.20	.10	.05	.02	.01	.001
26	31.795	35.563	38.885	42.856	45.642	54.052
27	32.912	36.741	40.113	44.140	46.963	55.476
28	34.027	37.916	41.337	45.419	48.278	56.893
29	35.139	39.087	42.557	46.693	49.588	58.302
30	36.250	40.256	43.773	47.962	50.892	59.703
32	38.466	42.585	46.194	50.487	53.486	62.487
34	40.676	44.903	48.602	52.995	56.061	65.247
36	42.879	47.212	50.999	55.489	58.619	67.985
38	45.076	49.513	53.384	57.969	61.162	70.703
40	47.269	51.805	55.759	60.436	63.691	73.402
42	49.456	54.090	58.124	62.892	66.206	76.084
44	51.639	56.369	60.481	65.337	68.710	78.750
46	53.818	58.641	62.830	67.771	71.201	81.400
48	55.993	60.907	65.171	70.197	73.683	84.037
50	58.164	63.167	67.505	72.613	76.154	86.661
52	60.332	65.422	69.832	75.021	78.616	89.272
54	62.496	67.673	72.153	77.422	81.069	91.872
56	64.658	69.919	74.468	79.815	83.513	94.461
58	66.816	72.160	76.778	82.201	85.950	97.039
60	68.972	74.397	79.082	84.580	88.379	99.607
62	71.125	76.630	81.381	86.953	90.802	102.166
64	73.276	78.860	83.675	89.320	93.217	104.716
66	75.424	81.085	85.965	91.681	95.626	107.258
68	77.571	83.308	88.250	94.037	98.028	109.791
70	79.715	85.527	90.531	96.388	100.425	112.317

Table abridged from Fisher and Yates, *Statistical Tables for Biological, Agricultural, and Medical Research*, published by Longman Group Ltd., London (previously published by Oliver and Boyd Ltd., Edinburgh), by permission of the authors and publishers.

Table 5 Distribution of F: .05 Level

df_2 \ df_1	1	2	3	4	5	6	7	8	9	10	12	15	20	24	30	40	60	120	∞
1	161.4	199.5	215.7	224.6	230.2	234.0	236.8	238.9	240.5	241.9	243.9	245.9	248.0	249.1	250.1	251.1	252.2	253.3	254.3
2	18.51	19.00	19.16	19.25	19.30	19.33	19.35	19.37	19.38	19.40	19.41	19.43	19.45	19.45	19.46	19.47	19.48	19.49	19.50
3	10.13	9.55	9.28	9.12	9.01	8.94	8.89	8.85	8.81	8.79	8.74	8.70	8.66	8.64	8.62	8.59	8.57	8.55	8.53
4	7.71	6.94	6.59	6.39	6.26	6.16	6.09	6.04	6.00	5.96	5.91	5.86	5.80	5.77	5.75	5.72	5.69	5.66	5.63
5	6.61	5.79	5.41	5.19	5.05	4.95	4.88	4.82	4.77	4.74	4.68	4.62	4.56	4.53	4.50	4.46	4.43	4.40	4.36
6	5.99	5.14	4.76	4.53	4.39	4.28	4.21	4.15	4.10	4.06	4.00	3.94	3.87	3.84	3.81	3.77	3.74	3.70	3.67
7	5.59	4.74	4.35	4.12	3.97	3.87	3.79	3.73	3.68	3.64	3.57	3.51	3.44	3.41	3.38	3.34	3.30	3.27	3.23
8	5.32	4.46	4.07	3.84	3.69	3.58	3.50	3.44	3.39	3.35	3.28	3.22	3.15	3.12	3.08	3.04	3.01	2.97	2.93
9	5.12	4.26	3.86	3.63	3.48	3.37	3.29	3.23	3.18	3.14	3.07	3.01	2.94	2.90	2.86	2.83	2.79	2.75	2.71
10	4.96	4.10	3.71	3.48	3.33	3.22	3.14	3.07	3.02	2.98	2.91	2.85	2.77	2.74	2.70	2.66	2.62	2.58	2.54
11	4.84	3.98	3.59	3.36	3.20	3.09	3.01	2.95	2.90	2.85	2.79	2.72	2.65	2.61	2.57	2.53	2.49	2.45	2.40
12	4.75	3.89	3.49	3.26	3.11	3.00	2.91	2.85	2.80	2.75	2.69	2.62	2.54	2.51	2.47	2.43	2.38	2.34	2.30
13	4.67	3.81	3.41	3.18	3.03	2.92	2.83	2.77	2.71	2.67	2.60	2.53	2.46	2.42	2.38	2.34	2.30	2.25	2.21
14	4.60	3.74	3.34	3.11	2.96	2.85	2.76	2.70	2.65	2.60	2.53	2.46	2.39	2.35	2.31	2.27	2.22	2.18	2.13
15	4.54	3.68	3.29	3.06	2.90	2.79	2.71	2.64	2.59	2.54	2.48	2.40	2.33	2.29	2.25	2.20	2.16	2.11	2.07
16	4.49	3.63	3.24	3.01	2.85	2.74	2.66	2.59	2.54	2.49	2.42	2.35	2.28	2.24	2.19	2.15	2.11	2.06	2.01
17	4.45	3.59	3.20	2.96	2.81	2.70	2.61	2.55	2.49	2.45	2.38	2.31	2.23	2.19	2.15	2.10	2.06	2.01	1.96
18	4.41	3.55	3.16	2.93	2.77	2.66	2.58	2.51	2.46	2.41	2.34	2.27	2.19	2.15	2.11	2.06	2.02	1.97	1.92
19	4.38	3.52	3.13	2.90	2.74	2.63	2.54	2.48	2.42	2.38	2.31	2.23	2.16	2.11	2.07	2.03	1.98	1.93	1.88

20	4·35	3·49	3·10	2·87	2·71	2·60	2·51	2·45	2·39	2·35	2·28	2·20	2·12	2·08	2·04	1·99	1·95	1·90	1·84
21	4·32	3·47	3·07	2·84	2·68	2·57	2·49	2·42	2·37	2·32	2·25	2·18	2·10	2·05	2·01	1·96	1·92	1·87	1·81
22	4·30	3·44	3·05	2·82	2·66	2·55	2·46	2·40	2·34	2·30	2·23	2·15	2·07	2·03	1·98	1·94	1·89	1·84	1·78
23	4·28	3·42	3·03	2·80	2·64	2·53	2·44	2·37	2·32	2·27	2·20	2·13	2·05	2·01	1·96	1·91	1·86	1·81	1·76
24	4·26	3·40	3·01	2·78	2·62	2·51	2·42	2·36	2·30	2·25	2·18	2·11	2·03	1·98	1·94	1·89	1·84	1·79	1·73
25	4·24	3·39	2·99	2·76	2·60	2·49	2·40	2·34	2·28	2·24	2·16	2·09	2·01	1·96	1·92	1·87	1·82	1·77	1·71
26	4·23	3·37	2·98	2·74	2·59	2·47	2·39	2·32	2·27	2·22	2·15	2·07	1·99	1·95	1·90	1·85	1·80	1·75	1·69
27	4·21	3·35	2·96	2·73	2·57	2·46	2·37	2·31	2·25	2·20	2·13	2·06	1·97	1·93	1·88	1·84	1·79	1·73	1·67
28	4·20	3·34	2·95	2·71	2·56	2·45	2·36	2·29	2·24	2·19	2·12	2·04	1·96	1·91	1·87	1·82	1·77	1·71	1·65
29	4·18	3·33	2·93	2·70	2·55	2·43	2·35	2·28	2·22	2·18	2·10	2·03	1·94	1·90	1·85	1·81	1·75	1·70	1·64
30	4·17	3·32	2·92	2·69	2·53	2·42	2·33	2·27	2·21	2·16	2·09	2·01	1·93	1·89	1·84	1·79	1·74	1·68	1·62
40	4·08	3·23	2·84	2·61	2·45	2·34	2·25	2·18	2·12	2·08	2·00	1·92	1·84	1·79	1·74	1·69	1·64	1·58	1·51
60	4·00	3·15	2·76	2·53	2·37	2·25	2·17	2·10	2·04	1·99	1·92	1·84	1·75	1·70	1·65	1·59	1·53	1·47	1·39
120	3·92	3·07	2·68	2·45	2·29	2·17	2·09	2·02	1·96	1·91	1·83	1·75	1·66	1·61	1·55	1·50	1·43	1·35	1·25
∞	3·84	3·00	2·60	2·37	2·21	2·10	2·01	1·94	1·88	1·83	1·75	1·67	1·57	1·52	1·46	1·39	1·32	1·22	1·00

Table 6 Distribution of F: .01 Level

df_2 \ df_1	1	2	3	4	5	6	7	8	9	10	12	15	20	24	30	40	60	120	∞
1	4052	4999.5	5403	5625	5764	5859	5928	5982	6022	6056	6106	6157	6209	6235	6261	6287	6313	6339	6366
2	98.5	99.00	99.17	99.25	99.30	99.33	99.36	99.37	99.39	99.40	99.42	99.43	99.45	99.46	99.47	99.47	99.48	99.49	99.50
3	34.12	30.82	29.46	28.71	28.24	27.91	27.67	27.49	27.35	27.23	27.05	26.87	26.69	26.60	26.50	26.41	26.32	26.22	26.13
4	21.20	18.00	16.69	15.98	15.52	15.21	14.98	14.80	14.66	14.55	14.37	14.20	14.02	13.93	13.84	13.75	13.65	13.56	13.46
5	16.26	13.27	12.06	11.39	10.97	10.67	10.46	10.29	10.16	10.05	9.89	9.72	9.55	9.47	9.38	9.29	9.20	9.11	9.02
6	13.75	10.92	9.78	9.15	8.75	8.47	8.26	8.10	7.98	7.87	7.72	7.56	7.40	7.31	7.23	7.14	7.06	6.97	6.88
7	12.25	9.55	8.45	7.85	7.46	7.19	6.99	6.81	6.72	6.62	6.47	6.31	6.16	6.07	5.99	5.91	5.82	5.74	5.65
8	11.26	8.65	7.59	7.01	6.63	6.37	6.18	6.03	5.91	5.81	5.67	5.52	5.36	5.28	5.20	5.12	5.03	4.95	4.86
9	10.56	8.02	6.99	6.42	6.06	5.80	5.61	5.47	5.35	5.26	5.11	4.96	4.81	4.73	4.65	4.57	4.48	4.40	4.31
10	10.04	7.56	6.55	5.99	5.64	5.39	5.20	5.06	4.94	4.85	4.71	4.56	4.41	4.33	4.25	4.17	4.08	4.00	3.91
11	9.65	7.21	6.22	5.67	5.32	5.07	4.89	4.74	4.63	4.54	4.40	4.25	4.10	4.02	3.94	3.86	3.78	3.69	3.60
12	9.33	6.93	5.95	5.41	5.06	4.82	4.64	4.50	4.39	4.30	4.16	4.01	3.86	3.78	3.70	3.62	3.54	3.45	3.36
13	9.07	6.70	5.74	5.21	4.86	4.62	4.44	4.30	4.19	4.10	3.96	3.82	3.66	3.59	3.51	3.43	3.34	3.25	3.17
14	8.86	6.51	5.56	5.04	4.69	4.46	4.28	4.14	4.03	3.94	3.80	3.66	3.51	3.43	3.35	3.27	3.18	3.09	3.00
15	8.68	6.36	5.42	4.89	4.56	4.32	4.14	4.00	3.89	3.80	3.67	3.52	3.37	3.29	3.21	3.13	3.05	2.96	2.87
16	8.53	6.23	5.29	4.77	4.44	4.20	4.03	3.89	3.78	3.69	3.55	3.41	3.26	3.18	3.10	3.02	2.93	2.84	2.75
17	8.40	6.11	5.18	4.67	4.34	4.10	3.93	3.79	3.68	3.59	3.46	3.31	3.16	3.08	3.00	2.92	2.83	2.75	2.65
18	8.29	6.01	5.09	4.58	4.25	4.01	3.84	3.71	3.60	3.51	3.37	3.23	3.08	3.00	2.92	2.84	2.75	2.66	2.57
19	8.18	5.93	5.01	4.50	4.17	3.94	3.77	3.63	3.52	3.43	3.30	3.15	3.00	2.92	2.84	2.76	2.67	2.58	2.49

20	8.10	5.85	4.94	4.43	4.10	3.87	3.70	3.56	3.46	3.37	3.23	3.09	2.94	2.86	2.78	2.69	2.61	2.52	2.42
21	8.02	5.78	4.87	4.37	4.04	3.81	3.64	3.51	3.40	3.31	3.17	3.03	2.88	2.80	2.72	2.64	2.55	2.46	2.36
22	7.95	5.72	4.82	4.31	3.99	3.76	3.59	3.45	3.35	3.26	3.12	2.98	2.83	2.75	2.67	2.58	2.50	2.40	2.31
23	7.88	5.66	4.76	4.26	3.94	3.71	3.54	3.41	3.30	3.21	3.07	2.93	2.78	2.70	2.62	2.54	2.45	2.35	2.26
24	7.82	5.61	4.72	4.22	3.90	3.67	3.50	3.36	3.26	3.17	3.03	2.89	2.74	2.66	2.58	2.49	2.40	2.31	2.21
25	7.77	5.57	4.68	4.18	3.85	3.63	3.46	3.32	3.22	3.13	2.99	2.85	2.70	2.62	2.54	2.45	2.36	2.27	2.17
26	7.72	5.53	4.64	4.14	3.82	3.59	3.42	3.29	3.18	3.09	2.96	2.81	2.66	2.58	2.50	2.42	2.33	2.23	2.13
27	7.68	5.49	4.60	4.11	3.78	3.56	3.39	3.26	3.15	3.06	2.93	2.78	2.63	2.55	2.47	2.38	2.29	2.20	2.10
28	7.64	5.45	4.57	4.07	3.75	3.53	3.36	3.23	3.12	3.03	2.90	2.75	2.60	2.52	2.44	2.35	2.26	2.17	2.06
29	7.60	5.42	4.54	4.04	3.73	3.50	3.33	3.20	3.09	3.00	2.87	2.73	2.57	2.49	2.41	2.33	2.23	2.14	2.03
30	7.56	5.39	4.51	4.02	3.70	3.47	3.30	3.17	3.07	2.98	2.84	2.70	2.55	2.47	2.39	2.30	2.21	2.11	2.01
40	7.31	5.18	4.31	3.83	3.51	3.29	3.12	2.99	2.89	2.80	2.66	2.52	2.37	2.29	2.20	2.11	2.02	1.92	1.80
60	7.08	4.98	4.13	3.65	3.34	3.12	2.95	2.82	2.72	2.63	2.50	2.35	2.20	2.12	2.03	1.94	1.84	1.73	1.60
120	6.85	4.79	3.95	3.48	3.17	2.96	2.79	2.66	2.56	2.47	2.34	2.19	2.03	1.95	1.86	1.76	1.66	1.53	1.38
∞	6.63	4.61	3.78	3.32	3.02	2.80	2.64	2.51	2.41	2.32	2.18	2.04	1.88	1.79	1.70	1.59	1.47	1.32	1.00

A P P E N D I X 2

Multivariate Statistics

BASICS OF MULTIVARIATE STATISTICS

■

MATRIX ALGEBRA

■

FOUR MULTIVARIATE PROCEDURES

■

OTHER MULTIVARIATE METHODS

■

REFERENCES AND SUGGESTED READINGS

The discussions of statistics in Chapters 10–12 dealt with *univariate* procedures, which are used to investigate the relationship between one or more independent variables and a single dependent variable. This appendix is a preliminary discussion of **multivariate statistics**, methods that allow analysis of several independent variables *and* several dependent variables in a single study.

The rationale for using multivariate statistics in mass media research is quite simple. Both human behavior and the media are complex systems of interacting variables. There are probably few situations, if any, in which one dependent variable accurately represents a phenomenon or is solely responsible for a particular attitude or behavior. Instead, a series of dependent variables, correlated to some degree, act together to produce or represent a phenomenon, or create an attitude or behavior.

Because they accept the idea of interacting variables affecting interrelated phenomena, many researchers select multivariate statistical methods to analyze data rather than the more traditional, and limited, univariate approaches. This does not mean that univariate procedures are invalid, but rather that multivariate statistics are generally more useful in media research.

The reliance on multivariate analysis in research is based on insights made several years ago: (1) any given experimental manipulation affects several different, but partially related, areas of an individual's behavior, and univariate analysis is capable of investigating only one of these relationships at a time (Harris, 1975); (2) because human beings are multidimensional, it seems reasonable to study them on several dimensions simultaneously, rather than to focus on a single, often arbitrarily chosen variable (Tucker, 1982); (3) measurements taken on the same individual are correlated by virtue of their common origin and thus lend themselves to simultaneous study (Tucker, 1982); (4) multivariate statistical methods are parsimonious and save time, money, and resources, since it is much simpler to investigate several correlated variables simultaneously than to study them one at a time; and (5) multivariate analysis allows researchers to investigate variables as *structures* or *constructs* rather than as the individual components of a structure or construct (Cattell, 1966).

Multivariate statistics, however, do have some disadvantages. First of all, they are difficult to use compared to univariate methods. It is not possible to sit down and learn the procedures involved in factor analysis, for example, as one can do with a *t*-test; multivariate methods

Figure 1 Study design to measure effects of TV viewing and newspaper reading on academic exams

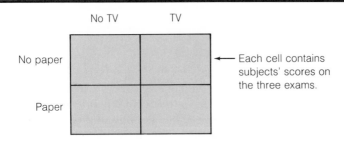

No TV   TV

No paper

← Each cell contains subjects' scores on the three exams.

Paper

require extensive reading and trial-and-error work with a computer. The interpretation of multivariate results is equally difficult in many instances. The results of a *t*-test are relatively straightforward; two groups are either similar or different. In multivariate procedures, however, researchers are often faced with dozens of variable combinations to interpret, and intuitive abilities may become taxed.

Another disadvantage of the multivariate approach is that it is easy to include so many variables that no sense can be made of the results. Although researchers are often tempted to include many potentially relevant variables in a multivariate study, guidelines must be established and followed to restrain this tendency. Finally, it should be noted that multivariate statistics are useful when a question calls for such analysis, but they are not a panacea for all research problems.

The bulk of this appendix is devoted to discussions of four of the most widely used multivariate statistical methods and examples of how they are used in mass media research. The simplified explanations ignore many controversial aspects of each method for the sake of brevity. Readers interested in learning more about multivariate statistics should consult works listed in the "References and Suggested Readings" section.

Basics of Multivariate Statistics

The usefulness of multivariate statistics can be demonstrated by an example using the method called **multivariate analysis of variance (MANOVA)**. Assume that researchers are interested in measuring the effects of television viewing and newspaper reading on academic exams in English, history, and economics. Their study design would look like Figure 1. This design offers four situations to examine: "no paper/no TV," "no paper/TV," "paper/no TV," and "paper/TV." More important, however, it allows the researchers to investigate the effects of the independent variables on all three exams simultaneously; univariate AN-OVA would require three individual studies of each exam. It is clear that the multivariate procedure represents a significant savings in time, money, and resources.

All multivariate statistics are designed to reduce an original "test space," or group of data, into a minimum number of values or dimensions that describe the relevant information contained in the data; this is in accordance with the principle of parsimony. Thus, instead of using 20 dependent variables to describe a phenomenon, a researcher might use multivariate methods to reduce the number to 3 summary variables (weighted linear combinations) that are nearly as accurate as the original 20. Data reduction involves little loss of information and makes the data easier to handle. It is an especially useful process in mass media studies dealing with almost limitless numbers of variables.

Matrix Algebra

Multivariate procedures solve the problem of comparing multiple criterion variables by establishing *weighted linear combinations* of two or more such scores. These composite scores are represented as lines in space called **vectors**. Thus in multivariate statistics one or more vectors are manipulated, usually in an attempt to predict an outcome or event through the **principle of least squares**. This manipulation of vectors requires a different type of analysis, involving what is known as *matrix algebra*.

Because all multivariate statistics deal with multiple measurements of data in multidimensional space, they depend on matrix algebra. A complete knowledge of matrix algebra is not necessary to understand multivariate statistics, but familiarity with several frequently used terms is essential.

A **scalar** is a single-digit number, such as 6, 9, or 7. A column of scalars is called a *column vector* and is denoted by a lowercase letter:

$$a = \begin{bmatrix} a_1 \\ a_2 \\ \cdot \\ \cdot \\ \cdot \\ a_n \end{bmatrix}$$

(The subscript represents the scalar's location in the column.) A row of scalars is referred to as a *row vector* and is denoted by a lowercase letter followed by a prime symbol:

$$a' = [a_1 \ a_2 \cdots a_n]$$

A **matrix** is a two-dimensional array of scalars, having p rows and n columns, and is denoted by a capital letter:

$$A = \begin{bmatrix} a_{11} & a_{12} & \cdot & \cdot & \cdot & a_{1n} \\ a_{21} & a_{22} & \cdot & \cdot & \cdot & a_{2n} \\ a_{p1} & a_{p2} & \cdot & \cdot & \cdot & a_{pn} \end{bmatrix}$$

The most common matrix used in multivariate statistics is the **intercorrelation** (or simply correlation) **matrix**, which is denoted as R. This matrix contains the coefficients of correlation between pairs of variables. For example, a 3×3 correlation matrix (the first number refers to the number of rows, the second to the number of columns) is used to display the relationship between three variables:

$$R = \begin{bmatrix} 1.0 & .64 & .29 \\ .64 & 1.0 & .42 \\ .29 & .42 & 1.0 \end{bmatrix}$$

This is a **square matrix**: the number of rows equals the number of columns. It contains the value 1.00 in the principal diagonal (top left to bottom right), since the correlation of a variable with itself is usually considered to be 100%. The term "usually" is necessary because in some multivariate models it is assumed that even a correlation of a variable with itself includes some error and hence must be valued at less than 1.00.

A **diagonal matrix** is a square matrix whose elements equal zero except in the principal diagonal. If in addition all the elements in the principal diagonal are 1, the array is known as an **identity matrix** and is denoted by a capital I:

$$I = \begin{bmatrix} 1 & 0 & 0 \\ 0 & 1 & 0 \\ 0 & 0 & 1 \end{bmatrix}$$

An identity matrix indicates that there are no correlations between the variables in the analysis except for the correlation of each variable with itself. Essentially, the identity matrix form implies that the data are of poor quality. Identity matrices are common in research studies that use random numbers (usually in demonstrations of statistical procedures).

Associated with every square matrix is a single number that represents a unique function of the numbers contained in the matrix. This scalar function is known as a **determinant** and is denoted as A. In addition, each square matrix has an associated characteristic equation that represents the information contained in the matrix. The results from the characteristic equation (when computed) reproduce the matrix from which the equation was developed. Several values can be used to calculate a characteristic equation for a matrix; each of these includes a value or number known as an eigenvalue. Each eigenvalue has an associated eigenvector (a column of numbers); the eigenvalue is actually the sum of the squared elements in the eigenvector. In short, eigenvalues and eigenvectors are used to construct a formula that duplicates the information contained in a matrix. Each matrix has a number of characteristic equations, but only one is appropriate for a particular type of analysis.

Multivariate statistics involve two basic algebraic operations. The first is *partitioning* of a matrix, whereby the original matrix is divided into submatrices for analysis. The second operation, *transposition*, involves changing the matrix columns to rows and the rows to columns for further analysis (Horst, 1966). For example, the "transpose" of Matrix A is Matrix A':

$$A = \begin{bmatrix} 1 & 4 \\ 2 & 5 \\ 3 & 6 \end{bmatrix} \qquad A' = \begin{bmatrix} 1 & 2 & 3 \\ 4 & 5 & 6 \end{bmatrix}$$

Four Multivariate Procedures

Although there are several multivariate statistics available, four methods appear to be used most often in mass media research. These are factor analysis, canonical correlation, discriminant analysis, and multivariate analysis of variance (MANOVA). Each method is discussed below in terms of how it works and what it can do in media research.

Factor Analysis

Factor analysis is a generic term for a variety of statistical procedures developed for the analysis of the intercorrelations *within* a set of variables. These relationships are represented by weighted linear combinations known as **factor scores** (or variates), which, in turn, are used in the development of constructs and theories. Factor analysis is divided into several techniques, each of which is appropriate to a specific type of investigation. However, two major techniques are used most often in mass media research: *R-technique* and *Q-technique*. The R-technique is used to factor a set of variables collected at the same time from a number of individuals. The Q-technique is used to factor a number of individuals from variables collected at the same time from those individuals.

Each technique includes a variety of approaches. Some types of R-technique factor analysis are: common factor analysis (CFA), principal components analysis (PC or PCA), and minimum residuals (minres). The most often used procedure in the Q-technique is cluster analysis, which seeks to identify types of individuals, not groups of variables as in the R-technique.

Factor analysis is the most widely used multivariate statistic in mass media research, due to its flexibility. Some of the more common uses for factor analysis include the following (Rummel, 1970).

1. Investigating patterns of variable relationships
2. Reducing data
3. Analyzing the structure of a phenomenon
4. Classifying or describing individuals, groups, or variables
5. Developing of measurement scales (see Chapter 2)
6. Testing hypotheses or research questions
7. Making preliminary investigations in new areas of research
8. Developing theories

As Rummel suggested, factor analysis is appropriate in any phase of research, from pilot studies to theory development. This is not true of other multivariate statistical procedures. The development of the LIS-REL program (Joreskog, 1973) has made factor analysis much easier to use.

Researchers who use factor analysis assume that any group of variables has some inherent order that, once discovered, can make the description of a concept or construct less complicated. As Thurstone (1947) noted:

> A factor problem starts with the hope or conviction that a certain domain is not so chaotic as it looks. Factor analysis was developed primarily for the purposes of identifying principal dimensions or categories of mentality; but the methods are general, so that they have been found useful for other psychological problems and in other sciences as well. . . . [F]actor analysis is especially useful in those domains where basic and fruitful concepts are essentially lacking and where experiments have been difficult to achieve.

As Thurstone suggested, factor analysis is useful in all types of scientific research. This does not imply, however, that the results of a factor analysis in any particular area are necessarily *meaningful*; any matrix of variables can be factorially analyzed, but not all will yield scientifically useful or meaningful information (Gorsuch, 1974). It is necessary to understand the purpose of factor analysis in order to determine its appropriateness for a specific mass media problem.

Factor analysis includes a wide variety of alternatives. Because of the complexity of many of these methods, it is not possible to discuss each one here. This is left to multivariate statistics books and other more detailed texts.

The two most widely used forms of factor analysis are *principal components* and *principal factors* (also called common factor analysis). The methods are identical except for the initial step: the principal components model uses *unities* (1.00) in the principal diagonal of the correlation matrix, while the principal factors technique assumes that each variable's correlation with itself contains some degree of error and

Figure 2 Example of correlation matrix (*R*)

	1	2	3	4	5
1	1.00	.92	.70	.38	.05
2	.92	1.00	.95	.71	.26
3	.70	.95	1.00	.88	.33
4	.38	.71	.88	1.00	.14
5	.05	.26	.33	.14	1.00

therefore cannot be 100%. These correlations, called *communalities*, replace the unities in the principal diagonal of the original matrix. Communalities are a bit more complicated than unities, since they are only *estimates* of the correlations of variables with themselves. Although choosing the communality estimates to insert into the principal diagonal may sound simple, it is one of the most controversial decisions in factor analysis.

A typical factor analysis begins with the collection of data on a number of different variables (usually at the interval or ratio level). These quantified variables are then transformed via computer into a *product–moment correlation matrix*, the matrix that is usually chosen for factoring. To illustrate, consider the problem of determining which medium, or combination of media, a subject uses for news and information. A questionnaire is designed to collect this information with regard to five media sources: (1) radio, (2) television, (3) magazines, (4) newspapers, and (5) books. The correlation matrix developed from these data may look as shown in Figure 2. The matrix shows the correlations between all five variables. The principal diagonal divides the matrix into two parts, each a mirror image of the other. The diagonal itself is composed of unities, indicating that the method of principal components is being employed.

Note that although any matrix can be factored, even a matrix of random numbers, there are procedures that can help researchers determine whether a particular correlation matrix is valid. Two tests are particularly useful: Bartlett's sphericity test and Kaiser's measure of sampling adequacy (MSA). Both are used to determine the quality of the correlation matrix and to indicate whether the information is adequate for analysis.

In mathematical terms, factoring a matrix consists of extracting eigenvectors and their associated eigenvalues. These two sets of values are used to mathematically reproduce the correlation matrix.

Table 1 Unrotated Factor Matrix

Medium	Factor 1	Factor 2	
Newspaper	.85	.53	
Magazines	.66	−.09	
Books	.37	.73	Eigenvectors
Radio	−.52	.34	
Television	.29	.63	
	1.65	1.33	Eigenvalues

Eigenvectors are factor loadings, or numerical values from − 1.00 to + 1.00, indicating the amount of contribution each variable makes toward defining a factor. A factor loading is a quantified relationship— the farther its value is from zero, the more relevant the variable is to the factor. The eigenvalues are used to determine which factors are relevant, and hence should be analyzed. (Recall that an eigenvalue is computed by squaring and summing the elements in its eigenvector.) One common procedure is to interpret only the factors with eigenvalues greater than 1.00 (although other methods are used).

The eigenvectors and eigenvalues for the hypothetical study are displayed in Table 1. This example shows that two factors "fell out" (were significant as determined by the eigenvalue cutoff of greater than 1.00) and may be used in explaining the media used for news and information. The eigenvalues are computed by squaring and summing each element in the eigenvector:

$$.85^2 + .66^2 + .37^2 + .52^2 + .29^2 = 1.65$$

The analysis does not stop with this initial extraction of factors; the initial factor loadings are generally too complex to be used for interpretation. Instead, researchers generally perform a second step, factor *rotation*, which essentially involves changing the multidimensional space in which the factors are located. Recall that eigenvectors (a vector of factor loadings) represent lines in space—a space visually constructed by *x*- and *y*-axes. The unrotated factor loadings are often in complex form; that is, there may be several complex variables such that one variable loads significantly on more than one factor. Rotation attempts to clear this problem by changing the space in which the factor loadings are placed. The new factor loadings are mathematically equivalent to the original unrotated matrix, but more often they represent a more meaningful set of factors—where the goal is to have each variable load significantly on only one factor. This additional ease of interpretation makes rotation appealing in behavioral research. A rotated factor matrix is shown in Table 2.

The rotated factor matrix is mathematically equivalent to the unrotated matrix, as witnessed by identical eigenvalues, and the factors are now easier to interpret. The first step in interpretation is to identify

Table 2 Rotated Factor Matrix

Medium	Factor 1	Factor 2
Newspaper	.87	.15
Magazines	.66	−.03
Books	.61	.22
Radio	.17	.85
Television	.20	.74
	1.63	1.34

the variables that are associated with one and only one factor. Here, it is evident that Variables 1, 2, and 3 "load" more heavily on Factor 1, while Variables 4 and 5 load more heavily on Factor 2. Three variables (1, 2, 3) are said to "define" Factor 1, and two variables (4, 5) define Factor 2.

The next step is to categorize the factors on the basis of the variables that define it. In this case, Factor 1 might be classified as "print media" and Factor 2 as "electronic media." In reality, however, Factor 2 might be eliminated altogether at this point, since it is defined by just two variables. It is customary when classifying factors to select only factors that have at least three variables with significant loadings. Some researchers consider this practice controversial, but three significant loadings are necessary to establish the direction of the factor. If a factor has only two significant variable loadings—one positive and the other negative—it cannot be determined whether the factor itself is positive or negative; a third variable is required to provide the direction. Even when both variables are positive or both are negative, however, a two-variable factor may be inadequate to explain the variance in the factor. As a general rule, it is best to consider only factors that are defined by at least three variables.

Researchers must also consider which type of rotation to use. There are many procedures available, but the two used most often by behavioral researchers are *orthogonal* and *oblique* rotation. The names refer to the angles of the axes on which the data points (factor loadings) are located. Orthogonal rotation keeps the angles at 90° and assumes that the factors are not intercorrelated (that is, orthogonal = uncorrelated). Oblique rotation allows the axes to take any angle that will produce the most interpretable results; researchers using this approach assume that the factors are correlated to some degree (that is, oblique = correlated). The choice of a rotation method depends on the researcher's likes and dislikes as well as the purpose of the study.

Of the many possible uses of factor analysis mentioned earlier, the three that are most prominent in research studies are data reduction, the search for order in variable structures, and the exploration of uncharted phenomena.

Data reduction, as noted earlier, is essential when investigating research problems that contain large numbers of variables. Factor analysis is often used as a preliminary narrowing device because it allows the selection of salient variables from a large group: it provides a simplification of a particular domain of variables by replacing them with a small number of hypothetical variates (weighted linear sums of the original variables, or factor scores). These variates can then be used in other analyses that employ different statistical methods without a substantial loss of information. For example, consider a 50-item questionnaire designed to measure attitudes toward commercials on television and their effects on buying habits. A factor analysis of the 50 variables would produce a substantially smaller number of representative variates, for factor scores, thus providing an opportunity for a much simpler explanation of the phenomenon being investigated.

The *search for order* in a domain of variables via factor analysis is referred to by several different names: it can be said that factor analysis identifies variable patterns, dimensions of variable domains, underlying constructs, factor dimensions, or factor structures. Whatever terminology is used, the meaning is the same: factor analysis allows the identification from a large group of variables of a smaller number of composite variables that help order and define the phenomenon under study.

A construct such as "program success" may be defined by an infinite number of variables. It may be difficult, if not impossible, to intuitively determine which variables contribute significantly to the construct. Factor analysis, by reducing the number of variables, makes it easier to identify patterns and underlying structures. However, one factor analysis does not produce conclusive results concerning the composition of a construct; different samples, different factor analysis methods, and different variables must be used to verify that the initial results were not sample- or method-specific. That is, replication is necessary to ensure that results are not dependent on some condition external to the relationship among the variables.

Finally, factor analysis can help to provide *explanations of previously unstudied phenomena*. Every research area has many concepts and constructs that have eluded investigation. One reason for this is that the concepts are obscured by large numbers of variables. An example is the question of what characterizes a successful television program. Television executives still do not know; there are simply too many variables. Factor analysis can play a significant (albeit preliminary) role in solving problems of this nature by isolating salient variables from those that will add nothing to the accuracy of a prediction.

Factor analysis allows researchers to take a panoramic view of a variable domain and to isolate important variables. However, it should be used only when a research project is well constructed and meets the prerequisite assumptions discussed above. It should *not* be used in an attempt to salvage a poorly planned study. As mentioned

Figure 3 R_c intercorrelation "supermatrix"

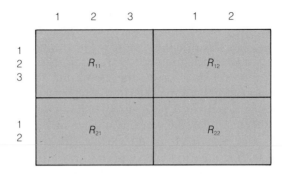

earlier, any matrix of variables can be factorially analyzed, but there is no guarantee that the results will be meaningful.

Canonical Correlation

Canonical correlation (R_c) is essentially multivariate extension of linear multiple regression: a group of independent variables is analyzed to predict multiple criterion variables. However, no distinction is actually made between independent and dependent variables; there are simply two *sets* of variables.

A canonical correlation begins with the formation of an intercorrelation "supermatrix" composed of both sets of variables. For example, if three variables are included in one set and two variables in the second set, the intercorrelation matrix is formed as in Figure 3.

Note that the correlation matrix is divided into four areas: R_{11} represents the intercorrelations among the elements of Set 1; R_{22} denotes intercorrelations among the elements of Set 2; and R_{12} and R_{21} are the cross-correlations between the elements of Sets 1 and 2. This "supermatrix" of intercorrelations provides the information necessary to compute the basic R_c relationship matrix by means of the formula:

$$R_c = [R_{22}{}^{-1}R_{21}R_{11}{}^{-1}R_{12}]$$

The canonical correlation matrix formed by the formula is a square matrix and therefore contains eigenvectors and eigenvalues (each unique solution is called a root; each root has a canonical correlation). A *pair* of eigenvectors is extracted from each variable set and normalized; the resulting scalar values are the sets' beta weights. Finally, for each variable set, the subject's standardized raw scores are multiplied by the beta weight and the products summed. This process yields a pair of scores called *composite canonical variates* (weighted linear combinations of variables). The R_c is the product–moment correlation between these variates.

A researcher interprets three basic values in canonical correlation analysis: the canonical correlation for each root, the canonical components, and the redundancy index. The canonical correlation, since it is merely a product–moment correlation, is interpreted in the same way as any correlation value: the closer the value to 1.00, the stronger the relationship between the composite variates (canonical correlations cannot be negative). The R_c model allows the extraction of as many roots as there are variables in the smaller of the two sets (in the example above, the researcher could extract two unique roots), and each of these is orthogonal (uncorrelated) to all other roots in the analysis. This can provide several possibilities for interpretation (although not all the roots may be statistically significant).

Interpretation of the individual variables in a canonical correlation involves analyzing their *canonical components*, that is, each variable's correlation with the canonical variate corresponding to its particular set. Thus, the canonical components are also correlations and interpreted as such: the components whose values are farthest from zero are considered most significant. However, not all researchers agree on what constitutes a significant component value; many consider .30 to be significant, while others use .35, .40, or some different value.

The **redundancy index** provides the direction in which the canonical results should be interpreted; that is, it determines whether the R_c is to be interpreted as "Set 1 given Set 2" or "Set 2 given Set 1," or, possibly, whether it should be interpreted in both directions. The redundancy index increases the interpretive value of canonical correlation by allowing researchers to interpret relationships within canonical components, as well as between the variable sets. In fact, relationships between sets should never be interpreted without first computing the redundancy index.

The formula for computing a redundancy index $(\overline{R})$ is simple: square each component value in a variable set, add the squares, divide the sum by the number of variables in the set, and multiply this value by the canonical correlation squared:

$$\overline{R} = \frac{\Sigma(R_{cc})^2}{M} (R_c^2)$$

where $\overline{R}$ = the redundancy index; R_{cc} = a canonical component; and M = the number of variables in the set.

The importance of these three values in canonical correlation analysis can be illustrated by a research problem shown in Table 3, which asked the question: "What, if any, relationship exists between the mass media actually used for political information and the media considered to be most informative?"

First consider the four canonical correlations for the four

Table 3 Canonical Correlation Example

Variables	Root 1 (R_c = .85)	Root 2 (R_c = .45)	Root 3 (R_c = .31)	Root 4 (R_c = .31)
	Left set (media considered most informative)			
Newspaper	.28 (1.00)*	−.63 (−.29)	−.33 (−.07)	−.06 (−.03)
Radio	.02 (.35)	−.08 (.01)	.42 (.50)	−.87 (−.84)
Television	.53 (1.30)**	.53 (.62)	−.30 (.10)	.01 (.02)
Magazines	.16 (.54)	−.46 (−.31)	.64 (.72)	.46 (.45)
Paper and TV	.07 (.27)	−.02 (.03)	−.15 (−.10)	.05 (.05)
2 Combination	.06 (.22)	−.10 (−.05)	.13 (.17)	−.10 (.09)
3 Combination	.04 (.13)	−.09 (−.01)	.10 (.12)	−.02 (−.02)
People	.01 (.08)	.06 (.09)	−.05 (−.03)	.01 (.01)
None	−.30 (.50)**	.49 (.65)	.46 (.59)	.19 (.18)
	Right set (media used for political information)			
Newspapers	.85 (.41)**	−.41 (−.82)	−.30 (−.99)	.02 (−.05)
Radio	.62 (.15)**	−.03 (.07)	.32 (.43)	−.70 (−1.10)
Magazines	.63 (.52)**	−.38 (.45)	.56 (.97)	.35 (.57)
Television	.90 (.52)**	.41 (1.10)	.02 (−.05)	.11 (.39)

Root 1: x^2 = 5,460.32; df = 36; p<.01
Root 2: x^2 = 1,358.26; df = 24; p<.01
Root 3: x^2 = 635.01; df = 14; p<.01
Root 4: x^2 = 313.93; df = 6; p<.01

Redundancy indexes

Left set		Right set	
Root 1:	.0470	Root 1:	.4308
Root 2:	.0273	Root 2:	.0258
Root 3:	.0117	Root 3:	.0126
Root 4:	.0111	Root 4:	.0154

*Canonical components are listed first with corresponding beta weights in parentheses.
**Indicates a significant canonical component value.

roots. Each root has a value of at least .30, indicating that all may be interpreted unless the component loadings and redundancy index indicate otherwise (.30 is usually the cutoff value for interpretation of a canonical root; however, this depends on the nature of the study and the requirements established by the researcher). In most cases the roots in a canonical analysis do not all have a value of .30 or higher, but such values are common in studies using extremely large samples.

The second step is to examine the significant canonical components, which are considered to be those with absolute values of .30 or greater (again, this limit is at the discretion of the researcher). Referring to Root 1, the variables in Set 1 (also known as the *left set*) show a high positive component value for television (.53) and a very low value for the variable "none" ($-.30$); the remaining variables have values too minimal to be considered significant. The left variable set of Root 1 thus suggests a degree of dichotomy: a great many subjects considered television the most informative medium for political information, but a smaller number indicated that none was most informative, possibly meaning that all were regarded as equally informative (the negative value means that those subjects who responded "television" as most informative did not respond "none"). All the variables in Set 2 (the *right set*) surpassed the .30 cutoff value for Root 1, indicating that the subjects in the study used all these media for political information.

Before the computation can be continued, redundancy indexes must be computed. Without redundancy figures, one can interpret only the relationships within sets, not those between sets. This point is repeated because of its importance: many researchers incorrectly interpret the relationships between sets because they have neglected to compute redundancy indexes.

The general cutoff level for redundancy is .05. That is, a canonical root must account for at least 5% of the variance in the set before interpretation can continue. The redundancy indexes displayed in Table 3 indicate that only Set 2 of the first root achieved a high enough value to qualify for further interpretation; this means that Root 1 is to be interpreted from the right set (media used), given the left set (media considered most informative).

The remaining three roots in the analysis did not receive significant redundancy indexes (even though their R_c values met minimum requirements); these roots must therefore either be eliminated from further discussion or interpreted for heuristic value only. This demonstrates how the redundancy index serves as a cross-validation for the canonical roots extracted from the analysis; it serves as a backup test for significance.

Applying this information to the data, the results show that individuals who used all the media for political information tended to feel that television was the most informative. In addition, a smaller group of individuals who used all the media felt that all were equally important.

Discriminant Analysis

Mass media researchers frequently are interested in examining or predicting the attitudes or behavior of subjects who are members of a particular group. For example, a researcher might wish to examine the differences between subjects who subscribe to certain magazines or newspapers, or to predict the characteristics of individuals occupying management level positions in the media. **Discriminant analysis** can be a useful tool in research situations of these types.

Figure 4 Discriminant analysis procedure

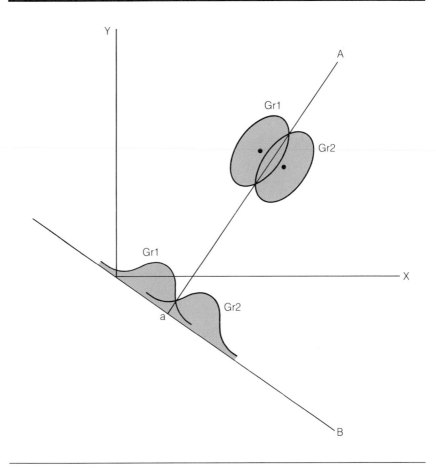

In discriminant analysis, linear combinations of continuously scaled variables are derived from measurements made on groups of subjects. The model is used to define a vector that represents the variables for each group so that the separation between groups is maximized. In other words, the researcher uses all the variables in the discriminant analysis to compute a weighted linear combination (variate) for each group, from which it can be determined which of the variables are most helpful in separating or distinguishing the groups. These variables are known as the *discriminating variables*.

The discriminant analysis procedure is shown in graphic form in Figure 4. Here, a *bivariate* example is used (two groups). The two ellipses represent data *swarms* for each group, and the dot at the center of each ellipse denotes the group mean, or *centroid*. The two points at which the ellipses intersect define a line, designated as *A*. If a second line, *B*, is constructed perpendicular to Line *A*, and the points from the intersection of Groups 1 and 2 are projected onto Line B, the overlap between the groups is smaller along Line B (indicated as a) than any other possible line (Cooley & Lohnes, 1971). The discriminant analysis procedure attempts to define this *true* line along which the groups are maximally separated.

Discriminant analysis can serve two purposes, analysis and classification. The data are analyzed by means of statistical tests designed to measure the significance of the combined variables. In classification, which takes place after the data have been analyzed, categories of membership are created for the subjects in the study. A particular study may involve one or both procedures.

Discriminant analysis is closely related to factor analysis and canonical correlation in that each model extracts "factors" from a battery of variables. The factors, which are linear combinations in all models, are referred to as *discriminant functions*. Each discriminant function is orthogonal to all others in the analysis; that is, each function is an independent representation of the analysis in question. In discriminant analysis, the number of functions is one less than the number of groups involved, unless the number of variables in the analysis is smaller. In that case, the number of discriminant functions is equal to the number of original variables.

Interpreting a discriminant analysis involves examining the discriminant functions and the weights assigned to each of the variables used in forming those functions. These observations taken together allow researchers to analyze the nature of group differences. As in factor analysis, the dimensions represented by the discriminant functions may be susceptible to meaningful interpretation. However, even if the interpretation is not meaningful, parsimony is achieved by reducing the original space in which the group differences existed (Tatsuoka, 1971).

Another procedure involved in discriminant analysis is plotting the centroids of the discriminant functions. Each group has a mean for the linear combination it creates; these means are plotted to determine the nature of the distance between the groups—the plot provides a visual representation of group differences. Tests are also available to indicate whether the distance separating the groups is statistically significant (Klecka, 1980; Tatsuoka, 1970).

Haynes (1978) used discriminant analysis to test two hypotheses related to children's perceptions of comic and authentic violence in cartoons. A "comic" cartoon was defined as one that portrayed a violent act in a comical manner, and the victim suffered no true or lasting ill effects. An "authentic" cartoon depicted a violent act as "true to life," with no comic effect intended. The two hypotheses were: (1) that children would perceive the violence in a comic cartoon as being more violent than that in an authentic cartoon, and (2) that females would perceive all the cartoons as being more violent than would males.

Table 4 Haynes's Discriminant Analysis of Male and Female Perception of "Comic" and "Authentic" Cartoon Violence

	Discriminant function coefficients	
	Function I	Function II
Perceived violence	−.997	.079
Acceptability of violence	.093	.994

DF I–perceived violence	Centroids
Male/authentic	.35
Female/authentic	.42
Male/comic	−.48
Female/comic	−.51

DF II–acceptability	Centroids
Male/authentic	.61
Female/authentic	.65
Male/comic	−.17
Female/comic	−.12

Source: Richard B. Haynes. "Children's Perception of 'Comic' and 'Authentic' Cartoon Violence." *Journal of Broadcasting,* Winter 1978, p. 68. Reprinted by permission.

Haynes's first step was to administer a 12-item questionnaire to a group of 120 children, asking them to describe how they felt about a cartoon they viewed in an experimental situation. These responses were factor analyzed and the factor scores used in the discriminant analysis to determine whether group differences existed. (In this study, Haynes used discriminant analysis solely as a classification procedure, since he had no knowledge about group membership beforehand.)

The first discriminant function (DF I, Table 4) revealed that the males and females who viewed the comic cartoons (Group 1) were most clearly distinguishable from the males and females who viewed the authentic cartoons (Group 2) in terms of a function described as "perceived violence" (so named because of the nature of the most significantly weighted variables in the function). The second discriminant function, DF II, showed that Group 1 was most different from Group 2 with regard to a function described as "acceptability of violence." The centroids for each group showed that no sex differences existed. However, Haynes did find that the comic cartoons were perceived as being more violent than the authentic cartoons, and that the comic violence was perceived as being more unacceptable than authentic violence.

Discriminant analysis is a useful research tool in all areas of mass media. The method is often used as a secondary phase of research, such as was done by Haynes: the researcher may conduct a factor analysis or other statistical procedure that produces summary

Figure 5 Simple ANOVA

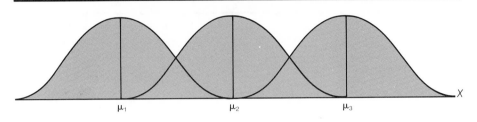

scores, and use these scores in a discriminant analysis to determine whether group differences exist.

Multivariate Analysis of Variance

Multivariate analysis of variance (MANOVA) was introduced briefly earlier to demonstrate the utility of multivariate statistics over univariate methods. As mentioned, MANOVA is an extension of the simple ANOVA model to situations involving more than one dependent variable. Specifically, MANOVA allows researchers to test the differences between two or more groups on multiple response data.

The distinctive feature of MANOVA is that the dependent variables are represented as a vector, or weighted linear combination, instead of as a single value, as in ANOVA. ANOVA involves testing for group differences along a continuum formed by the dependent variable, as is shown in Figure 5 (Cooley & Lohnes, 1971).

The MANOVA model extends this idea by testing for group differences in a multidimensional space, as depicted in Figure 6.

The test used in MANOVA to determine the equality of centroids (compared to the test for equality of group means in ANOVA) involves forming an *F*-ratio between the within groups' and total groups' *dispersion matrices*. This concept is beyond the scope of an introductory text; suffice it to say that the procedure is similar to that used in ANOVA except that matrices are used instead of sums of squares.

Lambert and his colleagues (1980) performed a study that illustrates how several dependent variables can be simultaneously analyzed using MANOVA. The project demonstrates that not only are time and resources saved, but also several characteristics of an individual can be considered simultaneously, thus providing a closer approximation of reality than could a univariate statistical approach.

Lambert and others were interested in examining the attitudes of consumers generally, and of the elderly in particular, toward

Figure 6 Simple MANOVA

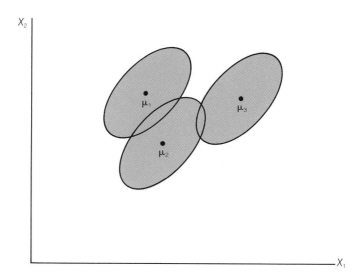

the exploitation of opportunities to save money by substituting lower priced generic drugs for brand name products prescribed by their physicians. The authors used a multistage quota sampling procedure to select 510 respondents from four cities in Florida. The subjects completed a questionnaire containing 18 dependent variables. An interesting aspect of the study was the refusal of several of the respondents over age 65 to cooperate with the researchers for one reason or another (such as poor eyesight or fear of being victimized by salespeople). The study offers excellent examples of the problems that can occur in some research studies.

The authors divided the sample into two groups: people who accepted the idea that generic drugs are equivalent to brand name drugs, and those who did not. The two groups were compared with respect to their scores on the 18 variables, which included demographics, mobility, general drug knowledge, age, and income. The design is illustrated in Figure 7.

The MANOVA results indicated a significant difference ($p < .0001$) between the two groups on the 18 variables taken as a whole. The study allowed the authors to discuss the influence of many variables on consumers' attitudes toward generic drugs and to make recommendations concerning how drug education programs might help individuals, especially older people, take advantage of the lower cost generic drugs that are available.

Figure 7 MANOVA example

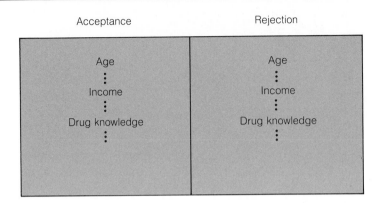

Other Multivariate Methods

We have described only four of the many multivariate statistical procedures available to mass media researchers. Several other statistics are appropriate for media researchers, some of which are presented briefly here. Researchers interested in these areas are urged to consult the "References and Suggested Readings" section.

Most researchers understand that human behavior and attitudes are comprised of a complex series of interacting variables, and that some variables are more important than others. In many situations, researchers may wish to define a series of steps involved in a decision or attitude and to "map out" the relationships between the relevant interacting variables. Path analysis is appropriate for this task.

Path analysis essentially creates a "causal path" to describe the relationship between the independent and the dependent variables. The method is particularly useful in situations involving decision-making processes or selections from among several alternatives that might be followed in a given course of action. Path analysis does not *demonstrate* causality; rather, it is a method for tracing a set of causal assumptions made by the researcher.

In *cluster analysis*, which is closely related to factor analysis, objects or persons are grouped together into "factors," or clusters, on the basis of their similarities and differences. A cluster analysis of variables is referred to as a V-analysis, and a cluster analysis of objects is called O-analysis.

Multidimensional scaling (MDS) is used to analyze judgments of similarity between variables in such a way that the dimensionality of those judgments can be measured. The idea behind MDS is relatively simple. If each variable is thought of as a point in space, the problem becomes one of finding the smallest dimensionality of that space and eliminating errors in prediction (Torgerson, 1958). In other words, one might conduct a research study of subjects' use of radio, television, and newspapers to predict product purchase behavior. The closer together these three variables can be defined as points in space, the better will be the prediction of purchasing behavior.

References and Suggested Readings

Cattell, R. B. (Ed.). (1966). *Handbook of multivariate experimental psychology*. Skokie, IL: Rand McNally.

Comrey, A. L. (1973). *A first course in factor analysis*. New York: Academic Press.

Cooley, W. W., & Lohnes, P. R. (1971). *Multivariate data analysis*. New York: John Wiley.

Duncan, O. D. (1966). Path analysis: Sociological examples. *American Journal of Sociology, 72,* 1–16.

Gorsuch, R. L. (1974). *Factor analysis*. Philadelphia: W. B. Saunders.

Harris, R. (1975). *A primer of multivariate statistics*. New York: Academic Press.

Haynes, R. B. (1978). Children's perceptions of "comic" and "authentic" cartoon violence. *Journal of Broadcasting, 22,* 63–70.

Horst, P. (1966). An overview of the essentials of multivariate analysis methods. In R. B. Cattell (Ed.), *Handbook of multivariate experimental psychology*. Chicago: Rand McNally.

Joreskog, K. G. (1973). A general model for estimating a linear structural equation system. In A. S. Goldberger & O. D. Duncan (Eds.), *Structural equation models in the social sciences*. New York: Seminar Press.

Joreskog, K. G., & Sorbom, D. (1984). *LISREL VI*. Mooresville, IN: Scientific Software.

Klecka, W. R. (1980). *Discriminant analysis*. Beverly Hills, CA: Sage Publications.

Lambert, Z. V., Doering, P., Goldstein, E., & McCormick, W. (1980). Predisposition toward generic drug acceptance. *Journal of Consumer Research, 7,* 14–23.

Rummel, R. J. (1970). *Applied factor analysis*. Evanston, IL: Northwestern University Press.

Tatsuoka, M. M. (1970). *Discriminant analysis*. Champaign, IL: Institute for Personality and Ability Testing.

Tatsuoka, M. M. (1971). *Multivariate analysis*. New York: John Wiley.

Thurstone, L. L. (1947). *Multiple factor analysis*. Chicago: University of Chicago Press.

Torgerson, W. (1958). *Theory and methods of scaling*. New York: John Wiley.

Tryon, R. C., & Bailey, D. E. (1970). *Cluster analysis*. New York: McGraw-Hill.

Tucker, R. K. (1982). *Basic multivariate research models*. San Diego, CA: College Hill Press.

Brief Guide for Conducting Focus Groups

PLANNING THE GROUPS

∎

CHOOSING A FIELD SERVICE AND A FACILITY LOCATION

∎

RECRUITING

∎

BEFORE THE GROUPS BEGIN

∎

CONDUCTING THE GROUPS

∎

HANDLING RESPONDENTS

Focus groups can be very valuable research tools; however, they are double-edged swords. The method looks deceptively simple: invite 6–12 people from a homogeneous group to a research location and have a 2-hour, controlled discussion. But despite their simplicity, focus groups have gremlins hiding behind dozens of corners. Researchers who are unaware of the potential problems in conducting a focus group may reap disastrous results. Even the simplest focus group topic can become impossible to handle. Here we discuss some of the problem areas that require consideration both before a focus group meets and while the group is in progress.

First, the investigator needs to be sure that the focus group methodology is the correct approach for the research problem at hand. Focus groups are intended to collect qualitative information and nothing more. But all too often this intention is altered, and people (including some researchers) attempt to interpret focus group data as quantitative information. Indeed, the most serious error associated with the conduct of focus groups is using the method for the wrong reason(s).

Planning the Groups

Any research project requires a great deal of careful planning. The best way to accomplish this task is to try to anticipate any condition or situation that might complicate the completion of the groups. Two important considerations in planning focus groups are date and time.

Date

Similar to surveys and experiments, focus groups must be planned with careful consideration of the groups' scheduling. Any conflict with major holidays or other officially recognized days away from work may create severe problems in recruiting participants. In addition to religious holidays, the Fourth of July, Labor Day, and other long-established holidays, researchers need to anticipate problems that may be created by less-well-known events.

Depending on the city and the time of year, some or all of the following may create havoc with recruiting: Monday Night Football, the World Series, the Stanley Cup, or even local high school or college games; blockbuster television shows or other widely publicized TV programs that create a great deal of viewer interest; county or state fairs; major musical events or concerts; and political elections.

Problems created by nature obviously cannot be controlled, but consideration should be given to the weather conditions that may exist at the time the groups are scheduled. For example, focus groups planned in the northern part of the United States from January to March have a good chance for cancellation due to snow storms. If research cannot wait until spring, it is wise to plan for an alternative day and possibly an alternative site. Experienced research companies that recruit for focus groups often ask the people recruited about their availability at a later time if the weather forces cancellation of the originally scheduled group.

Friday focus groups should be attempted only in an emergency. Most people do not want to give up one of their weekend nights to participate in a research project. Indeed, few recruiting companies in the country will accept a job of assembling a Friday night focus group. It isn't impossible to conduct Friday night groups, but researchers should plan to pay people more money for their participation and should expect to make many more recruiting phone calls than are normally required.

Time

The time selected to conduct focus groups depends completely on the type of person whose participation is desired. If housewives are needed, late morning or early afternoon is satisfactory. People who work outside the home are best scheduled for evenings. In most cases, back-to-back night focus groups begin at 6:00 P.M. and 8:30 P.M. Since most groups last about 2 hours, the extra half-hour between groups (if two groups are conducted) allows for cleanup of the facility and resetting of tape recorders (if used). Also, it gives the moderator a few minutes to relax before the second group starts.

Just as the date of focus groups can affect the turnout, so can the time. If business travelers are the target group, it might be wise to schedule their group to begin at 8:30 P.M. Researchers need to put themselves in the position of the type of person who is being recruited and try to anticipate the time that would be most convenient.

Choosing a Field Service and a Facility Location

Researchers who frequently conduct focus groups in the same city tend to use the same field service for respondent recruiting and facility use.

In addition to establishing a rapport with the company, the researcher is accustomed to the facilities and is not surprised by anything when the groups begin. It is vitally important to make a complete investigation of *any* company used for the first time. Researchers who do not follow through on this simple task may be headed for serious consequences in the long run.

Veteran researchers have learned very early that just because a company calls itself a "research" firm does not mean that the people who own and operate the firm know what they are doing. There are incompetents and charlatans in the research field, just as in any other business. Many researchers who plan to use a company new to them consult the lists of affiliates prepared by various marketing research organizations. For example, the American Marketing Association publishes a list of its members. To the untrained researcher, membership in such an organization may imply that the affiliates listed on the roster are accredited in some way or have passed a series of competence tests. However, the only requirement for listing is payment of annual membership dues. Thus the first caveat in the research field is: beware of any marketing, research, or consulting group that members can join for a fee.

The best way to investigate a field service, although even this is not 100% effective, is to ask for references and check them out. In addition, one can make one's own inquiries. Veteran researchers have contacts throughout the country and usually can find out about any research company or recruiting firm in one or two phone calls. The value of developing such contacts becomes clear to the novice almost immediately. The truth of the matter is that one can't be too careful. Recently we witnessed a supposedly respected professional research company convince subjects who were recruited for focus groups to lie about their names, relationships to other members in the group, and addresses. The company apparently had had difficulty in recruiting the required subjects for the groups and committed fraud to save the contract. All researchers, pros as well as novices, need to remember: *do not rely on any type of membership list as a sign of competence; ask others who have used the firm or know of its operations.*

Once satisfactory references about a field service have been received, it is necessary to investigate the facilities provided by the firm. Is the meeting place easily accessible, or will focus group participants have difficulty finding the building? Is parking nearby and safe? If the groups are to be held in a motel room, it is important to find out about the motel itself. Obviously, a rundown and poorly located motel will hinder recruitment.

Any facility that is used for the groups should be clean and neat. It can be very embarrassing for a researcher to attempt to moderate a serious discussion among strangers who have been invited to an unkempt location. Respondents will base their perceptions on the status of the research project, and on the quality of the facilities, so every effort should be made to select a facility that enhances the professionalism of the effort.

The focus room should provide enough seating space for up to 14 adults, and the table should allow for easy discussion among all members of the group. The viewing room should have comfortable seating for the observers.

Finally, the researcher must find out about the recording equipment the research company plans to use. The microphones must be sensitive enough to pick up all levels of sound in the room, and a backup system should be provided in the event that the main recording system fails during the groups.

Recruiting

The recruiting questionnaire, or the **screener**, used to select people to participate in the groups is one of the most important aspects of the focus group methodology. The screener defines who will and who will not be allowed to participate. If the screener questions do not adequately identify the type of person who should attend, the results of the research will probably be worthless.

Researchers usually work very closely with the recruiting firm in the development of the screener. Every characteristic desired for the participants needs to be covered (age, sex, race, location of residence, type of employment, knowledge of the topic under discussion, and so on). All relevant characteristics must be addressed by the questions in the screener, and the people who will make the recruiting phone calls must understand the requirements precisely. Good research companies will carefully review the screener with their recruiting staff, but it never hurts to ask whether the procedure is planned.

Some guidelines for recruiting include the following.

1. Always overrecruit. The number of excess people generally depends on the type of person desired. There is no rule of thumb, but if a researcher needs 10 participants in a group, 14 or 15 should be recruited.

2. Determine the amount of co-op money to be paid during the initial discussions of recruiting with the research company. As mentioned earlier, co-op fees can range between $10 and $100. Most research companies ask that the co-op money be provided in advance; this is standard procedure. The respondents, however, are always paid after the group, not before or during the session.

3. Make sure the guidelines for recruiting participants are clearly understood by the field service. These companies often use lists of names in recruiting for focus groups, and it is best to spell out in detail that only one person from each such club, organization, or other group will be allowed to participate. (An unscrupulous field service might simply call the local PTA and ask for volunteers.) In addition, it must be emphasized that relatives of participants will not be allowed in the groups. Finally, it is usually good practice to insist that no person be recruited for a group if he or she has participated in related focus groups during the past year (or other time period the researcher feels is appropriate). This restriction serves to eliminate the "professional" focus group member—the person who is constantly called by the field service to participate.

4. Always ask the field service for the screeners used in recruiting the groups. Professional field services will have no hesitation about providing the researcher with the screeners; the companies that claim the screeners are private property, have been destroyed, or are proprietary information, are generally trying to hide something (such as the practice of recruiting members from the same club or organization).

Before the Groups Begin

The major items researchers must attend to before the focus groups begin are enumerated below. Some jobs involve a great deal of time; and others can be completed in a few minutes.

1. Prepare the moderator's guide. The moderator uses the guide to be sure that all relevant questions are asked, but not to force a group into a set pattern of questioning and answering. Researchers must be prepared to skip around the prepared questions depending on how the group reacts.

2. Make arrangements with the field service for any audio or video taping that will be required. Audio taping is generally considered compulsory; video taping is an option. Most research companies do not charge for audio taping, but there is usually a substantial additional fee for video taping.

3. Check all electronic equipment and other mechanical devices that will be used during the groups. Assume that nothing will work and check everything. The items (for example, tape machines) that aren't checked are the ones that will not work when they are supposed to (Murphy's law).

4. In most focus group situations, respondents are offered a light dinner or snack. Catering arrangements need to be discussed with the recruiting company and depend on how much money the client wishes to spend.

5. Although respondents are reminded several times of the group's starting time, one or two people are sure to arrive late. It is the researcher's responsibility to instruct the recruiting company how

to handle late arrivals. Some focus groups may suffer no harm if one respondent arrives a few minutes late. If, however, the session begins with the playing of informational audio or video tapes, a late respondent cannot participate meaningfully in the group. In such cases, it is best to pay the late respondent the co-op money and allow him or her to go home.

Many "professional" focus group respondents have learned that if they arrive about 15 minutes late they will still receive the co-op money. It is up to the researcher to decide the time limit; in most cases, people who are more than 15 minutes late for the session should not be paid co-op.

6. Researchers need to establish with the recruiting company the course of action when there are not enough respondents for a group. The course of action (such as not paying for the recruiting of the group) depends on the reason for the low turnout. If bad weather or other unpredictable natural event makes it difficult for people to get to the facility, the research company should not expect to avoid paying the recruiting fee. However, if the weather is fine, and there are no unexpected disrupting influences, the researcher may request that recruiting charges be waived. Fortunately for researchers, good field services who face shortfall problems generally offer to reschedule the groups for no additional charge.

7. There is one basic rule for the people who will view the groups behind the two-way mirror: no loud noises. The only thing that separates the viewing room from the focus room is a thin sheet of glass, and loud talking, laughing, or other noises from behind the barrier are very annoying to the moderator as well as to the respondents. Viewers should also refrain from lighting cigarettes, cigars, or pipes if the flame may be detected by those on the other side of the mirror. This sounds like a minor detail, but the quick flash of light can distract a respondent who is unaware of the presence of viewers behind the mirror. Other rules for the viewers are established by the moderator on an ad hoc basis.

Conducting the Groups

The type of introduction to a focus group, and the amount of information provided to the respondents, depend on the purpose of the group and the sponsor of the research. In some cases it is important for the respondents to have no preliminary information in the introduction; in other cases concepts or procedures must be explained before actual questioning can begin.

Most focus groups start by allowing each respondent to give a very brief self-introduction. Then the moderator generally identifies the purpose of the group and summarizies the goals of the project. Some guidelines for preparing an introduction to a focus group are as follows.

1. Explain that there are no right or wrong answers to the questions that will be asked. Respondents should feel free to make relevant comments, whether positive or negative.

2. Advise respondents that the session is being taped for future reference. If the explanation of the taping procedure is handled quickly and professionally, most respondents will be unconcerned with the process.

3. Be prepared to mention the two-way mirror. Some researchers immediately explain that the respondents are being watched; other researchers believe that the mirror and the viewers should not be discussed except in response to a specific question. If someone does ask whether there is a two-way mirror, a brief answer along these lines is appropriate: "The people who are sponsoring the research have told me that they may view the group, to get as much information as possible. At this time, I cannot really say whether the sponsors are in the room." (This is not lying, since sponsors enter and leave the room periodically, out of sight of the moderator.)

4. Remind the respondents that they should treat the discussion as a very informal gathering; they should not hesitate to ask questions, and they should feel free to speak up without being invited. The more relaxed the respondents are, the more responsive they will be to the questions asked of them.

5. Listen closely to respondents' answers, to ensure follow-up on potentially relevant information. The researcher should not be restricted to the order of questioning in the moderator's guide if respondents are providing comments that are relevant to the questions developed before the group began.

Handling Respondents

All things considered, there are basically five types of people who participate in focus groups:

1. The active participant who is interested in providing relevant answers to the moderator's questions.
2. The shy person who is embarrassed to speak out or feels inhibited for some reason.
3. The person who knows too much or has answers to every question. Such people tend to try to dominate the group.
4. The person who rambles on and gives a speech with every response. The "overtalker" will answer a question adequately and then forge ahead: "By that I mean. . . ."

5. The obnoxious person, who does not really wish to participate and attempts to hinder the moderator by making sarcastic remarks or irrelevant comments.

People of the first two types are easy to deal with in a focus group. Even the shy person can be coaxed to provide valuable information by a good moderator. The last three types, however, can ruin a project, and they must be eliminated from the group before they can affect the other participants.

Getting people out of a group that is already in session calls for a prior arrangement with the field service. For example, it may be agreed that when the moderator believes it is necessary to terminate the participation of a group member, the moderator will leave the focus room and give the name of the offending person to the field service representative. A few minutes after the moderator has returned to the group, the unwanted group member is summoned for a phone call. Outside the focus room, the company representative very politely dismisses the person. ("You seem to be an expert in the area, and your input may affect the other respondents' answers" is one approach.)

The goal is to eliminate the know-it-all, the overtalker, or the bully as soon as he or she is identified as a problem. The moderator cannot allow an individual to destroy the group. Speed is most important in getting rid of an unwanted respondent.

acoustic modem (coupler): a device used to allow remote access to a main frame computer via a telephone receiver hookup

advertising element research: a type of copy testing; each component of an advertisement (for example, headline, illustrations, typography) is tested for effectiveness

agenda setting: the theory that the media provide topics of discussion and importance for consumers

aided recall: a survey technique in which the interviewer shows the respondent a copy of a newspaper, magazine, television schedule, or other item that might help him or her to remember a certain article, program, advertisement, and so on

algorithm: statistical procedure or formula

American Standard Code for Information Interchange (ASCII): the standard machine language used by microcomputers; each letter, number, or special character is represented by 7 bits of information

analysis of variance (ANOVA): a statistical procedure used to decompose sources of variation in two or more independent variables

analytical survey: a survey that attempts to describe and explain why certain conditions exist (usually by testing certain hypotheses)

antecedent variable: (1) in survey research, the variable used to predict another variable; (2) in experimental research, the independent variable

applied research: research that attempts to solve a specific problem rather than to construct a theory

area of dominant influence (ADI): a region composed of a certain number of television households; every county is assigned to one and only one ADI

artifact: a variable that creates a rival explanation of results (a confounding variable)

audience turnover: in radio research, an estimate of the number of times the audience changes stations during a given daypart

audimeter: an electronic television audience measurement device used by the A. C. Nielsen Company to collect data

available sample: a sample selected on the basis of accessibility

average quarter-hour (AQH): the average number of persons or households tuned in to a specific channel or station for at least 5 minutes during a 15-minute time segment

beta weight: a mathematically derived value representing a variable's contribution to a prediction or weighted linear combination (also called *weight coefficient*)

bit: a single piece of information in computers; 8 bits typically represent one character or number, called a *byte*

bit processing: term used to identify the type of information processing system used by a computer; most common is the 8-bit processor in microcomputers

buffer: a block of memory a computer uses to store information until ready for use by peripherals

byte: a unit of computer storage, which is typically one character or number; a byte consists of 8 bits

call-out research: a procedure used in radio research to determine the popularity of recordings; see also *hook*

canonical correlation: a multivariate statistic used to investigate the relationship between two sets of variables

case study: an empirical inquiry that uses multiple sources of data to investigate a problem

catch-up panel: members of a cross-sectional sample done in the past who are relocated for subsequent observation

CATI: computer-assisted telephone interviewing; video display terminals are used by interviewers to present questions and enter responses

census: an analysis in which the sample comprises every element of a population

central processing unit (CPU): the control and coordination system of a computer that decides the order in which computations are made and where to store information, sends information to peripherals, and regulates the entire system operation

central tendency: a single value that is chosen to represent a typical score in a distribution such as the mean, the mode, or the median

checklist: a type of questionnaire in which the respondent is given a list of items and is asked to mark those that apply

chi-square statistic: a measurement of observed versus expected frequencies; often referred to as *crosstabs*

circulation: in the print media, the total number of copies of a newspaper or magazine that are delivered to a subscriber plus all copies bought at newsstands or from other sellers

circulation research: (1) a market-level study of newspaper and magazine penetration; (2) a study of the delivery and pricing systems used by newspapers and magazines

close-ended question: a question the respondent must answer by making a selection from a prepared set of options

Cloze procedure: a method for measuring readability or recall in which every *n*th word is deleted from the message and readers are asked to fill in the blanks

cluster sample: a sample selected in groups or categories

coding: the placing of a unit of analysis into a particular category

coefficient of determination: in correlational statistics, the amount of variation in the criterion variable that is accounted for by the antecedent variable

coefficient of nondetermination: in correlational statistics, the amount of variation in the criterion variable that is left unexplained

cohort analysis: study of a specific population as it changes over time

communication audit: in public relations, an examination of the internal and external means of communication used by an organization

complete execution: a form of testing in which an entire advertisement or commercial is used as a stimulus

computer cards: rectangular cards used to input data into a computer

concept: a term that expresses an abstract idea formed by generalization

confidence interval: an area within which there is a stated probability that the parameter will fall

confidence level: probability (for example, .05 or .01) of rejecting a null hypothesis that is in fact true (also called the *alpha level*)

constitutive definition: a type of definition in which other words or concepts are substituted for the word being defined

construct: a combination of concepts that is created to describe a specific situation (for example, "authoritarianism")

constructive replication: an analysis of a hypothesis taken from a previous study that deliberately avoids duplication of the methods used in the previous study

continuous variable: a variable that can take on any value over a range of values and can be meaningfully broken into subparts (for example, "height")

control group: subjects who do not receive experimental treatment and thus serve as a basis of comparison in an experiment

control variable: a variable whose influence a researcher wishes to eliminate

copy testing: research used to determine the most effective way of structuring a message to achieve desired results (also known as *message research*)

cost per thousand (CPM): the dollar cost of reaching 1,000 people or households by means of a particular medium or advertising vehicle

criterion variable: (1) in survey research, the variable presumed to be the effects variable; (2) in experimental research, the dependent variable

cross-lagged study: a type of longitudinal study in which information about two different variables is gathered from the same sample at two different times. The correlations between variables at the same point in time are compared with the correlations at different points in time

cross-sectional research: the collection of data from a representative sample at only one point in time

cross-tabulation analysis (crosstabs): see *chi-square statistic*

cross-validation: a procedure whereby measurement instruments or subjects' responses are compared to verify their validity or truthfulness

cultivation analysis: a research approach that suggests that heavy television viewing leads to perceptions of social reality that are consistent with the view of the world as presented on television

cume: an estimate of the number of different persons who listened to or viewed a particular broadcast for at least 5 minutes during a given daypart (see also *reach)*

data archives: data storage facilities where researchers can deposit data for other researchers to use

data base: the entire collection of information that is available for analysis

daypart: a given part of the broadcast day (for example, prime time = 8:00 P.M.–11:00 P.M. EST)

demand characteristic: the premise that subjects' awareness of the experimental condition may affect their performance in the experiment (also known as the *Hawthorne effect)*

dependent variable: the variable that is observed and whose value is presumed to depend on the independent variable(s)

descriptive statistics: statistical methods and techniques designed to reduce data sets to allow for easier interpretation

descriptive survey: a survey that attempts to picture or document current conditions or attitudes

design-specific results: research results that are based on, or specific to, the research design used

determinant: a scalar that represents a unique function of the numbers in a square matrix

diagonal matrix: a square matrix whose elements all equal zero, except for those along the principal diagonal

discrete variable: a variable that can be conceptually subdivided into a finite number of indivisible parts (for example, the number of children in a family)

discriminant analysis: a multivariate statistic used to classify groups according to variable similarities or to analyze the statistical significance of a weighted linear combination of variables

disk drive: the portion of the computer that either reads information from a disk or writes information to a disk

dispersion: the amount of variability in a set of scores

distribution: a collection of scores or measurements

double-barreled question: a single question that in reality requires two separate responses (for example, "Do you like the price and style of this item?")

double blind experiment: a research study in which experimenters and others do not know whether a given subject belongs to the experimental or the control group

dummy variable: the variable created when a variable at the nominal level is transformed into a form more appropriate for higher order statistics

editor–reader comparison: a readership study in which the perceptions of editors and readers are solicited

environmental monitoring program: in public relations research, a study of trends in public opinion and events in the social environment that may have a significant impact on an organization

equivalence: the internal consistency of a measure

error variance: error created by an unknown factor

evaluation apprehension: a fear of being measured or tested that may result in invalid data

evaluation research: the process of judging the effectiveness of program planning, impact, and implementation

exhaustivity: a state of a category system such that every unit of analysis can be placed into an existing slot

experimental design: a blueprint or set of plans for conducting laboratory research

external validity: the degree to which the results of a research study are generalizable to other situations

factor analysis: a multivariate statistical procedure used primarily for data reduction, construct development, and the investigation of variable relationships

factorial design: a simultaneous analysis of two or more independent variables or factors

factor score: a composite or summary score produced by factor analysis

feeling thermometer: a rating scale patterned after a weather thermometer on which respondents can rate their attitudes on a scale of 0 to 100

filter question: a question designed to screen out certain individuals from further participation in a study

Flesch reading ease formula: an early readability formula based on the number of words per sentence and the number of syllables per word

floppy disk: an external computer storage device

focus group: an interview conducted with 6–12 subjects simultaneously and a moderator who leads a discussion about a specific topic

Fog Index: a readability scale based on sentence length and the number of syllables per word

follow-back panel: research technique in which a current cross-sectional sample is selected and matched with archival data

forced-choice question: a question that requires a subject to choose between two specified responses

forced exposure: describing the test situation in which respondents are required to be exposed to a specific independent or dependent variable

(to) format (a disk): to initialize, or prepare, a floppy or hard disk for use with a specific computer

frequency: in advertising, the total number of exposures to a message that a person or household receives

frequency curve: a graphical display of frequency data in the form of a smooth, unbroken curve

frequency distribution: a collection of scores, ordered according to magnitude, and their respective frequencies

frequency polygon: a series of lines connecting points that represent the frequencies of scores

gross rating points: the total of audience ratings during two or more time periods, representing the size of the gross audience of a radio or television broadcast

group administration: conducting measurements with several subjects simultaneously

hard disk: an external computer storage device capable of storing several million bytes of information

hardware: any type of computer equipment; the physical components of a computer

histogram: a bar chart that illustrates frequencies and scores

homogeneity: equality of control and experimental groups prior to an experiment (also called *point of prior equivalency*)

hook: a short representative sample of a recording used in call-out research

hypothesis: a tentative generalization concerning the relationship between two or more variables that predicts an experimental outcome

identity matrix: a square matrix whose elements equal zero except for those along the principal diagonal, which equal one

incidence: the percentage of a population that possesses the desired characteristics for a particular research study

independent variable: the variable that is systematically varied by the researcher

inferential statistics: statistical methods and techniques that allow a researcher to generalize sample results to a population within a given margin of probable error

instrumental replication: the duplication in a research study of the dependent variable of a previous study

instrument decay: the deterioration of a measurement instrument during the course of a study, which reduces the instrument's effectiveness and accuracy

interaction: a treatment-related effect dependent on concomitant influence of two independent variables on a dependent variable

intercoder reliability: in content analysis, the degree of agreement between or among independent coders

intercorrelation matrix: a matrix composed of correlations between pairs of variables

internal validity: a property of a research study such that results are based on expected conditions rather than on extraneous variables

interval level: a measurement system in which the intervals between adjacent points on a scale are equal (for example, a thermometer)

isomorphism: similarity of form or structure

item pretest: a method of testing subjects' interest in reading magazine or newspaper articles

item-selection study: a readership study used to determine who reads specific parts of a newspaper

kurtosis: the degree of "peakedness" in a frequency curve; curves can be *leptokurtic* (large number of scores around the center), *platykurtic* (spread over a wide area), or *mesokurtic* (two or more areas having a high concentration of scores)

leading question: a question that suggests a certain response or makes an implicit assumption (for example, "How long have you been an alcoholic?")

literal replication: a study that is an exact duplication of a previous study

longitudinal research: the collection of data at different points in time

mailing list: a compilation of names and addresses, sometimes prepared by a commercial firm, that is used as a sampling frame for mail surveys

mail survey: the mailing of self-administered questionnaires to a sample of people; the researcher must rely on the recipients to mail back their responses

main effect: the effect of the independent variable(s) on the dependent variable (no interaction is present)

marker variable: a variable that highlights or defines the construct under study

masked recall: a survey technique in which the interviewer show respondents the front cover of a newspaper or magazine with the name of the publication blacked out to test unaided recall of the publication

matrix: a two-dimensional array of scalars

mean: the arithmetic average of a set of scores

measurement: a procedure whereby a researcher assigns numerals to objects, events, or properties according to certain rules

measurement error: an inconsistency produced by the instruments used in a research study

media efficiency: reaching the maximum possible audience for the smallest possible cost

median: the midpoint of a distribution of scores

medium variables: in a content analysis, the aspects of content that are unique to the medium under consideration (for example, typography to a newspaper or magazine)

method of authority: a method of knowing whereby something is believed because a source seen as an authority says it is true

method of intuition: a method of knowing whereby something is believed because it is "self-evident" or "stands to reason" (also called *a priori reasoning*)

method of tenacity: a method of knowing whereby something is believed because a person has always believed it to be true

method-specific results: research results based on, or specific to, the research method used

metro survey area: a broadcasting region representing one of the Consolidated Metropolitan Statistical Areas (CMSA), as defined by the U.S. Office of Management and Budget

microcomputer: a small computer made possible by the development of microprocessors (chips)

mode: the score that occurs most often in a frequency distribution

modem: an electronic device used to transfer computer data via telephone lines (acronym for *mo*dulate-*dem*odulate)

monitor: a television-type screen that allows a user to view what is entered into the computer as well as the results of any calculations or word processing; also known as a *CRT* (cathode ray tube)

mortality: a problem in panel studies and other forms of longitudinal research caused by original sample members who drop out of the research project for one reason or another

multiple regression: an analysis of two or more independent variables and their relationship to a single dependent variable (used to predict the dependent variable)

multivariate analysis of variance (MANOVA): an extension of analysis of variance used to study more than one dependent variable

multivariate statistics: statistical methods that investigate the relationship between one or more independent variables and more than one dependent variable

mutually exclusive: a state of a category system such that a unit of analysis can be placed in one and only one category

nominal level: the level of measurement at which arbitrary numerals or other symbols are used to classify persons, objects, or characteristics

nonparametric statistics: statistical procedures used with variables measured at the nominal or ordinal level

nonprobability sample: a sample selected without regard to the laws of mathematical probability

normal curve: a symmetrical, bell-shaped curve that possesses specific mathematical characteristics

null hypothesis: the denial or negation of a research hypothesis

objective function: a mathematical formula that provides various quantitative values for a given media schedule of advertisements; used in computer simulations of advertising media schedules

open-ended question: a question to which respondents are asked to generate an answer or answers with no prompting from the item itself (for example, "What is your favorite type of television program?")

operational definition: a definition that specifies patterns of behavior and procedures in order to experience or measure a concept

operational replication: a study that duplicates only the sampling methodology and experimental procedures of a previous study

optical character reader (OCR): an input device that electronically reads information from a printed page for entering into a computer

ordinal level: the level of measurement at which items are ranked along a continuum

overnights: ratings surveys of a night's television viewing computed in five major U.S. cities by the A. C. Nielsen Company

panel study: a research technique whereby the same sample of respondents is measured at different points in time

parameter: a characteristic or property of a population

parametric statistics: statistical procedures appropriate with variables measured at the interval or ratio level

parsimony principle: the premise that the simplest method is the most preferable (also known as *Occam's razor*)

partial correlation: a method used to control a confounding or spurious variable that may affect the relationship between independent and dependent variables

path analysis: a multivariate statistic used to create a "causal path" for dependent variables and their relationships to independent variables

people meter: an electronic television audience data-gathering device capable of recording individual viewing behavior

periodicity: any form of bias resulting from the use of a nonrandom list of subjects or items in selecting a sample

peripheral: any add-on device to a computer system such as a printer

personal interview: a survey technique in which a trained interviewer visits the respondent and administers the questionnaire in a face-to-face setting

pilot study: a trial run of a study conducted on a small scale to determine whether the research design and methodology are relevant and effective

population: a group or class of objects, subjects, or units

population distribution: the frequency distribution of all the variables of interest as determined by a census of the population

power: the probability of rejecting the null hypothesis when an alternative is true

predictor variable: see *actecedent variable*

prestige bias: the tendency of a respondent to give answers that will make him or her seem more educated, successful, financially stable, or otherwise prestigious

principle of least squares: a mathematical procedure used to determine a prediction line or vector through a set of data points

printer: a typewriterlike device controlled by a computer

probability level: a predetermined value at which researchers test their data for statistical significance

probability sample: a sample selected according to the laws of mathematical probability

programmable read only memory (PROM): information stored on a computer chip that is used over and over again, as in cable television channel converters

proposition: a statement of the form "if A then B," which links two or more concepts

proprietary data: research data gathered by a private organization that are available to the general public only if released by that organization

protocol: a document containing the procedures to be used in a field study

psychographics: an area of research that examines why people behave and think as they do

public relations audit: a comprehensive study of the public relations position of an organization

purposive sample: a sample deliberately chosen to be representative of a population

qualitative research: a description or analysis of a phenomenon that does not depend on measurement of variables

quantitative research: a description or analysis of a phenomenon that does involve specific measurements of variables

quota sample: a sample selected to represent certain characteristics of interest

random access memory (RAM): a computer's main memory that is erased when the computer is turned off

random digit dialing: a method of selecting telephone numbers that ensures that all telephone households have an equal chance of being selected

random error: error in a research study that cannot be controlled by the researcher

random sample: a subgroup or subset of a population selected in such a way that each unit in a population has an equal chance of being selected

range: a measure of dispersion based on the difference between the highest and lowest scores in a distribution

rating: an estimate of the percentage of people or households in a population that are tuned to a specific station or network

ratio level: a level of measurement that has all the properties of an interval level scale and also has a true zero point

reach: in advertising, the total number of people or households exposed to a message at least once during a specific period of time (see also *cume*)

reactivity: a subject's awareness of being measured or observed and its possible impact on that subject's behavior

readability: the total of all elements in a piece of printed material that affect the degree to which people understand the piece and find it interesting

reader–nonreader study: a study that contrasts nonreaders of newspapers or magazines with regular readers

reader profile: a demographic summary of the readers of a particular publication

read only memory (ROM): permanent memory stored in a computer

recall study: a study in which respondents are asked to remember what advertisements they remember seeing in the medium being investigated

recognition: a measurement of readership in which respondents are shown the logo of a magazine or newspaper

redundancy index: a mathematical procedure used in canonical correlation to aid in interpreting relationships between variable sets

region of rejection: the proportion of area in a sampling distribution that equals the level of significance; the region of rejection represents all the values of a test statistic that are highly unlikely, provided the null hypothesis is true

reliability: the property of a measure that consistently gives the same answer at different points in time

repeated measures design: a research design wherein measurements are made on the same subjects

replication: an independent verification of a research study

research question: a tentative generalization concerning the relationship between two or more variables

retrospective panel: a study in which each respondent is asked questions about events and attitudes in his or her lifetime

rough commercial: a "first draft" of a television or radio commercial that uses amateur actors, low-cost equipment, and rough editing

rough cut: a model or simulation of a final product

sample: a subgroup or subset of a population or universe

sample balancing: see *weighting*

sample distribution: the frequency distribution of all the variables of interest as determined from a sample

sample-specific results: research results that are based on, or specific to, the research sample used

sampling distribution: a probability distribution of all possible values of a statistic that would occur if all possible samples of a fixed size from a given population were taken

sampling error: the degree to which measurements obtained from a sample differ from the measurements that would be obtained from the population

sampling frame: a list of the members of a particular population

sampling interval: a random interval used for selection of subjects or units in the systematic sampling method

sampling rate: the ratio of the number of people chosen in the sample to the total number in the population (e.g., if 100 fraternity members were systematically chosen from a sampling frame of 1,000 fraternity members, the sampling rate would be 10% or 1/10)

scalar: a single digit (used in matrix algebra)

scattergram: a graphic technique for portraying the relationship between two variables

scientific method: a systematic, controlled, empirical, and critical investigation of hypothetical propositions about the presumed relations among natural phenomena

screener: a short survey or portion of survey designed to select only appropriate respondents for a research project

secondary analysis: the use of data collected by a previous researcher or another research organization (also called *data reanalysis*)

semantic differential: a rating scale consisting of seven spaces between two bipolar adjectives (e.g., "good __:__:__:__:__:__: __ bad")

share: an estimate of the percentage of persons or households tuned to a specific station or network

sigma (Σ): the Greek capital letter symbolizing "the sum of"

skewness: the degree of departure of a curve from the normal distribution (curves can be positively or negatively skewed)

SMOG Grading: a measure of readability based on the number of syllables per word

social audit: in public relations research, an analysis of social performance of an organization

software: any type of ready-to-use computer program designed for mathematical computations, word processing, graphics, spreadsheets, and so on

spreadsheet: computer software designed for mathematical and statistical calculations as well as graphic representations of those data

square matrix: a matrix in which the number of rows equals the number of columns

stability: the degree of consistence of the results of a measure at different points in time

standard deviation: the square root of the variance (a mathematical index of dispersion)

standard error: an estimate of the amount of error present in a measurement

standard score: a measure that has been standardized in relation to a distribution's mean and standard deviation

stratified sample: a sample selected after the population has been divided into categories

structured interview: an interview in which standardized questions are asked in a predetermined order

summary statistics: statistics that summarize a great deal of numerical information about a distribution such as the mean and the standard deviation

sweep: a nationwide survey of every television market conducted by A. C. Nielsen Company and Arbitron

systematic sampling: a procedure to select every *n*th subject for a study, such as every 10th person in a telephone directory

systematic variance: a regular increase or decrease of all scores or data in a research study by a known factor

telephone coincidentals: a broadcasting research procedure in which random subjects or households are called and asked what they are viewing or listening to at that moment

telephone survey: a research method in which survey data are collected over the telephone by trained interviewers who ask questions and record responses

theory: a set of related propositions that presents a systematic view of phenomena by specifying relationships among concepts

total observation: in field observation, a situation in which the observer assumes no role in the phenomenon being observed other than that of observer

total participation: field observation in which the observer becomes a full-fledged participant in the situation under observation

total survey area (TSA): a region in which an audience survey is conducted

tracking study: a special readership measurement technique in which respondents designate material they have read (using a different color of pencil for each reading episode)

trend study: a longitudinal study in which a topic is restudied using different groups of respondents (for example, the Roper studies on the credibility of the media)

triangulation: using a combined quantitative and qualitative approach to solve a problem

t-test: a statistic used to determine significance between group means

Type I error: rejection of the null hypothesis when it should be accepted

Type II error: acceptance of the null hypothesis when it should be rejected

unit of analysis: the smallest element of a content analysis; the thing that is counted whenever it is encountered

unstructured interview: an interview in which the interviewer asks broad and general questions but retains control over the discussion

uses and gratifications study: a study of the motives for media usage and the rewards that are sought

validity: the property of a test of actually measuring what it purports to measure

variable: a phenomenon or event that can be measured or manipulated

variance: a mathematical index of the degree to which scores deviate from the mean

vector: a series of data points represented by a line in space

volunteer sample: a group of people who go out of their way to participate in a survey or experiment (for example, by responding to a newspaper advertisement)

weighting: a mathematical procedure used to adjust the sample to meet the characteristics of a given population (also called *sample balancing*)

NAME INDEX

Hatch, D., 174, 191
Hatch, M., 174, 191
Hawkins, D., 163, 342, 370
Hawkins, R., 392, 393, 401
Haynes, R., 172, 191, 478, 479, 483
Hays, W. L., 136, 242, 244, 264
Hecht, T., 290, 304
Heeter, C., 66
Heller, M., 374, 401
Hency, T., 162
Hennessee, J., 169, 191
Henningham, J., 66
Herzog, H., 6, 15, 381, 401
Hess, R., 398
Hezel, R., 181, 189
Higginbotham, J. B., 162
Hilker, A., 388, 402
Himmelweit, H., 139, 162
Hirsch, P., 390, 402
Hocking, J., 395, 396, 400
Hogan, L., 167, 191
Holly, S., 257
Holsti, O., 168, 181, 190, 191
Hoofnagle, W., 350, 370
Horst, P., 467, 483
Hoskins, R., 300, 304
Howard, D., 54, 67
Hoyt, J. L., 263, 380, 405
Huesmann, L., 378
Hughes, M., 390, 402
Humphrey, R., 191
Hursh-Cesar, G., 114, 125, 135
Husson, W., 281
Hvistendahl, J. K., 289, 304
Hyman, H. H., 23, 38, 42, 196, 208

Idsvoog, K. A., 263, 281
Iyengar, S., 388, 400

Jackson, K., 289, 305
Jackson-Beeck, M., 169, 190, 291, 305
Jacobs, J., 50, 67
Jacoubovitch, D., 289, 305
Jeffres, L., 281
Jeffries-Fox, S., 190
Johnson, D. K., 163
Johnston, J., 260
Joreskog, K. G., 194, 206, 208, 468, 483
Joslyn, R. A., 257

Kahn, S., 169, 190
Kang, N., 291, 292, 303
Katz, E., 6, 15, 194, 208
Katzman, N., 42, 167, 191, 373, 376
Kearney, K., 445
Keir, G., 292
Keith, P., 204, 208
Kelly, C. W., 39, 42
Kelman, H., 436, 445
Kendzierski, D., 200, 208, 375, 401
Kenny, D., 203, 208
Keppel, G., 99

Kerlinger, F. N., 8, 16, 45, 48, 55, 67, 136,
   166, 191, 277, 281
Kessler, R., 67, 206, 208, 375, 403
Kintz, B. L., 99
Kish, L., 69, 86
Klapper, J., 6, 16, 373, 402
Klecka, W. R., 478, 483
Knop, J., 200, 209
Kohn, P., 396, 402
Kraus, S., 42
Krekel, T., 290, 305
Krippendorf, K., 166, 181, 185, 190, 191
Kroeger, A., 369
Krull, R., 281
Kubas, L., 55, 66

LaChance, C., 370
Lafky, S., 293, 304
Lambert, Z. V., 480, 483
Lang, G., 385, 389, 402
Lang, K., 385, 389, 402
Larkin, E., 304
Larson, C. U., 385, 402
Larson, M., 367
Lasswell, H. D., 6, 16
Lazarsfeld, P. F., 6, 15, 16, 194, 208
Leckenby, J., 343, 361, 362, 370
Lefkowitz, M., 194, 204, 208, 378, 402
Lerbinger, O., 364, 366, 370
Lesser, G., 398, 400, 402
Leuthold, D., 54, 66
Levin, S. R., 445
Levinson, D., 395, 404
Levy, M., 385, 401
Lewis, C., 158, 162
Leyens, J., 378, 403
Liebert, R., 376, 401
Linz, D., 381, 402
Lippmann, W., 385, 402
Little, J., 356, 370
Lodish, L., 356, 370
Lohnes, P. R., 478, 483
Lometti, G., 168, 190, 375, 389, 405
Long, J., 206, 208
Lorch, E. P., 445
Lorr, M., 179, 191
Love, B., 301, 304
Lowery, S., 194, 208
Lowry, D., 144, 162, 169, 191
Lubitt, A., 370
Lueptow, L., 438, 445
Lull, J., 145, 147, 162
Lykken, D. T., 39, 42
Lyle, J., 381, 403
Lynch, M., 187, 191
Lynn, J., 290, 304

MacDonald, G., 391, 393, 401
Magid, Frank N., & Associates, 103, 333
Marketing Evaluations, Inc., 334
Markham, D., 59, 67
Markus, G., 206, 208

Mason, K., 197, 208
Massetti-Miller, K., 367
Mathiowetz, N., 133, 135
Mayes, S., 391, 400
McClure, R., 386, 403
McCombs, M., 42, 292, 296, 300, 304,
    386, 389, 402
McCormick, W., 483
McCullough, B., 206, 208
McIsaac, R., 350, 369
McLaughlin, H., 299, 304
McLeod, J., 377, 378, 384, 387, 388, 402
McNair, D., 179, 191
McNemar, Q., 57, 67
Mednick, S., 203, 209
Meringhoff, L., 398, 402
Merritt, S., 168, 191
Mertz, R., 169, 191
Messick, J., 436, 445
Metallinos, N., 281
Milavsky, J., 64, 67, 194, 202, 208, 375,
    379, 403
Milgram, S., 143, 163, 374, 378, 403
Miller, D. C., 90, 99, 123, 136
Miller, M., 282
Miller, S., 191
Minton, J., 375, 403
Moore, G., 159, 163
Moore, R., 290, 305
Moran, W., 355, 370
Morgan, M., 169, 190, 390, 393, 401
Mueller, C., 381
Mullins, E., 388
Mullins, L. E., 296
Murphy, J. H., 16
Murray, J., 375, 403
Myers, J., 355, 370

Nafziger, R., 304
Naples, M., 340
National Association of Broadcasters, 136
Nestvold, K., 299, 304
Newcomb, T., 194, 208
Newcombe, H., 67
Newspaper Research Council, 290
Nicholson, J., 169, 191
Nicolich, M., 370
Nicosia, F., 369
Nie, N. H., 266, 281
Nielsen, A. C., 83, 103, 202, 308, 309,
    310, 311, 314, 316, 319, 327, 328,
    331, 337, 340, 350, 360, 410
Noble, G., 398, 403
Norlen, V., 204, 208
Nunn, C., 295, 304
Nunnally, J. C., 9, 11, 16, 57, 67, 86, 91,
    100, 233, 244

Ogan, C., 293, 304
Oppenheim, A. N., 136, 139, 162
Orenstein, F., 350, 369
Orne, M. T., 37, 42

Osgood, C., 58, 67

Paisley, W., 181, 190
Palmgreen, P., 384, 403
Palmore, E., 200
Parke, R., 378, 403
Parker, E., 381, 403
Patterson, T., 386, 403
Pedhazur, E., 55, 67, 277, 281
Peirce, C. S., 8
Pekurny, R., 145, 163
Penrod, S., 381, 402
Peters, T. J., 157, 163
Peterson, T., 194, 208
Pezdek, K., 247, 257
Piaget, J., 398
Piele, L. J., 42, 425
Pines, A., 375, 403
Pingree, S., 392, 393, 401
Poindexter, P. M., 136, 291, 300, 301, 304
Polsky, S., 374, 401
Powers, E., 204, 208
Presser, S., 282

Rainbow, C., 178, 190
Raj, D., 69, 72, 73, 81, 86
Ravage, J. W., 145, 163
Reale, G., 395, 404
Redding, C. W., 138, 139, 163
Reeves, B., 278, 281, 282, 396, 400
Reid, L. N., 24, 40, 42, 163, 445
Reide, P., 292, 305
Rentz, J., 200, 209
Research Group, The, 333
Reymer-Gersin, 103
Reynolds, F. D., 163, 200, 209
Richman, S., 178, 190
Ries, E., 8, 16
Roberts, D., 42, 386, 388, 403
Robertson, L., 142, 163
Robinson, J., 59, 67
Roscoe, J. T., 57, 67, 100, 219, 244, 261,
    267, 282
Rosenberg, M. J., 37, 42, 100, 136
Rosengren, K., 384, 403
Rosenthal, R., 37, 42, 72, 86, 100
Rosnow, R. L., 72, 86, 100
Rossi, P., 366, 370
Rothschild, W., 393
Rouner, D., 391, 393, 403
Roy, R., 370
Ruben, J., 298, 305
Rubens, W., 67, 375, 403
Rubin, A. M., 42, 56, 67, 159, 382, 383,
    403, 425
Rubin, H., 163
Rubin, R. B., 42, 425
Rubinstein, E., 375, 378, 404
Rummel, R. J., 243, 244, 428, 445, 468,
    483
Runco, M., 247, 257
Russial, J., 24, 42

Ruth, M., 287, 304
Ryan, M., 257

Sanders, K. R., 281
Schenck-Hamlin, W., 56, 66
Schramm, W., 286, 304, 381, 403
Schreibman, F., 167, 189
Schulsinger, F., 203, 209
Schuman, H., 191, 282
Schwartz, E., 67
Schwartz, H., 50, 67
Schwartz, S., 290, 305
Scott, W., 184, 191
Sechrest, L., 67
Sellitz, C., 445
Seltzer, R., 247, 257
Semlak, W., 55, 67, 387, 389, 405
Senter, R. J., 100
Sewell, W., 122, 136
Sharp, L., 118, 136
Shaver, P., 59, 67
Shaw, D., 122, 191, 291, 304, 386
Shaw, M., 136
Sherrill, K., 180, 191
Shotland, R., 143, 163, 374, 378, 403
Shrader, R., 168
Siegel, A., 233, 244, 389, 403
Signorielli, N., 169, 190, 390
Silbert, M., 375, 403
Silverstein, S., 435, 445
Simmons, K., 167, 191
Simon, J., 156, 163
Simon, R., 370
Singer, D. G., 29, 34, 42
Singer, E., 439, 445
Singer, J. L., 29, 34, 42
Siskind, T., 297, 305
Skinner, B. F., 10, 16
Slater, D., 66, 247, 257, 391, 393, 403
Smart, R., 396, 402
Smith, E., 299, 300, 303
Smith, R., 300, 305
Sobal, J., 291, 305
Soldow, G., 399, 403
Soley, L. C., 24, 42, 163
Solow, N., 298, 305
Sorbom, D., 483
Sparkes, V., 191
Sprafkin, J., 375, 378, 398, 404
Stamm, K., 289, 305, 369
Stanley, J. C., 35, 38, 42, 99
Stempel, G., 163, 174, 191, 287, 298, 303, 305
Stipp, H., 67, 375, 403
Stone, G., 295, 296, 305
Stone, P., 181, 190
Stout, R., 200, 209
Stricker, L., 436, 445
Stroman, C., 247, 257
Suci, G., 58, 67
Suedefeld, P., 435, 445

Surrey Consulting & Research, Inc., 103, 333
Swanson, C., 287, 305
Swift, C., 398, 404
Sybert, P. J., 16
Szybillo, G., 163

Tada, T., 398, 404
Tamborini, R., 391, 404
Tan, A. S., 25, 42, 141, 163, 374
Tannenbaum, P., 58, 67, 187, 191, 380, 392, 404
Tatsuoka, M. M., 478, 483
Taylor, W., 148, 162, 299, 305
Television Audience Assessment, 327–328, 340
Termini, S., 370
Thomas, S., 203, 208, 257, 375, 401
Thompson, T., 247, 257
Thorburn, D., 67
Thorndike, R. M., 276, 282
Thurstone, L. L., 468, 483
Tiemens, R., 281, 399, 404
Tillinghast, W., 295, 305
Tipton, L., 386, 404
Tolley, S., 350, 369
Torgerson, W., 483
Trotter, E., 296, 305
Trout, J., 8, 16
Tryon, R. C., 483
Tucker, R. K., 39, 42, 256, 257, 463, 483
Tukey, J. W., 23, 42, 246, 258
Tull, D., 163, 342, 370

Venus, P., 96, 97, 99
Vial, V., 393, 404
Vince, P., 139, 162

Wackman, D., 395, 397, 399, 404
Wakshlag, J. J., 136, 282, 393, 404
Waldner, L., 378
Walizer, M. H., 37, 42, 69, 86, 100, 136, 166, 191
Walter, B., 189
Ward, S., 394, 395, 397, 398, 399, 404
Wartella, E., 396, 398, 399, 404, 405
Washington, R., 370
Waterman, R., 157, 163
Weaver, D., 292, 296, 304, 305, 389, 405
Weaver, R. M., 3, 16, 291
Webb, E., 67
Wedding, N., 343
Weinstein, C., 91, 99
Weinstein, S., 91, 99
Weisberg, H. F., 136
Wertham, F., 373, 405
Westley, B. H., 138, 163
Wheaton, B., 206, 209
White, M., 397, 401
Wienir, P. L., 37, 42, 69, 86, 136, 166, 191
Wilhoit, G., 180, 191, 292, 305

Wilkinson, M., 290, 303
Williams, F., 244, 249, 258
Williams, W., 55, 67, 386, 387, 389, 405
Williamson, L., 394, 405
Wilson, C., 54, 67
Wimmer, R. D., 24, 40, 42, 105, 135, 136, 162, 163, 172, 191, 445
Windahl, S., 381, 385, 402, 405
Winer, B. J., 282
Winick, C., 394, 405
Winkler, R. L., 136, 264, 282
Winter, J., 386, 389, 401, 405
Winters, L., 362, 370

Woodside, A., 160, 163
Woodward, B., 160, 163
Wrightsman, L., 445
Wurtzel, A., 168, 172, 178, 190, 191, 375, 389, 405

Yin, R., 156, 157, 159, 163
Yu, J., 118, 131, 132, 136
Yule, G., 191

Zillmann, D., 113, 136, 169, 181, 189, 191, 207, 209, 380, 381, 383, 391, 400, 404, 405

computer assisted telephone interviewing (CATI), 133, 493
computer cards, 420–421, 494
computer systems, 410
concealment, 436
concept, 45, 494
concurrent validity, 63, 186
confidence interval, 83, 242, 494
confidence level, 83, 494
confounding influences, 91
confounding variable, 247
conseffects, 382
Consolidated Metropolitan Statistical Area (CMSA), 319
constitutive definition, 11, 494
construct, 45, 494
constructive replication, 39, 494
construct validity, 63, 187
content analysis, 165–192, 364
  analyzing data, 181
  coding, 179–180
  constructing categories, 175–178
  defining the universe, 172
  definition, 166–167
  exhaustivity, 177
  interpreting results, 181–182
  limitations, 170
  quantification system, 178–179
  reliability, 182–183
  selecting a sample, 172–173
  steps in, 171
  unit of analysis, 174
  uses of, 167
  validity, 186–187
contingency table analysis, 264–266
continuous variable, 57, 494
control group, 36, 267, 494
control variable, 47, 494
co-op payments, 332, 448
copy testing, 342–351, 494
  affective dimension, 346–349
  cognitive dimension, 344–346
  conative dimension, 349–351
correlational statistics, 229–233
correlation coefficient, 61, 62, 229–233
cost per thousand (CPM), 318, 319, 354, 494
criterion variable, 47, 494
Cronbach's alpha, 61
cross-lagged correlation, 195, 494
cross-sectional research, 194, 494
cross-tabulation analysis (crosstabs), 264–266, 494
cross-validating, 37, 147, 494
cultivation analysis, 169, 389–393, 494
cumulative audience (cume), 321, 351, 494
curvilinear relationship, 229

data analysis, 33–38
data archives, 22, 103, 428, 495
data base, 410, 495

data distribution, 213–217
  frequency curve, 216
  frequency distribution, 214
  frequency polygon, 215
  histogram, 215
  normal curve, 217
data reduction, 471–472
data transformation, 242–243
day-after recall, 345
daypart, 316, 321, 495
deception, 436
degrees of freedom, 263
demand characteristics, 37, 495
dependent variable, 46, 103, 297, 495
descriptive statistics, 213, 495
descriptive survey, 102, 495
desensitization, 380
designated market area (DMA), 319
design-specific results, 39, 495
determinant, 466, 495
deviation scores, 222
diagonal matrix, 466, 495
diaries, 202, 311, 328
  in-tab, 326
dichotomous response, 110
  data, 241
discrete variable, 57, 495
discriminant analysis, 476–480, 495
  function, 478
disk drive, 413, 495
disk operating system (DOS), 414
dispersion, 221, 495
  matrices, 480
  range, 221
  standard deviation, 224–226
  variance, 222–223
distribution, 495
diversification analyses, 336
double-barreled question, 108, 495
double bind, 109
double blind experiment, 37, 495
dummy variable, 54, 495

editor-reader comparisons, 292–293, 495
effects size, 255
eigenvalue, 466, 470
eigenvector, 466, 470
Eisenhower Commission, 374
Electronic Media Ratings Council, 83
electronic media research, future of, 336–339
empiricism, 10
environmental monitoring program, 364, 495
equal differences, 55
equivalence, 55, 495
equivalence reliability, 60–61
equivalent forms, 62
error, 31, 48, 248, 252–254
  measurement, 69
  random, 82
  sampling, 69, 70, 82–85

standard, 82
Type I, 253–254
Type II, 253–254
evaluation apprehension, 37, 495
evaluation research, 366, 495
excitation transfer, 380
executions, 330
exhaustivity, 54, 495
expansion boards, 413
experimental design, 30–32, 92–96, 495
  defined, 30
  factorial studies, 95–96
  posttest only, 94
  pretest-posttest, 93–94
  repeated measures, 93
  Solomon four-group, 94–95
experimental research, 296
experimental treatment, 35
exploratory research, 246
extended focus groups, 152
external validity, 27, 38, 91, 147, 495

face validity, 62, 186
factor, 95
factor analysis, 467–473, 495
  rotation, 470
  scores, 467, 495
factorial design, 95, 495
factorial studies, 95–96
Federal Communications Commission, 13,
  28, 336, 337
feeling thermometer, 113, 297, 495
field experiments, 138–144
  advantages, 139–140
  disadvantages, 140
  examples, 141–144
  types of, 140–141
field observation, 144–151
  advantages, 146
  analyzing data, 150
  collecting data, 149–150
  disadvantages, 147
  exiting, 150–151
  gaining access, 148
  participant observation, 145
  sampling, 148–149
  techniques, 148–151
  total observation, 145, 501
  total participation, 145, 501
field service, 32–33, 486–488, 489, 490,
  491, 492
fill-in-the-blank, 112
filter questions, 107, 495
Flesch reading ease formula, 298, 495
floppy disk, 414, 496
focus groups, 151–155, 334–335, 496
  advantages, 151–152
  conducting, 485–492
  disadvantages, 152–153
  extended, 152
  individual, 155
  methodology, 153–155

planning, 485–486
recruiting, 488–489
selecting field service, 486–488
Fog Index, 299, 496
follow-back panel, 204, 496
forced-choice question, 112, 496
forced-exposure, 348
format (disk), 414, 496
F ratio, 271–273
frequency, 351, 496
frequency curve, 216, 496
  kurtosis, 217, 496
  skewness, 217
frequency distribution, 214, 496
frequency polygon, 215, 496

gross rating points (GRP), 321, 351, 496
group administration, 104, 129–130, 496
  advantages, 130
  disadvantages, 130

hard disk, 414, 496
hardware, 412, 496
histogram, 215, 496
homes using television (HUT), 316
homogeneity, 36, 76, 496
hook, 332, 496
hypodermic needle model, 6, 9
hypothesis, 29, 247–249, 496
  criteria, 248–249
  null, 249, 255, 273
  purpose of, 247–248
  testing for significance, 242, 249–252

identity matrix, 466, 496
incidence, 76, 496
independent variable, 46, 103, 496
index, 57–59
individual focus group, 155
inferential statistics, 237–242, 496
  defined, 237
informed consent, 434
instrumental replication, 39, 496
instrument decay, 36, 496
in-tab diaries, 326
interaction, 274, 496
intercoder reliability, 60–61, 177, 183–
  186, 496
intercorrelation matrix, 466, 496
internal validity, 34–38, 496
  demand characteristics, 37
  evaluation apprehension, 37
  experimental mortality, 36–37
  experimenter bias, 37
  history, 35
  instrumentation, 36
  maturation, 35
  selection, 37
  statistical regression, 36
  testing, 36
interval data (level), 55, 233, 261, 496
intervening variable, 247

operational definition, 11, 25, 48–49, 175, 498
operational replication, 39, 494, 498
optical character reader, 412, 498
ordinal data (level), 53, 261, 498
orthogonal rotation, 471
outliers, 36, 220, 243
overnights (ratings), 309, 498

panel studies, 200–203, 364, 498
  analyzing causation, 205–206
  catch-up panel, 204–205
  continuous panel, 201
  defined, 200
  follow-back panel, 204
  interval panel, 201
  retrospective panel, 203–204
parameter, 498
parametric statistics, 56, 260–261, 267–280, 498
  analysis of variance, 270–275
  multiple regression, 275–278
  partial correlation, 278–280
  t-test, 94, 181, 260, 267–270, 501
parsimony principle, 28, 498
partial correlation, 278–280, 498
path analysis, 195, 482, 498
Pearson r, 230–233
people meters, 48, 327–328, 337, 338, 498
performer Q, 334
periodicity, 76, 498
peripheral, 412, 498
personal interviews, 104, 127–129, 498
  advantages, 128–129
  disadvantages, 129
  procedures, 127–128
  structured, 127
  unstructured, 127
persons using radio (PUR), 316
photomatics, 330
pi index, 184
pilot study, 32, 118–119, 158, 182, 498
platykurtic distribution, 217
point of prior equivalency, 36
population, 69, 498
  distribution, 238, 498
  parameters, 70
positioning, 7
posttest, 35, 349–350, 362
power, 255–256, 498
predictive validity, 63, 187
predictor variable, 47, 498
prestige bias, 132, 498
pretest, 35, 362
primary source, 103
principal components, 468
principal factors, 468
principle of least squares, 234–237, 276, 465, 498
printer, 415, 498
private sector research, 6, 12–14, 18

probability, 238–240
probability level, 250, 498
probability sample, 70–71, 498
  random, 73
programmable read only memory (PROM), 413, 498
program testing, 330–331
  animatics, 330
  executions, 330
  photomatics, 330
  rough cut, 330–331
  storyboards, 330
proposition, 11, 498
proprietary data, 13, 498
prosocial effects, 372–381
protocol, 158, 498
psychographics, 85, 208, 498
public relations audit, 365, 498
public relations research, 363–368
pupillometer test, 349
purposive sample, 72, 498

qualitative research, 49–50, 286, 328, 499
quantitative research, 50–51
questionnaire design, 114–118
  instructions, 114–115, 499
  introduction, 114
  layout, 177
  length, 118
  question order, 116–117
questions, types of, 105–106
quota sample, 72, 499

RADAR, 309
Radio Expenditure Reports (RER), 361
random access memory (RAM), 413, 499
random digit dialing, 73–74, 127, 499
random error, 82, 499
random sample, 73, 499
range, 221, 499
rank ordering, 111
rating scales, 57–59, 111, 365
rating, 4, 82, 316, 499
ratings, interpreting, 316–325
  area of dominant influence (ADI), 319
  audience turnover, 321–322
  average quarter hour, 321
  cost per thousand, 318, 319
  cume, 321
  daypart, 316
  designated market area (DMA), 319
  homes using television (HUT), 316
  metro survey area (MSA), 319
  people using radio (PUR), 316
  rating, 316
  total survey area (TSA), 319
ratings research, 308–329
  methodology, 310–315
  National Audience Composition, 308
  National Station Index, 308
  National Television Index, 308
  overnights, 309

social audit, 366, 500
software, 416, 500
Solomon four-group design, 94–95
sources of variation, 271
Spearman's rho, 233
split-half reliability, 62
spreadsheets, 419, 500
SPSS-PC, 417
SPSS-X, 417
square matrix, 466, 500
stability, 61, 500
stability reliability, 60–61, 500
stand-alone system, 410
standard deviation, 224–226, 237, 500
standard error, 82, 240, 268, 325–326, 500
standard scores, 224–226, 500
station image research, 335
statistical significance, 255
stepwise analysis, 355
stereo AM radio, 338
storyboards, 330
stratified sample, 76–77, 500
   advantages, 77
   disadvantages, 77
structured interview, 500
subject recruiting, 332–333
subscription television (STV), 35
summary statistics, 218–226, 500
   central tendency, 218
   mean, 219–221
   median, 219
sum of squares, 222, 268, 271, 277
supermatrix, 473
survey research, 102–133
   advantages, 103
   constructing questions, 104–114
   disadvantages, 102–103
   general problems, 132–133
sweeps, ratings, 309, 500
systematic sampling, 75–76, 500
   advantages, 76
   disadvantages, 76
   periodicity, 76
systematic variance, 271, 500

t-distribution, 269
telephone coincidental, 314, 500
telephone surveys, 104, 123–127, 500
   advantages, 126
   disadvantages, 126–127
   procedures, 124–125
Television Audience Assessment (TAA), 328–329
television meter (Arbitron), 311
terminal emulator, 412
Testsight, 331, 344, 349, 351
theory, 11, 500
time sharing, 410
total observation, 145, 500
total participation, 145, 500

total survey area (TSA), 319, 500
tracking studies, 361–362, 364, 500
trend studies, 195–196, 500
trial-and-error research, 247
triangulation, 51, 501
true zero point, 56
t-test, 94, 181, 260, 267–270, 501
two-factor design, 95
two-tail test, 250, 269
Type I error, 253–254, 501
Type II error, 253–254, 501
typography research, 296–298

unaided recall technique, 344
unit of analysis, 174, 290, 501
universal product code, 327, 351, 362
unrepresentative samples, 325–326
unstructured interview, 501
USA Today, 288, 298
uses and gratifications, 291–292, 381–385, 501

validity, 31, 34–38, 59, 62–65, 186–187, 501
   concurrent, 63, 186
   construct, 63, 187
   defined, 62
   face, 62, 186
   predictive, 63, 187
variable, defined, 46, 501
   antecedent, 47
   continuous, 57
   control, 47
   criterion, 47
   dependent, 46, 103
   discrete, 57
   dummy, 54
   independent, 46, 103
   marker, 46
   medium, 167
   predictor, 47
   transforming, 54
variance, 222–224, 237, 501
   error, 271
   systematic, 271
vector, 465, 501
Verified Audit Circulation, 358
Violence Index, 50, 59, 196
volunteer sample, 72, 501

weighted linear combinations, 275, 465
weighting, 326, 501
word processing, 418–419

x-axis, 215

y-axis, 215

z score, 224–227
zapping, 338
zipping, 338

514   SUBJECT INDEX